Dorothy Papini
9 Timber Acre Dr
Livingston N J
992-0970

The
GREATER JUDAISM
in
THE MAKING

THE
GREATER
JUDAISM
IN THE
MAKING

A STUDY OF THE MODERN
EVOLUTION OF JUDAISM

by

MORDECAI M. KAPLAN

THE RECONSTRUCTIONIST PRESS

New York

Designed by Harvey Satenstein
MANUFACTURED IN THE UNITED STATES OF AMERICA BY
BOOK CRAFTSMEN ASSOCIATES, INC., NEW YORK

IN LOVING MEMORY
OF
LENA KAPLAN

Preface

With the removal of Medieval disabilities, Jews began to experience Judaism as a far heavier burden than did their ancestors throughout the centuries of subjection to inhuman treatment by the rest of the world. One fact which rendered their sufferings endurable was their implicit belief that they belonged to a People which had been chosen by God to proclaim His greatness. Despite dispersion, the Jewish People had a definite status as a nation in exile, expecting to be restored some day to its ancestral land. Today such terms as "nation" and "exile" are misnomers when applied to world Jewry. Jews do not form an organic, interactive community. They are at best only like veterans of a disbanded army, without any specific purpose to live for as Jews, and without any reason for transmitting their Jewish heritage to their children.

What specifically has brought about loss of status and the consequent deterioration in the Jews' attitude toward Judaism? The answer is that, in the past, the very challenge which Jews encountered from their Christian environment *confirmed* them in their Jewish loyalty. Christianity then taught, and its adherents actually believed, that the Jews had originally been God's Chosen People, a privilege they had forfeited when they repudiated Jesus as the incarnation of God. The idea that they might regain that privilege by accepting Christianity—which was then the only alternative to remaining loyal to their own People—seemed to make no sense, as far as the Jews were concerned.

Nowadays, however, the challenge to Jews and Judaism comes from modern naturalism. Naturalism is not in conflict with religion as such. Its conflict is with the supernaturalism inherent in the traditional religions and with their doctrine that salvation is achievable only in the hereafter and not in this world. The truth is that modern naturalism is at present in conflict also with Christianity. Consequently, the faith which Jews had in their being God's Chosen People is being undermined not only directly by modern naturalism, but also indirectly by the fact that their neighbors are being de-Christianized. Though many Jews still insist on using the formula of chosenness when they are called up to the reading of the Torah, very few of them take it seriously; it does not make the least difference in their way of life. All that is left of Christianity that might reenforce the attachment of Jews to the Jewish People is the denigration of Jews. That is certainly not enough to elicit their self-respect, or to prevent them from trying to escape Judaism.

There are incidents in the life of a people which are symptomatic of much that is wrong with it. That is the case with two incidents that occurred in the year 1958 in the State of Israel during the tenth anniversary year of its establishment. One was a ruling issued by the Ministry of Education to all elementary and secondary schools of the country that they make a point of teaching subject matter to be known as "Jewish consciousness."

The second incident was the crisis in the Israeli Government which led to the resignation from the Cabinet of the Minister of Religion because of his refusal to recognize the Government's prerogative to decide the question of "Who is a Jew?" In his opinion such prerogative belonged to the Orthodox Rabbinate, which bases its authority on ancient Rabbinic law.

What occasioned the issuance of the ruling that the Jewish schools in Israel make a point of inculcating in their pupils Jewish consciousness? The realization that the rising Jewish generations in Israel were losing the sense of unity with the rest of world Jewry, and that they tended to repudiate the history of the Jews since the destruction of the Second Commonwealth in the year 70 C. E., if not all post-biblical history.

What occasioned the Government crisis over the question of "Who is a Jew?" The need for knowing who is entitled to the special privilege of being admitted to Israeli citizenship immediately upon entry to the land, and who may be registered as a Jew on the cards to be carried by all persons in the land for purposes of military security.

Both of these incidents reflect a very serious condition in the soul and the body of the entire Jewish People, which is in need of being attended to if it is not to prove fatal. They point up in unmistakable fashion the process of social and spiritual disintegration which has been going on in world Jewry for the last century and a half, ever since Jews have begun to be admitted into the body politic of the modern nations—and have been exposed to the intellectual revolution which has been undermining all traditional religions.

What renders these two incidents particularly ominous is that they should have occurred in the newly established State of Israel. They frustrate the one expectation which all Jews who had the least concern for the well-being of the Jewish People shared—the expectation that the fulfilment of Zionist aims would strengthen the bonds of Jewish unity and would normalize the place of religion and religious authority in Jewish life. Instead, these two incidents, by bringing to the surface the disruptive forces both social and spiritual, not only in Israel but in world Jewry as a whole, have rendered them more poignant.

If the Jewish People is to survive neither as a phantom nor as a fossil, but as a living and creative world community, opinion-molding Jews will have to rethink the contemporary Jewish being and situation. They will then recognize that what is actually happening to the Jewish People is a radical transformation which is nothing less than metamorphosis. It is evolving a new social structure for its body, and a new perspective on life for its soul. These cannot be created out of nothing. The Jewish People does have a viable tradition, a spiritual heritage on which it can draw in remaking itself—and it can remake itself consciously by exerting what is left of its will-to-live.

To acquire, however, the necessary self-knowledge in terms of the present, Jews have to become knowledgeable in terms of the past. They must not only realize what Judaism was like immediately before its present critical stage. They must also be aware that the Judaism of tradition had itself been the product of metamorphosis, as was the Judaism of the Second Jewish Commonwealth which was destroyed in the year 70. The capacity of the Jewish People for retaining its sense of identity amid different stages of metamorphosis is not just an accidental trait. On reflection, that capacity has tremendous import for the understanding of human life in general, particularly for that aspect which makes life distinctively human. Should the Jewish People succeed in negotiating the transition to the new stage in its being, it would throw new and welcome light on the meaning and purpose of its own will to live as well as that of other historic societies or peoples.

Our spiritual leaders have certainly not ignored the problem we are discussing. In their effort to help Jews meet the challenge of the modern world they have proposed four different solutions: Reform, Orthodoxy, Conservatism and Zionism. Reform stresses the need for change, Orthodoxy the need for tradition, Conservatism the need for tradition and change, and Zionism the need for the return of the Jews to their ancient homeland.

All this is tantamount to saying that, if Judaism is to survive, it will have to emerge as a Greater Judaism, and that the present chaos in Jewish life is the process of creation which should properly be described as "the Greater Judaism in the making." In the words of Meir Ben-Horin, the contemporary condition of Judaism is one of "ferment of creativity which begins with decomposition and culminates in reconstructive action." With that as a clue, the treatment of the problem which forms the subject-matter of this book will proceed along the following lines:

First comes a synoptic presentation of Traditional Judaism before it encountered the challenge of Western thought, and as it was actually lived by those who disregarded that challenge.

That is followed by a summary of Medieval theology, both philosophic and mystical, in terms of which Judaism figured in the minds of those who effected a synthesis of Traditional Judaism with currents of thought which derived from Hellenic sources.

Then comes a brief description of the cultural revolution in the civilization of the West beginning with the Renaissance and culminating in the scientific and cultural revolutions of the last two centuries. The resultant of those revolutions is the naturalist approach to reality, in contrast with the thought-world of supernaturalism and otherworldly salvation.

Far more significant than the stupendous technological development which is the practical outcome of modern naturalism is modern democratic nationalism. This new political pattern of human society is still in the process of finding the most suitable economic forms for its functioning as a means to freedom, justice and peace. Nevertheless, it has in some countries, particularly the United States, reached the point where it competes with both Christianity and Judaism for the idealistic interests of the citizen. Hence questions which never could have been conceived before, like "How and why be a Christian?" or "How and why be a Jew?" are now in the air.

The four above-mentioned responses to the challenge of both modern naturalism and modern nationalism are summarized in the description of the four contemporary trends or versions in Judaism. Each of these responses is described in detail, and both the strong and the weak points carefully noted. This is done not only with a view to objectivity, but also in order to prepare the reader for the concluding chapter on "The Greater Judaism" which sets forth a new approach to the entire problem of Judaism. That approach calls for a reorientation to the Jewish tradition, a restructuring of the body of the Jewish People, and a rethinking of the belief in God.

All this can be compatible with the continued functioning of the four main groups in contemporary Jewish life, provided they learn to identify in their respective versions some unifying factor which transcends their differences. That means that they have to learn to accept the principles of unity in diversity and of continuity in change as integral to the next stage in Judaism. It is, indeed, possible to combine whatever is valid in each of those four versions into a rational and inspiring way of life. The main prerequisite to such a development in Jewish life is that all Jews learn to view that which has united the generations of the Jewish People into a living historic entity—as an evolving religious civilization, and the present predicament in Judaism as marking the transition to the next stage in its evolution. At that next stage it will make as great a contribution to universal civilization as it made in its first creative stage, which is reflected in the Hebrew Bible.

Grateful acknowledgement is hereby made to the publishers of Philosophical Library, Inc. for permission to include in the final chapter entitled "The Greater Judaism" the selection which appeared as a chapter on "Reconstructionism" in *Religion in the*

20 *Century*, and to Monde Publishers, Inc. for permission to include the selection on "Judaism as a Modern Religious Civilization" which appeared as a chapter in *Two Generations in Perspective*.

I wish above all to express my heartfelt thanks to the friends of the Reconstructionist movement in Chicago, whose generosity made possible the publication of this work.

February 1960

M.M.K.

Contents

CHAPTER NINE

THE REFORM MOVEMENT IN THE U.S.A.   273

CHAPTER TEN

ORTHODOX JUDAISM   316

CHAPTER ELEVEN

CONSERVATIVE JUDAISM   350

CHAPTER TWELVE

ZIONISM   381

"But this is the covenant which I will make with
the House of Israel after those days, says the Lord:
I will put my law within them, and I will write it
upon their hearts, and I will be their God, and they
shall be my people."

JEREMIAH 31:33.

"Man, and indeed the whole stream of life, has
thrived on crises, evolving out of their novel adap-
tations and enhanced survival power."

J. H. RUSH, in The Dawn of Life.

CHAPTER ONE

The World of Traditional Judaism

WHAT IS TRADITIONAL JUDAISM?

The overwhelming majority of Jews have become modernized, or westernized, as a result of their integration into the body politic of the various European and American nations of which they are citizens, and of their self-adjustment to the cultural climate of their surroundings. This process of westernization began during the latter part of the 18th century almost simultaneously among the Jews in France, Prussia, and Austria. Western mankind was then undergoing a transformation which heralded changes that were certain to take place in the world outlook and in the social structure of Jewish life.

Individual Jews had begun to be westernized intellectually some decades before they were westernized politically and socially. Wherever Jews lived in considerable numbers, the more ambitious among them undertook to help their fellow-Jews to be integrated culturally into the general body politic. They would first westernize their own lives, and then seek to influence their fellow-Jews to follow their example. The process of westernization would usually begin, as it did in Prussia under the leadership of Moses Mendelssohn and his followers, with the effort to have the Jews exchange their own Yiddish dialect—or as they then termed it

3

"Jüdisch-Deutsch"—for the native vernacular, and to take up secular studies which were the hallmark of culture.

Thus arose *Haskalah*, or the militant Jewish Enlightenment movement. From Prussia of the end of the eighteenth century the movement passed within less than a generation to Austria and, soon after, to Poland and Russia. Despite the long time that has elapsed since the beginnings of the westernizing process among Jews and the numerous catastrophic changes and vast migrations since then, there are still islands in Jewry in all parts of the world which have remained immune to modern cultural influences. Sooner or later even these islands are bound to disappear. Their places will be taken by various Jewish groups which identify themselves with one or another of the existing trends in modern Judaism.

Each modern trend in Judaism represents a specific version, or interpretation, of pre-modern Judaism. The Reform version, which is the first to have been formulated, emerged during the forties of the nineteenth century. The Conservative version, known at first as "Positive Historical Judaism," and the Orthodox version likewise arose then as counter-movements to Reform at about the same time. Orthodoxy and Conservatism treat Traditional Judaism as normative for all time. Orthodoxy strongly deprecates all deviation from Traditional Judaism. Conservatism, however, is prepared to sanction innovations, provided they can be kept within the framework of traditional law. Even the Reform version, which avowedly departs both in belief and practice from Traditional Judaism, maintains, as a rule, that its deviations are only from the letter, and not from the spirit, of Jewish tradition. Whatever in that tradition it rejects Reform treats as only incidental to the inner spirit of ancient Judaism, and as generally the product of abnormal conditions of life during the pre-modern centuries which a hostile world imposed on the Jews.

In evaluating the trends in contemporary Judaism, we need to know as accurately as possible what pre-modern Judaism had to say concerning God, the Jewish People, the Torah, and the destiny of human life. We have to recapture as much of its original spirit as possible. All too often tradition is invoked to validate as authentic whatever derives its authoritative character from its connection with the past. It is then that appeal to tradition is popular, intended to lead us into believing that nothing really catastrophic has happened to sever that connection. We are lured into assuming that we can go about our business as of old, without having to resort to any drastic measures to set things right. That is why we should be on our guard against forming a distorted picture of Traditional Judaism. Such a distorted picture would minimize the effort which has to be exerted in rendering Traditional Judaism relevant to the spiritual needs of Jews of today.

The findings of an *objective* study of Traditional Judaism, summarized in the first part of this book, unmistakably point to the following conclusion: *The conceptions of God, Israel, Torah, human nature, sin, repentance, messianic redemption and the world to come in pre-modern or Traditional Judaism belong to a radically different universe of thought, or world outlook, from that of the average westernized Jew*. This means that every one of the modern trends in Judaism, insofar as it is articulated by Jews who have come under the influence of modern thought, cannot possibly be the original Judaism of tradition. It can only be an adaptation of it to the spirit of the times, whether that fact is recognized or not. The scholars and theologians who sponsor these trends are generally tempted to force the tradition into a mold that will resemble their own adaptation of the tradition to the contemporaneous needs of Jewish life. Consequently, their histories of the Jewish People and of its religion are more often idealizations than a recording of facts.

RABBINIC JUDAISM

Traditional Judaism[1] is the religious culture, or civilization, of the Jews, as they lived it before they felt the impact of Western thought through the medium of Arabic culture in the Middle East during the tenth to the twelfth centuries of the common era. The salient character of Traditional Judaism was the pervasive awareness on the part of every Jew that his People had been covenanted to God, or committed to the task of making Him and His will known to the rest of mankind. The account of the enactment of the covenant and the duties that it imposed on the Jews were to be found in the Torah which God had revealed or dictated to Moses. Those duties, however, were spelled out with great detail in the patterns, ideals, institutions and norms of conduct formulated by the Sages of the Talmud.

"The Sages of the Talmud" is a term used to denote the *Tannaim* and the *Amoraim*. The *Tannaim*, all of whom were Palestinian Jews, were the authors of the various laws included in the *Mishnah*, which was adopted as an authoritative code by Rabbi Judah the Prince at the end of the second century. The *Amoraim*, some of whom were Palestinian and others Babylonian Jews, were the scholars whose interpretations of the *Mishnah* and the Bible, both legalistic and homiletic, are contained in the *Gemara* and the *Midrashim*. They flourished from about the beginning of the third century to the end of the fifth century, C. E.

That pattern of Traditional Judaism was maintained essentially intact until the invasion of Jewish life by modernism. The finality of Talmudic law formulated by the *Amoraim* was never questioned. "Rav Ashi and Ravina," we are told, "represent the consummation of authoritative teaching." [2] That implies that no one has any right to change that teaching, "whether in substance or in form." [3]

The sharply discerning eye of the scholar may perceive slightly different shades of belief and practice in the Rabbinic pattern, slight changes in emphasis under the influence of varying conditions. But by and large that pattern remained unchanged during the seventeen centuries that elapsed between R. Yohanan ben Zakkai and Moses Mendelssohn. The slight changes in outlook and in social structure of Jewish life which took place in the course of those centuries were so gradual as to be imperceptible. They certainly were not deliberate. To the ancient mind any deliberate change was considered subversive of tradition as a whole, and therefore dangerous.

To the generations of Jews whose mode of life was regulated by the Talmud, all the teachings of the Sages appeared inherently consistent. A considerable portion of the post-Talmudic writings is devoted to the reconciliation of contradictory statements in the tradition itself. Very seldom was a traditional text interpreted in the light of either literary or historical context. Whenever new conditions arose, it was tacitly assumed that they had been provided for in the tradition, since the tradition was assumed to have been revealed by God to Moses simultaneously with the written

Torah.[4] That is the assumption on which the entire Rabbinic literature is based. The discussions recorded in the Talmud were carried on in the Rabbinic academies of Palestine and Babylonia over a period of about five centuries. Their purpose was a twofold one; first, to arrive at an inherently consistent interpretation of the tradition as it had come down from the *Tannaim,* and as recorded in the *Mishnah, Tosefta* and other sources; and secondly, to relate that interpretation to the written Torah.

Except for the large-scale revolt against Rabbinic Judaism known as Karaism which flourished for a long time during the ninth to the twelfth century in the Middle East, and the extreme antinomian wing of the Shabbatean sect which arose in Smyrna in 1665, the Talmudic tradition was universally regarded as the norm of Jewish life. "The positive influence of this way of life (the Mosaic and Rabbinic Law) over the Jewish mind had been so great," writes G. G. Scholem, "that for centuries no movement, least of all an organized movement, had rebelled against the values linked up with the practical fulfillment of the Law." [5]

During the three centuries between the tenth and twelfth inclusive, the rising tide of rationalism, which derived from Greek culture, had invaded the Moslem countries where most of the Jews then lived. It also seeped into Jewish life, and for a time jeopardized not only the authority of the Talmudic tradition but the very existence of Judaism, especially among the intellectual elite and the well-to-do. But before long, that threat was offset by a succession of writings which countered successfully the challenge of rationalist thought. Those writings were of two types, philosophic and mystic. Of the two, the mystic writings were by far the more potent in fortifying the Talmudic tradition. The mystic writings kept growing in scope and influence, while the philosophic writings remained limited in both.[6] By the time Traditional Judaism began to feel the impact of modernism, there were but few extant copies of Maimonides' *Guide for the Perplexed,* and the interest in Medieval Jewish philosophy was at its lowest ebb, whereas the study of the *Zohar* received a new impetus with the rise of the Hasidic movement during the middle of the eighteenth century.

Another remarkable fact is that, in the pre-modern era, faith in Traditional Judaism was shared alike by all classes, regardless of their general educational background. Due to the fact that, with few exceptions, neither the philosophic nor the mystic writings seemed to challenge Traditional Judaism, there was little discrepancy in world outlook between the masses and the learned among the Jews. A Jewish woman like Glueckel of Hameln, though more literate than the majority of her kind, was nevertheless typical. Through the medium of the Judeo-German version of Rabbinic teachings she acquired a world outlook that contained virtually all the fundamental concepts and values articulated by the ancient Jewish Sages.

What Judaism as a whole meant to the Jews in the pre-modern era of Jewish history may be inferred from what the term "Torah" meant to them. There is, indeed, no Hebrew term for "Judaism" in the entire literature of that period. *Yahadut,* by which Judaism is designated in modern Hebrew, always meant in the past "Jewishness" or Jewish practice.[7] The term used throughout that period as summing up the entire substance and import of Jewish life is "Torah." For the Jews before modern times *the* Torah consisted essentially of the Pentateuch as interpreted by the oral tradition, *Torah she-be-al-peh.* The authorship of the Pentateuch and of the traditional interpretations of its text was ascribed, in all literalness, to God. Unlike the other parts of the Bible, which were regarded as having been written under the inspiration of the Divine Spirit, but which also reflect the thought and personality of those who wrote them, the text of the Pentateuch was regarded as free from any human admixture.[8] This assumption was so self-evident to the Sages that they did not hesitate to use a Pentateuchal text as source of verification or refutation, in the same way as we would use a logical or mathematical axiom.

The following passage from *Sifrē,* a collection of Tannaitic interpretations of Numbers and Deuteronomy, is a typical illustration of that sort of reasoning: *"I, even I am He, and there is no God beside Me."*[9] This verse is an answer to those who say, *"There is no Power in heaven,"* or to those who say, *"There are two Powers in heaven."*[10] "One can imagine," C. G. Montefiore and H. Loewe comment, "that this verse might be used against those who say that there are two powers, because such persons might also acknowledge the divine authority of Scriptures. But it is exceedingly curious that the Rabbis, who are not wanting in great acuteness when it comes to making legal distinctions or indeed to anything juristic, should not have seen that for those who deny that there is any God at all . . . the verse is valueless, as such people would obviously deny any authority to the book from which the verse comes." [11]

Another example of how literally they took the tradition that the precepts in the Torah were authored by God is the following: Yehudah Halevi in his *Al-Khazari* has the Rabbi say to the Khazar king: "What is now your opinion of a select community which has merited the appellation 'people of God' and also a special name called 'the inheritance of God,' and of seasons fixed by Him, not merely agreed upon or settled by astronomical calculations, and therefore styled 'feasts of the Lord?' The rules regarding purity and worship, prayers and performances, are fixed by God, and there-fore called 'work of God' and 'service of the Lord.' " [12] It is not easy for a modern person to recapture that complete sense of acceptance of whatever was stated in the Torah as absolute truth. Such acceptance was possible only so long as Jews had implicit faith in the divine authorship of its contents.

Throughout the centuries of Traditional Judaism, the doctrine, or dogma, that the Torah had been dictated directly by God to Moses during Israel's sojourn at Sinai, was the cardinal principle to which every Jew had to give assent, or else he was read out of the fold. "He who says that the Torah is not from heaven forfeits his share in the world to come," [13] that is, he is deprived of salvation. When the Sages said of the Torah that it was "from heaven," they were not speaking in metaphors. Heaven was to them a place actually above the earth. Just as literally as they be-lieved in the existence of waters in the upper regions, so literally did they believe that the Torah emanated from the upper regions[14] that is, from God who dwelt in the heavens above.[15]

Moses' relation to the Torah was nothing more than that of an amanuensis, according to Rabbi Meir[16], who used as an illus-tration the instance of Jeremiah's dictating his prophecies to Baruch. "Whoever says that Moses himself wrote even one word of the Torah, of him it is said that he holds God's word in contempt. He forfeits his share in the world to come." [17] The only question was whether God dictated the contents of the entire Torah at one time, or in sections at different times.[18] Some Rabbis maintain that it is forbidden to write the Pentateuch on the same scroll with the rest of the Scriptures, because of the superior sanctity of the former. For the same reason it is not permitted to place a scroll containing the writings of the Prophets and the Hagiographa upon one containing the Pentateuch.[19]

If it were not for Israel's sins, we are told, only the Pentateuch and the parts of Joshua which indicate the boundary lines of Eretz Yisrael would have constituted the Sacred Scriptures.[20] The benediction, *"Blessed art Thou . . . for having given us Thy Torah"* may not be recited before reading any section of the Scriptures outside the Pentateuch, though it may be recited before a passage from the *Mishnah*. In the future, according to R. Yohanan, when Israel's sins have been eliminated, the Pentateuch alone will continue to be studied, to the exclusion of the Prophetic writings and the Hagiographa.[21]

The importance which Traditional Judaism attaches to the Oral Law may be gathered from the fact that it views the Oral Law not merely as coordinate with the Written Law, but as related to it organically. The Sage whose function it is to transmit the Oral Law is deferred to more implicitly than the Prophet. That is why the Oral Law is more authoritative than the Prophetic writings.[22] The relation of the Oral Law to the Written Law is indicated in the story of Hillel and the would-be proselyte. The latter at first refused to accept the Oral Law. Hillel, however, convinced him by means of a lesson in the Hebrew alphabet that the Oral Law was as indispensable to the Written Law as was the tradition concerning the name and pronunciation of each letter of the alphabet to the letters themselves.[23]

The Palestinian *Amoraim* of the third and fourth centuries[24] advance the opinion that the Oral Law is that element of Torah which renders it the unique possession of Israel. This Amoraic conception of the Oral Law is, no doubt, intended to offset the claim of Christianity to the effect that, in adopting the Jewish Scriptures, including the Torah, as part of its sacred writings, it embraces all the revealed truth of which Judaism claims to be the sole possessor. The inclusion by non-Jews of the Pentateuch among their sacred scriptures was resented by the *Tannaim*, as is evident from the following passage in a Tannaitic *Midrash*: "The Torah is betrothed to Israel, and cannot therefore be espoused by any other people." [25]

THE TWOFOLD FUNCTION OF
TRADITIONAL JUDAISM

The Torah, in the sense of the Oral and the Written teaching and legislation, performed a twofold function in the life of the Jews: It served as an instrument of national and of individual salvation. The verse in Deuteronomy which reads: "That your days may be multiplied and the days of your children, as the days of the heavens above the earth" is commented upon in *Sifrē*, as follows:[26] 'That your days may be multiplied,' in this world; 'and the days of your children,' in the Messianic era; 'as the days of the heavens upon the earth,' in the world to come." Among the various petitions which the Jew has been wont to recite at the end of the prayer of thanksgiving after a meal is one which reads: "May the All-merciful make us worthy of the days of the Messiah and of the life of the world to come." This petition sums up in succinct fashion the two goals which Traditional Judaism sought to help the Jew attain. "The days of the Messiah" refers to national redemption, to freedom from oppression at the hands of other nations, and to the return of the Jews to Eretz Yisrael, their ancestral land. "The life of the world to come" refers to the life of bliss which awaits the individual Jew who, while in this world, lives in comformity with the will of God as expressed in the Torah.

The Torah, or Traditional Judaism, must therefore be understood as having made of the Jews both a nation (ummah) *and an ecclesia* (K'nesset Yisrael). As a nation, the Jews developed all those institutions which were essential to the conduct of everyday affairs in men's relations to one another and in their relations as a group *vis-a-vis* other groups. A nation is a political group. Before the modern era the Jews were a political group insofar as they always enjoyed a measure of autonomy. On the other hand, they were also an ecclesia or *K'nesset*. "Ecclesia" is a distinctly religious concept, religious in the *traditional* sense of being based upon some supernatural revelation of divinity. An ecclesia is a *corpus mysticum*. Its members are united by the common bond of allegiance to some specific instrument of a supernatural character. That instrument may be a sacred text, or it may be a sacred personality. By means of that instrument, it is assumed, men learn what God would have them do in order to achieve salvation.

Of the two functions of the Torah, that of maintaining the solidarity of the Jews as a People was expected to lead to the advent of the Messiah. The other function, that of uniting them into a holy nation, or ecclesia, designated as *K'nesset Yisrael* was expected to enable them, as individuals, to achieve salvation, or a share in the world to come. Those two functions were not inherently integral to each other,[27] though, before Rabbinic Judaism became crystallized, they gradually fused into the one eschatological hope of a miraculously bright future for the entire People.

However, the belief in the hereafter, or in the world to come, because of its reference to the destiny of the individual, was bound to play a greater role in the Jewish consciousness during the centuries of exile than the Messianic expectation, which had to do with the destiny of the nation. This is apparent from the tendency of the Sages to reinterpret scriptural passages which unmistakenly refer to the future destiny of the nation as referring to the world to come. Thus the teaching of the Mishnah that "All who are of Israel have a share in the world to come" [28] is based upon the statement in Isaiah [29] which reads: "*Thy people are all righteous; they will inherit the land* (eretz) *forever.*" Even if *eretz* means "the earth," it could mean that only in the same sense as in Psalm 37:11, where the poet wishes to affirm his faith in the ultimate survival of the meek and humble instead of the aggressive and violent ones. In any event, the Prophet is concerned with the destiny of the entire People and not merely with that of the individual. Moreover, the *Chapters of the Fathers*, which have as their central theme the importance of Torah study, and the reading of which is preceded by the foregoing *Mishnah* about the world to come, do not treat that study as a means to national redemption but to a share of the individual Jew in the world to come.[30]

If we call to mind the difference between the origin of the belief in the advent of the Messiah and of the belief in the world to come, we sense the difference in the connotations of those beliefs. The belief in the Messiah stems directly from Biblical sources. It is indigenously Jewish. On the other hand, the belief in the world to come, with its concomitant belief in bodily resurrection, is an importation mainly from Zoroastrian civilization.

In the Bible, the People of Israel, after having undergone divine chastisement, is assured of its return to its land and of the attainment of bliss. Every such assurance became part of the pattern of hope in which the central figure was a scion of David, known as the Messiah. The prophecies of Balaam, the concluding verses in the farewell song of Moses, the prophecy in Isaiah and Micah concerning "the latter days," the description of the Messiah given in *Isaiah*, Chapter 11, the entire collection of consolatory prophecies in the second part of Isaiah, those in all the other prophetic books from Jeremiah through Malachi, the allusions in the book of Psalms, and the concluding chapter in Daniel—all were uniformly interpreted as referring to the Messianic era which awaited the Jewish nation.

On the other hand, the belief in bodily resurrection and the belief in the world to come stem from non-Jewish sources. It was accepted by the Jews to meet a spiritual expectation which had arisen during the period of the Second Commonwealth. That expectation was to find some correspondence between the merit and the lot of the individual. Experience seemed to refute the principle of reward and punishment stressed in the Torah. The Jews therefore had recourse to the same solution as all other religions which stressed the salvation of the individual. That solution posited another world wherein the inequities of this one were righted. Thus the belief in the world to come is essentially motivated by the desire to vindicate the principle of individual retribution. Both the Messianic hope and the expectation of bliss in the world to come are voiced in the traditional liturgy, as in the following: "May it be Thy will that we keep Thy statutes in this world, and be worthy to live to witness and inherit happiness and blessing in the days of the Messiah and in the life of the world to come." [31]

TRADITIONAL JUDAISM AS REFLECTED IN JEWISH MEMOIRS [32]

To form a correct idea of Traditional Judaism as it actually functioned in the past, before the advent of modernism, we must consider the testimony of those who themselves either lived their whole lives, or spent at least their early years, amid old-time Jewish surroundings. Only with the aid of such first-hand accounts of pre-modern Judaism can we form a true mind-picture of its inner intent and outward expression. Such first-hand accounts are to be found in the autobiographies of two men and two women which are here summarized. These autobiographies throw much light on the way Traditional Judaism actually functioned while it was still in its heyday, just before it met the challenge of Western civilization. They reflect the inner life of Jews prior to their emancipation from the Medieval status of alienage.

GLUECKEL OF HAMELN (1645-1724)

Glueckel [33] lived the greater part of her life in Hamburg, but her story [34] takes the reader to a number of cities in Germany, where the many branches of her family lived. Her household, with its wide circle of acquaintances, typified the most prosperous element in German Jewry of the period between 1650 and 1725. Her memoirs are written in that mixture of old German and Hebrew which later developed into Yiddish.

Throughout her book one gets the impression of Jewish life as virtually homogeneous, and free from all inner conflict or self-doubt. She has occasion to mention "the heretical sect of followers of the false Messiah Shabbetai Tz'vi," but that sect had cut itself off from the main body of the Jewish People. The only case of conversion to Christianity recorded in her book is that of one of two Jewish thieves who were about to be hanged. (The other thief did not care to save his life at the price of conversion.) There is not a single mention of any heretic or doubter either among the worldly successful or the learned in any one of the many communities she had visited.

The only jarring note is the one she recorded after her second visit to Metz about 1715. "When I first came here," she writes, "Metz was a very beautiful and pious community, and the *parnassim* were all worthy men who verily adorned the council room. In those days not a man who sat in the council room wore a perruque, and no one heard of a man going out of the *Judengasse* (Jewry) to bring a case before a Gentile tribunal. When differences arose, and there were many, as there always are among Jews, they were one and all settled before the communal or rabbinical courts. No such arrogance reigned in the old days as now, and people were not wont to eat such costly meals. The children applied themselves to learning, and the elders time and again had the ablest rabbis serve the community." [35]

A striking illustration both of the sense of kinship with Jews of other countries and of the selfless spirit of hospitality manifested in aiding them is Glueckel's description of how her parents' home would be turned into a hospital whenever Jewish refugees from Poland happened to come to Hamburg. "At least ten of them, whom my father took under his charge, lay on the upper floor of our house. Some recovered and others died. My sister Elkele and I both took sick. Nothing could stop her (my grandmother) from climbing to the garret three or four times a day in order to nurse them. At length she too fell ill. After ten days in bed she died." [36]

Glueckel was not given an intensive training in the Hebrew texts, either Biblical or Rabbinic, "because Jewish tradition did not expect the woman to study Torah." But Glueckel was by no means illiterate. Besides being able to read and understand Hebrew prayers, which she recited thrice daily, she read much and often from the considerable number of books of devotions and homiletic-ethical collections in Judeo-German. One of these collections *Tze-ena u'Re-ena* is a running homiletic commentary on the Pentateuch, arranged according to the weekly pericopes. It contains a large number of the characteristic sayings of the *Tannaim* and *Amoraim*, strewn throughout the Talmud and *Midrashim*. This homiletic commentary served as the chief source of religious inspiration to Jewish women throughout the length and breadth of European Jewry, during the two centuries preceding the invasion of Jewish life by modernism. How thoroughly permeated Glueckel's mind was with what she read in those books is evidenced in her *Memoirs*, nearly every other page of which contains some quotation, phrase, or turn of thought, taken from them, all quoted in their original Hebrew.

The keynote of all her ideas about life is that God exercises His providence over the destiny of every human being and decrees what shall befall him. She assumes that, on the whole, there is an understandable correlation between the extent to which human beings conform to God's will as expressed in the Torah and their lot in life. There are, to be sure, apparently sufficient deviations from that rule to render God's ways with man mysterious. But whether those ways were understandable or mysterious, Glueckel, whose mind was formed on the Rabbinic teachings quoted in her devotional readings, was convinced that whatever happened was divinely ordained. If a marriage is arranged and it falls through, if one goes on a journey and is set upon by robbers or killed, if the thief is found out, if one makes money at the fair, if one's child dies, if one is a victim of ingratitude, if one recovers from sickness or dies of it—no matter what happens, the thought that chance or nature might have contributed to the event never entered her mind. "Wish as we may, the Most High has already decreed whatever shall come to pass." [37]

Solomon Schechter thinks "her reasoning is as little cogent as that of all other theodicies." [38] But the one to blame is not Glueckel, but the Rabbis of the Talmud, whose vindication of God she restates with the utmost fidelity. Having at her command a knowledge of how the ancient Prophets and Sages had accounted for Israel's sufferings, she can easily account for the fiasco of the movement of Shabbetai Tz'vi, the false Messiah. "Full well we know," she writes, [39] "the Most High has given His word, and were we not so wicked but truly pious from the bottom of our hearts, I am certain God would have mercy on us; if only we kept the commandment, 'Thou shalt love thy neighbor as thyself.' But may God forgive us for the way we keep it. No good can come from the jealousy and uncaused hate that rule our lives." One recognizes at once the well-known Rabbinic teaching that the Second Temple was destroyed because of the sin of uncaused hate. [40]

The questions which we should want answered are: What did Jews live by? What constituted the substance of their literacy and their education, the source of their knowledge of God, of man, and of the world? On what did they base their communal life, and how did they regulate their personal and public affairs? To all these questions Glueckel's *Memoirs* give a clear answer. She does not exaggerate in the least when, in her opening words, she makes use of the Rabbinic metaphor to describe what the Torah meant to the Jews then. "We have our holy Torah in which we may find and learn all that we need for our journey through this world to the world to come. It is like a rope which the great and gracious God has thrown to us as we row in the stormy sea of life, that we may seize hold of it." [41]

She was married at the age of fourteen, and went to live with her husband and his parents in the town of Hameln, where there were only three Jewish families. Among her fondest recollections is one about the way she delighted in the piety of her husband and the male members of her household, who never omitted their daily chore of Rabbinic studies. In describing her husband's brother she uses the Rabbinic phrase, "full of Torah as a pomegranate is full of seeds." In her own milieu it was assumed that a son who showed any inclination for learning must be given an opportunity to become a rabbi or rabbinic scholar. Poland was then the center of Jewish learning. Although the journey was not without danger, young sons of the well-to-do would be sent there to become expert in the knowledge of Torah. Only those who had "no itch for learning" were put to a trade or went into business. But even being in business did not exempt one from the duty of studying Torah. After the day's work at the Bourse was over, the men would get together in one of their homes to study a chapter of *Mishnah* or a page of Talmud.

There is no intimation in her *Memoirs* of any non-Jewish source of literary or general knowledge. Only once does she have occasion to mention the fact that her sister studied French and knew how to play the piano. Those fashionable attainments of young women in the homes of the well-to-do were apparently already in vogue then.

SOLOMON MAIMON (1746-1800)

Solomon Maimon[42] was born in Nieszwicz, Lithuania, in 1746. Undeterred by the greatest difficulties, he succeeded in negotiating the transition from the pre-modern world of Traditional Judaism to the modern world of late eighteenth century German culture. He was impelled by an inordinate hunger for knowledge, which he at first tried in vain to satisfy through the study of *Kabbalah*. Before long, he reached out for the scientific and philosophic works that had come from Germany, whither he migrated later and where he spent the rest of his life. So thoroughly did he assimilate the learning of the day that he wrote many works in German and Hebrew on the most recondite philosophical themes. He did not hesitate to criticize the popular philosophy of Christian Wolff, or take issue with the new critical philosophy which Kant was then expounding. But of main interest, from the standpoint of Jewish life on the verge of the modern era, is his *Autobiography*. There we learn about the conditions under which he was born and received his early Jewish training.

The Jews in Poland then constituted the overwhelming majority of the Jewish population in the world. Although the picture Maimon gives of them is largely subjective, enough of objective fact emerges to reflect the same ardent devotion to Rabbinic learning which we found recorded in Glueckel's *Memoirs*.

"The majority of Polish Jews," he writes, "consist of scholars, that is, men devoted to an inactive and contemplative life, for every Polish Jew is destined from his birth to be a rabbi, and only the utmost incapacity can exclude him from the office." [43]

The ancient Rabbinic world outlook was in those days inculcated in the Jewish child at an early age. This we gather from the following story: Solomon Maimon's father was reading with him from the Pentateuch about Jacob and Esau. The father gave that story the traditional, or Rabbinic, interpretation. According to that rendering, Jacob and Esau divided between them all the blessings of the world. Esau chose the blessings of this life; Jacob chose those of the hereafter. "Since we are descended from Jacob," his father added, "we must give up all claim to the temporal blessings of this world." [44]

Solomon Maimon was then little more than a child and completely immured within the narrow confines of the Jewish enclave. It would never have occurred to anyone in that environment to question the wisdom and holiness of Israel's Patriarchs. Yet, as though the far-away spirit of free inquiry mysteriously invaded that obscure little town, young Solomon dared to say to his father that Jacob should not have been a fool; he should have chosen the blessings of this world. "Unfortunately," adds Maimon, "I got for answer 'You ungodly rascal!' and a box on the ear. This did not of course remove my doubts." [45]

A second incident which Maimon records illustrates to what

extent the Talmud then filled the entire mental horizon of the Jews. As a child, Maimon was fond of drawing. One day he showed his father some pictures he had copied from a book of animal stories. "You want to become a painter?" cried his father, "You have to study the Talmud and become a rabbi. One who understands the Talmud understands everything." [46] The all-dominating influence of Rabbinism on Maimon's environment is reflected in the following: "Riches," he says, "bodily advantages and talents of every kind have indeed in their eyes a certain worth and are esteemed in proportion; but nothing stands among them above the dignity of a good Talmudist. He has first claim upon all the offices and positions of honor in the community. He is mentor of the conscience, lawgiver and judge of the common man." [47]

Solomon Maimon was precocious as a child. At the age of eleven, he knew almost as much Talmud as a full-fledged rabbi in those days. While still in his teens he began to experience the intellectual stirrings of the modern spirit. "I found pleasure (in the Talmud) merely in view of its form," he writes, "for this calls into action the higher powers of the mind, but I took no interest in its matter. It affords exercise in deducing the remotest consequences from their principles and in hunting out the finest distinctions. But as the principles themselves merely have an imaginary reality, they cannot by any means satisfy a soul thirsting for knowledge." [48]

At times Maimon cannot restrain himself from holding the Talmud responsible for having narrowed the mind of the Jews. "This religion," he says, "which by the intention of its founder should have formed the Jews into the wisest and most intelligent of nations, made them by its injudicious applications the most ignorant and unreasonable of all." [49] Though Maimon speaks disparagingly of the contents of the Talmud which have to do with the guidance of conduct, whether religious or secular, he credits the Sages with having possessed the true wisdom of life, which they conveyed in their theological and ethical teachings. "It is remarkable," he says, "that with all Rabbinical extravagances in the practical department, namely the laws and customs, the theoretical department of Jewish theology has still always preserved itself in its purity." [50] He then proceeds to give an idealized description of the Jewish way of life which is entirely the product of the Talmudic discipline and world outlook.

"The influence of these (Talmudic-moral) doctrines in practical life is also unmistakable. The Polish Jews who have always been allowed to adopt any means of gain, and have not, like the Jews of other countries, been restricted to the pitiful occupations of *shacher* or usurer, seldom hear the reproach of cheating. They remain loyal to the country in which they live, and support themselves in an honorable way.

"Their charity and care for the poor, their institutions for nursing the sick, their special societies for burial of the dead, are well enough known. It is not nurses and grave-diggers hired for money, but the elders of the people, who are eager to perform these acts. The Polish Jews are indeed for the most part not yet enlightened by science, their manners and their way of life are still rude, but they are loyal to the religion of their fathers and the laws of their country. They do not come before you with courtesies, but their promise is sacred. They are not gallants, but your women are safe with them from all snares. Woman, indeed, after the manner of Orientals in general, is by them not particularly esteemed, but all the more on that account are they resolved to fulfill their duties toward her. Their children do not learn by heart any *forms* for expressing love and respect for their parents—for they do not keep their French *demoiselles*; but they show that love and respect all the more heartily.

"The sacredness of their marriage, and the ever fresh tenderness which arises from this deserves especially to be mentioned. Every month the husband is wholly separated from his wife for a fortnight (the period of monthly separation in accordance with the Rabbinical laws); they may not so much as touch one another, or eat out of the same dish or drink out of the same cup. By this means satiety is avoided; the wife continues to be in the eyes of her husband all that she was as a maiden in the eyes of her lover. Finally, what innocence rules among unmarried persons! It often happens that a young man or woman of sixteen or eighteen years is married without knowing in the least about the object of marriage. Among other nations this is certainly not the case." [51]

We may perhaps regard this picture of the Talmud Jew as entirely too idyllic. But what is of main interest historically is that, before the Jew was confronted with the problem of adjusting his life to his new status and new outlook, his mentality and character were fashioned by Rabbinic law.

Before Solomon Maimon came into contact with secular education, he tried to slake his thirst for the kind of knowledge which he hoped would prove more fruitful than that which he had obtained from the Talmud and the Codes; he turned to the study of *Kabbalah* or Jewish mysticism. Mystic lore had always formed part of Judaism, but it remained an esoteric pursuit until about the middle of the eighteenth century, when it began to be fostered by the adherents of Hasidism, which arose about that time. In Maimon's day that movement had already made considerable headway. Maimon compares the *Hasidim* to the "Illuminati" of Bavaria, a group which regarded itself as divinely inspired.[52]

Maimon's interest in *Kabbalah*, however, had nothing in common with that which it had for the *Hasidim*. They were entranced by it because of their faith in its theurgic formulas. He, on the other hand, was for a time held spellbound by it because he hoped that it would satisfy his eager curiosity concerning the factual reality behind appearances and conventional ideas and beliefs. Needless to say, he was soon disillusioned and turned elsewhere in quest of the truth. His spiritual odyssey, which is recorded in his autobiography, gives the reader a vivid picture of the shattering effect which the impact of modernism must have had on those whose early thinking had been circumscribed by Talmudic lore.

PAULINE WENGEROFF (1833-1916)

In Pauline Wengeroff's *Memoirs*[53] we get a picture of the Jewish life of three generations of a very limited but influential number of Russian Jews, from about 1830 to 1905. It is a picture which may be summed up in the words of the author's mother. "I am certain I will live and die a Jewess, my grandchildren will not live and die as Jews. As for my children, I find it hard to guess what they will be." [54] These memoirs have a special significance from the standpoint of the transformation which took place in the life of the Jews as a result of their being Europeanized, because those memoirs were written mainly with the purpose of describing that transformation, and not merely, as in Glueckel's case, to inform her children of their antecedents.

Pauline Wengeroff was born in Bobruisk, Russia, in 1833, and spent the first eighteen years of her life there. Her story takes us to a number of widely scattered localities, most of which were within the Pale of Jewish settlement. The only two localities in which she lived outside the Pale were St. Petersburg and Helsingfors, during the reign of Alexander II. She also had her home for a time in Volhynia, where the Jews had become adherents of the Hasidic movement, and in Lithuania, where the *Haskalah* (Jewish enlightenment) movement was making itself felt. The class of Jews to which she belonged, being among the first to engage in large-scale transactions with non-Jews, were therefore among the first in Russian Jewry to break with the traditional customs and beliefs, and to lend the weight of their influence to assimilationist tendencies. Of main concern for us, however, is Pauline's description of Jewish life before the assimilationist tendencies began to assert themselves.

The *Memoirs* open with a statement about Pauline's father. "My father," she says, "would rise daily, summer and winter, at four in the morning. He took care not to walk four ells from his bed without first washing his hands. Before he tasted anything he recited devoutly the early morning prayers and then went to his workroom. Built around the walls were shelves which contained various editions of the Talmud, together with other Hebraic and Rabbinic works. . . . Into this room my father went, taking with him the candle which had been prepared by the servant. He would open up one of the volumes which lay on the desk from the previous day ready, as it were, to be reopened, and he began to study aloud in his usual sing-song. Thus the hours passed till 7:00 in the morning. He then drank his tea, and went to the synagogue for the morning prayers." [55]

That morning routine belonged to a life context which was given direction and meaning by the Torah, as interpreted by the *Tannaim* and *Amoraim*. The study of Rabbinics, the observance of the detailed precepts *(Mitzvot)* in the spirit inculcated by the Rabbis of old, filled the entire horizon of Jewish existence. Jewish solidarity was based upon the actual need for one another, due not merely to the natural interdependence of human beings, but to the religious and national unity promulgated by the Torah. Jewish communal life was culturally and spiritually self-sufficient. It had all that was necessary to satisfy the needs of the individual. In the social circle of his widely ramified family the Jew felt a sense of security. That sense of security stood him in good stead whenever a turn in the wheel of fortune deprived him of the means of self-support. The round of Sabbaths, festivals and half-holidays supplied sufficient opportunity for his leisure, enjoyment and play. Judaism was uniform, self-sufficient, and in no need of reckoning or competing with non-Jewish culture or religion.

Pauline's education as a child was limited to the elementary study of mechanical reading from the prayer book, and probably included the translation of the narrative parts of the Pentateuch. This was all the formal education a girl would receive. But with the kind of spiritually informed environment which the Jews generally succeeded in creating, despite their limited numbers and resources, text knowledge was not the principal means of inculcating loyalty to tradition. This is seen in Pauline's case. Her limited knowledge of Jewish lore did not prevent her from cherishing a sensitive and passionate love for the Jewish People and its traditions. The man she married broke with Jewish tradition, yet she struggled hard to keep her home traditionally Jewish. She really has herself in mind, when she describes the Jewish woman as "hanging on to the tradition with every fibre of her being, eager to transmit it to her child, but being rebuffed by her husband and having all her pleadings silenced with the statement that 'the children do not need religion.' " [56]

Pauline derived this devotion to Judaism from the daily life in the home of her parents which, though abounding in wealth and comfort, was as intensely Jewish as any of the poorer homes. There was then as yet no class distinction, so far as devotion to the Jewish way of life was concerned. The lullabies to which her mother or nurse would rock a baby to sleep were the same as those which could be heard in every Jewish home. Their themes were the ideals cherished by the Jewish People, such as the great merit of Torah study, its high rewards in this world and in the next, the coming of the Messiah, and the Rabbi as the source of authority in matters practical and spiritual.

These lullabies were the woman's oral tradition which directed her thinking into the groove of the Rabbinic spirit, and which expressed itself in a routine of ritual observances and prayer-recitals, and conscious obedience to Rabbinic law. The multitude of precautions pertaining to the *kashrut* of food, the proper observance of the Sabbath and festivals, or even such an out-of-the-way law as that which prohibited the introduction of flax material into woolen garments or any other objects made of wool—all these rendered the study of the Talmud an indispensable guide and inspiration for living as a Jew.

Time and again Pauline had occasion to experience in a practical way the high esteem in which the study of the Talmud was held in her surroundings. The most vivid of her recollections, in that regard, is that of the examination to which her father subjected the young man who was to be married to her, to see whether he had as much knowledge of the Talmud as the matchmaker had ascribed to him. Such knowledge constituted one of the principal qualifications which the young man had to meet if he was to be her husband.[57] More than once Pauline Wengeroff alludes to the change which had come over her husband. Though he kept up his study of the Talmud, he no longer pursued that study in the spirit of a religious duty, but of a purely cultural interest. She well knew that only when studied as a religious duty did the Talmud lead to religious observance and to the conservation of Jewish life.

SHMARYA LEVIN (1867-1935)

When we turn our attention to a section of Jewry which was comparatively untouched by the influence of modernism as recently as the eighth and ninth decades of the nineteenth century, we find the same unswerving adherence to the Talmud. The person who furnishes us with a vivid account of East European Jewry just as it was emerging from the Medieval way of life—about three quarters of a century after Western Jewry had emerged from it—is Shmarya Levin. He was born in Swislowitz, Russia in 1867.

"The years of my childhood and my early boyhood," says Levin,[58] "were passed in a narrow but consistent world, in a world entirely permeated by the traditional Jewish spirit, devoted to Jewish interests, and filled with Jewish sorrows and hopes. A tiny world which was yet big enough for me; close and confined, but within, organically independent, almost autonomous. And within that world, I moved and developed, a stranger still to violent inner conflict and revolution. The non-Jewish half of the little town took up only a small fraction of my consciousness, and had no share at all in the process of my soul. I was unaware of love and hatred toward it, it was only alien to me, and I remained indifferent." [59]

We can form a conception of the kind of world in which Shmarya Levin's childhood was spent from the kind of schooling he received, and from the pattern of ideas which gave him his mental cast, before he came into contact with the outside world. As soon as a Jewish child would reach his sixth year, and if he was bright even before that, he would be placed together with about fifteen or twenty other boys in charge of a teacher to learn to read Hebrew and to follow the *Siddur*, or order of prayers.

One of the two or three rooms which constituted the teacher's home served as classroom. There, for a period of one to two years, the teacher drilled the children in mechanical reading. The last few months were devoted to the reading and translation of the first few chapters in Genesis into Yiddish, which was the vernacular of the Jews in the Jewish Pale. The following two years, the child studied, under a different teacher, the text of the Pentateuch with Rashi's commentary, which contains in large measure Rabbinic interpretations, and was introduced to the other books of the Bible. After that, the child would be sent to a teacher of Talmud with whom he usually studied to about the age of thirteen, when he became *bar mitzvah*, that is, obligated to perform all ritual practices. As part of the *bar mitzvah* celebration of a bright lad, he was expected to deliver a casuistic address on some legal problem of the Talmud.

Only during the first year of his school life was the child permitted to have one or two hours of play in the afternoon. After that he spent in the *heder* ten hours daily during the summer, and twelve hours during the rest of the year. It is difficult for those who were brought up in a modern school, especially if they have some idea of the amount of thought which is being given to the problem of education, to conceive it possible for children to be confined in one room, for hours on end, studying the same subject day in and day out. Yet that was the way the Jewish People succeeded in transmitting its spiritual heritage from generation to generation.

The attitude of his parents toward secular education is described by Levin in the following words: "The reasons that lay behind my parents' reluctance to let me study (that is to say, to acquire a Western secular education) are instructive. There was in our family no tradition of secular study. We were a good, middle-class Jewish family, with a high tradition of Jewish education. It was not easy to overcome the inertia of generations. Furthermore, it was a well established fact that children who left Jewish homes and threw themselves into secular studies, at the high schools and universities, almost invariably became alienated. . . . In no Western country did the education of Jewish youth create so hopeless a break between the two generations. . . . A professional man—a doctor, lawyer or engineer—who still retained a sort of relationship with Jewish religious traditions was, in the Russia of the sixties and seventies, a very rare phenomenon." [60] The concentration on the Bible and the Talmud, to the exclusion of virtually any other kind of study, laid the foundation of the East European Jew's universe of thought, prior to the modern era.

The effect of so intensive an education, especially with an efficient teacher and a sensitive child, was to render the child oblivious to his actual environment and to transplant him into a mentally different world from the one in which he lived physically. "With every new chapter of the Bible learned," writes Levin, "with every new hero I came to know, with every incident that I lived through, I was drawn one step further from the soil into which I was born, and closer to the sacred soil of ancient heroes and ancient heroines. And when the books are closed and the *heder* is shut, and with my rabbi or my companions I walk homeward, I must exert myself to return to this world of reality. . . . So day by day I am drawn more deeply into this double existence—the material world of Swislowitz and the dream-world which issues from the books of the Bible." [61] Comparing this kind of an education with the classical one given to non-Jewish children in the Humanist period, Levin points out how incomparably more effective the *heder* education was in imbuing the Jewish child with a vivid appreciation of the classic age of his own People.

A Jewish educator most perceptively characterizes the traditional type of education, as it was conducted during the centuries when Jewish life was self-contained. "The method of Jewish education," writes Leibush Lehrer, "rested upon a foundation of the merging of time dimensions into a sort of dramatic immediacy, at the sacrifice of the child's developing sense of history, within the frame of Jewish experience. . . . Actually the child in the *heder* was taught not history but drama, the dramatic unfolding of a story·on a vast scale, a story which involved God, the world, His people,—all these constituting the source of his spiritual sustenance." [62]

At the age of fourteen, thanks to the Crimean War, Shmarya was brought closer to the realities of Russian life. A new world opened up before him. He discovered that he could no longer find himself at home in the mental world of his early training. He then began to look for ways of entering this new world, and he asked his father to increase his Russian lessons to two hours a day. "But even then," he writes, "the center of gravity of my education still remained with my Jewish studies. It only shifted from the Bible to the Talmud. . . . From my tenth to my fourteenth year, the Talmud was my chief study, taking up five hours daily. . . . As my mother had spoken to my heart, and my father to my mind, so now the Bible appealed to my emotions, the Talmud to my intelligence." [63]

A highly important educational influence in the life of the Jewish child was exerted by the Sabbaths, the holidays, festivals, half-festivals and fast days. They served as occasions for dramatizing the main episodes in the early history of his People. Around them were organized all the fun and the play which the child was allowed to indulge in. In the drab life of the Jews who lived in the Pale of Settlement, the preparation for Sabbaths and festival days afforded the main source of joyful activity. The child would sense that a new spirit entered his home with the cleaning, the scrubbing, the whitewashing, the baking, the cooking, and the putting on of new shoes and new clothes. The most thrilling of the festivals was, of course, Passover, for which the preparations had to be more extensive than for the other festivals, because it necessitated the thorough removal of all traces of unleavened bread. The children were given either whole or half-time off from the *heder* for the entire two weeks before Passover to help their elders usher in the festival.

Shmarya, at the age of fourteen, had already outgrown the Jewish schooling he could obtain in his native town. His parents debated what to do with him next. The father, warned by the example of his own son-in-law, who was a great scholar but "utterly at a loss in worldly matters," did not want to send his son to a *Yeshivah*, for fear that it might prevent him from becoming a successful merchant. Already we discern a taint of modernism in this calculation of the father. Not so the mother. She still cherished the traditional hope of every Jewish mother, which was to have her son become a rabbi. A compromise was arrived at. Shmarya was put under the charge of the rabbi of the local community, who guided him in the advanced study of Talmud and Codes.

As in the case of Solomon Maimon more than a century before, Shmarya Levin when still a child was troubled by religious questions and doubts which could not have been entertained in premodern times. That happened to him, despite the segregated character of Jewish life in which he had been brought up. The questions that troubled Levin were of a somewhat different nature from those that had troubled Maimon. He, too, found the story of Jacob and Esau a stumbling block, but for a different reason. The unethical conduct of Jacob annoyed him, and he had to wait till he was mature to find in non-Jewish sources a satisfying explanation.

He also records a rising spirit of revolt against the legal fiction to which Jews resort in connection with the *hametz* (unleavened bread) in their possession when Passover comes around. By going through the formality of selling the *hametz*, his father did not need to destroy the barn full of *hametz*. This formality passed young Shmarya's understanding, and together with the four questions which he asked that night at the *Seder* there arose in his mind other questions which he did not dare to express.

By the age of sixteen, though Shmarya was still confined to the narrow traditional environment of his small town, reports of what was happening to the Jews in the great outer world had already begun to reach him. Despite his mother's fond hopes for him, he confesses that neither the Talmud nor the *Yoreh Deah*, the Jewish code which he had been studying as part of the rabbinic training, any longer gave him mental satisfaction. He wanted to serve his People, but not in the capacity of the traditional rabbi. He had heard the voice of a modern Jewish prophet, Peretz Smolenskin,[64] calling upon the Jewish People to liberate itself from the age-old dispersion. The rest of his life-story belongs to one of the modern trends in Judaism.

CHAPTER TWO

The Ethnic Aspect of Traditional Judaism

ᒎ INTRODUCTION

To realize how the Torah functioned in the life of the Jewish People as an instrument of ethnicity, we must have a clear idea of the distinction between what nationhood meant to the ancient man and what it means to modern man. To modern man it means being part of a political society whose unity derives mainly from territorial proximity, a common language and culture, and a common government. To ancient man it meant being part of a kinship society whose unity derived from the consciousness of a common past, a common way of life, and a common destiny. The common way of life was always of a religious character. We shall therefore henceforth use the concept of peoplehood rather than nationhood to designate the type of ethnic relationship that bound Jews to one another, and speak of the Jews as a People in the sense of the Hebrew term *am* as used in the Bible. According to Gesenius the original meaning of that term was probably "connected, united, related."

The Jewish People seem to have achieved a more intense and permanent ethnic consciousness than any other ancient people. Of the many historical factors which contributed to the exceptional character of Jewish peoplehood, the most important is undoubtedly the rise of a line of spiritual geniuses, beginning with Moses. Their genius consisted in the capacity to incarnate in their own being the collective consciousness of their People, and to treat that capacity as granted them by God for the sake of their People.[1] Such was the genius of a Moses, a Samuel, an Elijah, a Hosea, an Amos, an Isaiah and a Jeremiah. The influence of that type of genius made itself felt in the obsessive sense of Jewish peoplehood which possessed the average Jew of pre-modern times.

Never until modern times did there exist any community, whether tribe, city-state, nation, or church, whose individuals were so preoccupied mentally with an awareness of the people to which they belonged. The entire education of the Jewish child was confined to writings which dealt with the Jewish People. The main purpose of that education was to cultivate in him a loyalty and devotion to Israel and Israel's God, and to teach him the facts he had to know and the duties he had to perform as a member of the Jewish People. The theme of Jewish education as of Jewish life was: "Hear, O Israel, the Lord our God, the Lord is one." What the Jew studied as a child he lived as an adult. The same is true of the traditional form of worship. Its obvious purpose was to have the Jew commune with God, to have him become aware of God's infinite power as creator of the world, as the author of the Torah with its teachings and laws whereby man was to fulfill the purpose of creation. That communion, however, was not in terms of an I-Thou but of a We-Thou relationship, the "We" being the Jewish People which God had chosen to make Him known to all the world. Thus it was only as a member of that People that a Jew was to experience his relationship to God. It was not the situation of the individual Jew that formed the subject-matter of the worshipful praise, thanksgiving and petition but the situation of the K'lal Yisrael, the totality of the Jewish People in time and in space. The required quorum of ten worshippers as constituting a congregation that symbolizes the totality of the Jewish People is an additional evidence of the extent to which the individual Jew merged his personal being with the collective being of his People particularly when he communed with God.

The uniqueness of the Jewish religion did not consist, as is often said, merely in providing precepts for the whole of one's daily life; all religions in the past, whether those of states or of churches, whether primitive or civilized, prescribed every detail in the daily regimen of their adherents. Jewish religion, however, was unique in raising every such detail to the level of national or ethnic significance. That significance was inherent in the Jewish tradition which fostered in the Jew an awareness of the following: 1) common ancestry, 2) the divine election of Israel, 3) the sanctity of Eretz Yisrael, 4) the divine election of the Davidic dynasty, 5) the Temple of Jerusalem as the seat of the Divine Presence, 6) the duty to cultivate a common religious culture, 7) the duty to exercise communal autonomy, and 8) faith in the Messianic redemption.

1. COMMON ANCESTRY

Traditional Judaism stressed the fact of the common ancestry of all Jews. This emphasis on their common ancestry did not necessarily imply that they were entirely free from the admixture of alien blood. In ancient times, there already existed the practice of adopting strangers and, by some legal fiction, making them members of the same blood-kinship. This shows that the sense of mutual kinship among Jews was not based entirely on an awareness of consanguinity but also on common life interests which grew out of living together over a long period of time.

The Torah tradition kept the Jews constantly in mind of such ethnic kinship. Year in and year out they read the Pentateuch, which reminded them that they were descendants of the Patriarchs Abraham, Isaac and Jacob. Whatever virtues and blessings they found in Jewish life they were wont to ascribe to *zekut avot,* "the merit of the Patriarchs." It was to their father Abraham that God had said: *"I will make thee into a great nation."* [1a] They did not regard the biblical stories as belonging to a remote past, about people with whom they had little in common. Nothing in their own contemporary world stood in the way of their identifying themselves with the world of the characters in the Bible. Nowadays such self-identification calls for deliberate educational effort on a level of mental maturity, and with the aid of modern archeological knowledge.

In the past, the Jew would recite thrice daily and four times on the Sabbath the *Amidah,* which opens with the solemn benedictions addressed to "our God and the God of our Fathers, the God of Abraham, the God of Isaac, and the God of Jacob." No matter how mechanically the Jew might have repeated these benedictions, they could not have failed to impress upon him the thought of his being descended from a great ancestry and of his belonging to the same human group as all who acknowledged that ancestry. Implicit faith in the historicity of the Pentateuchal narratives, together with the practice of referring to them daily, could not but make of the awareness of physical and spiritual descent from the Patriarchs a determining factor in the Jew's struggle for survival, a factor that conferred both an obligation and a privilege. Only in a rare moment of dark despair did R. Ishmael ben Elisha counsel national suicide when he said, "Let us not marry, nor have children; thus will the race of Abraham perish of its own accord." [2]

The traditions concerning their common past were to the Jews a sort of extension of their personal memories. They were enjoined not only to remember the exodus of their forefathers from Egypt, but to relive it as though it had happened during their own lifetime. "In every generation, a person is obliged to regard himself as though he himself had gone forth from Egypt." [3] By identifying himself with the past of his People, the Jew accepted the ancestral commitment to the covenant with God, as though he personally were a party to that covenant. *"Not with you alone do I make this covenant and this oath, but with him who is standing with us here today before the Lord our God and with him who is not here with us."* [4] What these words meant to our forebears is conveyed in the Rabbinic statement that the souls of all unborn generations of Israel were present when Israel accepted the Torah, and bound themselves to live by it.[5] When in 1172, Maimonides wrote his famous *Iggeret Teman*, the letter addressed to the Jews of Yemen, who were then in a great spiritual plight, he reminded them of the saying that a Jew who acted shamelessly (i. e., became an apostate) thereby proved that he was not a lineal descendant of the Israelites who had been vouchsafed the divine revelation of Sinai.[6]

Though the sense of kinship with his People which the Jew experienced was a spontaneous reaction to the memories of a past shared with his fellow-Jews, it was not conceived primarily as a matter of physical heredity. Rabbinic law makes provision for the admission of proselytes. According to the theory of that law, the proselyte ceased to be the child of his parents; he was regarded as having been born anew when he was adopted into the kinship of the Jewish People.[7] To such an extent was this legal fiction taken seriously that even the prohibition of incestuous marriage did not apply to a proselyte in relation to his kindred, though the Sages retained the prohibition in the case of kindred from the same mother.[8]

In keeping with this attitude toward the proselyte, the Sages consider fatherhood essentially not as a physical, but as a spiritual, relationship. One who teaches a child Torah, or brings up an orphan, or converts a heathen is as though he had begotten him.[9] Abraham is, therefore, called "the father of the multitude of nations," [10] and every proselyte is considered a descendant of Abraham.[11] Modesty, compassion and benevolence are assumed to be characteristic traits of those who are descended from Abraham. On the strength of this assertion, the opinion is expressed in the Talmud that certain wealthy but uncharitable Babylonian Jews must have been descended from the "mixed multitude" which accompanied the Israelites when they left Egypt.[12]

This sense of kinship persisted far into modern times. It was stressed by the modern scholar S. D. Luzzatto of Padua, as a means of counteracting the likely effect of the Jewish emancipation. "The fortunes of our People do not depend upon emancipation," he wrote, "but upon our love for one another and upon our being united with ties of brotherhood like children of one family. That is one advantage which we are apt to forfeit because of the emancipation." [13]

2. BELIEF IN DIVINE ELECTION

God had sent His servant Moses to redeem the Israelites from slavery, to lead them to their land, and to give them laws, and He had sent his messengers, the prophets, to anoint their kings, to exhort, to castigate and to console them. In that way God proved to the Israelites that they were His Chosen People. They were told, however, that they owed that privilege to no merit of their own but to the divine love earned by their ancestors, Abraham, Isaac and Jacob.[14] That privilege was retained by their descendants, the Jews.

Even later, when the God of Israel came to be acknowledged by other nations, the fact that only the Jews were in possession of the Torah, which was universally believed to have been dictated by God, fortified them in their belief that they were God's Chosen People. This conception which the Jews had of themselves permeates their entire written and oral tradition, and finds repeated expression in their traditional prayers. *"Blessed be our God,"* runs the text of one of these prayers, *"who created us for His glory, separated us from them who err, and gave us His Torah."* [15]

By itself, however, the belief in being chosen would not have had the unique impact which it had on the entire history of the Jewish People. Taken out of the context of monotheism, being divinely chosen was a matter of course and made no more and no less difference than having religion in general. Callimachus of Alexandria, the chief librarian of the famous Alexandrian library during the third century B.C.E., remarked, "Even the Jews call themselves the 'Chosen People.' "

For the Jews, however, the idea of being divinely chosen carried with it the assumption of being the center of world history. In the Bible the conception of world history as centering around Israel underlies the account of the creation of the world and of man. History, throughout the Bible, is God-centered, in that it is a history of God's activity and self-manifestation. It is in a sense, however, also man-centered, in that man is represented as the purpose of creation and the chief occasion for God's self-manifestation. On the other hand, of all the descendants of Adam, only Israel is considered capable of fulfilling God's purpose in having created man. *"Ye, my flock, are men"* says God of Israel, according to the Prophet Ezekiel.[16] In the Talmud and in the Midrash, the Israel-centered view of history is made strongly articulate. Israel is there declared to be not only the purpose of creation, but also the source of the world's stability.[17] Both the general prosperity and the general adversity of mankind are said to be related to the conduct and destiny of the Jewish People.[18]

The doctrine of divine election functioned most effectively as a means of keeping alive in the Jewish People the awareness of their peoplehood. It must be remembered that, for the pre-modern, God was not a vague abstraction, but a personal being. Whatever was associated with God was felt most keenly, and whatever was felt most keenly was associated with God. That Jews assumed their peoplehood to have been divinely ordained simply means that Traditional Judaism succeeded in fostering in them an ethnic consciousness which, for intensity and far-reaching consequences in their lives, was without a parallel in the life of any other people.

The divine election of ancient Israel is accepted as a historic fact both by Christianity and Islam, but is regarded by them as having been superseded by the advent of Jesus, in the one case, and by the advent of Mohammet, in the other. Thus we are told that a heretic (probably a Christian Jew), said to R. Hanina, "Now that you (Jews) are in exile, you are evidently unclean, as it is written. *'Her uncleanness is in her skirts.'* [19] How then can you still claim that the Shekinah abides with you?" "Come and see what is said of them," replied R. Hanina. "In Leviticus, we read, *'He who dwelleth among them in their uncleanness.'* [20] This implies that God abides with Israel, despite their unclean (sinful) state." [21]

The Sages allude to the Gentiles as trying to argue the Jews out of the belief that they are still God's Chosen People. "We read in Scripture: *'Many waters cannot quench love, neither can the floods drown it; if a man would give all the substance of his house for love, he would utterly be condemned.'* [22] *Many waters* refers to the nations that seek to extinguish the love which obtains between God and Israel. Likewise, *the floods* allude to the nations that strive to alienate God from Israel. But their effort will be frustrated." [23]

The following is a comment upon the verse: *"O ye sons of men, how long shall My glory be put to shame, in that ye love vanity, and seek after falsehood?"* [24] "This text alludes to the Gentiles," add the Sages. "God says to them, 'Why do you delude yourselves, and assume that I have forsaken and forgotten My people, and that My Shekinah will never return to them? You are misled; because I have removed My Shekinah from My People for a while, you imagine that I intend to remain away from Israel forever.'" [25]

The Sages reacted passionately to the Gentile claim that God had repudiated the Jewish People. This is evident from the parable based on the verse: *This I recall to my mind, therefore, have I hope.*[26] "Said R. Abba bar Kahana, in the name of R. Yohanan: God, in his relation to Israel, may be compared to a king who, after marrying his queen and giving her a marriage contract in which he had promised her a great dower, departed to some distant land and remained there for a long time. Thereupon, the queen's neighbors taunted her, saying that her husband, the king, had left her and would never return. She wept and sighed. But, when she went to her room and reread her marriage contract, she was comforted; she was certain that the king would return to her. When, finally, he did return, he said to her, "My beloved, how could you have waited for me patiently all these years? She answered, 'O my royal master! If it were not for the marriage contract which you had given me, my neighbors would have been the death of me.'" [27]

In like manner, the nations of the world keep on taunting Israel and saying, "Your God has hidden His face from you, and removed His Shekinah from among you, never to return." The Jews are grief stricken. But, as soon as they enter the House of Prayer and of Study, and find that it is written, *I will turn to you, and fructify you,*[28] they are consoled. "When the redemption takes place, the Holy One, Blessed be He, will say to Israel, 'My children, I marvel how you could have waited all these years for Me.' 'O Master of the Universe!', they will reply. 'If it were not for the Torah which Thou hast given us, the nations would long ago have put an end to us with their taunts.'" [29] The more violently the nations challenged the doctrine of Israel's divine election, and the more they accompanied their challenge with threats and persecutions, the more firmly did the Jews hold on to their faith in that doctrine.

The apparent paradox of a universal God historically identified with a particular people did not escape the notice of the Rabbis. A typical Rabbinic comment calls attention to the fact that both the universality of God and His special relation to Israel are implicit in the ancient affirmation of Israel's faith in the unity of God. "We read, *"Hear, O Israel, the Lord is our God."* [30] Why does the Torah add, *The Lord is One?* Because '*The Lord is our God*' means that His name has been made to rest particularly on Israel; *The Lord is One* means that He is the God of all the inhabitants of the world." [31]

The seeming paradox is thus resolved by means of the assumption that, though God singled out the People of Israel for the knowledge of His will, whether as an act of grace or of merited privilege, He offered salvation to all men who wished to identify themselves with the People of Israel and to accept its Torah. The absence of proselyting efforts during the centuries of exile was not due to exclusiveness on the part of the Jews, but mainly to the prohibition of conversion to Judaism issued by the Church, and only secondarily to their own struggle for survival.

In the mind of the Jew, national or ethnic self-awareness expressed itself as God-consciousness. Thus the most potent motive for performing an act that would reflect honor on the Jewish People was *kiddush ha-shem*, "the sanctification of the Divine Name," and the most effective inhibition upon disgracing the Jewish People was *hillul ha-shem*, the fear of "profaning the Divine Name." The Prophet Ezekiel had taught that the honor of God's Name rendered Israel's restoration from their Babylonian captivity inevitable. Thus we read: "*When they* (the exiles from Judea) *came into the nations whither they came, they profaned My Holy Name, for it was said of them: 'These are the people of the Lord, and are gone forth out of His land. . . .' Wherefore say unto the House of Israel: Thus saith the Lord God: 'I do not do this for your sake, O House of Israel, but for My Holy Name, which ye have profaned among the nations, whither ye came. And I will sanctify My great Name, which ye have profaned among the nations.' " [32]

In the Rabbinic writings, the correlation between the prestige of God and the greatness of Israel is further elaborated. Thus runs a well-known Rabbinic statement: " '*My salvation is near to come.*' [33] . . . My salvation, not *your* salvation. Had not Scripture said so explicitly, it would be unthinkable. God says to Israel, 'If you have no merit, then I will do it for My own sake.' As it is said: *I am with him in distress*,[34] and, *Behold thy King comes to thee: He is righteous and saved.*[35] It does not say *moshia* (a Savior), but *nosha* (saved). Even if you have no good deeds to your credit, God will bring salvation, for His own sake." [36]

The greatness of Israel, however, with which God's prestige is correlated is not material but spiritual. The fear of causing *hillul ha-shem*, or committing sacrilege, would inhibit a Jew from acting dishonestly in his dealings with Gentiles. The opportunity to add to the glory of God's Name was a strong incentive to worthy behavior. The honor of the Jewish People and the glory of God thus came to be synonymous. This is how in Traditional Judaism the ethnic consciousness and the God consciousness, or religion and peoplehood, confirmed and re-enforced each other.

Throughout the past, in keeping with the prevailing religious climate of opinion, the ethnic consciousness which the individual Jew shared with his fellow-Jews could not but be viewed as religious experience. Throughout the centuries of exile, the Jewish People had no government or representative body to speak in its name. Yet that People was, in a sense, as real to the individual Jew as his own person, and, in addition, the source of his certainty concerning the existence of God and His providential care. The tradition, which was the one medium through which the Jew acquired literacy and knowledge, was preoccupied with the vicissitudes of his People and with its responsibilities. He was thus led to see the meaning of life not in the order and beauty of the external world, but in the collective experience of his People, as reflected in the episodes in its career which he never tired of recalling. Hence he could not help being conscious of God, more through history and the interplay of human affairs than through theological mysteries or philosophic speculations, as was the case with his Christian or Moslem neighbors.

No ancient people, culture or civilization possessed so vast a religio-ethnic literature, with which not merely the pundit or priest, but every individual, was expected to be familiar. The individual Jew was thus made aware of God through the medium of his People in which he had a personal stake. Nor was he allowed even for one moment to forget that involvement. As soon as he went outside the "Jewish street" and faced the scowls and jeers of the Gentiles, he realized that the prayers for redemption and the outcries against the suffering, which he had voiced in the synagogue, did not refer to other-worldly longing for salvation or fear of hell, but to this-worldly realities which he confronted daily.

The Jew did not pray or worship, or perform some rite or sacrament, as did the Christian or Moslem, merely for his own individual well-being and redemption from sin. Constantly, the theme of his worship was the well-being and redemption of his People. That was the case, not because the Jew was inherently more socially-minded, but mainly because he was made keenly aware that his own fate and fortune were inextricably bound up with those of his People.

In the light of the foregoing facts, the vast mass of the Jewish literature of prayer known as *piyyutim* and *selihot* becomes highly significant. That literature is a liturgical hymnology which is unique among the religions of mankind. The Christian layman could never identify himself with the Church, or the Moslem layman with the "Body of Believers" in Islam in any such intimate and completely absorbing fashion as did the Jew with his People. The Church as a collective unity, or divine ecclesia, figured mainly in the consciousness of the hierarchy. For the Moslem, the text of the Koran was basically a magic means of achieving his heart's desire. Except when engaged in a *Jihad*, or a holy war, there existed for the Moslem only the small world of his own clan or tribe. The same was true for the lay Christian, who needed a crusade to create in him a corporate Christian consciousness. The Jew needed no holy wars or crusades. His People was engaged in a defensive war every day of its life. In that war the only weapons were the Jew's faith in his cause and his power of endurance.

3. THE SANCTITY OF ERETZ YISRAEL

Traditional Judaism taught the Jew that Eretz Yisrael was not only his homeland, but the land which God had chosen for His People. Only there could the Jewish People achieve its destiny. Thrice daily, after every meal, and on every occasion of thanksgiving, the Jew was expected to thank God for the gift of Eretz Yisrael which had been bestowed on his ancestors, and to pray that his People be restored to it. Never did he observe a Sabbath or a festival without voicing his yearning for Israel's return to their homeland. Danton of French Revolution fame is credited with saying that a man does not take away his country's soil on the soles of his feet. The Jew, however, wherever he wandered, did carry with him the soil of Eretz Yisrael on the soles of his feet. He treasured above great wealth the handful of Eretz Yisrael earth which he owned and kept for interment with his body.

In Jewish tradition, Eretz Yisrael is the Chosen Land, in a sense similar to that in which Israel is the Chosen People. It had been promised by God to Abraham, the father of the nation, who is known in later tradition also as the discoverer and first apostle of monotheism. It was a holy land. There only was it possible for the Jew to enter into direct communion with God.[37] By virtue of that quality, Eretz Yisrael was believed to be incapable of harboring a sinful or unworthy people. Exile, in consequence of Israel's sins, is referred to as tantamount to being "vomited out" by the land. *"Ye therefore shall keep My statutes and Mine ordinances, and shall not do any of these abominations; neither the homeborn nor the stranger that sojourns with you—for all these abominations had the men of the land done, that were before you, and the land was defiled—that the land vomit not you out also, when ye defile it, as it vomited out the nation that was before you."*[38] Even when the Prophets stress the universal sovereignty of God, they associate the principal manifestation of that sovereignty with Eretz Yisrael.[39]

The conscious relationship of the Jews to Eretz Yisrael has no analogue in the relationship of any other people, ancient or modern, to its land. That is why the Jews were the only people which, in all its wanderings, sojournings, and settlements never took root in any other land. No matter how long they might have lived in a land, or how strongly entrenched they might have felt as a result of political rights and privileges extended to them, they never considered that land their permanent abode. The prayer in which they acknowledged that they were in exile because of their sins, and in which they voiced the hope of being gathered back to their land, never ceased to be part of the Jewish active consciousness.

The belief that the land on which a people dwelt was the possession of the people's god was a common one in the ancient world. But the fact that the God of Israel to whom the land belonged was the only God gave that belief a radically different significance from that which it had for the other peoples of antiquity. To use a modern analogy, *it gave to Israel's settlement in, and possession of, the land the character of a pilot experiment in developing a way of life in accordance with the will of God, and therefore one which was calculated to enable man to fulfill himself as a human person.*[40]

Numberless passages in Rabbinic literature express the belief in the sanctity of Eretz Yisrael. The following is typical: "One should always live in Eretz Yisrael, even in a town most inhabitants of which are idolators, and not live outside Eretz Yisrael, even where the majority of the inhabitants are Jews. We read in Scripture: *To give you the land of Canaan, that I may be your God.*[41] Does this mean that whoever does not live in the Land of Israel is without a god? Obviously not. The text is meant to teach that whoever lives outside of Eretz Yisrael is to be regarded as though he worshipped idols. David said: *'For they have driven me today from sharing in the inheritance of the Lord, saying: Go serve other gods.'*[42] Who ever said to David, 'Serve other gods?' That verse is therefore intended to teach that whoever lives outside Eretz Yisrael is to be regarded as one who worships idols." [43]

Another Rabbinic passage tells us that when R. Eleazer ben Shamua and R. Yohanan ha-Sandlar arrived at Sidon on their way to Nesibin, in Babylonia, to study under R. Judah ben Batira, their eyes filled with tears, and they rent their garments. They recalled the verse: *"And ye shall inherit it* (Eretz Yisrael) *and dwell in it, and take heed to do all the statutes."* [44] They inferred from that verse that to live in Eretz Yisrael was equivalent to fulfilling all the precepts of the Torah. They then gave up their purpose of leaving Eretz Yisrael.[45] Another Rabbinic saying reads: "Whoever walks four cubits in Eretz Yisrael may be assured that he is destined to have a share in the world to come." [46] This implies that the land itself is intrinsically holy.

Among the inferences Rabbinic Judaism drew from assumptions like the foregoing concerning the role of Eretz Yisrael in the life of the Jewish People are the following: The authentic observance of the *mitzvot* is possible only in Eretz Yisrael.[47] No community outside Eretz Yisrael has authentic status.[48] Maimonides, in *Yad ha-Hazakah*,[49] states: "No attention should be paid to those who live outside Eretz Yisrael, for only Jews in Eretz Yisrael can constitute a *kahal.*" In the Middle Ages the outstanding authorities who ascribed to Eretz Yisrael a holiness that is charismatic were Yehuda Hallevi and Nachmanides.[50]

In view of all this, we can understand why the Jews never became reconciled to being separated from their ancestral home. Even after centuries of living in other lands, they still regarded themselves as in temporary exile. Among the Jews, the natural sentiment of love for their ancestral land was raised to the high pitch of spiritual fervor, by reason of the place it occupied in Jewish religion. At the same time, loyalty to the religious obligations of Judaism was intensified by making the beloved land itself a symbol and instrument of the Jewish People's consecration to God and His Torah.

In the words of a medieval Jewish authority, "Eretz Yisrael is the eternal possession of the Jews. Though they are exiled from it, they are certain to return to it, for it belongs to them forever, and to no other nation." [51] This was not merely esoteric doctrine, or the fantasy of isolated visionaries; it was an *idée force* which dominated the Jewish consciousness. There being no prospect of a return to Eretz Yisrael by natural means, the Jews looked to some miraculous event to bring about their return.

In a series of solemn fasts culminating in the one on the ninth of Ab, the Jews commemorated different events connected with the destruction of the First and the Second Temple. Those who were inclined to practice supererogatory deeds of piety would rise every midnight to mourn for "the exile of the Shekinah." Most Jews, to this day, conclude the Yom Kippur service and the Passover *Seder* with the devout prayer: *Next year in Jerusalem!* The hold which Eretz Yisrael had on the Jews was demonstrated time and again, when some self-deluded visionary claimed that he was the long-awaited Messiah. He would always be sure to get a following, despite the tragic consequences in the wake of the many false Messiahs who had preceded him.

The most spectacular of these pseudo-messiahs, and one whose movement had repercussions for more than a century after his adventure, was Shabbetai Tz'vi (1626-1627). His followers, who numbered by the thousands, were to be found among the most learned and pious, as well as among the most humble, in the wealthy communities of Amsterdam and Hamburg, as well as in the most out-of-the-way villages of Carpathia. Well-to-do- Jews of Poland, Germany, and Italy left their homes and made perilous journeys to greet Shabbetai Tz'vi and to join him in his expected march to Jerusalem.

Despite the bitter disillusionment which followed the collapse of the hopes raised by Shabbetai Tz'vi, the yearning of the Jews for Eretz Yisrael became more intense than ever. From then on, all Jewish writings evince a marked impatience with the state of dispersion, and allude to the restoration of Israel to its land as no longer remote. The negotiations which Menasseh ben Israel carried on with Cromwell, and the petitions addressed by him to the English Parliament, were based on the conviction that the Messiah was certain to appear before long. What stood in the way of his advent, according to Menasseh ben Israel, was the fact that England was the one country where there were no Jews at the time, for the Messiah could not come so long as the dispersion of Jewry was incomplete, so long as there was a single nation which did not harbor any Jews.[52]

From that time on emigration to Eretz Yisrael of men and women who wanted to spend their last years there was a familiar phenomenon in the life of Diaspora Jewry. Those who remained behind had to contribute toward the maintenance of those who migrated to Eretz Yisrael, because the existing regime there did not permit the Jews to acquire land and to develop a self-sustaining economy. This interest in those who migrated to Eretz Yisrael, though philanthropic, reflected the traditional belief that the national redemption could not take place, unless the Messiah would find Jews there to acclaim him.

It would, on the other hand, be untrue to maintain that all Jews without exception regarded their situation as abnormal, or experienced a sense of exile. There were at all times a few whose material success was such as to render them so contented with their lot that they had no Messianic yearnings whatever. Yehuda Hallevi, in twelfth century Spain, complained that his contemporaries repeated prayers for return to Eretz Yisrael merely in parrot-like fashion.[53]

4. LOYALTY TO DAVIDIC DYNASTY

Among all peoples the sense of nationhood manifests itself not only as love for one's native land, but also as loyalty to one's government. When sovereignty is vested in hereditary rule, loyalty to the person of the king and to his dynasty is an expression of love for one's people. The Jews were no exception. But with them, loyalty to a royal dynasty was raised to a new level of spiritual significance, because that dynasty was regarded as having been divinely ordained.

No one who reads the historical books of the Bible can fail to be impressed by the idealization which the character of David undergoes at the hands of their authors. The critical reader may see in David a courageous tribal chieftain who succeeded eventually in uniting all the tribes of Israel under his rule and in extending their territory. But tradition invests David with additional qualities of a high order. He is primarily the zealous servant of YHWH. He dances with joy before the Ark of YHWH when he brings it to Jerusalem, the new capital of his kingdom. He is a friend of prophets. He submits to the rebuke for his sins by the Prophet Nathan in the spirit of an humble penitent. He is the *sweet singer of Israel*, glorifying God in psalmody.[54] In reward for his piety, God promises him that *"There shall not fail thee a man in My sight on the throne of Israel, if only thy children take heed to their way, to walk before me as thou hast walked before me."*[55]

In the later history of the Kingdom, a prophet might question the legitimacy of the ruling house,[56] but he would never impugn the Davidic dynasty.[57] Though he felt that kings were failures as leaders,[58] he nevertheless pictured the ideal state as headed by a descendant of David, who would rule, like David, in accordance with the will of God.[59]

When the Kingdom of Judah was destroyed by Babylon, the loss of the monarchy, with which the memories of Israel's past glory and the hopes of its future were associated, was as much occasion for lamentation as the loss of the land or Temple. The captured king is described as *"the very breath of our lives, the anointed of the Lord . . . . of whom we said, 'Under his shadow we shall live among the nations.'"* [60] When the Jews returned from captivity, they expected to re-establish the monarchy under Zerubbabel, but they were doomed to disappointment.

Nevertheless, loyalty to the dynasty of David was so strong and had developed such sacred associations through the teachings of the Prophets that, during the entire era of the Second Commonwealth, the actual governments were regarded as in a sense provisional, until such time as God would reinstate the Davidic rule in the person of the Messiah.[61] The unpopularity of the later

Hasmoneans and of the Herodian dynasty only intensified the hope that the Davidic dynasty would be reinstated through some divine manifestation.

When the Second Jewish Commonwealth was destroyed, the scattered communities of the Jewish People were certainly not inclined to transfer their supreme loyalty to the governments under which they lived in dispersion. *Fealty to the expected Messiah who was to be none other than a descendant of David continued to function as a bond of national unity.* There were few centuries in the history of the Jews after the destruction of the Second Commonwealth when the faith in the coming of the Son of Jesse did not. flare up in some parts of the Diaspora into a Messianic movement which generally ended in tragic disillusionment.

By the same token that the belief in the re-establishment of the Davidic dynasty intensified national loyalty, it also served as a means of keeping alive the belief in the ultimate establishment of God's Kingdom, to which all nations would render fealty. David Ben Gurion, the Prime Minister of Israel, was entirely correct when he said that, "The State of Israel arose by virtue of the Messianic vision that lived within our People through the generations." [62]

5. THE TEMPLE AS INSTRUMENT OF PEOPLEHOOD CONSECRATED TO GOD

Like the Land of Israel and the Davidic dynasty, the Temple, too, with its priesthood and the sacrificial cult, has to be viewed in the light of the unique interaction in Traditional Judaism between the God-consciousness and the ethnic-consciousness of the Jews. Originally, the Temple in Jerusalem achieved its holiness, which excelled that of other sanctuaries, by reason of its association with the Davidic dynasty. This is evident from the prayers which the author of the Book of Kings ascribes to King Solomon on the occasion when the first Temple was dedicated.[63]

The site of the Temple originally possessed no greater sanctity than the sites of the other local sanctuaries where the God of Israel was worshipped. But it acquired added prestige from the role played in its selection by David,[64] and it, in turn, conferred prestige on his dynasty. When Jeroboam led the secession of the Ten Tribes of Israel, he found it expedient to glorify the sanctuaries at Beth El and Dan, which had been sacred sites from of old. During the entire period of the divided kingdom, the prestige of the Temple of Jerusalem hardly exceeded that of the other sanctuaries. But, with the destruction of the Northern Kingdom, the Temple in Jerusalem, having no rival, became the symbol both of the unity of God and of the unity of the nation. During the reigns of Hezekiah and Josiah, the effort to centralize all sacrificial worship in the Temple at Jerusalem was accompanied by the attempt to abolish all idolatrous rites.

Thus the Temple of Jerusalem became the visible symbol of the One God to whom Israel, as a united nation, owed exclusive allegiance. It was the Palace of the Invisible and Divine King of Israel, in whose name and by whose authority the human kings held sway. It was, therefore, as much a national as a religious shrine. In it, all important public assemblies took place. There the supreme court of justice met. In the open precincts surrounding it, the Prophets would frequently address the people. When the armies of Sennacherib besieged Jerusalem, and every circumstance pointed to the destruction of the city, the Prophet Isaiah was certain that the city would be spared, because it was the capital of God's Kingdom, from which God ruled the world. Its destruction would inevitably be construed as not only Israel's defeat, but as the defeat of Israel's God.[65]

Despite the impending destruction of the Kingdom of Judah by the Babylonian army, the Prophet Jeremiah could not make the Jews realize that the City of Jerusalem and its Temple were doomed. They regarded his warning as sacrilege, for they had been accustomed to think that Jerusalem, being the dwelling place of YHWH's Presence, could not but be invulnerable.[66] Only the immunity which a prophet enjoyed saved Jeremiah from being slain for his insistence that the national sanctuary would be destroyed.

When his dire prophecy was fulfilled, the people were at first stunned. The destruction of the Temple seemed to have cut them off from communion with God. They could not offer sacrifices to God elsewhere, and any other form of worship was deemed ineffective. *"How shall we sing the Lord's song in a foreign land?"* [67]

one of the Temple psalmists complained. The Prophet Ezekiel made it his task to exorcise this feeling of being forsaken by God. He not only predicted the return to Jerusalem and the rebuilding of the Temple, but also described in detail the sacrificial cult which would be instituted in the rebuilt sanctuary.

The vision of Ezekiel was, in essence, fulfilled in the Second Commonwealth. That Commonwealth was a theocracy, in that the High Priest who officiated in the Temple was also the head of the state. Even under the Hasmonean and Herodian rulers, although the priesthood had lost much of its prestige, the Temple continued to be the center of the political as well as of the religious life of the Jews. All important public functions were conducted within the Temple precincts. There, in the "chamber of Hewn Stone," the Sanhedrin held its sessions. It is noteworthy that, although the Synagogue provided for the ritual expression of Jewish religion wherever Jews might reside, it did not replace the Temple. The Temple became the *national* institution *par excellence.* In the Jewish mind, the concepts "one People," "one Temple," and "one God" came to be mutually related as part of one spiritual pattern.

Although the Jews of that time regarded God as governing the world not from the Temple in Jerusalem, but from somewhere in heaven, they still felt that Jerusalem, the Holy City in which the Temple stood, was directly beneath the heavenly Jerusalem from which God ruled the world. Another Rabbinic saying expresses the thought that the Temple was the very center of the world and its foundation: "The Land of Israel is the navel of the earth because it is the earth's central land. Jerusalem is the center of the Land of Israel. The sanctuary precincts are in the center of Jerusalem, the Temple is in the center of the sanctuary precincts; and the Ark is in the center of the Temple. In front of the Temple is the 'Foundation Stone,' 'which is called by that name because that is where the world had its foundation." [69]

When the Temple was destroyed, Yohanan ben Zakkai found it difficult to establish the authority of the new *Bet-din ha-Gadol* (Supreme Court) on which the continuity of Jewish national life depended. A court that met outside the Temple could not be considered as divinely inspired in its decisions, and hence lacked authority. It was with the utmost difficulty that the Jews, under his guidance, finally adjusted themselves to the loss of the Temple. That loss had left them with the same feeling of being exiled from God's Presence that their forefathers had experienced when the First Temple was destroyed. Ben Zakkai, however, succeeded in imbuing them with the hope that the Temple, as they remembered it, would soon be restored. Since that time, prayers for its restoration have been included in the daily worship of the Synagogue. In most synagogues even to this day, these prayers are an essential part of the daily ritual. The traditionally-minded Jew, devoted though he was to the synagogue, never felt that it had the same sanctity as the Temple, because only the Temple could serve as a symbol of the will of the entire nation to serve God.

The Jews have, therefore, always associated the end of their exile and their eventual restoration to Eretz Yisrael not only with the advent of a Davidic Messiah, but also with the restoration of the Temple together with the priesthood and the sacrificial cult. Hence, worship in the synagogue was rendered as reminiscent as possible of the sacrificial worship in the Temple.[70] The statement in the Talmud that the three-fold system of daily prayers is intended to correspond to the sacrificial system, though not literally true, indicates how eager the Sages were to make it correspond. The "Eighteen Benedictions" of the weekly *Amidah*, the most important series of prayers, are said to correspond to the eighteen times that the expression *"as the Lord had commanded Moses"* is repeated in the account of the sanctuary in the Wilderness.[71]

The "additional service" (*Musaf*) on Sabbaths and festivals was no doubt instituted for the purpose of keeping alive the remembrance of the Temple and the yearning for its restoration. Passages from the Mishnah, dealing with the daily sacrifices were incorporated into the daily prayer book, and petitions for the restoration of the sacrificial cult recur throughout the liturgy. Thus, the synagogue came to be not merely a place where the individual Jew communed with the God of the world for the salvation of his individual soul. It was essentially intended as a means of having the individual Jew merge with the rest of the Jewish People in a spirit of communion with God and dedication to His Torah.

The method of substitution frequently employed in cults was also prevalent among the Jews, especially in the matter of the sacrificial cult and the Temple. Throughout the Diaspora, during the centuries preceding the modern turning point in Judaism, the portions of the Torah which deal with the building of the Tabernacle were read for the purpose of having the Jews live through, in imagination, the actual process of its construction. Likewise those laws which deal with the sacrificial rites were read on Sabbaths, New Moons and festivals as a surrogate for the performance of those rites. R. Eleazar, in a play on the word *mizbe'ah*, teaches that the sacrificial altar had manifold potency. It removed God's evil decrees, it caused fertility, it rendered Israel beloved, and it wiped out Israel's sins.[72] The continuance of the traditional division of Jews into the castes of *Kohanim*, *Leviim* and *Yisraelim* has helped to keep alive the memory of the Temple and its sacrificial cult.

The dominance of Temple worship as a motif is further strikingly illustrated in the case of the Passover *Seder* service. That entire service is so arranged as to recapture as far as possible the actual regimen and spirit of the Paschal sacrifice in Jerusalem while the Temple was still in existence. The various symbols of the *Seder* point to that sacrificial rite, and the recitation of the *Hallel* is intended as a reminder of the actual psalm-singing which accompanied that rite. Accordingly, the concluding prayers of the Seder service reads: "As we have been privileged to observe the order of the Pesah Seder rite with all its laws and prescriptions, may we again be privileged to observe the actual sacrificial rites of the Pesah."

6. A COMMON RELIGIOUS CULTURE

The Jews, during the centuries of their dispersion, were faced with the problem of having to acquire the various languages of the countries in which they sojourned, while retaining Hebrew as their own ethnic language. They solved that problem by using the vernacular of the country for every-day purposes, and retaining the Hebrew for their cultural and spiritual interests. The Hebrew language served as a medium of religious self-expression. It was also the principal medium of all important documents, and of the large literature of legal *responsa*. It was, in addition, the means of communication between the different Jewish communities. The decisions of the Jewish courts in Poland prior to the dissolution of the "Council of the Four Lands" were written in Hebrew.[73]

There were periods, however, when Hebrew came to be fashionable. "At that time," complains Shmarya Levin, referring to the sixties and seventies of the nineteenth century Russia, "the Hebrew language played a much more important role in the daily life of the Jew than it does today. All Jewish shopkeepers kept their accounts in Hebrew. Jewish merchants corresponded in Hebrew, and, among the latter classes, bride and bridegroom exchanged notes in the same language. If they could not write in Hebrew, they could have their love letters written for them by their teachers or by special scribners." [74]

But most important of all, Hebrew was the language which every Jewish boy was expected to learn to understand, to some extent at least, as a prerequisite to literacy and to social recognition. Every Jew was expected to make daily use of it as part of his life as a Jew. To be ignorant of Hebrew was to be regarded as a boor (am-ha-aretz). Though Hebrew was limited in its uses, those uses were common to everyone. It, therefore, cannot be compared to Latin, which, during the Middle Ages, was in Christian Europe the language only of the learned, particularly the clergy.

Because Hebrew was the medium of the Jewish religious regimen, which extended to every phase of life and which penetrated into the furthest recesses of the Jewish consciousness, it succeeded in keeping alive the sense of peoplehood among Jews throughout the world. Herder wrote: "Has a people anything dearer than the speech of its fathers? In its speech resides its whole thought domain, its traditions, history, religion and basis of life, all its heart and soul. To deprive a people of its speech is to deprive it of its one eternal good." [75] "Language," adds Carlton Hayes, "is probably the chief factor in forming and sustaining a nationality. Uniformity of language tends to produce like-mindedness, to provide an inclusive set of ideas as well as of words, and like-minded persons tend to develop group consciousness, to experience a sense of common interest, to constitute a tribe or nationality." [76]

Along with language there was a number of customs, some of which were part of the legal aspect of Judaism, while others re-

tained their character as folkways, without thereby being deemed
less obligatory. An outstanding instance of obligatory customs was
the Jewish calendar. Before it became fixed, the naming of the new
month was jealously guarded as the prerogative of the academies in
Eretz Yisrael, as a means of preserving Jewish ethnic unity and
the spiritual hegemony of Eretz Yisrael Jewry. So long as traditional
Judaism functioned, the Jewish calendar was the only one used by
the Jews in their daily life.[77] The time of the day would be designated in ordinary parlance by its relation to the morning, afternoon or evening prayer, and the time of the year by its relation to
the various festivals.

The customs which were most effective in keeping Jews aware
of their peoplehood were the inhibitions which had religious
sanctions. Many practices which Jews deliberately avoided were
in themselves not contrary to traditional law, but were forbidden
because they were known to be characteristically Gentile. There
were times when even the adoption of Gentile names, the
wearing of a non-Jewish style of dress and manner of coiffure were
regarded as improper. Pauline Wengeroff has a great deal to say
in her *Memoirs* about the consternation which the decree of Czar
Nicholas I issued in 1845 ordering Jews to westernize their dress
threw into the life of Polish-Russian Jewry.[78]

If a particular language is the *form* of self-expression by which
a people becomes aware of itself as distinct from other peoples,
culture furnishes the *content* of that self-expression. The culture
which articulates the individuality of a people is the entire manifold of religious and ethical teaching, social expectation, legal
maxims and esthetic creations which reflect its experiences and its
values. The most noted modern Jewish historians at first wrote
Jewish history as though it were essentially a history of a national
literature or of a national culture. The element of truth in this
conception of Jewish history is that, for the Jews more than for any
other people. literature and culture played a highly important role
in maintaining and articulating their peoplehood.

As a rule, no people deliberately plans its culture. An ethnic
culture evolves spontaneously. Those who possess a gift for articulating any of the cultural values do not require official stimulation.
If their contribution happens to answer the generally felt need for
self-expression, it becomes part of the cultural capital of the peo-

ple. It is transmitted from generation to generation, and is regarded as a means of imbuing both the child and the adult with the collective consciousness of the people.

With the Jews, however, whatever cultural expression answered their collective needs came to be viewed as something more than the wisdom or insight of those who uttered it. The original creators of its culture, its lawgivers, priests, prophets and sages were convinced that they were merely the instruments for transmitting wisdom and inspiration beyond the power of man to originate. They, therefore, ascribed to God whatever they contributed to the enrichment of their people's life. Even when they sang of the glory of God, or prayed to Him, they were certain that they did so under the impact of divine afflatus. This is why with the early Israelites, as with all ancient peoples, the spontaneous generation of culture was interpreted as divine revelation.

In course of time, whatever survived of those ancient revelations of the spirit came to be canonized, that is, accepted as permanently authoritative and binding upon the entire people. For many centuries thereafter, whatever anyone added to the sum of the cultural values, in line with those which had been thus canonized, also received the stamp of authority. Such was the case with the two Talmuds, i.e., the Mishnah, together with the two collections of the discussions and applications based on it, the Palestinian and the Babylonian, the large collections of *Midrashim*, both Halakic and Aggadic, the commentaries thereon, and the vast mass of *Responsa* which were based on them. This deliberate nationalization of the products of the Jewish spirit is reflected in the saying, "Whatever teaching any devoted disciple of the Torah evolves is part of what was originally revealed at Sinai." [79]

That ancient method of signalizing a nation's attitude toward what expressed its innermost self points to the fact that cultural content did more than imbue the Jewish People with an ethnic consciousness. It individuated that consciousness. *It also rendered their common culture operative by placing a premium upon the study of it.* The Bible and the Talmud, with their commentaries, were enough to supply the young Jew with subject matter for years of study. Those studies gave him literacy and sharpened his intellectual powers. A fact seldom noted about the Talmud is that its *method* has done as much for the intellectual life of Jewry as its *content* has for the social and spiritual aspects of that life. Its method is that of argument and reasoning, and calls for the exercise of a high degree of intellectual acumen. The mere task of following an argument through labyrinthine windings of reasoning taxes the mental grasp of the most keen-minded. There is constant call for noting differences and resemblances. The purpose was less to arrive at a conclusion than to tarry over the steps in the argument.

The education of the child was compulsory. *"And thou shalt teach them diligently to thy children."* [80] Either the father himself had to teach his children, or he had to get a teacher for them. The poor as well as the rich had to be trained in the knowledge of Torah. "Take heed of the children of the poor, for from them will come forth Torah." [81] A Jewish scholar was duty-bound to teach. [82] The process of transmitting the national culture to each succeeding generation was not left to the initiative of the individual parent, but was treated as an imperative duty of the community.[83]

Maimonides, in his Code,[84] brings together the educational rules from the Talmud, among which are the following: "Teachers must be appointed in every province, district and town. Any town which has no children at school should be excommunicated. At the age of six, every child must be introduced to formal study. No more than 25 children should be entrusted to a teacher. If he has more than 25, and less than 40, he should be given an assistant. If there are more than 40, an additional teacher must be provided." Provision was made in every community for the collection of a special tax for the maintenance of schools for the children of the poor. Where only two or three Jewish families lived in an outlying district, the teacher had to be engaged cooperatively.

An interesting document which has come down from the thirteenth century Jewry of France gives an educational plan known as *Hukē ha-Torah*. It is modeled very much after the educational procedure of the Church of that period, with its three types of school— the cathedral schools, the parochial schools, and the elementary schools. The influence of the Church went so far as to lead to the suggestion of training *perushim*, almost a Jewish replica of the Catholic priests. The training was to last seven years. Every family was to have one of its sons become a *parush*.[85]

How organic a part of Jewish life educational activity was, prior to the beginning of the modern era in Judaism, may be inferred from the fact that every community in Poland of any standing had a *Yeshivah*, which was a school for advanced studies of the Talmud and commentaries. The community would provide board and lodging for both local and out-of-town students. The rule was that a community of 50 householders had to support a minimum of 30 students. There was scarcely a home in Polish Jewry that did not have at least one who was learned in the law. Out of 50 house-holders, 20 had the title either of *morenu*, or of *haber*, the equiv-alent of a master's and a bachelor's degree respectively. As late as 1792, when the Berlin Jewish community found itself heavily in debt, it passed an ordinance that it would support no more than 40 young men engaged in study of Rabbinic lore.[86] The practice of having the rabbi of the town, who was expert in expounding Talmudic lore, conduct a *Yeshivah* was current throughout Eastern Europe until the beginning of the twentieth century.

The maintenance of the students was shared by all those who could afford it, and was regarded as a great privilege. Nevertheless, many a student suffered want. If he persisted in his studies, it was because he was reminded in the *Mishnah* that, "This is the method of acquiring the knowledge of Torah: Eat bread with salt and sleep on the floor." [87] Isaac Hirsch Weiss, the author of the classic work *Dor Dor V'dorshov*, records in his autobiography his wan-derings from one town to another, and makes mention of a large scale exodus from one of these *Yeshivot*, because of the discontent which had arisen among the more advanced students on account of the poor treatment accorded them.[88] Similar incidents are known to have occurred in the Medieval Christian universities.

The study of Torah was not undertaken, as in our day, mainly for the purpose of qualifying for the field of Jewish scholarship or for the rabbinate. Whatever personal ambition it may have ful-filled, it was never devoid of the religious purpose of performing the first of the three cardinal duties as a Jew.[89] This zealous pursuit of study gave the Jews during the pre-modern centuries a sense of cultural superiority over the non-Jews among whom they lived, and counteracted whatever sense of inferiority the Jews, as a per-secuted minority group, might have experienced. Class for class, the Jews were more literate than their neighbors. Every Jew, virtually without exception, was able to read, and, in the main, to understand, the contents of the prayer book and the Pentateuch, the Psalms and certain sections from the Prophetic books. The more well-to-do among the Jews excelled by far their peers among the non-Jews in ability to comprehend ideas of an abstract character. The rabbis were, as a rule, both intellectually and morally superior to the Christian clergy. They contributed to the morale of the Jews and enabled them to endure the oppression and persecution which were their lot in life.[90]

7. AUTONOMY BASED ON A COMMON CODE OF LAW

"Like the other corporations," wrote Salo Baron, "the Jewish community enjoyed full internal autonomy. Isolated and alien, it was left severely alone by the state. Thus the Jewish community of pre-Revolutionary days had more authority over its members than the modern Federal, State and municipal government combined. Education, administration of justice between Jew and Jew, taxation for communal and State purposes, health, the control of markets, public order, were all within jurisdiction of the community-corporation. In addition the Jewish community was the fountain-head of social activity, which was of a quality on the whole superior to that carried on by the non-Jews. The Jewish self-governing bodies issued special regulations and enforced them through their own officials. Communal statutes were re-enforced by religious, supernatural sanctions as well as by public opinion. For example, a Jew who was excommunicated by a Jewish court was a lost man. Excommunication was a fairly common means of imposing the will of the community on the individual. All this self-governing apparatus, however, disappeared, when the Revolution brought equal rights to European Jewry." [91]

The toleration of Jewish autonomy was not due to the recognition of minority or group rights. It was motivated by the material benefit which the local authorities, whether king, prince or bishop, expected to derive from Jewish self-government. Such self-government exempted those authorities from the need of providing special machinery for collecting taxes from the Jews, since the responsibility for the payment of those taxes devolved upon the Jewish communal leaders. Nevertheless, *the effect which Jewish self-government had in keeping Judaism alive is incalculable.* But what rendered such self-government not only possible but beneficent was the traditional code of law to which the Jews adhered with unsurpassed fidelity.

Throughout the centuries between the fall of their Second Commonwealth and the French Revolution, the Jews constituted a nomocracy, that is, a society held together and governed by laws which were enforced without the aid of a central government. *The sense of common peoplehood among the scattered Jewish communities survived because of the effective system of decentralized self-government which the Jews had evolved.* The particular function which a central government performs in the life of a nation was, in the case of the Jews, fulfilled by an autonomous legal system that was capable of being enforced wherever there was a quorum of ten Jews. That code laid down the procedure for collective self-discipline, thereby making possible the decentralized form of self-government which the Jews maintained throughout the centuries of enforced dispersion. The Jews possessed an adequate instrument of peoplehood in their autonomous system of civil and marriage laws. These laws provided the means of social control in the area of economic and sex relationships, where conflicts of interest were apt to wreak havoc.

To evaluate properly the significance of a common legal code for Jewish survival, we have to bear in mind that the Rabbis of old succeeded in formulating a code which fulfilled the following functions:

1) It provided the scattered communities of the Jewish people with a sense of unity and solidarity.

2) It called for the leadership of those who were expert in the knowledge and application of Jewish law, and who were authorized to use sanctions as means of enforcing their decisions.

3) It led to the establishment of courts of law which, being sufficiently flexible in structure, were able to adjust themselves to the various contingencies in the life of the Jewish People.

4) It helped to foster a conscious ethnic will which deprecated resort to non-Jewish courts as treason and sacrilege.

The Rabbis were on the alert against any tendency that might have led the Jews to avail themselves of the code law or of the common law by which their neighbors had their litigation adjudicated. In the second century (C.E.), R. Tarfon laid down the principle that Jews were not permitted to litigate in non-Jewish courts, even though those courts rendered decisions according to Jewish law.[92] That principle was stringently enforced down to modern times. When Jews in thirteenth century Spain showed a tendency to defy that law, Solomon Adret (Rashba) complained bitterly. "Of what use would the most holy writings then be to us, the Mishnah compiled by R. Judah, and after him the Talmud compiled by Rav Ashi and Ravina? Would Jews teach their children the laws of the Gentiles and build themselves altars of the uncleanness of the heathen? Far be it! It shall never be thus in Israel! Shall the Torah gird itself in sackcloth?" [93]

"Any Jew," wrote Bachya ben Asher, toward the end of the thirteenth century, "who resorts to a civil court, thus evidencing greater esteem for secular than for divine law, is guilty of profaning God's name. . . . For a Jew to refuse to submit to the legal decisions of the Torah and choose to abide instead by the verdict of alien courts, is to proclaim his abandonment of the belief in its divine authority." [94] On the other hand, the highest approval is accorded to those who function as judges: "When three sit and judge, the Shekinah is in their midst." [95] That this norm survived until recently is borne out by the following: "The practice of appealing to the Russian courts for the settlement of cases between Jews," writes Shmarya Levin, "did not exist in those days (in the 70's of the last century). The appeal was made instead to the Torah, to Jewish law, as interpreted by the Rav of the town." [96]

Due to the existence of Jewish self-government, the poorest was never without an opportunity for legal redress. This was made possible through a practice known as "the interruption of the Torah reading" during the Sabbath services in the synagogue. Any Jew, no matter what his station in life, who felt himself aggrieved could go to the synagogue and hold up the services, until he was promised that his grievances would be looked into. That practice is described by Shmarya Levin as follows: "The high officials of the synagogue make ready to bring out of the Ark the scroll of the Torah . . . . and suddenly a Jew appears in the pulpit where the scroll is to be laid down, delivers a resounding blow and cries out 'I forbid the reading.' The effect is electrical. First there is a gasp of astonishment; then a mutter of angry voices . . . . and then silence. The Jew in the pulpit waits, and when the silence is complete, he voices his complaint. He knows that he is secure. He is exercising an ancient privilege which it would be blasphemy to challenge." [97]

Thus did the commonly accepted code of law serve as the basis of Jewish peoplehood during the many centuries after the destruction of the Second Commonwealth. "Since the time," says Solomon Maimon, "when the Jews lost their own national position and were dispersed among the nations . . . . they have had no national form of government but their religious constitution, by which they are held together and still form in spite of their political dispersion an organic whole. Their leaders, therefore, have allowed themselves to be occupied with nothing so much as with imparting additional strength to this, the only bond of union by which Jews still constitute a nation." [98]

As an instrument of peoplehood, the legal code based on the Written and Oral Torah functioned in the double capacity of fostering culture and maintaining social order. This twofold function gave rise to the two main social institutions in Jewish life, the court and the academy. The rabbi, throughout the period of Traditional Judaism, likewise served in the twofold capacity of head of academy and judge in the civil court, enabling the academy and the court of justice to be mutually complementary. The Talmud itself is the product of this unique correlation of the theory and the practice of law.

Not long after the final redaction of the Talmud there arose the need for applying and organizing its laws. This led to the development of a vast legalistic literature consisting of legal *responsa*, of which there are about 1300 volumes, and codes of different types, ranging from monographs dealing with one or more branches of the law to all-inclusive compendia.

The Babylonian Talmud which received its final redaction about the end of the fifth or beginning of the sixth century C.E. was accepted by the Jews as the authoritative guide to Jewish belief and conduct. The principal codes which served Jewish life during the Middle Ages down to our own day were the *Yad ha-Hazakah* by Maimonides (1135-1204), the Semag (*Sefer Mitzvot Gadol*) by R. Moses ben Jacob of Coucy (circa 1250), the *Turim* by R. Jacob ben Asher (about 1269-1340), and the *Shulhan Aruk* by R. Joseph Karo (1488-1575). Of these the *Shulhan Aruk* was the most influential in molding the life of the Jews along traditional lines. The more recent codes not only facilitate the finding of the particular laws which apply to specific situations; they also indicate which opinion to follow in the case of conflicting views, and incorporate additional decisions and customs which have accumulated in the course of time.

From the standpoint of Jewish law as an instrument of Jewish peoplehood, the civil and marriage laws of the Talmud were most effective. These form the subject matter of the two orders of the Talmud known as *Nezikin* and *Nashim*. The Jewish civil law covers a wide range of problems, such as loans, property, obligations, inheritance, damages, torts, fraud and errors, assault and battery, hiring and letting, employer and employee, partnership, usury, taxation, trusts and trustees and agency. The marriage laws deal with subjects like the following: adultery, widow and *agunah* (the deserted wife or one whose husband's whereabouts are unknown), betrothal, divorce, dowry, *ketubah* (marriage contract) and seduction. The study of all this subject-matter in all of the Jewish academies produced in the Jewish consciousness an attitude of deference to the authority of the Talmud that was far more effective than any outward pressure which could be brought to bear even in a highly organized state.

Solomon Maimon in his autobiography states that it was usual in his day for a well-to-do merchant or farmer who had a daughter to make every possible effort to get a learned Talmudist as a son-in-law. It was customary for the father-in-law to make provision for maintaining his son-in-law from six to eight years, during which time the latter continued his studies. At the end of that time the son-in-law would either receive a call to the rabbinate or would continue his studies, while his wife not only attended to the affairs of the house but also ran a small store. Her reward consisted in sharing the reputation and the other-worldly bliss of her husband.[99]

In the field of human relations, those which come under the category of "family" constitute the particular object of solicitude in any national system of law. Those relationships are basic to the character and welfare of the individual and to the health and integrity of the community. The main prerogative of a people is the power it exercises in giving status to the family. The family is not merely a group that exists by virtue of the consent of those who compose it; it is a cell in the context of the ethnic organism which holds it together, and which gives it social status. In return for such status, the family submits to the laws whereby the people exercises control over its individual members in their relations to one another. In these laws are reflected some of the most significant aspects of a people's individuality. "Judaism got its lofty moral tone," says Charles A. Ellwood, "from the projection, idealization and spiritualization of the values found in the ancient Jewish family. The concepts and phraseology of Judaism can indeed be understood only through understanding the Jewish family." [100]

We can, therefore, understand why Traditional Judaism regarded the entire range of family relationships as entirely its domain, and resented violently any interference with them by non-Jewish authorities. It gave sanction to the marriage formula. The significant phrase "according to Mosaic and Jewish custom (k'dat Moshē v'Yisrael)" in that formula emphasizes that the validity of the marriage depends upon its being performed in accordance with the Jewish religio-ethnic practice. Thus did every Jewish home realize from the moment of its establishment that it owed its status and permanence to the authority of the Jewish People, which guaranteed the enforcement of the mutual obligations of its members. *It is significant that the laws dealing with the family relationships take up practically as much space in the Talmud as the rest of the civil law.*

The Jewish consciousness, in addition to being conditioned to submit to the authority of the civil and marriage laws formulated in the Talmud, was also conditioned to submit to the jurisdiction of the Jewish courts which put those laws into effect. The sanctions at the disposal of the Jewish court by means of which it could enforce its decisions consisted of "corporal punishment, outlawing by proclamation throughout the Jewish communities, complete religious ostracism by major or minor excommunication in which not only the culprit but all his family were involved, disqualification as witness, declaring one's oath as untrustworthy, and exile." [101]

The communities throughout the Diaspora had organs of self-government with legislative assemblies and courts of their own. In Eretz Yisrael, under Roman-Byzantine rule, the Jews had their Sanhedrin, their academies and their Patriarchs. In Babylonia, they had their Exilarchs, *Geonim* and legislative academies. In Spain, they had their *Al-jamas* and Congresses of Communal Delegates. In Poland and Lithuania they had their *Kahals* or communities. Their *Vaadim* were Diets consisting of *Kahal* representatives.

Thus the stateless type of peoplehood which the Jews maintained was rendered feasible through their unanimous acceptance of the Torah, both the Written and the Oral, as a divinely given ethnic code. But it was the personality of the rabbi that actually made Jewish self-government possible. That had not always been the case. In the early stages of Traditional Judaism, as it existed in Babylonia, Spain and the Mediterranean countries, the tendency had been for the "goodmen of the town" to exercise executive authority and to utilize the services of the rabbi only for judicial purposes. He was merely a functionary. Thanks to the efforts of Rashi and his successors in Franco-German Jewry, the status of the rabbi assumed far greater importance. After being appointed by the "goodmen of the town," he was vested with full executive authority.[102] That change in the status and function of the rabbi ·may have been due to the influence of the Roman Catholic Church environment.

The Rabbi of the Talmudic period, as described by Claude G. Montefiore,[103] was a type of Jewish spiritual leader whose like one may still meet in densely populated Jewish neighborhoods, where as Talmudic scholars some of them still live the sequestered form of life of the Medieval ghetto. "Here were men," says Montefiore, "who had undoubtedly a tremendous love for God and for His Law: a complete readiness to sacrifice for God and for His Law, if need be, their very lives. Yet withal, these men were by no means anxious for martyrdom. On the contrary, they wished to avoid it wherever or whenever they legitimately could. They desired, if at all possible, to live their lives in peace and quiet, studying the Law, practicing as judges the most scrupulous justice, and showing in the intervals of study and as leaders of the Jewish Communities in Babylonia or Palestine charity, kindness, and consideration to those around them."

The knowledge of the Torah carried with it the moral duty of acting in the twofold capacity of teacher and judge,[104] provided, of course, the scholar had received authorization to do so from one who himself enjoyed such authority. According to the "*Takkanot* of the Province of Moravia*,*" every community that had thirty families or more was obligated to maintain a rabbi and a *Yeshivah* in which at least a dozen young men studied Torah. As late as the first part of the nineteenth century, it was customary in many instances to include among the duties of the rabbi, which were enumerated in the contract between him and the community, that he conduct a Talmudic academy or *Yeshivah*. The function of the *Yeshivah* was not to train rabbis, but merely to familiarize those who studied there with the teachings and practices of Judaism as set forth in the Torah, both Written and Oral. The notion of utilizing the knowledge of the Torah as a means to a professional career was strongly deprecated.[105]

The regional court *(Bet Din)*, or the chief rabbi of the region, would see to it that the communities in small towns had rabbis who were duly qualified. The State, or the Church, often tried to meddle with the appointment of the rabbi. To prevent such interference, Rashbam and Rabenu Tam, during the twelfth century, together with one hundred fifty associates, passed an ordinance, confirmed by a ban, prohibiting the acceptance at the hands of non-Jewish authorities of any office empowering its incumbent to exercise coercion over his fellow-Jews.[106] Among the rights accorded to Jews in Poland during the sixteenth and seventeenth centuries, there was the stipulation that the Jews should be free to elect their rabbis. The Rhineland Government, which always treated the Jews with exceptional harshness, meddled with the office of the rabbinate by exacting a fee for confirming the right of the incumbent to exercise his office.[107]

The outstanding example of Jewish self-government, which functioned for almost two centuries, and which ceased to exist in 1764, not long before the beginning of the era of Jewish emancipation, was the "Council for the Four Lands," namely, Lesser Poland, Greater Poland, Galicia and Lithuania.[108]

On the whole, however, the autonomous organization of the Jews was entirely at the mercy of the Christian authorities. As soon as the local government realized that it could exact more taxes from the Jews by collecting directly from each individual Jew whatever taxes it imposed, it forbade the continuance of any permanent authoritative Jewish body. So long, however, as a body like "The Council for the Four Lands" functioned, the Jews interpreted even the limited measure of social autonomy which they then enjoyed as evidence of their continued existence as a nation. "The representatives of the Four Lands," says an annalist of the first half of the seventeenth century, "reminded one of the Sanhedria, which in ancient days assembled in the 'Chamber of Hewn Stones' of the Temple." [109]

8. FAITH IN THE MESSIANIC REDEMPTION

To appreciate the full significance of the belief in the advent of the Messiah, we should take note of what constituted for Jews of the pre-modern era, first, national redemption, and secondly, the cosmic significance of that redemption.[110]

a) Return to Eretz Yisrael

There is nowhere any intimation that, after the advent of the Messiah the Jews would continue to dwell outside Eretz Yisrael. Throughout the centuries of pre-modern Judaism, even under the best circumstances, dispersion was invariably considered undesirable. This at once rules out from the conception of the Messianic age any prospect of conquest or empire, since that would necessitate the residence of Jews outside their own land. There would be no need for military bases, nor occasion for an army of occupation, since that age would be one of universal peace. Moreover, Eretz Yisrael meant for the Jews much more than a national territory. They regarded it as that part of the world where God's Shekinah was manifest to a degree unequaled elsewhere.[111] Although the Shekinah was said to have accompanied the People of Israel wherever they were exiles, its power and glory suffered diminution outside Israel's land.

b) The Restoration of the Temple and the Sacrificial Cult

The whole of Eretz Yisrael was God's Chosen Land; Jerusalem was the most sacred city; and the Temple with its Holy of Holies the place of divine manifestation.[112] The rebuilding of the Temple and the reinstatement of the sacrificial cult were viewed as an indispensable part of national restoration. That belief was a survival of the universally held notion in ancient times that a tribe, a city state, or a people required a visible symbol of its deity or guardian spirit to maintain and protect it. Since the God of Israel was invisible, a kind of substitute symbol had to be used to meet that requirement. Before the Babylonian captivity, the Ark with its Cherubim served that purpose. After the return from captivity, the Temple itself became the needed symbol. Its destruction, therefore, constituted the supreme tragedy in the life of the Jewish People, and its rebuilding the supreme hope.

c) Restoration of Judicial and Legislative Authority

So important was this deemed that the prayer for it was included in the daily *Amidah*. That prayer reads as follows: *"Restore our judges as at first and our counsellors as at the beginning . . . . Blessed art Thou, O Lord, the King who lovest righteousness and justice."* [113] We realize the full significance of that prayer when we recall the prophecy of Isaiah: *I will restore your judges as at first.*[114] Isaiah regarded the just functioning of the law and of the courts as the most important expression of Israel's obedience to the Law of God. The abuses of justice by rulers and judges called forth his sharpest rebuke, and the re-establishment of conditions that made for the exercise of justice was to him one of the crowning glories of the restored nation. Thus reinstatement of judicial and administrative authority was a highly integral part of national redemption.

d) The Reinstatement of Torah

The Jews looked to national restoration as liberating them for the study of Torah and the practice of the *Mitzvot*, or divine precepts. The era of redemption was pictured as one in which the entire nation, having learned from bitter experience the consequences of having abandoned the Torah, would repent and return to it. This is implied in the prayer in the *Amidah*, which reads: *Cause us to return, O our Father, unto thy Torah; draw us nigh, O our King, unto thy service, and bring us back in perfect repentance unto Thy Presence. Blessed art Thou, O Lord, who delightest in repentance.*[115]

In keeping with this hope was the fantastic conception that the academies and synagogues which were established in Babylonia would be transferred to Eretz Yisrael.[116] This indicates how far the idea of national restoration was conceived as the complete ingathering of all Jews in Eretz Yisrael. Report of the ideal life which the restored Jewish nation would lead in Eretz Yisrael was expected to reach the other nations, so that they would come to Jerusalem to submit to the sovereignty of the God of Israel and to learn from Him how to lead a life of justice and peace.

The Cosmic Significance of the National Redemption

The national redemption was viewed as being of cosmic significance. According to that conception, the People of Israel is the principal figure in the world drama of the nations. In this drama, the People of Israel is the protagonist of the only true God, in contrast with the other nations which have broken away from His rule. In the *denouement* of this drama, the nations recognize the People of Israel as God's protagonist, thereby repudiating their own deities and accepting the authority of Israel's God. This consummation of human history was expected to come about through divine intervention. God, who created the world for His own glory, has given man considerable latitude, so that he is free to choose the manner in which he is to play his part. But if man persists in defying God's will, God has to bring him to his senses. That applies to Jews as well as non-Jews.

The Rabbinic Sages conceived the ultimate redemption of the Jewish People from exile and their restoration to Eretz Yisrael as an unquestionable certainty. It was taken for granted that the redemption would resemble the exodus from Egypt, and be accompanied by miracles which would display the power of God. According to the generally accepted view of the *Amora* Samuel, who flourished during the first half of the 3rd century (C.E.) in Babylonia, the present physical world order would continue unchanged during the era immediately following the advent of the Messiah.[117] If the People of Israel would obey God, the Messiah might appear any day,[118] but if they remained obdurate, God would send against them tyrants to afflict them, and, in their agony, they would turn to God in repentance, whereupon their redemption would follow. Commenting on the verse: *"In due time, I will hasten it*," [119] the Sages added, "If they (the Jews) will deserve it, I will hasten the redemption, but if they do not, it will come in due time." [120] All attempts, however, to foretell the specific time of its coming were severely frowned upon.[120a]

The Rabbinic tradition is mainly responsible for the attitude of passive waiting for the Messianic redemption. In the verse in Canticles: "I *adjure you, O daughter of Jerusalem, not to arouse not to stir up love till it please*," [121] various *Tannaim* and *Amoraim* find a basis for what they regard as an oath by which God had bound the People of Israel to refrain from rebelling against their Gentile rulers, and from migrating en masse from the lands in which they dwell.[122]

The foregoing attitude made it possible for a conquered and dispersed people like the Jews not only to survive, but to maintain its unity and retain its confidence in the ultimate fulfillment of its Messianic hope. There can be no doubt that the attitude of passive waiting had a survival value in the pre-modern world, though it has lost that value in the modern world. That attitude was a variation of the well-known saying: "He that fights and runs away/May turn and fight another day/But he that is in battle slain/Will never rise to fight again."

The certainty that the Jews would ultimately be restored to their ancestral home derived also from the assumption that the prestige of Israel's God demanded it. This thought long antedated the Rabbinic ideas concerning the redemption. It pervades many of the Prophetic writings, particularly the Book of Ezekiel. *Due to the fact that the monotheism of the Jews was not part of a philosophical, but of a historical pattern of thought, the very idea of godhood implied that God was the sovereign and protector of His people. Whatever fortune befell God's People was considered an index of the extent to which God's glory was manifest in the world. That idea was never outlived in Traditional Judaism.*

The foregoing correlation between God and the People of Israel takes the chauvinistic sting out of the traditional expectation that the People of Israel would exercise spiritual hegemony over the other peoples of the world.[123] The expected hegemony of Israel was conceived entirely in spiritual terms, as a manifestation of God's power and a source of blessing to the world. It meant that mankind was ultimately to be rid of the worship of false gods, including deified potentates. That could take place only with the downfall of "the kingdom of arrogance," which, to the Sages of the Talmud, always meant the Empire of Rome.

The apocalypse in the book of Daniel served as the pattern of world history, which was destined to terminate with the establishment of God's Kingdom on the ruins of the four world kingdoms. It was assumed that those kingdoms defied the will of God and therefore spelled *hubris* or presumption against God. God's Kingdom, however, would be represented by the People of Israel, as described in the book of Daniel: "*And the Kingdom and the Dominion, and the greatness of the kingdoms under the whole of heaven shall be given to the people of the saints of the Most High; their Kingdom is an everlasting Kingdom, and all dominions shall serve and obey them.*" [124]

During the Rabbinic period, the foregoing passage in the Book of Daniel became the basis of the Rabbinic interpretation of history.[125] According to that interpretation, four human kingdoms are destined to arise, one after the other, before the establishment of the Kingdom of God. The last and most powerful of those kingdoms was Rome, whose heavy hand on the Jewish People almost crushed it body and soul. Why, indeed, does God permit the hegemony of Rome to endure so long? Why does He not redeem Israel from servitude to Rome, even though that servitude prevents His own sovereignty from being recognized? The Sages suggested various answers, which fall into two categories: One was that Rome was living off the merit of the blessing which the Patriarch Isaac had bestowed on Esau, the alleged ancestor of the Roman People. The other was that the Jewish People was still unworthy of the redemption.[126]

The latter answer has been by far the more popular and authoritative. That derives from the belief throughout the Rabbinic tradition that the dispersion of the Jews was a state of exile and, as such, a punishment for their sins past and present. "*And because of our sins are we exiled from our land*" [127] is one of the chief refrains in the traditional liturgy. Consequently the principal means of redemption from exile is recourse to repentance. "Great is (the power of) repentance, for it can bring about the redemption." [128]

A clear statement of the cosmic significance assigned to the national redemption of Israel is contained in the prayer ascribed to the *Amora* Rav, a contemporary of Samuel. That prayer is recited at the end of every worship service thrice daily, according to the traditional ritual. It reads thus: *"We therefore hope in thee, O Lord our God, that we may speedily behold the glory of thy might when thou wilt remove the abominations from the earth and the idols will be utterly cut off, when the world will be perfected under the Kingdom of the Almighty and all children of flesh will call on thy name."* [129]

How was it possible for the Jews to cherish the hope of national redemption at times when every circumstance pointed to what should ordinarily have produced national despair? That hope was never dimmed, because it was accompanied by a saving formula, whereby it managed to outlive the worst disasters that befell the Jews. That formula was: *hevlo shel mashiah,* "the travail of the Messiah." [130] It is based on the idea that "labor pains" are part of the birth of a new era, and on biblical texts which represent Mother Zion as a woman in travail, as she is about to give birth to the Redeemer. [131] Moreover, the Book of Daniel, which is one of the main sources of the traditional conception of the Messiah, states that prior to the redemption, the Jews will experience *"a time of trouble such as never has been since there was a nation."* [132]

This idea is further elaborated in the Apocryphal books. [133] In the Talmud and Midrash, numerous passages detail all the woes and calamities that are destined to mark the period immediately preceding the advent of the Messiah. [134] One of these passages reads: "The Son of David will not come until the redemption is despaired of, for it is written, *"when he sees them that their power is gone, and there is none remaining, bond or free,"* [135] as though to say, Israel had neither supporter nor helper." [136] All of the foregoing references indicate how deeply rooted was the faith of the Jews in their ultimate redemption, and how ineradicable it has remained, despite insufferable persecutions. Some Jewish martyrs of World War II, as they were being led to Hitler's gas chambers, chanted the part of the *Ani Maamin* credo which proclaims faith in the ultimate advent of the Messiah.

CHAPTER THREE

The Salvation Aspect
of Traditional Judaism

OTHER-WORLDLY SALVATION

Together with the intense feeling of Jewish peoplehood which Traditional Judaism inculcated in the Jew, it also imbued him with a keen *yearning* for individual salvation, or fulfillment of his destiny as a person. Along with the hope which it held out for the advent of the Messiah, it fostered in him a striving for "a share in the world to come."

The belief in individual salvation seems to have become an integral part of the Jewish tradition not long before the Maccabean era. During the first Commonwealth era the lines between the individual person and the People as a whole were not sharply drawn. Exhortations in the second person singular might refer to the individual or to the People as a whole. Such is the case in the Ten Commandments. Likewise when the Psalmist speaks in the first person singular, it is not always clear whether he speaks for himself or whether he speaks in the name of his People. The fact, for example, that punishment is meted out by God to the third and fourth generations, and mercy extended to the thousandth generations, implies a continuity of being among the generations of a People. In such a continuity, the individual person had not as yet fully come to his own.

Only when we are told *"children are not to be put to death for*

70

their father's sins," [1] do we begin to discern a regard for the individual human being as such. That such doctrine was novel is evident from the way the historian in the book of Kings[2] calls attention to the fact that King Amaziah, in sparing the sons of his father's assassins, acted in keeping with the above ordinance in the *Book of the Law of Moses.* In Babylon, the Prophet Ezekiel had to labor with his fellow-Jews in captivity to persuade them to stop repeating the cliché about the children's teeth being set on edge because their fathers had eaten unripe fruit.[3]

The exception to the tendency of absorbing the individual in the social aggregate was of course a leading personality, a ruler, a king or a prophet. In accordance with ancient thinking, God meted out to the elite their deserts. But even they were not dealt with purely as individuals. They were, after all, representatives of the People; hence the People was dealt with in accordance with the merits of these leading personalities. Thus when King David committed the sin of taking a census of the Israelites, God sent the plague on the entire land.[4] The writer in the Book of Chronicles, which is generally assigned to the fourth century B.C.E., seems to have sensed the anomaly of collective responsibility. He therefore represents King David as having prayed to God, when the plague broke out: *"Was it not I who gave the command to number the people? It is I who have sinned and done very wretchedly. But these sheep, what have they done? Let Thy hand, I pray Thee, O Lord my God, be against me and against my father's house; but let not the plague be upon Thy People."* [5] Even in this prayer, the individual is inseparable if not from the People, at least from his family.

The principle of responsibility, whether in relation to God or to fellow-man, implies the self-transcendence of the individual, and therefore tends at first to merge the individual with the group. The Jews had to pass through a rather long transition period before they learned to think in terms of individual responsibility even in relation to God. In that transition period, they were very much troubled by the problem of accounting for the seeming lack of correlation between a person's conduct and his condition. The pious were all too often in trouble, while the wicked were prosperous. In one of the psalms, the author, noting the prosperity of the wicked, consoles himself with the thought that in the end God will send upon them the retribution they deserve.[6] But it is hardly convincing. The

Prophets Jeremiah [7] and Habakkuk[8] wrestled with that problem, but left it unsolved. The Books of Job and Ecclesiastes make that problem their main theme, but in the end leave the reader as perplexed as ever.

A solution finally presented itself in the dominant civilization of the Achaemenian Empire, of which the Second Jewish Commonwealth was for a time a satellite province. Under the influence of Zoroaster, who had reformed the ancient paganism that had held sway in Persia, the life of the individual human being came to be viewed as transcending the limits of this-worldly existence. The belief in the bodily resurrection of the dead, and in the ultimate triumph of Ahura Mazda, the God of righteousness, contributed to an enlarged conception of the human person. Those beliefs are first heard of in the Jewish tradition at the time when the Jews found themselves within the orbit of Iranian civilization. That is a good reason for assuming that those beliefs came to the Jews from Iran.

Not all the Jews, however, were willing to accept those beliefs. The ruling element, known as Sadducees, during the two centuries preceding the destruction of the Second Temple, were conservative, and resisted all ideas that deviated from the letter of the Written Torah. Since there was no basis in the Torah for believing either in resurrection or in a world to come, they considered those beliefs heretical. The rising class of Pharisees, however, who made the study and teaching of the Torah their preoccupation, and who took issue on many matters with the ruling class, thought otherwise. They sensed in those beliefs the possibility of finding at long last a solution of the most troublesome problem in personal religion—the apparent inequity that inheres in human life. With the resurrection and a share in the world to come to look forward to, that problem was regarded as solved. The reward which a person merited through his good deeds, but missed in this life, awaited him in the world to come.

Insofar as the Pharisaic view-point came to predominate, the Jews, as a corporate entity, acquired a new character. In addition to continuing as a nation, they became an *ecclesia*. They no longer knew themselves merely as an *Am*, or, *Goy*, as was the case in biblical times, or as an *Ummah*, in post-biblical times. Henceforth they considered themselves a dedicated People, a conception which later was embodied in the designation *Kenesset Yisrael*. *Kenesset* is the Hebrew equivalent of "Synagogue" which came to be a term applied to the entire body of the Jewish People, in the same way as "Church" came to be applied to the entire body of Christian believers.

Originally, the term "Kenesset" was applied to a group of people gathered in one place for prayer and study. Such places were fostered by the Pharisees. The fact that the entire Jewish People came to be known as *Kenesset Yisrael* meant that as a corporate entity it undertook the mission of enabling each individual Jew to achieve his destiny through worship of God and the study of Torah for which each synagogue provided the opportunity. Thus while the Temple, even after it was destroyed, continued to serve as a symbol of God's ever-abiding Presence (*Shekinah*) in Israel, the synagogue as an institution provided the means necessary for the salvation of the Jew as an individual. Thus, the *Bet ha-Kenesset*, the synagogue as an institution, became the symbol of the *Kenesset Yisrael*, the Synagogue as the Jewish collectivity.

Again, as with so much in biblical religion that underwent metamorphosis through the unconscious process of reinterpretation by the time it became post-biblical religion, so with the concept of salvation. In the Bible, the Hebrew word *teshua* or *yeshua*, which is commonly translated "salvation," has in its context an altogether different meaning from the one generally associated with the term "salvation." Biblically, it refers mainly to deliverance from enemies, to victory over foes bent upon the destruction of the one "saved." Since God alone was the source of man's strength, deliverance from enemies constituted a manifestation of God's help.[9] But there are other evils, like national calamities, sickness or famine, from which man has to be saved. Those who are saved from those evils also experience salvation. Hence, in the Bible, salvation is always associated with life and bliss in this world.

When the Jews living in Alexandria during the reign of the Ptolemies translated the Bible into Greek, they used for the Hebrew words *teshuah*, and *yeshuah* the Greek word *soteria*. In the Hellenic environment in which they moved, that word had acquired from the mystery religions the special significance of deliverance from death. Those mystery religions grew in influence during the one or two centuries prior to and after the rise of Christianity, because they claimed to help their adherents transcend death. They consisted of mystic rites and rituals which were believed to be a potent means of achieving immortality. That was the conception of salvation which the Jewish Hellenists read into the Bible. Thus salvation came to mean the bliss of the soul in the hereafter.

The Pharisees who read the Bible in the original Hebrew had no occasion to reinterpret *yeshuah* or *teshuah* as salvation in the hereafter. Having accepted, however, the belief in the hereafter, which they later expressed through the concept of a "share in the world to come," they, too, had to find for their belief a basis in the Bible. That they did by means of artificial exegesis. To prove, for example, that the Torah took the belief in bodily resurrection for granted, the Rabbis pointed to the grammatical form of the Hebrew of the verse: *"Then Moses and the Israelites sang"* [10] as being in the imperfect, or future, tense. Ordinarily that is the grammatically correct tense to be used with the adverb "then" when referring to the past. But they read into it the meaning: "Then (i.e., in time to come) Moses and the Israelites *will* sing." [11]

In the case of the belief in the world to come, those Sages resorted to a different method of exegesis. The story is told [12] of a father who asked his son to climb to the roof of a house on which a bird had a nest with fledglings, to set free the fledglings and to bring down the mother bird. The son obeyed his father, but on his way down from the roof, the ladder broke, and he fell down and was killed. "How could his death be reconciled," the Sages asked, "with the promise of long life, which accompanies only two precepts in the Torah, the one commanding the honoring of parents and the other commanding that, if a nest containing a mother bird and its young be found, the young should be set free and only the mother bird taken?" Their answer is that the long life promised in each case refers to eternal life in the hereafter.

Salvation, as redemption from death and the other evils of this earthly existence, and as the achievement of bliss in the hereafter, was thus equated by the Hellenist interpreters of Judaism with the bodiless immortality of the soul, and by the founders of Rabbinic Judaism with a share in the world to come. This twofold interpretation persisted in Traditional Judaism down to modern times. Those whose mental horizon was confined to Rabbinic teaching retained the other-worldly version; the Jewish theologians like Maimonides and Albo who had come in contact with Greek thought generally reinterpreted *ha-olam ha-ba* to mean the immortality of the soul. The latter, however, are in this respect unrepresentative of the main stream of Jewish tradition.

Few Rabbinic sayings have so impressed themselves on the Jewish consciousness as the well-known saying of R. Jacob b. Korshai[13] which describes this world as a vestibule before the world to come, and which urges that we should spend our days on earth with a view to meriting a share in that world. [14] When R. Eliezer took sick and his disciples came to visit him, they said to him: "O our master, teach us the ways of life, so that we may attain through them the life of the world to come.[15]

THE WORLD TO COME

The belief in the world to come is, in Rabbinic Judaism, seldom, if ever, confused with the belief in the coming of the Messiah. That is because in the minds of the Talmudic Sages, the two aspects of Judaism—the national and the individual—were accorded distinct, though equal, significance. R. Eleazer of Modiin is quoted as saying: "If you will succeed in keeping the Sabbath, the Holy One, blessed be He, will give you six good portions: the Land of Israel, the world to come, the new world, the Kingdom of the House of David, the priesthood, and the Levitical offices." [16] "The world to come" or *ha-olam ha-ba* is the one in which the individual is granted his due reward; "the new world" refers to the Messianic age, when the Jewish People is destined to experience redemption from exile.

The belief in the world to come was another one of the main issues on which the two ancient sects, the Sadducees and the Pharisees, were divided. To the Sadducees, the Torah was fundamentally an instrument of national life and not of individual salvation. They could, therefore, have but little sympathy with the Pharisaic interpretation of the Torah which regarded it as being also an instrument of individual salvation. This function of the Torah figures prominently in the Mishnaic treatise known as *Pirke Abot*.

That treatise is not intended, as is generally assumed, to be merely a random collection of ethical teachings; it is a collection of statements by the greatest of the *Tannaim* on the primacy of the study of the Torah. Nothing can be more important than a share in the world to come; the best means to achieve it is through the study of Torah. That is the main *motif* of *Abot*. The custom of reciting a passage from the *Mishnah Sanhedrin* before reading on Sabbath afternoons a chapter of *Abot* emphasizes this *motif*. That passage states: "All who are of the People of Israel have a share in the world to come." [17] The reason for granting them this special privilege is that they accepted the Torah, which is a means to the attainment of life eternal.

The spirit of Tannaitic sayings collected in *Abot* is one of exhortation to the individual to make the best use of the means at his command to achieve salvation. Hillel urges the learned man to love peace and strive for peace, and to love his fellow-men. The most concrete way such a man can show his love for them is by bringing them nigh to the Torah,[18] for "he who has acquired words of Torah has acquired for himself the life of the world to come." [19] "A share in the world to come" is the term used for the reward which awaits the individual after death. Thus when we read, "R. Eleazer said: 'Be thou alert to study Torah. . . . and know before whom thou laborest and who is the master of thy work to give thee the wages of thy toil,' " 'wages' refers to salvation in the world to come for the individual who has labored in the study of Torah.[20]

How great their share is depends upon how much of the study of Torah and the practice of the *mitzvot* they engage in while they are still in this world. "If thou hast learned much Torah" says R. Tarfon, "they give thee much wages, and faithful is the Master of thy work who will pay the wages of thy toil. And know that the giving of the reward to the righteous is in the time to come." [21] R. Akiba is no less emphatic as to the bliss which awaits those who have lived up to the duty of engaging in the study of Torah and the performance of *mitzvot*. "They have whereon to rely," he says, "and the judgment is a judgment of truth, and all is made ready for the banquet." [22]

The analogy of the world to come to a banquet is a favorite one in Rabbinic literature. It is the basis of the above-quoted statement by R. Jacob: "This world is like a vestibule before the world to come; prepare thyself in the vestibule, that thou mayest enter into the banquet hall." [23] The underlying assumption is that this world is a place where men should strive to do the will of God and that the world to come is one for enjoying the reward of that striving.[24] This distinction between the two worlds gave rise to the comparison of the world to come to the Sabbath. The enjoyment of the Sabbath is but a minute fraction (a sixtieth) of the enjoyment in the world to come." [25] On the principle that only he who has prepared enough for the Sabbath has enough to eat when the Sabbath arrives, we are told that he who has laid up deeds of piety in this world may expect the bliss they will yield in the world to come.[26] Even in the statement of Abba Arika (Rav) which says that in the world to come there will be no eating nor drinking, the simile of the banquet recurs again. Thus we are told that, "The righteous sit with their laurels on their heads and enjoy the splendor of the Shekinah." [27] This refers to the custom in vogue among the ancients of having the guests wear laurels at banquets.[28]

The Sages themselves were doubtful as to what would happen to the world and to man after the advent of the Messiah. Neither Samuel's statement concerning the Messianic age,[29] nor Rav's statement concerning the world to come helped to remove that doubt. Maimonides tried to square the views of both Rav and Samuel with his own philosophic assumptions. He assumed that the present world order was not likely to be changed. For that reason he welcomed Samuel's statement that there was to be no distinction between the present world order and the one which would obtain during the Messianic era, the only difference being that during the Messianic era the Jews would be freed from foreign rule.

Maimonides assumed that no physical body could possibly be immortal, since, as a compound, it must in time disintegrate.[30] That led Maimonides to conclude that those who would be resurrected would die again; only their souls were immortal. There is, of course, an evident contradiction in his reasoning. By the same token that bodies could be resurrected, they could be kept alive eternally. We must remember, however, that Maimonides sought to reconcile tradition with reason. By this compromise he managed to pay deference to both reason and tradition.

According to the view predominant in Rabbinic Judaism, the "Messianic Age" is that era of *this* world which will begin with the advent of the Messiah. That advent marks an end to "this world" or the present age. On the other hand, the term "world to come," or as some render it, "the age to come," denotes the eternal life of those who have been resurrected. Thus a familiar prayer reads: *"There is no one to be compared to Thee, O Lord, in this world, neither is there any beside Thee, O our King, in the world to come. There is none but Thee, O our Redeemer, for the days of the Messiah; neither is there any like unto Thee, O our Savior, for the resurrection of the dead."* [31] In that prayer, each appellation for God denotes a different manifestation of His divinity.

Those who will have died before the advent of the Messiah, and had lived a fully worthy life, will be resurrected when his advent takes place. They are destined to enter forthwith *ha-olam ha-ba* (the world to come). All others, however, on being resurrected, will be judged on the Day of Judgment. Those found incorrigible will be utterly destroyed. The rest, known as "the one-third," mentioned in Zechariah 13:8, will pass through the ordeal of purgation by fire, and thereafter live forever. This is, in simplified form, the tradition concerning the resurrection. That tradition did not attain as definitive a form as have most of the theological concepts in Rabbinic lore.[32]

Ha-olam ha-ba, the world to come, is the present world re-created. This is unmistakably evident from the following saying: "The division in the world to come will not be like the division in this world. . . . In the world to come every one will own land that is situated on mountainous ground as well as on a plain and in a valley.[33] The imperfections of this world, which are the consequence of Adam's sin, will be eliminated. In that re-created world, Eretz Yisrael will abound in those extraordinary blessings which were foretold by the Prophets Isaiah[34] and Ezekiel." [35]

The *Amora* Rav's conception of the world to come is radically different, and does not seem to have been shared by the other Sages. "In the world to come," he said, "there will be neither eating nor drinking, no begetting of children, no business transactions, no envy, no hatred and no rivalry; but the righteous will sit with laurels on their heads and enjoy the brightness of Shekinah." [36] The general opinion, however, seems to have been that even in the world to come the human being will retain his physical nature with its needs, though he will be free from the domination of the

Evil *Yetzer* (the inclination to evil). It was assumed that mankind would then achieve the perfection which Adam originally possessed before he committed the sin that corrupted the human race.[37]

Thus, to have a share in the world to come meant being eligible for the life of eternal bliss.[38] That is the ultimate destiny of the individual human being, as a person in his own right. On the other hand, the conception of "the Messianic Age," refers to the future of the nation. *Traditional Judaism in all its teachings and precepts aims simultaneously at the twofold goal of national redemption and individual salvation.* Corresponding to those two goals are the two aspects of its life-pattern, the national and the individual, according to which the Jew is expected to order his own life.

At the basis of the other-worldly conception of salvation, or human destiny, is the belief that this world is intrinsically marred by sin and suffering. It therefore is altogether unfit to be the scene of man's self-fulfillment. In this vale of tears, life at best is merely like a fleeting shadow. The words: *"which I command thee this day to do them"* [39] are interpreted by R. Joshua B. Levi as follows: *This day,* refers to man's life in this world, as the time for *obeying* God's commandments. As for the *reward,* that will come on "the morrow," when man enters the next world.[40] That world is not the spiritual heaven which, according to the Medieval philosophers and theologians, is the abode of divinity, the ministering angels, and the souls of the righteous. It is none other than the world we live in, re-created and restored to the condition it was in when it first came from the hand of God, and when *"He saw everything that He had made, and behold it was very good."* In that re-created world, *"The light of the moon will be as the light of the sun, and the light of the sun will be sevenfold, as the light of seven days."* [41]

To effect the transition from this world to the next, man has to pass through the ordeal of death. Nothing perhaps so characterizes the ancient mind as its bizarre notion of death. It seemed unable to regard death as a normal part of the world order. In Rabbinic writings, for example, it was assumed that *man was not meant to die, but to live forever.* "The whole effort of philosophical thought," writes Ernst Cassirer, "is to give clear and irrefutable proof of the immortality of the human soul. In mythical thought the case is quite different. Here the burden of proof lies on the other side. If anything is in need of proof, it is not the fact of immortality, but the fact of death." [42]

According to R. Judah bar Ilai, it was Adam who brought death on mankind.[43] Elsewhere he mentions the fact that Elijah did not suffer death. This should prove that if Adam had not sinned, he would not have died.[44] The *Amora* Rav Ami states that every death is caused by sin, and that sickness is a punishment for transgression.[45] This statement gives rise to a discussion in which various Tannaitic passages are introduced to prove that it was Adam's sin that had brought death on mankind. There is no dissent from this assumption.[46] We are told [47] that, when the Israelites stood at Mount Sinai, God wanted to exempt them from death, but was prevented by His irrevocable decree, which had imposed death on Adam and his descendants.[48]

According to R. Yosē, exemption from death was the condition on which Israel was willing to accept the Torah.[49] R. Hama bar Hanina said, "Adam would not have experienced the taste of death, if not for the fact that some of his descendants were bound to consider themselves gods." R. Jonathan said to him, "If that were true, only the wicked should suffer death and not the righteous." To which R. Hama replied: "That would lead the wicked to practice insincere repentance and to perform *mitzvot* for ulterior motives." According to R. Jonathan, "The reason the wicked die is that they might cease provoking God. The reason the righteous die is that they might rest from their continual struggle with the Evil *Yetzer*." According to R. Shimeon ben Lakish, "The wicked die because of their sins. The righteous, on the other hand, accept death willingly so as not to appear to be motivated in their righteousness by the fear of death; for that they will be rewarded doubly in the world to come." [50]

Not a single one of the foregoing *Amoraim* seemed to have conceived death as a normal phenomenon. Those who take that view of death cannot possibly regard the troubles of human life as purely accidental, or the destructive forces of nature as part of the original creation. They invariably look to a future in which the present condition of the world will be replaced by one in which there will be no suffering nor death.[51]

The Jews, moreover, developed an elaborate eschatology with

regard to the soul. It dealt with the state of the soul during the interim between death in this world and life in the world to come. It also included accounts of *Gan Eden*, *Gehinnom*, and the Day of Judgment.[52] In Rabbinic times the Garden of Eden, or Paradise, was conceived as the region on earth where God had placed Adam. Though the rest of the earth had deteriorated since the days of the Flood, the Garden of Eden was believed to have remained in its original state of perfection somewhere on earth. The waves of the great Flood stopped at its gates. In *Gan Eden* the souls of the dead are said to abide after having undergone their purgation in *Gehinnom*, which was supposed to be situated somewhere beneath the earth's surface. The Sages assumed that one of the three entrances to it was near the Hill of Zion, in the historical Valley of Hinnom.[53] Whatever sins man commits during his life have to be expiated during the interim existence in *Gehinnom*.[54]

In *Shevet Mussar*, an ethical treatise which appeared in 1712,[55] the author gives the following detailed description of *Gehinnom*: "The lower (i. e., earthly) *Gehinnom* is a vast space extending over myriads of acres. The more the wicked increase in numbers, the larger it grows. It is divided into many regions where suffering is meted out in varying degrees of severity, so that every sinner may have meted out to him the punishment he deserves. The fire which exists there is sixty times as hot as the fire in this world. There are coals as large as entire mountains. In the midst of *Gehinnom* there are rivers of pitch and sulphur, which well up from the deeps. Moreover, all kinds of evil demons and devils are begotten by the evil deeds of the wicked. Our Sages say: 'Every transgression one commits becomes an accusing angel.' These accusing angels are added to the evil spirits which have been in *Gehinnom* since its creation. All of them inflict different kinds of wounds on the body of the wicked. Some hang and choke the wicked, others gouge out their eyes. The torture depends upon the gravity of the sins committed."

The fact that, in Talmudic Judaism, other-worldliness does not take the form of asceticism, or that it does not imply that the present world is hopelessly beset by sin, has led many modern Jewish and non-Jewish theologians to maintain that Judaism, in contrast to Christianity, is mainly concerned with this world. That contrast is entirely unwarranted. A small treatise on conduct which dates probably from the Geonic period prescribes the way of life which a scholar should pursue. Among other things it says: "A scholar should act on the thought: 'I take no pleasure in the good things of this world, since life here below is not my portion.' " [56]

Christianity has added to the otherworldliness, which it emphasizes in common with Traditional Judaism, the disparagement of the bodily functions. Indeed, Traditional Judaism itself was not entirely averse to asceticism. On the contrary, there were times in Jewish life when asceticism was the vogue. R. Shimeon ben Yohai and his son lived for twelve years in a cave to avoid the Roman terror. They spent those years in mystic contemplation. When they finally emerged, they saw with astonishment and dismay a farmer tilling the soil. " 'The people neglect eternal life,' cried the Rabbi, 'and busy themselves with temporal life.' So great was his anger that wherever he turned his gaze, the crops withered. But a voice from Heaven protested: 'Have you come to destroy my world? Go back to your cave!' " [57] This Talmudic passage reflects an ambivalent attitude toward asceticism.

OTHER-WORLDLINESS AS A SURVIVAL VALUE

The other-worldly conception of salvation has undoubtedly been one of the main factors making for Jewish survival. It enabled the Jew to endure with resignation the suffering and martyrdom at the hands of mobs and potentates. Solomon Maimon in his *Autobiography* tells of his having stared, as a young child, in wonderment at the beautiful Princess Radziwill and her splendid retinue, when she happened to stop over for a day at his father's little farm, in the course of a hunting expedition. His father, noting young Solomon's amazement, whispered into his ear, "You little fool, in the next world this princess will tend the fire in our stove." [58] Claude G. Montefiore evaluated the traditional belief in the world to come as follows: "It fortified in days of trial. It stiffened endurance of persecution. It enable hundreds to undergo martyrdom. It constituted a powerful motive for the avoidance of sin. It explained away all difficulties in the otherwise unequal distribution of prosperity and adversity. It prevented scepticism, and it stimulated, while it purified, the hope of reward." [59]

The belief in the world to come as the *locus* of ultimate reward and punishment had a decidely pervasive influence down to our own day on the life of every Jew from the most learned to the most ignorant. This is evident from the study which is recorded in *Life is With People*.[60] Whatever action was motivated by that belief was socially and psychologically so gratifying as almost to over-shadow the role of the belief itself. That explains why modern Jewish scholars and theologians keep on insisting that traditional Judaism deprecated other-worldliness.

Of utmost significance is the fact that this other-worldly outlook was by no means confined to Jews. It was but part of the common consciousness of the Western world, before the era of the En-lightenment, the basis of the conception of salvation, upon which the pre-modern theocratic Christian and Moslem civilizations were erected. To survive in the midst of both those civilizations, the Jewish People had to meet the challenge implied in their respective claims that they alone possessed the effective means to the sal-vation of the individual. This the Jewish People could do without difficulty, since it accepted the same *major* premise as those civili-zations did with regard to the other-worldly character of salvation. As for the *minor* premise, with regard to the means of salvation, the burden of proof lay on Christianity and Islam that their respective means superseded those which were stressed in the Jewish tradition.

The main issue on which Christendom, Israel and Islam were divided was: What constituted the final and authoritative revela-tion of God's will, obedience to which was a prerequisite to sal-vation, and which body of believers could claim that it was in pos-session of the final and authentic revelation? Both Christians and Moslems agreed that the Jews had once been in possession of an authentic revelation which later was superseded by a more author-itative one. The integral relation of the New Testament to the Jewish Scriptures stems from the fact that Christianity sought to prove that it had its roots in Judaism. Though no such integral relationship exists between the Koran and the Jewish Scriptures, nevertheless even Mohammed sought to prove that his advent had been foretold to the Jews. He claimed[61] that many passages in the Torah referring to him had been deliberately altered or eliminated. Islam regards the passage in Deuteronomy 33,2 as adumbrating the final revelation to Mohammed. It reads thus: *"The Lord came from Sinai; He dawned from Seir upon us, and He shone*

forth from Paran." In this passage Seir is taken to refer to the
Christian revelation, and Paran to the mountain near Mecca
where God is alleged to have revealed Himself to Mohammed.[62]

Both Christianity and Islam, however, assumed that the Jews
had forfeited the key to salvation; according to the former, by refusing to acknowledge Jesus as Messiah, and, according to the latter, by refusing to recognize Mohammed as "the seal of prophecy."
The Jews, on the other hand, could not but feel that, since according to the very admission of their adversaries, their Jewish ancestors
had been the original possessors of the key to salvation, their adversaries were at a disadvantage.[63]

Thus the very consensus in regard to the meaning and method
of salvation served as the bone of contention among the three
monotheistic religions, to the point of fostering in them mutual
contempt and hatred. Moreover, all the three religions assumed
that only those who were qualified for salvation, or life eternal,
were truly human. Christianity taught, "No salvation outside the
Church." [64] Islam likewise assumed that only those who accepted
the gospel of Islam were qualified for salvation.[65] Christians and
Moslems regarded each other as doomed to perdition. Both groups
regarded the Jews as outside the pale of salvation. What effect
this assumption was bound to have on the political and social
status of the Jews is apparent. Having been regarded as of a lower
species, or as spiritually depraved, the likelihood of their being
dealt with on an equal footing with either Christians or Moslems
was out of the question.

This, however, did not shake the Jews in their faith that they
alone possessed the true means to salvation. The specific meaning
which salvation had for the Jew was determined by the teachings
of the *Tannaim and Amoraim.* Those teachings molded the
Jewish consciousness during the eighteen centuries prior to the most
recent turning point in Judaism. *That Judaism did not have any
synods to work out creeds to which Jews had to subscribe does
not mean that Jews were free to believe anything they chose. It
simply means that the Jews differed from the Christians in the
way they arrived at a consensus in regard to what was authoritative.*
The Moslems had a still different way. But all three groups were
equally insistent on the acceptance by the individual of the
authorized beliefs concerning the meaning of salvation and the

nature of man, and concerning God and the kind of world in which salvation was to be achieved.

* * *

The problem of contemporary Judaism is far from being grasped in all its complexity even by some of the outstanding Jewish thinkers and theologians. There are many reasons to account for this anomaly. But one reason, certainly, is the failure to perceive the *significance* of the fact that other-wordly salvation does not figure in the religion of the Bible. Jewish scholars know, of course, that the religion of the Bible, and particularly of the Pentateuch, displays no concern with what happens to the human being after he dies, though it voices the belief in a *Sheol*, a nether world, in which the dead are assumed to be leading a kind of shadow existence. They know, too, that the entire Bible text was later reinterpreted in terms of the belief that man's life on earth was only a preparation for life in a better world to come. But for some strange reason, they have failed to draw such conclusions from those facts as might have a bearing on Judaism for our day.

The very fact that the text of Scripture may be interpreted to mean, in terms of the most basic ideas concerning God, man and the world, something radically different from what it had meant originally should have led to the following conclusion: That a religion can retain its identity, despite changes in some of its fundamental doctrines, provided its adherents retain their sense of group continuity by treating as sacred the same texts, persons and events as that group did in the past.

Secondly, the fact that the Jewish religion underwent so radical a change in its doctrines in the past without a break in its continuity, indicates that it might again undergo a radical change in some of its basic beliefs without losing its identity. Indeed, it might even acquire new vitality as a result of such change. What is needed is a method of reinterpretation, whereby the sacred texts of Judaism might be made relevant to the most urgent religious and moral needs of current human life.

Thirdly, the other-worldly outlook on life, God, and man which became an integral part of the Jewish tradition was not originally a part of that tradition, but came to it from without. This shows that a religious tradition, no matter how sacrosanct, cannot remain uninfluenced by a dominant world outlook, however alien to the tradition's original character. Naturalism has become as dominant a world outlook as other-worldly supernaturalism was in the days when the Pharisees had to reinterpret the Torah in keeping with the then prevailing other-worldly outlook. If, therefore, the Jewish religious tradition is to function in our day, it has to come to terms with naturalism. That is the next metamorphosis it has to undergo.

The failure of modern Jewish thinkers and theologians to reckon fully with the implications of the changes in the Jewish religion during the latter half of the Second Commonwealth era is largely due to an inadequate understanding of the function of religion in general. Religion in general is usually regarded and studied as a distinct system or way of life, comparable to a system of philosophy. It is thus divorced from the society which it unites, directs and inspires. Viewed in that abstract form, its existential reality escapes the observer. What he centers his attention upon is unlike religion in the process of operation, as the footprints of a person are unlike the person himself.

GOD AS THE SOURCE OF SALVATION

To achieve salvation we have to assume that salvation, or the fulfillment of human life, whether in the here and now or in the hereafter, is achievable, and that the world is so constituted as to enable man to make the most of his capacities and opportunities. This is one way of describing the belief in God. Essential, therefore, to an understanding of traditional Jewish teaching concerning salvation is a knowledge of its conception of God. That conception, not being the result of intellectual reflection, is not given in Rabbinic thought the form of abstract categories. It is latent in the symbolic significance of the religious practices which evoked deep feelings of fear, love, trust, and a sense of compulsive duty. It is implicit in the vivid imagery of the biblical narratives, which give body to the anxieties and hopes of the generations of Jews.

"Without drawing a sharp distinction between religion and theology," wrote the late Louis Ginzberg, "it would be good to remember that the Rabbis were as little theologians as the prophets philosophers. As the latter did not reason out, but experienced, the truths to which they gave utterance, so the theology of the former is not based upon speculation, but upon warm feeling. The most characteristic feature of the rabbinical system of theology is its lack of system. With God as a reality, revelation as a fact, the Torah as a rule of life, and the hope of redemption as a most vivid expectation, one was free to draw his own conclusions from these axioms and postulates in regard to what he believed!" [66]

Traditional Jewish religion teaches that God created the world and all that is in it, and that He expects man to love, fear and obey Him. He is called God of Israel, because He revealed Himself through the vicissitudes which constituted the history of Israel. His glory, however, fills the entire world; there is no other God beside Him. What the Jew felt when he turned his gaze toward the world of nature is summed up in the following Rabbinic statement: "His power and His might fill the universe. He was before the universe came into being, and after all things have come to an end He will still exist . . . . He stretched out the heavens and the earth. His voice cleaves flames of fire, splits the mountains, shatters the rocks. His bow is fire and His shafts are flashes of fire. His javelin is flame, and His shield the clouds. His sword is the lightning. He formed the mountains and the hills. He covers the heavens with clouds. He sends down the rain and the dew. He makes the grass to grow, and He causes the fruits to ripen. He causes kings to pass away and sets others in their place." [67] Thus the affirmation that God exists was intended to negate the idea that the physical world was self-caused.[68]

The foregoing, however, represents the way in which the Jews of ancient times assumed that the power of God manifests itself in the orderly processes of nature. That was not for them the most significant manifestation. Far more significant for them was the manifestation of God in the history of their People. There the processes of nature were set aside to give way to demonstrations of God's most characteristic power. There God displayed that uniqueness which distinguished Him from all other superhuman beings, real or imaginary. "Who is like unto Thee, O God, among the gods? Who is like unto Thee, glorified in holiness, revered in praises, doing marvels?" [69] It was this God with whom Jews communed in worship, rather than the God of the orderly course of nature.

How did the Sages of the Talmud conceive God? *The oft-quoted saying of R. Yishmael [70] that "the Torah speaks in the language of men" has been repeatedly misinterpreted in Jewish theological writing as implying that any passage in the Bible which offends reason is not to be taken literally.* That includes passages in which God is referred to in anthropomorphic terms. This, however, is an unwarranted use of R. Yishmael's saying. The ancient Rabbis were not troubled by the anthropomorphic conception of God. They could easily conceive God as residing in a particular portion of space. The throne and the angels and the various heavens were to them not mere metaphors, but space-occupying entities.[71]

Being accustomed to expect consistency in conceptual thinking, we find it difficult to recapture the idea which the ancients had of God. Our Sages found nothing in the anthropomorphic idea of God incompatible with what they expected of a God who was the Creator of the world and the Arbiter of human destiny. They did not hesitate, for example, to say that once, when R. Yishmael ben Elisha went into the innermost sanctuary, he beheld "Yah, the Lord of Hosts." [72] A Palestinian *Amora*, R. Abahu, who frequently engaged in controversies with heretics, stated that the Shekinah dwelt in the West, whereas his colleagues maintained that it dwelt in other parts of the universe.[73] There can be no mistake about the anthropomorphism of the statement that man compared with the Shekinah is like an ape compared with man.[74]

The very concept of the Shekinah is extremely puzzling. It may originally have had no more significance than the term "His Majesty" when applied to a king. As such an expression, Shekinah may have been intended merely as a substitute for the term "God," to avoid the too frequent use of the latter term. On the other hand, it may have been devised to satisfy the psychological demand for some visible manifestation of God. In fact, the Jewish theologians in the Middle Ages regarded the Shekinah as a kind of physical entity which God had created to act as intermediary between Himself and His creation.[75] Actually, the use of the term Shekinah enabled the Rabbis to overcome their reluctance to ascribe to God human traits and actions. R. Meir, for example, alludes to the Shekinah as suffering pain of the head and arms.[76] Outside philosophic circles, the anthropomorphic conception of God was unquestionably dominant in Jewish life until modern times.[77]

The solity of God did not exclude the existence of superhuman beings like angels or demons, who acted as messengers of God's will throughout the universe. They helped maintain the physical world order and the order of human life. They were God's creatures, and never set themselves up in opposition to God. Whatever evil or destruction some of them wrought, including Satan, the greatest among them, it was always in obedience to God's will. The one passage in the Midrash[78] which depicts the Serpent in the Genesis story as "slandering God" is not typical. In Jewish theology, the Serpent never assumed the demonic proportions of the Christian Satan, who is a slightly revised version of the Zoroastrian deity, Ahriman. No idea was so vigorously combatted by the Rabbis as the Zoroastrian dualism. It served as a background against which the solity of the God of Israel came to be passionately affirmed. The avowal of that solity stamped one a Jew.[79]

The solity of God, as the Creator of the world and as the Redeemer of Israel, was given special emphasis, particularly to offset Christian doctrine. R. Abahu said: "An earthly king has a father, a brother or a son; with God it is not thus. God says, 'I am the first,' for I have no father; 'I am the last,' for I have no brother; 'for there is no God beside me,' for I have no son." [80] "When Jacob was on his death-bed," we are told, "he wanted to reveal to his sons what would happen in the end of the days. But at that moment the Shekinah left him. Therefore he said; 'Perhaps there is some flaw in my household. Ishmael was a flaw in Abraham's household, and Esau in Isaac's.' Then his sons said, 'Hear, O Israel, the Lord our God, the Lord is One. Even as He is the Only One to you, He is the Only One to all of us.' " [81] This passage indicates that the solity of God had an ethnic, not a metaphysical connotation. The solity of God was understood by the Sages not as reflecting the unity that underlies the whole of nature but as reflecting the solidarity of the Jewish People.

We cannot go wrong in the understanding of Jewish monotheism, if we keep in mind the following prayer: "Thou art One and Thy name is One, and who is like Thy People Israel, one peo-

ple on earth." [82] The solity of Israel's God reflects the solity of Israel's peoplehood. As Israel's peoplehood is based on the Torah, so is God's divinity based on the Torah. Since the Torah represents Israel's twofold method of salvation, national and individual, we should likewise try to understand, from the standpoint of both national and individual salvation, what the Jewish tradition affirms concerning God.

Another basic idea which is stressed in the traditional view of God is His unchanging identity. The world is various, and life displays many contradictory aspects. This, to the ancient mind, implied the existence of various and conflicting powers. The philosophic notion of the inherent unity of the world through the interaction of endless series of causes and effects was entirely unknown. The heterogeneity of life was the outstanding fact. All the more significant, therefore, is the Rabbinic emphasis upon the sameness of God in the manifold ways in which life is experienced.[83] *"The Lord is His name"* is thus interpreted as follows: "God is the same both in Egypt and at the Red Sea; both in the past and in the future; both in this world and in the world to come. We read accordingly, *"See now that I, even I, am He,"* [84] and *"I the Lord am the first, and with the last I am the same."* [85] [86]

GOD'S PRESENCE

In the Rabbinic tradition, it is assumed that earthly beings partake of the physical character of the earth, and heavenly beings partake of the spiritual nature of God. Man is the only exception; he combines in himself both body and spirit. The spirit in man is his soul. In contrast with the origin of the body, which derives from the earth, the origin of the soul is in heaven.[87] Like spirit in general, man's soul, too, is regarded as an entity which occupies space.

The souls of human beings were believed to have been created together with the world, and to have their original abode in the seventh of the heavens, which is named "Araboth." [88] In its pre-earthly existence, the soul possesses high gifts of knowledge and insight, which it loses when it enters the human body.[89] That view is expressed in Plato's *Phaedrus*,[90] which must have been the source from which it seeped into Rabbinic teaching. The religious attitude associated with the traditional conception of the soul is best expressed in the daily prayer which is based on a passage in the Talmud.[91] "O my God, the soul which Thou has given me is pure. Thou didst create it, Thou didst breathe it into me. Thou preservest it within me, and Thou wilt take it from me, but Thou wilt restore it unto me hereafter." [92]

The Rabbis were inclined to draw many parallels between God and the soul. "As God fills the whole world, so does the soul fill the whole body; as God sees without being seen, so does the soul see without being seen; as God feeds the entire world, so does the soul feed the entire body; as God is pure, so is the soul pure; as God dwells in innermost chambers of the world, so does the soul dwell in innermost chambers of man." [93] "Someone asked R. Gamaliel where does God reside? In reply he said, 'You aske me about God, who is removed from us a distance of five hundred years' journey. Let me ask you about the soul, which abides with you day and night. Tell me in what part of the body the soul resides?' " [94]

Jewish tradition was not in any way the result of scientific observation or metaphysical reflection. It, therefore, was not inhibited from ascribing contradictory attributes to God. Its interest in contemplating the nature of God was motivated by the desire to know how that nature had to be reckoned with in man's efforts to achieve salvation, or bliss in the hereafter. On the principle that every affirmation concerning God in Rabbinic literature is to be understood from the standpoint of salvation, the omnipresence of God is to be interpreted as a reminder that man is watched by God's all-seeing eye. Nothing man does, thinks or feels escapes God's observation. Again, the fact that God is omnipresent means that man is cared for; consequently, if man obeys God's will, he will not be forsaken.[95]

That is the reason the Rabbis stressed God's omnipresence. "Why is God called *Makom* (*Place*)? Because He is the place of the world, but the world is not His place." [96] It is doubtful whether the author of this statement was aware that it sums up the modern conception of God as expressed in panentheism, the doctrine that "the world is not identical with God (Pantheism) nor separate from God (Deism), but in God (Theism), who in His divine nature transcends it." On the other hand, the Rabbis assumed that God's transcendent Presence was capable of manifesting itself locally. Simeon ben Azzai said: "It is said of God, 'The heavens and the earth do I fill.' [97] Note how great is God's love for Israel. He crowded Himself for their sake into the narrow space between the two cherubim." [98]

The belief that God can, and does actually, manifest Himself by means of some identifiable experience, whether sensate or psychic, constitutes the essential difference between philosophic and historical religion. To this day that belief functions in the life of millions who subscribe to the traditional Christian doctrine of the Eucharist. In Rabbinic Judaism, that belief is implied in a multitude of teachings and laws concerning the Temple in Jerusalem.

How difficult it is for modern scholars to think in terms of the ancients is illustrated by the controversy between C. G. Montefiore and H. Loewe. [99] Referring to the rule that when a man prays he must turn toward Eretz Yisrael, Jerusalem, and the Temple, Montefiore remarks. "To us moderns all this seems very needless, as if it mattered a pin whether our bodies face one way or another." H. Loewe finds it necessary to controvert this opinion on the ground that "We must resort to symbolism in religion as in all activities."

The truth is that conscious symbolism is modern. Whatever the ancients were unable to account for rationally they ascribed to God's will or they associated with the actual Presence of God. The latter is undoubtedly the reason for the rule concerning the direction in which one should turn during prayer. The Temple was accepted by all Jewry, without a dissenting voice, as the indispensable means of experiencing the "real Presence" of God. The Shekinah is the term used to denote God's "real Presence." We have in the idea of Shekinah, in addition to its use as a metonymy for "God," an analogue to the Christian conception of Incarnation. The traditional assumption was that for human life to function normally, God's real Presence had to be in its appropriate place on earth. Accordingly, so long as the Temple was in ruins, God's Presence was "in exile," and human life could not but be distraught.

This notion of Shekinah is one of those ancient Jewish beliefs which most of us find it difficult to assume were meant to be taken literally. Yet it is a fact that the outward, or sensate, manifestion of Divinity plays an important role in Jewish tradition.

Such manifestion is what gives some religious rites a sacramental character. Such was, indeed, the character of the sacrificial cult. According to Tannaitic teaching, "ten miracles were wrought" in the Temple. These occasions, which marked the suspension of the natural order, constituted a sensate evidence of God's Presence.[100] The restoration of the sacrificial cult has remained an object of petition thrice daily and in the thanksgiving prayers after each meal. The description of the sacrificial cult is still included in the traditional prayer book. One who observed a voluntary fast would recite the prayer asking God to accept his loss of "fat and blood" as though it were the "fat of the sacrifice" laid on His altar.

GOD'S POWER AND PROVIDENCE

The knowledge that the world was governed by a Creator who was all-wise and all-powerful had a bearing on the problem of human salvation, since the Creator was regarded as using His transcendent power in the interest of man. The main evidence that God used His power in that way was, for traditional Judaism as well as for Christianity and Islam, the occurrence of miracles. The specific miracles which are recorded in the Biblical narratives have the definite function of proving that the God of Israel is the only God, since it is taken for granted He alone possesses the power to suspend the regular course of nature. *The attempt to explain away the miracles recorded in the Bible by interpreting them as naive versions of natural events is, from the standpoint of Traditional Judaism, not only uncalled for but heretical.*

The most important inference from the assumption that God employs His power for man's good is the efficacy of prayer. The belief that prayer and fasting can bring rain, ward off pestilence, or cause God to change the plans of some evil despot, is based upon the acceptance of daily miracles as an integral part of the world order. The non-occurrence of miracles was viewed as evidence of divine displeasure, due to man's sins of omission or commission. The greater part of the treatise *Taanit* is devoted to various procedures to be followed by individuals and communities in a time of drought. Rabbi Meir taught: "Two people suffer from the same ailment, one recovers the other dies. That is because the first one prayed devoutly, but the second one did not." [101]

We must realize that the ancients lived in a thought-world in which the only notion they had of power was that of power moved by a purposeful will. God's power in the world was to them entirely analogous to that which a king exercised over his subjects.[102] The notion that the world is governed by impersonal forces which act with unalterable uniformity was entirely alien to the Rabbinic mind. *Any version of Rabbinic Judaism which fails to note that the element of miracle is for the Sages of the Talmud the chief evidence of God's existence and power is a distortion.* To ignore the fact that to them prayer had a theurgic significance is to misrepresent the part played by prayer in the spiritual life of the Jew of the past. Prayer is described by the Rabbis as a "hereditary occupation, the occupation of Abraham, Isaac and Jacob." [103] The reason the People of Israel is likened to a worm[104] is that "just as the worm uses it mouth to bore into the cedar tree, so the People of Israel uses the power of prayer at its command." [105] Prayer is Israel's only weapon against its enemies.

Part of God's power over the world is His power over man, which manifests itself in His prescience of man's doings and His omniscience of all that goes on within man's mind and heart. "Before a thought is framed in a man's heart, it is already known to God. Even before a man is fully formed, his thought is made manifest to God." [106] This is stated expressly in Ps. 139:4.

With bliss in the world to come as the goal of human fulfillment, God has to determine who shall have a share in it, and how great that share shall be. R. Eliezer ha-Kappar said: "They that are born are destined to die; and the dead are to be brought to life again; and the living to be judged, to know, to make known, and to be made aware that He is God, the Creator, the Discerner, the Judge, the Witness, the Complainant; He it is that will in the future judge, blessed be He." [107] The thought of God as the Judge of mankind should dispel from the mind any apprehension based on the seeming lack of correlation between men's deeds and their fortunes in this world. "Everything is given on pledge," said R. Akiba, "and a net is spread for all the living; the shop is open, and the dealer gives credit; and the ledger lies open; and the hand writes; and whosoever wishes to borrow may come and borrow, but the collectors regularly make their daily round, and exact payment from man whether he be content or not; and they have that whereon they can rely in their demand; and the judgment is one of truth; and everything is prepared for the feast." [108]

A much-misunderstood doctrine is that of reward and punishment. According to Traditional Judaism, God metes out to man both rewards and punishments. This doctrine is often adduced as an evidence of a mercenary streak in Jewish religion. Such an inference is unwarranted. The Rabbis emphasized the doctrine of reward and punishment not with the object of bribing or intimidating one into virtue. Their purpose was to inculcate the teaching that God exercised His providence over each individual life. They were intent upon emphasizing that nothing that happened in the world was due to chance. This is in accord with the saying, "No human being strikes his finger, unless Heaven has decreed it." [109] All physical and mental suffering, sickness and disease were regarded as penalty for sin, whether overt or secret, conscious or unconscious. In the prayer of the *Amora* R. Hammuna which is recited on the Day of Atonement, the concluding words are: "As to the sins I have committed, purge them away in Thine abounding compassion, though not by means of afflictions and sore diseases." [110]

The same urge to find the world consistent and dependable that led the philosophers to arrive at the idea of natural law led the Rabbis to arrive at the idea of retribution.[111] What the law of gravitation means to the occidental man, the divine attribute of justice meant to those who thought in terms of the Jewish tradition. R. Oshaiah states that, from the time that God finished the work of creation, He has been engaged in meting out justice to the righteous and the wicked.[112] The religious philosopher was interested in emphasizing that God had established an immutable order, since in His perfect prescience He must have made provision for every possible contingency. When Papos, a friend of R. Akiba, intimated that the verse: *"He is at one with Himself, and who can turn Him?"* [113] implied that God's decrees were arbitrary, R. Akiba silenced him, for he would not brook the thought that God acted arbitrarily.[114]

Until the middle of the eighteenth century the Talmudic doctrine of divine reward and punishment was still accepted without reinterpretation or modification by the religious authorities. Jonathan

Eybeshuetz (1690-1764) did not hesitate to tell his community: "We are humbled and dispossessed by the nations of the earth, and our humiliation goes unavenged, because we have ceased to guard zealously the honor of God and His law." [115] The influence, however, of the Enlightenment must have begun to make itself felt already in his day, since he found it necessary to rebuke his community for ascribing the ill-fortune that befell them not to divine Providence but to circumstances, bad luck or inefficiency. "When sickness overtakes a person," says Eybeschuetz, "he attributes it to overfeeding, or the unwholesomeness of the climate or the like. When he fails in business, he blames his own laziness on the negligence of his employees. That God, the molder of his destiny, may have had something to do with all these, never occurs to him." [116]

How all-important the Sages considered the problem of divine justice is shown by the fact that they interpreted the prayer of Moses, *"Make known unto me Thy ways"* [117] to mean that Moses asked God to explain to him why the righteous suffer and the wicked prosper.[118] While R. José is of the opinion that Moses was given a satisfactory reply, R. Meir maintains that Moses was put off with an evasive answer. For not even Moses was privileged to understand the mystery of divine justice; why then should the ordinary man expect to penetrate that mystery?

Faith in God's justice is perhaps the main pragmatic test of the vitality of a religion, and that test Rabbinic Judaism withstood most successfully. "R. Berekiah said in the name of R. Levi: 'It is written, *Thou, O Lord, art ever on high.'* [119] That means, God is always right. When a human sovereign who sits in judgment pronounces acquittal, he is applauded; when he convicts, no one praises him, for it is assumed that he was led to do so by anger or prejudice. Not so with God; whether He acquits or He punishes, He is known to be always right. R. Huna, in the name of R. Aba, interpreted the verse, *'I will sing of mercy and judgment, unto Thee, O Lord, will I sing'* [120] to mean that David said: 'Whether, Thou, O God, dost acquit or convict me, I will sing, O Lord, to Thee'. R. Judah b. Ilai explained Job's saying, *'The Lord gave, the Lord took; may the name of the Lord be blessed,'* [121] to mean that, when God gave, He gave in mercy, and when He took, He took in mercy.[122]

These sentiments are an elaboration of the Mishnaic teaching: 'One should bless God for the evil even as one blesses Him for the good.' " [123]

The doctrine that "whatever God does is for the best" [124] was not merely an official dogma; it permeated the entire mentality of the Jew and supplied him with moral stamina during the most critical periods of his life. In the house of mourning, R. Akiba would have the one who recited Grace add the words, "God, who is good and does good unto all." The majority opinion among the Sages was in favor of the following benediction: "God is a just judge, He governs His works, He exercises judgment throughout all generations with righteousness. All of us are His people and His servants, and are in duty bound to thank Him and bless Him for everything that befalls us." [125]

The noteworthy fact about Rabbinic Judaism is that, although it stressed God's transcendence, it nevertheless took every opportunity to emphasize God's proximity and intimate relationship with man. God's transcendence derives from the fact that He is the Creator of the world. That, however, does not preclude His abiding within the world among the humblest of His creatures. Said the *Amora* R. Ammi: "From the very moment that the Holy One, blessed be He, created the world, He longed to enter into relationship with man." [126] Although the chasm that separates God from man was sensed more vividly during the Rabbinic than during the Biblical era, it was nevertheless bridged. This was due to the fact that *both Prophet and Sage conceived God not in in terms of general ideas, but in terms of those needs which arose from the urge to salvation*, regardless of how they conceived salvation, whether in national or in individual terms.

The Sages of the Talmud succeeded in teaching the Jew to obey God not only out of fear but also out of love. Although they assumed that the fear of God was necessary to help one withstand temptation, they attached supreme worth to conduct that was prompted mainly by love for God. The Scriptures supplied them with numerous allusions to God's beneficent care of His creatures, to His readiness to pardon sin, and to His championing the cause of the oppressed. Bringing to bear upon these allusions a spirit of pious fervor, the Sages elaborated them with a great deal of imaginative detail. The Scriptures, thus illumined by the Rabbinic conception of divine love, became an inexhaustible source of solace to the Jew during the centuries of unrelieved tragedy.

Rabbinic teaching gives to the aspect of divine benevolence a threefold meaning. In the first place, it beholds that benevolence in the fact that God is the sustainer of all living beings, "At all times the Shekinah provides sustenance for all the inhabitants of the world according to their need, and satisfies every living thing, not only the pious and the righteous, but also the wicked and the idolaters." [127] Thrice daily the Jew recited in the *Amidah* his idea of God in the following words: "Thou sustainest the living with lovingkindness, quickenest the dead with great mercy, supportest the falling, healest the sick, loosest the bound, and keepest the faith with them that sleep in the dust." [128]

Secondly, the divine attribute of mercy is shown as functioning particularly in the exercise of forgiveness. The classic text in the Torah which is the basis of the oft-repeated allusion to the thirteen attributes of mercy reads as follows: *"The Lord, the Lord, is a merciful and gracious God, long-suffering, abundant in lovingkindness and truth, keeping mercy to a thousand generations, forgiving iniquity, transgression and sin and rendering acquittal."* [129] The last two words in the Hebrew, which convey the meaning—that He does not altogether acquit—are omitted in the liturgy.[130]

Thirdly, Rabbinic teaching beholds God's benevolence in His condescension and humility, in that He enters intimately into human life, and sympathizes with man in his trials and sufferings. The Palestinian *Amora* R. Yohanan said: "Wherever you find in Scriptures any mention of God's greatness, there, too, you find mention of His humility.[131] His younger contemporary R. Elazar b. Pedat said: "You can find seven passages wherein God Almighty puts Himself on the same level as those of humble heart. First, He is spoken of as '*the God of Gods and the Lord of Lords.*' [132] And then we are told '*He does justice for the fatherless and the widow.*' " [133] In every such instance, the humility of God manifests itself through His redressing the wrongs of the oppressed.

To what extent the Sages went beyond the Bible in affirming the divine attribute of mercy may be inferred from the following: "When Abraham interceded for the people of Sodom, he spoke thus: 'Oh Master of the world! If Thou seekest strict justice, there can be no world. But, if Thou desirest the world to endure, there cannot be strict justice. Wouldst Thou hold the cord by both ends? Dost Thou want both a world and strict justice? If Thou wilt not relent, Thy world cannot endure.' " [134] Another Rabbinic saying reads: "When God wanted to create man, truth protested that man would be steeped in lies. But God cast truth to the earth, so as to be able to carry out His intention of creating man." [135] Thus the Rabbis voiced, in their way, the common experience of all who reflect upon life and find that it is possible to account for the survival of the human race and to entertain any hope for its future, only on the assumption that divine patience and love inhere in the world as well as justice.

Nowhere does the contrast between the metaphysical and the religious approach to the conception of God stand out so clearly as in the case of the divine attribute of mercy. The metaphysician regards compassion as incompatible with divine perfection. Compassion is a mark of weakness, since it implies being subject to emotions.[136] The metaphysician who is also a believer is therefore compelled to give an allegorical interpretation to the numerous passages in the Bible which dwell on the mercy of God. On the other hand, from a religious point of view, compassion is a distinctively divine trait. In Scriptures we read: *"My heart recoils, all my compassion is enkindled; I will not execute my fierce anger, nor will I again destroy Ephraim, for I am God, not man."* [137] "When Moses remonstrated with God for having provoked Pharoah to increase the burden of the Israelites," say the Rabbis, "the Attribute of Justice was about to strike him, but God interceded, saying: *'Am I man that I should have no compassion?'* " [138]

The Rabbis explain, in a spirit of childlike piety, how God can afford to exercise infinite mercy. A human being who wishes to be obeyed is apprehensive of any leniency that he might show toward those who disobey him. No human law would be effective, if mercy were to be accorded a place in it. This fear, however, of giving way to compassion is a sign of weakness. Only the strong can afford to deal generously with offenders and enemies. Lest any show of kindness on the part of a sovereign render his subjects unafraid of him, he has to possess extraordinary power. Accordingly, only God, who is omnipotent, does not need to have recourse to strict justice, in order to have His will carried out in the world.[139] R. Levi interprets the verse, "*Keep back Thy servant also from presumptuous sins, that they may not have dominion over me*," thus: "Said David: 'O Master of the universe! Thou art a great God, but as for me, my sins are great. It befits a great God to forgive great sins, as it is written, 'Pardon my guilt, for it is great.' " [140]

THE MEANS TO SALVATION

1. The Study of Torah

What the study of Torah meant to the Jew may be inferred from the following saying of R. Berekiah and R. Hagiga of Kephar T'humin: "The whole world is not equal in value to one word of the Torah. All the *mitzvot* are not equal to one word of the Torah." [141] The verse in Proverbs, "*Wisdom is better than jewels*," [142] is interpreted as implying that neither *mitzvot* nor good deeds can compare in value with the study of Torah. The Torah was to the Jew not a mere series of narratives and ordinances which had come down from the past, nor was its divine authorship assumed in the ancient conventional manner of ascribing to the god of the nation whatever code was authoritative. In the words of the Rabbis, "The Torah was not to them like an ancient edict with which no one reckons, but like a recent one which everyone is eager to read." [143]

Despite the frequent reiteration of the contrast between the God of Israel, the sole Creator and Maintainer of the universe, and the false gods of the other nations, it never lost its edge. Fully conscious as the Jew was of belonging to the only People that worshipped the true God, he could not but thrill to the possibility of communing with Him in the course of learning what God would have him do. When a man reads a letter from his beloved, he does not only read what it says, but, pondering over every word, imagines her communing with him. Likewise when the ancient Rabbis studied Torah, they relived the experience of divine revelation.

The study of the Torah was never treated as a burdensome duty. In the school of R. Ishmael they taught: "Do not consider the study of Torah as a mere duty." [144] Neither the prospect of reward in the world to come nor the expectation of social status in this world could have provided that inexhaustible stimulus which kept alive the study of Torah for so many centuries. That study generated in the Jew a sense of beatitude, and, in the case of some, even a state of divine ecstasy, akin to that which the Israelites had experienced at Mount Sinai.[145] "He who always engages in the study of Torah," we are told,[146] "is endowed with the Holy Spirit." According to R. Hiyya, speaking in the name of R. Abba, God is present whenever two disciples sit and argue with each other a matter of law. "He not only listens to what they are saying," adds R. Abba, "but He even corrects their mistakes." [147] When Babylon became a center of Jewish learning, the *Amoraim* Samuel and R. Huna wished to emphasize the importance of the study of the *Mishnah*. They likened it to the offering of sacrifices in the Temple.[148] What this comparison implies becomes evident when we recall the sacramental conception of the sacrificial cult.

Another factor that helped to render the study of Torah a means of communing with God was the suspension of the sacrificial cult. When the Temple was destroyed the Jew felt deprived of the most effective means of communion with God; a substitute had to be found for the Temple cult. That need was met in the study of Torah. The command to "worship" God wholeheartedly is interpreted both as study and as prayer.[149] Study thus functioned as a means not only of learning God's will, but also of obeying it "wholeheartedly."

Thus did the study of the Torah prevent the religious life of the Jew from becoming a deadening routine. It enlivened the scrupulous observance of the *mitzvot* with the experience of divine communion. "The Torah," says R. Judah, "becomes as dear to those who study it as it was on the day that it was given at Sinai." [150] The repeated emphasis upon the importance of accuracy in the knowledge of what one studies, and of readiness in quoting from it correctly, arose from the conviction that each word in the Torah had been dictated by God. "Let the words be as beloved to you as though you first received them this day. . . . Let them be as ready on your lips, as though you heard them this day." [151] On the other hand, those who fail to occupy themselves with the Torah do not merely disregard an ancient revelation, but deliberately turn a deaf ear to the heavenly voice which goes forth every day from Mount Sinai, proclaiming "Woe to those who suffer the Torah to become an object of contempt." [152]

Every possible opportunity should be utilized to engage in the study and discussion of the subject-matter of the Torah. The Torah should be the principal vocation of the Jew. R. Meir said, "Lessen your toil for worldly goods, and busy yourself with the Torah." [153] The first question that is put to a man on the Day of Judgment is, "Have you busied yourself with the study of Torah?" [154] One should take advantage of every opportunity, and not postpone that study for some more leisurely time, is Hillel's advice. [155] Every time two people sit down to converse, they should, according to R. Hananiah b. Teradyon, look for an occasion to refer to the Torah; otherwise they belong to the class of scorners. [156] Likewise, according to R. Simeon, when three people sit down to a meal, they should exchange some "words of the Torah"; otherwise they are like pagans eating of the offerings to idols. [157] Sabbaths and festivals during which no time is devoted to the study of Torah are opportunities wasted. [158] If physical suffering does not divert a person from the study of Torah, it should be considered not as punishment but as divine discipline administered in a spirit of love. [159]

The Torah is not merely a mass of doctrines, exhortations and laws from which, once mastered and committed to memory, one can then turn to other intellectual pursuits. "Do not say, 'I have acquired the wisdom of Israel. I shall now apply myself to the wisdom of the other nations.'" No other study must interfere with, or usurp, the place of Torah. [160] When Ben Damah asked his uncle, R. Ishmael, whether after having learned the entire Torah he might take up the study of Hellenic culture, R. Ishmael replied, "We are commanded, *'Thou shalt meditate thereon day and night'.* [161] If you can find a time which is neither day nor night, you can use it for other studies." [162] Had Ben Damah done what he had intended, he would have been guilty of a sin no less heinous than that of apostasy; [163] Besides, Ben Damah had the wrong idea of Torah, in assuming that there was nothing more for him to learn. Said Ben Bag Bag: "Turn it and turn it over again, for everything is in it, and contemplate it, and wax gray and old over it, and stir not from it. Thou canst have no better rule than this." [164]

The Torah, say the Rabbis, has been compared to a fig tree. The fruit of all other trees, such as the olive tree, the date tree, and the vine, is gathered all at once, whereas that of the fig tree cannot be gathered all at once. Likewise, the Torah; a man learns a few laws one day, a few more the day following, and so all his years. Torah is not something that can be acquired in a year or two.[165] Of course, one keeps on forgetting, but forgetting has its compensation, in that it keeps one constantly occupied with study.[166]

In view of the vast amount of subject-matter contained in the Torah, both Written and Oral, the intense application necessary to discover new meanings in the text, and the ease with which we are apt to forget what we have learned, the study of Torah cannot be pursued successfully if we pamper ourselves, or insist upon having all our physical wants met. We must be willing to forego many comforts. We must even be prepared to endure physical hardship. After all, was not the Torah originally given to the Israelites after they had experienced many a hardship? Why then should we want to enjoy the benefit of communion with God through the study of His words, without having to pay a similar price? "This is the way to acquire Torah," we are told. "A morsel of bread with salt thou must eat, and water by measure thou must drink, thou must sleep upon the ground, and live a life of hardship the while thou toilest in the Torah." [167] If a man fails to be cruel to himself and to his family, he cannot earn the privilege of mastering the words of the Torah.[168] The verse,"This is the law, if a man die in a tent," [169] suggests to R. Yonathan that a man should not refrain from study even when on the point of death, and to R. Simeon b. Lakish that the knowledge of Torah is retained only by those who sacrifice their lives for it.[170]

All efforts and sacrifices for the sake of becoming proficient in the knowledge of Torah, however, are of no avail, if one lacks certain indispensable moral traits. The privilege of knowing the Torah is greater than that of the priesthood and of royalty, and therefore requires more qualifications than either. Among the forty-eight qualifications which are a prerequisite to a knowledge of Torah are moral traits like the following: reverence, meekness, cheerfulness, sedateness, moderation, patience, kindliness, faith, acceptance of chastisement, contentment, modesty, sympathy, charity.[171] No trait is so obstructive to the knowledge of Torah as self-assertiveness. Humility to the degree of self-effacement is necessary to those who wish to benefit from their study.[172]

The main reward of whole-hearted devotion to the study of Torah is salvation, or a share in the world to come. That devotion is rewarded also in this world. If the stock laid up in the world to come, as a result of study of Torah, is greater than that attained by other meritorious effort, so also are the fruits thereof which are enjoyed in this world greater than those earned by good deeds.[173] It is generally assumed that the study of Torah leads to physical well-being, despite the opinion of R. Hanan that the effort involved in the study of Torah enfeebles one's health and despite the instances, recorded in the *Midrash*,[174] of men of great physical strength who lost their strength, after they took to the study of Torah. The dominant opinion is that the study of Torah is effective in curing bodily ailments, and is therefore prescribed for the relief of pain.[175]

Of far greater importance, however, is the effect of Torah upon one's inner life. The study of it is a most potent means of overcoming one's evil desires. "It is true," says God, "I created the Evil *Yetzer* which continually prompts you to sin. But I have also created the Torah to counteract the power of the Evil *Yetzer*." [176] The Evil *Yetzer* should not be allowed to have its way. We should incite the good *Yetzer* to fight against it. If we find that the Good *Yetzer* is being worsted, we should resort to the study of Torah.[177] All impure thoughts are dispersed when a man applies his mind to the study of Torah.[178] "The Evil *Yetzer*" says R. Simeon b. Elazar, "is like iron which has to be cast into the fire before it can be shaped into any kind of a vessel. The Torah, which has been compared to fire, is the only thing that can enable a man to subject the Evil *Yetzer* to useful purpose.[179]

R. Meir said, "Whoever labors in the Torah for its own sake merits many things; yea the whole world is indebted to him. He is called friend, beloved, a lover of the All-Present, a lover of mankind. It clothes him in meekness and reverence; it fits him to become just, pious and faithful." [180] And he continues in that vein to point out that the entire spiritual status of the man is raised. When a man utters the words of Torah, he is transfigured and becomes like a ministering angel. On the other hand, without Torah he is like an ordinary beast of the field, which does not recognize its master.[181] A man's spiritual status is in no way determined by his birth, but by the extent to which he gives himself to the study of Torah. This is evident from a statement made by R. Meir that even a Gentile who engages in the study of the Torah ranks higher than a high priest who is ignorant.[182]

It was hardly feasible, however, for the majority of the Jews to live up to the exacting demand of making the Torah their main, if not their only, calling in life. The early *Tannaim* who were content to lead almost ascetic lives are characterized in later Talmudic sources as having made the study of Torah their sole vocation. R. Elazar said, "Israel complains to God. 'We should like to devote all our energies to Torah, day and night, but we have not the time.' Thereupon, the Holy One, Blessed be He, replies: 'Observe the *mitzvah* of *tefillin*, and I shall account it to you as though you were engaged in the study of Torah day and night.' " [183] This is typical of a number of sayings in which the limited time and opportunities of the average person are taken into account. Thus we find that, in actual practice, those who divided their day into three parts, devoting one-third to study, one-third to prayer, and one-third to work, were considered a "holy congregation." [184]

Other and far more lenient compromises were adopted. According to R. Joshua b. Hananiah, a man who learns two laws in the morning and two in the evening, and attends to his business the rest of the day, fulfills the duty of Torah study.[185] R. Shimeon b. Yohai, who is described as one of those who made the study of Torah his sole vocation,[186] is quoted as saying that the mere recital of the *Shema* morning and evening is considered fulfillment of the duty to study Torah.[187] When the ideal of Torah study was thus reduced to various minima, the question arose whether it was advisable to inform those who were ignorant *(amme ha-aretz)* concerning those minima. Rava thought they should be informed; they would at least maintain the practice of reading the *Shema*. That would prevent them from regarding themselves as being outside the pale of Jewish life.[188]

To the Rabbis the survival of the People of Israel depended on the study of Torah. If this, however, meant that every Jew was expected to study Torah, the People of Israel would long have disappeared. Therefore we read in Scripture: *"It is a tree of life to them who lay hold on it."* [189] Had it said: "to them who toil over it," the People of Israel would have been in a perilous state. Though the average Jew finds it almost impossible to engage in study, he can at least contribute to the support of those who do study.[190]

On the principle that those who are not in a position to carry out a certain duty should at least help others in the fulfillment of that duty, women, too, are in a position to further the study of Torah. The social status of women in ancient times made study infeasible for them. Consequently, what was a product of social conditions came to be justified as a matter of law. The Sages found in the Torah itself a basis for exempting women from the commandment, *"Ye shall teach them to your sons."* [191] That implies, they maintained, that daughters need not, or should not, be taught. How then were the women to earn their share in the world to come? As mothers, by taking their children to school, and as wives, by sitting up late, waiting for their husbands to come from the houses of study.[192]

Thus was the study of Torah prevented from becoming the exclusive pursuit of the few. It was an object of concern to all and sundry, to men, women and children, to the ignorant no less than to the learned. As every ideal that is exalted to a position of vital importance undergoes the process of apotheosis, so the ideal of study of Torah attained a significance which found expression in the conception of God as engaged in studying and teaching Torah.[193]

2.   *The Observance of* Mitzvot

With all the emphasis that was placed on the study of Torah, and with the opportunity that it afforded the keener minds to display their mental power in hair-splitting arguments, the danger that it might become an end in itself was all too imminent. Hence the numerous warnings sounded against forgetting that "not learning but doing is the chief thing." [194] R. Hanina b. Dosa said, "He whose works exceed his learning, his wisdom will endure, but he whose learning exceeds his works, his learning will not endure." [195] That learning and works are to each other respectively as branches and roots is carried out in a lengthy analogy by R. Elazar ben Azaria.[196]

A most striking paradox in the Rabbinic literature is the one which was formulated at the end of the protracted discussions on the part of R. Tarfon, R. José and R. Akiba as to which was more important, study or works. They finally came to the conclusion that study was more important, because it led to works.[197] The Rabbis state distinctly that the reward for study and the punishment for neglecting it are greater than the reward for performing works of piety and punishment for neglecting them. The consensus, however, is that study is a means to works.[198] Even R. Meir, who is the greatest advocate of study, advises, "Let thy works exceed thy learning." [199]

R. Shimeon b. Halafta said, "Whoever studies and does not practice is liable to suffer greater punishment than he who has not studied at all." [200] This he illustrated by a parable. A king who had an orchard brought to it two caretakers. One was in the habit of planting trees and hewing them down, and the other neither planted nor hewed. Certainly the former is more deserving of punishment. Elsewhere we are told: "He who only studies Torah but does not engage in pious works is as though he had no God." [201]

Obedience to God's will is regarded as leading to individual and collective bliss, both in this world and in the next, but that is neither the purpose for which the *mitzvot* are intended primarily nor the main reason why they should be obeyed. That is the idea underlying the oft-quoted teaching of Antigonos of Soko, "Be ye like servants who minister to their master without thought of reward."[202] Those who observe the *mitzvot* for the sake of material advantage or personal aggrandizement are denounced. Said Rabbi, "A man who observes the *mitzvot* for an ulterior purpose had better not been born." [203]

We are so accustomed to think of human welfare as the purpose of ethical and spiritual conduct that we find it difficult to enter sympathetically into the state of mind of the ancients. To them human welfare, though undoubtedly important as a criterion of value, never figured consciously as such, when the question of God's will was involved. The welfare of others was a motive for doing good to them, not because of any altruistic considerations, but because putting at the service of others whatever one possesses, be it wealth, learning, or energy was itself deemed a great blessing. To do good was a blessing, because it expressed compliance with the will of God. In Scripture, conformity to God's will is assumed to be a sufficient sanction for all the laws, statutes and ordinances associated with His name.[204]

Nevertheless, neither in the Pentateuch nor in the Prophetic writings do we note any tendency to minimize expectation of reward or fear of punishment. Material advantages are frankly promised as a consequence of doing God's will. There is not slightest intimation in Scripture that obeying God for the sake of reward is unworthy of man's highest loyalty to Him. On the other hand, though the Sages of the Talmud stress no less emphatically the principle of reward and punishment,[205] they frequently deprecate making the expectation of reward or fear of punishment the main motive of conduct.

We are told that the resistance which we often experience when we try to live in accordance with the precepts of the Torah is to be welcomed, because it affords us the opportunity to subordinate our own will to the will of God. Hence the feeling of being weighed down by the will of God as by a yoke is not deplored; it is treated as the normal state of mind in man's relation to God. If the performance of the *mitzvot* were easy, or if they did not run counter to man's will—in other words, if they were not felt to be a yoke—how would one know that they really represented the will of God? *Being sure that the* mitzvot *express God's will and obeying them because of that fact are of the very essence of Rabbinic Judaism.* Not that God is arbitrary in His precepts, or that there is no intrinsic purpose to them. Even a law like that of the red heifer has a reason. God simply did not want that reason to be generally known; He revealed it only to Moses.[206]

R. Nahman b. Isaac attached such importance to obeying the will of God as the all-controlling motive of the practice of the *mitzvot* that he put the matter paradoxically by saying: "A transgression performed with the intention of serving God is better than a *mitzvah* performed with no such intention." [207] This urge to perform the will of God has given rise in Rabbinic literature to the metaphor, "to afford delight to the Holy One, blessed be He." The true saint is he who so loves God that his one purpose in life is "to afford God delight." Every Jew felt it incumbent upon him to give heed to the teaching of Judah b. Temma, who said: "Be bold as a leopard, swift as an eagle, fleet as a gazelle and strong as a lion to do the will of thy Father in heaven." [208]

The conception of the *mitzvot* as affording man the opportunity of deliberately obeying the will of God enables us to understand the attitude of the Rabbis toward what we ordinarily call the ethical laws. The Rabbis evaluated human conduct differently from the way we do. They regarded the opportunity to do the will of God as the highest privilege granted to man, to which all else was secondary. *They were religionists first and foremost, and nationalists and moralists only secondarily.* They were in all literalness God-intoxicated. Hence, we must not at all be surprised that they considered the *mitzvot* "between God and man" as ends in themselves, and the *mitzvot* "between man and his neighbor" as indispensable means to those ends.

Ahad Ha-Am was mistaken in assigning to the Jewish People an inherent tendency to treat ethics as occupying a position of primacy in Jewish religion. The entire Rabbinic and philosophical tradition is opposed to that assumption.[209] The primacy of ethics in man's relation to God is compatible only with man-centered religion, the kind of religion that was unthinkable in pre-modern times. *The shift in Jewish religion of the center of gravity from ritual observances to ethics is at the very heart of the metamorphosis which Judaism is undergoing.*

There can be no question that the *mitzvot* "par excellence," or those which, according to R. Shimeon b. Yohai, may be termed "messengers of the Holy One, blessed be He," are the commandments pertaining not to human relations but to ritual observances.[210] When the Sages interpret the verse, *"Thou art beautiful, my beloved,"* as referring to the *mitzvot* insofar as they confer beauty on Israel, the *mitzvot* which are singled out are the following: the heave-offerings to the priest, the tithes, the gleanings, the corners of the field for the poor, the fringes on the corners of the garments, the phylacteries, circumcision, *mezuzah, sukkah, lulav, ethrog,* prayer, the reading of the *Sh'ma.*[211] In addition to these, also the following are enumerated elsewhere: the prohibition against an ox and ass plowing together and the one against sowing mixed seeds, the commandment to offer certain portions of the animals to the priest, the prohibition against shaving the hair of the head and of the beard, the commandment to build a parapet to the roof.[212] All those *mitzvot* God bestowed upon Israel in order to afford them the opportunity to earn their share in the world to come.

Moral actions assume a new significance insofar as they confer glory upon the Name of God for having commanded them. They are regarded as means of sanctifying God's name—*kiddush ha-shem*—because they lead even the ignorant and the non-Jew to acknowledge the greatness and goodness of the God of Israel. On the other hand, immoral conduct that leads to the profanation of God's name—*hillul ha-shem*—subjects one who is guilty of it to far greater punishment than if he were judged merely on the basis of the harm he does to his fellow-man.

Rabbinic literature abounds in moral teachings which inculcate honesty, humility, peace, forgiveness, lovingkindness and similar traits. The Sages declare the sin of pride as tantamount to displacing, as it were, God from the world; the penalty is that the sinner will have no share in the resurrection.[213] The reason probably is that one who is proud plays the god and thus sets himself up as the rival of God. Breaking a promise is equivalent to the sin of idol worship.[214] Sycophancy and flattery consign one to *Gehinnom*.[215] *Derek Erez*, in the twofold sense of morals and manners, is declared to have preceded the Torah by two thousand years.[216] An entire treatise by that name is devoted to a detailed enumeration of moral laws. Yet it cannot be said that Rabbinism considers the most scrupulous fulfillment of these moral laws the acme of human attainment; Though, to be sure, they are an indispensable prerequisite to communion with God, which can be achieved only through the study of Torah and the observance of the ritual *mitzvot*. In this regard the Rabbis merely reflect the Psalmist's idea that to be "*clean of hands and pure of heart*" makes one worthy of ascending the mount of the Lord.[217]

As a rule, we are more likely to appreciate a good which we alone happen to possess than one which we share in common with others. The moral laws of the Torah were known to be common to civilized mankind, and their possession did not distinguish the Jews from other peoples. Only in rare instances, as with the feeling of shame or pity, is there a suggestion of a specifically Jewish trait.[218] The ritual laws, on the other hand, were confined to Israel. Believing as the Sages did that Israel was God's Chosen People, they could not but see in the ritual *mitzvot* an irrefutable proof of that belief. "Beloved are the Israelites, whom the Holy One, blessed be He, has surrounded with *mitzvot* by bidding them to place phylacteries on their heads and arms, a *mezuzah* on their doorposts, fringes on the four corners of their garments. . . . The matter may be compared to a king who said to his wife, 'Adorn yourself in all thy jewels in order that you may please me.' So did God say to Israel, 'Be distinguished by means of the *mitzvot* in order that ye may please Me.' " [219]

* * *

The foregoing summary of Rabbinic, or Traditional, Judaism is no more than a meagre sketch of those teachings of the *Tannaim* and *Amoraim* which have served until modern times as the source of whatever has been consistently authoritative in Jewish life down to the end of the eighteenth century. We have stressed only those teachings that counteract a misleading contemporary tendency: that of attempting to minimize the present crisis in Judaism by minimizing the gulf between the thought-universe of Traditional Judaism and that of the major trends in Modern Judaism.

Before describing those trends, however, we have to treat, even if only sketchily, the developments in Judaism which took place after the creative period in Rabbinism came to an end. Finding itself in the midst of the newly risen empire of Islam, the Jewish People felt the impact of the Greek thought which had helped to intellectualize the civilization of that empire. In meeting the challenge of Greek philosophy, the Jewish People evolved two medieval trends in its theology, the rationalist and the mystical. These we shall discuss in the next chapter.

CHAPTER FOUR

Trends in Medieval Judaism

MEDIEVAL JEWISH THEOLOGY

It is impossible to have a proper understanding of the Jewish tradition as it has come down to us without taking into account the two distinct trends that developed in it during the Middle Ages, namely, rationalism and mysticism. Gershon G. Scholem does not exaggerate in the least when he says: "Undoubtedly both the mystics and the philosophers completely transform the structure of ancient Judaism; both have lost the simple relation to Judaism, that naïvete which speaks to us from the classical documents of Rabbinical literature." [1] Both philosophy and mystic lore were esoteric disciplines. Nevertheless, insofar as they permeated the teachings of many outstanding leaders in Jewish life, they exerted a powerful, even if indirect, influence on their followers. Only in the recent East European Hasidic movement did mystic lore, known as Kabbalah, come to have a direct bearing on the lives of the Jewish masses.

Rationalism invaded Rabbinic thought with R. Saadia's *Emunot ve-Deot* (The Book of Beliefs and Doctrines), in the tenth century. It had its heyday in what is known as the "Golden Era" of the Jews in Spain, during the period between the twelfth and fifteenth centuries. It flourished to a limited extent in Italy during the Renaissance of the sixteenth century and in Holland in the eighteenth century, but was either ignored or referred to only disparagingly by East European Jews before the rise of *Haskalah*.

The Jewish rationalist writings were intended to fortify the loyalty to Judaism of those Jews whose knowledge of the writings of some of the Greek philosophers tended to shake their religious faith. Those writings were based on the assumption that mankind could have arrived at the truth concerning God by way of the intellect as well as by way of revealed tradition. Revelation was a short-cut for what was intellectually a long and difficult pursuit which only a gifted few were capable of undertaking.

As far as the Jews were concerned, the Torah which God had revealed to their ancestors was for them an adequate and unfailing source of salvation. There were, to be sure, many teachings in that Torah which were evidently in conflict with those of reason, as expounded by the great philosophers. Theologians, like Saadia and Maimonides, regarded such conflict as only apparent. They were certain that both Torah and reason originated from the same divine source, and therefore concluded that a proper method of interpreting the teachings of the Torah would eliminate the seeming conflict.

It is certainly far easier to bring the teachings of the Torah into harmony with the conclusions of reason than vice versa. Only a bold thinker like Isaac Albalag (second half of the thirteenth century) ventured to suggested that Torah and philosophy belonged to different universes of thought. In any event, the recognition of philosophy as a possible source of salvational truth gave validity to the ideas or beliefs which certain great thinkers had arrived at as a result of rational reflection. Such validity, however, was likely to weaken the Jews' sense of complete dependence upon the Torah and their adherence to its precepts. The theologians, it is true, did all in their power to reinterpret the statements in the Torah that were in conflict with reason. Maimonides went even further in catering to the demands of reason; he tried to justify the ritual laws in the Torah on rational grounds, by stressing their practical value. But the more plausible became the attempts of Jewish theologians at harmonizing tradition with reason, the greater grew the prestige of reason at the expense of tradition.

Men render unswerving loyalty to tradition so long as they lack confidence in the ability of the human mind to help them find the true way of life. As soon, however, as they begin to rely on their own thinking, they are inclined to challenge the tradition in which they have been brought up, especially when it is the tradition of a minority group. In the Diaspora, Jews have always been outnumbered in power and influence; hence, they suspected the tendency to defer to reason as likely to undermine loyalty to their tradition. That suspicion inhibited the development of philosophic studies.

That accounts for the at best merely grudging reception accorded by the main body of the Jewish People and its spiritual leaders to philosophical or theological writings. It is true that some of the most important results of the rational approach to the conception of God ultimately found their way into the normative Judaism of pre-modern times. The negation of all human attributes applied to God in sacred scriptures and the deprecation of literal rendering of spiritual concepts became an integral part of the Jewish theology. That was indirectly due to the influence of Philo's writings. Those writings were known only in Christian theological circles, but their influence reached the Jewish theological writings of the Middle Ages. It is interesting to note the difference between Judaism and Christianity, from the standpoint of how they assimilated Greek philosophic thinking. Whereas the synthesis of the early Christian tradition with Aristotelianism, effected by Thomas Aquinas in the thirteenth century, became the official and authoritative doctrine of the Roman Catholic Church, the synthesis of Jewish tradition with Aristotelianism effected by Maimonides never received official sanction, and was for the most part resisted rather than welcomed.

Jews first encountered philosophy in Alexandria. They lived there in considerable numbers during the four centuries between 200 B.C.E. and 200 C.E. Though they retained their Jewish identity and group life, they were completely Hellenized. Their vernacular was Greek. The most intellectually alert among them came into contact with Greek culture, which was then dominant in Alexandria. The Bible and the observance based on the laws in the Torah were all that bound those Jews to Judaism. For the Bible to function in their lives, it not only had to be translated into Greek; its teachings had also to be made compatible with the assumptions concerning God and man which they had acquired from Greek culture. Thus began the process of reinterpretation of traditional values in terms of the dominant world outlook of the

Hellenist world, a process which culminated in the writings of Philo.

That process of reinterpretation of the Jewish tradition contributed perhaps more than any other factor to the spread of early Christianity beyond Jewish circles, and to the viability of that tradition in the Gentile world. It also laid the foundation for the synthesis of early Christianity with Greek philosophic thought for mankind. For when the Arabs conquered Syria, the part of the world where this synthesis had been achieved, they took over the entire scientific and philosophic heritage of the Greeks and incorporated it into Moslem culture. From there Greek philosophy passed on to the Jews.

The majority of the Jews happened to live then in the Moslem empire. Before long they found themselves so adjusted to the life of their Arab neighbors that they gave up the Aramaic language they had been using for centuries and adopted Arabic as their vernacular. Their cultural and spiritual leaders acquired the philosophic learning which had become part of Arabic culture. During those centuries (800-1200), the foremost men in Jewry wrote most of their important works in Arabic. But what is more significant is that they had to reconcile once again the teachings of Judaism, as Alexandrian Jews before them had done, with the teachings of Greek philosophy and ethics.

The outstanding thinker whose writings were regarded as authoritative, second only to divinely revealed teachings, was Aristotle. He was referred to as "the philosopher." According to Maimonides, all that Aristotle had taught concerning the sublunar universe was unquestionably true.[2] The four outstanding works in Jewish theology which are a product of the contact with Greek thought through the medium of Arabic culture are Saadia's *Beliefs and Doctrines*, Bahya's *Duties of the Heart*, Halevi's *The Kuzari* and Maimonides' *Guide for the Perplexed*. These four works, written originally in Arabic, were later translated into Hebrew for the Jews who lived in Provence during the thirteenth century.

The awareness of having drawn on non-Jewish sources for his philosophic ideas is clearly indicated in the statement of Maimonides. "You will find that, in the few works composed by the Geonim and the Karaites on the unity of God and such matters as are connected with this doctrine, they followed the lead of the Moslem Mutakalimun. It also happened that at the time when the Moslems adopted this method of Kalam, there arose among them a certain sect called Mutazila." [3] Maimonides himself, though as much influenced by non-Jewish thought as the other Jewish philosophers, speaks rather contemptuously of the tendency among the latter to adopt the first philosophy they come upon.

The purpose of Jewish philosophic thought during the Middle Ages was to effect a *modus vivendi* between two such apparently incompatible approaches to reality as those of Greek philosophy and Rabbinic Judaism. The two outstanding arguments whereby the Medieval Jewish philosophers justified the need for revealed truth, without implying that such truth in any way conflicted with reasoned truth, were the following: In the first place, revelation makes accessible to the multitude, in a form adapted to their understanding, such truth as, in its reasoned form, would be capable of being grasped only by a few intellectuals. Secondly, revelation supplies the knowledge of truths which the most intellectually gifted could arrive at only after arduous study and reflection.

To what extent Rabbinic Judaism underwent metamorphosis when synthesized with Greek philosophy may be seen from the following teachings of Medieval Jewish theology:

1. According to Rabbinic Judaism, salvation (or the fulfillment of human life) can be achieved only through the study of Torah and the practice of the *mitzvot*. According to Medieval Jewish theology, it can be achieved only through contemplation of the truth concerning the nature of reality or of the Divine government of the world; this is what the Jewish theologians understood by study of Torah in its esoteric sense. They accepted Aristotle's view of the moral virtues as being, in the words of Matthew Arnold only "the porch and access to the intellectual, and with these last is blessedness." At the hands of the Jewish theologians, also the conception or prophetism underwent a radical change. In Rabbinic writings, the prophet is conceived merely as the "messenger of God," or *malak*,[4] whose intellectual powers had nothing to do with his being selected by God to exhort and instruct. In philosophic writings, however, the prophet is viewed as a great thinker whose intellectual powers were so extraordinary as to render him qualified for his prophetic mission.[5]

2. Rabbinic Judaism is not troubled by the anthropomorphic conception of God. But Medieval Jewish theology's principal task is the vigorous deprecation of anthropomorphism. It explains away the anthropomorphisms in the Bible as purely metaphorical, on the Rabbinic principle of "the Torah speaks in human idiom." That principle was intended originally to apply only to the legalistic rendering of the Torah text. As such, its purpose was to offset the tendency to derive legal conclusions from what appeared to some *Tannaim* to be verbal redundancies; it had nothing to do with questions of theology.

3. Rabbinic Judaism was not in the least disturbed by the problem which miracles presented from a philosophic point of view. Now, philosophically, miracles imply changes in God's will in accordance with circumstances occasioned by man. That conception of miracles is incompatible with the assumption that God's will is immutable. Those statements in Rabbinic writings which have a bearing on the miracles of the Bible are not motivated, as is wrongly assumed, by the foregoing consideration. To the Rabbis, the miracles are part of their Israel-centered view of the world, and their comments on miracles have to be understood in that light. For the theologians, however, the philosophic considerations are primary. Maimonides, therefore, treats the miracles as having been built into the structure of the world when God created it.[6] Gersonides, who tries to steer a middle course between tradition and reason, arrives at a highly sophisticated explanation of miracles which seems to satisfy the demands of neither.[7]

4. Rabbinic Judaism sees no contradiction between the conception of God's infinite power and the many attributes ascribed to Him such as those in Exodus 34:6-7, which imply that He is influenced by factors outside Himself. On the other hand, Jewish theology, finding it necessary to describe God in negative terms, gives a negative meaning to the attributes ascribed to God in the foregoing verses in Exodus, since their affirmative meanings imply limitations on God's being and power.

5. Rabbinic Judaism is unaware of any contradiction between God's foreknowledge and man's free will. The usual interpretation given to R. Akiba's statement in *Abot* III, 19 as implying an awareness of such contradiction is incorrect. The phrase *Hakol tzafui* in that statement does not mean "everything is foreseen,"

but "everything is beheld." Hence what R. Akiba says is not "Everything is foreseen, yet freedom of choice is given," but "Everything is beheld *and* freedom of choice is given." What he wishes to emphasize is not God's foreknowledge but God's *knowledge* of whatever man does or thinks. Jewish theology, on the other hand, never wearied of seeking a solution for the apparent contradiction between God's foreknowledge and man's freedom to choose between obeying and disobeying the will of God.

6.   Rabbinic Judaism sees no need for attaching any meaning other than a literal one to biblical stories in which human traits are ascribed to God. Jewish theology either interprets those stories allegorically, or it considers them as visions or dreams. It does not regard them as accounts of objective events. This applies especially to stories like those of Creation, the Garden of Eden, the Tower of Babel, the three divine visitors to Abraham, and Jacob's struggle with the angel. In the case of the theophanies recorded in the Bible, Medieval Jewish theology resorts to the novel concept of *kavod nivra*, a kind of visible being created for the occasion, or an existing light too dazzling for human eye to behold, except after it has passed. The basis for this novel view is the biblical term "the glory of the Lord" and the Rabbinic term "*Shekinah*."

7.   Rabbinic Judaism recognized only one kind of authoritative law, namely, the supernaturally revealed law contained in the Torah. It regarded that law as intended to help the Jew attain his well-being in this world and bliss in the hereafter. Jewish theology, on the other hand, as represented by Joseph Albo in his *Ikkarim*, which is a kind of abbreviated Jewish *Summa Theologica*, accepts the classification formulated by Thomas Aquinas of three kinds of law—namely, natural law (the medieval equivalent for our term "moral"), positive law (formulated in some human code), and divine, or supernaturally revealed, law. According to this classification, the Torah as supernaturally revealed law is contrasted with moral and humanly formulated law. This classification has given rise to the modern distinction between religious and secular, a distinction which has only helped to confuse thinking and darken counsel.

8.   Rabbinic Judaism deprecates the interpretation of the *mitzvot* as having a purpose other than that of affording the opportunity to serve God.[8] It insists on their being observed as divine

decrees, or as means of teaching man to obey God's will without any ulterior purpose. Jewish theology, on the other hand, takes it for granted that ritual practices have the additional purpose of improving man's character. Ritual practices which seem devoid of such purpose are regarded as inferior in sanctity or importance.[9]

Rabbinic Judaism has a special category for duties pertaining to interpersonal relations. It assumes, however, that the Torah lays down in each case what is right and what is wrong. Jewish theology introduces an additional ethical norm which emanates from reason. That norm is usually the one suggested by Aristotle's "Golden Mean." According to Maimonides, who makes a point of stressing the "Golden Mean," it is identical with whatever conduct the Torah prescribes. He considers it the principle underlying the Mishnaic treatise of *Abot*.

9.   Rabbinic Judaism sees no difficulty in conceiving God as exercising individual providence over the life of every human being. Jewish theology regards such providence as being exercised in accordance with the intellectual development of the individual. If the individual has failed to develop his intellect, divine providence knows him only as a member of the general species "man." To be an object of God's special care, a human being must develop his intellectual powers.

10.   Rabbinic Judaism accepts the principle of reward and punishment. Jewish theology finds it necessary to retain the belief in divine retribution, but, in doing so, it draws a sharp distinction between the body and the soul, insofar as they are objects of reward or punishment. The soul is conceived in philosophical terms suggested by Aristotle. According to him, man possesses three souls— the vegetative, the animal and the human. Of these, the human soul, which is synoymous with the intellect, is the only one that survives the body. But its survival consists in being united with what is termed the Active Intellect of the world, third in the order of spiritual beings, of which the first two are God and the Separate Intelligences. Maimonides, Hillel ben Samuel (1220-1295) of Verona, Italy, in his *Tagmulē ha-Nefesh*, and Hasdai Crescas (1340-1410) of Barcelona, Spain, in his *Or Adonai*, explain allegorically the statements in Rabbinic writings concerning *Gan Eden* and *Gehinnom*.

11.   Rabbinic Judaism assumes that in the world to come the

human body will be so perfected as not to be subject to the hunger, ailments, and deterioration which mark its present life. We seldom meet in Rabbinic writings any attempt to describe in detail the process of bodily resurrection. Otherwise, that belief is accepted as a matter of course. The theologians, on the other hand, find resurrection a troublesome belief. Admitting that it has to be accepted on faith, they recognize that it calls for stretching that faith. Maimonides, however, is the only one who refuses to accept unqualifiedly the traditional idea concerning the resurrection. Though he accepts that part which affirms the reunion of the soul with the original body, or with a new body, at some time after death, he cannot accept the traditional assumption that this re-union is to be eternal. The body, being a compound substance, must ultimately disintegrate and fall away from the soul.

All of the foregoing deviations from Rabbinic Judaism show that Medieval Jewish theology evolved a radically different universe of thought from that of the Rabbinic tradition. Medieval Jewish theology was based on an attempt to reconcile authoritative tra-dition with the conclusions of reasoned thought. The Jewish theologians themselves were unaware how radically different their own point of view was from that of tradition. This unawareness was due to their lack of historical perspective. One has only to read Maimonides' Introduction to his Commentary on the Mishnah and the one to his Code, for his account of the transmission of the Torah from Moses to his successors, to realize how uncritical of tradition Maimonides was, from the standpoint of objective history.

In contrast with the Jews who lived in Moslem countries, those who lived in Christian countries did not have the opportunity to come in contact with philosophic thought. The reason for this was that the medium of philosophic thought was not any of the vernac-ulars of the populations in those countries, but Latin, which was the language used by the functionaries of the Church. Those ver-naculars were the incipient languages of modern Europe, and were also familiar to the Jews, but they were not used as a means of philosophic discourse or writing. Hence, in Christian Europe, prior to the Renaissance, the Jewish authorities did not encounter the challenge of philosophy. That accounts for their resistance to philosophic studies, as exemplified by the ban against them issued by R. Solomon ben Adret of Barcelona in 1304.

The influence of the early opponents to the study of philosophy went beyond their own original intent. What they combatted was mainly the attempt to deal with the belief in God from a meta-physical standpoint. But more recent imitators have banned all secular studies. "What matters it," said R. Ezekiel Landau (1713-1793) of Jampol, Poland, "that logic is necessary for acquiring the wisdom of the Torah? Since the original purpose of logic was to aid one in acquiring secular knowledge, one should have nothing to do with it." [10] The theological writings of the Jewish thinkers in the Western world fell into neglect and would have been com-pletely forgotten were it not for Maimonides' Code known as *Yad ha-Hazaka* and his Commentary on the *Mishnah*, and the Medieval exegetical and homiletical commentaries on the Bible, which contain philosophic material. Even those commentaries, however, were not always viewed with favor. R. Nachman of Bratzlav (1770-1811) said of *Akedat Yitzhak*, which is a collection of philosophic homilies on the Pentateuch by R. Yitzhak Arama, a Spanish rabbi of the fifteenth century, that although it is a *sefer kasher*, it should not be studied because it contains statements by philosophers and the questions they raise.

An incident which illustrates how antagonistic Jews were to the study of philosophy during the sixteenth century is the following: In the course of a response to a question pertaining to *kashrut*, R. Moses Isserles (1520-1572) happened to quote Aristotle's opinion concerning a certain disease to prove that it was not fatal. For this he was roundly denounced by R. Solomon Luria. R. Moses Isserles found it necessary to appease his disputant with profuse apologies for having introduced Aristotle's name into a question of Jewish law. "Although I have quoted some words of Aristotle, I take heaven and earth to witness that I have never in all my days busied myself with any of his books." [11]

R. Joel Sirkes (1561-1640) of Poland, the author of a famous commentary on the *Arbaah Turim* of Jacob ben Asher, characterizes philosophy in the following words: "Philosophy is the essence of heresy and 'the strange woman' against whom King Solomon warned man." [12] R. Solomon Luria (1510-1573) of Lithuania assails

Maimonides for having advised his own son to study the writings of Ibn Ezra.[13] Solomon Maimon (1754-1800) was not admitted into Berlin, because the rabbi of the Jewish community of that city refused to vouch for his character. The reason for this refusal was that Maimon had written a commentary on Maimonides' *Guide for the Perplexed*. When the commentary was published, it appeared anonymously. "The Rambam," said R. Elijah, the Gaon of Vilna, to his disciples in a fit of anger, "was allured by the cursed philosophy. Its sophistry misled him into interpreting the *Gemara* as though it were a jest, and tearing away the aggadic passages from their literal meaning." [14] In Russia during the middle of the nineteenth century there were many large Jewish communities where not a single copy of Maimonides' *Guide* was to be found.[15]

It is not necessary to give more than a brief sketch of those philosophic problems and conceptions which, despite the prejudice against philosophy, were kept alive in the various writings that shaped the Jewish consciousness before the end of the eighteenth century.

First and foremost was the problem of explaining the anthropomorphic allusions to God. The creed of Maimonides had found its way into the daily prayer book. So did some of the religious poetry of Ibn Gabriol and of the anonymous author of the "Song of Unity." These reminders of the importance of having the right conception of God helped to keep alive the doctrine that it was sinful to conceive God as having bodily form, or as subject to human emotions. Despite the many naïve-minded authorities in Rabbinic Judaism who voiced their opposition to Maimonides, he did succeed to a large degree in impressing upon the Jews the idea that to think of God as though he were a magnified man was to be a heretic and to forfeit one's salvation.[16] Despite that prohibition, however, the average Jew found it necessary to form some mental image of Deity. Only in intellectual circles was the anthropomorphic conception of God taboo.

Related to the problem of anthropomorphism is that of the numerous passages in the Bible where God is represented as harboring such emotions as pity, anger, delight, or regret, and acting as though he possessed human traits. All these are explained away by means of the principle that "the Torah spoke in human idiom."

Another principle which survived from Medieval Jewish theology was *creatio ex nihilo*. Insistence upon the doctrine that the world was created out of nothing was due mainly to its pragmatic significance. For only on the assumption that God had created the world out of nothing was it possible to understand how He could suspend the routine order of the world from time to time for the sake of Israel. To assume with Aristotle that matter was eternal was to ascribe limited power to God, since the existence of primeval matter necessarily put a limit to what God might want to do. *The need for stressing the historicity of the miracles may have been felt because the increasing awareness of a fixed order of nature tended to undermine belief in the religious tradition.* Besides re-enforcing the belief in the historicity of the miracles recorded in Scriptures, the assumption that God created the world out of nothing was necessary to fortify one's faith in the resurrection of the dead—a miracle, as it was then believed, essential to the future redemption of Israel.

A third principle which survived from the philosophic age in Judaism was that the text of the Torah was intended to convey more than the surface meaning, or *Peshat*. Not even the Rabbinic interpretation, or *Derush*, was regarded as exhaustive of the significance of the text. There was, in addition, the allegorical meaning, or *Remez*, which could be ascertained only after one had developed his intellect and acquired a need for a rational approach to tradition. And finally, there was *Sōd*, the mustic or esoteric significance, which was reserved for those who were spiritually qualified. The first two types of interpretation were exoteric, i.e., intended for everybody; the last two were esoteric, i.e., intended only for the intellectual élite.

More important, however, than these specific principles which came down from Medieval Jewish theology to modern times was the basic assumption that the demands of reason must not be disregarded, and that traditional beliefs and practices have to be interpreted in compliance with those demands. That attitude of Jewish rational thought not only held its ground, but received new impetus with the rise of the modern *Haskalah*, the Jewish Enlightenment movement.

MEDIEVAL JEWISH MYSTICISM

Unlike philosophy, whose study tended to alienate Jews of a reflective turn of mind from the Jewish tradition, mysticism exercised an attractive influence on them. Jewish mystics were unaware of any challenge to the authority of the Torah. They did not recognize any source of knowledge concerning God, man, and the world, outside the tradition. Unconsciously, however, Jewish mystics did draw upon ideas concerning reality which were current in the non-Jewish environment. Some of those ideas were of a highly intellectual character, and others were of a folk character. In the same way as the Hasidic "masters" of Eastern Poland and the Ukraine in the nineteenth century created melodies and songs in the genre of the folk music of their part of the world, so did Jewish mystics of preceding centuries absorb ideas and habits from the folklore and folk practices of the neighboring peoples. Most of the superstitions and theurgic practices which have since crept into Jewish life originated in that fashion.

What is more striking is that even the pronouncedly intellectual elements in Jewish mysticism, such as those which have to do with the conception of God, of the world, or of the soul, are definitely extraneous in origin. Yet, those elements were never recognized as such, and therefore never constituted a challenge to the Torah. Alien notions, such as those concerning the resurrection of the dead, or of the world to come, unconsciously transformed the thought-pattern of Biblical religion during the era of the Second Commonwealth. So did alien notions about emanation, "sparks," and metempsychosis, which unconsciously found their way later into the Jewish tradition as interpreted by the mystics. The *Tannaim* of the *Mishnah* were so certain that the doctrine of resurrection was contained in the Torah that they consigned to perdition anyone who denied such origin. The Jewish mystics would similarly have condemned anyone who would have questioned the Torah origin of such beliefs as those concerning the *Sefirot* or concerning metempsychosis.

The reason Jewish mysticism exercised an attractive influence on Jews of a reflective turn of mind is that it conceived its problem as not being how to reconcile the teaching of the Torah with those derived from reason, but how to discover the hidden meaning of what the Torah itself taught. Nor did mysticism try to find a rational explanation for the ritual *mitzvot* in the Torah. It sought in those *mitzvot* that theurgic significance, or sacramental character, which it assumed they had always possessed. The mystics were entirely unaware that they were reading anything *into* the Torah; they were always certain that they were reading meanings *out of* the Torah which had always been there. Jewish mysticism is inherently the continuation of the same method whereby the Oral Torah came to be regarded as essentially the interpretation of the Written Torah. The same kind of attractive influence that was exercised by the development of the Rabbinic Oral Law was later exercised by Kabbalah.

Due to this approach, which Jewish mysticism had in common with Rabbinic lore, it intensified the Jew's devotion to the study of Torah and the observance of *mitzvot*, and augmented his sense of privilege in being identified with the Jewish People. "Woe unto the men who see in the Torah nothing but simple narrative and ordinary words," says the *Zohar*. "Were this so, we could even today compose a Torah which would equally be worthy of our esteem. But this is not so. Every word of the Torah contains an elevated sense and a sublime mystery. The narratives of the Torah are the garments of the Torah itself." [17] That fact of itself is sufficient to account for the high regard in which mysticism was held by the Jews throughout the ages, in contrast with the ill-repute in which philosophy was held by the large body of the Jews and their leaders, especially during the years immediately prior to the modern era in Judaism. A philosopher like Maimonides regarded the cultivation of philosophy as indispensable to the immortality of the soul. No wonder he was suspected of setting up philosophy as a rival to the divine teaching revealed by God in the Torah.

The rationalist trend in Traditional Judaism was limited during the Middle Ages to small groups, living in countries where Moslem culture was dominant; and even there that trend lasted only three or four centuries, principally during the brief periods when Jews enjoyed comparative peace. With that exception in mind, we may say that rationalism, as represented by the Jewish philosophers in the Middle Ages, was on the whole treated with aversion in pre-modern Judaism. On the other hand, Kabbalah enjoyed great prestige. There were times when its study was taken up by people who had not the necessary knowledge or character qualifications. This irked many ardent Kabbalists. These mystics were especially disturbed by the fact that the interest in mysticism had diverted many from the basic study of Jewish law.

Strong protests were then heard against the misuse of Kabbalistic studies which had fallen into the wrong hands. R. Moses Isserles complained, "Many among the masses venture into the study of Kabbalah . . . Lay people who are so illiterate as not to be able to understand a chapter of the Pentateuch even with the aid of Rashi's commentary, undertake the study of Kabbalah." [18] In the same spirit, R. Solomon Luria thus addresses would-be students of Kabbalah: "Recent upstarts want to belong to the group of Kabbalist and esoteric scholars. My friend, do not walk in their way, and keep away from mysticism." [19] Yet the very authors of those protests were themselves not only masters of Kabbalah, but also wrote extensively in its spirit.

What especially contributed to the hearty welcome which Judaism extended to mystic lore, in contrast with the antagonism toward philosophy, was the central place assigned in that lore to the People of Israel. The very opening chapter of the Zohar dwells at length upon the supernatural powers wherewith the People of Israel is endowed. The centrality of Israel did not remain merely an exalted abstraction. It was made the basis of the very practical hope which kept the Jewish People alive, the hope that the promised Messiah would appear and redeem it from exile and subjection. Jewish mysticism interpreted this redemption of the Jewish People as synonymous with the redemption of the Shekinah, thus giving to that redemption a cosmic dimension. It taught, furthermore, that the advent of the Messiah depended upon the conduct and inner life of every Jew. When a Jew kept his inner life free from sin and obeyed the mitzvot of the Torah, he brought about those changes in the very nature of the universe which speeded the redemption of his People.

According to the Zohar, the mitzvot are a part of the very process whereby the world came into being.[20] To be sure, all rational philosophies likewise stress self-discipline as indispensable to the attainment of that clarity of mind which is necessary for the per-ception of the truth and for the unclouded judgment that can distinguish clearly between good and evil. On the other hand, the observance of ritual precepts lies outside the domain of rational philosophy. Indeed, they even have to be apologized for, and their value defended on grounds which often seem far-fetched. Quite often, these very grounds serve as a reason for their non-observance, because once their purpose is recognized, it seems attainable without all the effort expended in their observance.

With mystic lore, however, the case is entirely different. In the first place, both ritual practice and self-discipline come to be indispensable means to the cultivation of that lore and to the attainment of the mystic state of mind or of soul. The sense of power, of being an efficient cause, is one of the most vital urges in human nature, and that urge is satisfied by the self-discipline which is a prerequisite to mystical speculation. Likewise, the ritual observances, upon which Jewish mysticism lays great emphasis, are not merely a means of securing reward in the hereafter. On the contrary, their reward is assumed to be near at hand, in the form of added power which the one who observes them acquires.

Jewish mysticism did not merely emphasize the importance of the ritual precepts; it assigned to them a theurgic function by ascribing to them meanings (*kavanot*) which were expected to endow one with the power to control, or manipulate at will, the forces of the cosmos. The Jewish mystics seemed to share with all other Medieval mystics the ambition to compete with alchemists and other dabblers in primitive science in their attempt to wrest from nature those secrets which place it at the command of the human will. "That the doctrine of *Kawwanah* in prayer" writes G. G. Scholem "was capable of being interpreted as a certain kind of magic seems clear to me; that it involves the problem of magical practices is beyond any doubt." [21]

Together with the observance of the *mitzvot*, the study of Torah and engaging in prayer are repeatedly stressed in Jewish mysticism. Whatever contributed to man's salvation or *tikkun ha-nefesh* (setting the soul in order) was regarded as contributing also to *tikkun ha-olam* (setting the world in order). *Tikkun ha-olam* was tantamount to the restoration of the original harmony of the universe, of the lower with the upper worlds, and of Israel with God.

In contrast with the theurgic potency associated in Jewish

mysticism with the traditional way of life, Jewish philosophy or theology saw the highest good in the realization of the Hellenic ideal of intellectual contemplation. The entire regimen of Torah, *mitzvot* and prayer had for the Jewish philosopher only the instrumental value of providing the environmental conditions necessary to enable the intellectual élite to achieve their self-fulfillment or salvation. It is no wonder, therefore, that philosophy did not have the slightest chance of appealing to the heart or mind of the average Jew.

The reason mysticism always exercises an attraction for the human mind is that it seems to hold out the promise of coping either theoretically or practically with the problem of evil. Apart from mysticism, all that traditional religion has to offer is the regimen of moral and religious duties, accompanied by the promise that those who lay up sufficient merit in this world will be amply compensated in the hereafter for the evils suffered in this world. Jewish theologians tried to argue evil out of existence. They took the position that existence was intrinsically and necessarily good. Hence evil was merely non-existence.[22]

Jewish mysticism, on the other hand, not only recognized the reality of evil, but was preoccupied with the problem of combatting it in *this* world. It viewed the evils that troubled man as rooted in the very constitution of the universe. To combat them, man had to measure himself against a foe of cosmic proportions. Having no conception of the possibility of resorting to the control of natural forces through scientific knowledge or their operation, the Jewish mystics concluded that for man to be equal to the combat, he had to be clothed with more than human power.

Medieval mysticism, whether Jewish or non-Jewish, represented in large measure animism, or the human tendency to project human traits into nature, both animate and inanimate. That tendency is bound to persist so long as the human mind has not acquired the full significance of the impersonal operation of events in nature. To the pre-scientific mind, all phenomena were the effect of some personal will, whether that of God or man, angel or demon. "There is not a blade of grass" we are told, "but has a constellation which strikes it and says 'grow.' "[23] The notion of natural law was as inconceivable to the ancients as non-physical reality is to most people even nowadays. So long as the mind is unacquainted with the concept of natural law, its tendency to think in terms of causal relations is continually misled by analogy and by the fallacy of *post hoc ergo propter hoc*. Its thinking is further vitiated by its tendency to reify or thingify its own abstractions and to treat them as separate entities. Thus, untrammeled by logical considerations, the primitive human mind, both ancient and contemporary, builds up entire systems of mythology to account for the various phenomena of nature and of human life.

These two factors—animism and an uncritical sense of causation—were shared by Medieval mysticism with all ancient religion. The only difference is that Medieval mysticism tried to come directly to grips with the problem of evil in the form of sin, suffering and death. It sought deliberately to lessen the measure of those evils in the present, and refused to take the attitude of institutional religion, which was satisfied with the prospect of having those evils removed by God at some distant future. That led the mystics to dabble in magic.

Mysticism also had as its purpose to foster inner states of mind which would enable the individual to transcend evil. To that end it tried to evoke a state of ecstasy, or charism. The formulation of all such ideas as have a bearing either on magic or on ecstasy gave rise to theosophy. Some mystics specialized in theosophy, others in the practice of ecstasy or charism, and still others in the practice of magic. Thus arose various types of mysticism, though not always were the boundaries dividing them clear.

Mysticism as such never functions in a vacuum; it presupposes the existence of a specific religious or philosophic tradition. Medieval Jewish mysticism accordingly, strove, in the first place, to combat evil with the theurgic means provided by Jewish tradition, and, secondly, to keep alive the inherited religious impulse by interpreting in its spirit the texts of the Jewish tradition. The Bible, the Talmud and *Midrashim* could not but be enchanced in importance and sanctity as a result of their being utilized for those two purposes. What seemed inert became vital with significance. The tradition, which might have become obsolete, thus acquired new life under the mystic touch.

When we compare the Medieval mystic's approach to tradition with that of the Medieval theologian, we can well understand why the Jews were attracted by the former and repelled by the latter.

The Jewish mystic regarded tradition as an inexhaustible mine of truths that might help the Jewish People recover its ancient glory materially and spiritually, as well as the individual Jew to fulfill the purpose of his own life on earth. The Jewish theologian, on the other hand, found it necessary to reconcile the tradition with the teachings he had acquired from non-Jewish sources. That purpose so preoccupied him that he failed to establish a clear connection between the tradition and salvation, whether national or personal.

The outstanding values or ideals which inhered in the Jewish tradition and which were strongly accentuated in Jewish mysticism were the redemption of Israel and the salvation of the individual Jew. Jewish mysticism aimed to convert both of these values or ideals into experienced realities. When we study the trends in Jewish mysticism from the standpoint of these two purposes, we discover a definite rhythm in its development from the earliest times to the present.

THE ORIGINS OF JEWISH MYSTICISM

The origins of Jewish mysticism go back to the first century B.C.E. Already then certain teachings concerning God, man, and the world were transmitted only to those who had led a distinctly holy life. We gather that from the story of the Essenes in Palestine and the *Therapeutai* in Egypt.[24] Through contact with non-Jewish mystics, Jewish mysticism absorbed many of the ideas which had been developed by Pythagoreans and Platonists and especially by Philo. During the first century of the Common Era there arose a kind of eclectic mystic lore which, in addition to those sources, drew also upon Zoroastrianism and Mithraism. That mystic lore which was fostered in and around Palestine during the early Christian centuries was known as Gnosticism. During the Tannaitic and Amoraic period, Gnosticism exerted considerable influence on a number of Jewish scholars who were susceptible to the mystic approach to life. The existence of esoteric teachings as well as the high values placed upon them may be inferred from the mention of the communication of *rāzē Torah*, or hidden meanings of the Torah, as a reward to the deserving scholar.[25]

In Rabbinic literature, we meet with two categories of mystic or esoteric teachings, or theosophy: *Maaseh Bereshit* and *Maasseh Merkabah*. Those teachings deal respectively with the story of Creation and the description of the Divine Chariot.[26] In the Mishnah we are told that the *Merkabah* and the *Maaseh Bereshit* must not be interpreted to more than one or two at a time, and only to those who have shown themselves worthy. The oft-repeated emphasis upon high moral and spiritual traits as a prerequisite to the study of mystic lore implies that, in the hands of someone lacking those traits, that study might lead to dangerous consequences. Rabbinic literature contains large areas of each of the three types of mysticism mentioned above: charism, magic and theosophy.

a) Charism, the gift of divine spirit, is that self-identification of the human with the divine which enables the human being to enjoy the experience of having transcended or transformed the evil in his own personality. It may express itself as a state of prophecy or of ecstasy. The passages in Rabbinic literature which bear on charism are statements about Shekinah, in which Shekinah has the special connotation of *ruah ha-kodesh*, or holy spirit. The statement, for example, that "The Shekinah does not abide with anyone who is in a state of idleness, sadness, levity, etc . . . but only with those who are in a state of ecstasy resulting from the performance of a *mitzvah*" [27] refers to charism. Here Shekinah is synonymous with the Divine Spirit.[28] R. Halafta's statement that "The Shekinah rests not only upon ten who occupy themselves with the Torah but even upon three, or two or even upon one," [29] implies that the study of the Torah can give rise to charism. Charismatic powers were ascribed to some of the Tannaim. Among them were R. Yohanan ben Zakkai and his noted disciples.[30] The reason is that the Torah is assumed to be literally the word of God. By becoming absorbed in it, a person relives, as it were, the experience of those who were present when God revealed Himself on Mount Sinai.

Faith in God, or in God's messenger, or the performance of a single *mitzvah* in the spirit of faith, is said to cause the *ruah-ha-kodesh*, or the holy spirit, to rest upon one.[31] In the *Baraita* of R. Pinhas ben Yair, saintliness is said to lead to *ruah ha-kodesh*.[32] In the world to come, we are told, all physical functions of the human being will undergo a charismatic transformation. That is implied in the saying: "The righteous will enjoy there the radiance of the Shekinah." [33] When the Israelites heard God's voice at Sinai, they experienced charism; during that time they became a nation of prophets. Then they were free from the power of the angel of death and of the Evil Yetzer.[34]

The foregoing are only a few of the numerous passages in Rabbinic literature which indicate that the mystic experience of ecstasy was regarded by the Sages as an attainable state, in the sense that one might have a foretaste of the heavenly bliss while still in this world. There was little in Jewish mysticism of the Middle Ages and the subsequent centuries that was entirely new, except, perhaps, the doctrine of metempsychosis, which was introduced by the mystics of Safed in the sixteenth century.

b) Similarly, we find in Talmudic writings large areas of theurgy, or magic, which figured in certain trends of post-Talmudic mysticism to a greater degree than in others. It is true that the Talmud definitely prohibited certain forms of magic which it describes as "the ways of the Amorites." [35] This is not at all surprising. In every ancient civilization we find both prohibited and permitted magic. A type of magic which for some reason is still recognized as of alien origin is always prohibited. On the other hand, magic which is believed to be of native origin is not only permitted, but even commanded as a religious duty. In this class of duties we must place the perfomance of all ritual actions which were believed to produce desired results in the physical world, such as health, prosperity or safety from enemies. There is reference in the Talmud to a "Book of Healing," [36] which contained prescriptions against diseases. Since the ancients regarded disease as due to demonic attack, the only prescriptions a book of healing was likely to contain were magic formulas.

The resort to incantations and invocations to produce preternatural effects is frequently referred to in Rabbinic writings as a normal procedure. The entire range of demonology and angelology is taken for granted in Rabbinic Judaism, and with it, the existence of occult practices by which the malign influences of the various demons were to be brought under control. In the New Testament, this kind of magic figures as a normal part of Jewish life. Adolph Jellinek in his Bet Ha-Midrash has collected writings which deal with magic and theurgy. According to Ludwig Blau,[37] those writings date from Talmudic and, in part, from pre-Talmudic times. R. Akiba is described[38] as worthy of "making use of My Glory." This means that R. Akiba was worthy of engaging in theurgical practices.[39] The various combinations and permutations of the four letters of the Ineffable Name of God constituted the main source of potency in Jewish magic.[40]

The Talmud refers to a work on magic named *Sefer Hilkot Yetzirah* (Book of the Laws of Creation.)[41] "On the eve of every Sabbath," we are told, R. Hanina and R. Oshaia, students of R. Judah ha-Nasi, would busy themselves with study of *Sefer Yetzirah* and create, by means of the directions contained in it, a grown calf, and eat it on the Sabbath.[42] Rabba said: "If the righteous wanted, they could create a world, for it is written, *"Your iniquities have divided you off from your God!"* [43] This means that, if man had not sinned, he would have shared with God the capacity to create worlds." [44]

The Torah is said to "have many mouths," because those who study it can impose their will on the creatures of the upper world and of the lower world. The verse, *"I have profaned the princes of the Sanctuary"* [45] is interpreted as referring to the children of Israel who, but for their sins, might have imposed their will on the creatures of the lower world.[46] Those who led the pious, saintly life were regarded as capable of changing even God's decree. The same thought is conveyed in a Rabbinic comment on the verse: *"He that rules over man shall be righteous, even he that ruleth through the fear of God"* [47] What does this mean? R. Abbahu said: "It means, I (God) rule over man; who rules over Me? The *tzaddik*; for I ordain a decree of punishment, and he annuls it by dint of his virtue or of his prayers." [48]

c) To furnish a rationale both for their theurgy and the experience of charism, the Jews developed theosophy. Evidences of theosophy in Talmudic Judaism are too familiar to need laboring. The Mishnah lays down special rules governing the exposition of the *Maaseh Bereshit* and the *Maase Merkabah*. These terms denote, respectively, cosmogony, which deals with the creation of the world, and theosophy, which deals with the nature of Deity. The Mishnah assumes the existence of considerable lore on both of these subjects. References are also found to other types of lore, such as the knowledge of the Ineffable Name,[49] and to eschatology, which deals with life after death of the individual and with the redemption of Israel.[50]

The general term by which theosophy was known was *Sitrē Torah* or *Razē Torah*, [51] i.e., esoteric lore of the Torah. During the first centuries of the Common Era, that lore became involved in Gnosticism, which had its origin in ancient Chaldean sources, and which had absorbed Pythagorean, Platonic and Stoic ideas. When that happened and Jewish mystic lore became known as *Pardes* (Heavenly paradise), it took on a speculative turn of a heretical character. So mentally upsetting and spiritually weird must that theosophy have been that of the four oustanding Tannaim who engaged in the study of it, only R. Akiba managed to come out unscathed; of the others, one died, one lost his mind and the third became a heretic.[52]

The first book to set forth the principles of Jewish mysticism in speculative form is the *Sefer Yetzirah*. The date and place of its publication are unknown. It was extant during the Geonic period. R. Saadia regarded it as so significant that he was impelled to write a commentary on it. Being anonymous, it was ascribed to Patriarch Abraham.[53] Although its content amounts to no more than a few pages, it exerted, according to Louis Ginzberg, a greater influence on the development of the Jewish mind than almost any other book after the completion of the Talmud.[54]

The *Sefer Yetzirah* deals with the creation of the universe by means of the ten basic categories, or *Sefirot*, and the twenty-two letters of the Hebrew alphabet. Such a conception of creation is reminiscent of the type of thought which had been inaugurated by the Pythagoreans. Pythagoras and his disciples were so amazed at their discovery of the properties of numbers, which were then designated by means of letters, that they came to regard both numbers and letters as possessing creative power. That belief continued to play an important role in Jewish mysticism.

By the same token, the spoken word came to be regarded as inherently possessing creative power. It was very natural, therefore, to conclude that all created things owed their coming into being and persistence to the power of the hidden combination of primal lingual elements. The universe as a whole was, accordingly, conceived as the outcome of the different combinations of the letters in the various ineffable Names of God. Thus it was assumed that by knowing the particular combination of the Divine Name which played a part in the creation of the world, the human being might also come to possess the power to create.

THE LATEST PHASE OF JEWISH MYSTICISM

As early as the eighth century, Jewish mysticism flourished in Italy, Spain and France. From Italy it was transported by the Kalonymides to Germany, where R. Judah ha-Hasid (died 1217) and his disciple R. Eliezer of Worms (died 1238) were its most noteworthy exponents. They were part of the religious movement in early Medieval Germany known as Hasidism. The term "Hasid" acquired a new and special connotation which it had not had in the writings of the Rabbis of the Talmud. "Three things above all others," says G. Scholem "go to make the true Hasid as he appears before us in the *Book of the Devout*: ascetic renunciation of the things of this world; complete serenity of mind; and an altruism grounded in principle and driven to extremes." The influence of the Christian environment on that type of Jewish mysticism is unmistakable.[56]

In Provence, Languedoc, from the twelfth to the fifteenth centuries, great literary activity in mysticism was developed in centers like Arles, Marseilles, Lunel, Posquieres, Toulouse. During the thirteenth century, the most important center in Spain for the cultivation of Kabbalah was Gerona. The outstanding Kabbalists of that period were Todros Abulafia, Abraham Abulafia and Moses de Leon. Abraham Abulafia was distinguished for having sought to utilize Kabbalah as a means to mystic contemplation and the attainment of prophetic illumination. Toward the end of the thirteenth century the *Zohar* appeared and soon became the Bible of Kabbalistic lore.

The *Zohar* ascribes itself to R. Shimeon ben Yohai and his disciples, who flourished in Palestine after the Hadrianic wars, during the second century. Critical scholarship, however, has established beyond all doubt that almost all of it is the work of Moses de

Leon (1250-1305) of Spain. Its contents are cast in the form of *Midrash*, in that they convey various teachings through the interpretation of scriptural texts.

During those years, the position of Jewish mysticism, or Kabbalah *vis á vis* the other currents in Traditional Judaism, became crystallized. Kabbalah began to assail Talmudism, or the unreflective Rabbinic attitude, because of its legalistic formalism and its tendency to engage in logomachies based on the text of the Talmud and its commentaries. These logomachies were characterized by the Kabbalists as devoid of any sense of piety, or yearning for God. On the other hand, though much indebted to rationalist thought, especially in its element of theosophy, Kabbalah also assailed Jewish rationalism for rendering man reliant upon his own thinking and leading him away from God and the Torah. *Kabbalah came to regard itself as more capable of giving man a knowledge of the truth and of enabling him to change the environment than were philosophy and the physical sciences of the time.* The ecstatic Kabbalah, which had been inaugurated by Abraham ben Samuel Abulafia (1240-1291?), combined with the "Permutation of the Letters" to lay the foundation for the psychomagical Kabbalah of the Safed school, which began its career with the arrival of Ibn Gaon in Safed in 1325.

A further development in Kabbalah took place as a result of the expulsion of the Jews from Spain. A number of the Jewish refugees settled in Palestine. Among those who settled in the picturesque town of Safed there was a new flowering of Kabbalistic lore. Kabbalah ceased being an esoteric discipline and became a great social and religious force. Scholem rightly characterizes the changes which Safed Kabbalah effected in Jewish life as nothing less than revolutionary. Attention was henceforth centered on achieving immediate and practical results—the coming of the Messiah and the redemption of the Jewish People from its state of exile. With Palestine as the center of study, Kabbalah came to dominate Judaism during the sixteenth and seventeenth centuries in Germany, Poland, Italy, Morocco, Turkey, Persia and Yemen. The outstanding personality who gave impetus to the new development of Jewish mysticism was R. Isaac Luria, known as Ha-Ari. His chief disciples were R. Hayyim Vital and R. Elijah Vidas.

The new development consisted not only in a new emphasis on the national redemption as the objective of the regimen of study and practice conducted in the spirit of Kabbalah. It also included the introduction of the following new elements: the doctrine of *tikkun*, the doctrine of metempsychosis, and the emphasis on asceticism. The doctrine of *tikkun* is a phase of theosophy which deals with world improvement based not on an empirical study of needs, but on the traditional conception of reality. That conception is elaborated and popularized by means of analogies. Analogic reasoning is the source of such fanciful explanations of good and evil as are found in the theories concerning the "broken vessels" and the "sparks." Those theories attempt to account for the existence of good and evil in terms of Divinity as both immanent and transcendent.

The tendency toward asceticism found expression not only in abundant prayer and meditation on repentance, but also in fasting, self-flagellation and all manner of self-torment. The purpose was to make atonement for those sins of the Jewish People that prevented it from being redeemed from exile. Instead of maintaining the attitude of passive waiting for the redemption, the "masters of Kabbalah" hoped by their piety and self-renunciation to force the hand of God, as it were, to "hasten the end." The ascetic regimen, the elaboration of angelology, and the new element of metempsychosis, were related to the prescribed ritual practices, to insure their most meticulous observance. A series of self-imposed penitential fasts was adopted.[57] Thus were set in motion the mental and spiritual forces which soon produced the Messianic movement of Shabbetai Z'vi. It may justly be said that he was the inevitable outcome of the Safed Kabbalah.

The reaction against the Messianic movement after its tragic failure did not lead to the denial of theurgic or mystic means of influencing God's will. It merely led to the assumption that the time for the redemption had not yet arrived. It did express itself, however, in a suspicious attitude toward too intense an interest in Kabbalah. Thus Moses Hayyim Luzzato (1707-1747) was suspected, and perhaps with good reason, of endeavoring to achieve messiahship. The feud between Jonathan Eybeschuetz and Jacob Emden during the eighteenth century shook the whole of European

Jewry. That feud broke out because Emden sought to prove that Eybeschuetz had written amulets in which he made use of Shabbatian Kabbalah.

The more recent the Jewish mysticism, the less was it influenced by the changes which took place in European civilization between the end of Medievalism and the dawn of the modern era. Actually, by reason of its apotheosis of the Jewish People, Jewish mysticism succeeded in immuring those who came under its influence in a world of their own, and immunizing them against the changes which were taking place in their non-Jewish environment. As a result, the Jewish mystical trend not only continued unbroken even after the rise of modernism, but by the beginning of the nineteenth century grew into the powerful mass movement of Hasidism.

Hasidism arose in pre-partition Poland during the latter part of the eighteenth century. That movement removed Kabbalah from the category of an esoteric pursuit and transformed it into a popular cult. It not only raised Kabbalah to the same status as that of the Talmudic studies, but it also assigned the *Zohar* to a place of primacy in post-biblical writings. This led Hasidism to develop what J. Abelson rightly described as "a new spirituality." This "spirituality," he says, "which derived from the *Zohar* consisted in the conviction that there was an unbroken intercourse between the world of divinity and the world of humanity; that these worlds have a reciprocal influence on one another; and that prayer should be an ecstatic communion with God, so as to unite the human life with Him Who is the life of all the worlds. . . . It is not given to all men to attain this exalted state. But the man who attains it is, in the Hasidic sense, the *Tsaddik* who, as a result, possesses a degree of prophetic insight and a power to work miracles." [58] Without the new institution of the *Tsaddik*, or the pious master, it is doubtful whether Hasidism, despite its popularization of mystic lore, could have made much headway. The *tzaddikim* were regarded as charismatic, i.e., endowed with magical powers. The above-quoted statement concerning the power which God has granted to the *tsaddik* to annul His decree was taken both seriously and literally.[59] That fact created a new genre in Jewish tradition: miracle stories and legends dealing with the *tsaddik*.

Those stories and legends constitute a religious mythology which fulfilled the same function as the religious mythologies of all primitive and ancient peoples. They helped to give the *tsaddik* the status of a superhuman being. His intercession with God was sought whenever a person wished to make sure that his prayer would be heard. Such mythology is the warm, live content of religious experience, before it is cooled by the breath of rational reflection. In a sense, therefore, Hasidism constitutes a more creative aspect of religion that even the development of Kabbalah. Hasidism through its very mythology created *new* content; Kabbalah only reinterpreted *old* content. Hasidism was as superior creatively to Kabbalah as R. Luria's theurgy was to R. Cordovero's theosophy.

In keeping with Rabbinic tradition, Hasidism regarded the condition of Jewry as being that of exile, both spiritual and physical. This was sufficiently confirmed by the political and economic status of Jews in Eastern Europe during the period in which Hasidism flourished. The Jews of Poland and the Ukraine were being ground between the upper millstone of central governments and the feudal masters and the lower millstone of the peasantry. They were continually being denounced by the clergy and were vilified by the merchant and artisan guilds, which sought to squeeze them out of all enterprises and gainful occupations.

The Jewish proletarian masses and the disinherited, the *Luft-menschen*, the people whose sustenance was precarious and who not only lived from hand to mouth, but had very little to put into their mouths, were, in addition, the victims of governmental discriminatory tax laws. These weighed more heavily on them than on the middle-class people. They owed the state nothing, but the state exploited them ruthlessly. Each government in whose jurisdiction there were members of the Hasidic sect made it a practice to persecute them. It accused them of refusing to give their children a secular education, of fostering superstition and isolating themselves from the rest of the population.[60] It is no wonder, therefore, that any Jewish diletante (*maskil*) who sought to acquire the culture of his persecutors was looked upon by the Hasidim as a traitor.

Hasidism and *Haskalah* may be regarded as having functioned in Eastern Europe during the greater part of the nineteenth century as mutual foils. Hasidism was in all respects a revival of Traditional Judaism, intransigeant and determined to defy Westernism and the Gentile world. It was true to the letter and spirit of Traditional Judaism, conscious of waging a life and death struggle against overwhelming odds. Hasidism, through its addition of new mystical content, actually gave Traditional Judaism a new lease on life.

Haskalah, on the other hand, was a more violent antagonist of Hasidism than of non-mystical Rabbinism. Hasidism lent itself to mass vulgarization. Apart from the superstitions which it countenanced and the "white magic" that it fostered, it encouraged a mass heartiness and gaiety which was often restorted to as an escape from responsible living. That is why the *maskilim* were intent upon combating it with ridicule, the only weapon at their disposal.

The *maskilim* were mainly concerned with modernizing the Jews, by rationalizing their religious beliefs and practices, stressing the use of the vernacular, and having them acquire non-Jewish culture. They wanted to see in Jewish life the adoption of non-Jewish values. Among those values which had lately come into fashion was the so-called "return to nature." To the *maskilim* that meant that Jews should turn to agricultural pursuits and renounce the economy based on petty trading and artisanship. The *maskilim* invariably regarded the Hasidim as obstructing the Jewish emancipation.[61] But there were among the *maskilim*, also, the forerunners of constructive trends in Judaism, men like Isaac Erter, Judah Ber Levisohn, Nachman Krochmal and Judah Leib Rapaport.

There was nothing new in such mystical assumptions as were dominant in Hasidism, namely, that the outer world is the outer garment of Divinity, or that the visible world is an emanation of God, or that this emanation consists of matter and spirit. The distinctive feature in Hasidism was the way in which it tried to stimulate the individual Jew to disengage the element of Divinity in the cosmos and in man, by freeing it from whatever obscures or obstructs it. The doctrine of individual Providence is as old as Judaism itself. But, once again, it is Hasidism's new emphasis on the ubiquity of God that translates the teaching of individual Providence into an effective means of inward monition and conscience. The idea of God in Hasidism is given a pragmatic significance by being made the basis of an optimistic attitude toward life. *That there is a God means for Hasidism that nothing can be so absolutely evil as to be incapable of being made into an instrument of good.*

The best illustration of how Hasidism merely revitalized tradi-tional values of long standing is what it did with the institution of prayer. Hasidism was not the first movement in Judaism to place a high value on prayer. It succeeded, however, in calling to mind various analogies and putting into practice numerous devices which helped to save worship from becoming a matter of routine and to make of it an experience of passionate and ecstatic piety. Its other great achievement was to raise the study of Torah once again to the level of communion with God.

Not the whole of Hasidism, however, was swept along with the tide of pious emotionalism. There arose in it an intellectualist trend known as *Ha Ba D* which is a mnemonic based on the first letters of the words, *Hokmah* (wisdom), *Binah* (understanding), and *Deah* (knowledge). The founder of that movement was R. Shneor Zalman of Ladi (1747-1812).[62] *Ha Ba D* is little more than a popular presentation of semi-poetic and amateurish philosophic notions about the relation of God to the visible universe. *Ha Ba D* deviated from the main stream of Hasidism in attaching greater value to study and to religious practices than to prayer. But it was not less intransigent than the rest of Hasidism in refusing to come to terms with the non-Jewish cultural environment and with the development of the human sciences.

It is generally assumed that Hasidism harbored two distinct trends, from an ideological standpoint. According to that view, there was, in the first place, the pantheistic trend represented by the thinking of R. Baer the *Maggid* of Mezeritz, "Baal Shem's most important follower" (1710-1772) and his disciple R. Shneor Zal-man. That trend stressed the fusion of the divine with the human, the optimistic evaluation of sin and evil, the ecstatic state in wor-ship, the fulfillment in the present of the significance of the past miracles, and finally the expectation of future redemption. In contrast, there was the transcendental trend represented by R. Nahman of Brazlav (1770-1811). According to him, the chasm between the divine and the human is impassable. Both God and man are conceived by him as personal, but in no way comparable, so remote is God in his holiness from man in his sinfulness. Prayer should concern itself with one's own personal needs, and those who pray should look to God to fulfill those needs as an act of grace. All of one's hopes should be centered on the future redemption and the world to come, for no salvation is possible in the present.[63]

Whatever ideology may be discerned in Hasidism seems to have been for the most part either an attempt at making the obvious seem mysterious, or vainly applying the imagination to problems which only the most highly trained rationalist thinkers are capable of grappling with. On the whole, it appears that Martin Buber, the exponent of Neo-Hasidism, sums up correctly the ideological contribution of Hasidism in the following statement: "Regarded by itself, the Hasidic teaching offers no new spiritual elements; it presents only a selection, which it has taken partly from the later Kabbalah, and partly from popular traditions among the people.."[64] This statement, however, is not intended to disparage Hasidism. To Buber, life means more than ideas. He views life as the source of ideas rather than the reverse. Hence he adds: "The decisive factor for the nature and greatness of Hasidism is not found in a teaching, but in a mode of life." [65]

Perhaps it would be more accurate to describe Hasidism as the expression not so much of a new teaching as of a new attitude toward divinity. Throughout the Rabbinic tradition the dominant tendency is to behold the manifestation of divinity either in the recorded miracles of the past or in the promised miracles of the Messianic era. Hasidism, without negating either the one or the other, stressed the need of beholding or experiencing the manifestation of divinity in the common every-day experiences. That attitude helped to dispel the gloom which attended the anxieties and fears that grew out of precarious existence, and to foster a feeling of ecstasy due to the sense of God's nearness. *"The Lord is near to the broken-hearted"* [66] was a teaching which Hasidism translated into life.

The revolutionary character of Hasidism had also its social aspect, in that it accorded to the illiterate Jew—the *am ha-aretz*— a spiritual dignity he had never enjoyed in Jewish society. Only those who were learned in the knowledge of Torah, or whose wealth gave them power in the community, possessed social status. The rest, who had neither learning nor wealth, had no standing whatever. A typical illustration of the way Hasidism reinterpreted the tradition, which had set a low estimate on the *am-ha-aretz*, the ignorant Jew, is a clever turn given by the Baal Shem Tov *(Besht)* to the following Talmudic passage: "Said R. Shimeon ben Lakish, 'This nation (Israel) is compared to a vine. It burghers are the vinerods, its scholars are the grape clusters, its am-ha-aretz (peasants) are the leaves, and those who lack all merit are the tendrils.' " [67] This passage was rendered by the Besht as follows: "Jews are compared to a vine. The scholars are the grape cluster, and the am-ha-aretz are the leaves. The leaves of the vine are essential to the growth of the vine, and they protect the grapes. They are more important than the grapes, for the status of the protector is greater than that of the protected.[68]

Once these humble people were admitted into the company of the tsaddik's adherents to drink in his words of mystical wisdom, they ventured to assert themselves even in the presence of men of learning or of wealth. That was the main cause of the feud which developed between the Hasidim and their opponents, who came to be known as Misnagdim. The establishment by the Hasidim of their own houses of prayer helped to intensify the feud. A contributary factor was the upsurge of miraculous cures and wonder-working prayers of the tsaddikim, who came to be regarded as intermediaries between God and man. From this there followed the cult of personality, with all its customary abuses. Faith in the tsaddik was raised to the level of faith in God.

No doubt, there was much in Hasidism that was a reaction against the exaggerated emphasis on the minutiae of ritual observances. Such over emphasis gave rise to scholastic debates concerning the meaning of Rabbinic texts on which the observances were based, and to a sanctimonious rivalry among Jews who sought to outdo one another in religious scrupulosity. Hasidism, however, over-reached itself in its efforts to translate the unbridled speculations of Kabbalah into a program of daily living. Those efforts came at the very time when the spiritual disasters due to the fiasco of Shabbetai's false Messianism were still fresh in the minds of Jews.

If, in this chapter which deals with Medieval Judaism, the story of Hasidism has carried us far into the modern era, it is because for the Jews the Middle Ages lasted virtually to the end of the eighteenth century.

CHAPTER FIVE

The Transition to the Modern Era

THE MEDIEVAL WORLD-OUTLOOK

Judaism in the Western world can be best understod when seen in the context of Western civilization. Jews were actually never so well oriented spiritually as they were during the pre-modern centuries. Though they were completely segregated from their neighbors, they and their neighbors lived in the same spiritual climate of other-worldliness and in the same thought-world of supernaturalism. Judaism actually supplied the basic texts for the beliefs concerning God, man and the world commonly held by all the three religious civilizations.[1]

The universe of thought of the Medieval man was based on the striving for other-worldly salvation as the chief goal of human endeavor. "Christianity," wrote Rousseau in his *Contrat Social*, "is an entirely spiritual religion, concerned solely with heavenly things; the Christian's country is not this world. He does his duty, it is true; but he does it with a profound indifference as to the good or ill success of his endeavors. Provided that he has nothing to reproach himself with, it matters little to him whether all goes well or ill here below. If the State flourishes, he scarcely dares to enjoy the public felicity. If the State declines, he blesses the hand of God which lies heavy on his people." [2]

Mozart at the age of thirty-one consoled his ailing father in a letter which said the following: "As death is the true purpose of

144

life, I have, for many years, made myself familiar with that best friend of man, and his face has now no longer any terror for me, but is, if anything, calm and consoling to look upon. I thank God for this blessing . . . And I never go to bed without thinking that perhaps on the morrow I may no longer be alive. And no one who knows me could say that I am sad or discontented." [3]

Other-worldly salvation was also to Jews the keynote to the meaning of life on earth. In some instances and in certain areas of life, Jews did not go to the extent of glorifying asceticism as the most appropriate means to the attainment of other-worldly salvation and did not resort to the mortification of the flesh, as did Christian hermits and self-flagellants. Nonetheless, they assumed that the fulfillment of human life could not possibly take place in the limited span of years allotted to man in this world.

Other-worldy salvation, which was accepted by Jews and Christians as the dominant motive of their respective life-systems, was the outcome of a complete pattern of thought to which Jews and Christians subscribed with passionate faith. It is well to keep that pattern in mind when we try to visualize the position of Judaism in pre-modern times. That is indispensable to a realization of how totally different is the position of the Jewish People in the world today from what it was then. Then, it was easy for the rest of the world to understand itself and the Jewish People. However bitter their mutual hostility, Jews and Christians still spoke a common language. Now, however, there is such a babel of tongues that neither non-Jews nor Jews understand themselves or one another. The two centuries between 1750 and 1950 were progressively marked for both Jews and non-Jews by what Emile Durkheim calls "anomie," [4] which is "a disintegrated state of society that possesses no body of common values or morals that effectively govern conduct."

The establishment of the State of Israel has only aggravated for the Jews the condition of "anomie." They find it difficult to define to themselves, and all the more to non-Jews, their status and role in the world. The only parallel to the present bewilderment of non-Jews concerning Jews is that which existed during the two or three centuries from 150 B.C.E. to 150 C.E. when the pagan nations could not understand why Jews persisted in refusing to mingle socially with Gentiles, or to be respectful of gods other than their own one God. But then at least the Jews themselves had no doubts as to the reality of their peoplehood and as to what it represented. This is not the case in the twentieth century, as far as the overwhelming majority of them are concerned.

The .thought-pattern of other-worldly salvation which the Church emphasized as the main purpose of human life derived from the following assumptions:

1. The Jewish Scriptures contain the sole authoritative information concerning the origin and constitution of the physical world and the beginnings and history of mankind.

2. Man's destiny is to be fulfilled in the hereafter.

3. To be worthy of bliss in the hereafter man has to live in accordance with the will of God.

4. The Jewish Scriptures are a basic source of man's knowledge of God's will.

These assumptions constituted a sufficient orientation to life and all its vicissitudes.

1. To take for granted that the world in which we live was created by God so that man might inhabit it, to believe that everything in the world has to fulfill some function which might help man achieve his destiny, and to assume that the earth, the sea and the sky, all living beings and all the heavenly bodies have their assigned tasks—all this must have generated in the mind of the pre-modern man a sense of security and at-homeness in the world which modern man can no longer know.

What a wonderful experience it must have been for the Medieval man, with the aid of the first eleven chapters in Genesis to be able to survey in his mind's eye at one sweep the entire history of the human race! Human life was not just a meaningless phantasmagoria of events, with kingdoms arising and falling without any plan or purpose. According to the Bible, man no sooner was created than he disobeyed God's will and became subject to frustration and death. God, therefore, initiated with Abraham the long-drawn-out drama of human salvation. In that drama, the People of Israel was the central figure, and continued to be such until the birth of Jesus. On this, Jews, Christians, and Moslems were of one mind.

From this point on, Jews and Christians diverged in their orientation. But this very divergence implied two further areas of agreement in outlook, one with regard to the *locus* of salvation, and the other with regard to the means necessary to achieve it.

2. There was not the least doubt in the mind of all pre-modern Jews and non-Jews alike that this world could not possibly constitute the *locus* of salvation, or the fulfillment of man's destiny. The reason for that assumption was that a world in which man was as mortal as all other living beings could not be the scene of salvation. Immortality was regarded as the unquestionable prerogative of man.

It will probably be a long time before the generality of mankind will be reconciled to death as setting absolutely final limits to the life of the individual. The life of man on earth will long continue to be treated merely as an episode in an endless career. All the more reason then why in pre-modern times Jew and non-Jews should have thought almost alike about immortality as the *sine qua non of* salvation, and therefore about the world of the hereafter as the only one in which salvation could take place.

3. From that common ground, both Jew and non-Jew had to take but one step to arrive at the identical conclusion concerning what man had to do to be worthy of salvation in the hereafter. That conclusion was that only by living in accordance with what God had planned for man from the very beginning, when He created the world, could man hope to merit salvation. Why did God reveal the story of creation of the world and of the origin of man, if not to unfold His purpose to man? God's purpose, then, was none other than that of saving man from the consequences of his corrupt and evil ways, so that he might regain the life of eternal bliss.

4. Jews and non-Jews agreed that the Law which God had revealed to the People of Israel at Sinai constituted at one time the only means to salvation. But for how long? At this point they parted company. The Jews insisted that God had never abrogated the revelation of the Torah. Christians maintained that, with the advent of Christ, and the Moslems that, with the advent of Mohammet, a new world order set in. Both Christendom and Islam regarded themselves as in direct line of spiritual succession from the People of Israel, whom God had first chosen to be his prized possession.

Due to the foregoing facts, the Jewish People during pre-modern times, *despite its dispersion and its segregation from the non-Jewish environment, was influenced in its outlook, practices and attitudes by that environment.* If that influence re-enforced the loyalty of Jews to their own People and their own religion, it was because the universe of discourse inhabited by Jews and Christians had derived in the main from the Bible, which even in its Christian section was authored by Jews. M. Guedemann's *Geschichte des Erziehungswesens und Kultur der Juden in Mittalalter* (1880) contains an extensive record of such influences, which were more than skin deep; they penetrated to the very soul of the Jew. A phenomenon like the early Hasidic movement of the thirteenth century in Medieval Germany was the effect of the same spiritual factors as those which produced monasticism in the Christian world.[5]

Medieval Judaism, in its very effort to meet the challenge of Christianity, assimilated some of the characteristics of the latter. Hasdai Crescas (1340-1410), for example, one of the most incisive Jewish thinkers, found it necessary to include among the dogmas of Judaism one which in its way stressed the efficacy of priestly mediation, as did the Church of his day. Thus he stressed as important the belief in the oracles imparted by the High Priest through the *Urim ve-Tumim,* and in the efficacy of priestly blessings. "It is in fact undeniable," says G. Scholem, "that certain popular religious and social ideas common to the Roman Catholic West after the Cluniacensian reform also filtered into the religious philosophy of some Jewish religious groups." [6]

When thinkers try to figure out the strange case of the Jewish People, they overlook the fact that *for fifteen centuries the peoples of Europe and the Mediterranean basin moved in a universe of discourse in which Christendom was obsessed with the existence of the Jewish People and with its vicissitudes.* That obsession was due to the thought-pattern of the Christian scheme of salvation. After a long-drawn-out struggle with various heresies, especially the Marcionite, the Church succeeded in establishing the principle that the People of Israel had been an indispensable instrument in the divine plan to redeem the world. That enabled the Church to consider itself in line of continuity with the Israel of the Bible. The promises of ultimate redemption and glory contained in the "Old Testament" were regarded as referring to the Church because the Church regarded itself as the true Israel. The Jewish People, in refusing to accept Christ, had ceased to be the true Israel. In continuing to lay claim to those promises, and in challenging the high destiny of the Church, the Jewish People, from the Christian viewpoint, was obstructing God's purposes on earth.

To appreciate what all this means, it is well to contrast the case of Christianity with that of Mithraism, which, during the first centuries of the Common Era, was Christianity's most formidable rival. Mithraism arose in Persia. When Mithraism was transferred to other parts of the world, it lost its local and national associations. The adherents of Mithraism outside Persia did not identify themselves as Persians. Abstracted from its native environment, Mithraism developed into a mystery religion. With its promise of immortality or salvation, it addressed itself to the individual, as individual, and not as a member of a sacred community. It was a nature religion, transposed into the key of a mystery religion.

Such, however, was not the development of Christianity. The Apostle Paul, it is true, was almost on the point of giving it the character of a mystery religion. But, by and large, Christianity developed as a historical religion. As such, it had to appropriate the entire history and destiny of the People of Israel. The Church, conscious of what it had done, had to keep on justifying its claim to Israel's patrimony. By the same token, it had to denounce the Jews of its day not only for having forfeited the original patrimony, but for constituting a hindrance to God's plan of redemption of mankind from its original sin. In Christian theology, the Jewish People figured as the Cain of history, doomed to be homeless and driven wanderers over the earth. A remnant was destined to persist in its blind stubbornness in order to testify to Christian truths until the second coming of Christ, when he would complete his work of redemption. This was the theory on the basis of which the Church considered it proper, on the one hand, to oppress and humiliate the Jews, and, on the other, to treat them as infidels to be tolerated. Such tolerance was not extended either to Christian heretics or to other non-Christians.

Typical of this ambivalent attitude of the Church toward the Jews is the following declaration,[7] which was drawn up by the Catholic Clergy in Plotzk, Poland in 1733: "We regret with all our hearts that, in our Polish province which is free from heresy and false doctrine, only the refractory Jewish religion, that is hated by God, occupies a place in the cities and endures alongside the Catholic faith. We know that the other provinces of our kingdom, and that other kingdoms beside our own, tolerate that people. But that is only in order that the remnant of Israel may ultimately enter the covenant. Their case may be compared to the stem of a tree that is preserved for the sake of the flower which it bears. It is necessary that the Jews should dwell among us to remind us of the sufferings of our Lord Jesus, so that in the miserable and wretched state of subjection in which they subsist one may behold at first hand the justice of God, and finally, in order that by being scattered throughout the world, they may serve as eye-witnesses to the truth of that religion which they detest." Thus did the Jews pay dearly for being a Christian obsession. The Jewish People was to be preserved as a lasting testimony of the sufferings of Christ, but it was to be degraded to the status of a pariah people.

That program, however, led not only to the incessant houndings and terrorizations. It also fostered in the Jewish People itself a confidence in its own cosmic significance, and strengthened its determination to go on living at all costs *Through the very thought-pattern by which Christendom lived the Jewish People was perforce made aware of its own individuality and worth*. If the Jews lacked a territory to give them the sense of being an independent people, the manner in which they figured in the consciousness of their neighbors was sufficient to make them aware of occupying *an area of life* not only distinct from that of the peoples among which they found domicile, but worthy of the Jews' whole-souled devotion.

The modern challenge to Judaism differs radically from the one which the Jewish People encountered in the past. That challenge emanates from the spirit of this-worldliness, or secularism, which permeates contemporary human life. The transfer of the center of gravity of human existence from the other world to this world is both the cause and the effect of modern man's passionate desire to acquire mastery over the forces of nature and his growing ability to render the world he lives in more habitable. The swift development of power-driven machines culminated in the industrial revolution of the nineteenth century. That revolution brought the promise of abundance within reach of the masses for the first time in the history of civilization. The production and distribution of goods, which made possible for the multitudes a standard of living formerly attainable only by the few, raised the improvement of this-worldly life to the status and dignity of human self-realization or salvation.

Formerly, the evils in the world, both natural and social, presented an impregnable wall against which man seemed to dash himself in vain. Hence, the more aware of his helplessness man grew, the more he found it necessary to look to another world than the present one for the meaning of his existence. This led him to conclude that affliction and misery were part of the divine plan as means of rendering man worthy of the bliss in the hereafter. According to Pascal, "suffering is the natural state of the Christian, just as health is that of the natural man." But once man realized what power he possessed to make this world more habitable by manipulating the forces of nature, he tended to abandon the idea that all of life's evils were inevitable. He began to think of eliminating those evils instead of trying to find some plausible explanation for them.

THE DAWN OF THIS-WORLDLINESS: ITS EFFECT ON THE STATUS OF JEWS

While West European mankind was in the process of outgrowing its Medieval state of mind, which had found embodiment in feudalism, ecclesiasticism and the guild system, and replacing them with free enterprise society, a progessive middle class and a balanced political system, the Western hemisphere was discovered. The impact of that discovery was probably as great in its day as would be today that of the establishment of contact with the planet Mars. Yet the actual results of that discovery have been incomparably more far-reaching than the achievement of the most fantastic gains in interplanetary travel. Apart from the new vistas opened up through commerce, exploration, colonization, growth of population and spread of civilization, the effect of that discovery on human life is incalculable. It shook the authority of the Church, undermined the credibility of its teachings and habituated man to rely upon his own initiative and intelligence.

Though we live on the same planet as did our forebears, we live actually in a different world. During the last three centuries, according to Stuart Chase, "the applications of science have quadrupled the population of Western civilization and greatly improved its health, released twenty billions of man-power of energy from coal, falling water and oil, created a vast collectivized, interlocked culture." [8] That was written in 1938. In view of the vast number of technical inventions since then, particularly those which have to do with automation, to say nothing of the opening up of new sources of energy, through discovery and exploitation of nuclear fission, the opportunities for the expansion of human life on earth seem limitless.

The thought formerly given to problems dealing with what one must believe and what one must do to earn salvation or a share in the world to come has been redirected and intensified a thousand-fold in the interests of this-worldly utlization of all that steam, electricity, petrol and the chemical laboratory can yield. A significant fact, which has often been stressed by students of society, but which is generally missed by those who reckon with the moral and spiritual destiny of man, is that improvement in technology transforms not only the economic system but also the entire scheme of human values.

"Authority may resist the frontal attack of heresy or repair the schisms that it causes," says R. M. MacIver, "but neither the secular nor the spiritual sword is potent against the habituations and attitudes that respond to new ways of earning a livelihood, or the manipulation of new mechanical powers, to the new resources, new luxury, new leisure, new freedom, and new servitude that their exploitation bring with it, and to the new relations between men and groups that they engender. It is not unreasonable to hold that in the course of Western civilization the line of technological innovators, from Roger Bacon to—shall we say—Henry Ford, have done more, unwittingly more than any other men to dissolve the sanctity of tradition and to transform the nature of authority. New schools and sects usually attack the established order from premises that belong within it. But new technology, by changing the basis of life, prepares for a change in the very basis of thought. It is thus of particular potency in undermining the established notions of authority held by the masses of men." [9]

The matter goes even deeper. The transition from Medieval to modern civilization, both general and Jewish, was effected not merely through the new technological improvements, but, and even more, by the altered attitude toward technology as such. Medieval civilization still labored under a general taboo against the very attempt to tamper with the established order of physical nature, a taboo which was carried over to, and intensified in, the attitude toward social change. In both areas, taboo was accounted for on religious grounds. All attempts to change the *status quo*, whether of nature or of society, were taken to be an implied criticism of God's work, and constituted an arrogant claim to being able to improve it.

At first sight, it might seem as though practical or magical Kabbalah, and its Christian analogue, ran counter to the feeling that it was wrong to meddle with the *status quo*. Their function was to bring about even more radical changes, especially in the physical world, than was contemplated by the most venturesome scientists of those days. The making of a Golem, in which Kabbalah played a role, though deemed an audacious act, was not regarded as an ungodly one. But on closer view, it becomes evident that the authors of the magical Kabbalah and their Christian compeers operated with means believed to have been divinely vouchsafed, or esoterically revealed by God Himself, to those who were "clean of hand and pure of heart." They fully realized the danger of entrusting the power to work changes in the world to anyone who was morally unfit, or spiritually undeserving.

Apart from the foregoing, the prevailing attitude in pre-modern times was one of resistance to meddling with the general order of nature. That attitude is reflected in a story which has come down from the Hasidic movement of a century ago. Its characteristic opposition to modernism may be said to be summed up in the following: "Rabbi Bunam was once walking outside the city with some of his disciples. He bent, picked up some grains of sand, looked at them and replaced them exactly where he had found them. 'He who does not believe,' he said, 'that God wants these grains of sand to lie in this particular place does not believe at all.' " [11]

The most widespread effect of the new secularist attitude which resulted from the development of technology has been the enlargement of the scope of economic activities. Improved technics have made possible unprecedented increase of production and wider distribution and exchange of goods and services. With the industrial revolution during the century from 1770 to 1870 opening up vast possibilities for raising the general standard of living, the millenium seemed to be close at hand. It was assumed man would be free to make the optimum use of his capacities. The unprecedented advances in science, communication and education seemed to promise the advent of a new day for mankind. The quantitative increase of life's scope and interests which the machine process made possible for the masses of men was regarded as certain to augment all human values. Only a few discerning people suspected the presence of new dangers that lurked in the machine process. So long as those dangers were hidden from the general view, there was the tendency to throw wide open the doors of economic opportunity to all who showed any ability to accelerate the economic expansion.

From an economic standpoint, the emancipation of the Jews meant making use of whatever money reserves a few of them may have amassed, and of their commercial contacts with fellow-Jews of the same economic status in other countries. Those few had developed the art of creating capital through combining small savings and utilizing their contacts with fellow-Jews of other countries to advantage in import and export activities. They were thus in a position to place their talents in commercial initiative and pioneering at the service of the state.

It is at this point that the economic expression of the new worldly spirit affected the Jew. Wherever that new spirit began to pervade economic life and the old restrictions of guild and state domination were relaxed, the Jews were permitted, and occasionally even invited, to add their capital and initiative to the promotion of industry. This was part of the post-Medieval policy known as "mercantilism." Two of its principles were: (1) Commerce and industry are more important than agriculture; (2) the state should foster national welfáre through economic expansion and power policy.[11] The granting of economic rights to a limited number of Jews did not come suddenly at the end of the eighteenth century. As far back as the seventeenth century, individual Jews who possessed exceptional ability were granted the right to organize and finance industries. But toward the last quarter of the eighteenth century their number and their economic usefulness, particularly to royalty in countries like Prussia and Austria, were such as to render the continuance of their inferior civic status impracticable.

As this-wordly advantage came to outweigh traditional religious scruples, Jews were allowed to prove how useful they could be to princes and high dignitaries by placing at their disposal vast funds and helping to organize various industries for them. From these occasional experiences with Jews on the part of the potentates was but one step to the conclusion that, if more Jews were given an opportunity to make use of their energies and abilities, the state as a whole might benefit from the removal of their Medieval disabilities.

This utilitarian argument, which had been sounded by Colbert in France during the seventeenth century, began to be advanced also by liberals in other countries during the latter part of the eighteenth century, in their plea for granting civic rights to Jews. Moses Mendelssohn himself resorted to that argument, and it undoubtedly weighed more than the appeal to the abstract principle of justice, or as they termed it then, "philanthropy." Mendelssohn alludes specifically to "the benefits which may accrue to the state which should succeed first in converting these native aliens (the Jews) into citizens, and in rendering serviceable a number of heads and hands born into it." [12] *Such an argument was unthinkable so long as the other-worldly conception of life dominated public policy.*

The limited number of Jews who, during the latter part of the eighteenth century, were the first to be integrated into the general economy, caught the fever of the growing eagerness to achieve success by availing themselves of the new economic opportunities that were opened up to them. With their newly awakened worldly interests, the traditional beliefs and hopes which had buoyed them up in the limited sphere of ghetto life gradually lost all meaning for them.

Moreover, as Jews learned to associate frequently and intimately with non-Jews in business and in social life, they found themselves inconvenienced by the traditional religious observances. In course of time, they began to neglect one observance after another, until their Jewish life became void of content, and therefore meaningless. At the same time, the writings of Voltaire and of the English Deists and sceptics, began to be known either at first-or-secondhand to the members of the well-to-do Jewish families, especially to the women. Whatever scruples they may have entertained about severing their bonds with Jewish life were dispelled by those writings.

What the advance of the worldly spirit—later identified as secularism—meant politically to the Jews at the opening of the modern era becomes apparent when we take into account the radical transformation which that spirit has wrought in men's attitude toward the State. An unmistakable index of the change from other-worldliness to this-worldliness, besides the economic one discussed above, was the shift of the dominant authority from the priest class to the laity. Among all ancient peoples, the priesthood, or that order of society which was expert in dealing with the divine powers, was the principal source of authority. Although the leisure which members of the priesthood enjoyed had enabled them to lay the foundations of organized human knowledge, the fear of losing their monopoly of power generally led them to become a hindrance to human progress. For some reason, the ancient Greeks were the only people in whose political life the priesthood played a subordinate role. That fact may have enabled Greek thinkers to make considerable headway with the natural sciences. To that exceptional trait of the ancient Greeks modern secularism owes its cultural origin. With the spread of Christianity and Islam, both of which are based on a supernaturally revealed tradition, the clerics, whether they were priest or imams, exercised cultural hegemony, with detrimental consequences to general culture. In Judaism, the hereditary priesthood was replaced by rabbis, who were in a sense lay clerics; but they, too, served as a brake on the slightest deviation from tradition.

The Fathers of the Church, especially Augustine, taught that the State was a realm of Satan and the arch-enemy of the Church, which they considered as the realm of God. They found adequate support in the Bible for that low estimate of the political State. Thomas Aquinas, living at a time when Aristotelian ideas began to pervade the minds of the higher Christian clergy, accorded to the State the indispensable function of enabling man to live as a social being. He maintained that it was natural for man to establish the State, as a means of acquiring the civic virtues. Man, however, needed something more than civic virtue, if he was to fulfil his destiny and achieve salvation. He stood in need of divine grace, and the only institution to mediate divine grace was the Church. Accordingly, he taught that the State must be subordinate to the Church.

Not long after Aquinas promulgated his doctrine of the State, Dante published his *De Monarchia*, in which he assigned to the State a position coordinate with that of the Church. According to Dante, the State, no less than the Church, derived its prerogative directly from God. These assumptions were in keeping with his daring suggestion that man's salvation was not intended to be confined to heavenly reward, but was to consist also of earthly happiness, which the State was duty-bound to promote. The Church, he maintained, should have nothing to do with temporal dominion. This marks the beginning not only of the secularist conception of salvation, but also of its translation into political terms.

The first rumblings in Christendom of an open challenge to the dominant authority of the prelacy were heard in England, in Italy and in France. In England, Henry II continually picked quarrels with papal Rome. He declared that the clergy should be subjected to secular penalties for crimes and misdemeanors. He was embroiled in strife with Thomas á Becket, the Archbishop of Canterbury, and was suspected of having encompassed his murder. This was the beginning of the struggle to wrest power from the priesthood. In France, Philip the Fair, as the champion of the laity, made it his policy to reduce the episcopacy to political impotence. This led to open conflict with Pope Boniface VIII, with whom Philip dealt violently and whose bulls he burned publicly, with the consent of his subjects.

Each revolt against the papacy on the part of king or prince to establish his supreme legal and political power over and against the Roman Catholic Church, marked the beginning of the struggle of the rising national secularist civilizations to emancipate themselves from the domination of Church politics and Church culture.

Those revolts against the Church, however, should not be identified with the earlier uprisings, like those of the Albigenses and

Lollards, which the Church finally crushed, or with the later Protestant uprisings which managed to survive. These uprisings were democratic movements within sacerdotalism itself and, therefore, cannot be viewed as challenging the fundamental principle of ecclesiastical hegemony. Calvin's theocracy, for example, called for an even greater concentration of power in the hands of those who ruled in the name of God than did the Roman Catholic Church.

The Renaissance, on the other hand, carried the secularization of the State still further. Machiavelli reduced the rank and authority of the Church by separating it entirely from the domain of the secular. Finally, with the beginning of modern thought as developed by Francis Bacon and René Descartes, and with the added sense of strength which society began to acquire through the new discoveries and inventions, the function of the State came to include helping the individual to pursue his worldly aims without Church interference. Thus arose the whole complex of problems centering about the doctrine of natural rights.

The principal factor that contributed to the gradual secularization of economic and political institutions was the rise of cities and of the middle class, known as "bourgeoisie." So long as the military power was confined to the lord in his castle, who was able to rally his serfs in defense of his holdings and to extend those holdings, he served as the secular arm of the Church. But when the tradesmen and the artisans of the growing towns grew sufficiently in numbers and power to wrest the military power from the feudal lords of the land, the ideals and discipline upon which the Church insisted as essential for salvation began to lose their hold on people's minds, and their place was taken by the newly awakened secular interests which town and city life helped to foster.

All this contributed to the rise of individualism and to the growing opposition to a universal Church. Other-worldly salvation, so long as it was believed in, offered a basis of catholicity which could be taken advantage of by the Church. But with the gradual insinuation of this-worldly salvation as the functioning goal of human life, that catholicity was undermined, and, with it, the universal authority of the Church. "Protestantism," as R. H. Tawney, Max Weber and others have shown, "expressed the aspiration of the rising bourgeoisie for *self-development*, for breaking the bonds of feudalism."

The main outcome of the new worldly interest in the individual human being and of the affirmation of natural rights was the promulgation of religious tolerance and civic equality. After having been aired in the writings of philosophers and men of affairs for over two centuries, the principles of religious tolerance and civic equality were finally given formal recognition. The establishment of the United States of America and the French Revolution translated those principles into constitutional law. In the wake of these revolutionary cultural and political changes in the Western world, came the emancipation of the Jews from Medieval disabilities.

One of the main consequences of the secularization of the State has been a change in the conception of equality. In the Middle Ages, spiritual equality was regarded as entirely compatible with civil, political or economic inequality. But with the advent of liberalism and its tendency to view the spiritual element in man's life as integral to the rest of his life, civic equality was accepted as the inalienable right of all human beings. Thus the need of emancipating Jews from Medieval disabilities became part of the new liberal creed.

THE CHALLENGE OF THE MODERN WORLD-OUTLOOK

The Emancipation, however, by no means put an end to the problem of Jewish status. The truth is that it created more problems for the Jew than it solved. This is the case because the secular conception of the State implies the principle that its function is to direct the cultural and economic activities of the nation, with a view to greater internal solidarity and to greater power in its relation to other States. These newly awakened needs gave rise to a new organization of society. In place of the heterogeneous mass of communities, classes and other political groups, each with its own system of law and mores and its own type of cultural life during the Medieval period, there emerged the modern homogeneously constituted and governed State. Whereas in the past a nation was a conglomerate of all kinds of groups and corporations, *it now seeks to achieve as tightly integrated a unity as possible.* To that end, the modern nation would have the State direct its energies.

Thus arose the modern type of State nationalism. The State has come to insist upon the exclusive allegiance of its citizens. It is apprehensive of any loyalty which might compete with the loyalty to itself. It wants all interests and affiliations of its citizens to be subject to its review and control. Whatever transnational historical groups or social organizations may survive in the nation must surrender all corporate rights and privileges that interfere with the centralization of the overall authority in the State. That insistence has developed in some countries into statism, or totalitarianism, .which promulgates the principle of absolute sovereignity of the State over the individual and over all groups within the nation.

With the increase of production as a result of technological development came increased competition for world markets and raw materials. That in turn gave rise to greater demands upon the State to protect the industries of the nation by means of tariff barriers, import restrictions, export subsidies, and in every other way to help the nation in its competitive struggle against other nations. Thus has the State become the sponsor of the most explosive form of nationalism, with all of its war-mongering tendencies. Nations which for their own true interests ought to collaborate economically are prevented from doing so by the trumped-up pride of absolute sovereignty. Thanks to these developments of modern nationalism, the State has come to interfere with all interests and loyalties that transcend national boundaries. It is quite evident how this absolutizing of the modern nation and its State is bound to create many difficult problems for a dispersed people like the Jews whose unity necessarily transcends national boundary lines.

Since the State has become secularized, it has taken over three important functions from the various corporate groups which were formerly part of the State. These are the administration of civil law, the prerogative of validating marriage and divorce, and the education of the child. Under the pre-modern organization of society these functions could be exercised by a minority group, so long as its presence in the land was tolerated. The modern

State, however, insists that its citizens submit to the laws enacted by it and that they resort to its courts for their litigation. Only courts for the arbitration of disputes may be established under private or voluntary jurisdiction. *That situation presented itself as soon as Jews were given civil rights, and has necessitated the suspension of all Jewish code law in civil matters.* The shock which this administered to the organic unity of the Jewish People was felt only by the generation in whose lifetime the suspension of Jewish courts was decreed. Before long, Jews grew insensitive to the disintegrative influence of that decree on their life as a People.

The modern State also assumes that to permit any of its subordinate groups the principal right to validate marriage and divorce would introduce confusion that would hinder the growth of the homogeneity which is essential to its power and the achievement of its purposes. It insists upon reserving to itself the prerogative of giving status to the family, thereby becoming indispensable to the individual at the most sensitive point in his career. Most important of all, however, is its prerogative to be the main educational agency in the life of the child. Even if it permits the establishment of school facilities under private auspices, it exercises the right to prescribe the curriculum of studies which the child has to be taught. In that curriculum, emphasis is placed upon inculcating in the child an awareness that his first duty as a citizen is to be loyal to his Government, and not to permit any other loyalty to come between him and his Government. Even in a country like the United States where the Constitution insists upon the separation of Church and State, the latter often creates difficulties for Jewish parents by encouraging the introduction of distinctly sectarian Christian teachings and celebrations into its public schools.

Most embarassing of all has been the challenge of the modern State to that element of international Jewish unity inherent in Jewish religion which had found expression in the yearning of Jews for return to their ancient homeland. The modern State is jealous of all other loyalties. It definitely deprecates, even if it does not actually prohibit, loyalties that transcend its boundaries, whether they be to universal ideals or to historical memories. What was then to become of the Messianic hope and of the whole mind-set which Traditional Judaism has fostered for centuries, and which pointed to Eretz Yisrael as the land of Jewish destiny? The lack of a clear answer has been the main source of many Jews' resistance to Zionism.

The secularization of the State has made itself felt not only in the altered status of the Jews in their relation with non-Jews, but also in their communal organization and in the role of their spiritual leadership. Until modern times the rabbinate had served the Jews in the two-fold capacity of Church and State. It functioned as the legislative and judicial areas of the autonomous Jewish community. It formed the Jews into a theocracy. The loosening of the bonds, however, which had united Church and State in the general population affected the Jews differently from the way it affected the non-Jews. The nature of the difference and the reason for it become understandable in light of the fact that France happened to be the first source of the modernizing influences on the Jews.

The most progressive ideas and arts cultivated in England and Italy found in France many ardent followers. There the reaction on the part of the Roman Catholic Church against those ideas was so violent that the possibility of any compromise between the intellectuals and the Church was precluded. Voltaire's dictum, "Ecrasez l'infame," reflects the wide gulf of mutual hatred that had sprung up between the Church authorities and the heralds of the Enlightenment. Instead of reformulating the meaning of otherworldliness so as to prevent its interfering with the needed political and social changes, as the intellectuals in the Protestant countries were inclined to do, the French intellectuals made it a point to keep at arm's length anything and anybody that had to do with traditional Christianity. Their antagonism and bitterness against clericalism was intensified during the eighteenth century, when the struggle of the third estate, or the bourgeoisie, against the social and economic privileges of the first estate, or nobility, reached its climax. The Catholic priesthood threw in its lot with royalty and the nobility, and lent the prestige of its authority to the prevailing misrule and exploitation of the peasantry. The result was that anticlericalism became an integral part of the movement for the Enlightenment which issued from France.

It was the French version of Enlightenment that reached in Central and Eastern Europe the rising Jewish bourgeoisie and the intellectuals who moved in its orbit. They, too, became anti-clericalist and vented their antagonism against Jewish religion by assailing the rabbinate, which had been the guardian of Jewish law, both religious and civil, and which had preserved the authoritative character of the Jewish community throughout the centuries. Rebellion against communal authority was to the Jewish intellectuals a way of expressing their hatred of clericalism, with all of the other-worldliness and supernaturalism which it upheld. *But, whereas among the non-Jews the intellectuals did not merely combat the clericals but also engaged in a vast campaign, both philosophical and political, to build up a social order and a national State founded on lay authority, the Jewish intellectuals did nothing of the kind for their own People. Their one ambition was to be integrated into the body politic of the country they lived in. That attitude on their part is responsible for the fact that the Jews in the Diaspora not only lack the very basis of permanent and creative unity, without which there can be no Judaism; they don't even miss it.*

The European Medieval system was dominated by an ecclesiastical culture which strove to become universal. It has since been replaced by the indigenous cultures of the various European peoples. The sixteenth-century Renaissance movements marked the beginning of that transition which culminated in the rise during the eighteenth century of Illuminism, or Enlightenment. The Enlightenment, insofar as it resulted in the secularization of morals and religion, derived from the newly formulated concepts of natural law and natural religion, or the religion of reason. Those concepts have since revolutionized men's ideas of human destiny, salvation or self-fulfillment.

Man has always tried to adjust himself to his natural environment. In the process of adjustment, he has accumulated a vast amount of empirical and practical information. Such information, though helpful in his daily living, was in pre-modern times considered irrelevant to the main purpose of human life. Only truths of an eternal character were deemed capable of furthering that purpose. The philosopers of the Greek classic age believed those eternal truths were discoverable through the exercise of reason, which enabled man to transcend the fleeting and the shadow-like experiences of his existence. A philosopher like Plato virtually reasoned himself into the same kind of other-worldly attitude toward human life as that professed in the Oriental religions. On the other hand, those who promulgated those religions argued that human reason was too much beset by uncertainty to arrive at a knowledge of the eternal truths that was essential to salvation. Only God, Who was the Creator of the world, could reveal them to man. Hence, the only knowledge worth cultivating was the knowledge of the revealed will of God. This attitude was reflected in the Medieval exaltation of theology as the queen of the sciences, and in the cultivation of all branches of knowledge, on the assumption that the revealed word of God was the only reliable source of truth.

The Jews of pre-modern times took a similar attitude toward matters of worldly interest. To them, the study of the Torah was the only means to salvation. It was the source of the eternal wisdom which alone was worth cultivating. Wisdom, which is the subject matter of the Book of Proverbs, was invariably identified with Torah. The reverence for the past stemmed from the assumption that those who lived then were nearer in time to those who had been vouchsafed, through divine revelation, the knowledge of God's will. They were, therefore, superior to those who came after them. "It is impossible," says Rashi, "that the later generations should equal the earlier generations."[13]

In spite, however, of the attempts on the part of Catholic and Protestant orthodoxy to suppress non-religious culture in the Western world, the mundane interests finally got the upper hand. The modern revolution in the cultural values of that world, which goes back to the Renaissance and the revival of interest in the literary and philosophic writings of the ancient Greeks and Romans, proved irresistible. A long time had to pass, however, before the forces of secular culture were strong enough to challenge the domination of the ecclesiastical authorities. Even in the seventeenth century that challenge was still underground. Open rebellion against the traditional supremacy of Church culture dates only from the eighteenth century.

The main contribution of ancient Greek culture to human life is the discovery that man and nature constitute an indivisible unity. In rediscovering Greek culture, the Renaissance rediscovered

the world and man. The most far-reaching change in man's thinking since those days came about as a consequence of the late
Renaissance realization that the only kind of knowledge which
can give man control over the forces of nature is that which is
based on careful observation and experimentation, and that the
most reliable results of both are those which can be expressed in
quantitative terms. Galileo, who conducted experiments for the
purpose of reducing the laws of motion to quantitative measure-
ment, inaugurated a new era in human thinking. It is true that
long before him Aristotle had stated that not to know the significance of motion was to fail to understand nature.[14] But Galileo
was the first to discover the mathematical version of motion without which modern technology is unthinkable. During the sixteenth
and seventeenth centuries, the invention of the telescope together
with new measuring instruments enlarged the scope of the quantitative study of nature. Thus came about the Copernican and
Newtonian revolutions in man's orientation to the cosmos.

The quantitative approach to nature gave a new direction to
man's striving for power, and to knowledge as the means of attaining it. In contrast with the verbal erudition of the Middle Ages,
which was fostered by each scholar in the privacy of his own study,
intellectual and practical craftsmen learned to work together. That
was even more significant than the organization of a number of
scientific organizations after the middle of the seventeenth century. As a result, the natural sciences were no longer cultivated in
a vacuum, but in close relationship with industrial production.
This combination of theory with practice ultimately replaced the
land economy of feudalism by the modern money economy of
capitalism.

Thus did the naturalistic and quantitative approach invade the
fields of economics. In 1662 Sir W. Petty drew attention to "the
vanity and fruitlessness of making *positive* law against the laws of
nature." On that basis, he combated all interference with free
trade. He was the first to deal with economic problems in mathematical fashion. He described his method as "not very usual; for
instead of using only comparative and superlative words and intellectual arguments, I have taken the course to express myself in
terms of number, weight, measure; to use only arguments of sense,

and to consider only such causes as have visible foundations in nature." [15] The scientific study of economics proceeded apace in the seventeenth and eighteenth centuries, and problems of money, taxation, rural economy, population, and foreign trade were no longer dealt with in haphazard and *ad hoc* fashion.

Simultaneously with the external changes which Western man underwent during the transition to the modern era, he also underwent internal changes. The human body, which since the days of ancient Greece and Rome had ceased to be an object of close scrutiny, began to be studied again both scientifically and esthetically. That led to the secularization of the plastic and pictorial arts. Throughout the Middle Ages, architecture, sculpture, painting and. dramatics had been motivated by the desire to express man's yearnings for other-worldly salvation. It was the secularist trend which put in place of that motive the conscious purpose of satisfying man's own creative promptings. "The religious scorn for the world of the here and the now," says Freeman, "with its correlate of a preoccupation with the other world, had profound consequences for art." [16] With the passing of that scorn, the preoccupation with this world gave rise to modern secularist art.

Likewise the scientific interest in outward nature was in time turned inward. Lewis Mumford sees in the effect of the sixteenth century invention of the silvered mirror the beginning of a new concept of human personality. "For perhaps the first time," he says, "except for reflections in the water and in the full surface of metal mirrors, it was possible to find an image that corresponded to what others saw . . . Self-consciousness, introspection, mirror-conversation developed with the new object itself." [17] The century following the invention of the silvered mirror witnessed the beginnings of modern psychology.

Since the beginning of the nineteenth century, industry has undergone enormous development. It has since raised the material welfare of human life to a level undreamed of before. The quickened pace of economic activity and its expansion over the entire world have improved communication and methods of exchange. Mass production and rationalization of industry have increased a thousand-fold the opportunities in the here and now for living a full and satisfying life, not only by the few but by the many. The growth in the internationalization of the world economy has

TRANSITION TO MODERN ERA

placed at the disposal of mankind an abundance of goods and services as well as sufficient leisure to enjoy them.

With all these revolutionary changes in man's outer and inner life, the traditional cosmic orientation could not but grow obsolete, despite the fact that it took a long time for the Copernican revolution to penetrate the mind of the average person. The Roman Catholic Church did not officially permit the teaching of the heliocentric conception of the universe until 1843. But once started on its way, this conception was bound to destroy the traditional world-outlook which was based on the Biblical account of the creation of the world and of man. *By the same token that man has been gradually weaned away from dependence upon religious tradition for his knowledge of the past, he has learned to depend upon himself for what he may expect of the future. Until a generation ago, the exit of religious authority meant the entry of intellectual freedom.*

This newly acquired intellectual freedom which came to be known as "Enlightenment" found expression in the emphasis on rationalism and universalism. The concept of natural law, instead of the classically reasoned *a priori* "laws of nature," began to permeate all human thinking. *The traditional universe of discourse, which had been common to Jews and Christians, no longer seemed habitable to the knowledgeable persons of either group.* It became necessary to achieve an affirmative orientation to this world because, in the words of R. H. Tawney, "to be at home in this world, it is not, unfortunately, sufficient to disbelieve in another." As soon as Renaissance humanism and Enlightenment rationalism began to undermine the belief in other-worldly salvation, the human mind began to explore the possibilities of this-wordly, or secular, salvation.

Among the first to gain the public ear for a new approach to the problem of salvation was John Locke. In his *Reasonableness of Christianity* published in 1695, he blazed a path for rational religion, which developed during the eighteenth century into what is known as Deism. This new approach to religion was based on the assumption that the only justifiable function of traditional religion was to act as a support and sanction for moral responsibility but not to spell it out in detail. Only tested human experience should provide us with the knowledge of what's right and what's wrong in each specific situation. A tradition which came into conflict with reason was in need of being apologized for or explained away. Miracles and prophecy had no intrinsic purpose other than that of furnishing external evidences to the truth of the claims of revealed religion. *The special privilege which revealed religion bestowed upon those to whom it had been vouchsafed was in need of being harmonized with the absolute impartiality of divine goodness, an impartiality which had now come to be taken for granted.*

In Germany, this kind of rational religion was promulgated during the first half of the eighteenth century by the philosopher Leibnitz and the theologian Reimarus. Lessing and Herder also contributed to the new development in the rational religion of that day. They taught that God had revealed Himself essentially through the education of the human race, which they conceived as a long-drawn-out evolutionary process. In a work entitled *Erziehung des Menschengeschlechts*, Lessing gave the first historical account of religion as reflecting the growth of the human spirit.[18] Every religion, he maintained, had its divinely appointed function to fulfil some need which had its roots in human nature.

The most significant step, however, in the modern rationalization of religion took place with the Kantian revolution in human thought. That thought heralded a new era in the understanding of the basic assumptions underlying man's intellectual, moral and spiritual strivings. It may best be described as having added a new dimension to the human spirit, alongside the previously recognized dimensions of sensation and reason. This is the dimension of intuition, which came to replace authority in the domain of moral and religious values.

Carl L. Becker sums up what he calls "the essential articles of the religion of the Enlightenment" as having been the following: 1) Man is not natively depraved; 2) the end of life itself, the good life on earth instead of the beatific life after death; 3) man is capable, guided solely by the light of reason and experience, of perfecting the good life on earth; and 4) the first and essential condition of the good life on earth is the freeing of men's minds from the bonds of ignorance and superstition."[19] *Each and every one of those principles has been contributing to the radical transformation of the inner and outer conditions of the life of the*

Jews as well as of the non-Jews. In the attempt to survive that radical transformation, Judaism is undergoing metamorphosis.

* * *

The European Enlightenment had been far advanced by the time it invaded the gloom and seclusion of the ghetto. It is true that the Enlightenment had reached Jewish life long before it reached Mendelssohn. But so long as it was not accompanied by actual or prospective emancipation, it resulted merely in widening the scope of cultural life for only a limited number of the intellectual élite among the Jews. That had been the case in Italy during the seventeenth century. But *Haskalah*, or the Jewish phase of the Enlightenment of which Mendelssohn was the protagonist, coincided with the nineteenth-century movement among the West and Central European States to emancipate the Jews from their Medieval disabilities, and with the efforts of the Jews throughout Europe to be intergrated into the body politic of the general population.

It is, therefore, futile to look for parallels to the Enlightenment era in the "Golden Era" of Jewish history in Arabic Spain, when the upper intellectual strata among the Jews succeeded in assimilating the general culture of the day without great detriment to Judaism. In those days Jews and non-Jews shared the same general other-worldly outlook. Mendelssohn, however, was the first Jew in whom Jewish traditional religion felt the impact not merely of the Enlightenment, but also of the modernist this-worldly striving for individual salvation. In common with the rest of the world, the Jews have come to regard such salvation as achievable only under social and political conditions which make it possible for all men, regardless of race, creed or nationality, to make the most of life, liberty and the pursuit of happiness.

Salvation, as the self-fulfillment of human life on this earth, is still, and will for a long time remain, an unsolved problem. The rise of modern nations is fundamentally part of man's search for a solution. That is why modern nationalism has all the impetus of a new revelation that is crowding out the old revelation. With the progressive replacement of other-worldly salvation, the function of institutional religion is being called into question. It will be a long time, however, before Western civilization will cease to be identified as Christian. In the meantime, the Jews, who are themselves of a divided mind between adhering to their tradition and rejecting it, are entirely confused as to their status as a People. The spiritual confusion under which non-Jews labor at present with regard to the Church-State relationship is even more troublesome to the Jews. They find it untenable to survive as a landless religious community, nor can they look forward for the solution of their dilemma to the State of Israel, in which only a limited portion of the Jewish People might be master of its own destiny.

CHAPTER SIX

The Impact of Modernism on Jewish Life

THE BEGINNINGS OF JEWISH EMANCIPATION

With the formal granting of political equality to the Jews and their incorporation into the Western nations, the history of the Jewish People begins to take on a new character. Until then it was the history of a people uprooted, without a central state, dispersed and driven from land to land. It has since become the history of a people, in part no less dispersed and driven, and in part accepted by the majority population in a variety of ways, ranging from an easy-going disregard of what such acceptance involves to a definite determination to tolerate Jews only as individuals, but not as members of an international People.

The modern upheaval in Jewish life reflects the revolutionary changes in the life of Western mankind, changes in social structure and in world outlook. The changes in social structure of the European peoples among which the Jews lived during the Middle Ages have culminated in modern nationalism. Nationalism is based on the conception of the nation as essentially a territorial unit. Physical propinquity and the common interests growing out of it supersede all affiliations, historical or purposive, as a uniting bond and as the essence of nationhood. Although a common history and a common culture give a modern nation its unity and individuality, they lack the sacrosanct character which suffusion with

171

religion gave to ancient histories and cultures. They, therefore, cannot exact the same exclusive loyalty as did the ancient civilizations. The secularized nationalism of our day which has made possible the Jewish emancipation represents, therefore, an entirely different constellation of society from the one which had kept the Jews in a condition of alienage.

Jewish life began to feel the impact of modern nationalism when Emperor Joseph II of Austria issued his Tolerance Edict in 1782. That edict was prompted by the desire to bring about some degree of national homogeneity and unity among the many ethnic groups that had kept the Austrian Empire in a state of continual turmoil. In accordance with that edict, Jews were placed in the same category as Christian dissenters from the authorized State Church. That constituted a break with the Medieval practice of treating Jews as complete aliens. In Austria, from that time on, they were not only permitted, but expected, to send their children to schools and universities, to engage in large-scale enterprise, and even to serve in the army. It was, however, only with the complete separation of Church and State, first effected in the American Constitution in 1787 and through the French Revolution in 1791, that the Jews acquired civil equality.

The first modern national State to be established on the continent of Europe was the First French Republic. The Declaration of the Rights of Man, which became the basis of the new State, necessitated the granting of civil rights to the 50,000 French Jews, most of whom then resided in Alsace-Lorraine. On the other hand, the few voices among the Gentiles raised in favor of emancipation were motivated by the assumption that it must lead to the complete assimilation of the Jews, even to the point of their ultimately adopting Christianity, and thus becoming entirely absorbed beyond all recognition by the rest of the population. Whenever the question of emancipating the Jews was debated, those who were in favor of emancipation always stressed the difference between the Jews as individuals and the Jews as members of the Jewish People. "To the Jews as a nation," declared Comte de Clermont-Tonnerre at the session of the Constituent Assembly on the 17th of December, 1789, "we refuse everything. To the Jewish citizen it is proper that we grant everything." In reply to that plea, Abbé Maury said, "The Jews are not a sect but a nation, with a law of their own which they have always followed and which they do not wish to abandon." The liberals, however, felt that they had to undo a historic wrong. Franz Grillparzer in his drama *Die Jüdin von Toledo* has the following lines:

> "Ich selber lieb es nicht, dies Volk, doch weiss ich
> Was sie verunziert, es ist unser Werk;
> Wir lahmen sie, und grollen, wenn sie hinken."

"We first lame them and then hate them for limping." Thus the liberals finally realized more or less clearly the truth that, if you deny freedom and responsibility to a group, you contribute to the conditions which you are then likely to advance as a reason for not entrusting the group with freedom and responsibility.

Those who opposed the granting of civil rights to Jews did so on the ground that they constituted a separate nation, and therefore could not be integrated into any other nation. Statesmen and publicists kept up a barrage of arguments against enfranchizing the Jews. In the early years of the first decade of the nineteenth century, Goethe, as representative of the old-time nobility, and Fichte, as spokesman of the newly rising nationalism, opposed all measures intended to give the Jews civil rights. In every national assembly or legislature where the question of emancipating the Jews from their Medieval status was suggested, the same argument about their being a nation apart was reiterated again and again. On the other hand, it did not enter the minds of men like Hardenberg and Metternich who, in 1815 at the Congress of Vienna, urged the humane treatment of the Jews, or of Alexander von Humboldt of Prussia, that the Jews might want to survive as a distinct group, even after they had become part of the body politic of the Western nations.

After all attempts under the Revolutionary regime in France to hinder the enactment of Jewish franchise had failed, they were revived when Napoleon came into power as First Consul. In 1802, he ordered Comte Joseph Marie Portalis, his minister in charge of religious affairs, to formulate a plan for finally determining the status of the Jews. Portalis, presumably after a careful study of the problem, reported that it was not feasible to grant the Jews civil rights, because they constituted a distinct nation and not merely a religious sect. Napoleon himself had by that time become prejudiced against the Jews, as a result of his contact with some of them in the course of his campaigns, and of the pressure brought to bear on him by the clerical reactionaries in his entourage. It was probably at their suggestion that Napoleon in 1806 summoned an assembly of Jewish notables for a preliminary inquiry to answer a number of pointed questions. Those questions placed the Jewish notables in the dilemma of either having to renounce Jewish nationhood or take the responsibility for the abrogation of even those rights which had at last been granted the Jews.

The notables chose the alternative of renouncing Jewish nationhood. "The Jews," they said, "do not constitute a nation any longer, since they have been granted the privilege of becoming a part of the great (French) nation. . . . There is no fraternity between Jews of different countries. A French Jew feels a stranger among English Jews. The Jews of France would willingly fight against fellow-Jews who served in the armies that fight against France."

Napoleon was so satisfied with their replies that he summoned in 1807, with great pomp and circumstance, what he termed a "Jewish Sanhedrin," in order that its members might give those replies the full weight of their authority. Thus, practically at the bidding of Napoleon, the Jewish notables, who came from the ranks of the rising bourgeoisie, surrendered as the price for civil rights all that autonomy and unity of the Jewish People which had enabled it to survive throughout the centuries of dispersion. It was among the few wealthy Jews chiefly that the attainment of civil rights had become an obsession. That was the form which the yearning for this-worldly salvation took on among them. They practically forced the poor Jews, who far out-numbered them, to accept civil emancipation against their will.[1]

The most significant part of their reply was their new and, from a traditional viewpoint, unwarranted application of the principle, "the law of the sovereign is law," which had been enunciated by Samuel Yarhina'ah, a Babylonian *Amora* in the third century.[2] They interpreted that principle to mean that Jews should renounce the right to juridical autonomy and recognize civil marriage between Jew and Gentile as binding, even from a Jewish point of view. Actually, all that the principle in question had meant to convey was that in all fiscal matters in sales and inheritances involving questions of State taxes and regulations, conformity to the State regulations should be practiced and assumed, and that all contracts confirmed by non-Jewish courts which were under State jurisdiction should be considered binding. There was nothing further from the mind of the author of that principle than that Jews should surrender the right to administer their own civil law. The first Rabbinical Conference, however, which officially inaugurated the Reform movement at Braunschweig in 1844, ratified this denationalizing resolution of the Paris Sanhedrin.

Napoleon's interest in the Jewish question was motivated, as his political enemies, in particular Metternich, surmised, not by an intrinsic interest in the fate of the Jews, and least of all by any ethical impulse to treat them on a footing of equality. It was part of his campaign to develop what is now known as "fifth columnists" in all countries which he wanted to bring under his rule. He, therefore, believed that the recognition accorded the Jews by the act of summoning a Sanhedrin would get them to regard him as a Messiah. In fact, when he invaded Russia, many of the Jews there believed that they would at last be redeemed by him from their age-long oppression and exile.[3]

Napoleon's ambivalent attitude toward the Jews manifested itself again in 1808 when he revoked the Emancipation Edict of 1791. The new disabilities deprived the 80,000 Jews under his rule of the freedom of trade and of settlement. Though the revocation was limited to a period of ten years, it served as a hindrance to the emancipation of Jews during 1815-1845, the period of general reaction in European affairs after the fall of Napoleon.

It is of utmost importance for the understanding of what has happened to Judaism since 1800 to note the influence which economic status exercised on the attitude of Jews toward their emancipation. Jews who were economically enterprising and who, by virtue of their success, came to exercise leadership in their respective communities cherished the ambition of attaining political equality. Likewise, the intellectually enterprising, who were restive under the restraints which prevented their sharing in the cultural progress of their day, looked to emancipation to open the gates to careers from which they had been excluded. These two groups persuaded the liberal statesmen to get their Governments to abolish the Jewish disabilities. But arrayed against them were the majority of the Jews, the scope of whose lives was confined within the narrow limits of a poverty-ridden existence.[4] The spiritual leaders of those Jews were generally men whose intellectual interests never strayed beyond the Talmud and its commentaries. It was, therefore, natural for them to discourage their followers from availing themselves of the advantages of emancipation. The acceptance of civil rights meant surrendering their communal autonomy and becoming identified with a culture which they still rightly regarded as Christian and, therefore, as hostile to everything Jewish.

Internal conflicts raged for a long time between the many who resisted the Europeanization of the Jews and the few who sought to promote it. In Holland, in Napoleon's time, the Jews for the most part resisted emancipation. In Poland, the Hasidic movement, which during the first part of the nineteenth century included the majority of East European Jews, had its face set against accepting citizenship in the State. R. Shneor Zalman, who stands out as the most philosophically-minded leader in modern Hasidism,[5] denounced the efforts of Napoleon I to force the enfranchisement of the Jews, on the ground that it was intended as a means of destroying Judaism.

When, after the fall of Napoleon, the province of Posen was annexed to Prussia, a number of traditionalist rabbis were consulted by the Prussian Government concerning the advisability of granting political rights to the Jews of Posen. Their reply was that they did not regard any country outside Eretz Yisrael as other than a place of temporary sojourn. They therefore did not want to accept those rights. The Rabbi of Posen is said to have replied: "We experience God's blessing in that all the enemies of our people have not succeeded in destroying us from off the face of the earth. But we also experience God's curse in that you are unable to give us permanent redemption." [6] The traditionalist rabbis in Hungary characterized the wish for political equality on the part of the Jews "as sinful and as inconsistent with Israel's hopes for the future." [7]

So long as Christianity continued to be the professed religion of the majority, it was natural for the majority to expect that the minority would ultimately become Christianized. Those Jews who were active in the process of Europeanizing their fellow-Jews were either unaware, or pretended to be unaware, of these ulterior motives, which were sensed by the plain people. Jews who were militant in the cause of Jewish emancipation and enlightenment often unwittingly became agents of the Governments and served as informers against their fellow-Jews. Such is the tragic concomitant of the struggle on the part of a minority group to achieve equality with the majority group.

CENTRAL EUROPEAN JEWRY DURING FIRST HALF OF 19TH CENTURY

The lot of the Jews during the first few decades of nineteenth century Europe was the outcome both of the new order which Napoleon was instrumental in imposing on the countries he conquered and of the reaction against it. In whatever country he conquered and occupied, he compelled the local Government to introduce a wider franchise and a greater measure of political equality for the general population. These changes included the granting of civil rights to Jews.

After the fall of Napoleon, however, when the conquered nations threw off the French yoke, a violent reaction set in against his political reforms. This reaction was called forth by the national resentment in the countries of Central Europe which Fichte knew how to fan to white heat. At the same time, their cultural leaders recoiled from eighteenth century rationalism; it had become associated in their minds with the political humiliation to which France had subjected them. The liberation of the masses came to be feared and hated as being the Jacobin heritage bequeathed by the French Revolution. German romanticism, as the counter-movement to French rationalism, spread rapidly and intensified the German national consciousness through its emotional appeal to racial and historical memories.

That period witnessed the beginning of the passionate agitation for German national unity. The entire cultural life of Germany was focused on her political status. Her foremost men of letters and her great thinkers and religious leaders were determined to foster her nationhood. The very division of her peoples into conflicting political states contributed to the conscious stimulation of nationalism—the movement to foster nationhood and to exalt its values. Statism was then becoming self-conscious, and the salvational aspect of Christianity was being reinterpreted in modern philosophic terms.

The romantic movement in Germany thus achieved a synthesis of modern nationalism with a reinterpreted Christianity, a synthesis which could not but react violently against the enfranchisement of the Jews. "Schleiermacher neatly anticipated the anti-Semitism of modern German fascism," says R. Niebuhr, "with the idea that once a people has arrived at a high state of development, it is disgraceful for it to embrace within it anything alien to it, no matter how excellent that may be in itself; its particular character it has received from God Himself." [8]

In Germany, where the new trends in Judaism were to arise, the Jewish communities felt the effect of the reaction which had set in as soon as the old order was restored. Anti-Jewish sentiment had been too deeply rooted to be affected by the marked intellectual progress which Germany then achieved. Even so enlightened a ruler as Frederick the Great could not shake off that sentiment. In a message in 1789 to his minister Von Hoym he stated, "If the Jews were expelled and Christians would take their place as innkeepers, it would be for the good of the country, and we would have more human beings and less Jews." [9] Consequently, as soon as the post-Napoleonic reaction set in, Jews were deprived of the rights that had been granted them. Though they had fought in the war against Napoleon, and though many of them had distinguished themselves by their valor, nothing could stem the tide of reaction. The commissions and other distinctions won by the Jews on the battlefield were cancelled. Books attacking the Jews in the most vituperative fashion began to pour forth from the presses. One of them was so vicious that the Prussian Government felt forced to make a gesture at prohibiting its distribution, only shortly thereafter to yield to public pressure and to withdraw its interdict. The populace was incited to raise once again the old pogrom cry of "hep-hep." Thus were the Jews of Germany thrust back into the old status of pariahs.

Underlying this reaction was the emphatic repudiation of the secular State and the revival of the theocratic notion of the State as Christian. There developed simultaneously a movement to proselytize the Jews. In order to make sure that Jews would avail themselves of the opportunity to accept Christianity, they were, on the one hand, offered positions in the Government if they were converted, and, on the other, were not permitted to introduce any changes in their own traditional beliefs and practices, so that they would not wish to remain loyal to Judaism. The Prussian Government went so far as to meddle in details of Jewish worship. With the purpose of maintaining the unesthetic form of the synagogue worship of those days, it forbade the introduction of choirs, of the clerical grab, of preaching in the vernacular or of any innovations in the ritual. Leopold Zunz's great work, *Gottesdienstliche Vortraege*, which was published in Berlin in 1832, was motivated largely by his desire to prove that preaching in the vernacular was nothing new.[10]

Despite the disabilities under which the Jews of Germany labored during the thirties and forties of the nineteenth century, they were certain that their complete emancipation could not be long delayed. Not only in Germany but even in Russia, and more so in Galicia, where Jews lived in large numbers, that was the conviction of the members of the growing middle class who succeeded in achieving economic competence that brought them special privileges and freed them from the burdens which the poorer Jews in the small towns had to bear. The wealthier Jews were able to exempt their children from military draft, because they could afford to send them to secondary and vocational shools.[11] They did not have to pay the special sales taxes imposed on the poorer elements. They cherished toward the Government a degree of love and loyalty scarcely matched by the non-Jewish citizens. They were convinced that the Government was genuinely interested in raising the standard of Jewish life both materially and morally. The fact that the Government placed a premium on the attainment of secular education was taken by them as proof of its paternal interest in the Jews. Even the oppressive measures against the poorer Jews, who were unable or unwilling to avail themselves of the opportunities to be westernized, were interpreted as proof of the State's desire to raise the level of Jewish life.[12]

Having only just begun their struggle for emancipation, the well-to-do and the middle-class Jews, both lay and learned, were certain that the dawn of their freedom and equality could not be long delayed. They assumed that they were entering an age of social

progress and cultural enlightenment, and that all Jews would before long be completely emancipated from their Medieval disabilities. Among the Jewish intellectuals, Joseph Perl, of Galician Poland, in 1837, and A.B. Gottlober, of Russia, in 1850, hailed the
new age as the millenium; the Jewish thinker Nachman Krochmal
was busy formulating, with the aid of Hegelian philosophy, the
place which the Jewish People would occupy in that millenium.

In 1838, the English translation of Mendelssohn's *Jerusalem* was
published in London, while the Jews of England were still regarded
as aliens. The translator, M. Samuels, after referring in his preface
to what the Jews had to suffer on account of their religion, adds:
"But wherefore these gloomy pictures of former ages? Let me
throw a veil over this horrid past, and skip that page in the records
of our hapless ancestors, lest I should again depress our spirits now
raised by modern and better scenes to the most pleasing expectation. A new chapter commences in the history of the Jews opening
with gladder events, and becoming more and more cheerful, as it
proceeds." He then goes on to give as the basis for his optimism
the fact that "*Humanity* is the watchword sounding from every
tongue and approximating to each other the hearts of all men . . .
Thank God! The times are over when the ideas of *Jew* and *Man*
are considered heterogeneous." Nevertheless, Samuels realized that
all obstacles had not yet been removed. The past had left its heritage of hate and misunderstanding and there was still "a world of
misapprehension to be explained and set to right."

Heinrich Graetz, in 1848, in a brief foreword to the Hebrew
translation of his *History of the Jews*, referring to the Jews who
had been accorded political equality, wrote: "There is good reason
to hope that their brethren who are still under the iron yoke will
also be redeemed without a price." Even the Governments that
withheld political rights from the Jews did not then dare to profess as a general principle that Jews were not entitled to those
rights. They tried to justify their retention of Jewish disabilities on
the purely practical ground that the Jews had not yet become sufficiently integrated into the life of the country, and would therefore
be subject to maltreatment at the hands of the non-Jews if they
were suddenly granted full equality.

The eagerness with which the more prosperous Jews looked
forward to the Emancipation began to undermine their attach-

ment to their own Jewish People. Even in Poland, where Jews were very far from having achieved any measure of political equality, they regarded as nothing less than anti-Semitic every practical suggestion made by well-meaning Polish political and cultural leaders to facilitate their settlement in Palestine, or in some territory where they would be able to lead an autonomous Jewish life. They looked to complete emancipation as the awaited millenium, without considering what effect it would have on their life as Jews.

Illustrative of the attitude of middle-class Polish Jews during the middle of the nineteenth century is the action they took in 1857. Pressure had been brought on Alexander II of Russia to consider the various proposals to solve the Jewish question in Poland by having the Government help the Jews settle in some territory of their own. To prevent any such consideration, the influential Jews brought in a petition in which they declared that, having lived for six centuries in Poland, they had become part of its life and indispensable to its economic national existence. Though they were believers in the "Old Testament," "they could nevertheless identify themselves completely with the native population." [13]

THE ROLE OF MOSES MENDELSSOHN IN
MEETING THE CHALLENGE OF MODERNISM

The secularist ideas and attitudes which radiated from the European civilization undermined the belief in the revelational basis of Judaism and in the other-worldly conception of salvation. In the past, that belief constituted the chief rationale for Jewish unity. At first, no attempt was made to evolve an alternative basis for Jewish unity. As a consequence, Judaism came to be regarded as a liability, and the tendency of Jews, particularly those in the upper brackets of wealth and influence, to escape it soon reached ominous proportions.

Modernist secularism invaded Jewish life, toward the end of the eighteenth and the beginning of the nineteenth century, with a disconcerting suddenness. It was not preceded by a transition period which might have mitigated the shattering effect of its impact on the accustomed ways of Jewish living and thinking.

Among the Western nations, on the other hand, the enlightenment made its appearance after three or four centuries of religious cultural evolution which resulted from the Renaissance and the Protestant movements. These were the centuries when Jews were made to feel their alienage in a way which only helped to intensify their adherence to their traditional values. The Jews then built more strongly the wall that divided their cultural and spiritual life from that of the Western world.

Following the expulsion from Spain in 1492, there arose a mystic movement which led to an intensified reliance on the hoped-for appearance of the Messiah—a movement that culminated in the Shabbatean fiasco in 1666. In the wake of the persecutions and massacres of the Polish Jews by Chmelnicki in 1648-55, there began to develop a new type of mysticism which widened still further the gulf between Judaism and the cultural life of their non-Jewish neighbors.

The outstanding Jew during the latter half of the eighteenth century, in whom the result of the sudden impact of modernist secularism on Traditional Judaism can best be seen and appraised, was Moses Mendelssohn. Though uncommonly gifted as a thinker and writer, he was unable to achieve a satisfactory ideological adjustment between Traditional Judaism and the European secular culture of which he was a leading spokesman. He would have preferred to keep his Jewish interests in a different compartment of his mind from that in which he cultivated his interests in general culture. Challenged to engage in the problem of reconciling his Judaism with his own modern world outlook, he was less successful in solving that problem than the Medieval Jewish theologians had been in their attempt to resolve the conflict between Jewish tradition and Greek philosophy.

Mendelssohn was not the first Jew to make his mark in modern European culture. Some of the more intellectually gifted among the Jews of Italy in the sixteenth century and among the Jews of Holland in the seventeenth century had come under the influence of Renaissance humanism. Leone Ebreo, who flourished during the first half of the sixteenth century, was an Italian writer and dramatic critic, author of many dramatic and poetic works in Italian, of which the *Dialoghi di 'Amore* is the best known. It is so completely devoid of any intimations of Judaism that he was assumed to have become a convert to Christianity. Azariah di Rossi (1513-1578), also an Italian Jew, was the first to apply the principle of modern historiography to the study of the traditional texts of Judaism, and to reclaim Philo for Jewish theology. The Sephardic Jews, in Amsterdam of the seventeenth century, conducted a school system in which secular studies were given an important place in the curriculm. The outstanding product of that school system was Baruch Spinoza. There were Jewish physicians, scientists, musicians and writers who played distinguished roles in the general European culture prior to the era of Mendelssohn.

In Mendelssohn, however, we have the first representative Jew who came under the influence of the particular type of eighteenth-century rationalism known as Enlightenment. It constituted a more adventurous reliance upon reason and experience and a more daring revolt against political and religious authoritarianism than mankind had ever known. Its revolt against the political regime prepared the way for modern nationalism and, incidentally, for the Jewish emancipation. The Enlightenment's revolt against the Church had repercussions in Jewish life in the revolt against the rabbinate, as the upholders of the authority of Traditional Judaism.

As in general life, so in Jewish life, Enlightenment meant reliance upon personal initiative and effort as a means of bettering one's lot, individually and collectively, instead of passively waiting for divine help. Jews looked to their emancipation as a means of improving their condition of life, and to Enlightenment as a prerequisite to emancipation. That is why the drive to achieve enlightenment took possession of the leading Jews in Central and Eastern Europe. Mendelssohn came upon the scene at the beginning of this Enlightenment Movement among the Jews.

Mendelssohn was born in 1729 in Dessau, Germany. At the age of fourteen he had already mastered considerable Jewish lore, both Rabbinic and Medieval. The only language he knew beside Hebrew was the Judeo-German dialect, which he was destined later to call upon his fellow-Jews to renounce in favor of pure German. The ambition to better himself intellectually impelled him to come to Berlin. With the aid of some Jewish students who gave him instruction in Latin, English, French, mathematics and science, he managed to master the higher learning of that day. In addition, he acquired the ability to write in a fluent and popular German on philosophy, literature and esthetics. By 1763, he was able to compete successfully for a high academic prize on a philosophic theme with no less a thinker than Immanuel Kant.

Mendelssohn's literary and philosophic abilities brought him into intimate contact with some of the prominent figures in Berlin, and his name became "open sesame" for Jews in Germany. It opened for them the doors of the rulers to whom they appealed for the grant of political status. Most Jews were then still largely subject to Medieval disabilities, though a small group of financially successful Jews enjoyed special privileges that almost placed them on a footing of equality with the upper circles of German society. Although intellectual fame placed Mendelssohn within the circle of these privileged Jews, he remained a practicing Jew in his personal life.

Mendelssohn might have had no occasion to state in writing how he had come to terms with Jewish tradition had he not been challenged by Johann Kaspar Lavater, a Christian friend and admirer who had tried to convert him to Christianity. In 1769, Lavater sent him a copy of his own work, *Untersuchung der Beweise fuer das Christenthum*, which was a translation of Charles Bonnet's *Idées sur l 'Etat Futur des Etres Vivants*, and which was dedicated to Mendelssohn. In the preface to the book, Lavater challenged Mendelssohn either to refute the arguments for Christianity advanced by Bonnet or "to do what Socrates would have done had he read the work and found it irrefutable." Mendelssohn took the challenge very much to heart and reluctantly made public a statement in which he defended his loyalty to Judaism, being careful at the same time not to offend Christianity.

From then on he applied some of his literary efforts to the exposition of Judaism. He translated the Pentateuch into German, first for his own children and later for general circulation, mainly with the view of having his fellow-Jews learn to replace their Judeo-German dialect with pure German. This brought him into conflict with prominent spokesmen of Traditional Judaism. The fact, however, that the King of Denmark had acquired a copy of Mendelssohn's translation silenced the main opponent, Rabbi Raphael Kohn of Altona, and the question of its legitimacy was no longer debated publicly.

Whatever further exposition of Judaism Mendelssohn engaged

in was the indirect result of his endeavor to help his fellow-Jews achieve some measure of civil freedom. First, he persuaded his friend, the Military Councilor of State, Christian Wilhelm Dohm, to write his *Ueber die buergerliche Verbesserung der Juden* (1781) which turned out to be the first public presentation in literary form by a non-Jew of the case for Jewish emancipation.

In this presentation, Dohm maintains that the Jews possess all the necessary qualifications for citizenship. They are industrious, sober, moral, and loyal to the country that harbors them. There is nothing in their religion to which anyone can object on moral grounds. Their exotic manners are due to segregation and discrimination. If the Government permits them to avail themselves of the opportunities for culture and education, either by establishing schools for them or allowing them to share the educational facilities of the country, they will soon be westernized like the rest of the population. Their loyalty to their religion should not be held against them. On the contrary, it shows what strong moral fibre they possess. His advice is that the Jews should be granted civil rights, *buergerliche Rechte*, not *buergerrechte*, or rights of citizenship. The distinction implies that Jews are not to hold office in the civil government, but are to maintain their own communal autonomy under government supervision.

Dohm's contention, however, that loyalty to Judaism did not warrant withholding civil rights from the Jews was challenged by his opponents on the ground that the main purpose of Judaism, especially in its ritual observances, was to segregate the Jews from their non-Jewish neighbors. To meet this challenge, Mendelssohn urged his Jewish friend Marcus Herz to publish a German translation of Menasseh ben Israel's *Vindiciae Judaeorum*, a defense of the Jews that had been addressed to Cromwell for the purpose of persuading him to permit Jews to live in England.

In a brief introduction to that translation, Mendelssohn took occasion to criticize Dohm's suggestion that Jews ought to be permitted, even after they were emancipated, to exercise autonomy to the extent of enforcing their own religious way of life. He took strong exception to that part of Dohm's plea for the Jews, because nothing less than complete equality as individuals with the rest of the population was acceptable to him. To grant to the Jews the right to exercise communal autonomy—as Dohm had expressly advised—would justify their exclusion from governmental positions. Mendelssohn exposed himself this time to an even more unfriendly challenge than he had encountered at the hands of Lavater. He, therefore, felt that he must make his position clear by publishing a full statement on the subject of religion and state. That led to his writing his brochure *Jerusalem, oder ueber religioese Macht und Judenthum.*

That brochure is significant in that it contains a warm plea for religious tolerance and an elaborate argument for the separation of Church and State. Mendelssohn's interest in advocating the principle of religious tolerance was motivated by his desire to help his fellow-Jews secure civil equality. He rightly assumed that the basic justification in Christian countries for keeping the Jews in a state of alienage was the prevailing idea that none but those who were affiliated with the Church were eligible to citizenship in the State. This close partnership between the Church and State, he maintained, had to be dissolved before Jews could be admitted to citizenship.

It required considerable courage for a Jew in Mendelssohn's position to come frankly to grips with the problem of Church and State, and to urge not only that they be separated, but also that the Church be deprived of all power to apply sanctions for disobedience or belief. Fortunately for him, the Church was not in high favor at the time he wrote *Jerusalem*. He could, therefore, allow himself to make statements of an uncomplimentary character about priests and Church authorities in general. He even dared to argue that the Church ought not possess any property, and that the clergy ought not be remunerated for their services. That would virtually have meant the end of established religion.

The truth is that, though Mendelssohn fully realized that the problem of the respective jurisdictions of Church and State was a complex one, he cannot be said to have contributed toward its solution. The main reason for his failure was that he operated with the conception of religion as entirely a matter between the individual person and God. As such, religion should be free from social coercion or sanctions. He had acquired that conception of religion from Leibnitz, Reimarus, Locke and the Deists. Religion, as a historical and social phenomenon rooted in the collective life of human society was entirely foreign to him and still is to most people who should know better. He assumed that a Church ought by right be nothing more than a kind of voluntary philosophical association. For such an association to employ the same means of enforcing its collective will as does a State seemed to him the height of absurdity.

The basic assumption which underlies Mendelssohn's position with regard to the mutual relations of State, religion and Judaism, is that the human being can reach a high point of spiritual development only when he is entirely free to choose his course of action. The State, which is inherently a coercive agency, fulfills a necessary function, but should have nothing to do with the spiritual life of its citizens. Religion, on the other hand, which is a means of rendering man spiritual, should not have to resort to coercion. Neither should Judaism, which is both a religion and a system of divine legislation, have to resort to coercive sanctions. Mendelssohn's failure to take into account the fact that religion functions as a social process, and not merely as a system of beliefs acquired through tradition or arrived at by the individual on the basis of his own experience renders his notions of Church-State relations unworkable. However, he is not always consistent. Though he would not have the State meddle with the religious beliefs of its citizens, he would nevertheless grant it the right to compel its citizens to believe in God, Providence, and immortality, on the ground that those beliefs are indispensable to the moral life. [14]

No less paradoxical than his rationalist view of the relations between Church and State is his attempt to interpret Judaism from the standpoint of his philosophic conception of religion, and to vindicate his adherence to Jewish tradition. He maintains that Judaism cannot be regarded as a religion, in the usual sense of the term. "I believe that Judaism," he writes, "knows nothing of a revealed religion, in the sense in which it is taken by Christians. The Israelites have a divine legislation: laws, judgments, statutes, rules of life, information of the will of God, and lessons on how to conduct themselves in order to attain both temporal and spiritual happiness. Those laws, commandments, etc., were revealed to them through Moses in a miraculous and supernatural manner, but no dogmas, no saving truths, no general self-evident assumptions. Those the Lord always reveals to us, in the same way as to the rest of mankind, by *nature* and by *events*, but never in *words* or *written* characters." [15]

The assumption implied in the foregoing passage is that reason, rather than revelation, is the source of those truths which are essential to salvation. Mendelssohn identifies salvation with bodiless immortality of the soul and its bliss in the hereafter. Such salvation is not the monopoly of any Church or religious communion. It is accessible to all human beings who cultivate their reason adequately.

To Mendelssohn, religion meant only that which reason revealed concerning God. The notion of a supernaturally revealed *religion*, therefore, appeared to him to be self-contradictory. Judaism, on the other hand, was to him, "revealed legislation," and not a religion. He may have derived that conception of Judaism from Joseph Albo's *Ikkarim*; to Albo, as well as to Thomas Aquinas in his *Summa Theologica*, conformity to revealed, or divine, legislation was a prerequisite to salvation, and only that religion's communion, or Church, which was in possession of such legislation, was qualified to be an instrument of salvation. To Mendelssohn, however, all legislation, whether divine or human, was intended to enable man merely to make the best use of what this world had to offer. On the other hand, salvation, or life eternal, was attainable only through the activity of reason. In that opinion one may discern the influence of Maimonides.

The conception of Judaism as "divine legislation" had led Spinoza to conclude that, with the destruction of the Second Commonwealth and the dispersion of the Jews, their divine legislation lost its authority. Mendelssohn, on the other hand, concluded that it was his duty to remain loyal to Judaism at all times. "Other nations," he writes in his reply to Charles Bonnet's *Palingenesie Philosophique*, "may alter their laws according to the times, circumstances and conveniences. But for me the Creator Himself dictated the laws. How then could I, a frail creature, presume to change at will those divine laws?" [16] It evidently takes a great man to be greatly inconsistent.

In attempting to harmonize the idea of supernaturally revealed legislation with religion based on reason, Mendelssohn imputed to historical Judaism tolerance of divergent beliefs, provided they did not deny the three fundamental principles recognized by rational religion—the existence of God, reward and punishment, and immortality. He maintained that Judaism exacted conformity to all its laws, and, at the same time, he emphatically opposed the imposition of sanctions for the violation of those laws. The enforcement of ecclesiastical law, he stated, should be unknown among Jews. Jews should constitute themselves into a voluntary society, and freely accept the obligation to obey the laws of the Torah.

In line with the foregoing rather inconsistent thinking, occasioned by the highly complicated situation with which Jews were confronted for the first time, is Mendelssohn's use of the well-known text in the New Testament: "Render unto Caesar the things which be Caesar's, and to God the things which be God's." [17] That reply, which is credited to Jesus, was an answer to an intrinsically difficult, if not an insoluble, problem. It is more evasive than illuminating. What Jesus said on that occasion may have silenced the hecklers who tried to implicate him in the guilt of rebellion against Rome, but it has contributed little to the ever-recurring problem of adjusting the competing or overlapping jurisdictions of Church and State.

Mendelssohn, however, was fascinated by that answer of Jesus. "A more wholesome advice," he writes, "could not have been given to the House of Jacob even at this very day. Comply with the customs and civil duties of the countries in which you are transplanted, but at the same time be constant to the faith of your forefathers. Bear the burden as well as ye can. It is true that, on the one hand, the burden of civil life is made heavier to you on account of the religion which you uphold faithfully, while on the other, the cultural climate in which you live and the times for the observance of your religious laws are more burdensome than they were originally. Hold out notwithstanding; remain immovable at the station which Providence assigns to you, whatever may befall you; which is no more than your prophets foretold to you long ago." In the same vein, he goes on to argue that the law under which Jews live, being divinely revealed, cannot be set aside except by God himself, "whenever the Supreme Legislator shall be pleased to make known to us His will thereon and make it known to us as loudly, publicly and utterly beyond doubt and hesitation, as He made known to us the Law itself." [18] All this is in line with what Joseph Albo says in his *Ikkarim*.

Mendelssohn's avowal of loyalty to Traditional Judaism, as he conceived it, was not mere high-sounding rhetoric. He took Traditional Judaism seriously. He did not recoil from the possibility that adherence to it might stand in the way of obtaining civil rights. "If civil union cannot be obtained on any other terms than that of departing from the law," he wrote, " we are heartily sorry that we deem it necessary to declare that we will rather renounce civil union. We cannot in conscience depart from the Law; and of what use would be to you fellow-citizens void of conscience?" [19]

When we remember that the purpose of the entire brochure was to make out as strong a case as possible for the removal of the disabilities under which the Jews had been living, and that Mendelssohn was liable to defeat that purpose by so outspoken an affirmation of loyalty to the traditional Jewish observances, we cannot but conclude that he was absolutely free of all mental reservations in his avowal of faith in the supernatural origin of the Torah. He expected his fellow-Jews to subscribe to that same faith. How that can be reconciled with his main thesis that Judaism knows no dogmas is quite unanswerable.

However, Mendelssohn retained his orthodoxy in the face of challenge. Nothing is further from the truth than to regard him as the father of the Reform Movement, or even as the first modern challenger to the rabbinate. Still, some of his disciples ascribed to him the inspiration for their own revolt against the rabbinate. Moreover, the early Reformists, who denationalized Judaism and deprecated the exercise of compulsory authority on the part of rabbis, likewise drew on Mendelssohn's arguments against Christian von Dohm.

So far as Mendelssohn himself was concerned, his main interest was to secure civil rights for his fellow-Jews. "Recognize in us," he pleads with the Gentiles, "fellow-men, even if not brothers, and give us the means to become better human beings. We cannot in good conscience remake our laws. Of what use to you are fellow-citizens without conscience?" [20] In addition, he strove to integrate the Jews into the cultural life of the majority population and to remove the moral and spiritual excrescences which had grown up among Jews as a result of their segregation and status as aliens.

THE DAWN OF JEWISH ENLIGHTENMENT

Mendelssohn died in 1786. The first decades of the nineteenth century witnessed in Government circles of Germany and Austria a reaction against the revolutionary tendencies in politics, religion and philosophy which had emanated from France. The effect of this reaction made itself felt, so far as the Jews were concerned, in the relaxation of the effort on the part of liberal-minded Gentiles to further Jewish emancipation. The Governments exacted exorbitant taxes from the Jews and, in some instances, imposed fines on the entire community for thefts and misdemeanors on the part of any one of its members. This treatment of the Jews, which in the main led to their further impoverishment, went hand in hand with the extension of privileges to a few Jews in each community—privileges for which they paid vast sums—to engage in industry, business or finance.

The families of these privileged Jews, by dint of their affluence and cultural attainments, were able to achieve social status in Gentile society. There were also some who, despite their ghetto background, were not only able to absorb the best in the Western cultures of the day, but also were eager to contribute the fruits of their own talents. They knew, however, that so long as they remained Jews, all careers were closed to them, and that they were condemned to a life of endless struggle against a hostile environment. They were unable to fall back upon the compensatory faith of their forebears. They had lost that faith through the very culture which they had hoped would open to them the doors of opportunity. Now all that was needed to open those doors was the formality of baptism. They had to possess, indeed, more than average strength of character to resist the temptation to embrace Christianity. Heine expressed what was true of most of those who were confronted by that temptation, when he said that he was not made of the stuff of martyrs. Like him, they renounced their Judaism.

There were, of course, exceptions. Some sought a way out of the dilemma in a more or less groping fashion. Such was Lazarus Bendavid (1768-1846) who had come under the influence of Mendelssohn. Being also an ardent disciple of Kant, he lectured in Vienna on his philosophy. Though his lectures drew large audiences, the fact that he was a Jew stood in the way of his being accepted as a member of the faculty of the Vienna University. The Austrian Government was displeased with the rationalist spirit of his lectures and with his efforts to introduce reforms into the Jewish religion, and ordered him to leave Vienna. When he came to Berlin in 1796, he applied several times for the right to engage in the practice of law, but was refused each time, though he had done nothing to offend the authorities. Their excuse was that if he were admitted to the bar, other Jews would soon apply for the same privilege. He was satisfied to eke out a precarious living by working as a grinder of lenses.[21] He did not renounce his Judaism for the sake of a career, but applied his proficiency in the secular studies to the problem of raising the intellectual and spiritual level of Jewish life. He wrote *Etwas zur Charakteristik der Juden*, (Leipzig, 1793) in which he advocated the abrogation of ritual observances and the concentration on ethical behavior.

Another disciple of Mendelssohn, whose sincere devotion to the cause of his fellow-Jews cannot be questioned, was David Friedlaender (1750-1834). He was a man of affairs rather than a scholar or writer. With considerable wealth at his disposal, he had no trouble in being admitted into the social life of wealthy Berlin circles. He might have preferred to be oblivious to the fate of his less fortunate brethren. Instead, he gave himself no rest in his efforts to ameliorate their lot. He tried every possible means to get the Government to lighten the burden it placed on them and to abolish the old discriminatory practice of holding the entire Jewish community responsible for misdemeanors of any of its individual members.

At one point, however, in the course of his endeavors in behalf of the Jews, he resorted to a quixotic remedy. In the name of a number of well-to-do Jewish families, he wrote to Councillor Oberconsistorialrath Teller, offering to accept Christianity, if they would be exempted from subscribing to the divinity of Jesus and the doctrine of the Trinity, and not be expected to take part in the celebration of Christian festivals. His proposal was rejected with the reply: "We have enough heretics of our own." Despite the failure of his pet project, Friedlaender continued to serve his fellow-Jews faithfully for more than three decades after that. Whatever reforms he urged cannot be regarded as having been motivated merely by practical considerations, for he unquestionably had at heart the spiritual as well as the physical welfare of his people.

Unmistakable proof, however, that the reforms advocated by men like Ben David and Friedlaender were dictated by a sincere desire to see Judaism function healthily in the life of their fellow-Jews was their vigorous opposition to reforms, whether educational or religious, in Jewish life which the State tried to impose. They continually stressed the importance of having all such reforms emanate from the Jews themselves. On the other hand, whenever the Government insisted in meddling in the inner life of the Jews, Friedlaender sought to persuade the Government at least to act in accordance with their highest interests. When Prussia granted civil rights to the Jews in 1812, he submitted a carefully worked out program of educational and religious reforms to the Prussian statesman, Prince Hardenberg, the Prime Minister of Friedrich Wilhelm III, who happened to be friendly to the Jews.

The Jews in Prussia who had come under the influence of Mendelssohn, especially those who had acquired considerable training both in secular subject-matter and in traditional Jewish lore, found themselves in a dilemma. Having received no guidance in dealing with the problems which arose in their minds from the mingling of the two cultures, the Jewish and the non-Jewish, they worked out various rough-and-ready schemes which could hardly bear the scrutiny of critical thought. The historian Isaac Marcus Jost, who was a contemporary of those early *illuminati*, gives us a glimpse of their inner confusion. On the one hand, we are told, they could not help finding the ideas of Christianity entirely bizarre and incapable of acceptance unless they abjured both reason and conscience. On the other hand, they felt that Judaism was still vigorous and capable of enduring. They took for granted the historicity of the supernatural revelations through which God had made known what man must do to achieve salvation. They believed in a hereafter and in the retribution which awaited the human being for the kind of life he had led on earth. They assumed that morality without the sanction of revelation was bound to break down, and that the Sacred Scriptures had, therefore, to serve as support of moral duty. They were fully aware of the various passages in Scripture which were in conflict with their own moral standards and philosophical assumptions, but they would always manage to find a way of reconciling those passages with their own beliefs.

"At all events," adds Marcus Jost, "a certain degree of vacillation is not to be mistaken. It was with the education of youth where they were most irresolute how to proceed. As to the ceremonial law, they never completely spoke their mind about it, but no one could help agreeing with Mendelssohn that they were nothing but the shell of the kernel. In sifting the enormous rabbinical additions, they soon began to make a distinction between what was essential and what was not. As they could not deny the Mosaic legislation a divine origin without upsetting Judaism altogether, all the additions foisted on it were discarded." [22]

Acting on the principle that most of the Mosaic laws were intended only for Eretz Yisrael, and that all laws intended to segregate Jews from pagans did not apply to Christians, the Jewish *illuminati* of Berlin managed to convince themselves that they were exempt from the observance of most of the ritual practices in Judaism. "In short," Jost goes on to say, "until the not-to-be calculated restoration of the Israelitish empire by the expected Messiah, only such precepts of the Law are to hold as tend to serve or to preserve the kernel of religion and as are adapted to form of its congregations a piously religious union, without their being hostile to existing relations or to the improvement of the mind. In this manner, the religion still continued orthodox although not in a rabbinical sense. They mainly adopted the maxim 'For the individual there is internal, living, spirit-and-heart-inspiring religion; for the congregation external worship and forms.' This was diamentrically opposite to rabbinism, and no less so to the not-altogether-absolvatory assertions of Mendelssohn, who maintained that in the present times and relations, the laws of the Jews are duties and obligations undertaken by every one of them individually." [23]

There were sporadic manifestations of the movement that later

crystallized as Reform in other parts of Europe. The most noteworthy were those in Hungary and Moravia. According to G.
Scholem,[24] the ground for those tendencies had been prepared by
Shabbatian circles which managed to maintain themselves, for the
most part secretly, far into the eighteenth century. Leopold Loew[25]
states that sons of families, on whom Shabbetai Tz'vi's messianic
claims had an impact, were encouraged in their non-observance
of Jewish ritual practices by what they had learned from Lessing
and other protagonists of the Enlightenment. Speaking of the
Frankists in Bohemia and Moravia, Hungary and Rumania, who
were the ideological successors of the Shabbetians, Scholem adds:
"It was the influence of these elements, which had not openly cut
themselves off from rabbinical Judaism, that, after the French
Revolution, became important in fostering movements towards
reform, liberalism, and enlightenment in many Jewish circles" [26]

Whatever may have been Mendelssohn's intention, it is a fact
that his writings did breach the wall of Traditional Judaism and
did undermine Rabbinic authority, which had guarded it throughout the centuries. That breach was widened by a group of his
disciples who collaborated on the first periodical that was published by Jews, known as Ha-Meāsef. That periodical began to appear in 1784 at Koenigsberg and lasted till 1811. It underwent
frequent changes in religious attitude and place of publication
during its existence.

The articles, essays, poems and stories were either original or
translations of selections from European literature. Great stress
was laid on purity of literary style. The main purpose, however,
was to introduce the Jewish readers into the Western universe of
thought. This was part of the movement inaugurated through
Mendelssohn's efforts to raise the cultural level of the Jews. That
is the movement known as Haskalah, or Jewish Enlightenment,
which spread almost immediately to the countries that were subject to German influence. "Throughout the greater part of my
native country, Moravia," writes Yizhak Hirsch Weiss[27] (1815-
1905), "wherever the spirit emanating from Germany penetrated,
the light of Mendelssohn of Berlin dawned. Many began to get
a taste of the secular sciences. Even in the hedarim where formerly
the main purpose was to teach Bible, Mishnah and Gemara, the
method of teaching was changed, the Bible was taught with the

aid of Mendelssohn's translation, and the better trained teachers expended much effort in teaching and discussing the science of Hebrew grammar."

Haskalah, as a sporadic venture of some intellectually enterprising individuals, antedated Mendelssohn. But as a movement inspired by Mendelssohn and his disciples, it was a large-scale process of Jewish self-adjustment to the new life upon which Jews were about to enter. It was a conscious attempt of the Jews to Europeanize or westernize themselves. They tried to fit their traditional values into the new universe of discourse which the Occident had been building up since the Renaissance. What the writers of the magazine *Ha-Meāsef* undertook to do culturally for the Jews was analogous to what the Encylopedists had done for the French people, though not in the same effective and systematic way.

Whenever the influence of the *Haskalah* movement made itself felt, spiritual unrest and inner conflict followed, especially among some of the more gifted youth who had studied in the talmudical academies. Many of them who surreptitiously got a taste of modern knowledge lost their spiritual balance and broke with Jewish life. They either openly flouted their heresies, or actually turned apostates. The contemporary rabbis noting this outcome for which they themselves were partly to blame, since they had declared all attempts to become Europeanized as disloyalty to Judaism, became even more intransigeant. This vicious circle was not broken at any point. If the attitude of the Traditionalist rabbis did not always alienate the aspirants to modernization, it all too often fostered the spirit of hypocrisy.[28]

The effect which *Haskalah* had upon the Jews was ambiguous. It either made for assimilation of the Jews and their complete absorption in the general population, usually through conversion to Christianity, or it deepened their national self-consciousness, transforming at the same time their traditional theocratic nationalism into modern and secular nationalism. Which of these effects *Haskalah* had upon the Jews depended upon their prospects of achieving civil status.

In countries such as those of Central Europe, where cultural progress was the avowed aim of the general population, and where Jews resided in limited numbers, *Haskalah* served as a transition stage to be quickly passed through and left behind on the way toward complete self-identification with non-Jewish culture. In the countries of Eastern Europe, however, where the prospects of Jewish emancipation were remote and Jews were massed in large numbers, *Haskalah* gave a new direction to Jewish cultural and spiritual activities. It sought to introduce into Jewish life Western standards of thought and behavior, without decreasing its scope and intensity. Thus, in Germany, *Haskalah* either led to the renunciation of Judaism, or it evolved into the Reform movement; in Poland, Austria and the Jewish pale in Russia, *Haskalah* continued in its career as an internal educational and cultural reform, with Hebrew as its medium.

In the process of serving as a medium for cultural reform, the Hebrew language began to burgeon forth anew, and Hebrew literature began to experience its modern renaissance. New Jewish cultural content came into being in the form of history, literary criticism, reflective writing, poetry, fiction. Thus, whichever form *Haskalah* took, it created a world of values that tended to render the world of Traditional Judaism and Rabbinic authority irrelevant.

In Germany, however, the Jews were so rapidly becoming culturally assimilated that, for those who wanted Judaism to survive, the problem arose how to stem the tide of assimilation. There was hardly any occasion to combat the traditional forces, because they were dwindling rapidly and were, for the most part, on the defensive. This explains why *Haskalah* as a movement was to be short-lived in the land of its origin. The movement, however, fared differently in the nearby countries, especially Galicia, which in 1792 was torn away from Poland and annexed to Austria. With Germanization dominant in Austria, it was natural for that part of Galician Jewry which resisted the Hasidic movement, then very much in the ascendant, to come under the influence of the Mendelssohnian school.

Joseph Peril and Herz Homberg, both ardent disciples of Mendelssohn, were engaged by the Austrian Government to help it with its plan to have the Jews use their schools as a means of teaching their children not only the traditional lore but also some secular subjects, including the German language. The immediate effect of contact with non-Jewish culture was the re-evaluation of the Jewish cultural values. Before that time, elementary Jewish education consisted merely of the study of the Pentateuch with Rashi's commentary, Advanced Jewish education was based on Rabbinic lore—the Talmud and the Codes. From that time on, the Bible, in its literal sense, became the principal study. The main stimulus to this radical departure was the translation, inaugurated by Mendelssohn, of the Hebrew text into pure German. This was supplemented by a new kind of commentary on the text. It dealt with problems of grammar, and attempted to recover the literal meaning of Sacred Scripture, which had become obscured by the midrashic interpretations of the ancient Rabbis.

This departure from the traditional method of Torah study met at once with very strong opposition, and in some instances led to the issuance of formal bans. Solomon Rapoport and his colleagues Isaac Erter, Samson Bloch, Jacob Samuel Byck and Judah Leib Mazer were excommunicated in Lwow "for reading the Bible publicly with the translation of the philosopher Moses of Dessau." The opponents of the *Haskalah* movement strenuously objected to the literalist approach to the Bible, because they sensed in that approach a repudiation of the Rabbinic tradition. They likewise condemned the study of Hebrew grammar, because it led to the use of Hebrew for secular purposes and to the production of literature which was bound to raise new problems and divert the Jewish mind from the study of Torah. Their prognosis proved to be true.

The *Maskilim*, or Jewish *illuminati*, who possessed creative ability found an outlet for it either in *belles lettres*, or in historical and theological disquisitions. Hebrew *belles lettres*, whether poetry or prose, dealt in part with ancient Biblical themes and in part with contemporary life and problems. It was at first quite amateurish and imitative of similar writing in contemporary literature, especially German, but it soon began to improve in content and style. The prose writings—fiction and satire—began to take on life when they concerned themselves with subject-matter drawn from daily experience.

Despite their tendentious character, these writings succeeded in mirroring Jewish life of that period and picturing distinctive types and characteristic manners. Jews were beginning to become self-aware in a deeper sense than ever before. They began to give thought to their future and to realize that they must take themselves in hand, if they wanted to improve their lot. Most of the self-criticism in this new Hebraic literature was directed against the human failings which Jews had in common with the rest of the world, but which had acquired added ugliness and viciousness due to the bitter struggle for survival. Jews had been subjected to that struggle by their non-Jewish rulers, who saw in the helplessness of Jews a profitable source of blackmail and exploitation. Much of that self-criticism, however, was directed against superstitious notions and practices which had sprung up in great abundance as a result of the Hasidic revival of mysticism.

Even though Hasidism did not *originate* as a counter-movement to *Haskalah,* the situation in which it soon found itself made it such. It came to be virtually the last concerted effort of Traditional Judaism to resist the invasion of Western culture and ways of thought and life. No wonder, therefore, that throughout the nineteenth century Hasidism regarded *Haskalah* as its mortal enemy. Among the outstanding writers of the early East European *Haskalah* period were the two satirists Joseph Peril (1770-1840) and Isaac Erter (1792-1841). Peril directed his shafts of satire mainly against the hypocrisies and venalities which corrupted the Hasidic movement, while Erter concerned himself mainly with the religious absurdities and superstitions to which Hasidism had given rise.

NACHMAN KROCHMAL (1785-1840)

For more directly formative influences in the remaking of the Jewish consciousness we have to turn to the writings which attempted to reconstruct the past of the Jewish people, or to reinterpret its theological concepts. Haskalah gave rise to very little in the nature of theological reinterpretation, but that little happened to be extremely significant. The outstanding and perhaps the only theologian of note whom the early Galician *Haskalah* produced was Nachman Krochmal. He was the first to take full cognizance of the inner conflicts which Enlightenment had caused in the mind of the Jew, and he labored hard and long to find a way of resolving them.

It was not safe in those days to express openly any idea that ran counter to the intransigeant traditionalism of the Hasidic environment in which Krochmal lived. In addition, he had to reconcile two such apparently incompatible universes of thought as those of Jewish tradition and modernism. He realized that he confronted a task no less difficult than that which had confronted Maimonides when he wrote his *Guide for the Perplexed*. He tried to formulate a conception of Judaism that would serve as a *Guide* for the perplexed of his day. Many years passed before he succeeded in putting his ideas into writing. Fortunately, however, his reputation as learned in Rabbinic lore, and as coping with the problem of Judaism, reached many talented young scholars who were in need of just such guidance as he could offer. They braved the hardships of distant travel to come to see him. To them he communicated orally the ideas that were taking shape in his mind. Some of those ideas played an important part in helping his contemporaries effect the transition from the ancient to the modern outlook while remaining loyal to Judaism. Krochmal did not live to publish his own writings. Before he died he willed them to Leopold Zunz, the founder of the scientific study of Judaism, who published them under the title of *Moreh li-Nebukē ha-Zeman* (A Contemporary Guide for the Perplexed).

Maimonides had been influenced in his thinking by the great Arab philosophers, chiefly Ibn Roshd (Averroes), who had helped to spread the Aristotelian philosophy and to reconcile it with the teachings of revealed religion. Nachman Krochmal, similarly, accepted the world-outlook which had been promulgated by the great German thinkers, principally, Kant, Schelling and Hegel. He was influenced by their method of reinterpreting traditional religion. To use his own analogy, *the problem of religion was principally one of removing from it the dross of erroneous notions which were the product of undisciplined imagination, and retaining the pure gold of reason.* That is indicated in the title he had given his writings: *Shaare Emunah Zerufah* (Gates of Purified Faith)—the title used in the Preface to his published work.

Krochmal maintains that erroneous notions have the effect of fostering the following of wrong kinds of religion: 1) that of the mystic visionary, who loses himself in wild speculations about the transcendent aspect of reality; 2) that of the magic-monger, who resorts to fetishes and incantations, in the hope of attaining his wishes; and 3) that of the pietist, who puts his faith in the inherent virtue of ritual practices, irrespective of their inner meaning. Those perversions of religion call forth bitter reaction, in the name of reason, which is only a pseudo-rationalism. Such reaction leads either to the denial of the reality of the spiritual, to the negation of both reason and tradition, or to the abandonment of ritual practices in favor of general truths of an abstract character.

In the opening chapters of his book, Krochmal gives an original interpretation of the "Golden Mean," and argues for the need of recognizing the role of purpose in the universe. To Krochmal, all organisms point to an aspect of reality which cannot be accounted for merely in terms of mechanical necessity, insofar as they display a certain degree of freedom from environmental factors. Every organism has a determining influence on each of its parts, and each part on the organism as a whole. That constitutes the organicity of living beings, which is a manifestation of purpose. Purpose, according to Krochmal, functions on a far larger scale in the life of a people; it reveals itself in that people's culture or civilization, which is tantamount to its consciousness.

As a result of the foregoing ideas, Krochmal arrives at a new conception of Godhood. *According to Krochmal, Godhood is the element of purpose manifest in a people's culture or civilization.* Purpose itself, however, functions on two levels, the conscious and the self-conscious. Only in the cultural heritage of the Jewish People, Krochmal maintains, did purpose achieve self-consciousness. Accordingly, only the Jewish People possesses a conception of God which, as compared with the conceptions of God promulgated by other peoples, is like self-conscious purpose as compared with merely conscious purpose. Self-conscious purpose, in the philosophic terminology of Krochmal's day, was termed "Reason" or "The Absolute."

Krochmal accepted the Hegelian principle that the clue to the interpretation of reality was spirit, or self-conscious mind. The activity of the mind is, according to Krochmal, present in all being, from the least significant creature to reality as a whole. The highest manifestation of that activity is reason. With that as a premise, Krochmal maintains that all cultures, no matter how primitive or corrupt, possess an element of truth. Religion, or the spiritual element of a culture, consists of whatever self-awareness those who live by that culture attain through that on which they rely as their mainstay in life. Judaism, the only culture in which the spirit reveals itself in all its potency, is free from all that is extraneous, conditioned or temporary, because the God in whom Jews put their faith, and to whom they give their unswerving loyalty, is none other than the Absolute. Judaism is thus the culture of reason *par excellence*. Hence, the basis of Judaism is faith in the primacy of reason. This means that, through the persistent application of reason to the teachings and practices of Judaism, one can arrive at the absolute spiritual truth which underlies them.

The fact that the Absolute, the self-conscious mind, or reason, has realized itself in Judaism more completely than in other cultures is only part of the larger truth that the nations are variously constituted, due to the differences in the inherent powers of their members, and in the extent of their associations and contacts with other nations. Mankind is thus providentially organized into nations. Each nation develops its own laws, customs, arts, attitudes and religious ideas and practices. The sum of them all gives rise to a life pattern which expresses the individuality of each nation. That individuality, when personified, is designated as its spirit, or god.

Krochmal adopted an additional important principle which he derived from the new universe of discourse of his day. That principle had been first clearly formulated by Giambatista Vico (1668-1744) and introduced into Germany through the translation, in 1822, of his *Principi de una scienza nuova interno alla commune natura delle nazioni* (1725) (Principles of a New Science Dealing with the General Nature of Nations). According to Vico, each nation passes through distinct stages of growth, equilibrium, and decay, in the course of its existence before it expires. The only exception to that process, Vico himself had intimated, was the Jewish People. He thus anticipated, by a century, the romantic interpretation of history, which substituted the concept of the spiritual cycle for the concept of rectilinear progress. According to Krochmal, the Jewish People is enabled to avert death through its extraordinary power of self-awareness, or reason. When the Jewish People reaches the end of one cycle, it exists for a time in a state of suspended animation. It later revives, however, and resumes its career, this time on a higher level of existence.

By a *tour de force*, Krochmal manages to divide the past of the
Jewish People into a series of cycles, and to identify the modern
period in Jewish history as one of rebirth and growth. The self-
awareness, or reason, which distinguishes the Jewish People from
other peoples is equated by Krochmal with the Absolute, or God,
manifesting Himself with unparalleled clarity. It is inevitable,
therefore, that the Jews should at present feel as strongly as ever,
if not even more strongly, that they are entrusted with a world
mission. They have to communicate to the other nations that intense self-awareness and reason which would ultimately bring
those nations under the sovereignty of the Absolute, and render
their spirit clear and undimmed by any taint of error and illusion.
Thus did Krochmal bring Judaism into the modern philosophic
universe of discourse and anticipate the main thesis of this book:
that *Judaism is at present undergoing metamorphosis, from which
it is likely to emerge as a greater Judaism.*

The foregoing, viewed objectively, is a radical recasting of the
traditional pattern of Judaism. Nevertheless, it has since helped
many spiritual leaders among the Jews to bridge the gap between
the ancient and the modern world by supplying them with an
orientation without which they would have felt intellectually and
spiritually lost. This is the first modern Jewish orientation which
reckons with the contemporary outlook on life, which saves the
primary traditional ideas from becoming defunct, thereby satisfying the psychological need for a sense of continuity, and which
provides Jews with a sense of spiritual purpose in the present.

We may question the validity of Krochmal's philosophy of
Jewish history. We may be sceptical of the Hegelian assumption
underlying that philosophy, namely, that history is the progressive incarnation of Reason, as the Absolute and as the Creator of
the universe. The entire approach is based on the doubtful assumption that the immanent and essential nature of things determines all human behavior and history. It ignores the law of cause
and effect in the empirical changes in human life, such as the
effect of technological progress on the entire pattern of human
life and human relations. It reifies the historical process and treats
it as a cause, instead of merely as a general and abstract term for
the way in which events take place. Moreover, Krochmal's application of Vico's principles to the different stages of Jewish history,

proves to be, on examination, far from tenable. Despite these challenges, however, *enough of the general structure of Krochmal's philosophy of Judaism remains strong to give support to the will of the Jewish People to survive.* That philosophy has inspired and guided all those modern trends in Judaism which have been most creative, and which hold out promise for a fruitful future for the Jewish People.

The specific merits of Krochmal's philosophy are the following: 1) It points the way to a conception of God that is the product of progressive human experience and knowledge as the basis of Jewish religion. It thereby frees Jewish religion from commitment to the doctrine of the supernatural origin of the Torah; 2) it shifts the center of Judaism from dogmas and rituals to the will-to-live of the Jewish People; 3) it frankly recognizes not only the legitimacy, but also the necessity, of studying the tradition in the light of so much historical context as it is possible to discover and reconstruct. This does away at one stroke with the oracular approach to the tradition, particularly the Bible. That approach has lent support to the most bizarre notions of commentators and interpreters. Krochmal's historical approach, on the other hand, establishes a rational basis for the modern historical study of the Bible, as well as of the post-Biblical writings.

Krochmal has thus laid the foundation of the historical approach to the Jewish tradition, which can help the Jewish People so to reconstruct and retrieve its past as to provide it with purpose and direction for its future.

YIZHAK BAER LEVINSOHN (1788-1860)

In the Russian Pale, Medievalism continued to hold sway, despite the hope which ran high during the reign of Alexander II that the lot of the Jews would be ameliorated. Here Traditional Judaism was challenged by those who came under the influence of the *Haskalah* movement in the Central European countries. A contemporary of Nachman Krochmal, Yizhak Baer Levinsohn, undertook a threefold task: 1) to persuade the traditionalists to cooperate with the Russian Government by reorganizing Jewish life, so as to render it economically productive and self-sustaining; 2) to have the *Maskilim* acquire a sympathetic appreciation of Traditional Judaism, and 3) to induce the Government to relax the pressure of its discriminating and exploitative laws against the Jews.

Levinsohn was born in Kreminitz, Volhynia, and lived there the greater part of his life. Belonging to a family of well-to-do merchants, he received in his childhood years a much broader Jewish education than that given in the usual type of *Yeshivah*, where the Talmud was virtually the only subject studied. He was taught Bible, grammar and the Russian language. As a young man, he was able to continue his general education, and he soon acquired proficiency in German, French and Latin. Although he wrote a satire against the Hasidim, his forte was not *belles-lettres*. He was mainly interested in demonstrating the compatibility of Traditional Judaism with enlightenment and with loyalty to the State. To that end he wrote a number of works, of which his *Teudah be-Yisrael* proved to be the most challenging, and his *Bet Yehudah* the most comprehensive.

Although intended mainly to foster an interest in the secular sciences and to evoke a sympathetic response to the efforts of the Russian Government of the time to westernize the Jews, Levinsohn's writings proved to be a defense of Traditional Judaism as well as of modernism. They expressed his reaction to the Jewish life around him. He lived in a small, segregated and inferior Jewish community, far from the mainstream of modern life. In addition, that community was for the most part identified with Hasidism, which by then had come to be an out-spoken counter-movement against *Haskalah*. Yet, even in that pietistic atmosphere there were some who secretly rebelled against the prevailing credulity and fanaticism which they regarded as stemming not so much from Hasidism itself as from Rabbinic lore.

Levinsohn knew of the inroads which the Enlightenment had made into Jewish life in Germany, and he very much feared that Jewish life in Eastern Europe might suffer a similar fate. He therefore devoted himself to the task of vindicating the Rabbinic tradition. He tried to prove that it had lost none of its validity in the light of modern knowledge. The outcome of his intellectual endeavors is a pattern of Jewish life and thought in which Traditional Judaism is interpreted as favoring collaboration with the State. He believed in the sincerity of the Russian Government's intentions to enable the Jews to avail themselves of the civil rights which would be granted to them. He was certain that the emancipation of the Jews in Russia depended entirely upon their becoming adequately westernized or enlightened. He therefore wished to forestall the possibility of their becoming dejudaized.

Levinsohn did not realize that the Russian Government was not at all interested in modernizing the outlook and education of the Jews. Its main purpose was to have them ultimately accept Christianity. He thought he was proving his loyalty to the Government, as well as helping the Jewish People, by acting as an intermediary between them. In that capacity, he had to render the ukases of the Government palatable to the Jews. But there were also occasions when he had to defend the Jews against the old charge of using Christian blood in their Passover meal. That is how he came to write his *Efes Damin* (1837), which has been translated into English and Russian.

We have seen[29] how Napoleon I, in 1806, put a series of questions to the Jews, the answers to which were to be the basis of the status which was to be accorded to them by the State. Those answers were intended to clarify the attitude of the *Jews* toward their *emancipation*. On the other hand, no one but a Jew was likely to take the initiative in defining the attitude of *Judaism* toward the *Enlightenment*. In *Teudah be-Yisrael*, published in 1827-28, Levinsohn undertook to answer a number of questions concerning the attitude of Judaism toward *Haskalah*, or Jewish enlightenment. Some of those questions were: 1) Is it essential for an adherent of the Jewish religion to study Hebrew in accordance with the rules of grammar? 2) Is an adherent of the Jewish religion permitted to study foreign languages? 3) May he study the secular sciences? 4) What benefit can he derive from the study of foreign languages and secular sciences? 5) Assuming that he himself may derive certain benefits, will not the detriment to religion and the weakening of faith outweigh those benefits?

The answers, which were intended to dispel the fears of the traditionalists who were apprehensive of the consequences of the spread of *Haskalah*, were the following: It is essential for a Jew to study the Hebrew language in accordance with the rules of grammar. It is equally essential for a Jew to be thoroughly versed in the Bible. Every Jew should known one non-Jewish language, especially the vernacular of the country. It is permitted to study other languages and literature and the secular sciences. Such study can bring only benefit, and will do no harm to religion. Levinsohn documents each of the foregoing affirmations from the Jewish traditional writings and from the lives of the long chain of Israel's spiritual leaders since Moses.

However, in spite of the strong support Levinsohn finds for his answers in Traditional Judaism, the application of those answers to the problem of modern life were bound to produce a Judaism in which the main interest was no longer the other-worldly salvation of the individual Jew but the mundane salvation of the Jewish People. He is convinced that the Jews have an inherent capacity for achieving a highly ethical and spiritual type of this-worldly life, by dint of their possessing advantages like the following: great antiquity, a highly ethical and spiritual code, reliability of their historic records, the divine origin of their laws and prophecies, a beautiful language, a long roster of sages, poets and prophets, a wonderful ritual, men and women of unusual beauty and strength. From these items it is quite evident that *the center of gravity in the discussion of Jewish life has shifted from the teachings of Judaism to the nature of the Jewish People.* This again points up the metamorphoses which Judaism is at present undergoing.

The *Bet Yehudah* (1857), from the introduction to which the foregoing items are taken, contains Levinsohn's most comprehensive discussion of Judaism, both past and present. In his survey of the Jewish past he displays a keen awareness of a long historical development in the attitude of the Jews toward the laws of the Torah. He tries to dispel the prevalent assumption that the Jews had always lived in accordance with a codified system of laws which has undergone no change. On the contrary, he points out that the uniform adherence to a code like the *Shulhan Aruk* came about only in recent centuries. Levinsohn's purpose in stressing that fact was undoubtedly to accustom the Jews of his day to the idea that changed circumstances necessitate changes in a number of the laws which had come down from the past. He even formulated the principles of change which he regarded as inherent in the tradition itself. Nevertheless all changes had to be authorized by a duly constituted *Bet-din* (judicial body).

Levinsohn classified the traditional laws into three categories: natural, civil and symbolical. When we compare his classification of the traditional laws with Joseph Albo's classification of laws in general, we note both points of resemblance and of difference. Albo divides laws in general into natural (i.e., moral), legislative and divine, or supernaturally revealed. Levinsohn, on the other hand, divides the traditional laws themselves into somewhat similar categories. In place, however, of the category "divine" he uses the term "symbolical." We thus note in Levinsohn's world outlook a radical departure from that of Albo.

Moreover, Albo and Levinsohn are worlds apart in the purpose for which they make use of their respective classifications. Albo was intent upon proving that Judaism was the only true religion, whereas Levinsohn was interested in arriving at the principle of change in Judaism. According to Levinsohn, no Jewish court is permitted to change natural (or moral) law, but it may change both civil and symbolical (ritual) law. In case a civil or ritual law is no longer enforceable, it should not be abolished, but circumvented by a legal fiction of some kind.

Of special significance as reflecting the new synthesis of tradition and enlightenment achieved by Levinsohn is his five-point program for social and cultural reforms, which includes the following measures:

1) The establishment throughout the Pale of Jewish Settlement of elementary schools for boys and girls, in which both religious and secular subjects should be taught according to the best pedagogic methods. In addition, all children should be taught some handicraft. It should not be the purpose of Jewish education to train all children to be rabbis, scholars or doctors. The emphasis in the teaching of religion should be upon its ethical aspect. In the four largest cities—Warsaw, Vilna, Odessa and Berditchev—higher academies of learning both of Jewish and general subject matter should be established for those who are qualified to pursue more advanced studies.

2) A regional chief rabbi should be elected, together with a high judicial body to assist him in carrying out his duties. He

should appoint local rabbis, preachers and *dayyanim* (judges) for each of the communities in his region, have charge of all the schools and synagogues in those communities, and make provision for uniform procedures in their respective functions.

3) Preachers should everywhere address the people on Sabbaths and festivals, principally on matters pertaining to ethical conduct in their dealings with one another and with their non-Jewish neighbors. They should avoid the discussion of *Kabbalah*.

4) The Government should be petitioned to grant farm and pasture lands to at least one-third of the Jewish population for agriculture and for raising cattle and sheep.

5) Jews should adopt sumptuary laws binding them to refrain from lavish spending on clothing and jewelry in general, and from all forms of ostentatious living.

The other-worldly approach which had dominated the Jewish outlook for the last twenty centuries is entirely absent in Levinsohn's perspective on Judaism. The Messianic hope that the Jews would return to their ancient land, the hope without which it is impossible to understand the entire pre-modern career of the Jewish People, no longer figures in his program. Instead, we read the following: "So long as the Jews lived under the protection of non-Jewish kings, they bore the burden of the State without complaint, as did its citizens, though they themselves were without any civil rights. They are remarkably steadfast in their allegiance, refusing to be among those who conspire against the Government. They are loyal to king and country, and, out of regard for their oath of allegiance, they refrain from any secular action intended to restore them to their ancient status, and resort neither to sword nor rebellion. They bide their time and wait only for divine help to bring them back to their original status."

Levinsohn's influence undoubtedly contributed to the spread of *Haskalah* among many who might otherwise not have had the courage to break out of the shell of traditionalism. But he also prevented *Haskalah* from serving, as it did for many German Jews in the generation after Mendelssohn, as a means of exit from Judaism.

SAMUEL DAVID LUZZATTO (1800-1865)

A different type of reaction to the secularist spirit of modern civilization from that of Mendelssohn, Krochmal, or Levinsohn is that of Samuel David Luzzatto, or *Shadal*. Having been born in Trieste and having come of an old Italian Jewish family, where there had been a standing tradition of an intellectually informed Judaism, he was bound to come in contact with Western culture independently of the *Haskalah* movement. It was natural, therefore, that the challenge to Traditional Judaism inherent in the Emancipation and the Enlightenment should have had an altogether different meaning for him from that which it had for those other pioneers of modern Judaism.

Luzzatto did not, like Levinsohn, have to convince a segregated Jewry that it ought to welcome the efforts of the Government to westernize it. The Jewish community of Trieste was small, and had yielded without resistance to the governmental reform of the Jewish schools. His own elementary education had been based on a seven-or eight-hour daily curriculum, two hours of which had been devoted to the study of German, Italian and mathematics. Even his Jewish studies had followed the more pedagogic system of Sephardic Jewry. He was well-grounded in Bible, Hebrew language and grammar, and in the *Mishnah*, before he began the study of Talmud. He thus received the methodical education which Sephardic Jewry in its best days in Spain, and later in Italy and Holland, had given its young. That should help us understand why, instead of being impressed by the prestige of the secularist or modern civilization, he was bold enough to assail and denounce it as a menace to humanity.

Luzzatto may, in a sense, be said not to have been catapulted into the modern world, but to have come to it gradually out of the best type of Medieval or Renaissance Jewish culture. When he became of age he, too, learned of the disintegrating effect of Western culture upon the Jews of Germany, and of the various innovations, both in practice and belief, which some of their principal leaders had proposed, in order to bring Judaism into line with the basic values of Western civilization. Due, perhaps, to the dominant Catholic spirit of the non-Jewish environment in which Luzzatto found himself, he was not at all smitten with any too great admiration for the spirit of modernism. Due to his own intrinsic insight into the spirit of Traditional Judaism, he was able to discern in it something that had been missed by all those who had studied it in the dry light of the intellect. Luzzatto maintained that the essence of Judaism was not to be sought in any abstract truth, but in the primacy it attached to *compassion* as the basic ethical trait of human conduct.[30] That was a highly significant discovery.

To prove his point, Luzzatto adduces numerous laws in the Torah as motivated by compassion for the weak and the helpless. The provisions in the Torah for the poor, the orphan and the widow, the wage earner and the slave, and even for bird and beast, imply a feeling of sympathy for those who are too weak to defend themselves against man's violence or cunning. In Rabbinic literature, likewise, the exercise of compassion looms large as a moral imperative. Luzzatto's irritation at the spirit of the West, and particularly at Aristotelianism which he considered to be its mainspring, comes through in the criticism which he directed against Maimonides. On two points in particular Shadal is unquestionably in the right. One is Maimonides' adoption of Aristotle's principle of the "Golden Mean" as the basis of ethical conduct. The other is Maimonides' view of the sacrificial cult in the Torah as a concession to the ineradicable habit of the ancient Israelites, who could not conceive a higher form of worship than that of animal sacrifice.

With regard to the "Golden Mean," Luzzatto quotes the definition given in Genesis (18:19) of what constitutes "the way of the Lord," namely "doing righteousness and justice." Abraham was not chosen to transmit to his children the kind of ethical life that Aristotle promulgated, a life that is intellectually planned with a view to self-interest and to the winning of respect from others. Shadal takes Maimonides to task for identifying such attributes as "long-suffering, abounding in mercy, righteous, holy, upright" ascribed to God with Aristotle's "Golden Mean." [31]

With regard to the sacrificial cult, Luzzatto maintains that bringing offerings to a deity was in ancient times considered the most appropriate form of worship. Had that form of worship been abolished and replaced by prayer, hymnology and the reading of the Torah, the ancient Israelites would not have revered God. That sounds even less plausible than Maimonides' rationale. However, Luzzatto has certainly the better of the argument in his explanation of what led to the centralization of the sacrificial cult at the Temple of Jerusalem and the destruction of the various altars throughout Eretz Yisrael. According to Maimonides, the purpose of that centralization was to wean the Israelites away from the sacrificial cult. According to Luzzatto, the purpose was to consolidate the unity of the People of Israel and to bring about uniformity in the cult itself.[32]

There is much in Luzzatto's interpretation of Judaism which is not strictly in keeping with the spirit of the tradition, and which is an idealization of it rather than an objective evaluation. That idealization enabled him to adopt a different tactic from any which his predecessors had taken in dealing with the problem of the relation of Judaism to Western philosophy and culture. To him, even Maimonides was merely an apologist for Judaism. Apologetics for Judaism, according to Luzzatto, are entirely gratuitous. Judaism is so much superior to modern, as well as to the most advanced ancient cultures, that it can afford to disregard them.

Luzzatto took it for granted that the most significant element in a culture or religion was its ethical teachings. From that standpoint, the best of Western civilization which derives its spirit and life pattern from Hellenic sources is inferior to Judaism. Western civilization is based on cold reason. The spirit of Hellenism is, according to Luzzatto, one of destruction rather than creation. In contrast with it is the spirit of Judaism, which is based on love and mercy. The fact that the first manifestation of that spirit took place in the Patriarch Abraham leads Luzzatto to designate it as "Abrahamism," which he contrasts with Hellenism. Concerning the outcome of the conflict which still rages between them Luzzatto had no doubt; Abrahamism would ultimately triumph.

Apparently Luzzatto was unaware of the reaction that was taking place in France, Germany and England against the rationalist Enlightenment. Louis de Bonald, Joseph de Maistre and Chauteaubriand in France had issued a call for a return to the religious tradition. In Germany, where there was good political reason for such reaction as a counter-move against what France had done to it, the philosophers Jacobi, Fichte, Schleiermacher, Schelling and Bader, and the romantic poets Novalis, Hölderlein, and Brentano outdid one another in the assault against the Enlightenment. England seconded its military victory over France with a barrage of counter-revolutionary sentiment through the writings of Blake, Coleridge, Wordsworth and Carlyle. But the process of cultural osmosis, which has operated in Jewish life for the most part unconsciously, must have reached Luzzatto as well.

In any event it was in the spirit of the foregoing reaction against the rationalist Enlightenment that Luzzatto took to task the Jewish scholars and thinkers of his day. He charged them with being dazzled by the outward splendor of Western civilization, and with making a futile attempt to assimilate Judaism to it. They seemed to him to be so fascinated by Hellenic culture, which he believed was the soul of Western civilization, that they looked to that culture for the absolute truth concerning God, man and the world. So far did Luzzatto go in his anti-intellectualism that to subscribe to the supernatural origin of the Torah and to the manifestation of divine providence through miracles was for him a necessary means of stressing Judaism's opposition to the cold rationalism of Western civilization.

Since one of the main miracles upon which Traditional Judaism bases its entire structure of belief is the power with which God endowed the Prophets of foretelling the future, he combated with all his zeal the scientific study of the Bible, which tacitly negated the miracle of prophecy. Great exegete though he was, he insisted on attributing the sections in the book of Isaiah which deal with the return of the Jews from Babylon to the prophet Isaiah, who flourished almost two centuries before that return. He thus demonstrated that it was possible to possess wide learning and be versed in the history of thought, and yet refuse to accept conclusions which have become synonymous with modernism. That fact, however, did not save him from being assailed by orthodox dogmatists. "It is not possible in this generation," he writes to a friend of his, "to fortify the faith for some people without weakening it for others." He then proceeds to quote from a letter which he had written to "one of the great men of the generation" as follows:

"You are right, my dear friend, in regarding the task I have chosen for myself a difficult and dangerous one, particularly if the writer intends to address himself in the same terms to all the different sects at the present time, which is a replica of the 'generation of confused tongues.' That is indeed an impossible feat. Even if God Himself were to come down on Mount Sinai and proclaim His will to the sons of Jacob, I doubt whether what He said would penetrate the minds of all who heard Him." [33]

The one apparent exception to Luzzatto's penchant for the supernatural as the basis of religious truth was his repudiation of *Kabbalah*. Indeed, besides the example of his father and the prevailing tendency among Italian Jews in general and his own family in particular, his own predilection should have led him to lean on *Kabbalah*. The probable reason for his repudiating it was that, in this instance, he allowed himself to be influenced by his exegetical researches. In the course of those researches he discovered anachronistic statements in the *Zohar*, and he became convinced that its claim to have been dictated or written by R. Shimeon ben Yohai was false. This set his mind against *Kabbalah*, and he gave expression to his views about it in his *Vikkuah al ha-Kabbalah* (Goritz, 1852). That is an extended dialogue which Luzzatto presumably carries on with a stranger, who tries to prove to him the fictitious character of the *Zohar*, as well as the falsity of some of the outstanding teachings of the *Kabbalah*.

HINDRANCES TO NORMAL READJUSTMENT

The Jews who counted on the Emancipation as about to be consummated were in a dilemma. They could neither remain segregated nor be absorbed by the majority population. The response to the strenuous efforts of Mendelssohn and his disciples and of men like Krochmal and Levinsohn to find some way out of the impasse in which Jewish life found itself during the early years of the Enlightenment and the Emancipation did not augur well for the coming years. The time was by no means ripe for anyone, however great as a scholar or thinker, to help the Jews of that era to negotiate effectively the transition from pre-modern Judaism to the Judaism that was to survive into the modern era.

1. In the first place, the solidarity of the Jewish People was

being shattered beyond repair. Other peoples, no matter how violently torn by inner dissensions, managed to retain enough of a sense of unity to weather the storms of cultural and religious change. In possessing a common territory, a common vernacular and common economic and political interests, the non-Jewish populations were able to surmount differences of class and creed. What had united Jews during the pre-modern centuries was exclusion from the Gentile world and enforceable adherence to tradition. Emancipation, however, or the prospect of obtaining it, and Enlightenment, or the pretense of possessing it, were enough to annul the sense of commitment to tradition. Consequently, there was no authoritative body that possessed either the power or the expertness to help the Jews pass over without loss of numbers and morale from the old order to the new.

Most Jews who first came into contact with the secularist trends in Western civilization naturally found the old type of authority irksome. But it did not occur to them to develop a form of organized Jewish life and a type of leadership that would meet the new needs which had arisen. Instead, there set in the process of social distintegration. Expecting to be incorporated into the general body politic, Jews lost the very capacity for any kind of "General Will" which is the generative force of a people's solidarity and creativity. With only voluntarism to rely upon, and with nothing to check the growing diversity of belief and practice, every undertaking of a collective nature had to be full of compromises and inconsistencies, in order to avoid giving offense to anyone who had to be counted on for cooperation.

When, for example, in 1819, in the Hamburg Temple, a new prayer book was to be drafted, the members of the commission to whom the task had been assigned found it necessary to offer an explanation which was typical of all attempts on the part of westernizing Jews, during the first decades of the nineteenth century, to resolve the dilemma in which they found themselves: "Had they (the members of the commission to draft the text of the prayer book) been truly and fully consistent," the statement read, "they would have had a book true to principle, but they would have had no congregation; even in the most favorable case, the congregation would have become entirely isolated from the rest of the Jewish community." [34]

That the liturgy and mode of worship should have been made the main controversial issue when the need for the Jews to survive as a distinct group was being challenged, indicates an unfortunate unwillingness on the part of Jewish leaders to come to grips with the basic dangers to Jewish survival. Instead of recognizing that the principal danger spot in the Jewish situation of that day was the disintegration of the communal solidarity of the Jewish People, and evolving new social and intellectual instruments for coping with that danger, the tendency was to view the problem as merely one of retaining such a minimum of the traditional ritual practices as would justify their identification as Jews without interfering with their integration as citizens of the country they lived in.

The need of guarding the continuity between the past and the present is part of the very effort of a people to survive. But prior to such an effort is the functioning of the will of the people to maintain its collective life. That involves creating social agencies and evolving social functions which help to keep alive a sense of mutual responsibility between the People as a whole and each individual who belongs to it. That need was entirely overlooked by the first Reformists. Thus men like Michael Creizenach (1789-1842) in Germany, and Aaron Chorin (1766-1844) in Hungary, and later, even Abraham Geiger, were at pains merely to point to Talmudic precedents for their proposed ritual modifications. All their argumentation on that score remained a dead letter, because it had no roots in any existing "General Jewish Will" such as had existed in the pre-modern era.

Before the rise of Zionism, the Jewish spiritual leaders interpreted the predicament of Jewish life as essentially theological in character, and to a large extent many of them still do, when as a matter of fact it has always been and still is socio-psychological. The question of religious belief and practice cannot and should not be evaded. But in order that Jews be interested in their religion, they must first want to maintain their solidarity with all Jews throughout the world. That requires a philosophy and a program for the social status of the Jews as a corporate entity. Lacking any such philosophy or program, the Jews who were eager to avail themselves of the opportunities that civil equality would open up to them grew indifferent to the entire matter of accommodating traditional beliefs and practices to the modern outlook.

Having become alienated from Jewish group life, they were bound to be indifferent to Jewish religion. But, unfortunately, the Jewish spiritual leaders of that time did not possess the necessary background that might have enabled them to see the predicament of their People in the light of the socio-psychological facts and forces that were undermining its collective existence.

2. Another handicap to the orderly adjustment of Judaism to the modern world was the interference of the State in the inner life of the Jews. Paradoxically, this interference was a concomitant of the process of emancipating the Jews from the Medieval status of alienage. Since they were to form part of the body politic, the State arrogated to itself the right to control the religious affairs of the Jews, on the ground that those affairs now had to be co-ordinated with the interests of the State. The precedent for this meddling had been set by Napoleon I. The Sanhedrin which he had summoned, and the questions he had put to its members meant that Jews were no longer autonomous, even in the matter of ritual observances. Jewish religion had to submit to the requirements of State policy. Though Napoleon's influence contributed to the emancipation of the Jews of Central Europe, it resulted in the policy that Jews must henceforth be answerable to the State for the way they conducted their religious affairs.

Thus the history of nineteenth century Judaism in France and in Central Europe is criss-crossed by all kinds of governmental edicts, for the most part obstructive and vexatious, and often mutually contradictory. The very first edict of this kind, issued by Frederick William III, King of Prussia, in 1812, which was hailed as a kind of Jewish *Magna Carta*, contained a clause abolishing all rabbinical jurisdiction, and decreed the governmental supervision of "the ecclesiastical conditions and education of the Jews" with the aid of Jewish representatives who were to be consulted.

After the downfall of Napoleon I and the resurgence of reaction throughout Europe, most of the Governments of the different kingdoms and duchies of Central Europe adopted the policy of prohibiting all innovations in Jewish public ritual and worship. That policy was largely motivated by the purpose of getting the more intellectually advanced Jews to be repelled by Judaism and to break down their resistance to Christianity. On the other hand, that policy was taken advantage of by the traditionalist Jews to obstruct the growth of Reform. Thus a practice was revived among European Jews during the nineteenth century which had been viewed with abhorrence by Jews in the Middle Ages—that of calling in the State to settle internal religious and communal disputes among Jews.

The Government policy of interfering with the conduct of the Jewish religion eventuated in a whole series of decrees. In 1817, for example, the Berlin Government decreed the closing of all private synagogues. That was aimed particularly at the attempt of a group of progressive Jews to conduct services on somewhat unorthodox lines and to introduce the preaching of sermons in German. Those Jews met at private homes. The 1817 decree was circumvented, but the opponents of Reform finally gained the upper hand. They succeeded in eliciting the well-known decree of 1823, which ordered "that the divine services of the Jews must be conducted in accordance with traditional ritual, and without the slightest innovation in language, ceremonies, prayers or songs." [35] That decree was reaffirmed in 1829 and 1836.

A series of decrees affecting Jewish worship emerged also from the Governments of Baden in 1824 and 1838, of the Duchy of Anhalt, in 1835, of Hanover in 1837, Bavaria in 1834 and 1835, of Franconia in 1838. In 1848 the Jewish community of Fuerth was enjoined against holding confirmation services, on the ground that they were a departure from Jewish tradition and an imitation of Christian practice. On the other hand, Duke Francis Frederick of Mecklenburg-Schwerin happened to favor reforms in the synagogue. Accordingly in 1839 his Government advertised for a rabbi and educator to head its newly organized Jewish community. In that case, the meddlesomeness of the Government helped to advance the cause of Reform.

In the main, Government control of Jewish religious affairs in the European countries prevented the Reform movement from making headway there. In Germany, before the Hitler regime came into power, every professing Jew had to pay a tax for the maintenance of the Jewish community. For that, he was given a seat in one of its synagogues and admitted to all the services he was in need of as a Jew. If he wished to belong to a congregation which the community refused to recognize, he would nevertheless have to pay the communal tax. Since no Jewish community in Germany, with the exception of the one in Berlin, recognized any Reform congregation, it was impossible for any such congregation to maintain itself in Germany.[36] Thus Government interference, though it may have aided the conservative, or middle-of-the-road, group to establish itself, prevented Jewish life from developing through free competition of alternative philosophies and programs.

3. A third factor which militated both directly and indirectly against the process of creative Jewish adjustment was the derogatory conception of Judaism which the French leaders of the movement for Enlightenment had disseminated. Voltaire, who was the spearhead of that movement, and who had become embittered against Jews and Judaism through some altercation he had had with some Jews concerning money matters, sought to defame both. He denounced Judaism in general, and the Talmud in particular, as a barbaric religion devoid of any high morality. When the Jewish aspirants for social status in Gentile society came upon these derogatory opinions about Judaism, they accepted them as authoritative, because of Voltaire's prestige, and because nothing in defense of Judaism from a modern standpoint had as yet been formulated. Marcus Jost's history of the Jews did not appear before the years 1820-1825. The scientific study of Judaism was still in the offing. The lack of an ordered presentation of the teachings of Judaism and its ethical spirit produced a sense of inferiority in the minds of the first two generations of Jews to whom Enlightenment and Emancipation came to be their most heartfelt *desiderata*.

Later, when the systematic approach to the study of Judaism resulted in a succession of scientific works of great merit, anti-Jewish agitation took the form of an open demand that the Jews renounce their ancestral faith. Baiting Judaism became the favorite indoor sport of Christian theologians in the universities. Their line of argument was, first, that Judaism was an inferior religion, secondly, that the Jews insisted on segregating themselves from their fellow citizens by a "barrier mistakenly considered essential."

The most prominent opponent in Germany to Jewish emancipation for both of these reasons was Bruno Bauer, whose article "Die Judenfrage" in *Deutsche Jahrbuecher* for November, 1842, caused a tremendous sensation in its day. The direct effect of both of the foregoing arguments was the creation in the minds of some of the most talented Jews of the feeling that all attempts to modernize Jewish life were futile. Indirectly, attacks like those of Bruno Bauer did much to nullify even the well-meant attempts at Jewish self-adjustment which sought to eliminate from Judaism whatever gave it individuality. The fear that such individuality might serve as a pretext for charging its Jews with ghettoizing themselves and secretly plotting world domination exercises to this very day a paralyzing influence on Jewish life, and has a devitalizing effect on Jewish religion.

CHAPTER SEVEN

Reform Judaism

THE BEGINNINGS OF THE
REFORM MOVEMENT

The modern trends in Judaism constitute the various responses of the Jewish People to the challenge to Jewish peoplehood and Jewish religion. Insofar as the collective will-to-live of the Jewish People calls for articulation through both peoplehood and religion, a challenge to either is a threat to Jewish survival. When, therefore, during the early part of the nineteenth century, Jews wished to obtain civil rights by becoming a part of the body politic without surrendering their historic group identity, they were forced to reformulate their conception of Judaism. They had to articulate clearly what was to unite them among themselves and to differentiate them from the rest of the world. They had to justify the maintenance of their corporate identity and individuality, without invalidating their claim to civil rights and to a status of equality with the other citizens of the country.

As soon as the Jews found themselves in need of redefining their status and clarifying their beliefs, they began to make changes in their traditional way of life and to introduce reforms in worship, education and community organization. Those efforts at reform were at first piecemeal and haphazard. The early sporadic changes which were sponsored, for the most part, by the laity were generally prompted by expediency. The more well-to-do had far more at stake economically in being emancipated from civil disabilities

221

than their poorer brethren, who still lived isolated from the rest
of the world. The rich were eager to be accepted by their neighbors,
without at the same time having to accept Christianity.

The more enterprising among the well-to-do-Jews usually organized themselves into a society, with the ultimate purpose of
forming a community of their own which would give them status
with the Government as Jews in good standing. The society would
look for a preacher, rabbi or theologian to lead them. If they were
unable to find the right man, the society would soon break
up. One such Jewish society in Berlin found an able leader and
thus managed to survive. On the other hand, a similar Jewish
society in. Frankfort died an early death, because it demanded such
radical changes in Judaism as no Jewish theologian was then willing to sanction. That was also the case with a number of other
Jewish societies in Germany, Hungary and England.

In the European countries, wherever the Government took an
active part in regulating the internal affairs of Jewish life, the early
attempts to introduce reforms failed. They were opposed not only
by the majority of Jews, but also by the Governments for reasons
of their own. Systematic Reform, however, was inaugurated and
developed by men in the rabbinate. *The Reform Movement, despite its apparent tendency to abrogate many traditional beliefs and
practices, was impelled primarily by a desire to stem the flight
from Judaism rather than by any light-hearted yielding to the
pressure of the environment.* Having made its appearance nearly
half a century after the Emancipation began to disrupt Jewish life,
Reform as an organized movement attempted to remotivate the
will-to-live as Jews.

If we wish to appraise the Reform movement justly, we must
take into account the magnitude of the problem that confronted
the first Reformists. The entire edifice of Jewish tradition was
crumbling, as a result of the political and intellectual cataclysms
that swept over Western mankind. Though Jews had been subject
to conditions beyond their control throughout the centuries of
their dispersion, there was always a sufficient element in those
same conditions which served to strengthen their resistance to
being absorbed by the rest of the population, and to re-enforce their
own determination to retain their corporate existence and their
traditional religion. That element has been lacking in the modern

world. So far, the political and cultural conditions with which Jews have had to cope have proved to be consistently and uniformly of a disruptive character. It is not surprising therefore that when the first Reformists sought to modernize Judaism, they encountered either intransigeant opposition or facile and undiscriminating acceptance. The combination of that kind of opposition and that kind of acceptance has tended to freeze Reform into a new orthodoxy instead of what it might have become—a method of objective experimentation with different ways and means of reconstituting the Jewish People and revitalizing its religion.

The opposition to Reform came from those who were so repelled by the extraneous and non-Jewish influences that had contributed to the rise of the Reform movement that they could see nothing good in that movement. For centuries on end Gentile learning had been engaged in the process of defaming the Jewish tradition. Consequently, the average Jew found it difficult to believe that his tradition would be enhanced as a result of being scrutinized by methods and ideas which had come from Gentile sources. On the other hand, those who wished to cast off their allegiance to Jewish tradition welcomed the adverse criticism leveled by non-Jews of scholarly repute against Jewish tradition, because they were thus provided with the excuse they needed to justify their defection from Judaism.

The early Reformists were not guided by a clear recognition of all that was involved in the attempt to re-form the historic structure of the Jewish People, the traditional theology, and the Rabbinic regimen of individual conduct. Very few of the Jewish spiritual leaders in those days had the insight, the courage, or the patience to face up to the seriousness of the situation which confronted their People. They could hardly realize that the very foundations of the House of Israel had been weakened by the shocks administered to it by Western civilization. They, therefore, could not at once devise the proper measures for strengthening those foundations and rendering them secure.

The first Reformists were by no means aware of the need of deliberately planning new instruments of Jewish solidarity and continuity to take the place of those which had become inoperative and defunct. They labored under the illusion that it was possible to maintain the sense of continuity with the Jewish past by

finding in the Talmud sanction for the reforms which they regarded necessary.[1] So long as the Jews constituted a corporate entity, the Talmud was regarded as authoritative even when, in emergencies, the machinery to mediate that authority was lacking.
Throughout that period the Jewish People was an identifiable reality which possessed what Rousseau termed a "General Will." But
for those Jews who renounced all group status or aspiration, the
Talmud ceased to be the source and instrument of authority.

Those Jews not only repudiated the doctrine of the advent of
a personal Messiah and the hope for the miraculous gathering in
of all Jews to Eretz Yisrael; they did not even contemplate a possible reinstatement of Jewish ethnic life. *The Reformists deliberately adopted the principle that the status of a land-rooted People
was an undesirable limitation on the spiritual potentialities of the
Jews, and should therefore be replaced by the ideal of a world
mission to be carried on in their dispersion.* Since the Talmud
was first and foremost an instrument of the Jews' survival as a
land-rooted People, it could not possibly continue to function as
an instrument of unity for those who had renounced the expectation of that kind of survival.

Actually, it was only for ritual purposes that the Reformists were
interested in emphasizing the sense of continuity with the Jewish
past by resorting to Talmudic sanctions. But so far as communal
antonomy was concerned, the Talmud had lost all significance for
them. When Frederick William III, King of Prussia, issued the Edict
of 1812, there was such jubilation among the Jews of Prussia over
the civil rights extended to them that they failed to realize what
a mortal blow those rights administered to Jewish life, in that they
called for the abolition of rabbinical jurisdiction in all matters of
civil law. That meant, in effect, the dissolution of the communal
solidarity which had been the *sine qua non* of Judaism as a way of
life.

The Orthodox managed to retain at least a token of rabbinic
authority. But the Reformists accepted, on principle, the dissolution of that authority. The very existence, however, of a collective
entity like a community or a people is inconceivable without some
degree of social structure, authority and discipline. So true is this
that to this day even the Reformists occasionally use the Talmud
as a guide in passing upon a moot question of Jewish prac-

tice.[2] On the whole, however, they treat Talmudic law as irrelevant.

Had the Reformists been aware that what they really needed was to create some new instrument of authority, they might really have given Judaism a new lease on life. They were, however, so obsessed with the desire to be integrated into the general body politic that they were fearful of any collective effort leading to the creation of communal authority on a modern basis, lest they be charged as clandestinely retaining the substance, if not the name, of the traditional Jewish nationhood. Hence, whenever they convened for group deliberation, they would take care to proclaim beforehand that they did not come together to take definite action or to make any binding commitments.

The fear of re-establishing genuinely binding authority was evident both at the very first rather informal conference called together in 1837 by Abraham Geiger, in Wiesbaden where he was rabbi, and at the more ambitious and carefully planned conferences in Brunswick in 1844, Frankfort in 1845 and Breslau in 1846. These were conferences of rabbis only and led to no satisfactory results. It then occurred to some who participated in those conferences that the Reform movement might make greater headway, if also laymen participated. To impress the public with the importance of these enlarged conferences, they were termed "Synods." The first Synod met in Leipzig in 1859, and the second in Augsburg in 1871. They proved even less satisfactory than the earlier rabbinical conferences. According to David Philipson,[3] much enthusiasm was evoked while those Synods were in session, but as soon as the delegates dispersed, they realized that very little, if anything, had been accomplished.

During the half century after Mendelssohn, various reforms were effected in Traditional Judaism, but there was still no Reform movement. The immediate effect of the impact of modernism on Jewish life was to express itself in haphazard changes in outlook and ritual practice. Such changes neither arose from, nor led to, the rethinking of the nature of Judaism, as a whole, or of the specific problems with which it was confronted.

Some time had to elapse before the very need for an intellectual reconstruction could even be recognized, and before the new intellectual and spiritual demands of the challenging environment could be sufficiently grasped to make possible a new Jewish orientation. During the half century after Mendelssohn, the changes which took place in ideology and practice were dictated for the most part by external pressure, such as that which Napoleon I exerted in spectacular fashion, or by a desire, on the part of occasional small groups to minimize the distinction between Judaism and the culture of the environment. In the meantime, the upper strata of German Jewry were rapidly disappearing from Jewish life, with or without conversion to Christianity.

It was for the purpose of halting the stampede from Jewish life that the two contemporaries, Samuel Holdheim and Abraham Geiger, undertook to formulate a consistent Reform ideology and system of practice, hoping in that way to resurrect the will to Jewish survival. Both of them assumed that Jews would be reconciled to remaining an identifiable group, and resist absorption in the general population, if they were to accept as a mission their function to uphold and promulgate the truth of ethical monotheism. On the other hand, they sought to remove all excuses for abandoning Judaism, on the ground that it demanded conformity to practices which interfered with free association with non-Jews. They went quite far in reducing the regimen of Jewish observances to a minimum. Holdheim was far more radical than Geiger in the reforms he proposed; he did not hesitate, for example, to sanction mixed marriages, without requiring the non-Jewish spouse to accept Judaism.

The elimination from Judaism of its ethnic element as the main purpose of the Reform movement during the first decades of its existence attained its climax in the effort of Samuel Holdheim. Although Abraham Geiger did his utmost to denude Judaism of its nationhood, he was prompted by different motives and resorted to different methods from those of Holdheim. Geiger was interested in proving that Judaism was a universal religion and as inclusive in its scope as Christianity. He realized that Christianity was still a vital force, and that, as the religion of the majority population, it offered great attraction to Jews to whom Judaism seemed an inferior religion because of the particularistic character which the element of nationhood imparted to it. Geiger, therefore, sought to prove that the ethnic element had persisted in Judaism mainly as a result of centuries of persecution, a result which the Emancipation made it possible to undo, thereby rendering Judaism a universal religion. As such, it was superior to Christianity, which was committed to dogmas that were an offense to reason. To achieve this interpretation of Judaism, Geiger evolved his philosophy of Jewish history.

On the other hand, Holdheim's purpose in denationalizing Judaism was to prove that it did not stand in the way of the Jews' integration into the body politic as loyal citizens of the State. His main objective was to counter the most potent argument advanced against granting civil rights to the Jews. The opponents of Jewish emancipation maintained that, even if the Jews officially surrendered their communal autonomy, they continued to function as a State within a State, by virtue of their own marriage laws and ritual practices. Jews, therefore, could not possibly serve their State with the same devotion as did the other citizens. In addition, Jews were prevented by their laws against intermarriage from being absorbed by the general population.

Holdheim thought that the most effective way of meeting these arguments was to eliminate from Jewish life all such laws as prevented the complete integration of Jews into the general body politic. Those laws, he recognized, had served a useful purpose so long as Jews retained their nationhood. However, now that Jews renounced their nationhood, those laws should be annulled. The method which he employed was the casuistical one he had learned in his early years as a student of the *Yeshivah* where the Talmud constituted his only field of study. He seriously tried to prove that the Talmud itself expected Jews to obey implicitly the laws of the State, even when those laws clashed with traditional Jewish practice.

SAMUEL HOLDHEIM (1806-1860)

Holdheim was born in 1806 in the town of Kempen, in Posen, which at that time was under Polish domination. He spent his early years in the study of the Talmud and its commentaries, and achieved a reputation as a prodigy in the dialectics of Rabbinic disputation. Having managed to learn the elements of the German language and literature, he made rapid headway as an autodidact in modern studies. He aspired to a rabbinic position through which he hoped to effect changes in the Jewish tradition and to transform the function of the rabbi from that of answering questions of ritual practice to that of teaching and preaching. The public discussions that were called forth by those who agitated for Reform, especially in the communities of Hamburg and Berlin, found in him an active participant in defense of the innovations they had introduced.

Samuel Holdheim ardently believed that the Jews must accommodate themselves to the new political order. That political order was regarded by him as providential. He was the first among the rabbinic spokesmen of Reform to adopt the German conception of the State, a conception which was part of a cosmic outlook. According to that conception, the State is the embodiment not only of the General Will of the people, as Rousseau had taught, but also of the highest purpose of God pertaining to man. Holdheim transfered the entire pattern of duties pertaining to human relations from the domain of Torah to the domain of the State, on the assumption that the new political status of the Jews demanded such transfer. The resistance which the process of emancipating the Jews from their Medieval disabilities met everywhere derived its strength from the claim that the Jews, who had lived apart from other peoples throughout their history, could not possibly so change themselves as to give up their own national solidarity. To refute that claim and to prove the capacity of Jews to merge with the nation that accepted them, many Jewish lay leaders made it a point of be quite demonstrative in their apotheosis of the State. The most prominent figure among the rabbinic leaders of whom that was true was Holdheim.

Holdheim did not treat accommodation to the new political order merely as a matter of expediency. On the contrary, he interpreted loyalty to the State as a *religious* duty on the part of the citizen, whether Jew or Gentile. He, too, seems to have labored under the illusion that the modern State was to be completely divorced from the Christian Church. The significance of the fact that Hegel had identified *Christian* Prussia as the supreme incarnation of the Absolute seemed to have escaped Holdheim. Holdheim naïvely idealized the State as seeking to promote the welfare of all its citizens, regardless of race or religious affiliation, in a spirit of universal brotherhood.

Realizing that the autonomous Jewish civil and marriage laws and the power of the Jewish courts to enforce them had constituted the foundation of Jewish nationhood, he made it his special task to remove from Judaism the last traces of juridical authority. To that end he wrote his book[4] *Ueber die Autonomie der Rabbinen und das Prinzip der juedischen Ehe.* His main thesis is that, in abrogating all rabbinic authority, the State is not only within its right, but is even acting in conformity with the spirit of the Torah. The Torah, even on the assumption of its divine origin, according to Holdheim, regards its own laws as valid only so long as the Jews have their own State. But once the Jews become part of a non-Jewish State, the authority of the latter is supreme, and only those Jewish laws which the State permits to remain in force are binding upon the Jew. These alone are valid in our day. The Mosaic law cannot function in Jewish life, unless the law of the State to which Jews belong expressly authorizes it. Fortunately for the continuance of Judaism in the past, the various States, despite their ill-treatment of the Jews, nevertheless permitted them to live in accordance with Mosaic law. In this reasoning, he drew heavily upon what Spinoza maintains in his *Tractatus Theologico-Politicus* (Ch. XIX), though he makes no reference to Spinoza.

Holdheim believed that the time was opportune for the concentration of Jewish spiritual energy on religion as such. He felt certain that the deepening of the religious element in Judaism could act as a bond of Jewish unity, and would more than compensate for the loss of national and folk elements. In all other respects, however, Holdheim upheld the primacy of the State, even when it came into conflict with the observance of Jewish ritual practice. According to him, the Jew who is in the service of the State, whether as soldier or as official, has no right to claim exemption from the performance of his duties on the Sabbath. He does not even draw any distinction between voluntary or compulsory service to the State. He points, for example, to the disregard of Sabbath laws in the Temple, and to one or two other instances of a similar character. It is not unreasonable to assume that this solution of the problem of the Sabbath influenced those rabbis who convened in Breslau in 1846, and who went so far as to declare working for the State on the Jewish Sabbath to be an act of *kiddush ha-shem* (santification of the name of God).

Holdheim applies the same principle to Jewish marriage laws. He draws the distinction between the religio-ethical character of the marriage and the legal forms pertaining to the confirmation or dissolution of the marriage. The rabbi should officiate at the wedding only as an authorized representative of the State, but should have nothing to do with the granting of divorce. That should be entirely within the jurisdiction of the State. This incidentally, came to be the established practice of Reform Judaism. That proves to what extent Reform Judaism is far from having renounced its radically denationalized position.

The main object of Holdheim's attack is what he designates as the aspect of particularism in Rabbinic Judaism. He takes Maimonides to task for having interpreted the Talmudic statement that "the pious of all nations have a share in the world-to-come" as implying that it is not sufficient for a non-Jew to obey the Noachian laws in order to be eligible to salvation, but that he must also believe that they have been revealed by God through the Torah.[5] In this, too, as, indeed, in his general outlook on Judaism, Holdheim echoes Spinoza.[6] Holdheim ascribes this opinion of Maimonides to the national spirit of the Jews, which permeates the whole of the Talmud, and which must now be eradicated, in keeping with the spirit of genuine Reform. He maintains that only in the unqualified acceptance of the universalism of the Bible does the hope of Judaism lie. The members of the Paris Sanhedrin, according to Holdheim, evinced a trace of the Jewish national spirit when they declared that a marriage between a Jew and a Christian, though valid from a moral standpoint, could not be given the sanction of Jewish law. He thus stopped at nothing in his effort to denationalize Judaism, and to reduce it to a purely religious creed.

From all of this it would seem that Holdheim would have the Jews constitute merely a voluntary communion of individuals professing certain ethico-religious principles in common. That had, indeed, been the conclusion at which Mendelssohn also had arrived in his *Jerusalem*. But, somehow, there was a tendency on Holdheim's part to recoil from this apparently inevitable conclusion. With all his radicalism, Holdheim found it necessary to maintain that being a Jew was also a matter of birth and, therefore, inalienable. This view is still the one that is generally professed by Reform authorities, though it can scarcely be defended either on logical or on scientific grounds, and confirms the suspicion that only the Germanic pride of race might have given sanction to this retention of race pride in the Jewish Reform movement.

ABRAHAM GEIGER (1810-1874)

Abraham Geiger was born in 1810 in Frankfort-on-the-Main. The Jews of that city were then still subject to Medieval disabilities, and were not permitted to leave the ghetto into which they were crowded. Nevertheless, they looked forward to better days, and already in 1804 had established the *Philanthropin*, a Jewish school in which secular studies formed part of the curriculum. They even went so far as to engage a non-Jewish teacher as a member of the teaching staff.

Geiger's education up to the age of eleven was the traditional one. It consisted mainly of the study of Rabbinics. From then on, without discontinuing his Jewish studies, he pursued secular studies and concentrated on the classic and Semitic languages. He continued those studies at Heidelberg, Bonn and Marburg, until he acquired a high degree of philological knowledge. His life during those years was agitated by violent inner conflicts as to the kind of Judaism he should advocate. There was a time when he wanted to eliminate the Talmud and to base Judaism entirely upon the Bible. Even the Bible, however, was not to serve as an authoritative source of belief or practice, but only as a great literary classic.[7]

In 1832, he entered on his rabbinic career at Wiesbaden where, after three years, he began publishing his magazine, *Wissenschaftliche Zeitschrift fuer Juedische Theologie*. In 1838, the progessive leaders of the Jewish community in Breslau extended a call to him to serve as rabbi. After he accepted it, he had to contend for a time with the traditionalists of the community who, with Rabbi Solomon Tiktin at the head, contested his right to function as rabbi because of the unorthodox views he had expressed in his writings.

Geiger served as rabbi in Breslau until 1863. During that period he was very prolific both in his philological and historical research and in his efforts to formulate an ideology for the Reform movement. His two outstanding works of that period are the *Urschrift und Uebersetzungen der Bibel* (Breslau, 1857) and the *Gebet-buch*. In the *Urschrift* he shows how the conflicts which raged during the period of the Second Commonwealth are reflected in the readings of the Bible text, which was finally made to conform to the beliefs and practices of the Pharisees, who won out in the end. The *Gebetbuch*, which he published in 1854, incorporated most of the changes made in the traditional text, in keeping with his Reform ideology. It also contains some original prayers in German and translations of the revised text.

Geiger cherished the ambition to organize the entire content of Judaism into subject matter on modern scientific lines, and to have it taught in systematic fashion as Jewish theology. In his early years he advanced the idea of having Jewish theology, in the foregoing sense, taught in the universities alongside Christian theology. He even went as far as trying to raise the necessary funds for that purpose. When that plan failed, because of the refusal of the universities to cooperate, he tried to interest some of his well-to-do friends in the establishment of a rabbinical school where Judaism would be taught in the spirit of what he regarded as the coming stage of its development. Without such a school, he believed, that development would be retarded, if not blocked altogether. One, can, therefore, imagine Geiger's disappointment when the funds which a former friend and sympathizer had bequeathed for a rabbinical school were applied by the executors of the will to the establishment of a school which was to foster a movement in opposition to Reform. The Jewish Theological Seminary, which was opened in Breslau in 1853, was headed by Zacharias Frankel, who on previous occasions had declared his strenuous opposition to Geiger's Reform proposals, and who was a leading figure in a counter-movement which he designated as "Historical Positive Judaism." That counter-movement gave rise in the United States about sixty years later to the "Conservative Movement."

The establishment of that Seminary prevented the Reform movement from making any headway in the Old World. The Seminary sent forth rabbis who formally met the requirements that Geiger had advocated as essential to the study of Judaism. It fostered a knowledge of modern historical and philological disciplines and the application of that knowledge to the traditional subject-matter.

Its graduates served as rabbis in the various Jewish communities in Central Europe, whenever Government regulation authorized the appointment only of rabbis who had received a modern academic education. They learned to preach in the vernacular and to use the terminology of university-trained men. They satisfied the wants of the overwhelming majority of the Jews in Central Europe who were affiliated with their local communities, and for whom the kind of ideological reconstruction advocated by Geiger seemed too radical.

Abraham Geiger did his share together with pioneer scholars like Solomon Rapoport, Leopold Zunz, Zacharias Frankel and Heinrich Graetz toward gaining a knowledge of the Jewish past subsequent to the return from the Babylonian captivity. But in addition, he tried to arrive at a new historic-religious orientation toward Judaism. This orientation is reflected in his *Zeitung fuer die Wissenschaft der juedischen Theologie* and in his *Juedische Zeitschrift fuer Wissenschaft und Leben*, particularly in his own contributions to them, under the title of *Das Judentum und seine Geschichte*. To appreciate the significance of Geiger's conception of Judaism, it is necessary to note the difference between the traditional approach to history and the approach which is characteristic of modern Jewish historiography.

Traditional Judaism is not based upon a series of abstract creeds or principles, but upon a religious interpretation of a series of noteworthy events beginning with the creation of the world. That interpretation is implied in the narrative parts of the Pentateuch and in the historical books of the Bible. Thus the Bible opens with stories and genealogies that bring into a view the whole of mankind, and then it focuses attention on the beginnings of Israel. It is apparent that the main purpose of the opening chapters in the Bible is to define the place of Israel in the world, and to recount the various manifestations of God's power and providence through Israel. It is strange, indeed, that in the endless discussions about what creeds are basic to Judaism, or whether creeds as such are at all essential, the learned disputants should have overlooked the crucial significance of the historical-religious approach which is set forth in the Bible and accepted implicitly throughout the Rabbinic writings. The only Medieval Jewish thinker who discerned the religious significance of the historical approach, though he did not state it is a formal principle, was the poet R. Judah Hallevi in his *Kuzari.*

With the advent of modernism, the historicity of the events which figure most prominently in Traditional Judaism began to be questioned. Consequently the religious interpretation given to them began to grow obsolete. But the Jewish scholars who were the first to foster the new knowledge of Judaism did not appreciate the significance of the historical-religious orientation which is basic to its tradition. They therefore failed to realize what it meant for that orientation to fall into desuetude. Nor did they try to replace it with an orientation that would be acceptable to a modern thinking Jew. The only exception was Nachman Krochmal. In his *Moreh Nevukē he-Zeman (Contemporary Guide for the Perplexed)* he pointed the way to a type of history writing that, as we have seen, was in accord with modern categories of thought, and free from the need of accepting as historic the miraculous events which form the basis of the traditional orientation. But those categories of thought, though modern, were not compatible with scientific objectivity.

The sustained Jewish historiography that has developed since, and that forms the lion's share of the *Juedische Wissenschaft,* is of the scientific type. It is assumedly free from any preconceived aim other than that of unearthing all the facts that might throw light upon significant persons, events or ideas that figured in the Jewish past. To reconstruct them in their context in time, place and social and cultural milieu has been the chief purpose of modern Jewish scholarship. Such scientific research has enlarged the horizon of Jewish cultural activity and has helped to retrieve in large part the forgotten past of the Jewish People. But *that knowledge by itself cannot be expected to yield much guidance or inspiration in coping with the problems which confront contemporary Jewish life. It is, indeed, apt to accentuate the difference between conditions in the past and those in the present. It might therefore render Jews so keenly aware of the unprecedented character of the contemporary crisis as to make them doubt whether the Jewish People can come out of it alive.*

Only after the role of Jewish peoplehood as the indispensable matrix of Jewish religion is fully understood and established, can the past of the Jewish People, retrieved through the arduous efforts of research scholarship, mean more than an addition to the science of archaeology. When such an understanding of Jewish peoplehood is achieved, every scrap of information that helps to bring to life the long-forgotten personalities and vicissitudes of Israel's career is invaluable. It helps to reinstate the existential reality of the Jewish People, a fact that far transcends any doctrinal belief or traditional practice in the capacity to motivate Jewish loyalty or elicit the need for identification with Jewish life.

Geiger saw the need of filling the void left in the soul of the Jew by the obsolescence of the historical-religious orientation of the Jewish tradition. He urged that the past of Judaism be re-read in the light of a conception of God which is derived from one's own deepest intuitions and is not merely a ritualistic hand-me-down or stereotype. In this approach to the belief in God, he seems to have been early influenced by Herder. Later, when challenged by a scientist who was an intimate friend of his to set forth his conception of God, he did so in terms which indicated that the reality of God was to him as immediate an intuition as the existence of his own personality. Part of that same intuition was his assumption that personality was an autonomous principle, independent of body. The reality of his own spirit was to him sufficient guarantee of the reality of the all-pervading transcendent spirit of God. Though the divine spirit pulsates in all human endeavors to achieve the highest and best, it so far transcends the spirit of man as to be infinite. That infinitude of the divine spirit is perceived intuitively by the human mind. Geiger recognized that such a conception of God bordered on the poetic, nevertheless it was to him the kind of conception without which life would be meaningless.[8]

Geiger attached no significance to the various cosmological and teleological arguments for the existence of God. "Religion," he says, "originates as an inner immediate illumination, a revelation of the divine aspect in the spirit of man. It so overwhelms the human being in his entire thinking and existence that it leaves him no freedom to formulate in detail each concept, for that would rob religion of its warmth and originality. Judaism made its appearance with its idea of the unity of God, and has been dominated by it ever since. Mankind could not have come upon that idea as a result of gradual evolution." [9] Geiger definitely accepts revelation as the source of man's knowledge of God, but not in the traditional sense of revelation. "Revelation," he says, "signifies the point of contact between human reason and the deep underlying ground of all things." [10]

The history of Judaism is, to Geiger, the story of the Jews as the People of revelation. As such, it is not only history, but also religion. The Jews were the only People among whom arose a long line of Prophets. To them was vouchsafed this unaccountable inner illumination and revelation. The Prophets had to labor hard and long before they could get their People to grasp their message. The way in which the People of Israel interpreted the God idea was necessarily conditioned by their cultural development during the different periods of their history. *The progress which the Jews achieved in their ethical and spiritual comprehension of God is their spiritual odyssey.*[11] *The awareness of that odyssey, according to Geiger, must henceforth constitute the Jewish historical-religious orientation, on the basis of which the Jews should plan their future.* This, he maintained, was the only conception of Jewish history which furnished the Reform movement with a philosophy and a program.

With this purpose in mind, he applied himself to the task of reconstructing the traditional orientation into one based on the assumption that God revealed Himself through the entire history of the Jewish People. In order, however, to interpret Judaism properly, he deemed it necessary to treat the Biblical period as of cardinal importance, for it was then that prophecy flourished. It was, therefore, the period of divine revelation *par excellence.* The first and most difficult step in the evolution of Judaism was to wean away early Israel from the heathen forms of divine worship, which included sacred prostitution and human sacrifice. To Geiger, the struggle that went on during the early centuries in the career of the People of Israel between the Prophets and their contemporaries, the former urging spiritual worship and the latter clinging to the barbarous practices of their neighbors, was a manifestation of the Divine Spirit striving to take possession of the collective Jewish consciousness.

A striking illustration of the method Geiger employs in reinterpreting the historical-religious orientation of tradition is his version of the story of the sacrifice of Isaac. The surface meaning of that story seems to be that Abraham's merit consisted in his obedience of God's command to sacrifice his son Isaac. According to Geiger, however, we have to understand that story differently, if we want it to serve as part of a historical-religious orientation. We have to learn from it that Abraham's merit consisted in his finally realizing the absurdity of worshipping God by so inhuman an act as human sacrifice, and in his refusal to go through with it.[12]

A far longer struggle, however, according to Geiger, had to be waged against the universal practices of worshipping God by means of animal sacrifice. Despite the pleadings and denunciations of the Prophets, the Northern Kingdom of Israel never succeeded in overcoming the influence of the priest-class, with its emphasis on sacrificial cult. The Southern Kingdom of Judah somehow succeeded in freeing itself from the spirit of heathenism. Though Judah, too, had its temple and sacrificial cult, it tended to restrict their importance. Even the priestly function was marked by a high degree of spirituality which had been lacking in Northern Israel. When the First Temple, however, was destroyed and the Judeans went into exile, the Zadokite priests helped to maintain the integrity of the nation through their loyal attachment both to the Davidic dynasty and to the sacrificial cult.

A new stage in divine revelation had been reached about two centuries before the downfall of the First Commonwealth, with the rise of a new school of Prophets who finally voiced the divine urge which had been struggling for expression within the People of Israel from its very beginning. That was the urge to announce to the world the message of universal religion, which was to bring salvation to all mankind. From that time on, the People of Israel has been aware of its mission and destiny. But many centuries have had to pass before it was in a position to translate that awareness into action.

With the rebuilding of the Second Temple and Commonwealth, subjection to Persian rule precluded the continuance of the Davidic dynasty. Instead, the priesthood came into power. Fortified by the authority of the Pentateuch, the priests might have hardened Judaism into a temple-and-cult-centered religion. Fortunately for its development, Judaism was challenged by Hellenism. The resulting crisis gave rise to a new type of spokesmen for the spirit of the Jewish People. Those were the Scribes, who were expert in the knowledge of Torah. These spokesmen revived the dormant spirit of the Prophets and combatted the cultic conception of Judaism which the Sadducees, or descendants of Zadok, had been fostering. Thus arose Phariseeism.

The Pharisaic movement restored to Judaism the capacity for evolving and bringing to ever greater purity and spirituality the religious teachings of the Torah. The Sages of the Talmud, especially the *Tannaim*, or the authorities mentioned in the Mishnaic code formulated by R. Judah ha-Nasi, continued the Pharisaic tradition of maintaining the conception of God in its purity, and preventing it from being corrupted by degrading influences. That tradition saved the Jews from yielding to the dominance of the various idolatries from which it was Judaism's mission to wean mankind.

Among those degrading influences Geiger included Christianity. Though recognizing its service in welding the barbarian races of Europe into a spiritual community and in imbuing that community with a common consciousness, he was quite outspoken in his criticism of its theology. Its central dogma which is stressed in the Gospel of John, that God sacrificed His son for the sake of mankind, was to him strongly reminiscent of the primitive ritual of human sacrifice. In fact, he strongly deprecated the various prayers in the Jewish liturgy in which the sacrifice of Isaac was made the basis of an appeal to God's mercy. He saw in those prayers the influence of Christian soteriology.

Geiger was convinced that it is both possible and imperative to have Judaism become a world religion, and, as such, to replace Christianity, which he regarded as marred by a wrong conception of God and of man. That God could become incarnate was to him nothing more than the worship of man as God, and therefore, on a par with idolatry. To believe that a single human being could have embodied in himself the perfection toward which the human race as a whole was striving he regarded as a hindrance to human progress. Both of these errors were absent in Jewish religion. It had been prevented, however, from becoming the religion of mankind, because it had been identified with a national life and a national land. By eliminating those national elements—a process made not only easy but also necessary by the incorporation of the Jews into the general body politic—the main obstacle, according to Geiger, in the way of rendering Judaism a universal religion was removed.[13]

Geiger hoped to bring the content and form of Jewish worship and ritual into line with his new orientation. At the various Reform Conferences and Synods in which he was one of the leaders, he pleaded passionately for changes in the traditional liturgy and in the conduct of religious services. He urged the substitution of the vernacular for the Hebrew, which he regarded as nothing more than a survival of Jewish nationhood. He conceded that, for the sake of continuity with the past, it might be necessary to retain the Hebrew text in the prayer book, but for the actual conduct of religious services he recommended resort to a modern version in the vernacular. He urged the avoidance of repetition, the formulation of new prayers and the shortening of the services. He favored the use of instrumental music, particularly the organ, as a means of rendering the services inspiring. He advocated the elimination of prayers which implied beliefs that were no longer tenable. Such were the beliefs in the bodily resurrection of the dead, the restoration of the Davidic dynasty, the coming of a personal Messiah, the rebuilding of the Temple, and the reinstatement of the sacrificial cult.

On the question of the Sabbath, Geiger was definitely opposed to the incipient tendency in radical Reform circles to observe it on Sunday. His contention was that the seventh day Sabbath constituted the outstanding symbol of whatever differentiates Judaism from Christianity. For Jews to adopt a Sunday Sabbath was tantamount to yielding the palm of spiritual victory to Christianity. That, of course, would be the death-warrant of Judaism. However, that did not mean for Geiger that the Sabbath had to be observed in accordance with all the restrictive regulations prescribed by tradition. Just how much latitude may be allowed, Geiger did not make clear. In the matter of the dietary laws, he saw no point to suggesting half-measures. If they could not be observed in their entirety, they ought to be abolished altogether. Although he himself, out of regard for the feelings of those to whom he ministered as a rabbi, observed the dietary laws,[15] he did not consider them as viable in modern Jewish religion.

The one point on which he displayed least scruple about breaking with the past and with deeply ingrained sentiment was the rite of circumcision. There he allowed himself to be swayed by the purely logical inference from what he believed was the history of that rite. He assumed, in the first place, that it had originally been intended as a substitute for human sacrifice. Secondly, he assumed that the Deuteronomist who represented the Judaic and, accordingly, the more spiritual conception of God, had deliberately omitted all reference to the rite of circumcision. Against this background, Geiger concluded that circumcision could be eliminated without any loss to Judaism.[16]

Of the traditional marriage laws, all that should survive, according to Geiger, is the requirement of a Jewish divorce, in addition to the divorce granted by the State, as necessary for the right to remarry. Such a divorce, however, may be granted by a rabbinical committee to the woman, if the husband refuses to grant it to her. This constitutes a radical departure from the traditional marriage law, which is partial to the man, in that it recognizes him as the only spouse authorized to dissolve a marriage. Geiger also proposed the abolition of the levirate divorce (halizah), and of the law forbidding one of Aaronic descent to marry a woman who was a proselyte, or one who had been divorced.

According to Geiger, reckoning with the growth of the human spirit was an inherent trait of Judaism. That trait had remained dormant for many centuries but was being reactivated by Reform. The scientific interest which he brought to bear on the study of Judaism was thus largely motivated by his desire to prove that it had been subject to the process of evolution throughout its entire history. Actually, however, Geiger confused two types of evolutionary process: one, the process of unconscious change which takes place in human society as a result of spontaneous responses to continually changing conditions in its environment; the other, conscious and planned effort to deviate from a habitual mode of living and thinking because the traditional assumptions are no longer tenable, nor the traditional way of life livable.

It is not true, as Geiger maintains, that this second type of conscious evolution has always existed in Judaism. Actually, resistance to change has always been its predominant characteristic. On the other hand, merely to say that traditional Judaism has undergone change in the course of its existence is to state a truism from which it does not follow that deliberate reform is legitimate.

Geiger's main point, however, that Judaism has evolved (even though he fails to stress that the evolution was unconscious) is not only valid, but may well be utilized in support of conscious and directed development.

In addition to stressing the past evolution of Judaism, Geiger was intent upon eliminating all vestiges of its national character. Jewish nationhood was to him nothing more than an historically conditioned outward form which the intrinsic spirit of Judaism had to assume in the past. According to Geiger, *Judaism addresses itself essentially to the individual. That makes it a universal religion.* Whatever in Judaism has only limited reference is unessential. Geiger admitted that Jewish nationhood originally had served a useful function, in that it had prevented Judaism from degenerating into a mystic, pagan-like cult. But nowdays nationhood could only be an obstacle to the full manifestation of the universal character which the Prophets had given to Judaism. Due to the segregation and persecution to which the Jews had been subjected in the Middle Ages, the universal teachings of Judaism had suffered eclipse. The time had come, however, for Judaism to bring them to light again.

Geiger's reinterpretation of Judaism is based on two assumptions. In the first place, a religion must lay claim to being the only true religion. It has to be capable of helping all human beings to achieve salvation. Secondly, Judaism is the only religion that can make good this claim, because it insists on an enlightened knowledge of God and on ethical conduct in all human relationships as prerequisites to salvation. It is now Judaism's mission to make known this conception of salvation. The existence of Christianity, in particular, makes it necessary for Judaism to adhere to its mission. Judaism, therefore, should do nothing that might be interpreted as surrender to the religion of the majority.

Geiger made it clear that he did not underestimate Christianity's service to mankind. "It were foolish and ridiculous," he says, "not to recognize a divinely willed mission in a religion which unfolded such great power. Christianity accomplished its mission, because it united nations which had lived in stupid isolation into a single totality and inspired them with common interests and with a great common human striving." [17] But in suggesting that Judaism should have the courage to counteract Christianity, Geiger was apparently also one of those who assumed that the Church would be completely separated from the State, and that Christianity would continue merely as a voluntary communion of the majority population out of force of habit and tradition. He little realized that while he was trying to eliminate nationhood from Judaism, Christianity was being integrated even more firmly into the State, thereby rendering the complete incorporation of the Jews into the State all the more difficult.

Geiger rationalized his opposition to the element of nationhood in Judaism on the ground that it prevented the universal element in it from coming into play. He therefore objected to any doctrine or practice which was conspicuously national. He expunged from the traditional prayer book all petitions for the restoration of the Jews to their ancestral land. Although he regarded the Talmud as having thwarted the Jews from living up to the universalism of the Prophets, he was happy to find in it a lonely saying to support him in his deprecation of the hope for the return to Eretz Yisrael. That saying is: "He who emigrates from Babylonia to Eretz Yisrael transgresses a prohibitive command." [18] To be properly understood, the saying has to be read in its historic context. Its author was the Babylonian *Amora* Rav Yehuda, who lived at a time when the academies in Eretz Yisrael had deteriorated, whereas those in Babylonia were at the height of their reputation for learning and influence. That Geiger should have used that saying as sanction for invalidating the historic yearning of the Jews for the recovery of their national home shows how determined he was to denationalize Judaism.

His pet aversion was the observance of the multitude of ritual prohibitions which stood in the way of free social intercourse between Jews and Gentiles. He did not hesitate to characterize circumcision and the dietary laws as barbaric relics. That they might have taken on in course of time a spiritual significance did not count with him. They emphasized Jewish individuality, and therefore had no place in a Judaism which aimed to be universal. He advocated the discontinuance of Hebrew in Jewish worship and the substitution of the vernacular. That Hebrew served as a bond to unite all Jews throughout the world was to him of no consequence. Indeed, there was a time in his life when he was willing to have the Jews of Germany officially repudiate the Talmud as their authoritative code, and formally constitute themselves into a Jewish Church that would be the analogue of the Lutheran Church.

The amazing paradox in Geiger's conception of Judaism is that, on the one hand, he regarded the Jewish People as the medium of divine revelation, and on the other, he viewed with apprehension the solidarity of the Jewish People, and with aversion whatever was calculated to maintain that solidarity. To such an extent did Geiger himself lose the sense of oneness with the body of world Jewry that he failed to react with bitter resentment toward the accusation of ritual murder in Damascus in 1840, though that accusation jeopardized the status of the Jews everywhere. He was said to have been more interested in having German Jews find for themselves careers as apothecaries and lawyers than in the fate of Jewry as a whole. *This lack of sensitiveness to the fate of world Jewry may perhaps be ascribed to the influence of Germanic abstractionism. It led him to transfer the essence of Judaism from the living People to abstract ideals and high-sounding universals.*

In all likelihood, it was also Germanic influence that induced Geiger to refurbish the traditional doctrine of Israel's election and give it the fresh modern sparkle of racial superiority. Fichte and Hegel had already raised the German race and nation to the status of God's Chosen People. Geiger was not going to let them take that title away from the Jews. Even though the Jews were no longer a nation, they still remained a unique race with a gift for religion that was tantamount to genius. By "a gift for religion" he meant the power of intuition which enabled the human consciousness to establish immediate contact with the very ground of reality. The Jews, in their collective capacity, according to Geiger, possess this remarkable sense of religion, or that intuitive capacity which enables them to cultivate more effectively than any other people the relationship between the human and the divine. He ascribed to that native faculty of the Jewish race the unique phenomenon of prophecy in ancient Israel.[19]

It is difficult to appraise the true significance of this teaching of Geiger's, which, until recently, was accepted in Reform circles as authoritative. To take it literally would mean that Reform lays claim to a unique character and status for the Jewish People with even more self-assertiveness than is warranted by tradition. For in tradition it is God's treatment of the Jews rather than their own worth or inherent nature that marks them out as unique. To ascribe, in all literalness, to the Jews as a race the possession of greater spiritual power than to other races or peoples is bound in the long run to be far more objectionable than the Jews' insistence upon retaining their group individuality, an ambition which is perfectly natural and understandable. In a world where presumably all human beings are considered equal before God, it seems arrogant for one group to lay claim to being more qualified for salvation than the rest of mankind. Yet this seemed to be the only way out of the dilemma in which the Reform leaders found themselves. On the one hand, they wished to maintain the individuality of the Jewish People, and, on the other, they did not wish that. individuality to retain the pattern of nationhood. The alleged unique Jewish endowment with a gift for true religion, and the inevitable inference that they were entrusted with the mission to spread it, seemed to satisfy both these needs.

In pre-modern times, a nation was regarded as essentially a homogeneous racial group. The very fact that this conception of nationhood no longer obtains makes of the assumption that the Jews are a race a convenient means of holding on to what is intuitively felt to be indispensable to Judaism—the assurance of their continuance as an identifiable group. Geiger's assumption that the Jews constitute a race has not remained an abstract doctrine in the Reform movement. It still serves in that movement, according to Kaufmann Kohler, who was a disciple of Geiger, as the powerful sanction of the interdict against intermarriage.[20] This interdict against intermarriage derives from Kohler's conception of Judaism, which is identical with Geiger's. "Judaism," says Kohler, "combines two widely different elements, and when they are brought out separately the aspect of the whole is not taken sufficiently into account. Religion and race form an inseparable whole in Judaism. The Jewish people stand in the same relation to Judaism as the body to the soul." [21]

Reform, however, went further in its efforts to denationalize Judaism than did Geiger and Kohler. Claude C. Montefiore, the founder in England of the Reform movement, which designates itself "Liberal," removed from Judaism all association with

Jews as a collective entity of any kind. Thus he draws a subtle distinction between the attitude of the modern Jew in his daily conduct and the attitude he assumes when he prays or worships God. "In the personal, individual, religious life of the modern Jew, the fact that he *is* a Jew may determine conduct. *Noblesse oblige*, the sanctification of the Name; these may become motives for resisting temptation and for a better life. But in his prayer to God, the modern Jew probably thinks of himself more as a human being than as an Israelite. He probably thinks of himself less as a Jew than the modern Christian thinks of himself as a Christian." [22]

In the United States, the official attitude of Reform with regard to Jewish nationhood was directed mainly against Zionism. "Reform Judaism contends," says David Philipson, "that the national existence of the Jews ceased when the Romans set the Temple aflame and destroyed Jerusalem. The career in Eretz Yisrael was but a preparation for Israel's work in all portions of the world. As the early home of the faith, and the land where they uttered their world-subduing thoughts and the psalmists sang their world-enchanting hymns, Eretz Yisrael is a precious memory of the past, but it is not a hope of the future. With the dispersion of the Jews all over the world, the universal mission of Judaism began. The Jews are citizens and faithful sons of the lands of their birth or adoption. They are a religious community, not a nation." [23] In a note to the foregoing, Philipson adds, "Though a number of Reform rabbis and writers are sympathetic with Zionism, the new nationalistic movement among Jews, there can be no manner of doubt that the position stated in the text expresses the true philosophy of the Reform movement."

The Reform movement, which flourished for a time in Germany, had its fellow-travelers among the Jews of Austria. Aaron Chorin (1766-1844) of Hungary may even be regarded as a forerunner of the movement. In Galicia, a group of writers associated with the scholarly periodical *He-Halutz* (between 1852 and 1859) used the rationalist approach in their critical analysis of time-honored Jewish beliefs and practices. The moving spirit of that group was Joshua Heschel Schorr (1812-1895). Associated with him was Abraham Krochmal (1820-1895), a son of Nachman

Krochmal. Though both of them were well-versed in traditional lore, they were not consistent in their treatment of contemporary problems of Jewish life.

Schorr came from a famous rabbinical family. In his youth, he received an intensive Talmudic training of the traditional type. Intellectually and temperamentally a rebel against what he regarded as the tyranny of tradition, which was especially oppressive in his environment, he utilized his knowledge of Rabbinic lore for the purpose of freeing his fellow-Jews from its authority. He tried to weaken the hold which the Talmud had on the Jewish consciousness, by exposing errors in R. Judah's codification of the *Mishnah* and in the Amoraic interpretations of the Mishnaic text. He made it a point to save the reputation of Medieval Rabbinic scholars like Aaron Abu al-Rabi and Yitzhak Albalag,[24] who had been in ill-repute because of their heretical views. He sought to shift Judaism's center of gravity from the Talmud to the Bible, by severing from Judaism the mass of Rabbinic tradition which, according to him, had transformed its entire spirit for the worse.

Abraham Krochmal did not engage in polemics as did Schorr. His interest in Judaism followed largely the same pattern as his father's, except that he stressed the theological aspect more than the national. Had he written in German instead of in Hebrew, he would undoubtedly have figured as one of the outstanding theologians of the Reform movement. The very titles of his works testify to his dominant theological interest, *Daat Elohim ba-Aretz* (Lemberg, 1863), *Iyyun Tefilah*, (Lemberg, 1885). He was so deeply influenced in his religious thinking by Spinoza, whom he regarded as a "God-intoxicated" man, that he wrote a commentary on the Bible in the form of a retrieved manuscript of Spinoza's.[25]

To Abraham Krochmal, the Reform movement itself was nothing less than a further manifestation of the Divine in the history of the Jewish People. That the Jews have been able to emancipate themselves from physical ties to their land, and that they have been able to reformulate their religious creed was to him a miracle. As for the creed, itself, it consisted for him of the following three dogmas: 1) The philosophic dogma of the unity of God, 2) the ethical dogma of the love of man, and 3) the theological dogma of the holiness of man.

CHAPTER EIGHT

Early Jewish Reform Theologies

REFORM THEOLOGY AND
THE GERMAN ZEITGEIST

The main contribution of Reform to the development of modern Judaism has been its attempt to reconstruct that aspect of the Jewish religious tradition which has a direct bearing on the life of the individual Jew. Reform has concerned itself with two problems: (1) What shall the Jew believe concerning God, man, the world, and Israel, that will justify his refusal to accept the religion of the majority populations, and that will validate the universal character and mission of his own religion? And (2) what forms of ritual observance and religious worship are best calculated to inspire the Jew to lead an ethical life?

One does not have to agree with the reinterpretation of Judaism as formulated by the early Reformists to recognize that they at least grappled with the problem of the God idea. Unlike Leopold Zunz, whose Jewish studies were centered on the reconstruction of the past, Abraham Geiger maintained an equal balance between the scholarly effort to retrieve the past and the philosophical effort to readjust Jewish thinking in the present. Geiger sought to arouse an interest in the theological problems of Judaism by establishing the first Jewish theological magazine, *Wissenschaftliche Zeitschrift fuer Juedische Theologie*. Currently with him, Solomon Formstecher, Samuel Hirsch and other Jewish thinkers laid the foundations of a modern Jewish theology.

One can understand why the Orthodox regarded all attempts to intellectualize the belief in God as gratuitous, since they assumed that the tradition concerning the supernatural revelation was the only reliable source of our knowledge about God. But those who realize that there is no future to a religion which fails to reckon with the modern orientation to nature, man and history, cannot but be grateful to the early Reformists for having inaugurated the effort to arrive in Judaism at a consistent philosophy of life and a program of salvation.

Those Central European Jews who had been culturally and spiritually conditioned against assimilation, but who were also alive to the changes taking place in the general world-outlook, had to find a way of so reinterpreting the Jewish tradition as to render it capable of being integrated into the new universe of discourse. That universe of discourse, or *Zeitgeist*, was evolved in the Germany of 1780-1820, the period during which Kant and his successors flourished. New systems of thought were then revolutionizing the modern mind. That is the period which is often compared, in the scope of its creativity, to the glorious Periclean era in Athens. The leaders of the Reform movement, finding themselves in the midst of the intellectual upsurge which followed that period, were completely carried away by it. Hence, the entire thought structure of *classical* Reform Judaism is practically little more than a Jewish version of the German philosophical idealism of which Kant, Herder, Lessing, Fichte, Schelling, Jacobi and Hegel were the architects.

German anti-Semitism, which was a concomitant of Germany's metamorphosis into a modern nation, made it a point to trump up the fear of a possible judaization of German *Kultur*. Only insane bigotry could have invented such a bogey. On the other hand, there can be no doubt that the reverse process did take place. German Jews became in time so thoroughly imbued with the German spirit that they were only too glad to place its stamp upon their own Jewish individuality. German Judaism underwent a thoroughgoing Germanization.[1]

That, however, did not satisfy the spokesmen of German *Kultur*. Even the most liberal among them counted on nothing less than the complete christianization of the Jews. Wilhelm von Humboldt and his colleagues in the Austro-Prussian cabinet during the second and third decades of the nineteenth century, who urged the granting of citizenship to the Jews, expected them to abandon their Judaism entirely, and made every effort to expedite that development.[2]

The first modern Jewish theologians took over the values and concepts that were alien to the Jewish tradition, and forced them into the mold of that tradition, much as Alexandrian Philo had done with Platonism and Saadya Gaon, Ibn Daud and Maimonides had done with Aristotelianism. The parallel extends even further. The Medieval Jewish philosophers had the ground prepared for them by the Moslem philosophers, who had synthesized Aristotelian thought with Islam. Likewise, the modern Jewish theologians had the ground prepared for them by the Idealist German philosophers, who reinterpreted Christianity in the light of the currently accepted philosophy. Unlike the French *illuminati*, who were fanatically anti-clerical, the German *illuminati* wished to see Christianity survive. The French experiment with the "Religion of Reason" had proved a fiasco, and the reaction against it contributed to a revival in Germany of interest in Christianity. Hegelianism, as the Prussian State philosophy, was enlisted in the service of the State religion.

To understand properly the development of the German *Zeitgeist* in the first decades of the nineteenth century, we have to take into account the nationalist sentiment which the Napoleonic wars had fanned into a flame among the conquered peoples, particularly in Central Europe. In addition, it must be remembered that in the period when the political fortunes of Germany were at their lowest ebb, German culture was at its zenith both in philosophy and *belles lettres*. Out of this unique combination of circumstances— political failure and cultural success—arose the compensatory notion that it was the destiny of the German nation to exercise moral and spiritual hegemony over the other nations of the world.

German culture, toward the last quarter of the eighteenth century, began to develop so rapidly that it became conscious of itself as a dominant influence in the world. This awareness contributed to the growing tendency in Germany to ascribe to culture whatever made man human. The entire trend of the Enlightenment in France had given rise to the tendency to see the best in man as native to him, and the worst as the product of civilization or culture. The outstanding German thinkers, on the other hand, reversed that assumption. Nurture rather than nature, they insisted, was that which made man human. When, in addition to this spontaneous glorification of culture, there came the political subjection to France under Napoleon, the repudiation of the basic notions of the Enlightenment became a matter of patriotism as well as of principle.

According to Benedetto Croce,[3] the fact that Germany's political development was behind that of France and England accounts for her failure to translate into action the logical consequences of the Enlightenment, which she at first shared with those countries. "The generous illuminist spirit of humanity to which Herder and other thinkers of the eighteenth century had been moved gradually disappeared under State influence, underwent disturbance and corruption in its own concepts, employing them for uses of servility toward the existing powers and the old regimes." Of this tendency Fichte and Hegel are themselves the best examples.

There was also a strong reaction against the new mechanical conception of the universe, with which Newtonian science had replaced the traditional one. That was the conception from which French rationalism had drawn its inspiration. In addition, there arose the desire to find new and tenable meaning in traditional Christianity. The outcome was speculative Idealism. It was intended to offset what was then called the "dogmatism" of the French "materialistic" civilization. "Dogmatism" was a term of reproach to characterize the belief in mechanical necessity and in the inexorable working of the law of cause and effect as having disoriented the human mind and having robbed it of all incentive for the higher life.

Idealist philosophy, on the other hand, was supposed to free the human mind from the law of mechanical necessity and to make it complete master of its own domain. The Idealist approach was clearly recognized as an act of the will rather than of reason. The analogue of that approach in the twentieth century is known as "the leap of faith." Fichte frankly admitted that the choice between "the dogmatic and the idealist approach depended 'on what sort of man one was' " ("was fuer ein Mensch man ist"). Since the choice of the Idealist approach was arbitrary, there was nothing to prevent its application to religious and social institutions from being arbitrary. Hence the German Christian thinkers found no difficulty in using Idealism to prove that Christianity was the one absolutely true religion and the last word in spiritual truth. Hegel believed he accomplished that purpose by reinterpreting its main traditional concepts or values. He reinterpreted the traditional conception of religion as revealed (offenbarte) into the philosophical conception of religion as revelation (offenbarung). He equated the Holy Trinity with "the dialectic of the Absolute Mind." To him Christ was the God-Man, who experienced complete identity with the Absolute. He interpreted the Holy Spirit as signifying the community spirit, which is the product of social life. He saw in the redemptive power of love the equivalent of what the Christian tradition speaks of as Redemption.

The German Jewish thinkers likewise utilized the Idealist philosophy to validate their own Jewish religion. The fact is that speculative Idealism, being a subjective method of evaluation rather than an objective search after facts, lends itself to a rationale for whatever one happens to regard as of supreme value. "The compelling power which Kant's philosophy exercised over the minds and hearts of men," says W. Windelband,[4] "was due chiefly to the earnestness and greatness of its ethical conception of the world." Hegel actually declared that philosophy and theology were synonymous. "Hegel was a sort of philosophic Augustine, says J. T. Shotwell [5] tracing through history the development of the realm of spirit. The city of God is still the central theme, but the crude expectations of a miraculous advent are replaced by the conception of the slow realization of its power, rising through successive states of civilization." According to John Dewey, "Hegel assumed the task of justifying in the name of rational Idealism the doctrines and institutions which were menaced by the new spirit of science and popular government." [6] Christianity, as a result of the new reinterpretation given to it by the German philosophers, was so revitalized that it became part of the entire "Restoration" psychology, as is evidenced by the formation of the Holy Alliance and the spread of the gospel of "Christian Nationalism" which followed the peace of Vienna.

The function of the Idealist German philosophy as the reinterpretation of the Judeo-Christian traditional orientation was most effectively formulated by Fichte.[7] Fichte maintains that Reality is intelligible, not from the standpoint of what is but from the standpoint of what ought to be. God is not, as with Spinoza, *natura naturans*, the eternal substance whence all that constitutes reality arises *more geometrico*, through inner necessity. God is *ordo ordinans*, the moral order, the goal or purpose which alone determines what is. Certainly no method of reinterpretation could be more congenial to the traditional religious values of Judaism and Christianity.

When, therefore, the Jewish thinkers of the nineteenth century undertook to restate the traditional Jewish orientation in modern terms, they could avail themselves of what the Idealist school of German thought had to say concerning the meaning of God as revealed in the functioning of the moral conscience. Salvation was reinterpreted to mean the conscious realization of moral freedom, and moral freedom was said to be the functioning of the Divine Spirit both in the universe and in man. The religious life came to be regarded as essentially the self-expression of the Divine in man. The life of the spirit was viewed as consisting in progressive achievement of moral freedom, which is the antithesis of the life of nature. Hegel operated with the old scholastic antithesis of nature and spirit. He interpreted human history as man's education for freedom, or for the life of the spirit.

Likewise, the Idealist interpretation of the traditional teaching concerning the supernatural revelation of God served for the Reform leaders and thinkers as the needed formula for religion. The Idealist reinterpretation negated the possibility of a rational demonstration of the existence of God. With Kant, the existence of God could be based only on the assumption of practical reason; with Fichte and Hegel, only on the intuition that reason was realizing itself in the process of history; with Schleiermacher, only on the psychological experience of the sense of need and dependence. The entire religious tradition of the Jews abounded in teachings which lent themselves most easily to reinterpretation in terms of all these ideas. *In the same way as Philo had reinterpreted Jewish religion in terms of the Platonic universe of discourse, so did the first Reform theologians reinterpret Jewish religion in terms of the thought realm of German speculative Idealism.* Speculative Idealism was the *Zeitgeist* of the first part of the nineteenth century, and the trends in Judaism that reckoned with it were *Haskalah* and Reform.

The very fact that the Idealist German philosophy furnished a common universe of discourse to Jews and Christians contributed to the carrying over from traditionalism to modernism of the age-old controversy between Judaism and Christianity. As a corollary of the new orientation achieved by German Idealism, in which Christianity was reinterpreted, the polemic against Judaism was renewed and clothed in modernist phraseology. Part of the reinterpretation of Christianity consisted in resharpening all its traditional weapons against Judaism. The principal contention, of course, was that Judaism was particularistic and exclusive in its conception of salvation. It had no salvation to offer the non-Jew. Christianity, on the other hand, was assumed to be universal.

This emphasis on the universal character of Christianity coincided with the emphasis on the doctrine of statism, economic and autarchic nationalism. Fichte raised German nationalism to a religion, and assigned to the German People the mission of bringing enlightenment and true culture to the world. He took it for granted that the German People was the elect of God, and far more eligible for salvation than any other People. In his *Addresses to the German Nation*,[8] he called upon Germany to create the true civilized State to establish "the kingdom of reason and freedom," the new term for what traditionally had been spoken of as the Kingdom of God. From what we know of Fichte's fervid advocacy of German nationalism, this glorification of reason and freedom may sound like a reversion to his own earlier revolutionary period. But the fact probably is that he, as well as all the other philosophers, assumed whenever they spoke of freedom that only a "State-building" race can have the right to live in freedom.

Judaism was subjected to a barrage of adverse criticism on the part of writers of standing, and of taunts and insults on the part of journalistic scribblers. Reform leaders and teachers tried to counteract the demoralizing effect of these onslaughts by finding a place for the Jewish People in the scheme of human history. It was only natural that they should employ the method and terminology of the new philosophy to discover in the process of Jewish history the evidence of Divine Reason, in the same way as the German Idealist school found such evidence in the trend of events that had led to their faith in ultimate German hegemony. Idealist philosophers of the type of Hegel and Schleiermacher tried to prove that Judaism represented an inferior type of religion, and the Jewish Reform theologians retorted by proving that Christianity was inferior to Judaism. Reformism had a difficult battle on its hands against the mighty intellectual forces of the German nation, which was then growing in self-conscious power. It fought for the equal rights of Jews not only to civil freedom and equality, but also to the maintenance of their religious individuality. That subjected the Reform movement to a storm of abuse which was let loose by philosophers, theologians, and publicists.

The Reformist leaders were confronted with a delicate and difficult task, which they tried to carry out with as much tact as possible. The Jewish tradition, as a result of the struggle for survival carried on by the Jewish People throughout the centuries of dispersion, had stymied what originally might have developed into a universal philosophy of history. The pre-exilic Prophets had practically attained a world-view in which the God of Israel came to be recognized as the God of mankind, without necessarily having all history Israel-centered. But, with dispersion, exile and unremitting presecution as the lot of the Jews during the last twenty centuries, the only means of defense and resistance at their disposal was a psychological one. Thus arose the particularistic history of philosophy which is writ large over the entire Rabbinic, philosophic and mystic literature of pre-modern Judaism.

The Emancipation promised to offer respite from the long career of suffering. It appeared to be not the result of some ruler's arbitrary whim, but the by-product of a new world-outlook and estimate of man. It was made possible through the tacit repudiation of Christian exclusivism, which had known no such thing as "inalienable human rights." Hence, to those Jewish theologicans who took the promise of the Emancipation seriously, there seemed to be no longer any need for stressing Jewish particularism. In fact, they regarded that particularism as a stumbling block to the extension of the Emancipation, and as invalidating their efforts to prove that Judaism was superior, ethically and philosophically, to all other contemporary religious and ethical systems.

SOLOMON FORMSTECHER (1808-1889)

Among the first formulations of the new Jewish outlook was that of Solomon Formstecher, whose *Die Religion des Geistes* appeared in Frankfort on-the-Main in 1841. He was born at Offenbach in 1808. After receiving his doctorate from the Giessen University in 1831, he was appointed preacher in his native city. In 1842, when the local rabbi died, Formstecher succeeded him as rabbi and held that post until his death in 1889. He participated in the various rabbinical conferences which took place in Germany for the purpose of reformulating the ritual practices in Judaism.

Formstecher was the first to attempt a comprehensive presentation of Judaism in the light of the new philosophic trends which were greatly the vogue in Germany since the days of Kant. He regarded the systematization of Jewish theology as a means of eliminating the unessentials in Judaism and bringing its essentials into bolder relief.[9] By adopting the basic ideas of the Idealist philosophers of his day, he sought to refute their exaltation of Christianity and their defamation of Judaism.

The philosopher on whom Formstecher leaned most was Friedrich W. J. Schelling.[10] From him he took over the conception of God as the free and self-determining Spirit behind the phenomena of nature. In man, the Divine Spirit functions as the Absolute and as self-awareness. By means of that Spirit, man learns to know both nature and his innermost self. His knowledge of outward nature leads to his recognition of the laws of logic and of natural necessity. His knowledge of the Divine Spirit itself leads to his recognition of the laws of ethics. Only in the domain of the Spirit should man's activities be designated as either good or evil, whereas in the domain of nature, it is only in the metaphorical sense of helping or hindering some desire that man's activities are so judged.

Formstecher distinguishes between the categorical imperative which recognizes only good and evil conduct, on the one hand, and revelation which recognizes also virtue and sin, on the other.[11] Reward and punishment, Formstecher maintains, should be ruled out from the motivation of conduct, if it is to belong

to the category of virtue. Yet, he accepts the functioning of retribution in human life as an objective fact. In monotheistic
religion, evil, as suffering, can have only relative existence. Theology
is to Formstecher synonymous with ethics, and the highest knowledge of God is the knowledge of the ethical attributes through which
God manifests himself. There is also a lower form of the knowledge of God, namely, the aesthetic, which deals with the self-
manifestation of God in nature. The latter is the knowledge which
the more advanced nations have cultivated. The Jews, on the
other hand, were the first to achieve ethical knowledge.

The knowledge of the right cannot be attained merely through
reflection or study, because ethical truth is different from mathematical or scientific truth. It has to be perceived intuitively, or
as Formstecher puts it, through revelation. Although he uses the
term "revelation," it has in common with the traditional use of
that term merely the negation of logical reasoning. "Revelation,"
as Formstecher understands it, is not to be identified as a supernatural event in history, but as an educative process within man's
spirit itself.

When the human mind first became spontaneously aware of
the specific content of the ethical ideal, it experienced a feeling
of ecstasy. That was the stage of prophecy. Later, that content
was set forth in Sacred Scriptures, of which God was conceived
as author. In both of these stages the human mind viewed the
ethical deal as coming to it from without. In the third, which is
the present, stage of its development, however, the human mind
recognizes the ethical ideal as its own creation. In this, the highest
stage, man discovers the truth of the Idealist interpretation of
experience. Thus the process of revelation is the progress from the
naïve belief which regards the ethical law, or ideal, as coming
from without, to the conscious recognition of the spirit within
man as its real source. At the same time, the ethical ideal comes
to transcend the narrow limits of its application to a particular
group, and its universal significance begins to be perceived.

The ethical ideal consists in the subordination of the universal laws of nature to the particular needs of the self-conscious
spirit. In ancient times, that ideal was achieved only by the People
of Israel, the people of revelation, whereas in the pagan world
God was worshipped as manifest, not in the spirit of man, but in

physical nature, or as revealing Himself not through the ethical ideal, but through the beauty of the physical world.

This identification of God with nature led the pagan world to view human life as governed by fate. Jewish religion, on the other hand, beheld in the history of mankind the working of a divine personal will. While the rest of mankind saw in the world only the functioning of the law of necessity, Israel discerned the functioning of divine freedom. Through its emphasis upon creation, freedom of the will and Divine Providence, the People of Israel earned the right to speak in the name of revealed truth.

There is still need for the Jewish negation of the pagan tendency to view life as subject to the law of necessity. Such a tendency may be discerned even in a work like Hegel's philosophy of history. Though it purports to be a description of the progress of the spirit, it nevertheless assumes that the law of inner necessity, like that of birth, growth and decay, or the dialectic of process, controls the course of the progress. Therein it merely repeats in different terms the fundamental error of paganism.

So long as Judaism was in danger of being swamped by the pagan world, Formstecher maintains, it elaborated its system of religious observances as a means of self-protection. Otherwise, it tries to be free of anything that is likely to narrow its scope. It is not even tied down to any particular country or State, because both its spirit and its message are universal.

The pagan nations, Formstecher maintains, were bound to develop to a point of self-consciousness, where they could no longer be satisfied with their limited knowledge of God, and they had to turn to Judaism for a truer knowledge of God. This accounts for the rise of Christianity and Mohammedanism. Christianity, on the one hand, liberated the Jewish ethical message from its particularistic shell, and on the other, compromised with the pagan conception of God as revealed in nature rather than in spirit. The doctrine of incarnation was a compromise to which Christianity acceded, in order to appeal to the pagan world, which was not yet ready for the complete adoption of the religion of the spirit.

Mankind, Formstecher holds, is still under the dominance of the pagan tendency to identify God with the inexorable law of nature. That is evident in the various formulations of world history as the working out of some iron law of necessity. So long as that is the case, it is Judaism's mission to emphasize the freedom of the spirit and to deprecate all speculations, whether religious or philosophical, which point to some inevitable eschatological outcome. To Judaism, this world is adequate for man's salvation. All speculations concerning the beyond which have come to be part of Traditional Judaism are really extraneous to it, and in conflict with its essential spirit.

SAMUEL HIRSCH (1815-1889)

In 1842, the year after the appearance of Formstecher's Die Religion des Geistes, came Samuel Hirsch's Die Religionsphilosophie der Juden.[12] Samuel Hirsch was born in Rhenish Prussia in 1815. After serving three years (1838-1841) in the rabbinate at Dessau, the native town of Moses Mendelssohn, he resigned on account of his unorthodox views. In 1843, he received a Government appointment as chief rabbi of Luxembourg, then a Grand Duchy of Holland. During that period he took an active part in the growing Reform movement and contributed to its literature. In 1866 he left for the United States, where he was appointed rabbi of the Reform Congregation, Keneset Israel, of Philadelphia. In 1869 he had occasion, as president of a rabbinical conference in that city, to draw up the principles of Reform Judaism.

Samuel Hirsch states in the Introduction to his Religionsphilosophie der Juden that he was prompted to write his opus magnum by the fact that Judaism was only tolerated, but not given the status of an authorized religion, as was Christianity. He also wished to refute the charge that the Jews were eager to obtain their emancipation mainly because of the material advantage they hoped to derive from it. He declares that "mere tolerance is intolerable." He expresses resentment at the royal decree of 1822 which forbade the rise of new sects among Jews, and their intermarrying with Christians, unless they pledged themselves to bring up the children as Christians.

In that same Introduction, he writes: "The Jews are not, as one often hears many Jews themselves say, a religious denomination (eine Confession). They constitute a nationality. A Jew is such by virtue of birth." He takes care, however, at once to qualify that statement by adding that the Jews are not a nationality like any other. Their nationality is purely spiritual in character. "We hope," he adds, "that in Jerusalem a House will again be built that will serve as a visible House of Prayer for all nations."

Approaching the problem of Judaism as a religion entirely from the standpoint of the Hegelian dialectic, Hirsch challenges Hegel's conclusions. Hirsch believes that progress in the consciousness of the freedom to choose between good and evil, which is the main evidence we have of the functioning of the spirit, is achieved as much through religion as through philosophy, whereas, according to Hegel, philosophy begins where religion leaves off. The Hegelians regarded religion as a less adequate means of knowing God, and its history as repeated on a higher level when it became the history of philosophy. The anti-Hegelians, on the other hand, maintained that religion was a higher form of the knowledge of God than philosophy, because based on conscience and intuitive ideas.

According to Hirsch, both are wrong. Philosophy is itself an integral part of religion, testing it by the highest standards of reason and conscience. To Hirsch it is not religion in the abstract that is a means to spiritual freedom. That is true, according to him, only of the specific religion of the Sacred Scriptures, to the interpretation of which he gives considerable attention in his book. Although that book is not intended to be a commentary on the Bible, it reminds one of Philo's writings. His interpretation of Judaism, however, does not confine itself to the Biblical text; it includes also vast segments from Rabbinic lore.

Hirsch accepts from the philosophic Idealism of his time the postulate that man's capacity for moral freedom is the source of his awareness of God. He therefore finds in the story of the fall of Adam the Jewish view concerning the origin of sin. That story, he maintains, implies that Adam acted on the false assumption that it was futile for him to try to oppose nature, since the human spirit was too weak to control it. That false assumption is symbolized by the temptation of Eve.

Here again Hirsch takes issue with Hegel. According to Hegel, man is destined ultimately to lose his natural freedom, or the capacity to sin. According to Hirsch, however, if man is to realize his spiritual freedom, he has to retain the capacity to sin. Man enhances his essential freedom whenever he uses his natural instincts in its service. Hirsch finds support for this idea in Rabbinic teaching that "everything is in God's hand, except the fear of God." [13] This is contrary to the Christian and the Hegelian assumption that man, under the curse of his original sin, must of necessity sin. That affords Hirsch occasion to emphasize the role of Judaism as being that of stressing man's inalienable freedom of the spirit.

Hirsch's conception of nature is somewhat different from that of Formstecher. To Formstecher, nature is synonymous with the entire manifold of physical phenomena. To Hirsch, however, nature is mainly the life of impulse, in contrast with the life of the spirit, or freedom. The reality of God is experienced whenever man succeeds in subduing his impulses and asserting his inner freedom. God is to be found everywhere and at all times, and all vicissitudes of fortune are an educational means of eliciting that inner freedom.

Hirsch takes issue with Formstecher also in his estimate of paganism. Whereas Formstecher, like Herder and other German thinkers, especially Schelling, treats paganism as the inevitable child-stage of humanity, Hirsch retains the Biblical evaluation of it as moral perversion and rebellion against God. He reads that interpretation of paganism also into the story of Paradise, thus once again discovering in paganism the mortal error from which it is Judaism's function to redeem mankind, the error of regarding sin as inevitable. He brackets the Greek and Roman religions entirely with paganism. In this, too, he differs from Hegel, who saw in those religions evidence of spiritual progress.

In a long dissertation on the history of religion for which Hirsch draws upon contemporary German anthropology, he discusses the growth of paganism from the standpoint of his initial assumption concerning the nature of sin and of moral freedom. He passes in review fetishism, shamanism, Chinese civilization and religion, Hindu civilization and religion, Buddhism and Brahmanism, the religions of Persia, Near East, Egypt, the religion of the pagan Semites, as well as the religions of Greece and Rome. He does not spare the pagan philosophies. In all of them he detects the fatal premise of the inevitability of sin. He then takes up the history of Israel, which begins with Abraham.

In Hirsch's opinion, only the People of Israel broke definitely with paganism. He derives this from the fact that the People of Israel has as its prototype Abraham who, having been born and bred a pagan, became an idol-breaker and a seeker of the true God. A man who achieves the moral freedom of true religion cannot rest until he communicates it to his fellow-men, intense love for whom impels him to bring to them the message of salvation. This kind of religion is communicated only by leading an exemplary life. Such is the mission which the People of Israel has inherited from its ancestors. In the fulfillment of that mission, it has had to endure great suffering. But even its suffering has not been in vain, for through its ability to survive in the face of all it has had to endure, the Jewish People demonstrates the limited power of evil.

In the evolution of religion, two things happened simultaneously. In the case of the People of Israel, the spirit of true religion attained a point where it could no longer remain confined to one people, but had to reach out to the rest of mankind. At the same time, the rest of mankind, which was pagan, came to a point where corruption could go no further, and, in order to save itself from extinction, it turned to the redeeming power of spiritual religion. It was just then that Jesus appeared on the scene. The place in Jewish history which Hirsch assigns to Jesus evoked opposition not only from Jews but also from Christians. He offended the latter by maintaining that the Gospel of Matthew was the only one which gave an objective account of Jesus, in that it was free from anti-Jewish bias. In that Gospel, Jesus appears as a full-fledged Jew.

Hirsch maintains that, because Jesus came from an intensely Jewish environment, his personality and fate constituted a turning point in the epic of the Jewish religion. Jesus realized in himself fully the ideal of the Jewish religion, which was that the Kingdom of God would be established when *every one* of the Jewish People became what the Jewish People *as a whole* was destined to become. Jesus wanted to be the first to set an example to the rest of his People. This is what Jesus meant by calling himself "the Son of God." He deprecated the attempt to regard his sonship as unique. Such was the Christianity of Jesus which, according to Hirsch, would never have broken with Judaism.

The tragedy of the break with Judaism came through the Apostle

Paul. Paul misunderstood and misrepresented Judaism when he insisted that it was opposed to the teaching of God as sin-forgiving love, or that it minimized the importance of faith as a prerequisite to the fulfillment of the Law. With his doctrine of original sin and redemption, Paul caused Christianity to place itself in opposition to reason. Origen, one of the Church Fathers of the third century still believed in individual responsibility, and not in the idea of original sin, as did later Augustine and Calvin. Pauline Christianity, instead of uniting man and God as Hegel had claimed, only widened the gulf between them. When Christianity is rid of Paulinism, Hirsch maintained, it will not only be again at one with Judaism, but come to be an adequate religion for the whole of mankind. That is the Messianic Era, for the sake of which the Jewish People must retain its individuality and be prepared to play the part of the Suffering Servant of God. Its individuality is not political, cultural or national in character. It is entirely spiritual, in that it serves as a symbol of human destiny in general. The example set by Jesus should be adopted by the entire Jewish People.

The philosophy of Judaism as formulated by Hirsch is marked by a spirit of fidelity to tradition as well as originality and daring. He maintained that the teachings of Scripture were inherently authoritative, and therefore unaffected by problems of date or origin of their formulation. He found no difficulty in accepting the historicity of the miracles recorded in the Scriptures. That acceptance he extended even to the New Testament, and felt no compunction, as a Jew, in regarding the resurrection of Jesus as actually having taken place.

Hirsch, however, attached no significance to the *occurrence* of miracles; he stressed rather their educational value. Thus, according to him, the reason God revealed himself to the People of Israel by means of theophanies was that He wanted to prove that nature was not all-powerful. The miracles in Egypt were meant to demonstrate the absurdity of glorifying nature, as the Egyptians had been wont to do. Likewise, the resurrection of Jesus is explained on the ground that God wanted the personality of Jesus to continue to influence the lives of his disciples. But once having learned the lesson of true religion, the Jewish People is in no need of miracles.

All the religious observances occupy an important place in Hirsch's version of Judaism of the future. Strangely enough, he does not find it necessary to eliminate from Judaism the Messianic hope of a return to Eretz Yisrael, though he definitely repudiates the other-worldly outlook of Rabbinic Judaism. That outlook, according to Hirsch, developed in Judaism when it came under Persian influence, and should be disassociated once again from it. Not other-worldliness, but Messianism, expresses the inherent goal of Judaism.

In the last part of his book, Hirsch comes to grips with Christian theology and modern philosophy. He is outspoken against the failings of Protestantism and the shortcomings of Kant, Fichte, Schleiermacher, Schelling and Hegel. He finally concludes with a conception of human history in which both Christianity and Judaism have their special tasks assigned to them. The main source of inspiration for Christianity should not be the Bible, but its own sacred history. Man was created free, but he sinned. Then came Abraham and made man free. Therefore, God elected his descendants as the instrument of His education through miracles, prophecy, punishments and rewards. When the Jews finally learned their lesson, Jesus, the man of perfect obedience to God, appeared. With him, sacred history came to an end. That sacred history is a microcosm of world history and is the main source of religious teaching. What educated one nation to value spiritual freedom can also educate the other nations.

The Catholic Church, writes Hirsch, should evangelize the heathens, and the Evangelical churches should evangelize the secular life. Neither, however, should attempt to convert the Jews. They were in possession of the truth long before Catholicism and Protestantism, and they have to live according to it in their own specifically Jewish way. The Hegelians are right in advocating that the State be Christian, provided it strive to emulate Jesus and it be not anti-Jewish. That is good Jewish doctrine, for according to Rabbinic teaching,[14] when the law of the State is not the arbitrary law of tyrants, but derives from a constitution, it is on a par with divine law.

The goal of human existence is the realization of spiritual freedom in this world. All relations among individuals and nations and classes must be based on justice. That is Messianism. When the Jews fulfil their vocation and lead a pure and holy life, the Gentiles will love them, follow their example and thus usher in the Messianic era. In that era, the Jewish People and the nations will profess alike the unity of God. Whatever distinctive cult the Jews will have will be respected and loved by the nations and may even be shared by them. The nations will restore the Jews to Jerusalem, not to set up a Jewish state—no special State will be necessary—but to establish the Jewish national cult which will symbolize the universal mission of Israel.

Both Formstecher and Samuel Hirsch were fully aware that their version of Judaism was a radical transformation of the traditional religion of their People. That did not deter them, however, from promulgating their own versions. They were convinced that they were revitalizing the Judaism of tradition, by accentuating what they regarded as the essential elements in it, and making it relevant to the prevailing mode of thought in their day. The part of the tradition which they renounced was, they believed, the expendable product of historical conditions. To both Formstecher and Samuel Hirsch, Judaism was inherently a *rational* religion. Formstecher's exposition of it implied a definite break with the traditional belief in the supernatural origin of the Torah and in the theophany at Sinai as historic. Hirsch's exposition is less frank on that point, but that it was no longer in line with tradition is quite unmistakable.

We should hardly expect that any Jew in the Germany of that period who was versed in science and philosophy, and who was on the point of accepting Christianity, would be deeply scandalized by these rationalizing efforts of men like Formstecher and Hirsch. Yet that was the case with Solomon Ludwig Steinheim, (1789-1865). He was a noted physician who, because of ill health, retired from his profession and devoted himself to the study of philosophy and religion. The result of his studies is embodied in four volumes on Judaism entitled *Die Offenbarung nach dem Lehrbegriff der Synagoge*. The first volume appeared in 1835, and the last in 1865.

Despite his having lived in a non-Jewish environment and his slender knowledge of Jewish sources, he writes with an air of dogmatic certainty about Judaism. He assails vehemently those with whose views he does not concur. He is as much displeased with S. D. Luzzatto and Samson Raphael Hirsch of the right wing as he is with Formstecher and Samuel Hirsch of the left wing. He charges Luzzatto and Samson R. Hirsch with substituting the law of God for the self-revelation of God, or orthopraxy for othodoxy, and Formstecher and Samuel Hirsch with catering to paganism though appearing to combat it. A philosophic religion is to him as absurd as a squared circle.[15]

Steinheim makes a brave attempt to prove that supernatural revelation can be verified by the same method as that employed in scientific and philosophic thinking. His main source for this affirmation is the negative element in the Kantian system of thought, in which pure reason is shown to be incompetent to deal with experience other than that derived from the senses. Instead, however, of going along with Kant in his conclusions concerning the "practical reason," Steinheim prefers to resort to supernatural revelation for the truths that are necessary for man's ethical and spiritual life. He finds in Judaism the supernatural revelation which is free of all such pagan notions as are essentially forms of fatalism, whether expressed as religion or as philosophy. Little force as there is to his critique of the modern reconstructions of Judaism, the alternative he offers is even less convincing. That alternative is to adhere to the belief in a supernatural revelation that transcends human understanding. It is no wonder, therefore, that Steinheim's was a lone voice.

JEWISH PEOPLEHOOD REDUCED TO INVISIBILITY

The Reformist theologians, realizing that they had deprived the Jews of outward and visible means of maintaining their group identity, went out of their way to stress what might serve as an inner and invisible means of achieving that purpose. In place of ethnicity with its social instruments of authority, such as code law, communal organization, and enforceable sanctions, they stressed the idea of Israel's Messiahship. This idea was intended to give the Jews something that was the analogue of the "Church Invisible," in which the bond of unity was none other than the state of mind, or subjective feeling, experienced in common by the members of a religious body. Thus the inner bond which Reform expected would unite all Jews was the consciousness of being identified with Israel, the Messiah People. "Reform Judaism has thus accepted the belief," says Kaufmann Kohler,[16] "that Israel, the suffering Messiah of the centuries, shall at the end of days become the triumphant Messiah of the nations."

The foregoing was the new function which the traditional belief in the election of the People of Israel assumed when the hope of a return to Eretz Yisrael was repudiated, and the ethnic character of Judaism treated as a particularistic element which had been rendered obsolete by the Emancipation. The function of being a "Messiah People" was not to be merely part of the general world-pattern in which the Jews were to take their place. It was regarded as the sum and substance of Judaism, as not only the one truly universal religion, but also as the only religion that was free from beliefs which offended either reason or the moral sense. Reform, in its classic expression, expected the Jews to be so imbued with the awareness of being dedicated to the Messianic ideal that they would not need the artificial or material bonds of either land or polity. Not always had the meaning of that ideal been stated in such specific terms as were set forth by A. Adler at the Frankfurt Conference in 1845. He defined the belief in the coming of the Messianic era as the assurance of the perfectibility of mankind on earth.[17]

It soon became apparent, however, to the leading Reformists, that the Messianic ideal, despite its grandiose character, was by itself not sufficently capable of giving a sense of corporate unity to the Jews. They, therefore, looked to certain ceremonial or ritual observances as a means of symbolizing various aspects of the Messianic ideal, thereby bringing it repeatedly to mind. At the Frankfort Conference, David Einhorn said: "The idea of the Messiah is most closely connected with the whole ceremonial law." [18] That principle supplied the leaders of Reform with the criteria which they needed for determining the place of Hebrew, the Sabbath and the festivals, circumcision and the regulations governing marriage and proselytism, in the scheme of Jewish living. Perhaps the clearest evidence of their subconscious desire to retain the sense of ethnic solidarity is to be found in their insistence on remaining *within* the frame of the organized local community. This contrasts sharply with the equal insistence of the Neo-Orthodox leaders on *seceding* from whatever community tolerated ritual innovations. The Orthodox leaders found sufficient basis for Jewish solidarity in the conformity to the *Shulhan Aruk*.

Reformism's efforts at de-ethnicizing Judaism transformed the pattern of Traditional Judaism almost beyond recognition. The essence of the traditional pattern consisted in the centrality, or primacy, of the Pentateuchal legislation, which included cult law as well as civil, administrative and criminal law. Whatever in the form of exhortation and instruction was contained in the Torah, and in the rest of the Sacred Scriptures, was regarded as a means of stimulating obedience to the laws of the Torah. Into this pattern Reform introduced two new categories: the particularistic and the universal. It treated the legislative part of the Torah as particularistic in character, and the hortatory and didactic parts of the Torah as universal.

Actually, however, those two facets of the Torah are inseparable and meaningless apart from each other. All life and action express themselves in the particular, and take on meaning when the particular is subsumed under some universal principle. *The particular without the universal is blind; the universal without the particular is empty*. Throughout the past, both the main stream of Judaism, as well as the deviations from it, were particular and universal at the same time. Even a deviation like Karaism retained the fundamental pattern of Judaism no less than did Rabbinism, in that it maintained the centrality of the Torah with its legislative aspect. Though it repudiated Rabbinic Judaism, Karaism nevertheless remained true to the *historic pattern* of Judaism.

This cannot be said of the modern Reform movement. It has reified each of the two aspects of Judaism, the ethnic and the religious, and treated them as though they could be severed from each other existentially. Having done that, it has arbitrarily transformed the historic pattern of Judaism. It maintains that the particularist element to be found in the Torah was conditioned by the circumstances that prevailed in ancient times and is therefore obsolete. Only the hortatory and didactic—or the Prophetic element—is eternal and, therefore the essence of Judaism. "The religious writings of Judaism" wrote D. Dérenbourg, "contain only in their hortatory and historical parts—or, in the prophetic parts, if we are to use 'prophetic' in a wide sense—revealed truth. Among the laws, on the other hand, are to be found formulas which have either disappeared, or will disappear in course of time." [19]

This distinction between the prophetic and the legal is not a revaluation, but a transvaluation of Jewish values. It is so definitely akin to the antinomianism of Paul of Tarsus that one wonders why the leaders of Reform failed to credit him with having anticipated them by eighteen centuries in what was, after all, according to them, the proper understanding of Judaism.

The fact is that the Reformist theologians labored under the illusion that the time had come for the Jewish religion to enter upon an active campaign against Christianity, which they regarded as in error because of its deification of Jesus. In order, however, to be qualified to carry on such a campaign, Judaism had to be able to prove that it was as antinomian and universalistic as Pauline Christianity claimed to be. To achieve that purpose, they tried to remold Judaism into a kind of Christless Christianity. They even took over the Christian interpretation of the first thousand years of Israel's history. Instead of regarding that period as the norm and ideal, which it has been for Traditional Judaism, Reform has been viewing it as a preparatory stage for a consummation which took place when the Second Temple was destroyed and the Jews were dispersed throughout all parts of the world. [20]

Although the Reformists renounced the ethnicity of the Jews, they could not entirely renounce their corporate individuality without reading themselves out of Judaism. However much they stressed the claim that Judaism was an idea—the idea of ethical monotheism, or of Messianism—they could not altogether ignore the fact that the Jews did constitute a corporate entity. They could not help sensing that the problem of Judaism was a problem of getting the Jews to know themselves as members of a body that had had a long history. They tried to find a suitable term for this corporate individuality which would differentiate if from a nation, but which would, nevertheless, help to maintain its unity and solidarity. That accounts for much in the Reform movement that seems inconsistent in its philosophy and program.

The basic assumption of early Reform was that nothing was as important for the salvation of the human being as the true conception of God, and that the Jews, being in possession of such a conception of God, held the key to universal salvation. The great interest in theology displayed by the spokesmen of early Reform derived from that assumption. Reform theology was marked by endless reiteration of its claim that the Jewish conception of God was superior spiritually and ethically to that of any philosophy or of any other religion. It can hardly be said, however, that it produced any profound scientific or philosophic evidence in support of that claim.

A most amazing development in Reform theology has been the gradual dessication of the belief in immortality. That belief has seldom received the serious discussion that its place in Traditional religion would seem to warrant. Outstanding theologians like Hermann M. Cohen and Claude G. Montefiore touch upon that belief only to dismiss it either as of secondary importance, as compared with the belief in a Messianic era, or as one without any significant content. "We, too, believe in a life to come," says Claude Montefiore, "but it is to most of us a wistful hope, the needful corollary of our belief in God. We are not greatly moved by any conceptions or anticipations of reward or of punishment. They have become unreal to us. The ideas of a final judgment or of resurrection have passed away. So, too, with the conception of a great catastrophe, a divine intervention, of a Messiah and of a prolonged Messianic age upon earth, when the people of Israel would be triumphant and the position of Top Dog and Under Dog (in relation to themselves and the nations) would be reversed."[21]

Classic Reform's attempts to prove the rational and ethical superiority of Judaism failed to impress even liberal Christians. Emil G. Hirsch, the son of Samuel Hirsch, was an outstanding leader of the Reform movement in America during the last two decades of the nineteenth century and the first two of the twentieth. In commenting on his exposition of Judaism as formulated in his posthumus *My Religion*, Dean Shailer Matthews of Chicago University notes that Hirsch's religion is essentially no different from that of liberal Christians, except in the display of an *ethnic* attachment and bias from which those Christians were free.[22]

The entire approach of the Reformist theologians to the interpretation of the Jewish religion is largely competitive and apologetic. In the light of their basic assumption concerning the nature of Judaism, it could hardly be otherwise. Judaism, as a religion pure and simple, has to justify itself on the ground that it is superior both rationally and ethically to other religions. This it cannot do without considerable idealization or distortion of the facts involved. Many a Rabbinic doctrine is pronounced by the expounders of Liberal Judaism as "childish, foolish and nonsensical." [23] Neither is it in keeping with truth to say, as Kaufmann Kohler does, that in each particular age Judaism was in the vanguard of moral and religious progress. It cannot be contended, for example, that Judaism of the age of Plato excelled in moral grandeur the ethical idealism of Plato in his "reasoned justification of goodness for its own sake and not for its rewards, his doctrine of the superiority of suffering over the infliction of it, or his doctrine of the imitation of God in the pursuit of justice, wisdom and holiness."

One need only read the summing up of the Reform version of Judaism, as given by one of its ablest and staunchest champions, to realize how near to bankruptcy Judaism was brought by the Reform attempt to reduce it to a system of individual salvation. What Claude G. Montefiore has to say in the "Epilogue to the Legacy of Israel," [24] amounts to a *reductio ad absurdum* of the basic assumption of early Reform. The following is a summary of the main points he stresses.

1. In spite of the apparent presumption on the part of the Jews that they are in possession of the truest conception of God, they persist in their claim.
2. The Jewish conception of God is still in the process of development.
3. The influence of the Jewish conception of God will begin to make itself felt after all artificial barriers between Jews and Gentile are broken down.
4. The Jews, ten million of them, should enlist in the defense of Theism against indifferentism and atheism.
5. The Jewish religion and the Christian religion do not contradict each other. On the contrary, they supplement each other. Both are one-sided. The concurrent existence of a certain one-sidedness may tend to enrich civilization.

Without entering into a detailed analysis of the foregoing theses and pointing out their remoteness from reality and their mutual

contradictions, it is sufficient to refer to Montefiore's own apprehension which, with his intellectual honesty and saintly character,
he could not withhold from expressing. He himself characterizes
the foregoing theses as "vague and shadowy hopes and anticipations which none beyond Israel can fully share, and few even can
adequately appreciate."

Perhaps the most damaging circumstance in Montefiore's conception of Judaism as a religion is that he, like his colleagues in
Reform Judaism, failed to reckon with the scientific approach to
the study of religion. This becomes evident when he gives away
the entire case for Judaism in a statement the main point of which
is that there can be no religion that is uniformly capable of serving the interests of all men and nations at all times. That in effect
denies that there can be a religion which is universally valid or
acceptable. How does that square with the contention that
Judaism is, or can become, a universal religion?

"It may well be," he says,[25] "that one religion, and even a particular phase or form of one religion, may be more suited to a given
age, a given nation, a given individual than another. Could any
kind of Christianity have been so suited to certain peoples or
races in the world as Islam has been or even still is? Could any
sort of Judaism have won such conquests as Christianity has won
and is still winning?" And later he adds. "In religions, as in human
characters, the words hold: *Suum cuique*, to each its own, its
excellences and qualities."

CHAPTER NINE

The Reform
Movement
in the U.S.A.

ટે THE PROTO-REFORM STAGE

The Reform movement encountered too many obstacles in Central Europe to make any headway there. In the course of a few decades, it virtually died out. Every one of the numerous Governments of Germany and Austria, with very few exceptions, had its own way of meddling in the religious affairs of the Jews, with the express purpose of hindering the introduction of any innovations in the Jewish way of life and worship. They expected that, as a result of such policy, the more ambitious and progressively-minded Jews might be driven to apostacy.

When David Einhorn (1809-1879), a noted scholar and theologian, was elected rabbi in Wellhausen, Bavaria, in 1838, the Munich Government refused to confirm his election. When in 1852 he was elected rabbi in Budapest, the Austrian Government closed the temple of the congregation. On the one hand, the Governments insisted that the rabbis should receive a modern academic training, and on the other, they inhibited the rabbis from carrying into effect the plans and hopes called forth by such training. The rabbis who advocated Reform were eager to find a way of enabling the Jews to survive as a distinct group, without affording the Governments any excuse for refusing to give the Jews full civil rights. But *the continued dominance of the Church in the*

European countries was responsible for the State's hampering of the free and untrammeled evolution of Judaism.

In the prevailing political structure of the States in Central Europe during the greater part of the nineteenth century, the Church continued to figure as an integral part of the State. Privileged status would be conferred on one of the Christian denominations, while the rest, by reason of their dissent, were given inferior status. The Jews, whose status was even lower than that of the dissenting Christian denominations, were treated as third-class citizens. Thus, despite some amelioration of their lot, the Jews continued to be segregated from the rest of the population and had to maintain their communal organization and unity. Those with Reform leanings were, in the nature of the case, very much in the minority. They could not organize for the purpose of introducing innovation without antagonizing the traditionalists, who could easily, and often did, invoke Government aid in resisting those innovations. Even if the traditionalists did not go that far, they refused to permit any of the communal resources to be used for activities of a Reform character. That discouraged those in the rabbinate who were sympathetic to Reform from advocating any changes. Young scholars with aspirations for the rabbinate who were convinced of the need of reforms could not look forward to any field in which to pursue their calling. That led many who wished to exercise spiritual leadership on Reform lines to migrate to the United States.

Some time before rabbis with Reform learnings began to migrate to the United States, several small Jewish communities there tried to introduce innovations in their mode of worship. The first such community was the one in Charleston, which consisted for the most part of descendants of Spanish-Portuguese Jews. For a long time they had made it a point to stress their provenance and to retain the Sephardic mode of worship. By 1824, however, when a number of them circulated a petition for some changes in their forms of worship, very few in that community had any appreciable knowledge of Hebrew or understanding of Judaism. The changes asked for involved not merely the occasional delivery of sermons and the substitution of the vernacular for Hebrew in the liturgy, but also the elimination of some traditional tenets, like the one concerning the resurrection and the advent of a personal Messiah.

The report of the current agitation for religious reforms in some of the German Jewish communities in Europe stimulated the petitioners to take action. When those in authority denied their petition, they seceded and organized themselves as "The Reformed Society of Israelites." That society did not last long, because it had no trained religious leader. By 1841, however, the original congregation, which had suffered loss through the secession, not only adopted the changes which had been requested, but also introduced additional ones. This action was taken under the leadership of Gustav Poznanski who had come under the influence of the Reform movement in Hamburg.

Similar unrest showed itself in a few other communities during those early years of the nineteenth century, but nothing came of it for lack of spiritual leadership. That leadership began to be provided, however, as soon as a number of rabbis and candidates for the rabbinate who held Reform views began to arrive in the United States. The most prominent among them were Max Lilienthal, Samuel Hirsch, Isaac M. Wise, Kaufmann Kohler, David Einhorn, Samuel Adler and Bernhard Felsenthal. These came during the fifties, sixties, and seventies of the nineteenth century. Though they all contributed, each in his own way, to the furtherance of the movement, is is doubtful whether they would have had a lasting influence had not Isaac M. Wise been one of them. He was the founder of the three institutions without which the Reform movement could not have made much headway. Those institutions are the Union of American Hebrew Congregations, founded in 1873, the Hebrew Union College, in 1879, and the Central Conference of American Rabbis, in 1889.

If we are to judge Reform from the point of view of its purpose to domesticate Judaism in the particular non-Jewish environment in which it happens to be, then Isaac M. Wise was only one of the group of rabbis who seemed capable of coping with the conditions in the United States. His colleagues were outstanding personalities and men of great learning and eloquence. But they brought with them the preconceptions and thought habits of their Central European nativity. "Reform Judaism is a German importation," said K. Kohler.[1] "Men unfamiliar with German philosophy and philology can have no real understanding of the development of the leading principles of the Reform movement." "Where German is barred," said David Einhorn, "Reform of Judaism is soul-less." [2]

The attitude implied in such sentiments made most of those who had come to the United States fully panoplied in the armor of Reform Judaism unfit for adjusting themselves to the situation which they found there. In Jewish, as well as in other cultural and religious respects, the United States was then largely frontier country. Isaac M. Wise, though possessing a well-rounded general and traditional Jewish education, did not consider scientific Jewish scholarship the prime requisite for the rabbinate. The fascination which the United States with its freedom and unexplored possibilities had for him led him to look to the fulfillment there of the dream which an Abraham Geiger and a Samuel Hirsch had cherished of a Judaism that would supersede Christianity as the universal religion of mankind.

ISAAC M. WISE (1819-1900)

Isaac M. Wise had received the old-time rabbinic training which enabled him to obtain the traditional *semikah*, or authorization to function as rabbi. In addition, he had received a literary training which gave him a facility for writing and speaking in both German and English. That facility stood him in good stead in the part he was to play as the founder of the Reform movement in the United States. The writings and endeavors of men like Geiger, Holdheim and Samuel Hirsch had shaped his thinking. The first community in Bohemia, however, which he had served as rabbi for three years was too set in its ways, and too far removed from the mainstream of the modern movements, to be amenable to religious reform. That, together with the inferior political status of Jews in his country, led him to migrate to the United States in 1846.

In the United States Wise found the Jewish life of those who had come over recently devoid of all culture and esthetic form. The interest in Judaism on the part of the long-established Jewish families was limited to a cold formal adherence to traditional observances that had lost all meaning for them. Among both the earlier and the recent arrivals he noted a decided materialistic and atheistic trend and a strong drift toward assimilation. But his was not the temperament to be disheartened by what he found. He realized that the New World was still inchoate. "The reforming spirit was in me," he writes in his *Reminiscences*. "It was my foremost characteristic. In addition to this, I was an enthusiast on the subject of America and freedom, and was convinced that everyone felt and thought just as I did. Consequently, I would begin at once to reform and improve the world." [3]

Wise had been only three years in this country when he sat for eight successive days in the Senate gallery, the first to come and the last to leave, in order to listen and absorb every word of the great debate concerning the conditions under which California was to be admitted as a State. "Since then," he writes, "I never neglected an opportunity to go to Washington and to form the acquaintance of the leading men of the nation." "These," he adds, "have been my best teachers and my instructive reading." [4] That perhaps more than anything else in his self-education furnishes the best clue to the extent to which the American background influenced the development of the Reform movement in this country.

Wise's strength lay in winning adherents who followed his leadership and who enabled him to withstand the storm of opposition which his ideas and suggested innovations aroused. Soon after he landed he received a call to the Congregation Beth El in Albany. Before long, however, as he began to unfold his program for Judaism, the lines of battle were drawn between those in his congregation who were with him and those who were against him. The struggle led to an open scandal, which ended with the secession of his followers and their founding a congregation committed to the principles of Reform. From there he received a call to the Congregation B'nai Jeshurun in Cincinnati, where he served as spiritual leader until his dying day. With the moral and financial support he received from that congregation, he was able to carry out his far-reaching projects in the upbuilding of Reform Judaism in the United States.

Wise clearly recognized that the future of Judaism in this country demanded that the individualism in Jewish life, which was then rampant, be replaced by some kind of institutionalized guidance and social control. He was fully aware of the void created by the destruction of the old type of Jewish community. He sought to fill that void with some form of social, or religious, organization that would avail itself of the freedom from governmental coercion or outside interference with the inner life of Jews. With that in view, he proceeded to establish congregations in various scattered communities for the purpose of carrying on Jewish religious activities. He agitated constantly for the establishment of Jewish educational institutions ranging from the elementary school to academies of higher Jewish learning. He utilized every possible opportunity of speaking and writing to urge concerted action among all Jewish organizations and institutions.

Although he himself minimized his executive powers, he actually possessed the creative ability to bring into being cooperative undertakings in behalf of the Judaism he fervently believed in. He was able to communicate to others his sense of urgent need for organized effort. His zeal refused to stop short of complete unification of American Jewry. In those early years he dreamt of uniting all the Jews in this country for education, philanthropy, and all other communal activities.[5]

In 1855 Wise was instrumental in having all of the nine officiating rabbis in this country issue a call for a conference to take place in Cleveland. He hoped that the conference would lead to the establishment of a modern type of synod. "This union," he said, "was to include all shades of Jewish belief and practice." To achieve that purpose he went so far as to yield to the insistence of the Orthodox signers to the call that the Talmud be recognized as the final authority. That meant that only those changes for which sanction could be found in Talmudic law would be permitted. His Reform colleagues denounced his compromise, and the Orthodox lacked faith in it. In time, Wise gave up the hope of achieving over-all unity in American Jewry, and he confined himself to those of outspoken sympathy with Reform. His efforts were finally crowned with success. 1855 was the year when he organized the Zion College expressly, as he put it, "to train Jewish ministers."

Although Wise's main contribution to the Reform movement lay in having provided it with the appropriate instruments for its functioning, it is doubtful whether he could have been as effective as he was had he not at the same time been animated by a faith and philosophy which were the driving force behind all his efforts, and without which he would not have been able to surmount the many obstacles he encountered. Wise had implicit faith in the Ten Commandments as the essence of all moral and religious truth which God had revealed to Moses. In 1880, he published a *Formula*, in which he summed up what he described as "The historical basis of Reform, progressive and 'law'-abiding, an outline of a guide for our future synod."

The following is his characterization of the "Ten Words": "Its laws are *categories*, its doctrines fundamental principles; in its logical order it is a *unit*, and in its totality it comprises the *entire* substance of *theology* and *ethics*, to which no new category of law can be added and from which none can be taken away, without destroying its harmony, its divine *perfection*. . . . The body of law contained in the *Pentateuch* is called *Thorath Mosheh*, the Law of Moses, which (a) reduces to practice the fundamental law of the Decalogue, (b) provides the legal means to enforce it, and (c) expounds and expands its doctrines. . . .

"The *Doctrines* underlying any of these laws (in the Pentateuch) and reduced to practice by them are *contained* in the Decalogue and are eternal like it, while any law itself is the temporary application of those doctrines to regulate emergencies which depend on time, place and other transitory circumstances, like which it must be temporary and subject to amendment or abrogation by the *Proper Authorities*.

"Inasmuch as the doctrines in the Law of Moses had *ideal existence* in the *Decalogue* before they were embodied in those laws and the law itself is a mere application thereof; and inasmuch, furthermore, as the Decalogue was taught Israel by the agency of *Moses*, *every law* of the Pentateuch whenever, and by whomsoever written may *justly* be termed a *law of Moses*, as the whole body may justly be styled the law of Moses. . . .

"The only problem to be solved is: who shall *decide* for the *Community* of Israel which law or custom is an embodiment of a doctrine contained in the Decalogue, which should be preserved and which amended. For the *Individual*, the Decalogue, Conscience and Reason must decide and guide him to Salvation by righteousness." [6]

To Wise, Judaism was Mosaism, a universal religion that had been divinely revealed to Moses. In the course of years, it assimilated numerous extraneous beliefs and practices. All those acquisitions had helped the Jews to create for themselves the shell of nationhood within which they had sought safety against the physical and spiritual onslaughts of the hostile world around them. With the advent, however, of the new era of enlightenment and freedom, particularly in the United States, with its Constitution to guarantee the permanence of that era, Judaism had the opportunity of becoming at long last what it was orginally intended to be. It could become "Mosaism in action." All that it needed was to rid itself of all those oriental elements in it that were narrowly national and intrinsically alien to its spirit. It should concentrate on the ethics and theology of the Ten Commandments which are the very basis of all civilization. "The religion of the future," he said, "will be Judaism in its pure and denationalized form."

His optimism was unbounded. He had not the least doubt "that his system will and must triumph all over this country, and is THE Judaism of the coming generations . . . *that before this century will close*, the essence of Judaism will be THE religion of the great majority of all intelligent men of this country." [7]

The foregoing was written in 1858. In 1888 he wrote: "The world, without knowing or professing it, Judaizes very rapidly in the very sense of the Law of Moses, so that *we in this country, religiously observing the law of the land*, actually observe the law of Moses."

Wise then goes on to point out that American law has adopted in spirit, and at times even in the letter, ordinances pertaining to protection of marriage, of property, labor, chastity and honor. Both in American legislation and in American sentiment he recognized the acceptance of the Mosaic law of charity to protect the poor and the helpless. Even "the dietary and hygienic law of Moses are no less rapidly becoming the law of the land. Every city has its health office and officers to enforce cleanliness, to protect against venomous contagion, unwholesome food and water just as Moses ordained it."

All that optimism sprang from a faith in America and love for its institutions which only one who had come from the oppressive and suffocating atmosphere of reactionary Europe of the thirties and forties of the nineteenth century into the freedom-loving sections of the United States could possibly experience. America spelled for

Isaac M. Wise the advent of the millenium and of the Kingdom of God on earth. "The dominion of popes and nobles," he wrote in 1852, "found its grave in the progress of civilization, being opposed to liberty; so the dominion of monarchs equally odious will also find its grave in the rushing wave of time." The main basis for his extravagant expectations for America was its Federal Constitution which separated Church from State. That fact, combined with the unity of language, the rapid growth in the means of transportation and communications, the freedom of press and the prevalence of common sense, he was sure, would make of the heterogeneous elements of this country, by the beginning of the twentieth century, "not only the most numerous and wealthiest nation, but also ONE nation." [8]

Two great obstacles stood in the way of the realization of his great hopes for America and Israel: Orthodox Christianity and Orthodox Judaism. Orthodox Christianity was to him little more than the perpetuation of paganism and the principal source of the world-wide defamation and persecution of Jews. Now that mankind was struggling to free itself from the incubus of superstition and hatred, Orthodox Christianity was putting up a strong resistance by engaging in missionary activity in which Jews were to receive special attention, and by resorting to every possible device to nullify the separation of Church and State, which Wise regarded as the sine qua non of human progress.

To engage in polemics against Traditional Christianity was to Isaac M. Wise a duty which devolved upon American Jews, both as Americans and as Jews. He threw himself into that campaign with all the vigor at his command. He held up the personality of Moses as by far of greater spiritual stature than that of Jesus. He contended that, "Nowhere in the Pentateuch does Moses protrude his own personality to any degree comparable with the way Jesus does in the Gospel. It is God and not Moses who teaches, ordains, decrees, threatens or promises. On the other hand, Jesus so far identifies himself with God as to state: "I am the life, I am the light, I and the Father are one; whoever receives me receives not me, but Him Who sent me." It is interesting to note that Spinoza, in his *Tractalus Theologico-Politicus*,[9] makes out a case for Jesus as against Moses, on the ground that Jesus did not have to resort to supernatural revelation. Thus in religious polemic, it seems, the polemist always manages to prove his case by resorting to Scriptures.

Wise assailed Orthodox Judaism not for its creed but for its religious regimen. He deprecated the emphasis which Orthodox Jews placed on the meticulous observance of dietary laws. He maintained that the prescribed rules of ritual practices often served as a means of salving consciences. Wise, nevertheless, recognized the role those observances had played in unifying the Jews and giving them a sense of solidarity, which he valued highly. But even that could not atone, in his opinion, for the moral and spiritual complacency and the cultural stagnation which were generally the concomitants of strict adherence to ritual observance. He attributed the failure of Judaism to become a universal religion to its fixation on ritualism.

Wise's philosophy of Judaism was unrealistic and inconsistent. The individual congregations which he had organized and the congregational union which he succeeded in establishing were actually the product of his own inner urge to have Jews aware of their corporate unity. But he knew too little of the socio-psychologic aspect of religion to understand the role of such corporate unity in religion, or the dependence of religion upon common secular interests which presuppose social interaction for other than specifically religious purposes. He therefore could see nothing in Zionism but a veritable threat to his life's work. He described those who wished to establish a State in Palestine as "pessimists who despair of human reason, the progress of humanity and the solidarity of mankind. We, the citizens of the United States," he declared, "who believe in Moses and the prophets, are and hope to remain citizens of the United States, an integral element of this nation and of no other, with no earthly interests or aspirations different from those who believe in Jesus and his Apostles." [10] He even stooped to vituperation. "We American Jews," he said, "have nothing to do with Zionism, or that nationality swindle, simply because we are Jews by religion only and exclusively untouched by nationality humbug or race sophistry." [11] He was too naïve to realize to what extent *non-Jews* were far from "untouched by nationality humbug or race sophistry," and that Zionism was the only means of saving the Jews and Judaism from the demonic frenzy which was ultimately bound to break out in the Old World against Jews, and even to have its repercussions in the New World.

CENTRAL CONFERENCE OF AMERICAN RABBIS

As we look back to the early years of the Reform movement in the United States, we note that it took three decades from the time that Wise arrived in 1846 for the movement to begin to take on momentum. That was because it had to contend against heavy odds. It encountered the resistance of the Orthodox, the unresponsiveness of the indifferentists, and the personal rivalries among the Reform leaders themselves. In the midst of it all came the Civil War, which necessitated the suspension of all public activities that did not have a direct bearing on winning the war. The three conferences that were called after the one in Cleveland in 1855—those in Philadelphia in 1869, in Cincinnati in 1871, and in Pittsburgh in 1885—ended with the passing of resolutions to revise Rabbinic law, and with the declaration of principles which were not followed up by action. Of the various declarations, only one made history. That was the "Pittsburgh Platform," which was formulated in 1885 at the Conference that had been called by Kaufmann Kohler. That Platform, though never officially adopted by the lay or rabbinical bodies in the movement, nevertheless served as an authoritative guide until it was replaced by a set of "Guiding Principles," which were formally accepted by the Central Conference of American Rabbis at its annual convention in Columbus, Ohio in 1937.[12]

The following, in substance, are the affirmations of the Pittsburgh Platform:

1. Though every religion is an attempt to grasp the Infinite, Judaism represents "the highest conception of the God-idea."

2. Though the Bible reflects "the primitive ideas of its own time," its validity as "the record of the consecration of the Jewish people to its mission as the priest of the one God" is thereby not impugned.

3. Though Mosaic legislation was necessary to train the Jewish people for its mission during its national life in Palestine, only its

moral laws and "such ceremonies as elevate and sanctify our lives" are still binding.

4. All laws regulating diet, priestly purity and dress are "apt to obstruct modern spiritual elevation."

5. "The universal culture of heart and intellect of our day" is the beginning of "the realization of Israel's great Messianic hope for the establishment of the kingdom of truth, justice and peace among all men." Jews are "no longer a nation but a religious community, and therefore expect neither a return to Palestine, nor a sacrificial worship under the sons of Aaron, nor the restoration of any of the laws concerning the Jewish State."

6. Judaism is a progressive religion "ever striving to be in accord with the postulates of reason." It is of the utmost necessity to preserve "the historical identity with our great past." Christianity and Islam, as daughter religions of Judaism, have "their providential mission to aid in the spreading of monotheism and moral truth. . . . The spirit of broad humanity of our age is our ally in the fulfillment of our mission, and therefore we extend the hand of fellowship to all who operate with us in the establishment of the reign of truth and righteousness among men."

7. The belief in the immortality of the soul is reaffirmed, but the belief in bodily resurrection, Gehenna and *Gan Eden* is rejected.

8. In the spirit of Mosaic legislation, Jews should help solve "the problems presented by the contrasts and evils of the present organization of society."

Of the three institutions which were established by Isaac M. Wise, and which have since sustained the Reform movement in the United States and Canada—The Union of Hebrew Congregations, the Hebrew Union College, and the Central Conference of American Rabbis—the last named has been the soul of the movement. The Proceedings of the C C A R, which have been published since 1891, two years after its establishment, reflect the best thinking that has been done by the ever-increasing number of rabbis affiliated with Reform. Their resolutions, addresses and deliberations reflect the efforts of the Reform rabbinate to maintain Jewish individuality amid centrifugal forces generated by the American civilization, with its freedom from the hegemony of the Church.

The problems dealt with at the annual sessions of the Conference have mainly been the following: worship and liturgy, ritual observances, religious education, marriage and divorce proceedings, intermarriage, proselytism, scope of congregational activities, the unsynagogued Jew, the separation of Church and State, and social justice. Running through all those problems, as well as expressed independently, are the ideological and theological questions pertaining to the place of religion in human life and to the status of Jews as a group in relation to non-Jews and to the State. It is in connection with the problem of Jewish status that the Zionist movement especially has been the subject of heated debate since the beginning of the twentieth century.

Despite frequent divergencies, which on occasions were quite sharp, the opinions expressed in the *Proceedings* which are reviewed here and which cover more than six decades of the existence of the C C A R reflect a high degree of homogeneity. With every participant free to voice his ideas and proposals, there nevertheless emerges from all the papers, resolutions, and debates a definite and recognizable pattern in the thinking of the Reform group, on matters theoretic as well as practical.

Of primary interest, of course, is the ideology of the movement. By adopting the usual division of Judaism into its three aspects of God, Israel and Torah, we shall try to find in that ideology the answers to the question: *How has the Reform movement, as represented by its spiritual leaders in the United States and Canada, interpreted each of those aspects?* What follows in a summary of views expressed in the course of the early years of the existence of the C C A R.

Basic to the ideology of Reform is the question: "What, to Reform, has been the ultimate source of authority? Reason, experience, tradition, or some synthesis of all three?" It may, indeed, be said that those who have participated in the proceedings of the C C A R have been virtually unanimous in the assumption that rational experience alone is the *final* authority in Judaism. Though admittedly the Prophets beginning with Moses had been vouchsafed divine revelation, the authority of what they taught derived from its inherent rationality.

"Divine revelation," said Isaac M. Wise, "is the twin sister of pure reason" (1891). "Whatever militates against reason," said Tobias Schoenfarber, "should be shelved" (1892). "Reason is the supreme test. No book, code or literature can be final authority," said Samuel Sale (1895). In describing, in 1901, the march of Reform as an unbroken series of triumphs, Solomon H. Sonnenschein added, "Ethics above ritual, science superior to tradition." In 1902 Joseph Stolz argued that freedom of thought had never been denied the Jew in the synagogue; the intolerance shown to a Spinoza, or an Uriel da Costa, had been acquired from the Christian environment. Though these facts are open to question, there can be no doubt that, to Stolz, Judaism was a religion based on reason. The supremacy of reason was taken for granted in all the deliberations of the CCAR. Only since the Second World War, when Existentialism began to seep into the thinking of some disillusioned intellectuals and some Christian and Jewish theologians, have irrationalism and mysticism crept into the deliberations of the Reform Conferences.

A possible exception, even in the early days of the CCAR, to the apparent unanimity on the supremacy of reason in Jewish religion might be deemed the attitude toward Biblical criticism. It is there that tradition and reason came into unmistakable conflict. We thus hear Julian Morgenstern in 1908 declaring that Biblical criticism should be hailed as "having made the Bible human, having reclaimed it for Judaism, and freed it from all Christology." He further maintained that far from being destructive and anti-Jewish, Biblical criticism is both constructive and Jewish. It is indispensable, in that it proves Judaism to be the product of historical evolution. From that fact Morgenstern drew the logical conclusion that the Bible was not to be treated as a source of authority but as a source of inspiration.

Morgenstern was far more consistent in his Reform thinking than Isaac M. Wise, who in 1895 had declared: "Our attitude toward post-Biblical literature is that of a religious treasure-house, not as binding authority. The Union Prayer Book declares that we are faithful to the Canon of Israel—the Bible." At the 1915 Conference, Morgenstern deplored the anomaly that Biblical science was neglected by Jewish scholars and rabbis. He pointed out that most non-Jewish scholars frequently employed Biblical scholarship as a means of venting their anti-Jewish prejudices. He therefore pleaded that rabbis and teachers of Judaism should be trained in the scientific approach to Bible and to Jewish history.

It would be caricaturing the Reform emphasis on the supremacy of reason to charge the Reform movement with having been devoid of emotion and a stranger to piety. That attitude toward reason had a bearing only on the authority of tradition but not on the spiritual realities which were the subject matter of the tradition. Faith in God, in the high destiny of Israel, in God's Kingdom on earth, these matters were expected to call forth a deep emotional response and were to be approached in a spirit of self-consecration. Kaufmann Kohler, who himself was an outstanding Jewish scholar, unquestionably stressed the need of rendering Judaism a soul-stirring religion. "I blame," he said, "the old-school theologians (since Zunz) for having made of Judaism an archaeological and philosophical science rather than a life force of human history, a system of ethical and spiritual life superior to any other. Our entire history and literature require reshaping and recasting in that spirit. Away with that insipid rationalism which chills and deadens life" (1894).

THE AVOWED AND THE UNCONSCIOUS AIM
OF THE REFORM MOVEMENT

Beginning with Isaac M. Wise's affirmation at the first session of the C C A R that "the Mosaic Jehovah is the highest conception of Deity attainable by man," every subsequent statement pertaining to the conception of God since then has stressed in one form or another the superiority, from a rational and ethical standpoint, of the conception of God in Judaism to that in any other religion. The freedom from dogmas that offend the reason is generally hailed as testifying to the rationality of Judaism. "We fear no modernism," said Harry H. Mayer, "we have no anachronism to apoligize for, no fall of man, incarnation, or resurrection" (1912). In Judaism, principle counts for more than personality, while in Christianity the personality is central (1913). Morris M. Feuerlicht (1920) still thought that the world wanted to be free from organized Christianity, was tired of the Church, but not tired of God. That was Judaism's opportunity to make its conception of God better known. At none of the Conferences was there any doubt that Judaism, in one form or another, was meant to be a world religion. The only one who questioned that assumption was Bernhard Felsenthal, at the 1904 Conference, when Max L. Margolis presented his plan for the formation of a Synod.

A division of opinion which was aired at those annual Conferences turned upon such questions as the following: "Which aspect of the God-idea is primary, the ethical or the metaphysical?" "Is the main message of religion social or individual?" "Is the function of religion to improve human relations or to save souls?"

According to Emil G. Hirsch (1895), the center of gravity of the Jewish God concept was not metaphysics but ethics. "Judaism began," he said, "with man, and from him rose to a cognition of God." When Solomon H. Sonneschein in 1901 interpreted revelation as synonymous with moral potentiality, and messianism with universal brotherhood, he evidently identified religion mainly with ethics. At the 1919 Conference, Judaism was defined as "a democratized ethics." William H. Fineschreiber (1920), discoursing on the "Decay of Theology in Popular Religion," deplored the fact that popular theology had very little place in contemporary Jewish life. The rationalist spirit, he maintained, had weakened the spirit of Jewish religion. The advance of the physical sciences had undermined the belief in things spiritual. Though the Jewish religious impulse had flowered forth in all kinds of humanitarian activities, Jews could not afford to have it lose its distinctive character as the source of faith in a living God. "Have all those activities," said Fineschreiber, "but see to it that they be hallowed through prayer and conscious religious sanctions." Meyer H. Simon, in his presidential message in 1923, hailed the lack of insistence on dogmatic theology and the greater emphasis on simple faith and righteous deed, because he believed that "thereby the wide chasms of religious hatreds may be lessened." Barnet Brickner (1931), likewise felt that the teaching of God must come through manifestation of godliness in human life rather than through definition.

Nevertheless, quite a few voices were raised in protest against all this theological vagueness. David Neumark in 1924 maintained that we must have a definite God-idea which is suitable for our time, and H. G. Enelow in the same year deprecated the social emphasis which had crept into Jewish religion. He therefore made a strong plea for the renewed cultivation of theology. These demands for theology were followed by sporadic attempts, like those of Leo J. Levinger in 1916 and Israel Mattuck in 1927, to reinterpret the God idea in terms of some recent philosophy, particularly that of Henri Bergson. Jacob Leonard Levy would even have Judaism stress in a Jewish way, as does Christian Science in its way, "the power of prayer as the greatest spiritual achievement" (1927). These attempts in turn were supplemented by a re-emphasis on the traditional conception of God, as a personal being with whom we should commune in prayer if we do not want prayer to be merely a form of auto-suggestion—by Samuel S. Cohon in 1928, and Bernard Heller in 1929.

It is quite apparent from the foregoing that, although the spokesmen of the Reform movement have maintained that the inner problem of living as Jews is one of so redefining or revitalizing the Jewish God idea as to constitute a valid reason for Jews' remaining a distinct religious group, they have hardly succeeded in proving their point. The sum and substance of all that was said in the course of the first sixty annual conventions of the Central Conference of American Rabbis on the meaning of God is far from being sufficiently enlightening or inspiring to answer the question which so many Jews ask: "Why remain Jews and bring up our children as Jews?" In all that discussion one misses any reference to so basic a problem as the one of the existence of evil both in nature and in man, or to the seeming contradiction between the reality of sin and suffering and the conception of a just and merciful God.

In the "Guiding Principles," adopted in 1937, the meaning of God is dealt with in the following paragraph: "The heart of Judaism and its chief contribution to religion is the doctrine of the One, living God, who rules the world through law and love. In Him all existence has its creative source and mankind its ideal of conduct. Though transcending time and space, He is the indwelling Presence of the world. We worship Him as the Lord of the universe and as our merciful Father."

If the "heart of Judaism" can be thus set forth in a single paragraph of four sentences which consist of phrases which are only timeworn stereotypes, how much vitality and drive can there possibly be in the rest of the body of Judaism?

The truth is that the spokesmen of the Reform movement have not been just to themselves, or to the movement. Their real concern is with something far more immediate and tangible than an abstract conception of God. Any such conception, however free from unreasonable dogma, must in the last resort be based on faith. Rare indeed is the person who is capable of unswerving loyalty to an abstract truth, even when it is supported by irrefutable experience; much more so, when it has to be accepted on faith. How then can the variety of persons who, with the usual foibles and failings of human beings, constitute the Jewish People be expected to endure the tension of belonging to a weak minority group, for the sake of an abstract theological doctrine? That question forces itself on the mind when the theological doctrine involved is as platitudinous as the one about God, which now forms the basis of the "Guiding Principles" of the Reform movement.

What the Reform movement has really been seeking to achieve is the conservation of world Jewry as an identifiable group with a collective consciousness of its own. That is the case, despite the asseverations of its leaders that its main purpose is to conserve and promulgate the Jewish teachings about God. The denationalization of Judaism, together with the renunciation of the hope for the reestablishment of a Jewish State, a renunciation which was for almost half a century the theme song of the Reform movement, was not at all what it was to be. It was not a means of serving notice on the Jews that they should disband as a People, nor a means of inviting non-Jews to accept Judaism. It was merely a formula devised by the early leaders of the Reform movement to meet the arguments used by the European statesmen and anti-Sermites generally against granting civil rights to the Jews. In the hands of the early Reform leaders, the denationalization of Judaism also supplied the rationale for rejecting ritual observances which, according to them, served no ethical or spiritual end. But apart from those specific applications of the denationalization of Judaism, the Reform movement has none the less sought in its way to reconstitute the solidarity of the Jewish People.

One has only to compare the "Guiding Principles" with the "Pittsburgh Platform" to note the change that has come over the

Reform movement, from the standpoint of the conservation of the corporate body of the Jewish People. In the "Pittsburgh Platform" the term "Jewish people" is mentioned in passing, as part of the formula concerning the Bible and Mosaic legislation. The existence of the People, as such, was either assumed, or not regarded as sufficiently important to be the subject of a distinct affirmation. On the other hand, in the "Guiding Principles," in the very definition of Judaism the Jewish People is given centrality. Judaism is no longer spoken of as a universal or a world religion. "Judaism," we are told, "is the religious experience of the Jewish people."

In addition, a special section in the "Guiding Principles" is now set aside for the *Israel* of history. It reads in part thus: "Judaism is the soul of which Israel is the body. Living in all parts of the world, Israel has been held together by the ties of a common history, above all, by the heritage of faith. Though we recognize in the group loyalty of Jews who have become estranged from our religious tradition a bond which still unites them with us, we still maintain that it is by its religion and for its religion that the Jewish people has lived."

In keeping with this new attitude toward the collective being of the Jewish People the "Guiding Principles" affirm the rehabilitation of Eretz Yisrael not only as a haven of refuge for the oppressed, but also as a center of Jewish culture and spiritual life. In recognizing group loyalty, even when not motivated by religion, as constituting a bond of unity with those who are motivated by religion, the Reform spokesmen now give evidence of having abandoned the slogan that Jews are merely a religious community. When, therefore, they go on to say that "it is by its religion and for its religion that the Jewish people has lived" they no longer really mean that the Jewish People has lived *exclusively* by and for its religion. Though they re-emphasize the centrality of Jewish religion in the life of the Jews, they by no means negate the importance of Jewish culture.

It is true, nevertheless, that a small but vociferous minority in the Reform movement has refused to go along with the majority, both lay and rabbinic, in the break with the "Pittsburgh Platform" and the adoption of the one formulated after considerable discussion at the Columbus, Ohio, Convention of the C C A R which took place in 1937. It is equally true that the Reform movement is far from having accepted the Zionist version of the Jewish People. Unlike the American Council for Judaism, it now recognizes the State of Israel as "*a* center of Jewish culture and spiritual life," but it parts company with Zionism which regards Israel as *the* center of Jewish culture and spiritual life.

"NO OTHER JUDAISM BUT RACE JUDAISM"

Long before the spokesmen of Reform came to their present realization of the peoplehood of historic Israel as basic to the survival of Judaism, they were engaged in developing a pattern of ideas for the purpose of fostering Jewish unity and solidarity. Those ideas, as we shall see, are the products of wishful thinking instead of being based on objective fact. They tend to be extravagant in their fanciful flight, instead of coming down to earth. That itself only proves how obsessed by the foregoing purpose they must have been.

The Reform leaders were apprehensive of avowing frankly the continuance of the corporate unity of the Jews as an end in itself, lest they be charged with accepting Jewish nationhood. They preferred to represent the continued existence of the Jewish People as a means to an end, and to draw from the past the rationale for that end. Nevertheless they laid great stress on the historic unity of the Jewish People. Even the "Pittsburgh Platform" states: "We are convinced of the utmost necessity of preserving the historical identity with our past." At the 1894 Convention, Kaufmann Kohler, quoting Abraham Geiger, stated the following: "The eminent power of Judaism consists in its being the direct outcome of national history, in its presenting a rare individuality of its own, a specific type of humanity, and not like Christianity a mere conglomeration of spiritual forces without a healthy national life as basis and background. But at the same time its purposes are broad and universal. . . . The psychic force of the Jewish religion lies in the Jewish race. The nation is the object of divine care in the great economy of the world. There is no other Judaism but race Judaism.

Jewish monotheism without the nation as a living and acting force is Theism or Deism, Pantheism but no Judaism. We must strengthen our racial individuality."

The year following, Emil Gustav Hirsch held forth in the same vein. "Judaism," he said, "is racial, tribal, national and universal. We are a Volk, no nation. Without race, we ossify in dogma. Without universal tendency, we are doomed to fossilization." In 1910 Kohler reiterated his own thesis: "We are not simply prophetic Jews who believe in proselytism. We believe in Torath Moshe. The whole congregation of Jacob lives in its spirit and is identified with its historical development." That same year David Philipson, quoting Geiger, said: "Every reform is a transition . . . does not break with the past, but rather preserves carefully the bond that connects the present with the past. . . . Such Reform proceeds not with inexorable logic; it follows the law of historical development."

If it were true, as Kohler maintained, that the Jews have been made by their national history into a race of "a specific type of humanity" which is chosen to be a Messiah People, or a Priest People, Jews could not want a more convincing reason and more compelling motive for remaining loyal to Judaism and maintaining their continuity with the past. It goes without saying that, when confronted with the implication of Jewish superiority, the Reform spokesmen are ready with their reply that the doctrine of election is one that implies responsibility and not privilege. They seem to forget, however, that *having greater responsibility is itself a special privilege.* In reply to Houston S. Chamberlain's racialist thesis in his *Foundation of the Nineteenth Century,* Max Heller in 1913 found it necessary to say that "the Jews are not a race in any hard and fast sense; they are a group unified by spiritual heritages, disciplines, life experiences and exalted hopes." But the assumption that the Jews are "a specific type of humanity" still stands, as well as the assumption that they constitute a Messianic or priestly type of humanity.

That kind of assumption belongs to what may be described as pre-Copernican theology. In our day, it may have relevance *vis-à-vis* the official Christian conception of the Church. According to that conception, there can be no salvation for any human being outside the Church. Kohler quoted David Einhorn as having said, "The idea of Israel's election should be retained, because it expresses an undeniable privilege; it engenders in the Jew a feeling of reassuring self-consciousness over against the ruling Church." [13] But that official Christian conception is itself, in the modern climate of opinion, so obsolete that any reply to it in its own terms cannot but deal in obsolete values.

Surely, the last thing the Reform movement should wish to be doing is transacting in obsolete values. Why then has it gone to such lengths in stressing the intrinsic chosenness of the Jewish *lineage?* Chosenness, in this narrowly ethnic sense, can hardly be accepted without qualification and apology. The only plausible explanation is that Reform has had to find a potent means of maintaining the historic continuity and unity of the Jewish People. Since all collective effort other than that which is of a distinctively religious character might be interpreted as political, and indicative of nationhood, and consequently, taboo, it seemed necessary to base that unity upon some inborn *differentia* in every individual Jew. Such is the *reductio ad absurdum* to which the Reform movement has been led by its urge to denationalize Judaism without at the same time destroying the corporate character of the Jewish People.

The *tour de force* involved in the doctrine of Israel's election as interpreted by Reform becomes apparent when the conflict between the intense particularism of being "a specific type of humanity" and the universalism of a mission which appeals to the highest moral and rational interests of the human being comes to the surface in a question like that of intermarriage. The Reform authorities then find themselves in a dilemma, not knowing whether to give greater weight to the particularistic or to the universalistic element in Judaism. According to Samuel Holdheim and Samuel Hirsch, Reform permits not only intermarriage in which the non-Jewish spouse is converted to Judaism, but also mixed marriage in which the non-Jewish spouse remains unconverted. According to Einhorn and Kohler, Reform prohibits mixed marriage. "Mixed marriages are a nail in the coffin of the small Jewish race," said Einhorn. The reason which Kohler gives sounds somewhat casuistical. "Just because of this universalistic Messianic hope of Judaism, it is still imperative, as it has been throughout the past, that the Jewish people must continue its separateness as a 'Kingdom of priests and a holy nation,' and for the sake of its world mission avoid intermarriage with members of other sects, unless they espouse Jewish faith." [14] From the standpoint of the Jews as a specially endowed race, it would seem to follow that even when the non-Jewish spouse is willing to embrace Jewish faith, intermarriage ought to be avoided.

At the 1937 Conference, Louis I. Mann argued just to the contrary effect. "Let us admit," he says, "that we who preach a complete and unqualified universalism, . . . if we refuse to officiate at a marriage between two young people deeply in love and sharing their highest aspirations and ideals, . . . we cannot help but feel an embarrassing contradiction between our words and our actions." Despite the resolution of the 1909 Conference, which had declared that "mixed marriages are contrary to the tradition of the Jewish religion, and should therefore be discouraged by the American Rabbinate," Louis I. Mann reported at the 1937 Conference that 45.5% opposed rabbinic non-participation, and that there were rabbis who officiated at mixed marriages even where there was no intention of bringing up the children as Jews. That division of opinion was out of keeping with the general unanimity which otherwise prevailed in the Conference. Though in 1947 the Conference again declared marriages between a Jew and an unconverted Gentile contrary to the tradition of the Jewish religion, and in need of being discouraged by American rabbis, it is doubtful whether the actual practice of Reform rabbis has undergone any change from that reported by Louis I. Mann in 1937.

REFORM'S RESISTANCE TO BECOMING A SECT

From the standpoint of the corporate status of the Jewish People, which would naturally be jeopardized by any internal separatist tendencies, it is noteworthy that the Reform movement, as it has developed in the United States, has not evolved into a distinct denomination, nor does it seem to have furnished even the Orthodox any ground for formally reading it out of Judaism. The unstable condition of the movement, especially as represented by the CCAR, may be due partly to the individualism of the rabbis, who would rather be free from authoritative control than submit to it, even if by submitting to such control they might gain in authority in relation to those to whom they minister. The resistance to authoritative control was in all likelihood motivated by the fear of transforming the Reform movement into a denomination which would monopolize the loyalty and interest that Jews owe to the entire Jewish People. That fear may well have been responsible for the rejection by the CCAR of two proposals which might have rendered the Reform movement distinctly sectarian. One was the suggestion that it form a Synod, the other that it formulate a definite creed.

The idea of convening a Synod goes back to Isaac M. Wise, who, as far back as 1848, had advocated a plan to unite all the Jews of America and to centralize the control of all their activities, including education, charities and other communal efforts. That ambitious plan did not have the least chance of succeeding even then. Nevertheless, in the early years of the CCAR, the possibility of bringing all Jews under one aegis reasserted itself. Thus in 1900, Enelow gave a historical survey of the various Synods that had functioned in Jewish history, and concluded with the recommendation that that institution be revived.

At the conventions of 1902 and 1903, the question of the Sabbath in general, and of Sunday services in particular, called forth various opinions which accentuated the lack of any authoritative statement by the rabbinical organization. That prompted Jacob Voorsanger to propose the creation of some kind of authoritative guidance within the Reform movement. He complained of the fact that the CCAR could only recommend but not legislate. "Congregational autonomy," he said, "leads to confusion and prevents unity. While we do not want unwieldly and unyielding authority, we do not want religious anarchy either." He therefore proposed the merging of the rabbinical Conference with the lay Union of the American Hebrew Congregations. "We must put more stress," he added, "on the fact that Judaism is more of a discipline and a factor for character building than an official system of theology." He then submitted a scheme for local State Conferences consisting of the rabbis and presidents of all the congregations in each state and meeting periodically as national Conferences, with an Executive Council consisting of nine laymen and six rabbis to function between conventions.

In 1904, Joseph Krauskopf in his presidential address also recommended the formation of a Synod. It was at that session that

Max L. Margolis unfolded his plan for a Synod, as a logical consequence of his proposal to formulate "A Creed for Reformed Judaism." "We must unify our societies," he said, "and place them under the roof of the synagogue. Whatever is inimical, or even indifferent, to the synagogue must be wiped out of existence. We are not ready for an episcopate; our big men lack the culture and the generosity and the piety . . . but we need a central organization . . . to create national movements for maintaining a Publication Bureau . . . for publishing works which shall set forth the truth about Judaism, for instituting lectureships under a Jewish Truth Society. Let us have a Synod as the key-stone of our Church." He then proceeded to outline a program for a Synod.

Hyman G. Enelow came out vigorously in support of Margolis' plan. "If Israel is a nation, it must be Zion," he said, "if Israel is a Church, it must be a Synod." But this time there were some who protested. Among them was Bernhard Felsenthal. He sensed that the establishment of a Synod was bound to lead to sectarianizing the Reform movement and making it into a Church. "Israel is no Church but a People," he maintained. "Judaism is the product of Jewish national life. Without Jews there can be no Judaism. So long as there are Jews there will be a Jewish religion. Jewish religion is not a synthetic world religion. It is adapted to our Jewish ethnic life. We need neither a Synod nor a formulated creed, and do not want coercion in matters of religion." When the proposal came to a vote, it was carried by a majority of one. That led to the reconsideration of the Synod idea, in both 1905 and 1906.

In the meantime, American Jewry was shocked by the Kishinev pogrom of 1905 into a sense of corporate Jewish unity. The Jews began to organize themselves for emergency needs of a temporary character. Out of the discussions ultimately came the ideas of having an "American Jewish Committee," the main function of which would be to protect Jewish civil rights and to combat anti-Semitism. That is the last we hear of the proposal for a Synod.

Similar was the fate of the proposal to formulate a specific creed for the Reform movement. It failed for the same reasons as did the suggestion to form a Synod. In 1903, there was a demand for "a system of theology, positive, clear-cut and adapted to our times." That was said in approval of the elaborate creed which had been presented by Max L. Margolis, entitled *Theological Aspects of Reformed Judaism.* "Without a creed," he had said, "we shall ever be vulnerable. We need a proper ecclesiastical organization." His creed dealt with the following four themes: "(1) *Theology:* God is holy, creator and sustainer of the world. (2) *Anthropology:* Man has the power to overcome evil, to come nearer to perfection and to commune with God in prayer. Man is subject to God's law and responsible to God for all his thoughts and deeds. He who confesses his sins and turns from evil will be forgiven by God. (3) *Psychology:* The pious and the true penitents share, as immortal souls, in the everlasting life of God. (4) *Ecclesiology:* Israel was chosen as God's annointed Servant to proclaim the truth. Though despised and rejected, he is to continue as God's witness until there come the Kingdom of Peace, and Moral Perfection, the fullness of the knowledge of God and the true community of the children of the loving God." As part of his plans for a Synod, Max L. Margolis suggested the appointment of a standing committee on creed and doctrinal matters.

Margolis' suggestion, that the Conference adopt his or any other creed, raised a storm of opposition. The keynote of the opposition was that any such catechism would lead to sectarianism. The very notion of a new theology was repugnant to many of his colleagues. Some of them regarded the adoption of a formal creed as alien to the entire Jewish tradition. "Judaism itself is a shifting religion, and its dogmas and doctrines are capable of contraction and extensions," said Marcus Friedlaender.

Max Heller (1906), as a member of a committee on Margolis' paper, summed up the objections against it as follows. "(1) Formulation of a creed is inadvisable in the interest of the union and gradual unfolding of Pan-Judaism. . . . (2) The basic principles of Reform Judaism forbid the hard and fast lines of a creed. (3) Our real need is a systematic exposition of the principles of Judaism." Margolis could not have used any worse argument in behalf of his proposal than the statement with which he closed the debate: "Let us have a strong ecclesiastical government, even at the risk of a few heresy trials." The mere spectre of such trials was enough to frighten the members of the Conference.

THE REFORM VERSION OF THE CONCEPT
"TORAH"

Jewish life has always owed both its substance and its form to that aspect of Judaism which is known as Torah. The definition given to Torah in the "Guiding Principles" which were adopted by the 1937 Convention reads in part as follows: "The Torah, both written and oral, enshrines Israel's ever-growing consciousness of God and of the moral law. It preserves the historical precedents, sanctions and norms of Jewish life, and seeks to mold it in the patterns of goodness and of holiness. Being products of historical processes, certain of the laws have lost their binding force with the passing of the conditions that called them forth. But as a depository of permanent spiritual ideals, the Torah remains the dynamic source of the life of Israel. Each age has its obligation to adapt the teachings of the Torah to its basic needs in consonance with the genius of Judaism."

Throughout the centuries before Jewish enlightenment the concept "Torah" referred both to the content and to the process of the following: education, civil law, religious rites, ethics and social customs. It was coextensive with the whole of a Jew's life, his world outlook, his emotional experiences and his higher strivings. As the culture of the Jewish People, Torah could afford to be self-contained, so long as it was not challenged by any rival culture. When it was challenged, it merely had to add to its own content that which might serve as a reply. Under the conditions of pre-modern times, the main problem which the Torah presented was how it might become the possession of the entire Jewish People and permeate its entire life.

Since the integration of Jews, however, into the general body politic, their lives have come to be pre-empted culturally by the native civilizations. To send their children to public schools was thus declared, at the 1893 Convention, to be the duty of the American Jews. "Jews do not and will not build parochial schools," we are told. "In spite of insult, we must send our children to the public schools. There they shall learn to love learning, law and humanity." Accordingly, education in Judaism, as interpreted by the Reform movement, comes to mean solely training in a religious tradition, and involves setting aside only a few hours during the week for attendance in religious schools under Jewish auspices.

"Teach our children," urged Maurice Harris (1893) at that same convention, "our faith, our history and the meaning of their separation." Ten years later (1903), Rudolph Grossman advocated the placing of Jewish history, instead of the Bible, at the center of the curriculum. By 1935, we are told that the high point of the Jewish cultural heritage is ethics and not history, and that altogether too much emphasis is being placed on history. In urging a reorientation in religious education, Abraham Franzblau at the 1936 Convention drew up an ideal program, which was to consist of the following: "The structure, organization and problems of present-day Jewish life, problems of personal religion and of modern ethical life, the enjoyment of religious participation, the enjoyment of Jewish fellowship, and the acquisition of knowledge." In view of the few hours a week, thirty-two weeks each year, to be given to religious training, Franzblau's curriculum sounds like offering a sybarite meal either to a person without appetite or to one who has to catch a train.

It hardly requires much imagination to picture the difficulties which Jewish education, or what should be more correctly designated, "Jewish religious training," is bound to encounter. A difficulty that is well nigh insurmountable is the fact that such training is no longer part of an indispensable education, but merely an optional addition. Though it might contribute to the Jew's moral or spiritual development, few Jewish parents are capable of appreciating that fact. With the progressive ignorance of Judaism on the part of each generation of Jewish parents, they are not very likely to retain sufficient interest in Judaism to make special provision that their children shall come to know it and want to transmit it to their children.

Jewish children whose entire mental horizon is pre-empted by the cultural values which permeate the public school, the home and the street, cannot but regard Jewish subject matter as an unwelcome intrusion into their play time. With most parents apathetic to Judaism as a whole, with only about 10 percent of the Jewish population affiliated with Reform Congregations, with those congregations spending on the average only 10 percent of their budget on youth education, with the entire period of attendance during the year amounting at best to about 75 hours, with long vacations between each school year necessitating annually the repetition of the same subject matter to the point of boredom, with no reason for anyone except top educational executives to specialize in the teaching of Judaism what more than headaches and heart-aches can the conscientious rabbi and educator expect from the most ingenious and resourceful attempts to transmit the Jewish heritage to the coming generations?

The Union of Hebrew Congregations, in cooperation with the CCAR and the Hebrew Union College, has been doing its utmost to achieve the maximum results within the limitations which all of the above-mentioned handicaps impose on the religious schooling of Jewish children. These three bodies have done yeoman service in trying to train teachers, organize curricula, foster the best peda-gogic methods and publish attractive textbooks. That the results have been meagre and disappointing can only be due to flaws that inhere in the entire Reform approach. All these facts are borne out by the testimony of the rabbis and educator members of the CCAR, in an evaluation in 1929 of the Reform religious schooling on the 40th anniversary of the founding of that rabbinical body. It had not succeeded, complained S. Fineberg, in promoting Jewish worship, in character training, or in arousing an interest in Jews and Judaism. "We have reacted too strongly against nationalism," he said, "and so failed to recognize the child's relation to living Jewry. We have created relations with the past but not interest in modern Jewish movements."

At the 1934 convention, Morton Berman struck a new note concerning the function of Jewish education. "If education be life itself, and if the Jewish child is to find a place in Jewish civilization, he must do so through living an active Jewish life. Education is not merely preparation for later living, but must be maximum living now. We should start with the needs and interests of the child, his skills and capacities, and seek to make them useful." This ap-proach marked a departure from the Reform outlook on Judaism, but it was not likely to bring about a change in the established educational routine of the movement without a radical transfor-mation in its ideology.

Lacking a sound and fruitful system of elementary Jewish

schooling, the Reform movement could not make much headway with its various endeavors to foster adult interest in Jewish studies or even in those which deal with the fundamental problems of ethics and religion. The Confirmation ritual with which the Reform movement has replaced the *bar mitzvah* ceremony, and by which it has succeeded in drawing the girl into the Jewish educational process, was intended from the very beginning to motivate the elementary training and to stimulate the continuance of Jewish studies at least through the early adolescent years. To assure both of these results, attempts were made to advance the Confirmation age of the adolescent two to three years. Undoubtedly, some improvement was effected through these and similar measures, but it was so minimal that it hardly retarded the progressive dejudaization of the home.

* * *

A second item which properly belongs to the category of Torah, or the third of the triad: God, Israel and Torah, is worship and ritual observances.

Neither in Germany, nor during the first decades of the Reform movement in America, was there any striving for a uniform or standard form of worship. Again it was Isaac M. Wise who, in the very first attempt at rabbinical cooperation sponsored by Max Lilienthal, brought out a text which he designated *Minhag America*. Wise hoped that it would be adopted by all Reform congregations and thereby constitute the basis of their unity. That hope, however, could not be realized, because other outstanding Reform rabbis also published their own prayer books. When Wise organized the CCAR, he expressed his willingness to withdraw his *Minhag America* if his colleagues would agree on one that they would all adopt. At the 1891 Conference, the resolution of the Committee for a *New Standard Union Prayer Book* contained the provision that the proposed prayer book should not only voice "sympathy with the ideal of a Religion for Humanity, but as firmly . . . adhere to the sacred language and living historical mission of Israel."

The history of the Reform *Prayer Book* in this country reflects the tension between the two conflicting tendencies in the Reform movement: on the one hand, the desire to give expression to the explicit avowal of having Judaism become the world religion, and on the other, the urge to reaffirm the corporate reality and continuity of the Jewish People. Those in whom the former tendency had the upper hand were dissatisfied with the prayer book. They accused it, as did Samuel H. Goldenson in 1924, of "suffering from senility." The burden of his complaint was that "there is too much particularism in our prayers." He was answered by Morgenstern, who said: "We cannot leave out of consideration the Jewish People." At the 1929 Convention, Abba Hillel Silver argued: "Unbroken continuity is a value. We must not change prayers so often. We Jews believe in ritual, not in improvising prayers. Prayer book revision will not save Reform Judaism."

The fact is that the *Union Prayer Book* has undergone revision with a view to bringing it nearer to its traditional form and content and rendering it more Hebraic in appearance, even if not in actual usage. The same tendency to reckon with the corporate reality of the Jewish People asserts itself in the *Union Hymnal*, where the outspokenly Zionist hymn of *Hatikvah* was introduced in the 1939 edition. Thus, while the Reform movement has found it impossible to agree on a theology or creed, it has assumed not only the feasibility, but even the indispensability, of a common prayer book. But the seeming paradox is resolved when we bear in mind that the most important theological doctrine in Judaism concerns the reality and continuity of the Jewish People. That doctrine was responsible for most of the content of the revised Reform prayer book published in 1950.

By the same token, the broad universalism so often proclaimed by the leaders of the Reform movement seems to have been overlooked, when the problem of Sabbath observance and Sunday services came to the fore. Why was that the case? As far back as 1896, the CCAR formulated the problem of the Sabbath in the following bold and logical fashion: "We should not acquiesce," said Israel Aaron, "in the existence of an emaciated Sabbath and a dissipated Sunday. The manly course is to decide upon a strong, heroic, self-sacrificing policy making toward a re-sanctification of Saturday, or obeying circumstances we seem unable to control, seek to invest Sunday with the spirit of the Jewish Sabbath. . . . No half-hearted allegiance and no half-way measures advantage Judaism." In 1903 the Committee on the Sabbath question proposed exactly such a half-way measure, by recommending Sunday services but leaving the traditional Saturday Sabbath intact. Solomon H. Sonnenschein warned that the Sunday Sabbath would lead to schism. The final vote was almost unanimous against the transfer of the Sabbath to Sunday. Only Hyman G. Enelow, in consonance with his creedal and churchly conception of Judaism which, if adopted by the Reform movement, would have transformed it into a Jewish Protestant sect, argued vehemently for making the transfer.

There is no doubt that the influence of Abraham Geiger, who had been decidedly opposed to a Sunday Sabbath (see above, page 239) had much to do with the action of the CCAR in 1903. Geiger, in contrast to Samuel Holdheim, had insisted that the future of Judaism was bound up with the retention of the historic Sabbath. He gave as his reason the fact that Christianity had rejected the historic Sabbath in order to render its break with Judaism final. Judaism would thus be surrendering to Christianity if it were to adopt the Sunday Sabbath. But even behind that rationale was undoubtedly the desire, more or less conscious, to do nothing that might jeopardize the corporate character and unity of the Jewish People.

With the years, the Conference tended to widen the scope of ritual practice. Even in the earlier years, K. Kohler, to whom Rabbinic ritualism "was as unbearable as sacrificial sacerdotalism," made an ardent plea for the elaboration of a modernized ceremonial system. He regarded ritual, as such, as indispensable. It was to him "the poetry of religion." He urged the observance of the traditional festivals in a new spirit (1907). That was in line with his advocacy, at the 1894 convention, of modern forms for the conservation of Jewish life. "Substitute better and more impressive for obsolete forms," he said. "We must surround the life of the Jew from the cradle to the grave, our festive seasons at home and in the synagogue, with symbols and signs expressive of Israel's great truth and mission." It is doubtful whether the Reform rabbis of Kohler's generation shared his enthusiasm for enlarging the regimen of ritual practice. Both laity and rabbis whose background was Central European, particularly German, were inclined to favor the elimination of distinctively Jewish ritual.

In course of time, the descendants of the original founders of the Reform congregations began to disappear gradually from Jewish life. Their places were taken, for the most part, by second-or third-generation descendants of East European Jews. A similar change took place in the Reform rabbinate, which by the middle of the twentieth century, if not much earlier, became predominantly of East European descent. These lay people and rabbis brought with them a nostalgia for the ritual observances they still recalled. That accounts for what came to be recognized as a trend toward, instead of away from, ritualism, particularly within the synagogue.

Thus by 1937, the Committee on Resolutions recommended the following: "Assuming (1) that the Conference is in accord with the trend of Reform Jewry to restore ceremonialism and ritual to Synagogue and home, and (2) that some degree of unanimity is desirable and essential in the achievement of the goal striven for, and (3) that the intelligent harmonization of tradition with modern living conditions is a *desideratum,* therefore, be it resolved that a permanent committee entitled 'The Committee on Practical Theology' be created, whose duties shall include: (1) a thoroughgoing study of existing practices in home and synagogue; (2) an intensive study of possibilities inherent in some of the traditional practices with a view to adopting them for modern use; (3) a series of experiments to test the validity and effectiveness of the adopted and advocated practices." The foregoing gave promise of a new attitude toward ritualism on the part of the Reform rabbinate. From what happened subsequently, one is inclined to say that the promise has met with half-hearted fulfillment.

* * *

In addition to education and ritual observances as the categories in which the Torah aspect of Judaism is stressed in the Reform movement, there is the category of ethics. The entire system of "Mosaic legislation" and juridical law had become inoperative as a result of the integration of Jews into the general body politic. The only way, therefore, in which Judaism could continue to make itself felt as a social force for the betterment of human relations was by deliberately enlisting its authority and sanctions in behalf of social justice and the establishment of righteousness in man's dealings with one another.

In the "Guiding Principles," the attitude of the Reform rabbinate toward social justice is set forth as follows: "Judaism seeks the attainment of a just society by the application of its teachings to the economic order, to industry and commerce and to national and international affairs. It aims at the elimination of man-made misery and suffering, of poverty and degradation, of tyranny and slavery, of social inequality and prejudice, of ill-will and strife. It advocates the promotion of harmonious relations between warring classes, on the basis of equity and justice, and the creation of conditions under which human personality may flourish. It pleads for the safeguarding of childhood against exploitation. It champions the cause of all who work and of their right to an adequate standard of living, as prior to the right of property. Judaism emphasizes the duty of charity, and strives for a social order which will protect men against the material disabilities of old age, sickness and unemployment."

Surely a more humane and comprehensive program in behalf of a just social order could hardly be conceived. Moreover it did not represent a mere prayerful wish of a few idealists. It detailed the objectives which had been formulated and stressed year in and year out by the CCAR through its standing committees on Social Justice, Arbitration, International Peace, and Church and State. Some notion of the wide range of interests into which the CCAR had reached out since 1908, both in statements of principle and in active efforts to remedy evils and effect improvement, can be had from the following partial list of matters that had been dealt with: child labor legislation, care for delinquents, white slave traffic, industrial conflicts and reforms, relations of capital and labor, immigration, prohibition, the New Deal, land reclamation, afforestation, highways, abolition of poverty, arbitration, the profit motive, good citizenship, industrial democracy, federal housing, civil liberties, cooperation, vocational guidance, international peace and atomic energy.

Anyone who imagines that the Reform spokesmen contented themselves with glittering generalities concerning righteousness will change his mind when he reads the remarkable "Declaration of Principles in Industrial Relations" in the Proceedings of the 1918 convention, or the reports of the Commission on Social Justice for 1932 and 1934. There is no mincing of words in what they had to say of the injustices of the profit system. They frankly advocated the socialization of such basic enterprises as banking,

transportation and power plants. They called upon the congregations as well as the rabbis to adopt active measures in behalf of
social justice.

Although Julian Morgenstern, at the 1933 Conference, tried to
keep his colleagues from allowing their enthusiasm for social justice
to run away with them by pointing out that it was not their task to
determine methods and details of the social program, he nevertheless admitted that, "It is our task as exponents of a religion
with a social message and social philosophy to call attention to
inherent wrongs and injustices and ask for their correction."

In line with the emphasis on social justice as an outstanding
expression of Judaism, Sidney E. Goldstein advocated at the 1932
Convention the general application of the principle underlying the
Free Synagogue, which Stephen S. Wise had established in New
York City. That principle, he said, consisted in making of social
service a department coordinate with the two other departments
of worship and education. "The synagogue will then become," he
significantly added, "an active agent in reconstructing the social
order, and create a system of society materializing Israel's social
ideals."

The intense interest displayed by the CCAR in the attempt to
translate the Jewish ethical spirit into specific programs of social
justice not only helped to fill the vacuum created in Judaism by
the replacement of its civil law with the law of the land. It also
demonstrated the extent to which Judaism could act as a humanizing and ethical influence on the law and the social order of the
land. In the struggle to keep sectarian influences out of public
schools, the CCAR took a leading part long before the Jewish
defense agencies made that struggle one of their main objectives.

This increasing tendency of the Reform rabbinical body to become involved in the social and economic problems of the general
community did not at all please the lay constituency of the Reform
movement. That was the one outstanding issue on which the
CCAR and the Union of American Hebrew Congregations did
not see eye to eye. "I think that in the past," said Robert P. Gold-
man, the president of the UAHC, at the 1938 Convention of the
rabbis, "many of your pronouncements on social, economic and
political questions have not had the consideration either by yourselves or by others that the importance of the pronouncements

deserved. Thus their effectiveness is minimized while their possibility for harm is increased. . . . You should not be untrue to your calling, if you would even call a moratorium on public pronouncements on social, economic and political affairs until the clouds roll by."

That "gentle" hint to the rabbis that they cease meddling in practical affairs was deeply resented by them, and received its appropriate reply. "The question of social justice," said James G. Heller, "is not a question of controversy with the Union, but a question of whether we are going to abdicate everything in our mission, in our claim to speak in the name of faith in God. . . . We could have spoken out boldly twenty years ago and the laymen would have said nothing. . . . There was no crisis in the life of humanity then. . . . Social justice today is not merely a question of collective bargaining. It is the crushing of the Spanish people; the brutality of Japan in China; the recrudescence of savagery." While now and then some member of the CCAR would protest against making social service, industrial progress and educational advance "superior to spiritual ministrations to our own people," James Heller undoubtedly then spoke for the overwhelming majority of the Conference.

The fact is that Heller and his colleagues came at that time into head-on collision with the powerful economic motive against which ethical idealism has always dashed itself in vain. Even people with a degree of moral sensitiveness, once they become involved in the conservation of the *status quo* become fearful of having it upset by any attempt to mix ethical ideals with business. In 1928 Joseph Stolz quoted his brother-in-law Louis Marshall as having said: "I like the *Union Prayer Book*, except the new Yom Kippur prayer for social justice." The Reform movement had so interpreted the problem of Jewish survival that the only justification for Judaism had to be some tangible evidence of its power to counteract the dominance of the economic motive in human life. If it failed to do that, the very *raison d'etre* of the movement disappeared. Yet that was just wherein its failure seemed most conspicuous.

There can be no more damning statement concerning wealthy American Jews, most of whom moved within the ambit of Reform Judaism, than the following, which we read in *Roosevelt and Hop-*

kins by Sherwood:[15] "The fear of anti-Semitism in America has often blinded the wealthy Jews to the fate of fellow-Jews abroad," he writes. "There were Jews, particularly in the upper economic levels, who supported the 'America First Committee,' because their fear of anti-Semitism in America far transcended their resentment of Nazi barbarism in Europe; and there were some Jews who were just as ready as anyone else to 'do business with a victorious Hitler!' "

The foregoing is not quoted to minimize the contribution which the Reform movement has been making to the ultimate emergence of Greater Judaism. No other version of Judaism would have been any more effective in arousing a sense of justice or compassion in Jews who were so dominated by the fear of losing their wealth. It takes much more than the preaching of ethics to tame what William James called the "bitch goddess Success." But the fact that the movement had undertaken a task which was beyond its power and on which it had staked the future of Judaism should have led its adherents to ask themselves whether they were not mistaken in assuming that the only justification for remaining Jews must necessarily be their mission to reconstruct the order of society. Perhaps the more modest aim of reclaiming Eretz Yisrael for a land-based Jewish Civilization might have enabled a considerable part of the Jewish People to create an ideal social order. Such a social order would demonstrate the possibility of actually making this world a fit place for man to live in and make the most of his life.

THE REFORM VERSION OF THE CONCEPT "ISRAEL"

What external conditions are best calculated to help Jews retain their corporate unity and continuity is a problem by itself. At this point, all that need be said is that the surest way to fail in creating those external conditions is to build a Jewish life in a country like the United States on the lines attempted by the Reform movement and imitated by both the Conservative and the Orthodox movement. Proceeding with Reform from the premise that Judaism is first and last a religion, and that the Jews are essentially a religious community, or a community bound together mainly by a common religion, it follows as the night the day that the only way to conserve Jewish life is for the Jews to organize into congregations, and for the congregations to unite for their common purposes.

The Synagogue, the institution through which the congregation functions, thus comes to be the central powerhouse of Jewish life. Even if the synagogue, as the Reform spokesmen claim, had occupied that position in Jewish life throughout the past, that would not by itself be sufficient reason for its occupying that position in the present. The entire structure of human society has been so transformed that many an institution which in the past answered the social or spiritual needs of the day has become obsolete. Moreover, to say that the synagogue was the center of Jewish life in the past without envisaging that life and the actual place of the synagogue in it is misleading. A synagogue then was not the property of a self-constituted group of families, but of the community as a whole. Those who worshipped in the Synagogue did not constitute an autonomous group independent of the community. The synagogue, as *bet hakneset* (house of assembly) and *bet hamidrash* (house of study) made it possible for the community to conduct its religious and educational activities there. Not the synagogue but the community was the central power house of Jewish life.

On the other hand, a modern congregation is merely a religious family club. It consists of a group of families which in practice are homogeneous socially and economically and in theory also religiously. They are banded together for the purpose of obtaining the means of meeting their own religious needs, such as worship and education, for themselves and their children. An aggregate of synagogues mutually independent can no more create a spirit of Jewish community than can an aggregate of privately supported schools create a spirit of civic community. However the Jewish community be conceived, whether as ethnic, theocratic, or humanist, it must normally be an agency that maintains the institutions which are expected to foster in the individual member loyalty to it and its ideals. The endless discussions which the Reform rabbis carried on at their conventions concerning the need of having more Jews affiliate with the synagogue and of widening the scope of its activities should have opened their eyes to this truth.

As early as 1895, we note an awareness on the part of Reform leaders that the fact that the Jewish People had survived to modern times was no proof that it was indestructible. "The conditions," said Isaac Moses, "that made the existence of separate ethnic groups within the national organization possible have disappeared. There is no reason and no prospect for the continuance of the Hebrews as such in the United States." So far the logic is quite incontestable. Then comes one *nonsequitur* after another. "The Jews," he adds, "can survive only as the bearers of a religious idea, a spiritual force. First we must judaize the Jews. We should give everybody a chance to become a member of a congregation, even if his money contribution is small. Congregations should do mission work outside their membership."

What basis is there for Moses' assumption that being the bearer of religious idea was the *only* factor that made for Jewish survival in the past? Is it not more logical to assume that having been segregated from the rest of the population was also a highly important factor? Moreover, if Jews themselves have to be judaized, what likelihood is there of Jewish survival, now that they do not need, or want, to be segregated? And most questionable of all is the assumption that congregations are qualified "to do mission work outside their membership," as though their own members do not need as much judaization as the unaffiliated. We can hardly believe that the payment of membership dues in a congregation qualifies one to missionize one's fellow-Jews. William H. Fineschreiber, in 1938, in pointing out that lay organizations, like the American Jewish Committee, the American Jewish Congress, and B'nai B'rith should be conceived as coordinate with, and not subordinate to the synagogue, added: "The synagogue cannot demand leadership. Millions of Jews have not yet achieved the Jewish faith."

In 1904, Joseph Krauskopf, in his presidential message, recommended the establishment of People's Reform synagogues "in the ghettos of our larger cities." Likewise at the 1909 convention, Solomon Foster advocated "branch synagogues for the poor, and additional Sabbath services very early in the morning or in the afternoon for those who have to go to work during the day." He also urged the publication of religious lectures and tracts in Yiddish. In 1917 the "Committee on Synagogue and Industrial Relations" recommended the democratization of the membership and the management of the synagogue. A more realistic note is struck by Samuel Koch in 1920, in his discussion of the "Problem of the Unsynagogued Jew." He points out that the public school is the greatest disintegrating force in American Jewish life. Though he deprecates all-day Jewish schools, he urges that "the synagogue should retain a more exclusive control of the education of its youth." Just what he meant by that is not entirely clear.

The ineffectiveness of the congregation as an instrument of religion was discovered a long time ago. Instead of merely increasing the membership of the congregations by finding ways of having all Jews affiliate with them, there was a trend toward enlarging the scope of the congregational activities beyond those of worship and elementary religious schooling. In 1889 on the question "How Can We Enlist Our Young Men?" Leo M. Franklin suggested having an "open synagogue." That meant making the synagogue a place for fellowship and social gatherings, for library and reading rooms and for meetings of various charitable organizations. These activities did not then have for Franklin an intrinsic Jewish significance. He recommended them because he believed that they could "make religion attractive." At the 1902 convention, however, the same rabbi came with a more carefully thought out plan on "Congregational Activities outside the Pulpit and Sabbath School." He then argued that "life is religion and that all secular activities must be sanctified." To meet the situation in which "the number of unaffiliated Jews number three to one," he would have the "open temple" outdo the club as a social center "to which nothing human would be alien."

Some of the synagogues in the larger cities proceeded to become "open temples" which were taken advantage of not by the members and their children but by the unaffiliated. The absence at services of those who were affiliated continued to be as conspicuous as ever. Before long, voices at the conventions were raised in protest against the "secularization" of the synagogue. "Today," Alexander Lyons protested at the 1916 convention, "social service tends to become an exclusive obsession. It may, as Solomon Schechter warned, turn our places of worship and religious schools into settlement houses in disguise. The mere social service program is an imitation of an Ethical Culture Society." [16] Leo Sharfman, in that same year, taking as his topic "Religion and the Synagogue," points out that "the establishment of numerous congregations, with large membership, beautiful temples, busy centers of social, philanthropic, literary, dramatic and musical activity cannot measure the essential religious influence of the synagogue." The implication, of course, is that the religious influence is minimal, if not nil.

A survey of religious conditions reported at the 1916 convention showed that, whereas among the older immigrants 47.5 percent had observed the Sabbath, the percentage of observance among their children had dropped to 29, and that 70 percent of the Jewish children were then untouched by religious education. In a study reported in 1925 as part of the effort to attract college youth to the synagogue, 60 percent of the students were said to have stated that their interest in Judaism ceased when they entered the university. In 1938, Edward Israel complained: "There is the feeling that we have neglected the religious training of our youth, and that we have built up a generation of unreligious people not prepared to cope with our problems of economic and political life."

Deliberate and direct striving for certain objectives in human life is known to be self-defeating. One such objective is happiness. It is a well-known psychological fact that the more one makes happiness the only purpose in life, the more one fails to secure it. The same is, in a sense, true of religion. That may well be what is wrong with the Reform philosophy of the synagogue. It is based on the mistaken notion that the way to foster religion is to organize congregations for the sole purpose of cultivating it. It is interesting to note that when a Reform congregation wants to hold its own members or to increase its membership it has to reckon with the foregoing psychological principle. In some of the congregations, a plan had been devised whereby young married couples were invited to meet within the walls of the Temple. The plan was called "Mr. and Mrs. Limited." Two rules were laid down by the inventors of that plan: (1) "Discreet relationship between the temple and the group." That meant that those who were invited must not suspect that the motive was to get them to belong to the temple. "No proselytism please!" (2) "Emphasis on sociability rather than religion and education." What that implies is indicated by the kind of activities in which the group was advised to engage. They were: a harvest party, a quiz show, truth and consequence show, dramatic production, magician's exhibition, with a few meetings "of a more serious nature," such as an address on the subject of "rent control." [17]

The foregoing travesty on the function of the synagogue is in a sense a *reductio ad absurdum* of the basic approach of the Reform movement to Judaism as nothing else than a religion, and to the synagogue as the end-all and be-all of organized Jewish life. The report delivered by Maurice N. Eisendrath, the President of the Union of American Hebrew Congregation in 1948, at its 40th biennial Assembly and the 75th year of its founding, contains sufficiently authoritative evidence of the failure resulting from Reform's basic misconceptions of Judaism and of the place of the synagogue in Jewish life.

The Reform movement in the future will scarcely be able to point with pride to the following rebuke to the UAHC. "Beginning with the decision of the United Nations last November," said Eisendrath "to recommend the partition of Palestine, through frustrating months of vacillation by our State Department and Government, and culminating in the proclamation of the State of Israel, your Union stood silently on the side-lines. Your Union, I believe, was just about the only organization that calls itself Jewish—with one exception—which was compelled by the demands of the neutrality resolution to seal its lips and stay its hand and heart from participating in the drama which the past year of Jewish history presented."

Of what value is the growth of the number of congregations now in the Union, when, after seventy-five years, there should be occasion for a statement like the following: "However, actual opposition has been voiced against this missionary movement (to organize new Reform congregations) arising from two sources. There are those who would keep all other would-be Liberal congregations from poaching upon their sacrosanct bailiwicks. Seemingly they would be happier in the formation of Conservative or even Orthodox congregations at their very doorsteps, than assist in founding another Reform congregation. These former, it ap-

pears, offer less competition." As a second source of opposition
to its effort to organize new Reform Congregations, Eisendrath
mentions the attitude of those "who would restrict our cause to
what they mistakenly believe is its uniquely mid-western character." It is no secret that he was referring euphemistically to the
attempt to keep the Reform movement "restricted" to Jews
descended from those of German origin.

In addition to the competitiveness and exclusive spirit which
marked Reform in this country to the same degree that they
marked non-Reform congregations, Eisendrath had occasion to
note with regret that when it came to carrying out the prophetic
mandate, "our contemporaries within the Church do not remain
quite as silent as some of our congregational leaders would wish
a religious organization to remain." Moreover, he refers bitterly
to the rejected offer of the president of CCAR to use his good
offices for the unification of American Jewish organizational life.
"He received the rejoinder that 'this subject is not primarily one
for religious leaders.' How empty," adds Eisendrath, "sound our
pretensions toward reestablishing the synagogue to a place of
primacy in Jewry, if we refuse to permit it to plunge into the
mêleé of Jewish life; to influence it, to direct it, to guide it, to bless
it!"

The fact is that those pretensions had always sounded hollow,
since the assumption that it is possible for a community spirit to be
generated by an aggregate of mutually independent religious family
clubs—such as American synagogues are, whether Reform, Orthodox or Conservative—or even by unions of synagogues, is contrary to all the laws of human nature and society.

What is wrong with Reform Judaism is perhaps best summed
up in an article entitled "Liberal Judaism as a Living
Faith," which appeared in the magazine *Commentary*. In that
article, Robert Langebaum, a member of the English Department at Cornell University, takes to task David Daiches, a
well-known literary critic, for having assailed Reform Judaism
for the wrong reasons. "The failure of spirituality ought to
have been the main object of Mr. Daiches's attack. . . . Our
reforms embarrass us because we know we have made them
not to promote a higher spirituality, but in order to get by
with as little spirituality as possible. . . . Worst of all is the

danger of second-rateness which threatens liberal Judaism as it must any attempt to tailor a tradition to our needs. . . . That may be why so few intellectuals can make a place for themselves in liberal congregations. . . . There is really, as things now stand, no place in our liberal congregations for anyone who, whether by choice or necessity, cannot live according to the routine assumptions of the middle class. . . . The case for liberal Judaism must in the end stand upon the extent to which it has kept alive the religious need by institutionalizing and cultivating it, and the extent to which it will in the future realize the possibilities of religious development." [18]

CHAPTER TEN

Orthodox-Judaism

૭ THE DIFFERENCE BETWEEN ORTHODOX AND TRADITIONAL JUDAISM

The Reform movement in Germany was inhibited from being institutionalized on the scale it achieved in the United States. It nevertheless was making sufficiently rapid strides in Germany during the thirties and forties of the nineteenth century to provoke its opponents into organizing a counter-movement which may be described as Orthodox. During those decades, the Reform ranks were still growing in numbers and influence. The traditionalists then realized that they could not stop the movement merely by engaging in vituperation against it. They had to find leaders capable of meeting the Reform leaders on their own ground.

The first outstanding person to meet the challenge of Reform was Isaac Bernays of Berlin (1792-1849). He had moved away from the isolated intransigent traditionalism which refused to have any truck with anything that smacked of modernism. Simultaneously with his Talmudic studies under the guidance of a noted Talmudist he pursued secular studies in the University of Wuerzburg. He acquired a fluent command of the German language, and became a distinguished orator. When the Hamburg Jewish community elected him as its Chief Rabbi, or as he preferred to be designated, its Hakham (a title used by Spanish-Portuguese Jews), he preached in the German vernacular instead of in the Judeo-German dialect. That itself was then a daring innovation. He had hoped thereby to forestall the demands for more radical innovations. That step taken by Bernays was indicative of the new policy which the opponents of Reform were beginning to adopt. What they combated was not the Germanizing tendencies inherent in the innovations. On the contrary, they, too, were eager to have the Jews Germanized. They were intent, however, upon keeping intact the traditional regimen of ritual practice and worship with all the *minutiae*.

Isaac Bernays did not content himself with engaging in polemics against the innovators. Instead, he tried to translate traditional Judaism into modern educational terms. He therefore undertook to introduce changes into the traditional type of Jewish education in order to qualify the young to be both pious Jews and loyal citizens, and, in addition, to fit them for some practical calling. This new conception of Jewish education, as well as his spirit of resistance to Reform, was transmitted by Bernays to his disciple, Samson Raphael Hirsch, who came to be the outstanding leader of Orthodox Judaism in nineteenth century Germany.

Samson Raphael Hirsch (1808-1888), like his teacher Bernays, received a thorough grounding in traditional lore and a modern university education. He was a prolific writer and a vehement polemist. In 1836 he published what may be regarded as the classic of Orthodoxy, *The Nineteen Letters of Ben Uziel*. In that book, we have in complete outline the ideology which has since been utilized by the Orthodox in their resistance to all innovation in Jewish religious beliefs and practice. Hirsch was the rabbinical head of the Jewish community of Frankfort-on-the-Main. In that position he was able to translate his ideology into a communal and educational program of Jewish living.

The term "Orthodox" is intended to imply a conscious reaffirmation of tradition in the face of challenge. The fact is that despite the intention of any orthodoxy to add nothing to, and to subtract nothing from, the tradition which it reaffirms, it inevitably interpolates nuances for which there is no warrant in the tradition itself.

In combating Reform, Orthodoxy could not afford to ignore the advantage which Reform, in apparently rendering Judaism compatible with complete integration into the non-Jewish culture of the environment, held out to its adherents. Reform possessed this advantage, in that it frankly renounced the element of Jewish nationhood, which had been an integral part of Traditional Judaism. Orthodoxy could not consistently defend Traditional Judaism against Reform while agreeing with it in the outright renunciation of Jewish nationhood. *What Orthodoxy did was to desiccate nationhood by treating it as a theological concept instead of as a concept of polity which calls for a specific organizational structure. Thus was the letter of Jewish nationhood permitted to remain, but its spirit was gone.*

According to Orthodoxy the principal reason for wishing to be identified as a Jew should be the belief that the miraculous events recorded in the Torah, and particularly the theophany on Mount Sinai, literally and actually took place. In addition, the entire text of the Torah should be accepted as having been dictated by God to Moses. No greater privilege could therefore be vouchsafed to any people than the obligation to conform to the precepts of the Torah. Orthodoxy thus availed itself to the utmost of what had actually until modern times constituted the most powerful motive for Jewish survival.

Nineteenth-century Reform in Germany had aimed at the following three objectives: 1) The substitution of a rationalist attitude to tradition for the one based on unquestioning faith; 2) the elimination of those religious observances and prayers which emphasized the particularistic aspect of Judaism; and 3) the shifting of emphasis from the legalistic to the prophetic aspect of Judaism. To counteract that threefold program, Orthodoxy proposed a program of its own, which called for the following: 1) faith in the supernatural origin of the Written and Oral Torah; 2) maintenance of all traditional observances and forms of worship; and 3) the continuance of the study of Torah in the traditional spirit. This program was intended to rule out any possibility of compromising with modernism. In practice, however, Orthodoxy did not shut out completely all tendencies that conflicted with tradition.

The entire style of thought in Reform bears the imprint of Protestant theology and philosophy. Jewish Orthodoxy, on the other hand, clearly reflects the style of thought characteristic of Catholic theology. That may explain in part why Orthodoxy attained its greatest strength in the Catholic part of Germany. The reaction of the Orthodox Jews against the modernist emphasis upon reason and the spirit of the times was very similar to that displayed by the Catholics among whom they lived. The spokesmen of Orthodoxy maintained that to recognize the primacy of reason was to place oneself outside of Judaism. They maintained that the authoritive character of Traditional Judaism should be sufficient to validate whatever demands it makes on the Jew. Those demands, they argued, are intrinsically meant to be a challenge to whatever happens to be the spirit of the times, rather than a concession to it. *For Samson Raphael Hirsch, the essence of modernity is the humanist assumption that salvation consists in the achievement of happiness and self-perfection.* That assumption, according to him, is morally and spiritually untrue.

From protestations like the foregoing, we might infer that Orthodoxy actually rode roughshod over the ideas and ideals of the *Zeitgeist*. This, however, was far from being the case. In the very act of challenging the *Zeitgeist*, something of its spirit inevitably clung to Orthodoxy. We should, therefore, not be surprised to find that the two aspects of Judaism, the collective and the individual, underwent at the hands of Orthodoxy considerable, though unrecognized, change. That change is so significant as to point definitely to the influence of the *Zeitgeist*.

As specific evidence of the influence of the *Zeitgeist* in Samson R. Hirsch's interpretation of the Jewish tradition, the following example out of numerous ones might suffice:[1]

The traditional *K'dusha* reads thus:

"We will sanctify Thy name in the world even as they (the angels) sanctify it in the highest heavens, as it is written by the hand of Thy prophet:

'And they called one unto another and said,

Holy, holy, is the Lord of Hosts; the whole earth is full of His glory'

Those (over) against them say, Blessed—

'Blessed by the glory of God from His place.'

And in Thy Holy Words it is written, saying,

'The Lord shall reign forever, Thy God, O Zion, unto all generations. Praise ye the Lord.'

Unto all generations we will declare Thy greatness and to all eternity we will proclaim Thy holiness and Thy praise, O our God, shall *not* depart from our mouth for ever. For Thou art a great and holy God and King."

The foregoing is interpreted by Hirsch as follows:

"We will sanctify Thy name as does the choir of creative powers who acknowledge that the All-Holy One who rules over His creation does withal reveal Himself in the laws of that creation. Whatever it contains proclaims His greatness and in unison with all else dedicates itself to His service. So also does the community of Israel dedicate itself to the service of Him who amid all vicissitudes abides as God, the ruler of the world, and is glorified as such throughout all the ages, abiding withal in every generation, also in exile as Zion's God. May Israel as the instrument of his glorification abide forever. Every congregation, as a member of the community, takes upon itself the fulfillment of this high calling."

The truth is that Orthodoxy's seeming defiance of the *Zeitgeist* was intended to be mainly a challenge to Reform, which went to the opposite extreme of apotheosizing the *Zeitgeist*. Both Samuel Holdheim and Samuel Hirsch, foremost spokesmen of Reform, had actually looked upon the *Zeitgeist* as a new divine revelation. That glorification of the spirit of the times provoked the Orthodox counterblast. This did not prevent the modern orientation to reality from insinuating itself into Traditional Judaism.

THE CONCEPT OF THE *YISROEL-MENSCH*

The outstanding trait of Orthodoxy is the clarity and forthrightness with which it affirms its theological doctrine. It *bases Judaism upon implicit faith in the Written and the Oral Torah as the supernatural revelation of God's will.* "The Torah," says Samson Raphael Hirsch, "is an eternal code set up for all ages by the God of eternity." Orthodoxy is at no point vague or half-hearted in its affirmation that the Torah does not belong to the category of human writing. It insists that the Jew must believe that Moses was merely a passive amanuensis, recording at divine dictation each word of the Pentateuch, and simultaneously learning those interpretations and laws which constitute the authoritative Rabbinic tradition. In that respect it reaffirms in unqualified fashion the teaching of Jewish tradition, both Rabbinic ꞏand Medieval.[2]

"Let us not delude ourselves," says Hirsch. "The entire matter reduces itself to this question: Is the statement, 'And the Lord spoke to Moses,' which introduces all the laws of the Torah, true or not? Do we not believe that God, the Almighty and All-Holy God, spoke thus to Moses? Do we mean what we say when, in the circle of fellow-worshippers, we point to the written word of the Torah and declare that God gave us these teachings, and that these teachings are the teachings of truth, and that He thereby implanted in us everlasting life? Is all this a mere mouthing of high-sounding phrases? If not, then we must keep those commandments, fulfil them in their original and unabbreviated form. We must observe them under all circumstances and at all times. This word of God must be accepted by us as an eternal standard, transcending all human judgment, as the standard according to which we must fashion all our doings. Instead of complaining that it is no longer in conformity with the times, we should rather complain that the times are no longer in conformity with it." [3]

In keeping with this literal understanding of the supernaturally revealed character of both the Written and the Oral Law, the spokesmen of Orthodoxy combated the new approach to the study of Judaism, which is known as Die Wissenschaft des Judentums (The Scientific Study of Judaism), and which is based on the attempt to explain the content of a teaching or tradition in the light of its historic context. Beside Samson Raphael Hirsch the most outstanding among those spokesmen were Israel Hildesheimer (1820-1899), founder of the Orthodox Rabbinical Seminary at Berlin, and Marcus Lehmann (1831-1890), editor of the Israelit of Mayence. They rightly sensed that any attempt to explain a religious practice or teaching in relation to its historical context detracted from its eternally binding character. As divinely enunciated teaching or established practice, the contents of the Torah had to be regarded as absolutely true, infallible and immutable.

* * *

From the assumption that the Torah is the record of the supernatural revelation of God's will a number of important corollaries inevitably follow: In the first place, the Torah provides the Jew with all that he needs to know for his world outlook, or orientation to life and reality. It contains torot or teachings which deal, from the standpoint of his salvation, with everything that he has to know, concerning God, the world, mankind and Israel. He does not need to resort to any philosophical inquiry to prove the existence of God, or to attain a knowledge of the divine attributes. Kant had proved beyond all doubt the futility of all purely rational attempts to demonstrate the existence of God. The mere fact, however, that Kant is invoked in so basic a matter as the existence of God is a gratuitous concession to the *Zeitgeist*.

Actually, the Orthodox thinker, fortified by the certainty which he derives from the Torah concerning the reality of God, considered the Kantian resort to practical reason to validate the belief in God as mere word-play. In the intensely Christian climate of opinion, supernatural revelation was considered a far more reliable source of belief in God than any argument based on reason or intuition. To the Catholics, in particular, the ever-present miracle of the Mass rendered superfluous the need of philosophizing about God. Hirsch probably felt that Jews could well afford, with even greater justification, to dispense with philosophic reasoning as a basis for the belief in God, since they had in the Torah itself a visible object which was not a human creation. For Samson Raphael Hirsch of the nineteenth century the recorded account of the revelation on Mount Sinai was just as unquestionable as it had been for Judah Hallevi of the eleventh century.

Orthodoxy recognized that merely to be convinced of the *existence* of God was not enough; Jews also had to know something about the *nature* of God. They were warned, however, not to make the mistake of trying to arrive at such knowledge by themselves, since they had in the Torah all that was either necessary or possible for man to know about God. The account of creation as given in the Torah should be read in the light of as much scientific knowledge about the world as we can gather. Its main significance, however, consists in revealing the two fundamental attributes of God: His love and His justice. The most careful study of the phenomena of nature, even with the aid of scientific method, reveals nothing of their inner being and meaning. The eighteenth century philosopher David Hume had proved how little we can rely even upon what has always been assumed as the immutable law of cause and effect, the fundamental basic category of all science, to inspire us with confidence in the stability and orderliness of the universe.

The most rewarding procedure, therefore, is first to acquire a knowledge of the natural sciences and then to turn to the Torah. There Jews can learn to view the phenomena of nature as part of an integrated cosmos, in which every part from the smallest to the greatest interacts with every other. Such interaction manifests God's *love*, which pervades every atom of His creation. The harmony which obtains in nature is due to the tendency on the part of every element in it to adhere strictly to the limits within which God would have it function. That fact represents God's *justice*. It is possible, likewise, to learn from the Torah concerning the other divine attributes with which human character and conduct should reckon. Those attributes, according to Hirsch, are: the unity, the infinity, and the immutability of the nature of God.

Thus, Orthodoxy did not deny to the Jew the right to avail himself of whatever knowledge the human mind was capable of achieving through its own efforts. It is doubtful, nevertheless, whether it would permit unlimited freedom of research, to say nothing of freedom of hypothesis or inference. By that time there was no way of ignoring the established facts of modern astronomy, which contradicted tradition. Orthodoxy had tradition somehow come to terms with those facts. It held out, however, against the conclusions of the biological sciences with regard to the origin of species; it treated them as mere hypotheses. Least of all could it sanction the scientific study of the Bible, for that would have led to inferences which were in conflict with the traditional belief concerning the events recorded there as historical.

We need the Torah, Hirsch argued, not only to help us understand the meaning of what we see in the world about us, but also to know what to make of our lives. The great thinkers, who relied upon their own reasoning, disagreed among themselves as to what should be the aim of human life, and even when they agreed that happiness was the highest good, they differed as to the means by which it was to be attained. Some recommended power, in the form of wealth, fame or influence, others pleasure, whether of the senses or of the mind. As for the ideal of perfection, or the harmonious fulfillment of all of one's potentialities, that is so far beyond the reach of the general run of human beings as to be hardly helpful. Hirsch therefore concluded that for the Jew the only aim in life worth pursuing was the one that was in keeping with the *intrinsic* nature of mankind as a whole, and of the People of Israel in particular. But how was one to know that universally intrinsic nature of man? Hirsch had a ready answer: Study the Torah and reflect upon all that is implied in God's being the creator both of mankind and of Israel. You will then realize the significance of the laws which God has revealed to both Jew and Gentile, and which they must live by if they wish to achieve the purpose of their existence.

*   *   *

For Jews, however, the Torah was intended to serve as a guide in developing a particular type of human being, a kind of ideal man or superman. Hirsch designated that type as *Yisroel Mensch*. Observance of the precepts of the Torah had the effect of transforming the ordinary person into that higher type of human being. "The moral law," said Hirsch, "makes animals into men, and the Torah makes men into Jews." It is not quite clear whether he actually expected that all mankind would ultimately adopt the Torah and become Jews, or that the non-Jews would be content with remaining ordinary human beings.

The truth, however, is that such was not the traditional conception of the Torah's function. According to the traditional conception, the purpose of the Torah was to further the establishment of the Kingdom of God. The traditional emphasis was on society and not on the individual. The concern of the Torah was that justice should prevail among all who belonged to the People of Israel, the justice which had been spelled out in the laws of God. Worship and ritual observances were apparently intended to keep every person within that People aware of God's sovereignty. In setting up the production of a new type of individual, instead of the divinely governed social order, as the purpose of the Torah, Hirsch unwittingly yielded to the *Zeitgeist*, with its ideal of the individual "superman," which Friedrich Nietzsche enunciated with all the pathos and drive of a new revelation.

Hirsch stressed the point that it was the duty of the Jew so to live as to exemplify the ennobling influence of the Torah and thus serve as God's witness. That was the mission of the Jew. In their collective capacity, according to Hirsch, Jews constituted a community of Torah devotees, whose special task it was to demonstrate the meaning of holy living and to counteract the idolatrous obsession with power and pleasure, which to him constituted the spirit of the times. With no less insistence than the Reformists did Hirsch base the continued existence of the Jews on the contribution which they were expected to make to the improvement of mankind in general. There was, however, more warrant in Reform for this version of the Jewish mission than there was in Orthodoxy, because Reform had transferred the center of gravity in Judaism from the Torah to the prophetic writings. In those writings we do come upon occasional references to a universal mission; that is not the case with the Pentateuchal Torah. Possibly Orthodoxy's zeal for the mission idea may be due to the tendency of an opposition movement to take over some of the aims and methods of the movement it opposes, in order to be able to compete with it successfully. We should therefore not be surprised that Orthodoxy often speaks in the idiom of Reform.

Nor does Hirsch's conception of what the Jew as an individual should strive for coincide entirely with that which is stressed in Traditional Judaism. The traditional teaching on that subject was far more accurately summed up by Moses Hayyim Luzzato, the mystic moralist of the eighteenth century. "Our Sages," he wrote, "taught us that man was created only to find delight in the Lord, and to bask in the radiance of His Presence. But the real place for such delight is in the world to come." [4] The *Yisroel-Mensch*, on the other hand, is essentially a higher type of *ethical* being who is able to conquer his natural inclination to amass wealth, to acquire power and to indulge in pleasure, and who succeeds in living a life of holiness and humility, of justice and love. To be sure, there is nothing in the ideal of the *Yisroel-Mensch* that negates other-worldly "basking in the radiance of God's Presence." Nevertheless Hirsch's ideal presupposes a different conception of "the highest good" from that which is implied in the traditional ideal of other-worldly bliss. The *Yisroel-Mensch*, the "Ideal Jew," is a *summum bonum* that definitely belongs to this world. In substituting it for the *summum bonum* of tradition, Orthodoxy unconsciously reckons with the spirit of the times.

* * *

The only way to become a higher type of human being, a *Yisroel-Mensch*, Hirsch maintains, is to live in accordance with the laws, both mandatory and prohibitory, contained in the

Torah. Those precepts constitute the will of God as do the laws of nature according to which the life of all subhuman creatures is regulated. The divine laws are, in a sense, extensions of the natural law in the spiritual world. Man, being articulate, is vouchsafed the knowledge of God's will in the articulate form of commandments. That privilege is accompanied by the endowment of freedom of will, or the power to choose whether or not to obey God. Had God, however, granted man the freedom to choose between good and evil without at the same time instructing him in what was good, man would have had to grope blindly for centuries on end before he would have come to know what was good, or what God would have him do.

A *mitzvah*, said Hirsch, should be fulfilled in the spirit of obedience to God for its own sake. No attempt should be made to justify it in terms of what seemed humanly desirable. If, however, we perform a *mitzvah* because of the physical or social good which might result from it, we are not obeying God, but ourselves.[5] To those who were acquainted with the Kantian thesis that anyone who did what was right because of the advantage he expected to derive from it did not obey the ethical law but merely pleased himself, this teaching of Hirsch did not sound bizarre, even from a rational standpoint. So insistent was Hirsch upon the motive being obedience to God's will that he resented the tendency to speak of the ritual laws in the Torah as "ceremonies." The truth is that Jewish tradition does bear out this emphasis on obedience to the will of God as the only worthy motive in the observance of religious practices.[6]

Hirsch did not shrink from the logical consequences of such emphasis, even in the face of the hardships which it entailed. It was at this point that he challenged Reform most vigorously. Reform did not originally arise as the deliberate result of a revolution in men's attitude toward tradition. It was originally a concession to expediency. It began with the tendency to grow lax in the observance of religious practices, and then finally to neglect them altogether, because they interfered with the uninhibited participation in the business and cultural life of the non-Jewish community. Only later did it achieve a rationale that was not based on convenience or expediency.

The most important group of ritual laws in traditional Jewish religion are those which have to do with the observance of the Sabbath. The few well-to-do Jews who had business transactions with non-Jews became restive under the restraints imposed by traditional Jewish law. It was this fact which had led Samuel Holdheim to suggest the transfer of the Sabbath to Sunday. Though his suggestion was not adopted officially, the observance of the seventh day Sabbath fell into desuetude among the well-to-do Jews to whom he ministered. Even for those who continued to observe it, it had lost its traditional rigor. The attitude of Orthodoxy, however, in this, as in all matters involving religious observances, was uncompromising. "Is not the God who ordained the Sabbath," asked Hirsch, "the same as the One who provides us with the means to live by? Did He not, by giving a double portion of manna on the sixth day, and none on the Sabbath day, prove that no one need be anxious lest, through the observance of the Sabbath, he be left without a livelihood?" [7] This kind of reasoning was evidently based on implicit faith in the historicity of the miracle of the manna as having fallen from the sky twice as much on Friday as on the other days of the week, and not at all on the Sabbath.

Hirsch classified the divine laws which a Jew had to obey, if he was to be worthy of being designated as Yisroel-Mensch, or "Ideal Jew," into the following five groups: 1) Mishpatim (judgments), precepts concerning justice toward our fellow-men; 2) Hukkim (Statutes), precepts concerning justice toward beings of lower rank, like the earth, plants, animals, material goods. Among them should be included one's own body; 3) Mitzvot (commandments), precepts concerning love toward all creatures, on the basis of divine behest and of the concept of the Yisroel-Mensch; 4) Edot (testimonies), precepts which signalize established truths by means of symbols or symbolic acts; and 5) Avodot (worship), precepts which aim to exalt and consecrate man. They were all intended to evoke those traits in the human being which led to his becoming the superman, or ideal human being. Hirsch seemed to overlook the distinction, which had been stated in the Mishnah, between duties toward God and those toward fellow-man. That distinction corresponded to the one between ritual and ethical observances.

Despite the high value which Orthodoxy placed on ritual

observances, it did not attach to them any sacramental potency, such as the Jewish mystics were wont to ascribe to them. Orthodoxy, in general, seemed to avoid mysticism, because the latter required on the part of those who cultivated it qualities of mind and character granted only to the superior Jew. It preferred to emphasize the fact that the spiritual good to be derived from the performance of the *mitzvot* was accessible to the average Jew. One might say that it regarded the joy emanating from the faith in the divine origin of the observance as the principal factor in elicting the higher traits of the "Ideal Jew," or *Yisroel-Mensch*. This was what salvation meant to Hirsch. He saw all the problems of human life entirely from the standpoint of the individual, as though he had anticipated A. N. Whitehead's conception of religion as "what the individual does with his solitariness." The Jew, indeed, did not need to be at a loss as to what to do with his solitariness, since God had placed at his disposal many precepts by which he could be guided in the ordering of his life.

*   *   *

The effectiveness of the *mitzvot* in eliciting the traits of the "Ideal Jew," or *Yisroel-Mensch*, may be augumented by learning their symbolic significance. The development of a new type of symbolism may be considered Hirsch's most creative contribution to modern Judaism.[8] It is a new attempt to arrive at the inner meaning of the prohibitory and mandatory laws of the Torah. The first one to make a systematic attempt at interpreting the contents of the Torah symbolically, or allegorically, was Philo of Alexandria. He sought to read into the Torah, into its narratives and into its laws, ideas of a philosophical character which he had derived for the most part from Plato and the Stoics. That type of interpretation, in turn, had been employed by Euhemerus and other Stoics in their attempt to reconcile the mythology of Homer and other Greek poets with philosophic rationalism. After Philo, however, allegorical interpretation of the precepts seldom played any part in Jewish life. The first one to revive it was Samson Raphael Hirsch.

In the Middle Ages, some Jewish theologians indulged in the allegorical interpretation of the narrative and poetic parts of the Bible. The first one who interpreted the *mitzvot* both from a pedagogic and utilitarian point of view was Maimonides. In his *Guide for the Perplexed*, he explains the entire sacrificial system as having been a means of weaning the Israelites away from the elaborate sacrificial worship which they had learned from pagan nations with which they had come in contact. He also accounts for the dietary laws on the ground that the forbidden foods have a stupefying effect on the mind and the sensibilities.

The Jewish mystics evolved a much more elaborate system of interpretation. The principle underlying the mystic approach was that by means of the *mitzvot* the human being entered into communion with the supernatural forces. The *mitzvot* were treated as invocations of the Divine Name. If accompanied by the proper mental concentration, they were expected to acquire supernatural potency. This was the attitude that was fostered by the Safed mystics of the sixteenth century, and later by the leaders of the Hasidic movement. Orthodoxy added a new type of approach to the performance of the *mitzvot*, one which may be designated as religio-ethical symbolism.

* * *

This religio-ethical symbolism fostered by Orthodoxy, having arisen in an environment of critical thought, was much more self-conscious than any of the previous types of interpretation. Hence its originator Hirsch deemed it necessary to formulate its methodology before proceeding with its application. In the first place, Hirsch pointed out that symbolism, as a method of interpretation, was not to be regarded as confined to matters of sacred import. Symbolism was an inevitable concomitant of human thought and communication. It applied to the entire range of human experience, and employed a large variety of means, of which language and gesture were the most common. Moreover, throughout the Torah we meet repeatedly with allusions to the ritual laws as intended to serve as symbols. Terms like "covenant," "memorial," direct our attention to the symbolic significance of various laws. Thus did Hirsch's system of symbolism seek to move within the sphere of contemporary experience in order to be intelligible to the average person. It was not meant only for the few who were specially qualified, by virtue of some special mental or physical self-discipline.

The methodology of this new type of symbolism consists, according to Hirsch, of the following three canons of interpretation: "1) Symbolism derives from the assumption that ideas are most emphatically and permanently expressed through outward actions. This applies especially to ideas which are intended as a means of uniting a group and fostering in them a collective consciousness. 2) The meaning which is to be read into those actions should not be arbitrary. It should be inferred from the nature of the circumstances under which those actions are performed, from the intent of the individual performing the action, and from the nature of the individual for whom the action is performed. 3) The ideas and ideals thus symbolized must be of a simple and popular character." [9]

Of the foregoing canons, the most significant is the second. It implies that the meanings which should be read out of the *mitzvot* should be such as are germane to Jewish tradition, and not those which belong to other thought-universes, as was the case with the Philonic, the Maimonidean and the mystic interpretations. Hirsch did not actually succeed in avoiding the tendency to read meanings into, instead of out of, the *mitzvot* he interpreted. Insofar, however, as he strove to keep within the framework of traditional teachings, he succeeded in discovering among them some very striking associations of ideas that pointed to hitherto unrecognized meanings. A concrete illustration of his method of symbolism will help to make this clear.

In the rite of circumcision, for example, Hirsch found two important rules, one of which was stated in the Written and the other in the Oral Law. The first rule is that the rite must be performed on the eighth day; the second rule is that it must be performed only during the day. "Why the eighth day?" Hirsch asked. He noted in that fact the evident purpose to differentiate this rite from those in which the number seven figured prominently, as in the case of the Sabbath, the Sabbatical Year, the New Year, etc. Moreover, if the eighth day of the newly born infant falls on the Sabbath, the law is that the rite must take place on it, even though it involves infraction of many sabbatical prohibitions. Hirsch tried to arrive at the significance of the eighth day by first trying to discover the meaning of the number seven, which was associated with other ritual observances.

Hirsch rejected as un-Jewish the usual explanation that seven had a mystic significance. He maintained that the meaning of that number must be the one which is assumed in the Bible itself. This led him to make a close study of the different contexts in the Bible in which the number seven figured. He then discovered the particular significance which each context derived from its association with the number seven. He finally concluded that common to all of them was the idea of completion, or rounding out, of some matter of import. The Sabbath day thus marked the completion of the six-day creation of the physical world. The additional, or seventh day, was thus dedicated to the awareness of God as the Creator. Without that awareness, the creation as a whole, and each part in it, would have remained unfinished and incomplete. It achieved completion through the observance of the seventh day as Sabbath. The Jews, however, represented a higher order of creation. They were subject not only to the laws that governed the physical world which belonged to the lower order of seven-day creation. The rite of circumcision was, therefore, set for the eighth day, to indicate the higher sphere of existence into which the life of the Jewish child must be ushered.

The other rule which has to be observed in the rite of circumcision is that it may be performed only during the day. Hirsch found that this rule applied to about twenty-four other ritual observances, most of which were enumerated in the Talmud.[10] In administering justice, for example, the same rule must be observed. This led him to survey from a spiritual point of view the various ideas associated in the Bible with day and night. With day is associated the world of conscious purpose, of the visible and the tangible, insofar as it is subject to human will and intelligence, the world in which man is the active agent. The night is the symbol of the dark, mystic, telluric influences, in the presence of which man, finding himself helpless, is driven into all manner of black magic. It was in this area of reality in which man was wont to lose himself that the pagan religions had taught man to look for God; not so Judaism. It taught man to seek God in the intelligible and the controllable forces of nature. That is the kind of world of which daylight is the symbol. This is why Judaism prohibits the practice of various rites after nightfall.

Hirsch thus opened up a fruitful field for the articulation of new Jewish spiritual values. To be sure, he read into the tradition much that was subjective and arbitrary, but it takes more than objective science or history to revitalize a tradition. Hirsch went too far when he condemned the results of the scientific study of Judaism as deadening rather than revitalizing. Actually the scientific study of Judaism had not yet fulfilled the possibility that inhered in it of becoming a modern embodiment of the traditional spirit of Torah study.

The scientific study of Judaism undoubtedly did more for the renascence of Jewish peoplehood than for the cultivation of personal religion. On the other hand, Orthodoxy was in a better position to bring about a revival of the traditional spirit of Torah study. With its type of symbolism, it might have achieved rich spiritual results; but unfortunately the efforts of Orthodoxy to make the most of the individual aspect of Judaism, to which aspect this new type of symbolism belongs, have been neutralized by its failure to develop a strong affirmative attitude toward Jewish peoplehood. As a result, the influence of Orthodoxy's most significant contribution has hardly been felt, even in its own group, much less in the wider circles of Judaism.

THE DESICCATION OF JEWISH PEOPLEHOOD

At no point did Orthodoxy deviate so far from Traditional Judaism, with which it was supposed to be identical, as in the matter of Jewish peoplehood. In the first place, it contributed to the desiccation of the idea of Jewish peoplehood, both theoretically and practically; and, secondly, it raised separatism within the Jewish People itself to a principle of Jewish religion, and thus added to the disruption of the unity of the Jewish People.

The theoretic phase of Orthodoxy's efforts to denationalize Judaism consists in its interpretation of the entire history of the People of Israel not as the history of a nation, but as that of divine Ecclesia. The Bible always speaks of Israel as an *am* or as a *goy*. It is therefore natural to infer that, from the standpoint of collective life, the Bible regards the forebears of the Jewish People as belonging to the same type of social organism as do all other nations. But Hirsch very strenuously opposed the tendency to draw any such inference. The very designation of Israel as "a nation" always irritated him. The collectivity of the Jewish People had no other significance for him except as the matrix for fostering the Ideal type of Jew—the *Yisroel-Mensch*. A sufficient variety of spiritual abilities, physical powers and material resources necessary for the production of this higher type of human being can be found only in a nation. That, and that only, was for him the meaning of Jewish nationhood. That the Jews had actually led a national life of their own for centuries, and that since the destruction of the Second Commonwealth they had never ceased praying for the resumption of their nationhood, had nothing to do, according to Hirsch, with the problem of the present status of Jewry.

In keeping with Hirsch's idea of Jewish nationhood was his idea of Eretz Yisrael. The Israelites, he maintained, had been a "nation," in the specific sense which he attached to the term, long before they entered Eretz Yisrael, and remained such after they were exiled from it. The ordinary secular functions of nationhood, which called for a land and self-governing institutions had, according to Hirsch, actually diverted the Jews from their religious commitment. On the contrary, the lack of the worldly essentials of nationhood was a blessing in disguise. For the sake of their mission, it was best that the Jews had on the whole been "poor in everything upon which the rest of mankind reared the edifices of its greatness and its power; externally subordinated to the nations, armed with proud reliance on itself, but fortified by direct reliance upon God." [11]

* * *

With the foregoing as a premise, the dispersion of the Jews among the nations took on a different meaning from the one it had had in tradition. To be sure, the traditional assumption that the dispersion was a punishment for sin was retained. But that assumption was virtually nullified by the novel significance assigned to the dispersion as a means of liberating the Jews from being engrossed in the pursuit of so worldly an aim as being a nation in their own land. "The dispersion opened a new, great and extensive field for the fulfillment of its mission. . . . Israel has accomplished its task better in exile than when it was in the full possession of good fortune." [12]

The lessons which the Jews learn in the Diaspora and which qualify them for their mission are conceived by Hirsch in terms of individual character—of *Yisroel-Mensch*. As Jews behold the various national States with which they come in contact disappearing from the stage of history, they learn that wealth and power are ephemeral, and afford no permanent security to human existence. They also learn the lesson of endurance and martyrdom for the sake of achieving the ideal type of man who fulfills the will of God.

As we read Hirsch's alluring appeal in his *Nineteen Letters* addressed to the "young Benjamin" to exemplify this ideal type of human being, we imagine we hear the voice of Jewish tradition appealing for loyalty to the People of Israel and commitment to that People's future. But this is only an illusion. The People of Israel is, for Hirsch, only the name for a loosely formed group of individuals who have the opportunity of becoming "ideal Jews" if they choose to obey the will of God.

That conception of society as consisting of disparate individuals, whose perfection or salvation is something that lies outside the sphere of political and social interests, was understandable when the individual human being was regarded as the possessor of a completely individualized soul, and when life's center of gravity was believed to be in the world beyond. That conception, however, flies in the face of reality. The individual human being is mentally and spiritually inseparable from the society to which he belongs, and is therefore incapable of achieving his own salvation apart from the salvation of his group. On the other hand, the salvation of the group is impossible without a sufficient measure of social and cultural autonomy to permit its distinctive character and its spiritual heritage to come into play. Since a land is essential to such autonomy; it is indispensable to the salvation of the society or group, and of every individual in it. Orthodoxy is thus an incongruous mixture of traditional other-worldliness and outworn psychological notions of human individuality.

Perhaps nothing so accentuates how far Orthodoxy has carried its reduction of Jewish peoplehood to an ideal and abstract concept as its failure to sense that, with all its passion for the conservation of Jewish tradition, it was contributing to the nullification of perhaps the most significant part of that tradition. We have seen in the earlier chapters[13] with what devotion and persistence Jews, throughout the centuries of dispersion, had clung to their juridical autonomy. The system of civil law, on the administration of which Jews vigorously insisted throughout premodern times, is, from the standpoint of Orthodoxy, no less divine than the entire complex of ritual observances. The *Mishpatim* are as integral a part of the Torah as are the other categories of Torah law. But Hirsch felt that to put them into effect might give rise to the charge that the Jews were a State within a State, and therefore not entitled to civil rights. He did not hesitate to ask the Jews to observe the laws of the Sabbath even at the risk of being deprived of their livelihood. Yet he seemed to be entirely reconciled to the complete elimination of the juridical autonomy of Jews. It is, indeed, amazing that he, too, like the Reformists whom he denounced, should also have taken shelter behind the much-tortured Talmudic aphorism that "the law of the Government is law." [14]

The only explanation is that to him *Mishpat* was not a social function which was performed by a people in its collective capacity. *Mishpat*, or civil law, was, to Hirsch, nothing more than the expected reaction of the individual to such obligations and responsibilities as arose from the fact that he was a member of society. Viewed thus, *Mishpat* was not important in itself. It was only the embodiment of the ethical attitude which the individual human being had to cultivate as part of his obedience to the will of God, in order to attain a higher level of human existence. That ethical attitude can be fostered independently of the specific civil laws which form part of the Torah.

This atomized conception of Jewish collective life accounts also for the spirit in which Orthodoxy viewed the Emancipation. It saw in Emancipation greater freedom for the Jew to fulfil the divine ordinances, and an unprecedented opportunity to achieve the "Ideal Jew" or *Yisroel-Mensch*. So far as the Jews' relation to the state was concerned, Hirsch found a ready answer in the overworked text from Jeremiah which reads: "Seek the welfare of the city where I have sent you into exile, and pray to the Lord on its behalf, for in its welfare you will find welfare" (29:7). "No less religiously binding upon Israel," commented Hirsch, "than any of the other holy duties ordained by God is that,

in whatever land they sojourn, they should not only fulfil all the
duties which the laws of the land expressly demand, but also that
they do whatever is conducive to the welfare of the land." [15] He
failed to realize that the situation in Babylon, where the Jews
formed a colony of their own, did not present an instructive
parallel for the situation in which modern Jews, who were integrated into the general body politic, now found themselves.

Hirsch overlooked the fact that the Emancipation placed in-
superable obstacles in the way of fulfilling those Jewish purposes
which could be achieved only through communal cooperation
among Jews themselves. He saw only the moral danger which
confronted Jews as individuals, the danger of being drawn into
the mad race for power and pleasure. This new temptation called
for a greater exertion of. self-control than had the persecutions
and torments of former centuries. If Jews would succeed in overcoming it, they would exemplify most effectively the kind of perfect life that resulted from following the will of God as set forth
in the Torah. "In the centuries of passion and scorn, our mission
was but imperfectly attainable," says Hirsch, "but the ages of
mildness and justice, now begun, beckon us to that goal, that
every Jew and every Jewess should be in his or her own life a
modest and unassuming priest or priestess of God and true humanity. When such an ideal and such a mission await us, can we
still, my Benjamin, lament our fate?" [16]

*   *   *

With all the optimism with which Hirsch regarded the future
of the Jews in the Diaspora, he could not, like the Reformists,
entirely abrogate the belief in the ultimate restoration of the
Jewish People to its ancient historic land. Not even the assumption that the land was only incidental to the fulfillment of Israel's
mission could justify him in explaining away the oft-repeated
promise of God that He would gather the People of Israel. from
the four corners of the earth to the land which He had promised
to the Patriarchs. Did that traditional belief force Orthodoxy
to reckon with Jewish nationhood, at least as a facet of the future?
Not at all. Orthodoxy did not consider the return to the
ancestral home as realizable through human initiative and effort

in which the Jew was expected, or even permitted, to engage. It was part of the supernatural plan which God was working out for the People of Israel, and must therefore await God's own time.

This negative attitude of Orthodoxy toward something so profoundly Jewish as the involvement in an effort to reclaim Eretz Yisrael calls for explanation. According to Hirsch, the high purpose which God had in store for the People of Israel, its return to Eretz Yisrael, constituted an award which God would grant to the Jews, if they would fulfill their part in the world. The prize which one receives as a reward for some extraordinary feat is not something which one can with dignity seek to obtain directly; all of one's thoughts should be on the performance of the feat through which the prize may be earned, and not on the prize itself. The realization of the future promised by the Prophets will come about in due time, and for that we must pray and hope. "But actively to accelerate its coming were sin, and is prohibited to us." says Hirsch. [17]

This interpretation of the faith in the ultimate restoration of the People of Israel to its historic home was calculated to silence all opposition to the granting of civil rights to Jews, on the ground that they could not really become Germans, Frenchmen, or Englishmen since they really wished to go back to Eretz Yisrael. This Jewish yearning, according to Orthodoxy, was not meant to be translated into practical politics. It belonged to the divine scheme of things, and called for no action on the part of the Jew that might impugn his citizenship. [18]

Consistent with the supernatural perspective from which the return to Eretz Yisrael was viewed in Orthodoxy, was its attitude toward the Temple and the sacrificial cult. No attempt whatever was made to give other than a literal interpretation to the traditional hope for the restoration of the Temple, the priesthood and the sacrificial system. [19]

How seriously the Orthodox Jews who constituted the organization known as Agudat Yisrael took this conception of the Jews' relation to Eretz Yisrael was later evinced in their attitude toward Zionism. They combated it no less strenuously than did the early Reformists who had completely eliminated Eretz Yisrael from their reckoning. They not only denounced Zionism as irreligious and un-Jewish, but until the establishment of the State of

Israel went so far as to agitate politically against Zionism. They kept up a barrage of protests against Zionism, both to the League of Nations and to the Mandatory over Palestine, and at times worked together with the Arab nationalists against the Zionist Executive.

*   *   *

However, perhaps the most conspicuous evidence of Orthodoxy's denationalization of Judaism was its policy of sectarian separatism known as *Trennungs Orthodoxie*, which it pursued consistently in Germany. With European Governments insisting upon being Christian, and refusing to separate the Church from the State, the Jewish Emancipation necessitated some arrangement whereby, for all collective Jewish purposes, religious and cultural, the Governments might deal with the Jewish community as an authoritative body representing Jewish interests, and allocate State taxes for the support of all Jewish communal institutions. The Governments could not be expected to have separate dealings with each of the various religious groups within Judaism. The majority of the Jews, therefore, of their own accord and in conformity with the wishes of the State authorities, were willing to sink their religious differences and to operate as a united community.

Samson Raphael Hirsch, however, strenuously opposed having his followers in the Orthodox group cooperate with the other religious groups. He contended that the gulf between the Orthodox and the non-Orthodox was greater than that between Catholics and Protestants. When charged with violating the principle enunciated by Hillel which urged Jews not to separate themselves from the community (*Abot* II, 5), he retorted that it was not he and his followers who separated themselves from the community, but those who were disloyal to what he regarded as the only true Judaism.

The controversy over the principle of Orthodox separation ended up in the litigation in the courts on the occasion of what is know as "The Kompert Trial." [20] The circumstances of that trial were the following: Heinrich Graetz, the historian, had published an article in the 1862 *Jahrbuch fuer Israeliten*, one of whose editors was Kompert. In that article Graetz interpreted the fifty-third chapter of Isaiah as referring to the People of Israel as the Messiah-People. For this, Kompert was charged by the State attorney with having reviled the messianic doctrine of the Synagogue.

The main issue at the trial was made to turn upon the question whether there were different sects in Judaism. Isaac N. Mannheimer, a famous Jewish preacher of Vienna, and Rabbi Lazar Horowitz, the Rabbi of Vienna, were called in as experts to testify on the question. Both maintained that, though Judaism insisted upon the belief in a personal Messiah, it permitted considerable latitude with regard to one's idea of the details of his advent. The reason for such latitude, they maintained, was that Judaism considered the unity of the Jewish People as of the essence, and did not encourage sectarianism. This testimony aroused the ire of Samson R. Hirsch and Israel Hildesheimer, then of Berlin, and, together with seventy other rabbis, they published a strong protest against it, on the ground that Mannheimer and Horowitz had misrepresented Judaism by maintaining that it regarded Jewish unity as of primary importance.

It was this separatist attitude that led the Prussian Diet in 1876 to pass a law which contributed to the further fragmentation of the Jewish community. The law declared that one could remain a professing Jew though he seceded from the community. The bill had been introduced by Edward Lasker, a Jewish member of the Diet who himself had no interest in Judaism, and was vigorously supported by Samson R. Hirsch.[21] The separatist attitude of the Orthodox persisted long after Hirsch's death. When in 1906 the Prussian Diet took up the question of religious education in the schools, again the Orthodox refused to be included with the other elements of the Jewish population in working out a common solution of the problem of Jewish religious instruction in the schools. But the separatist spirit showed itself at its worst in Eretz Yisrael before the establishment of the State of Israel. The members of Agudat Yisrael then refused to be included in the *Knesset Yisrael* (General Jewish Community) which the British Mandatory had recognized as the official body representative of all elements of the Jewish population in Eretz Yisrael.

Isaac Breuer, one of the leaders of Agudat Yisrael developed an elaborate rationale in defense of Orthodoxy.[22] His main point is that the history of the Jews is totally and essentially unlike that of any other people. Theirs is a meta-history, in that it belongs to the supernatural order of existence.[23]

The 26th chapter of Leviticus and the 28th in Deuteronomy, which foretell with uncanny precision the fate of the Israelites among the nations, the suffering which they are destined to endure and the expiation they will have to undergo for their sins in failing to obey God's commandments, prove, according to Breuer,[24] that the career of the Jews is not governed by the ordinary laws of cause and effect, but by a higher law which reveals the working out of a divine purpose. Only those who acknowledge this conception of Jewish history, he contends, have the right to call themselves Jews. Those who act on the assumption that Jews are like everybody else read themselves out of the Jewish People, and should not expect that their cooperation for Jewish objectives would be desired or welcomed by those who can act on the principle that they are a meta-historical or supernatural People.

The Orthodoxy of Samson R. Hirsch met with far greater success in the Old World than any other modern synagogue movement in Judaism. There it achieved well-knit organizational form with the rise of the Agudat Yisrael. The Agudat Yisrael has branches all over the world, and thanks to the influx of refugees from Germany and Poland, it exercises considerable influence among American Jews.

Chaim Weizmann in his autobiography [25] describes a Dr. Barness, who was a typical product of Orthodoxy. This Dr. Barness was head of a Jewish boarding-school in Pfungstadt, not far from Darmstadt, Germany, where Weizmann at the age of eighteen was engaged to teach Hebrew and Russian. Weizmann found this Barness "even more bewildering to me than German gentiles. He was pious in the extreme, that is to say, he practiced the rigid formal piety of Frankfort Jewish Orthodoxy. But it was not the orthodoxy I had known and loved at home. It was stuffy, it was unreal, it had no folk background. It lacked warmth and gayety and color intimacy. It did not interpenetrate the life of the teacher and pupil; it was a cold discipline imposed from without. Dr. Barness was completely assimilated, and described himself as 'a German of the Mosaic persuasion.' He took his Judaism to mean that in all respects, save that of a religious ritual, he was as German in culture, background and personality as any descendant of the Cerusci." [26] That is as far as Orthodoxy got with its ideal of the *Yisroel-Mensch*.

THE ORTHODOX MOVEMENT IN THE UNITED STATES

The Orthodoxy which was developed in the United States had its beginning with the arrival of Isaac Leeser.[27] Contemporaneously with Samson Raphael Hirsch, who was the founder of the Orthodox movement in Germany, Isaac Leeser (1806-1868) promoted that movement in the United States. Born in Neuenkirchen in Westphalia, Prussia, he came to this country in 1824. He brought with him impressions of the conflict which began to be waged in Westphalia between the new movement of Reform and the upholders of tradition. Abraham Sutro (1784-1869), the Chief Rabbi of Muenster and Mark, had championed the cause of tradition in a work called *Milhamot Adonai* (Hanover 1836). He made a deep impression on Leeser while Leeser was still a child, and imbued him with zeal for Traditional Judaism. Although Isaac Leeser was not as learned as either Bernays or Hirsch, either in Jewish or in general studies, his training and cast of mind paralleled theirs, and his restless activity and zeal in combating the Reform movement earned him a place alongside them.

When Leeser came to this country in 1824, the Jewish population did not amount to more than twelve to fifteen thousand. The Jews had no precedent to guide them in their communal and educational activities. They adopted the congregational form of organization, a form most congenial to the environment which, theoretically at least, sought to conform to the principle of separation of Church and State. At that time, however, the scope of a congregation's activities was far larger than it came to be in later years. There was no social agency to take care of the poor, the orphaned and the sick. Moreover, public education was still unknown. Education, both elementary and advanced, was for the most part a function of the various religious denominations. A Jewish congregation, to meet the needs of its members, had therefore to do much more than provide facilities for worship and ritual observance. It had to be an organic community on a small scale. On the other hand, with the increase in the number of congregations, it was impossible for each of them to engage in multiple activities without duplication and overlapping.

The first one to meet the mounting organizational and religious chaos in the growing Jewish population of the United States was Isaac Leeser. He tried to meet it on virtually the same lines as did Samson Raphael Hirsch. Like the latter, he tried to build Jewish life from the very foundation. He established Jewish schools, both elementary and advanced; he organized philanthropic societies, established the first Jewish publication society, and published, wrote for and edited the magazine *The Occident*, the first Anglo-Jewish periodical in America. He published his sermons, translated the Bible into English, and wrote text books for religious institutions. He even engaged for a time in a project of establishing Jewish agricultural colonies.

All these undertakings were carried on by Leeser in the spirit of the Jewish Orthodoxy which flourished in Germany. Nevertheless, he was fully aware that the problem which Jews confronted in the United States was not whether they should be Orthodox or Reform, but whether they should remain Jews. With so many of them living out of touch with Jewish communal institutions, and incapable of forming any of their own, assimilation and conversion had already begun to decimate the limited number of Jews who then lived in the United States.

Leeser hoped to strengthen American Jewish life by organizing all the Jewish congregations in the United States into one body. He did not expect that body to engage in problems of theology or ritual. He urged the constituent congregations to undertake various projects, such as helping other small congregations to establish themselves, instituting a uniform system of philanthropy to take care of the needy, finding ways and means of preventing the growth of crime among Jews, publishing books of Jewish interest, and training young men for the ministry. He saw no purpose in raising questions of doctrine or practice, since he assumed that those were all amply answered in the Jewish tradition.[28]

Isaac Leeser was succeeded in the leadership of American Orthodoxy by Sabato Morais, who was more of a scholar and less intransigeant than his predecessor. Morais was at one time ready to collaborate, in his efforts to perpetuate Judaism in America, with so outspoken a Reform leader as Kaufmann Kohler. Later he actually collaborated with spiritual leaders who belonged to what may be described as the right wing of Reform. With their aid he laid the foundation of the Jewish Theological Seminary, which in time became the stronghold of Conservative Judaism. Nevertheless, Morais cannot be classed with the leaders of the Conservative movement which, under the name of "Positive-Historical Judaism," had been fought vigorously from its very beginning by Samson Raphael Hirsch. Morais may be said to have represented the transition stage from Orthodoxy to Conservatism.

Sabato Morais was born in Leghorn in 1823, and studied for the ministry under Chief Rabbi Piperno. As a young man, he took an interest in the Republican movement of Italy and came in contact with its political leaders, chiefly Joseph Mazzini. The friendship between him and Mazzini deepened when both had occasion to live in London for a time. While head instructor of the Hebrew Orphans' School, between 1845-1850, and private instructor of the children in the home of the Montefiores, Morais acquired a knowledge of English. That, together with his native oratorical gifts, won him in 1851 the position of *Hazan* and preacher of the Portuguese Congregation Mikvē Israel of Philadelphia, which he served until he died in 1897. Mikvē Israel, which was the first Jewish congregation in the city of Philadelphia and in the State of Pennsylvania, had been established in 1782, and numbered among its leaders men of influence and wealth.

The political interests of Morais during the Civil War took the form of strong Unionist sentiment and opposition to slavery. His talents as a scholar and teacher found a field in formal and informal instruction for all who wanted to learn. In 1873, the Maimonides College, an institution for the training of rabbis, was opened, and during the five years of its existence, Morais was professor of Bible and Biblical literature. For many years he agitated for a union of congregations with the view of effecting cooperation among them and bringing about changes in some of the religious practices that had no actual basis in traditional Jewish law. He hoped that such improvements would counteract the growing disregard of Jewish observances and indifference to Jewish religious belief. In these efforts he looked for assistance to Isaac M. Wise and Kaufmann Kohler, because he recognized in the former great ability for organization and in the latter great scholarship.

When, however, they placed themselves at the head of the Reform movement, with its open disavowal of the dietary laws and of the traditional manner of Sabbath observance, Morais rallied those who were revolted by these radical reforms. He met with a response from two prominent rabbis, Marcus Jastrow and Benjamin Szold, and later from the recently arrived Alexander Kohut. With their assistance, he succeeded in organizing the Jewish Theological Seminary Association of New York, for the training of rabbis in what he regarded as the spirit of Traditional Judaism. He worked indefatigably for the establishment of a "seminary of learning where all the ordinances of the Pentateuch compatible with our state of dispersion might be taught and enforced, in obedience with the demands of an enlightened Orthodoxy." [29] The Seminary opened on January 7, 1887, with a class of eight fourteen- and fifteen-year-old youngsters. One of them was Joseph H. Hertz, who later became Chief Rabbi of Great Britain.

What made it possible for Morais and his colleagues to be the forerunners of the third synagogue trend in Judaism becomes clear when we note in him the stirrings of ideas and attitudes that were not conmpatible with Traditional Judaism; this despite the fact that he regarded himself as a staunch traditionalist, and was regarded as such by the Jewish community. His son, Henry Morais, describes him as follows: "To the radical (i.e., Reform Jews), he was ultra-Orthodox as the most pronounced of that type could possibly be; to the ultra-Orthodox, the over-doing pietists, the bigots, he was not Orthodox." [30] He explains what it was that rendered Sabato Morais unacceptable to both extreme groups. It was because Morais ventured to intimate that, though Rabbinic Law was just as authoritative as the Written Torah, it was not as unalterable as the latter. He felt that changes in the conditions of life, especially those growing out of better relations with Gentiles, had rendered certain ritual practices required by Rabbinic law too difficult to be observed. Those laws, he thought, should be amended in accordance with the methods and principles inherent in Rabbinic law itself. That, he believed, required the calling of a

Synod consisting of "representative men of God-fearing Jews. . . . A synod clothed with authority, composed of men officially recognized in Israel." [31]

However, by that time the possibility of assembling a Synod that would be homogeneously constituted was out of question. Morais, however, "had faith in the people and thought that the great diversity of opinion would merge into a general acceptance of what is Jewish from a Biblical and traditional standpoint." [32] Though he was convinced of the need of certain changes in the ritual, he refrained from introducing them lest his action serve as a dangerous precedent for changes dictated by personal taste. He corresponded with scholars in England and Italy, in the hope of bringing about the organization of an ecumenical council which might institute necessary changes in the practice of Judaism. He was opposed, however, to having any local body arrogate to itself the right to tamper with traditional practice, for fear that such an attempt might give rise to schism.

Scarcely realizing the underlying causes of disintegration at work in American Jewish life, Morais adopted the conventional attitude of the pietist who can see in the laxity of his neighbors nothing but moral weakness. He regarded the desire to compete with non-Jews for temporal success as the main cause for the failure of Jews to observe the Sabbath. It did not seem to occur to him that possibly the very need of earning a livelihood might compel Jews to work on the Sabbath. He attributed the violation of the Sabbath to the hunt for luxuries.[33] But the mere fact that he recognized so much as the slightest need for change was sufficient to render him suspect with the strict traditionalists.

As a matter of fact, Morais did not stop with merely voicing demands for change. He even wished to find some way of cooperating with those who later organized the Reform Movement. He indicated time and again that what mattered mainly was the practice of the *mitzvot*, whereas belief was secondary. "We Hebrews have no dogmas to swear by, excepting 'Adonai Echod.'" [34] On the other hand, he insisted on the dogma of revelation and its inseparable accompaniment, tradition.

As a student of the Bible he could not help encountering the modern scientific study of its text. That study, together with the theory recently advanced at the time, of biological evolution, was already undermining religion in general. He conceded the possibility of errors in Biblical chronology and inaccuracies in transcription, but he did not dare to question the historicity of the miracles and of the Sinaitic theophany recorded in the Book of Exodus. He regarded preachers of religion who subscribed to the conclusions of modern Biblical scholarship represented by men like Wellhausen, Kuehnen, or Robertson Smith, as heretical and false to their charge. One of the main functions of the Seminary which he was instrumental in organizing was to combat modern Biblical science, which he considered as a blight upon faith in God, to say nothing of loyalty to the traditional way of life.

He subscribed, of course, to the general doctrine of reward and punishment, but he tried to formulate a rational conception of that doctrine. He grappled with the fundamentals of theology—the ideas of God, immortality and revelation. Though he did not contribute anything new to the understanding of these ideas, he at least tried to express some of his own thinking about them. He did not take the traditional beliefs for granted, nor did he regard them as above the need of logical demonstration. As for the idea of God, his main argument was centered upon negating Spinoza's identification of God with nature. His conception of immortality was no longer identified with the naïve belief in a bodily resurrection and in a hereafter in some heaven, or on a physically transformed earth. He did believe, however, in the personal survival of the soul after death. Though he realized that we could at best have but a vague idea of the soul, he, nevertheless, argued that the soul was capable of independent existence and was indestructible.

It is evident that neither his idea of God nor his idea of the soul was identical with traditional Jewish teaching. These ideas resembled those held by the Medieval Jewish theologians who had reinterpreted the traditional beliefs in terms of a rational world outlook. The same is true of Morais' conception of revelation. It was by no means the naïve notion of a theophany as described in the Torah, but a sophisticated idea, which reduced revelation to a higher type of inner experience, a type which could not be attained with the aid of reason.[36] Therein we note the influence of Maimonides.

These theological ideas, as expounded by Morais, did not arouse much interest or debate. They reflected, however, a significant change which had begun to take place within American Orthodoxy. It was showing signs of veering away from the strictly consistent course pursued by German Orthodoxy. This fact is substantiated by actual concessions which Morais was willing to make to the exigencies of the times. He was ready to collaborate with rabbis who were known to hold what to him were heretical views about the Bible, provided they would retain what he regarded as the basic observances in Judaism, primarily the Sabbath and festivals, circumcision, the dietary laws and the essentials of the traditional liturgy.

Morais admitted that he found the prayers for rebuilding of the Temple and the resumption of sacrifice incompatible with a rational conception of God, and that he was as emotionally repelled by the sacrificial cult as was Kaufmann Kohler. "Brother and Colleague," he addressed Kohler in one of his overtures to him, "with men of your calibre on the side of sensible conservation, what ought to be mended, could by sober caution, undergo a happy change. . . . Those who are conservatives because they recognize in 'orthodoxy' the depository of eternal principles, do not claim for each Jewish practice a Divine origin and immutability; but neither do they cast aside olden ritualism without the certainty that its absence can be supplied by what exceeds it in fitness and sterling worth." [37]

To that appeal Kohler replied that Morais was inconsistent. "Once renounce the idea of sacrifice by Aaronitic priesthood, and not only Mishnah and Talmud and the entire old synagogue ritual are mercilessly shattered, but the very Pentateuch for which you plead so fervently is put in abeyance." [38] Two years later, Morais was still courting Kohler and pleading with him to give up his "championship of a pseudo-Reform," stating that "the burning question of the hour was neither the *Chalitzah*, as you suggest, nor the acceptance of the work of Karo and Isserles in its entirety, nor even the restoration of a Hebrew nationality at the advent of a Messiah." [39]

This time Kohler was sharper in his refusal. "If I understand you well, you draw the line between *theory* and *practice*. In theory we might be extreme radicals, if we but observe and practice the Mosaic law in its entirety. But my dear brother colleague, do you not yourself distinguish between practice and practice, between law and law? You waive the question of '*Chalitzah*,' perhaps also the future obligation regarding animal sacrifice. Yet with what other authority than your own reason, which militates against some of the Mosaic laws?" [40]

Kohler put his finger on the weak spot in Morais' argument. Morais' attitude could no longer be accounted Orthodoxy, whether old or new. It came to be characteristic of what was later termed "Conservative Judaism." To be sure, in actual practice, Morais was scrupulous in adhering to the very letter of the traditional law. He made much ado against officiating at weddings after sundown, just because it did not happen to be a custom among Sephardic Jews, and he entered into a correspondence about it with rabbinic authorities in the old world.[41]

The one respect in which Morais differed from the Reformists, and in which he held a position identical with Orthodoxy, was in the matter of Jewish nationhood. He combated the tendency of Reform to universalize Judaism by removing the element of nationhood as emphasized in the system of observances which set the Jews apart from the rest of the world. But the nationhood which Morais insisted on preserving had nothing of the modern worldly spirit. It was entirely traditional and theocratic. In fact, he was very strongly opposed to Zionism, which meant the translation of Jewish nationhood into a program of political action for the return of Jews to Eretz Yisrael. He even went out of his way to take Emma Lazarus and others to task for favoring Jewish migration to Palestine and colonization of it on a large scale.

Whatever self-assurance and logical consistency the original Orthodoxy may possess, it certainly precludes the possibility of ever having the Jews, with their increasing diversity of opinion and attitude, achieve any kind of creative unity, whether it be political, cultural or religious. To be sure, Orthodoxy can find in traditional Judaism adequate authority in support of its intolerance of divergent beliefs and practices. But, on the other hand, if one looks hard enough, one can discover authority in support of the principle of Jewish unity as capable of being sufficiently broad to include even those who depart from what is regarded as the norm.

The question, however, is not one of texts authorizing diversity in belief and practice, but one of Jewish survival. From all appearances, it does not seem likely that inflexibility and intransigeance like that displayed by the Orthodox can help the Jews, with their widely different backgrounds and cultural development, to find a way out of their present spiritual impasse. It must be admitted, however, that Orthodoxy has succeeded in eliciting from its adherents far greater self-sacrifice for Judaism than have the two other synagogue trends, namely, Reform and Conservatism. Moreover, if Judaism is to survive as a social and spiritual life pattern for a variously minded Jewry, there must be a place in it for those who cannot do without the certainty that goes with the belief in supernatural revelation, and who cannot tolerate the doubt that often shadows even the deepest human convictions. For such as these, Orthodoxy's message is indispensable.

CHAPTER ELEVEN

Conservative Judaism

"Conservative Judaism" is a term that has been applied rather loosely to that trend in Judaism which is regarded as holding a midway position between Reform and Orthodoxy. It was used by Sabato Morais, who was himself virtually as orthodox in his theology as Samson Raphael Hirsch, to describe the congregation Mikve Israel of Philadelphia as the citadel of Orthodoxy.[1] In his first appeal for the founding of the Jewish Theological Seminary of New York in 1896, Morais used the terms "Orthodoxy" and "Conservatism" interchangeably.[2]

The Conservative movement marks a trend in American Jewish life which seems to approximate more closely than any of the other trends the dominant pattern which Judaism may finally assume in the free countries of the Western world. Like the other trends, it arose during the forties in nineteenth century Germany, where it later flourished under the name of *Liberal Judentum* until the liquidation of German Jewry under Hitler's regime. It was known at first as "Positive-Historic Judaism," a term coined by Zachariah Frankel (1801-1875). In America the movement acquired the name "Conservative" more through popular consensus than through official designation or approval.

This third synagogue trend was transplanted to the United States by Solomon Schechter and other scholars, for whom the ground had been prepared by a group of rabbinical leaders headed by Sabato Morais. The members of that group can scarcely be identified with the Orthodoxy of Samson Raphael Hirsch, or even with that of Isaac Leeser. They differed considerably.

among themselves in the theory and practice of Judaism. Among them were Marcus Jastrow and Benjamin Szold, who were moderate Reformists, and Alexander Kohut, who was moderately Orthodox. But they were all of one mind in considering the official Reform movement, with its antinomian tendencies, as detrimental to Judaism's future, and were therefore strongly opposed to it.

The general pattern of the Conservative movement was conceived in Germany where it first arose. Like the two other synagogue movements, it was the outgrowth of a desire on the part of Jewish spiritual leaders in Germany to stem the rapid decline of Judaism. *Reform tried to motivate the will of Jews to foster Judaism by holding up to them the glory of its mission to mankind. Orthodoxy tried to achieve that purpose by emphasizing the unique privilege of being in possession of the supernaturally revealed Torah. Conservatism sought to save Judaism by evoking in Jews the sense of belonging to a people that is destined for moral and spiritual greatness. Its first designation as the "Historical School" pointed to its apotheosis of the history of the Jewish People as the primary incentive to living as a Jew.*

The Conservative trend in Judaism further resembles Reform and Orthodoxy in being largely influenced by the *Zeitgeist,* or the spirit that prevailed in the environment in which it arose. That *Zeitgeist* then was the product of romanticism which found its embodiment in a chauvinistic German nationalism. One of the manifestations of that romanticism was a fervent interest in history and tradition and a zeal for the conservation of national traditions and institutions. The beginnings of that manifestation may be discerned during the latter part of the eighteenth century in men like Herder and young Goethe, who in their writings threw new light on the significance of individuality, whether personal or collective, and of the historical, or evolutionary, approach to the understanding of human behavior. This historical approach became so obsessive as to gain the epithet *"Historismus,"* or "historicism." In the nineteenth century it attained aggressive self-consciousness, when it was employed as a means of fanning German national sentiment into a flame of patriotism and bitter hatred of France and all her works.

As part of the German nationalist reaction to the reverses and humiliation which Germany had suffered at the hands of revolutionary France, romanticism served as the antithesis of the rationalist spirit which had spread throughout Europe in the wake of Napoleon's career of conquest.[4] Romanticism therefore deemed it as its mission to undo the evils wrought by the spirit of rationalism. Those evils were presumably centered in the disregard of national differences, and the flouting of traditional values which had been sanctified by history. Cosmopolitanism, the primacy of universals, the equality of nations and races, the application of abstract reason to social and religious sanctities, were all part of that spirit of rationalism which was held accountable for the havoc wrought by the Napoleonic wars.

It was therefore necessary to educate every German to an appreciation of his historical tradition and valuation of the uniqueness of his culture. Germans were to be redeemed from bondage to alien culture by means of a proper historical orientation. History as a body of specific facts about the life of peoples in their internal and mutual relations, and a philosophy of history in which one's nation was assigned a central place, came to be viewed as indispensable to Germany's recovering her self-respect. This development had a far-reaching effect on the Western world to such an extent as to warrant the following statement by Ernst Cassirer: "In the culture of the nineteenth century history began to take a leading part. After a short time it had replaced and almost eclipsed all the other intellectual interests."[5]

The philosophers elaborated grand *a priori* theories, in the light of which all history was to be read. Scholars, with their meticulous plodding, were engaged in systematic and tireless research to unearth the detailed facts of Germany's past. From the rationalist point of view that entire procedure seemed absurd and fraught with danger. "The Romantic writers," says Lord Acton, "relieved present need with all abounding treasure of other times, subjecting them to the will and the conscience of the dead. . . . They were strong by the recovery of lost knowledge and by making it possible to understand, to appreciate and even to admire things which the judgment of rationalism condemned in the mass of worthless and indiscriminate error."[6]

On the other hand, the romanticists congratulated themselves on their superiority to the light-minded and superficial rationalists. "What a blessing it is for a people," says Schleiermacher, "to possess in its home and surroundings, in its customs and usages, in its whole way of life that which has come down from ancient times! . . . When a people respects reverently and preserves faithfully what has survived from the earliest past through the stream of time . . . , when it concerns itself with the sources of its contributions and customs, preserves the knowledge of its antiquities, and through it looks ahead, yet always continues to cherish faithfully the memory of the old, such a nation is provided with a glorious foundation for a serious and worthy life. . . ." [7]

Concentrated interest in a national tradition, even if it is motivated chiefly by the desire to reconstruct the past of one's people, naturally produces the tendency to conserve the spirit of the past and to be distrustful of any changes which are dictated by practical or rational considerations. Those who display such interest are, indeed, the first to be aware that all life, whether of a people or of an individual, undergoes change. But, wishing to make sure that the particular national life in which they are concerned will retain its identity amid the changes which it must necessarily undergo, they act on the principle that change is normal only so long as it is imperceptible and evolutionary. *Any attempt deliberately to plan and execute change is regarded as rationalistic and revolutionary, and therefore as destructive of the higher values of life.* Thus, the *historical* comes to be invested with the sanctity of the *eternal*.

This resistance to deliberately planned change in social institutions was practically accepted as a guiding principle in the political and social philosophy of the German People. It was made an issue by the famous German jurist, Carl von Savigny, in 1814-1815. Germany had been in a state of confusion because of the heterogeneous character of the different law systems which prevailed in its various Governments. Those systems were not only in mutual conflict, but were also largely out of date within their own territories. Anton F. J. Thibaut, a professor of law in the University of Heidelberg, published a pamphlet in which he suggested that all those systems should be replaced by a uniform civil law for the whole of Germany.

Savigny was at that time professor of law at the newly founded University of Berlin, which was then the center of a recently awakened spirit of nationalist Germany. Sensing in Thibaut's pamphlet an echo of the rationalism which was then considered the chief menace to the welfare of the German people, he published an answer entitled *Von Beruf unserer Zeit fuer Gesetzgebung und Rechtwissenschaft*, the purpose of which was to prevent Thibaut's suggestion from being accepted. Savigny maintained that law should not be codified in rationalist fashion, because law was an organic growth, an emanation of the *Volksgeist*, and courts of law acted not as the exponents of universal reason, but as representatives of the *Volksgeist*. In the debate between the two scholars, Savigny and romanticism came out victorious. It is noteworthy that the concept of the *Volksgeist* provided the basis for a compromise between the rising nationalism and the reactionary legitimism of the post-Napoleonic restoration period.[8]

Concern with the preservation of one's national tradition and conservation of the traditional institutions of one's nation, which are the two factors of nineteenth century nationalist German romanticism, went into the making of Conservative Judaism. The first factor found expression in the newly evolved scientific study of Judaism known as *Wissenschaft des Judentums*. Zacharias Frankel, (1801-1875),[9] alludes specifically to the fact that the Jews, having noted the growth of the spirit of historic research which had penetrated all the fields of knowledge, felt the need of applying the same approach to their own tradition. The second factor, conservation of the traditional institutions of one's nation, gave rise to the norm formulated with regard to changes in Jewish law, first by Zacharias Frankel under the slogan of "Positive-Historical Judaism," and later reaffirmed by Solomon Schechter under the slogan of "Catholic Israel."

Romanticism, properly viewed, represents a second stage in the process of shifting the center of gravity of life from other-worldliness to this-worldliness. The first stage was rationalism. It is evident that rationalism, with its acceptance of natural law as all-dominant in the universe, and human welfare or utility as the criterion by which to determine what in the tradition to keep and what to reject, is motivated entirely by this-worldly considerations. On the other hand, romanticism, superficially regarded, seems to disregard immediate concern, and therefore seems to have much in common with the other-worldliness which rationalism seeks to undermine. The fact, however, is that romanticism is no less this-worldly than rationalism.

The difference between these two philosophies of life is only in what they regard as most likely to help man fulfil himself. Rationalism believes that reason is a constructive force in human life. It assumes, therefore, that man's salvation depends upon his exercising his reason to the utmost. Romanticism assumes that man is essentially a being actuated by will, instinct, or feeling, and therefore concludes that his fulfillment can come about only through the harmonious gratification or realization of his basic desires.

Conservative Judaism, in adopting the two principles of romanticism, by fostering an interest in national Jewish history and by upholding the conservation of Jewish law, far from being a mere continuation of Traditional Judaism, has been a creative adjustment to the mundane spirit of modern times. Conservative Judaism may therefore be described as a romantic this-worldly adaptation, in contrast with Reform, which began essentially as a rational-idealistic adaptation of Traditional Judaism. "To be miscellaneous, to be indefinite, to be unfinished, is essential to the romantic life," says George Santayana. "May we not say that it is essential to all life in its immediacy; and that only in reference to what is not life—to objects, ideals and unanimities that cannot be experienced but may only be conceived—can life become rational and truly progressive." [10] That contrast which Santayana drew between romanticism and rationalism was conspicuous in the contrast between Reform and Conservatism in the first stages of their development.

The Conservative movement was at first identified with the Historical School in Judaism, the members of which were among the principal founders of the scientific study of Judaism. The historical approach to Judaism is basically a secularization of Jewish learning. It applies to Jewish learning the objective historic-critical approach. Before the nineteenth century, that type of Jewish scholarship was unknown. The one outstanding exception was Azariah di Rossi, who flourished in Italy during the latter half of the sixteenth century. The spirit of the Renaissance had then penetrated the inner life of Italian Jewry. Di Rossi, however, was the only outstanding Jew in whom that Renaissance spirit awak-

ened a sense of historical and critical method in the study of the
Jewish past. That approach constitutes a break with tradition,
despite the attempt of most of those who have employed it to make
it appear as in reality a continuation of the ideal of learning which
prevailed in the past. Di Rossi's classic work *Meor Enayim* was
anathemized and ordered burned by Rabbi Joseph Karo, the author
of the *Shulhan Aruk*.

The chief founders of the *Wissenschaft des Judentums* were:
Isaac Marcus Jost, Solomon Rapoport, Nachman Krochmal,
Samuel David Luzzatto, Leopold Zunz, Abraham Geiger, Zacharias
Frankel, Heinrich Graetz, Isaac Hirsch Weiss, and Solomon
Schechter. Of these, Geiger was the only one who took a leading
part in the Reform movement. Most of the others might well
be claimed as having contributed to the version of Judaism which
Frankel fostered in the Old World and Schechter in the New
World.

Geiger was interested mainly in a rational scientific overhauling
of the traditional regimen which had derived its sanction from the
belief in its divinely revealed character. The only way to transform
that regimen, he believed, was through the medium of historical
study of Jewish antiquities. To a large extent this also motivated
Zacharias Frankel, but Frankel was too timid to translate into
practice his own inferences from historical research.

Virtually all those scholars began their intellectual career in
the *Yeshivah*, with its concentration on the study of Rabbinic
writings, principally the *halakah*, or Rabbinic legalism. This was
as much the case with Schechter as it had been with Rapoport.
Their earliest intellectual activity consisted in the casuistical study
of Talmudic lore. In terms of creative or reconstructive thinking,
such study had little to offer. Most of those who had been subjected to the traditional *Yeshivah* training broke away from Judaism
as soon as they got a smattering of Western culture. Those great
scholars, however, who had imbibed deeply of Western culture were
impelled to apply the modern scientific methods of research,
analysis, and interpretation to the great mass of Rabbinic tradition.
That enabled them to reconstruct in true scientific fashion the
main outlines, and in some cases even the details, of Jewish life of
bygone centuries.

The aim of the historical study of Judaism, as set forth by

Immanuel Wolf in the first issue of the *Zeitschrift fuer Wissen-schaft des Judentums*,[11] was to evolve a knowledge of past Jewish achievement in the field of intellectual, ethical and spiritual values, and to relate those values to the historic background and the specific environmental conditions under which they arose. It was expected that such knowledge would open the eyes of non-Jews to the fact that the Jews, throughout their historical career, had been creators of significant cultural values, and that they did not have to justify their continued existence as a People on the ground of their belonging to a supernatural order of reality.

It was assumed that non-Jews would change their attitude toward Jews as a result of this new knowledge concerning them. Thus not only would Jews gain the good-will of their Gentile neighbors, but they themselves would also arrive at a better understanding of their own People and its past. They would be cured of the sense of inferiority to which they had become subject, as soon as they ceased to believe in the literal account of the events recorded in the Torah. The claim of the Reformists that the Jews were entrusted with the mission of keeping alive the cause of true religion somehow failed to strike a responsive chord. There was need for something that was in keeping with reality, with the way Jewish life had actually functioned, to revive in the Jew his waning self-respect. *The Jew had to be made to feel that the People he belonged to had a significant history which reached down to his own day. By becoming aware of that history, his People would cease to have for him a kind of ghost-like character, and would acquire all the traits of a living, normal people.*

THE HISTORICAL APPROACH TO THE CONCEPTION OF JUDAISM

Heinrich Graetz gives a striking analogy to illustrate the function of the scientific study of Judaism. "Imagine," he says, "that in the unearthing of Pompeii and Herculaneum not only the streets, houses and furniture could be reconstructed, but also that the people who were encrusted in the lava could be resurrected and could recall all that they had experienced of the glory of Roman life and institutions which they and their ancestors had created. Assume, furthermore, that they felt they were still in complete possession of the vital powers which they had originally. They would then, indeed, have good reason to experience confidence in themselves. Nothing less than this far-fetched supposition has actually come true in the case of the Jewish People. The scientific study of Judaism has brought that People back to life. It has awakened the dormant powers of Judaism and inspired it with the confidence that it can play a role in the future as it did in the past. Thus has this scientific study of Judaism enabled an ancient nation to take its place among those newly risen." [12]

Graetz is by no means alone in this evaluation of the scientific study of Judaism. Every great contributor to its development has ascribed to it the power of resurrecting Jewish nationhood. "If the science of history," says Louis Ginzberg, "is the pride and ornament of a people, it is Israel's weapon and shield, a bulwark against enemies, a stronghold against derogation and misrepresentation, but also a source of our rejuvenation." [13]

This estimate of the part played by what is apparently little more than a suddenly aroused literary activity that has produced biography, bibliography, philology, and archeology is entirely warranted. The scientific study of Judaism constitutes a radical transformation in the perspective of Traditional Judaism on the nationhood of the Jewish People. Instead of eliminating Jewish nationhood, as did the Reformists, or desiccating it, as did the Orthodox, the Conservatives have sought so to reconstruct the very consciousness of Jewish People as to experience it as the source and inspiration of its religion with its passion for righteousness.

In Traditional Judaism, the national consciousness is articulated in theocratic other-worldly terms, in terms of miracle in the past and world-cataclysm in the future. That kind of national consciousness singles out from the career of the Jewish People only the few events and personalities that figured in the divine drama, of which God was the author and the People of Israel the central hero. Most of what there is of history in the Biblical and post-Biblical writings does not belong to objective fact. Yet it cannot be treated as mere legend or phantasy. To use a category suggested by Benedetto Croce, "it is a movement of moral conscience; it is a history in the making." Whatever historical truth is present there is at best expressed only episodically. Accordingly, when, as a result of the mundane spirit of the modern *Zeitgeist*, the nations formulated their own histories in terms of the secular processes of social life, the Jews were in danger of finding themselves devoid of a national history. Such lack could not but lead to the collapse of the ethnic Jewish consciousness.

The Jews who came under the influence of modern civilization found it incongruous to express their sense of oneness with their People by means of the *traditional* conception of Jewish nationhood. If Jews could at least have retained the traditional instruments of their nationhood, their juridical autonomy and an adequate system of education, the loss of the traditional conception of Jewish nationhood might not have left such a spiritual void in their lives. But all tangible institutional forms of Jewish nationhood were precluded by the strategy of the struggle for emancipation.

One need only recall the pathetic effort initiated by three Jewish young men in 1819 in Berlin to grapple with this problem for the first time. Leopold Zunz was one of them. They established a society which they called *Verein fuer die Kultur und Wissenschaft der Juden*. Before long the society grew to seventy men. Among those who joined was the famous German Jewish poet Heinrich Heine. However, the careerist interests of many of them, including its organizer Edward Gans, proved too strong for them to be able to withstand the waves of apostasy from Judaism in the Jewish circles of Berlin. Zunz was the only one who persisted in his efforts to achieve an objective or scientific method of research into the Jewish past.

At the same time, in other parts of Central Europe which had come under the influence of the German renaissance, Jewish young men who possessed a more intensive Jewish background grappled with the problem of reconstructing the consciousness of Jewish nationhood into modern mundane terms. Outstanding among them were Nachman Krochmal, Solomon Rapoport, and a host of others. They began searching for historic content to fill the long gaps in the account of the Jewish past; they sought for recognizable persons to emerge out of the long stretch of anonymity. Old texts began to be studied from a new point of view. Details of customs, events and people that had been considered too trivial to be noted began to be recorded and brought together into organic relationship. Manuscripts that had been mouldering in the great European libraries began to be published. Inexhaustible mines of secular information about the inner and outer aspects of Jewish life were opened up. "What lent these studies particular value," says Graetz, "and distinguished them from mere pedantry was the warmth and love with which they were undertaken. They are to be regarded, therefore, as national achievements, and not as the product of leisurely learning." [14]

"A society without history," said Gilbert Murray of Oxford on the occasion of his seventieth birthday, "cannot understand what it is doing; and history without scholarship cannot understand itself. For scholarship is just the understanding, the intimate understanding with imagination and with love of the noblest things of the past, the great thoughts, writings, doings, aspirations, which still live, but live precariously, because they will die if they are not understood, die if they are not loved."

Thus, for the first time, Jews came to possess a mundane history. They began to realize that their history was not merely a series of miracles, sins, backslidings and divine punishments, but a natural succession of human events that could be placed in a pattern dominated by the principle of cause and effect. The traditional values of Jewish nationhood which had been integral to the thought-world of pre-modern terms were thus replaced by values of nationhood which were relevant to the modern thought-world. Josephus had secularized to a large extent the history of his People mainly for Roman readers; the modern Jewish scholars have been secularizing Jewish history for Jewish and non-Jewish readers. Such works are Isaac Marcus Jost's voluminous writings on Jewish history and Graetz's monumental work, *Die Geschichte der Juden*, and Yitzhak Hirsch Weiss' *Dor Dor v'Dorshov*, which is a history of Jewish Tradition.

The effect of the historical approach upon the conception of Judaism may be illustrated by what Judaism came to mean to Graetz, the greatest Jewish historian. To him Judaism was a national unity, a State law (eiu Staatsgesetz). In his introduction to the fifth volume of his history Graetz asserts that "the history of the post-Talmudic period continued to have a national character; it is in no way the history of a religion or a Church, since it deals with the development of a people and not with the history of learning."

The foregoing makes it evident that the scientific study of Judaism constitutes nothing less than a radical self-transformation of the Jewish consciousness, in order that it might feel itself at home in the modern world, with its emphasis on this-worldly salvation. "The Renaissance," says Schechter, "is usually described as the moment in history in which man discovered himself. In a similar way, the Jew will also have to rediscover himself. This discovery, which should be undertaken with a view to strengthening the Jewish consciousness, can be made by means of Jewish literature, which retains all that is immortal in the nation." [15]

What then is to account for the comparative neglect of the scientific study of the Biblical writings, especially the Pentateuch, on the part of most of those Jewish scholars? It is evident that they were largely inhibited by apprehension of shocking the traditionalists. Even their attempts at textual emendation were regarded as "a dangerous amusement, and were viewed with uneasiness by Orthodox exegetes." Moreover, those scholars were intent upon something more immediate than what a scientific study of the Bible might have yielded. Such a study might produce at best an objective view of the early history of Israel and Israel's religion, but it would still leave the last 2500 years a blank. That blank had to be filled in with historic fact, in order that the continuity of the Jewish People, as a living social organism throughout that long interval since Bible days, might be established beyond all doubt. Hence *the chief interest of the Jewish scholars was centered on recovering the history of the post-Biblical and medieval period.*

In addition, the Jewish scholars were spared from engaging in polemics with the German Biblical scholars, whose research was impelled by the preconceived assumption that the entire career of the People of Israel had been merely a prelude to the advent of Christ, and who, for the most part, did not omit any opportunity that presented itself, in the course of their exposition, to defame the character of the Jewish People. This is why Schechter, an outstanding pioneer of Conservative Judaism, justly characterized Higher Criticism as "Higher anti-Semitism." [16]

If modern Jewish scholarship will continue to develop along the lines laid down by its pioneers, it will ultimately have to reckon with the scientific study of the Bible, and probably contribute to the solution of some of the most complex problems so far left unsolved by Higher Criticism. One does not have to be a follower of the Wellhausen school of Biblical criticism to attach little scientific value to such elaborate arguments as those which the Orthodox scholar David Hoffman advanced to prove the validity of the traditional conception of the Torah as having been dictated by God to Moses. To be sure, David Hoffman displayed great ingenuity, and actually won many a battle in his polemics with the critics, but he lost the war. The other outstanding Jewish scholars indicate more or less frankly in their various writings that they have parted company with the traditional conception of the Torah. But, except for strong affirmations of the need of maintaining the revelational view of the Torah, they have not made any serious attempt to bridge the gap between that view and their own by any historical or philosophical formula that might leave the authority of the Torah intact. George Foot Moore is correct in saying that the evolutionary study of a religious tradition "is an abandonment of the very conception of revealed religion as entertained by the teachers of Judaism on the basis of revelation itself." [17]

*   *   *

The one great drawback to the scientific study of Judaism is that the reworking of the contents of the Jewish literary heritage into the modern type of systematic presentation is a slow process, and can be carried on only by a small group of scholars and specialists possessed of a sacrificial devotion to their respective specialties. First, the most important part of the historic and literary material has to be properly systematized and published; then comes the process of popularization and interpretation of that material, with a view to developing in the reflective Jew an integrated, well-informed Jewish consciousness. This is a work of decades.

In the meantime, one generation of youth after another that cannot be reared any longer in the traditional type of education and presentation of Jewish subject matter grows up with little understanding of what constitutes being a Jew, and in what concrete way to express their Jewish individuality. "Theology and all that is connected with it," complained Schechter, while he was still in England, "has become with us a closed profession of no mortal interest to those who are not in it, which a gentleman may tolerate and even contribute toward maintaining, but which he must never enjoy personally." [18] The situation in that respect has improved relatively little since that day.

The Reform ranks have not been troubled by that problem. While their leaders were talking about a Jewish mission, the laymen were merely concerned with confining all their Judaism within the four walls of the synagogue, and giving Jewish worship all the possible appearance of a replica of a Protestant Church service. The Orthodox, on the other hand, by stressing the performance of the *mitzvot* and the study of the traditional texts, both Biblical and Rabbinic, as constituting the most active expression of fealty to Judaism, have virtually solved the problem of assigning to every Jew specific and feasible tasks, and thus providing definite content for those who wish to live and act as Jews. The type of study, however, which the Conservative school of thought calls for is still confined to rabbis and scholars, and has not yet been brought down to the level of the laity. When, therefore, Zacharias Frankel, the founder of what later came to be the Conservative movement, formulated the principle that the *cultivation of the scientific study of Judaism can furnish the only dependable criteria for Jewish life,* he only made it more difficult for Jewish life to meet those urgent needs that could not wait for the conclusions of scholarship. That these conclusions themselves are all too often dictated by personal bias, and are by no means unanimous, is a familiar fact which raises doubts as to whether they are worth waiting for.

Actually, no specific guidance in the daily conduct of Jewish life has resulted from the scientific study of Judaism. Its greatest contribution has consisted in keeping alive merely the *mood* of Jewish peoplehood. The only concrete results of that mood have been the following: 1) Insistence upon maintaining Jewish unity by refraining from any type of organization that might fragmentize the Jewish People into different regional and mutually unrelated groups or sectarianize them into different denominations; 2) opposition to all attempts to minimize the importance of Hebrew in religious ritual and prayer. It is true that prayers which are not understood are virtually meaningless; moreover even from the legalistic standpoint, the use of Hebrew in prayer is rarely treated as essential. Neither of these considerations, however, has prevailed against the strong feeling that the abolition of Hebrew from worship would mean the ultimate disappearance of Jewish life in the Diaspora; 3) retention of the prayer for the restoration of the Jewish People to its ancient land. This issue was fought out when, in 1840, the new Reform congregation in Hamburg issued a new prayer book in which that prayer was omitted. Needless to say, this omission was vigorously denounced by the Orthodox, on the ground that it was an act of disloyalty to traditional Judaism. Zacharias Frankel, however, did not approach the issue of the controversy in the manner of the traditionalists, or of the Orthodox school. He did not denounce the proposed change on the ground that it was wrong to break with tradition. He tried to prove, first, that without the hope of becoming a People once again in the land to which Jews were bound by imperishable memories, they were certain to lose the respect of the other nations and their own self-respect; secondly, that no fair-minded person could find fault with Jews for continuing to cherish that hope.

Frankel did not treat the return to Eretz Yisrael in the spirit of Orthodoxy, as part of God's miraculous dealings with the People of Israel. According to Orthodoxy, as stated above (page 337) the Jews, as a body, were not permitted to engage in political action leading to the establishment of a Jewish State in Eretz Yisrael. Jews should wait for the Messiah whom God would send to lead them back to Eretz Yisrael. Frankel, however, saw in the liberation of Greece from Turkish rule, and in the recovery of its nationhood, an example to be emulated by the Jews. He denounced as opportunist rationalization the cosmopolitanism of those who repudiated Jewish peoplehood. The Jewish People would be morally degrading itself, he maintained, if it were to give up its hopes and prayers of national restoration.[19] Elsewhere, Frankel wrote: "Jewish nationhood is imposed from without. When the State repels the Jews, when it refuses them rights and freedom, and the Jew experiences through its law, by reason of fact that he bears the name Jew, oppression and neglect, is he not plainly told by the State that he is regarded as the member of another nation?" [20]

Nothing practical, however, was done by Frankel and his colleagues to implement the sense of Jewish peoplehood which the scientific study of Judaism was recovering for the Jew through its recovery of the Jewish past. As a consequence, Jewish peoplehood, with the adherents of the Historical Positive School before Schechter openly came out for Zionism, did not become a program of action but remained a state of mind. As such, it served as the basis not of any collective social or political movement, but of the reinterpretation of the eschatological teachings of Traditional Judaism. The salvation of the individual Jew came to be regarded as bound up with that of the entire People of Israel. Whatever a Jew did for his own individual salvation had to contribute at the same time to the unity and solidarity of his People.

Jewish peoplehood, for the predecessors of Schechter, remained merely an idea concerning a way of praying and did not become the basis for a program of action. The Jewish People thus continued during the proto-historical era of the Conservative movement to be identified mainly as a religious communion, or as the *Kenesset Yisrael* of Rabbinic lore. Schechter, in the introduction to his first volume of *Jewish Studies*, which he wrote in his pre-Zionist days, says that those studies are based on a conception of the Synagogue which "for brevity's sake, I will call the High Synagogue, though it does not correspond in all details with what one is accustomed to understand under the term High Church." Elsewhere he has occasion to speak of the universality of Judaism and "what it meant to the Prophets and their *Jewish* successors." [21] According to Schechter, it meant "that the whole world should become Jews, not that Judaism should fade out into the world." That indicates that during its proto-historic stage the Conservative movement still hankered after the traditional conception of Jewish nationhood. According to that conception, the return of the Jewish People to its ancient homeland was compatible with the ultimate adoption of Judaism by the whole world. After Schechter himself had come under the influence of Ahad Ha-Am and his version of spiritual Zionism, the Conservative movement abandoned the eschatological conception of the Jews' return to their ancient homeland. But, so far, it has not yet fully integrated the mundane implications of Zionism into its conception of Judaism as a whole.

THE JEWISH PEOPLE AS WITNESS TO
DIVINE REVELATION

What must one do as a Jew to achieve the good and abundant life? This is the question which Jewish religion as a means of individual salvation seeks to answer.

According to Reform Judaism, the answer of Jewish religion is: "Let the Jew realize that God is the life of the spirit within man, and let him find in the past of his people the imperative to live this life of the spirit as a means to the salvation of mankind. That is his mission." Pragmatically, however, there is no specific guidance implied in this answer. It leaves the Jew entirely to his own conscience in all matters of social responsibility, and makes no specific demands upon him as a Jew, except that he worship with Jews instead of with adherents of other religions.

According to Orthodoxy, what the Jew must do to achieve salvation is clearly set forth in the supernaturally revealed teaching of the Torah, as interpreted by the Sages. Orthodoxy demands absolute faith in Jewish tradition. In return, it provides the Jew with a detailed regimen of conduct. According to Conservatism, the Jew should so identify himself with the Jewish People, or with the "Synagogue," that he will become imbued with its historic consciousness and its world-outlook, and will express his yearning for God through the performance of the duties prescribed in the Torah.

The way to identify oneself with the Jewish People, according to Conservatism, is to live the Jewish life, which is conceived entirely in terms of religious practices such as the Sabbath, circumcision and other observances aiming at the perpetuation of the Congregation of Israel. The main value of the religious observances in Judaism is that they promote in the individual Jew an awareness of his belonging to the Jewish People. That awareness is not attended by a depressing sense of inferiority, as when it is produced by anti-Semitism. On the contrary, it serves as a stimulating challenge to worthy living. Out of this awareness in action arises the collective Jewish consciousness.

For that reason any deviation from the established norm of

religious observance defeats the principal purpose of that observance. No wonder, therefore, that, according to Schechter, "the keeping of the Sabbath, even if a man stays at home and does not attend a service, because he happens to have no synagogue in his place, does more for Judaism and for the cause in general than the musical programs, gilded temples and unctuous addresses will ever accomplish on a Sunday." [22] Incidentally, it is interesting to note that *of the three modern trends which may be identified as Synagogue movements, Conservatism has been the only one which emphasizes the survival and enhancement of the Jewish People as the main problem of contemporary Judaism.*

What such emphasis can come to mean is well illustrated by the case of Leopold Zunz. He started his career as a Jewish scholar with the intention of completely westernizing Jewish life. His cultural interest in Judaism was based on the desire to discover in the Jewish heritage those universal elements which would assimilate Judaism to Western culture. As a result, however, of his researches he became so aware of the individuality and uniqueness of Jewish life that the fostering of it became with him an end in itself. He no longer asked for universal meanings to justify its characteristic practices. Thus we find him defending the ritual practice of wearing *tefillin* during weekday prayers, in refutation of the argument raised by Geiger that *tefillin* were originally nothin but pagan amulets.[23]

Conservative Judaism, in common with Traditional Judaism and with traditional religion as a whole, assumes that man is in need of divine revelation in order to know what constitutes salvation and how to achieve it. But being the creation of the Historical School of thought, Conservative Judaism's conception of divine revelation is a far cry from that of traditional religion. In Traditional Judaism, the guarantee of such revelation was the sacred and unimpugned text of the Torah and other holy writings. In Conservative Judaism the witness to that revelation is the *living*, continuing People.

The Bible text, by very reason of its fixed character, may be undermined as a source of authority as a result of some scientific or historical discovery. Not so the changing and evolving tradition of Israel, which expresses Israel's inherent religious response to the experience and challenge of each age. From this it follows that "the center of authority is actually removed from the Bible and placed on some *living* body. . . . This living body, however, is not represented by any section of the nation, or any corporate priesthood, or Rabbihood, but by the collective conscience of Catholic Israel as embodied in the Universal Synagogue." [24]

If one were to have asked Schechter how he expected the modern Jew to bridge the gap between the traditional conception of the written word as the witness to divine revelation and the new conception of the living body of the Jewish People as the witness to divine revelation, he would probably have answered that this is where "a touch of mysticism" is indispensable. He was certainly hopeful that the Jewish consciousness acquired through self-identification with the living body of the Jewish People would enable the Jew to attain salvation. "Being in communion with his Synagogue," he said, "we may also look hopefully for a safe and rational solution of our present theological troubles." [25]

Such "a safe and rational solution" may be said to have been attempted by Herbert Loewe. Like Schechter, whom he succeeded, he was a reader of Rabbinics in the University of Cambridge. Though he called himself "an Orthodox Jew, but one who is not a fundamentalist," he really belonged to the Conservative school in Judaism. His method of reinterpretation is set forth in his Introduction to A *Rabbinic Anthology*, which he edited together with Claude G. Montefiore (London, 1938). He assumed that both Liberal and Orthodox (Conservative) Judaism subscribe to the belief in divine revelation and in a Mosaic Torah as the embodiment of such revelation.

The term "Mosaic Torah," as Loewe used it, had but little in common with what the term denoted for Traditional Judaism, or with what it still denotes for the Orthodoxy advocated by Samson Raphael Hirsch. He found the acceptance of the documentary theory entirely compatible with the belief in a Mosaic Torah, for did not Abraham ibn Ezra hint broadly that the present text of the Torah contained minor additions by a hand other than that of Moses? And once you can believe that even a single iota, or vowel, is not divinely authored, and still remain a good Jew, then what is there to prevent a person from being a good Jew, even if he goes to the limit of denying that the bulk of the text comes from Moses, so long as he grants that one or two verses might be genuinely Mosaic. This is the argument in logic known as *sorites*, where the questioner is supposed to pull out single hairs from the horse's tail and ask after each one: Is it still a tail?—until the one who answers finds it difficult to know when to stop answering, "Yes."

Likewise with the doctrine of divine revelation. At first Loewe gives the impression that he is going to insist on the acceptance of "hard doctrine." He promises to indicate the scope of revelation and its content, assuming the immutability of revealed truth. The reader expects to be offered the choice between surrendering his right to reason, or being read out of Judaism in the challenging manner of Samson Raphael Hirsch. Instead, Loewe manages by a clever process of sleight-of-pen to convince the reader that no such alternative is placed before him. All that is necessary is to change the meaning of words gradually instead of suddenly, so that before long you find yourself subscribing to what you originally regarded as incredible doctrine. "All that revelation means," says Loewe, is "the silent imperceptible manifestation of God in history. It is the still small voice: it is the inevitableness, the regularity of nature. . . . It is the denial of chance." Since, then, revelation may be equated with the regularity of nature, it is almost tautologous to speak of revelation or the Torah as immutable. So why object to Maimonides' dogma: "The Torah, which is in our possession, is the same as that given to Moses our Teacher, peace be unto him?" This kind of reasoning has become current coin in the teaching and preaching of the current Conservative movement. One is reminded of what Edmund Wilson says of T. S. Eliot: "We feel in contemporary writers like Eliot a desire to believe in religious revelation, a belief that it would be a good thing to believe, rather than a genuine belief." [26]

THE SHORTCOMINGS OF CONSERVATIVE JUDAISM

The fact is that the underlying principle of Conservative Judaism, which would have the salvation of the individual Jew depend upon his fostering an intensive Jewish consciousness by identifying himself with the People of Israel, promises more than it fulfills. That principle sounds as though it really affords both inspiration and guidance to the modern Jew, as though it provides the way to his self-fulfillment, in that it enables him to achieve the synthesis of what is best in his tradition with what is best in the modern world. Upon careful scrutiny, however, that principle turns out to be a method of salvation by evasion. It evades outward difficulties and inner conflicts, instead of coming to close grips with them.

Conservative Judaism possesses that trait in common with romanticism, by which its beginnings were largely influenced. Romanticism is known to seek an anchorage in some calm water rather than ride the rough seas. It is especially fond of retiring into memories of the past, and it usually manages to select such memories as are pleasant and capable of affording a sheltered retreat. When the high hopes we place on man's reason and initiative to redeem himself from the evils that beset him are frustrated, and we find that the main result of the exercise of reason and initiative has been to despoil society of faith and idealism, and to give added stimulus to selfishness and aggression, we naturally yearn for the good old days of simple faith and unsophisticated morals.

No amount of wishing on our part, however, can actually bring back the conditions which obtained in the past. Not even the most vigorous efforts to create them artificially are of much avail. The result is that we spend our days mostly in nostalgic yearning for the past. Since we fail to achieve the object of that yearning, we conclude that the nostalgia is a spiritual experience, worthwhile in and for itself. We nurse our inner malaise and actually come to enjoy it. Needless to say, it renders us impotent to deal effectively with present realities. The old fable about the mountain's shaking and trembling only to produce a mouse is enacted time and again, particularly in the area of *halakah*, or Jewish law. During Prohibition days in the United States, *halakic* interpretation was restorted to in order to permit the use of grape juice when reciting the *Kiddush* benediction over the Sabbath. Currently it is being resorted to in order to permit the inclusion of an unenforceable clause in the outdated type of marriage contract (*ketuvah*), in the vain hope of overcoming serious divorce complications which are the result of the inferior status assigned to the woman in traditional law.

We would not be telling the whole story of modern Jewish scholarship, if, in addition to stressing its original motivation and its successes in re-creating the Jewish past, we were to overlook the fact that, occasionally, that scholarship shows signs of decadence. It tends to share the fate of literature and art when they lose contact with the realities of life, and are cultivated for their own sake. Many a modern Jewish scholar, despairing of a future for Judaism, but having devoted the best years of his life to the acquisition of Jewish knowledge, is naturally loathe to let that knowledge lie idle. He thereupon turns it to archaeological uses. The famous Jewish scholar, Moritz Steinschneider, in the nineteenth century, justified his devotion to research in the field of Judaism on the ground that he was helping to give Judaism "a decent funeral." Fortunately, this decadent cynicism has been halted by the Hebraic renaissance, for which every recovered item of the Jewish past is additional seed of new Jewish life.

The tendency to escape the need of grappling with the harsh realities of life is not new. Traditional religion, with its otherworldliness, which placed the purpose and center of human life in the hereafter rather than in the here and the now, offered that type of escape. "The safest refuge from time" it has been said, "is eternity." But now that the ideal of eternity has lost its hold on the human mind, another method of escape from the world which is too much with us is being tried. That is the salvation through history. The safest refuge from the present has come to be the past.

There is a very important difference, however, between the foregoing two types of escape from reality. When in ancient times the Jews took refuge in the ideal of eternity, it never occurred to them that they were running away from the present. On the contrary, they were certain that they thereby *conquered* the present, and that the eternity they believed in was sure of attainment. Moreover, since the ideal of eternity was believed in universally, it was, so to speak, part of the prevailing climate of thought. When nowadays, however, we indulge in nostalgic regrets for the assumed lost glories of the past, we know full well that the stream of life cannot be turned back. Hence we deliberately take shelter in an artificially fostered state of mind that is self-negating. Scholars who devote themselves to the study of the past naturally have their thoughts and emotions shaped by what they study. They live themselves so thoroughly into the past that it functions for them as a continuing force and authority with which they defy the present. But the average layman cannot be expected to be so immured in the past as to overcome the mighty pull of the present.

* * *

The only way it might be possible to have the past become a living force in the present would be not merely by wishing to see its desirable moral and spiritual qualities, its faith, piety, holiness and humility, reproduced in the present, but also by accepting the beliefs which made those qualities possible. Schechter, like another great Jewish scholar before him, Leopold Loewe of Hungary (1811-1875), was in keeping with history and with logic when he stressed the importance of dogma in Jewish religion, Moses Mendelssohn to the contrary notwithstanding. Schechter had no patience with the type of Conservatism which regarded itself as compatible with disbelief. The assumption that it was possible to fulfill every commandment in the Torah without believing that the Torah was given by God he dismissed as "diplomatic religion," or a form of hypocrisy. "Is Judaism," he asks, "as some platitudians think, a mere national institute with some useful dietary and sanitary laws, but with nothing that makes for the sanctification of man, with no guidance to offer us in the great problems of our life, and in the greatest anxieties of the human soul?" [27] What then, are the dogmas to which the Jew must subscribe?

Orthodoxy is at least specific. It insists on the entire Maimonidean creed. By accepting that creed as it stands, one might conceivably acquire the ethical and spiritual qualities which all Jews admire, and which many Jews actually achieved in the past. Orthodoxy is especially insistent upon the belief in the supernatural origin of both the Written and the Oral Law, and upon the observance of all the religious practices in the spirit of that belief. Any attempt to treat the Torah as a human document which may be studied and analyzed in a historical spirit is considered dangerous heresy. It is equally heretical even to question— as did Zacharias Frankel or Isaac Yizhak Weiss, both of whom were among the pioneers of the Historical School—the Rabbinic tradition which describes certain laws not contained in the Torah as having been given by God to Moses. But Conservative Judaism, despite the importance it attaches to dogma in general, is too sophisticated to commit itself to any dogma that would involve the renunciation of the modern historical approach to any element in the Jewish tradition, be it event, belief or practice.

Although those who belong to the Conservative school of thought, including Schechter,[28] insist upon divine revelation as a basic and indispensable dogma in Judaism, they find it difficult to give any but the vaguest idea of what they mean by that dogma. Moritz Guedemann[29] of Vienna resorted to the view that the voice on Sinai was not physically audible. "*Offenbarungen sind innere Erlebnisse.*" It was, according to him, a subjective experience. H. Loewe says: "Though the method of Revelation be hidden from us, we cannot think of it save in metaphor, each according to his own ways of thought; of the central, unalterable fact of Revelation, none has any doubt. This is what we mean by *Torah min-ha-Shamayim.*" How a metaphor which every one is at liberty to interpret as he chooses can be of any help in identifying a "central fact," and be set up as a dogma is, indeed, baffling.[30]

The article of faith which Schechter proposed for modern times reads as follows: "Judaism is a proselytising religion, having the mission to bring about God's Kingdom on earth and to include in that kingdom all mankind." [31] The main purpose of a creed or dogma should be to indicate wherein the religion which it helps to define adds to, or improves upon, what other religions profess. Judged from that standpoint, Schechter's proposed article of faith does not indicate wherein Judaism contributes anything that is not effectively promulgated and lived by any other religion. In 1911, after Conservative Judaism had been functioning for almost three-quarters of a century, Schechter still had occasion to write: "The Historical School has never, to my knowledge, offered to the world a theological program of its own. By the nature of the task, its labors are mostly conducted in the field of philosophy and archaeology, and it pays but little attention to purely dogmatic questions. On the whole, its attitude toward religion may be defined as an enlightened skepticism combined with a staunch conservatism,

which is not even wholly devoid of a certain mystical touch." [32]
And he then proceeds to define the theological position of the
school.

The most important corollary of that theological position is the
one that has a bearing on the regimen of observances. Though
never stated in clear and unmistakable terms, that corollary is one
which pervades the entire thinking of the Conservative trend. It
affirms the principle that Jews must continue to regard Rabbinic
Judaism as the authoritative norm of Jewish life. Whatever change
or innovation they find it necessary to adopt, they should do so
within the framework of Rabbinic Judaism itself. The spokesmen
of Conservatism, however, have thus far been unable to prove how
any vital change which circumstances call for can be adopted in
accordance with this principle.

*   *   *

Some of the scholars who were identified with the Historical
School sensed the fact that the lack of the traditional unsophisticated faith in the supernatural origin of the Law presented a
formidable challenge to the philosophy of Conservative Judaism.
Louis Ginzberg met that challenge by maintaining that while it
was true that "the task of the historian is to examine into the
beginnings and developments of the numerous customs and observances of the Jews, practical Judaism is not concerned with origin,
but regards the institutions as they have come to be. Judaism is a
religion of deeds, expressing itself in observances which are designed to achieve the moral elevation of man and give reality
to his religious spirit."[33] That kind of argument is tantamount
to basing the authority of the Jewish law not upon the belief in its
supernatural origin, but upon the fact that it has served as an
effective method of fostering in the Jew loyalty and devotion to
his religious tradition. The same scholar states that Zacharias
Frankel "never deduced the authority of the law from the plenary
inspiration of the Bible as the word of God." [34]

According to Louis Ginzberg, religion is like music. What
sounds musical to one race may sound harsh to another. Likewise,
"the forms in which religious feeling is expressed are not universal
but racial." [35] Other peoples may find the law a repellent method

of giving expression to their deepest religious feelings. Paul, who was less of a Jew than a Roman, voiced the attitude of those who failed to find the Law a fitting instrument of religious expression. Not so the Jew. His is an "active religion, falsely designated legalism." [36] This kind of active religion, argues Louis Ginzberg, "obviously met some of the deepest needs of human nature, and met them in a striking way, and for that human type which attained sharply defined characteristics in the course of a long historic process nothing can-take its place." [37] The implication in all this is that *one can dispense with the belief in the supernatural origin of the rites and observances, and yet feel duty-bound as a Jew to adhere to them, because in that way only can he share the Jewish consciousness and its religious spirit.* "One may, for instance, conceive of the origin and idea of Sabbath rest as the professor of Protestant theology at a German university might conceive it," writes Louis Ginzberg, "and yet minutely observe the smallest detail of the Sabbath observance known to strict Orthodoxy." [38] Hence "the contradiction between the theory and the practice of the positive historic school" is according to him only "apparent." [39]

The foregoing arguments which would identify Conservatism with Orthodoxy are scarcely convincing. In the first place, it is doubtful whether the assumption that throughout the past the Jews expressed their relationship to God by means of legalistically regulated actions, can have as impelling a force as did the wholehearted belief that those actions were literally commanded by God. That assumption is not likely to impel the Jew to keep the Sabbath, the dietary laws, the laws of ritual purity, as did the traditional dogma of the supernatural origin of the Torah in the past. Those who have devoted their lives to the study of those laws are emotionally conditioned in such a way as to find it difficult *not* to practice them. But most Jews who find that the observance of the seventh day Sabbath, for instance, prevents them from earning their livelihood, and who lack the impelling force of early upbringing or of intellectual conditioning, cannot be expected to make the sacrifices involved nowadays in keeping the Sabbath merely because their ancestors found it necessary to express their religious yearnings in strict legalistic fashion. If the leaders of Conservative Judaism, who believed that observances regulated by law were fundamental to Jewish life, had at the same time reckoned with the exigencies of the present situation, and had deliberately so adapted the laws pertaining to the religious observances as to render them capable of being kept, Conservative Judaism would have revitalized Jewish life.

*   *   *

Unfortunately, Conservative Judaism seemed unable to out-live the blight of the romantic influence of early nineteenth century Germany. The teaching of Savigny (*Vom Beruf unserer Zeit fuer Gesetzgebung und Rechtswissenschaft*), one of the anti-Semitic professors of the Berlin University, who ruled that the Jews of Frankfort-on-the-Main were not entitled to civic rights,[40] was in-directly responsible for the principle enunciated by Zacharias Frankel concerning reforms in Judaism. That principle is that "no practice should be considered obsolete because there happen to be a number who do not observe it. The criterion should be the attitude of the community as a whole." That principle has been repeated by every one of Frankel's successors in the leader-ship of Conservative Judaism. Perhaps more than anything else, it has proved the greatest stumbling block that Conservatism could have placed in the way of any intelligent solution of the practical problems involved in living as a Jew. It precludes deliberate change of law, and, above all, any legislation which might abrogate laws which have become irredeemably obsolete. There is in Conserva-tive Judaism no valid reason for this attitude, since the dogma of the supernatural origin of the law is no longer as seriously invoked as it is by the Orthodox. The only justification for this at-titude is the sentimental, romantic feeling that man-made laws must somehow grow of themselves, like Topsy, and that it is sacrilege to tamper with them.

A concrete illustration of how far this tendency went in its insistence upon conformity to tradition in practice, despite latitude in belief, is the elaborate defense of the traditional ritual by so notable a historian of Jewish thought as Manuel Joel (1826-1890), Geiger's successor as Rabbi in Breslau. In keeping with the spirit of the Historical School fostered by Zacharias Frankel at the Breslau Theological Seminary, Joel argued that the prayers for the restoration of the sacrificial cult, for the coming of a personal Messiah and for the bodily resurrection must be retained, even though we no longer believed in their possibility or desirability. Apparently, individual conviction and intellectual honesty counted for little, compared with the monolithic front which it was deemed necessary for "Catholic Israel" to present.[41]

"The crude unhistorical rationalism of Bentham" says Morris R. Cohen, "stirred into life reformative forces in all branches of common law, but the Anglo-American Historical School (founded by Maine) has not a single reform or conservative piece of legislation to its credit. Indeed, the Historical School has been a positive hindrance to any improvement or enlargement of the law, precisely because those who think of new problems in terms of historical analogies get tangled up in their own traces and think that what has been must remain forever." [42] The Historical School of law in Germany is described by Bentham as behaving like someone who does not give the cook the order of meals, but gives her instead the cost of the meals of the previous years.[43]

The attitude of the Historical School of thought has a paralyzing effect on any attempt to cope realistically with an unprecedented situation. This was amply demonstrated by what happened to the United Synagogue in 1918, when it was proposed to organize an authoritative council that would interpret Jewish law in accordance with the spirit of Historical Judaism. [44] Nothing came of that proposal. The reason for its failure may be traced to the statement which was intended to serve as a frame of reference. That statement was so ambiguous and inhibiting as to preclude helpful guidance in the functioning of an authoritative body.

On the one hand, the statement read: "We who stand on the firm ground of Historical Judaism must insist on the immutability of the Torah." On the other hand, it said: "Neither the physical nor the spiritual world presents us with any instance of absolute fixities or absolute mobilities, and to eliminate human agency from the workings of Jewish law would lead to Karaism of the worst kind." This apparent paradox was by no means resolved by the following definition of Jewish Law: "What constitutes Jewish Law is the interpretation and application of the words of the Torah by an authoritative body." How does that coincide with the immutability of the Torah? But even if this seeming contradiction were to be ignored, who or what can determine what are the qualifications of a body needed to render it authoritative? What kind of law does the Historical School expect the Jews to live by if no one is qualified to interpret it? Such law must, indeed, be either "in heaven" or "beyond the sea."

The spokesmen of Conservative Judaism repudiate indignantly the charge of failing to reckon with the principle of development. They maintain that Jewish law has been developing since its very inception, and that it has always reckoned with changed conditions of life and thought. They keep on repeating Geiger's discovery that Pharisaism represented the principle of development, in contrast with the attitude of the Sadducees, as Rabbinism did later in contrast with Karaism. Upon examination of those claims, however, it turns out that the conception of development of Jewish law which is thus read into the Rabbinic tradition and held up by the Conservative movement as offering practical guidance in our day is virtually the same as that of which the Roman Catholic Church boasts. It is merely a mechanical process of defining and explicating in detailed terms what is implied in revealed doctrine, which is necessarily immutable and forever authoritative. There is in this conception no place for a living interaction of a tradition with advancing thought and experience, no room for criticism, modification or amendment. In actual practice, the principle of "Catholic Israel" operates like the turnstile which, in *Mother Goose Rhymes*, says of itself: "I am in everyone's way, but no one I stop."

A more fundamental question, of course, is the one whether Louis Ginzberg's assumption that the observance of religious rites in the spirit of law is a unique Jewish trait is true to fact. The merest acquaintance with the literature of anthropology would seem to dispose of such an assumption as entirely unfounded. The truth is that all peoples, down to our own day, have performed all manner of religious rites, involving the most meticulous regard for rules and laws, the transgression of which in many instances was deemed fatal. Of the Egyptians, Herodotus says, "They are religious to excess, far beyond any other race of men." After mentioning a number of their religious practices, among which circumcision figured most prominently, he adds, "besides which they observe, so to speak, thousands of ceremonies." The Romans, who are always held up as a people devoid of the sense of religion, have given us the very word "religion," which etymologically means not abstract belief or faith, but essentially the binding duty of ritual observances. Seneca who, as a thinker, did not subscribe to popular beliefs about the gods, maintained that "religious usages should be observed not as pleasing to the gods, but as commanded by the laws."

It is high time that the legend about one people being more religious than another were exploded. *The truth is that all peoples are religious, if we understand by a religion an orientation and way of life subscribed to by a group or community. The real question is: What kind of religion do they believe in and practice?* The answer is to be found not in the claims which they advance concerning their religions, but in their general outlook on life, and in their conception and practice of social responsibility, or in the extent to which they reckon with reality and experience.

In all their discussions of the legalistic phase of Jewish ritual practices, the members of the Historical School assume that there are only two possible alternatives: Either ritual practices are observed in the same spirit and with the same meticulous regard for the letter of the law as civil and marriage laws, or they are treated as superfluous, if not a hindrance to spiritual life. They fail to reckon with the possibility of a third alternative: that of observing ritual practices in the spirit of religious poetry in action, or as "action symbols." In a modern orientation, the legalistic spirit is appropriate in jurisprudence, but is incongruous, to say the least, in one's relationship to God. So long as God was conceived in quasi-anthropomorphic fashion as a Lawgiver, religious rites might well have been observed in the same spirit as a law in jurisprudence. With the more spiritualized conception of God, however, that attitude is entirely unwarranted.

On the other hand, there is no reason why religious emotions and attitudes should not find expression in an abundance of religious observances. These are far more effective than the most plausible philosophy in eliciting a sense of life's worthwhileness and a spirit of dedication to life's supreme values. The Jewish religious regimen possesses great spiritual possibilities which, for the modern minded person, remain unfulfilled when associated with legal sanction. To be sure, the symbolic significance of ritual practices, without sufficient uniformity in their observance to enable them to serve as a common language of the spirit, would be lost.

Motivated by meaningful ideas, ritual practices are likely to evolve a high degree of uniformity of their own accord, without necessarily arousing a sense of guilt in case of occasional nonconformity. Conservative Judaism, noting the futility of its attempts hitherto to motivate the observance of the ritual practices by treating them as "laws," may ultimately learn to treat them as a poetic way of articulating the beauty of holiness.

*   *   *

Despite all its shortcomings, however, the Conservative movement in Judaism has served a useful function in the process of metamorphosis which Judaism as a whole is undergoing at present. It has made it possible for a large segment of Jewry to negotiate, without a sense of shock, the transition from the static to the dynamic conception of Jewish life. By insisting on the existential reality of the Jewish People as basic to the survival of Judaism, it has prevented the modern synagogue trends from fragmentizing the Jewish People and tearing *the* Synagogue or *Knesset Yisrael* into a multitude of mutually contending denominations.

CHAPTER TWELVE

Zionism

MODERN NATIONALISM
A THREAT TO JUDAISM

Modern nationalism presents a far more serious threat to the survival of Judaism than does modern rationalism. The challenge of modern rationalism is fully recognized and the Synagogue movements are attempting, each in its own way, to counter it. But the far greater danger that modern nationalism holds for Judaism is scarcely recognized and would be entirely ignored if it were not for Zionism. What renders modern nationalism so serious a menace to Judaism is that its main function is to act as a cultural melting pot. Modern nationalism seeks to fuse the cultural individualities of the minority groups in each nation with the culture of the majority. It therefore expects Jews who are citizens of the modern nations to renounce their own historic nationhood, which has been the main source of their sense of unity and solidarity throughout the centuries. True, modern nationalism formally permits Jews to retain their Jewish religion; but of what use is that permission, when, in the modern climate of opinion, religion acts as a divisive rather than as a unifying force? Unless the unity of the Jewish People itself is to be given the status of Jewish religious dogma, it is doubtful whether Judaism, or Jewish civilization, can survive anywhere.

Modern nationalism is more than a new constellation of political

381

forces. That constellation is itself largely the product of the intellectual revolution which culminated in eighteenth century Enlightenment. The acceleration of scientific and technical progress since the sixteenth century increased the range of mundane interests; there was a growing awareness that those interests could best be served by configurations of political groupings different from those which had obtained throughout the Middle Ages. Feudal regionalism, with its nobility and serfdom, had long been disintegrating, as a result of the rise of cities, of royalty, and of mercantilism. Even the Church, though dealing with men's other-worldly interests, which presumably transcend regional, cultural and political differences, no longer provided the appropriate social frame for the peoples of Central and Western Europe; the Church was in large part fragmentized into various Protestantisms.

These various factors largely explain the end of religious war in Europe after 1648. The Church had lost its power to excite men's loyalties. Beginning with the establishment of the United States and the Napoleonic crusade to spread French republicanism in the last quarter of the eighteenth century, nationalism came to the fore as a new gospel bringing the promise of a new age for mankind. It was to be an age in which men's mundane interests would be satisfied, their fears of injustice, violence and war would vanish.

The new gospel of modern nationalism had its apostles in France, Germany, England, Italy and America. Rousseau, Fichte, Burke, Mazzini, and Jefferson, each developed a grandiose ideology concerning the nature, the duties, and the benefits of nationhood. Each apostle seemed to find only in his own nation the possibilities for developing a type of nationhood which was bound to be universally adopted.[1] They all agreed in advocacy of conscious effort and deliberate planning to turn nationhood into a form of group solidarity that was total, homogeneous and indivisible. Nationhood was to be total, in that it was to involve all the interests of human life: political, cultural, social, and spiritual. It was to be homogeneous, in that all citizens of a nation were to share in all of those interests. It was to be indivisible, in that national allegiance was to be supreme, and not to be divided with any coordinate loyalty. Nationhood was thus raised to the status of a religion which the citizen had to accept and live by, or else suffer exile or some other form of punishment. Ideally, those apostles would have preferred religion to be based on the events, heroes, experiences, and cultural life of the nation itself. Practically, however, they realized that the masses were unprepared for such a national religion. They were, therefore, willing to accept a version of Christianity that would take on a modern national character.

The mere mention of the foregoing traits as characterizing modern nationalism is sufficient to point to its marked resemblance with the age-old nationhood of the Jewish People. Indeed, that resemblance went even further. Modern nationalism arrived of its own accord at two additional ideas which had characterized Jewish nationhood also, namely chosenness and messianism. Only England, under Cromwell and the Puritan regime, the first country to usher in modern nationalism, consciously drew on ancient Israel for its ideas of chosenness and of messianism. In France, the United States, Italy and Germany, however, the same ideas emerged; all felt an urgent need to break with the old order and to set up a new order that promised a wholesome, just, and peaceful way of life for their respective citizens.

It must be remembered that the Jewish Emancipation itself was an integral part of the process whence modern nationalism evolved. In breaking the Church's strangle-hold on the political life of the Western peoples, modern nationalism opened the door to Jewish citizenship. At the same time it placed the Jews, whose own nationhood was basic to their religion, in a more difficult predicament than the Church had ever done. Yet modern nationalism acted not in a spirit of malice to the Jews, but out of its own inner necessity. It happens to be entirely in keeping with the laws of individual and social human nature in its insistence upon being politically total, culturally and religiously homogeneous, and mundanely indivisible.

Modern nationalism is thus an expresion of the same type of collective will-to-live as that which had kept Judaism throughout the centuries a total, homogeneous, and indivisible religious civilization. Like pre-modern Judaism, which managed to keep the Jewish People alive, united, and on the highest level of human attainment, modern nationalism aims by similar collective means to enable the individual to achieve his fulfillment or salvation. In both cases those collective means have to be of a mundane nature and part of the very warp and woof of *social* life.

Historic Judaism and modern nationalism are so similar because both conform to the principle that human life, whether in the individual or in the group, is at its best when it is organic and not divided or schizoid. Only when all the elements of a civilization are organically related to one another, and likewise when all the elements in the life of an individual are organically interactive, can there be that wholeness of life which gives meaning to every part.

The truth of this proposition may be illustrated by the following analogy: The bow, the bow-string, the arrow, and the target together constitute an organic situation. Each element of the situation derives its meaning from all the other elements. Depriving the situation of any one element destroys it and leaves behind a meaningless mess. Similarly, a civilization, to be organic has to be rooted in a homeland, which is analogous to the bow. It has to have government or coercive power; the analogue of that is the bow-string. It has to possess a culture; that corresponds to the arrow. And finally, it must have a mission or destiny: the target.

These four elements—homeland, self-government, culture and mission—are both basic to the normal functioning of national life and must function in a mutually organic relationship: that is the sum and substance of modern nationalism. At first thought it might seem strange to think of the Jewish People, which has been without a land and a government of its own for almost nineteen hundred years, as having anything in common with modern nationalism. On second thought, however, we discover that actually both homeland and self-government played a greater role in the life of the Jewish People during those centuries of exile than the same elements did in the life of any other people in the world.

A home that one misses may have a more determining influence on one's life than a home that one possesses and takes for granted. That the Jews missed their homeland is of course attested by the fact that, on every possible occasion, they bemoaned their exile, no matter how actually welcome they were when they happened to be, or how comfortably situated. In addition, they never missed the opportunity to express the hope that they would in time be restored to their homeland. This awareness of a state of exile, this yearning for return, became part of their *religious* consciousness through reiteration several times daily in their prayers. Nor were these sentiments merely prayer forms such as are generally ignored in the business of living; they deeply affected the lives of untold generations of the Jewish People. This influence throws light on an otherwise inexplicable fact, to which Simon Dubnow calls attention. "Europe has been the home," he writes, "of the majority of the Jewish people for two thousand years. The remains of our fathers and grandfathers have found their last resting place in its earth. Here, as Roman colonists we witnessed the growth of Christian civilization. Here we developed our own spiritual and economic civilization whose influence extended also to our Christian neighbors. After all this we are called foreigners and strangers." [2] Dubnow forgets, however, that, unlike the other Roman colonists who regarded the land they lived in as home, the Jewish-Roman colonists regarded Eretz Yisrael as their real home, so intensely attached were they to their ancestral homeland.

In the same way, it is a mistake to consider the Jews' lack of a central government after the destruction of the Second Commonwealth as depriving Judaism of the character of a national civilization. The truth is that, despite their dispersion, wherever an appreciable number of Jews happened to live, in mutual proximity, the Jews developed a form of self-government that was more effective in keeping them united than could have any central government possessing police and military power. This was, of course, due to their acceptance of their Written and Oral Torah as absolutely authoritative and binding on all Jews throughout the world.

Culture, as an integral element of nationhood, consists of those means of communication which foster in the members of a nation a sense of solidarity and a feeling of love for, and pride in, national existence. Hence, the language of a people and those of its writings which set forth its struggles, its achievements and its hopes, are of basic importance. To the early Moslems the Jews seemed a remarkable phenomenon, in that they evidently derived their unity and common way of life from the Scriptures. The Moslems regarded the Jews as "the people of the Book," or as we would say nowadays, a people by virtue of possessing a common culture.

There is, of course, no gainsaying the fact that the elements of messianism and chosenness loomed large in Jewish nationhood. Both of these doctrines bespeak an intensive group self-awareness and a collective will-to-live. They usually accompany a state of exultation due either to a sense of power achieved through victory in war or prosperity in commerce, or a state of depression caused by military defeats and economic crises. There were sufficient occasions for both exultation and depression during the biblical career of ancient Israel. Those in ancient Israel who so identified themselves with its career as to become its spokesmen (which is the literal translation of *navi*) used the doctrines of chosenness and messianism either to inflate the pride and self-confidence of their people in times of euphoria, or to castigate their people for its sins. The inflators came to be known in Jewish history as "false prophets," the castigators as "true prophets." Latter day spokesmen of modern nationalism are rarely castigators. On the contrary, using the doctrines of messianism and election in the interests of national megalomania, they fostered the mad aberrations of Fascism and Nazism which have cut a wide swathe of devastastion in the world.

So long as modern nationalism was confined to its promulgation by its first apostles, the possibility that it might clash with the nationalist character of historical Judaism was unthought of. When, however, modern nationalism began to be translated into practical politics in parliamentary debate and governmental policy, it became clear that, if Jews were consistently to adhere to Traditional Judaism, its nationalist character would make them ineligible for citizenship. In the National Assembly of France the Girondist Clermont-Tonnere drew a clear and sharp distinction between equality of rights for Jews as individuals and rights for them as part of a Jewish nation.

What alternatives had the Jews under those circumstances other than frankly and sincerely to renounce their historically national character, or retain their solidarity under the guise of religion? That meant either abandoning the hope of renewing national life in Eretz Yisrael, or stressing the supramundane character of that hope as part of an order of reality which was irrelevant to the practical issue of Jewish emancipation. Reform cut the Gordian knot by declaring that Jews in their dispersion had nothing in common but ethical monotheism. Orthodoxy was content to treat the prayers for return to Eretz Yisrael as awaiting God's answer in God's own time. And Conservatism, insofar as it had a chance to flourish in the Old World, was equally averse to viewing those prayers as an incentive to human initiative. What the synagogue movements propose in place of the traditional hope for a return to Zion is like amputating a broken leg and giving the patient a matchstick to hobble on.

Those synagogue movements did more than de-activate the hope for return to Eretz Yisrael. They surrendered the age-old group autonomy of the Jewish People and the authority of Jewish code law in all matters arising out of economic and social conflicts. Evidently they had no alternative, if they were to avert additional repressive measures against the Jews in the countries which harbored them. That, however, does not excuse the failure of the leaders of the Orthodox and Conservative movements to give formal notice to the world that the elimination from Jewish life of group autonomy and national code law was carried out under duress. They should have declared openly that, while emancipation from the medieval disabilities was a welcome relief, it was being carried out at the expense of the very substance of Judaism—its civilizational content—leaving only the shell. That no such declaration was issued was probably due in part to the fear of encouraging the opponents of Jewish emancipation. More largely, however, it proceeded from the assumption that Judaism was essentially a religion concerned with beliefs about God and salvation and with ritual practices as a means of keeping those beliefs alive.

Opposition to Jewish emancipation far more bitter and violent than that displayed in the legislative halls or at sessions of government cabinet meetings of the aspiring modern nations was stimulated by the molders of public opinion. It was popular, not political, opposition that gave rise to anti-Semitism. Itself a product of modern nationalism necessarily based on total, homogeneous, and indivisible solidarity, anti-Semitism singled out the Jews as the chief hindrance to the development of that solidarity. It so happened that economically and culturally that growing solidarity worked to the advantage of the upper middle class of the nation. The lower middle-class, and more particularly the depressed classes were, by contrast, led to feel their economic and social impotence more keenly than in the past. The conspicuous prosperity of a few Jewish families, and especially the tremendous success of the banking firm of the Rothschilds, as a result of efficient handling of international finance, supplied the sensational hatemongers with ready explanation for the failure of national solidarity to materialize, and for the economic and social malaise of the masses.

By reason of its disunity, Germany had suffered most from the impact of the Napoleonic wars. It felt most keenly the need for the solidarity advocated by the apostles of modern nationalism. Hence, Germany became the mother-country of anti-Semitism, which Theodor Mommsen aptly described as "an abortion of nationalism." As early as 1810 Frederich Ludwig Jahn formulated his conception of German folkdom. He stressed biological *Volk*, or folk purity, as a prerequisite to nationhood. According to Jahn, the Jews, whom he put in the same class with the Gypsies, were contaminating the purity of the German nation.[3]

A half-century later, Richard Wagner described the 1848 revolution as a "Jewish importation of French rationalism." So passionate was his hatred of Jews that he incorporated it in his *Ring der Nibelungen*, where the dwarf, Alberich, who symbolized the lust for gold, was the antithesis of Siegfried, the symbol of the German Messiah. Infuriated by the French Jewish composer Myerbeer, who had patronized him, Wagner described all Jews as lacking "any touch of originality or creative genius." The philosopher Eugene Duehring called the Jews an inferior and depraved race. Eduard Von Hartmann claimed that they were a branch of the International Freemasons.

In 1879 Wilhelm Marr, an obscure journalist, issued a pamphlet, *The Victory of Judaism Over Germanicism, (Der Sieg des Judentums ueber das Germanentum)* that brought him world fame. It is here that the term "anti-Semitism" first saw the light. Sometime after, Adolph Stecker, court chaplain to the Austrian Emperor, founded the first anti-Semitic political party. In the 1880's Paul de Lagarde, professor of Oriental languages at Goettingen, inaugurated a new interpretation of the Bible, according to which the Jew was the archfiend of history and Christianity the curse of the Nordic super-race. Thus Bible criticism became an instrument for spreading anti-Semitism. W. M. I. De Wette, and E. Reuss labored the point that an impassable gulf lay between the Old and the New Testament.

But the climax of the anti-Semitic literary campaign in Germany against the Jews was the publication of a series of vicious articles

in the *Preussiche Jahrbuecher* by the historian Heinrich von Treitschke. There he described anti-Semitism as a "natural reaction of
German national feeling against a foreign element which has
usurped a large place in our life." He was also the author of the
slogan, "the Jews are our misfortune," which the Nazis used in
their campaign against the Jews. The one work, however, which
aroused the fierce indignation of even the alienated Jews was
Eugene Duehring's *The Jewish Problem as a Problem of Race,
Morals and Culture*, which appeared in 1881. Herzl recorded the
effect which that book had on him in the following words: "An
infamous book . . . If Duehring, who writes with so much undeniable intelligence and with so much universality of knowledge,
can write like this, what are we to expect from the ignorant
masses?" [4] At the time Herzl reacted thus to Duehring's book, he
was out of touch with Jewish life.

Anti-Semitism's main effect on the Gentile consciousness was to
nullify the most studied and drastic efforts of some Jews to denationalize and transform themselves into a religious community,
analogous to a Christian Protestant sect—their only bond of unity
was to be a series of dogmas about God, man, and immortality.
The fact is that even those Jews refused to forget their common
ethnic origin; it provided them with a solidarity that reached out
beyond their own lifetime and into areas of life beyond religion.
This affirmation of origin was in keeping with the spreading conscious, or subconscious, assumption that what really united a people or nation was common descent or blood kinship. Jewish ethnic
identification therefore acted as a double-edged sword. It helped
the Jews maintain their unity without which there could be no
Jewish religion; but it also served as a weapon in the hands of the
anti-Semites, who contended that the Jews were an unassimilable
group, and therefore an undesirable element in the modern emergent nations.

The anti-Semitic doctrine of Jewish unassimilability rendered
futile even the efforts of those Jews who, breaking with Jewish religion, tried to erase their Jewish identity through intermarriage and
conversion. Indeed Christianity itself played a dubious role in this
situation. If what it represents had been taken seriously by the non-
Jews, Christianity might have served as a buffer to absorb the
anti-Semitic attack, insofar as it called for an allegiance that was

supernational as well as supernatural. However, the Church's traditional condemnation of the Jew as anti-Christ reinforced the poison of anti-Semitism. Since Christianity's supernationalism was not taken seriously by the non-Jews, Christianity was no protection against the exclusive and total nationalism which served as a rationale for anti-Semitism.

It must also be remembered that even in those countries where Christianity was not taken seriously, it was so reinterpreted as to ride the rising tide of modern nationalism. Christianity in those countries became nationalized, each nation adopting its own national version of the religion. This development certainly was not calculated to give the Jews a feeling of home even in those countries in which they had been granted civil equality.

With the usual human tendency to refuse to believe that the worst may happen, the Jews regarded anti-Semitism as no more than a passing phobia. The Jews in France and Central Europe expected presently to enjoy to the full the benefits of the emancipation. The Jews of the Slav countries, particularly Russia, which contained in her Pale of Settlement what was then the bulk of world Jewry, were certain during the three decades between 1850 and 1880 of being granted emancipation soon. During those same decades, however, both modern nationalism and its concomitant anti-Semitism were being imported into the Slav countries from Germany. The Jewish masses in Russia continued to live communally, culturally, and religiously as they had lived in the Middle Ages. Only among the Jewish intellectuals were there stirrings of a broader-visioned and fuller life.

A considerable number of those Jewish intellectuals saw the possibility of a better future for the Jews only if they became an integral part of the majority population, and the majority achieved total solidarity, emancipating itself from the domination of Christian religion. Certain that the advent of such an era for the Slavic peoples was in the offing, some Jewish intellectuals abandoned Judaism, placing their own hopes on, and giving their talents to the service of the revolutionary movements. Most Jewish intellectuals, however, sought to help the Jews improve their own human lot by qualifying to live as Jews in the expected era of the emancipation to be extended them by the Slav governments. These "Enlighteners" concentrated on modernizing Jewish culture, fostering the Hebrew language and literature, revaluating Jewish religion in mundane ethical terms, and, most of all, on redirecting the economic pursuits of their own people into productive channels. They wished to transform the Jewish economy from a concentration on business or industry to an interest in agriculture, as a more "primary" social basis.

There was, then, no occasion for Jews in the Slavic countries to denationalize their Jewish heritage, for they were as yet not even being offered civil and political emancipation. Hence the traditional nationalist aspect of Judaism in those countries lost none of its momentum. Certain Jewish intellectuals preferred to canalize the momentum of traditional Jewish nationhood into a movement to reconstitute Jewish national life along the same lines as those which the emergent modern nations were following. The Jews were to become a territorial nation once again. But where was the necessary territory to be found? The possibility of securing some uninhabited land for that purpose suggested itself to some; but to most Jewish nationalists, Eretz Yisrael, with its historic associations, was the only psychologically eligible land. Thus arose the movement of *Hovevei Tsiyyon*.

It was not, however, until anti-Semitism grew to proportions which made it evident that modern European nationalism would not make peace even with minimal Jewish life, that modern Zionism came into being. Zionism is a modern Jewish mass movement to have the Jews foster their own autonomous life in their ancestral home. It proposes a radical solution to the problem of the future of the Jewish People with its social and religious heritage in a world where the climate of thought is modern naturalism and modern nationalism the dominant social pattern.

Two violent outbreaks of anti-Semitism, one in the East and the other in the West, were irrefutable evidence that continental nationalism was intent on making the European continent *Judenrein*. The first was the series of Russian Government-instigated pogroms in 1881, the second the anti-Dreyfus plot hatched in the early 90's by the top echelons of the French army to prove that the Jew was ready to sell his country to its enemy for a price. The Elizabethgrad pogrom in 1881 led to the organized effort of Jews to resettle in Eretz Yisrael. The Dreyfus Affair started Theodor Herzl, an assimilated Jew, on his dramatic career as the founder of Political Zionism.

Any measure less radical than Zionism could have made no headway toward the solution of the problem of Jewish nationhood. This was demonstrated by the failure of an alternative solution proposed by the historian and social philosopher Simon Dubnow. Dubnow assumed that the Jews could retain their nationhood despite their dispersion. Wherever they lived in considerable numbers they could foster their unique culture, provided the governments of the countries they lived in recognized their status as a minority nationality and granted them cultural autonomy. The Jewish community would be authorized to levy taxes and to regulate its own cultural, welfare, social and educational affairs.

During the early stages of Zionism, it seemed less likely that Jews would succeed in acquiring territorial rights in Eretz Yisrael than that they would obtain cultural autonomy in the countries where they had been living for centuries. After all, they were not alone in demanding minority rights. Central Europe during the decades prior to World War I was seething with the unrest of many nationalities spilling over their own territorial borders to form minority groups in neighboring territories. Great political thinkers of the time were led to develop a political theory of national self-determination which they applied to minority nationalities. Only in matters of common interest to the entire nation, they maintained, should minority nationalities be expected to cooperate with the majority nationality.

That theory had a great vogue prior to and during World War I. President Woodrow Wilson of the United States strongly influenced the acceptance of the principle of national self-determination by those who framed the peace treaties after the conclusion of the war. The Jewish representatives of the East European countries demanded minority rights for the Jewish population living there, and their demands were formally acceded to, despite the fact that no territory outside Eretz Yisrael was home to the Jews. Yet Simon Dubnow's contention can hardly hold water. He wrote: "If . . . territorial nationalities that are deprived of their political independence are still entitled to retain their nationality, then the same right also belongs to the Jews, since they are definitely a territorial nationality, except for the fact that their territory in Europe is divided into small fragments instead of being concentrated into one province. The Jews are inhabitants of Europe since ancient times and their territorial rights are based not on a property title but on colonization and cultural influences." [5] But, as we have noted, Jews have no claim on any lands in Europe they may have colonized in the distant past, for the simple reason that they never treated the lands they colonized as home.

Before long, the Jews who were among the beneficiaries of the "Minorities Treaties" were forced to realize that their never having been a majority in any European state took them out of the class of the "strong" minorities whose grievances the League of Nations could not afford to disregard. In fact, the Jews were reluctant to submit their grievances to the League lest they antagonize the state government. The "Minorities Treaties" as a whole turned out to be a failure. At the First Congress of European Nationalities which met in 1925 a resolution was passed declaring that "National cultural freedom is no less a spiritual possession of a civilized mankind than religious freedom. This principle shall be acknowledged as an ethical tenet for the relations between peoples." In December, however, of the same year the League Council heard two of its outstanding statesmen declare that the object of the Minorities Treaties was not to safeguard the rights of minorities, but "gradually to prepare the minorities to be merged in the national community to which they belong." This was said by Sir Austen Chamberlain and approved by Dr. Eduard Benes. Although Chamberlain retracted that statement three years later, the consensus among the ruling statesmen was that the Minorities Treaties were unworkable.[6]

In the meantime the entire theory of minority national rights, particularly as applied to the Jews, had become obsolete. Those rights were not found workable even in Poland and Lithuania, where Jews then lived in large numbers.

Soviet Russia, with her numerous minority nationalities, is a special case. In the first place, each such nationality is identified with a particular territory. For a time it seemed that Soviet Russia was willing to solve her Jewish problem; she offered Soviet Jews Biro-Bidjan in Siberia, near the Manchurian border, where they could establish themselves as a territorial nationality. Secondly, her entire policy with regard to minority nationalities was conceived only as a temporary measure to facilitate the spread of Communist gospel. "Nationalist in form and socialist in content," the motto of that policy, betrays the Soviet disparagement of minority nationalism in general. That, of course, is part of Marxist philosophy, according to which the proletariat really has no fatherland. What has happened to Biro-Bidjan proves that the Jews of Soviet Russia are not likely to be the beneficiaries of minority rights in Soviet Russia. They are less likely to get such rights anywhere else. For that reason Dubnow's thesis that Jews should everywhere contend for minority national rights has turned out to be completely unrealistic and utopian.

Zionism has thus been vindicated as the only movement capable of saving the historic nationhood of the Jewish People from the danger of being lost in modern nationalism's melting pot. Zionism is far from having arrived at a way of life whereby Jews who remain in the Diaspora might retain more than a nominal vestige of their historic nationhood. So far it has not contributed to the continuance and enhancement of Jewish life in the Diaspora. But there can be no question that the establishment of the State of Israel has given Jewish nationhood a new lease on life. That is an epoch-making achievement, the full significance of which will become apparent in time.

Zionism, as a movement to resurrect Jewish nationhood through the return of the Jews to Eretz Yisrael where, by constituting a permanent majority, they would be politically, economically, and culturally autonomous, was spelled out in various ideologies long before the term "Zionism" came into general usage. The rest of the chapter will summarize only those Zionist ideologies which have contributed to the enhancement of Judaism as an evolving religious civilization. Those are a) Pre-Messianic Zionism, b) Spiritual Zionism, and c) Political Zionism.

Pre-Messianic Zionism addresses itself to traditionalist Jews. It is based on the assumption that the advent of the Messiah will take place as foretold in the tradition. It adds, however, that as a prerequisite to the appearance of the Messiah, the Jews themselves must take the initiative by resettling in Eretz Yisrael.

Spiritual Zionism addresses itself to those Jews whose world outlook precludes the belief in the traditional conception of the

Messiah, but includes faith in the spiritual destiny of the Jewish People. Moses Hess views the spiritual aspect of that destiny as manifest in a socialist economy; to Ahad Ha-Am, Spiritual Zionism is manifest in a society dedicated to the ideal of social justice.

Political Zionism addresses itself to all Jews who wish to be free from the insufferable condition of belonging to a people that is homeless and subject to the prejudices and phobias of their host nations. Before the establishment of the State it called upon the Jews of the world to enter into negotiations with the leading statesmen of the world for the purpose of regaining their right to their ancestral land and establishing there a sovereign commonwealth of their own. At present, however, its function is problematic.

It is evident that Political Zionism is motivated primarily by the ineradicable character of anti-Semitism and the threat it holds to the physical survival of Jewry. On the other hand, Pre-Messianic Zionism and Spiritual Zionism appeal to the Jewish People's inner will-to-live and its unappeased yearning to resume the normal and creative life of a people in its own land.

A. PRE-MESSIANIC ZIONISM

The wholesale characterization of religion as an opiate for the masses is unwarranted on a number of counts. That does not mean that it can be dismissed as completely without foundation. There are emergencies when a patient has to be administered an opiate, if he is not to succumb to his agonies. There certainly are many situations in the life of peoples when without the consolation of religion they would be unable to withstand inhuman treatment. That certainly was the case with the Jews through the centuries of exile and persecution. In their state of helplessness, of what avail would it have been to urge them to help themselves? Had they shown the least sign of insurrection against their tormentors who outnumbered them, they would have been wiped off the face of the earth.

Nothing but implicit faith in the ultimate advent of a miracle-working Messiah sent by God to redeem His Chosen People could have mitigated their agonies. During World War II there were groups of Jews who while being led to the gas chambers chanted the credo: "I believe in the coming of the Messiah." Those episodes dramatize how Jews managed to endure for centuries the worst that their enemies could inflict on them. Thus traditional messianism of the Jews, with its promise that God would ultimately redeem them, saved them from despair when there was nothing they could do to help themselves.

The outstanding change in men's thinking and attitude toward life which is the result of all that we associate with modernism is that neither persons nor peoples dare resign themselves to the fact of helplessness. That is largely due to the sceptical attitude toward the miracles in which the historical religions abounded, the implication being that once man is on good terms with Deity, he can count on divine help to get him out of all kinds of scrapes without any exertion on his own part. Such scepticism, however, invaded only the circles of the intellectual élite among the Jews. The Jewish masses in Eastern Europe and their rabbinic leaders in the early decades of the nineteenth century neither questioned nor doubted any of the traditional teachings, least of all those pertaining to the Messiah. Moreover, they had become so inured to the habit of passivity from the centuries of their utter helplessness that they could not break with it even when they began to be in the position to help themselves. The habit of passivity, which began as a necessity, developed into a religious duty which it was as wrong to violate as any of the divine ordinances of the Torah.[7]

If that attitude of traditionalist Jews had persisted, the world Zionist movement would have been entirely in the hands of Jews who, as a result of modern nationalism or enlightenment, would have established a State from which religion would have been completely separated. Actually, modern Zionism has almost from the beginning included a Mizrahi wing; Mizrahi now is entirely responsible for the political role which traditional Jewish religion plays in the political and judicial aspects of Jewish life in Israel. The Mizrahi party in Zionism owes its existence entirely to two eminent traditionalist rabbis who at about the same time, yet independently of each other, inaugurated a conception of Zionism that seemed compatible with traditional messianism. They were Zvi Hirsch Kalischer and Judah Hai Alkalai. Both Kalischer and Alkalai wrote books, brochures, articles, personal letters, and traveled widely in the interest of the Jewish colonization movement which was their specific objective. Both men succeeded in winning sanction for their ideas and programs from outstanding traditionalist rabbis of the time. The opposition, however, which they encountered from the majority of traditionalist masses and their leaders was far greater than the approval and help they succeeded in securing. No less striking than the resemblance of their campaigns in behalf of their objectives was the fact that both Kalischer and Alkalai were impelled in their course of action primarily by the rise of modern nationalism. So ingrained, however, had become the traditional taboo against a public effort to reclaim Eretz Yisrael that, although the fact that those two rabbinic leaders had declared themselves for active colonization, they failed to win general support.

ZVI HIRSCH KALISCHER (1795-1874)

Kalischer was born in 1795 in Lissa, a town near Posen. He studied at the Talmudical academies of Lithuania and with Rabbi Akiba Eger of Posen, a world-famous Talmudic authority. In Thorn, Prussia, where he was married, his great learning was soon recognized by the Jewish community and he was appointed acting rabbi. That meant that, although he attended to all the expected duties of the rabbi, he refused to draw any salary. His wife owned·a business which supported both of them.

Kalischer became a master not only of rabbinic lore but also of Jewish and general philosophy. In his early years he wrote in defense of Maimonides whom Samuel David Luzzatto (*Shadal*) had assailed for succumbing to the influence of Aristotle. The very defense bespoke a rationalist and enlightened attitude on the part of Kalischer. His philosophic interests did not leave him in old age, as is evident from the fact that he published his *Sefer He-Emunah Ha-Yesharah*, which appeared in two parts, the first in 1843 and the second in 1871. The theme of that book is the superiority of faith over reason. Appended to it are commentaries on the books of Job and Ecclesiastes.

On the other hand, Kalischer attacked the rising movement of

Reform in Germany, because he regarded it as an unconscionable break with tradition. "God forbid," he wrote, "that we Jews should desecrate what is holy by saying that Europe is our Jerusalem." [8] He realized however, that merely proving that Reform was in the wrong would not stop it. Kalischer sensed fully the significance of the growth of national sentiment in the European countries. He knew that it would expedite the Jews' inevitable integration not only in the body politic but in the entire cultural and social life, and finally in the religious life of the majority population. It was, no doubt, this realization that led Kalischer to conclude that the only way to conserve Jewish life was for Jews to migrate to Eretz Yisrael, where they would be free to retain their traditional way of life. He used the example of the emerging nations as an argument to shame the Jews out of their national apathy. Kalischer was a clear enough thinker to reason out for himself that what had saved Judaism in the past was as the sense of ethnic kinship which in the modern world would have to find political as well as religio-cultural expression. Once Jews renounced or de-activated their sense of nationhood, which was inseparable from their yearning to return to Eretz Yisrael, nothing could prevent them from ultimate absorption into the general population.

In the first extant letter written by Kalischer in 1836 to Ascher Anschel Rothschild, the son of the founder of the famous banking house, he pleads for establishment of agricultural settlements for the poor Jews in Palestine. Palestinian Jews were dependent on *Halukah*, i.e., the charity that came from the well-to-do Jews in Europe. Kalischer's purpose was not to effect a more efficient way of helping the poor, but to start what he hoped would become a world-wide Jewish movement for Jews to resume life as a people on their own land. In that letter Kalischer states the thesis upon which he based all his subsequent writings and efforts: *The Jews must themselves take the initiative in resettling Eretz Yisrael.* "As for the redemption of Israel and the coming of our saintly Messiah, whose advent we await hourly," he writes, "let no one think that of a sudden the Holy One will descend from above and say to His people 'Go forth!' The beginning of the redemption will come about in a natural way through human initiative and the consent of the reigning powers to the ingathering of the dispersed Jews in the Holy Land." [9]

The two main works of Kalischer which bear on Zionism are his *Derishat Tsiyyon* (*"The Yearning for Zion"*), published in 1862 and *Sh'lom Yerushalayim* (*"The Welfare of Jerusalem"*), published in Thorn, 1868. The opening passage of *Derishat Tsiyyon* reads: "Since my youth I have been sorely troubled that ever since the Temple was destroyed and the sacrifices were suspended most Jews are apathetic [walk in darkness], doing nothing for one reason or another to reclaim the Holy Land. Some say 'Why should we look to Zion? What does the Holy Land mean to us? We lack nothing where we live among the nations.' These Jews are perfectly content. They love the countries where they live, renounce the holy and eternal values, and know not the heritage of our fathers. Others, again, say 'We believe in God. Our souls yearn for the love of His holiness, but why should we spend our lives in grieving over the loss of the Temple? When the time comes, God will proclaim freedom and will blow the great trumpet that will be a signal proclaiming: Leave your exile, come and take possession of the Holy Land, in accordance with the great promises of the Prophets.' As a result there is no one who cares for Zion. I have therefore made up my mind to agitate against these two groups." [10]

Later in the book, he writes: "Dear reader! Break away from the popular habit of assuming that at any moment our Saintly Messiah is liable to blow the trumpet and cause all the inhabitants of the world to tremble. Nothing of the kind. The redemption will begin through the spiritual awakening of the well-to-do (among us) who are generous, and through the consent of the governments to the ingathering of Jews in Eretz Yisrael from the rest of the world." [11]

The rest of the book is, except for practical matters, devoted to validating this contention by means of various texts drawn from all of traditional literature. Without a pre-Messianic era of planned effort on the part of the Jews to resettle in Eretz Yisrael, the promised Messianic era cannot come about. The pre-Messianic era to be enacted through human agencies must of necessity be one of gradual accomplishment.

Kalischer finds support for that assumption in the following texts in the prophecies of Isaiah: "On that day, Israel will blossom and bud; and they will fill the face of the earth with fruit . . . .

On that day will the Lord thresh out the ears of corn from the River Euphrates to the Brook of Egypt and you will be picked up one by one, O children of Israel! On that day will a blast be blown on a great trumpet, and those who were lost in the land of Assyria and those who were outcast in the land of Egypt will come and worship the Lord on the holy mountain in Jerusalem." (27:6, 11-13). This is only one sampling of the numerous texts from the entire biblical and post-biblical literature which Kalischer quoted to disprove the authoritative character of the few texts on which is based the traditional taboo against taking the initiative in the redemption from exile.[12]

Kalischer resorts to logic as well as to tradition to prove that there is need for a first stage of pre-messianic era of human effort in the process of Israel's redemption. Man should attempt to recognize, in whatever befalls him, the hand of God. The need for such attempt implies that the hand of God is far from being evident. If the redemption from exile were to be attended in the first instance by miracles, which would be an unmistakable evidence of divine intervention, what opportunity would the Jews have to prove their faith in God?[13]

Why then have the Jews hitherto failed to carry through that first stage of the redemption? Kalischer has a ready answer: The Jews have been in too helpless a state. They never in the past had either the good will of the governments or the kind of Jewish leadership which was influential with governments; but these they now have.[14] Kalischer is convinced that if the Jews were to reclaim their homeland they would elicit the respect of the other nations. He appeals to the Jews themselves to follow the example of those nations. "Why do the people of Italy and of the other states sacrifice their lives for their fatherland, whereas we stand aside, as though lacking the energy or the will? Are we really inferior to the other nations, which esteem life and possessions of far less value than love of people and country? Note how Italians, Poles, Hungarians risk their lives and their possessions for the reputation of their countries. Only we Jews, who are heirs to a land which is the glory and joy of all the world—a land deemed universally holy—have nothing to say, and act like a man who has no courage. Should we not be ashamed? Whatever the other nations do is after all only for their own glory. In our case, it is not a matter of saving the honor of our ancestors, but of saving the honor of God, who has chosen Zion to be His dwelling place." [15]

Kalischer himself was, without doubt, completely unaware that he was motivated less by his own reading and interpretation of the tradition than by the general climate of opinion, which was electric with national aspiration. So certain was he that the tradition itself demanded what he was proposing that he took issue with other great traditionalists, both past and contemporary, in the matter of reintroducing forthwith the sacrificial cult on the ancient Temple site. That is the theme of his *Sh'lom Yerusalayim*. In addition, he urged the revival of the practice of those religious ordinances which traditionally had been suspended because their enactment was assumed to depend upon a fully restored national life in Eretz Yisrael—such as only the Messiah himself could make possible. These ordinances were the heave offering, tithes, Sabbatical year, the prohibition of sowing mixed seed and of eating the fruit of trees during the first three years. Kalischer was convinced that all those ordinances ought to be put into effect at once, and that such a step would restore to the Jews the lost feeling of their nationhood. He thus anticipated, in traditional terms, the truth that Ahad Ha-Am stressed in psychological terms—namely that the national redemption of the Jewish People could not take place until the Jews themselves recovered their lost sense of nationhood.

How could the restoration of the agricultural ordinances by a few farmers in Israel help the Jews who remained in the Diaspora recover their lost sense of Jewish nationhood? In answer, Kalischer suggested a practical measure by which the main purpose of promoting Jewish settlement in Eretz Yisrael would be achieved; at the same time the Jews in the Diaspora would share the fruits of the restoration of the agricultural ordinances. He suggested that investment companies be organized for the purchase of land in Eretz Yisrael to be cultivated by the Jewish settlers. If these settlers observed the agricultural ordinances, the investors would earn a share in the merit of such observances.[16] Jews who invested in land in Eretz Yisrael, Kalischer maintained, would not love the land where they lived the less. Here we encounter a display of his naivete: "Did not Czar Nicholas," says Kalischer, "who has his own palaces in St. Petersburg, buy a palace in Berlin? Why may not then many of our great Jewish princes acquire houses and orchards in our ancestral land? That would raise the prestige of Jerusalem and prepare the way for its final redemption." [17]

There could be no more striking illustration of the difference between Traditional Judaism and modern Neo-Orthodoxy, despite their outward similarity, than Rabbi Samson Raphael Hirsch's comment: "Regarding the late Rabbi Zvi Hirsch Kalischer, nothing is known to me or my people; evidently I was his opponent in this matter regarding which he wrote me three or four times, sending me his books and urging me to head the work for the settlement of Eretz Yisrael. Until finally he censured me severely, as if I were delaying the Redemption, and I asked him to desist." [18] That statement foreshadowed the conflict which later developed between Agudath Yisrael and Mizrahi, each of which claimed to be the only movement in line with authentic tradition.

JUDAH HAI ALKALAI (1798-1878)

Judah Hai Alkalai was born in Sarajevo, Serbia in 1798. While still a child, his father moved with the family to Jerusalem. There, in addition to his studies in rabbinic lore, Alkalai delved into the study of Kabbalah, paying special attention to what it had to say concerning the advent of the Messiah. In 1825 he accepted the position of *Hakam* of the Sephardic community in Semlin, a town near Sarajevo. There he served until his return to Jerusalem toward the close of his life.

During Alkalai's incumbency in Semlin he came under the influence of its chief rabbi, Mordecai Massad, who encouraged him to widen the scope of his knowledge and interests. That saved Alkalai from being dominated by the mysticism and thaumaturgy of the Kabbalah. He did, however, retain from his study of the Kabbalah the apotheosis of the Jewish People; this imbued him with a passionate devotion to a self-imposed mission of saving his People from disintegration. But the mysticism of the Kabbalah did not reinforce Alkalai in the traditional attitude of waiting for the Messiah; rather, he derived from the Kabbalah the incentive to resort to measures of a naturalistic and practical character to hasten the advent of the Messiah. He also managed to find in the tradition warrant for disregarding the taboo against active campaigning for large-scale colonization of Eretz Yisrael.

The first public expression of Alkalai's mission appeared oddly enough in his introduction to a text on Hebrew grammar. The text, written in Hebrew, was called *Darkei Noam*, and it was published in Semlin in 1839. There can be no question that what motivated Alkalai in his Zionist campaign was the awakening of nationalism in the Balkan states, whose effects were strongly felt in Semlin. That such was the case may perhaps be inferred from the fact that, in the introduction to his Hebrew grammar, he expresses the wish that Hebrew might soon become the vernacular of the Jews. That wish was in keeping with modern nationalist sentiment.

Alkalai was confirmed in his determination to arouse the Jews to return to their mother country and resume their national life by the anti-Jewish atrocities which broke out in Damascus in 1840 in the wake of a blood-ritual libel. It was not so much the need for Jews to be secure from such outbreaks of religious fanatacism that accentuated the timeliness of Alkalai's plea. Rather, the Damascus scandal brought to light the great influence which, for the first time in centuries, men of the type of Adolphe Cremieux in France and Moses Montefiore in England could wield in international affairs. Alkalai was convinced that those men, and others like them, could negotiate with the Sultan of Turkey to allow the Jews to come to Eretz Yisrael in large numbers and to acquire all the land they needed for agricultural purposes. That realization prompted him to write his *Minhat Yehudah* (Vienna, 1843) lauding Cremieux and Montefiore for their efforts in behalf of the victims of the Damascus atrocities and of the general Jewish population in the Near East. He hoped his book would move them to start large-scale action in behalf of Jewish settlement.[19]

Moses Montefiore was the only one to respond. He had been urged also by Kalischer to take a leading part in the movement for the return of Jews to Eretz Yisrael. But all that Montefiore did was to make provision for the housing of some of the poor Jews of Jerusalem. Virtually all Alkalai got for his pains was to be berated by one of the ivory-tower Jewish scholars for having spread such mad ideas and having tried to persuade the rich and influential Jews through flattery to put those ideas into effect.

Like Kalischer, Alkalai was not content with the written word as a means of spreading his message. He travelled to some of the important Jewish communities in Central Europe where, like Kalischer again, he contacted Jewish leaders, in the hope that they might carry out some of his practical suggestions for the financing and administering of a vast undertaking. Alkalai insisted that the practical work of settling the Jews in Eretz Yisrael in large numbers should not be undertaken without the cooperation of the leading European governments, particularly those of France and England.[20] He regarded the redemption from the Babylonian Captivity with Cyrus as offering a precedent for modern times. He even went in person to Constantinople to try to persuade the Sultan, Abdul Medshid, to transfer Eretz Yisrael to the Jews as a tributary country. When that attempt failed, Alkalai tried to persuade the Oriental Jews, who were subjects of the Sultan, to migrate to Eretz Yisrael, since they were not likely to be prevented by the Turkish Government from settling there.

Alkalai realized, however that, without the large funds which the Jewish masses would have to supply for the project, it should not even be attempted. He therefore elaborated the idea of imposing a tax on all Jews that would be the modern equivalent of the tithes of produce which in ancient times all Jews had to pay to the Levites. Alkalai deprecated the notion that the project could be financed by voluntary contributions.[21]

Far more important than Alkalai's active campaign in behalf of Zionism and the practical measures by which he sought to promote it, is the rationale through which he, an authentic traditionalist Jew, sought to motivate it. Alkalai's rationale, though developed independently of Kalischer's, entirely coincided with it. It was based on the assumption that the traditional belief in the coming of a personal Messiah was not to be impugned in any way. On the other hand, the Messiah would not come unless the Jews on their part proved themselves worthy of redemption, by doing everything in their power to resume their national life in Eretz Yisrael. This, by the way, is still the assumption underlying the Mizrahi movement; it is responsible for the political power exercised in the State of Israel by Traditional Judaism.

Alkalai elaborated this assumption in a number of writings. The most important of them are: 1) *Sh'lom Yerushalyim*, published in

Budapest 1840. That is the tract in which Alkalai replies to a traditionalist who assailed him for his introduction to *Darkei Noam*; 2) *Minhat Yehudah*, Vienna, 1843; and 3) *Goral la-Adonai*, Vienna, 1857. In these works, Alkalai quotes widely from the entire traditional literature to drive home his conception of two stages in the redemption of the Jews from exile, one natural, the other supernatural. He bases that conception, in the first place, on an idea expressed in the Rabbinic tradition and further stressed in Kabbalah, to the effect that the authentic Messiah will be preceded by a precursor known as *Mashiah ben Yosef*, who is to be a descendant of the tribe of Joseph.

Thus he writes in *Sh'lom Yerushalayim:* "What I have to say about the redemption as taking place as a result of naturally planned action cannot be refuted by the statements of our Rabbis which speak in terms of miracles. Those statements refer to the Messiah who is a descendant of King David, whereas my statements, which speak in terms of literal fact, refer to the Messiah who is a descendant of Joseph." [22] Later he adds: "The redemption must be started by the nation itself. Those who assume that it will be started by the Messiah, who is a descendant of David, amid great signs and wonders such as appeared when we went forth from Egypt, believe what is absolutely false. Those who hold that belief are guilty of sin. That wrong notion has been only a stumbling block to the Jewish People. The Torah was not given to angels. What is desirable is achieved only as a result of effort." [23]

A second line of argument which Alkalai developed to support his position that redemption would take place in two stages is based on his interpretation of *teshuvah*—a term usually translated as "repentance," but which, properly understood, means "return to God." *Teshuvah* is one of the unique religious concepts in Jewish religion. It implies a different relationship between man and God from that found in any other religion. The chief mission of the prophets is to call upon their people to return to God; *teshuvah* has nothing of the idea of punishment or expiation implied in the Latin term *poenitia*, the origin of the word "repentance."

Alkalai points out that there are two ways of returning to God —as an individual, and as a member of the Jewish People. For the Jew as an individual "return to God" spells the resumption of ritual observances and the study of Torah. For the Jew as a member of the Jewish People, "return to God" means return to Eretz Yisrael. As evidence, Alkalai cites the Talmudic dictum: "Whoever lives outside Eretz Yisrael is as though he had no God." [24] In the light of his interpretation of *teshuvah*, Alkalai arrives at a radically different reason for the Jews' protracted state of exile from that which is given in the tradition. According to tradition, the long exile is both an expiation for past sins and a punishment for the failure to carry out properly the ritual practices and the study of Torah. According to Alkalai, exile is a punishment for the failure of the Jews to return to Eretz Yisrael and to reclaim it by resorting to natural means. [25]

To Alkalai, as to Kalischer, the return of the Jews to Eretz Yisrael was the only proper reaction of the Jews to the spirit of the times in which both men then lived. Both men condemned Reform as being the wrong kind of reaction. "The spirit of the times," Alkalai wrote, "has nothing whatever to do with Torah and religious practices, and those who make changes in the name of the spirit of the times are on the wrong track and do not realize that they are merely panicky. The spirit of the times demands liberty and freedom for each people to prosper, so that all the inhabitants of the earth may enjoy freedom wherever they happen to live; it demands that everyone be free to travel from one country to another. The same spirit of the times calls upon us Jews to leave our prisons. It requires all the states to set their countries in order and to give official status to their respective languages. Likewise, it calls upon us to put our own homeland in order, and to revive and give official status to our language." [26]

B. SPIRITUAL ZIONISM

MOSES HESS (1812-1875)

Spiritual Zionism found its first expression in the tract *Rome and Jerusalem* published in 1862 by Moses Hess. That tract may well be considered the greatest Zionist classic because it reckons with virtually every aspect of the Zionist movement, whether

theoretic or practical, which has come to the fore since Hess' day.
Apart from the intrinsic merit of Hess' argument, *Rome and
Jerusalem* carries added weight because Hess had become estranged
from his people and had returned to it only when convinced that
there was no other feasible or justifiable course of action for a Jew.
Hess' philosophy of the Jews' return to Eretz Yisrael, however, is
spiritual in character. To Hess, the chief motivation for the Jewish
return was not to enable the Jew as an individual to survive in the
economic and national struggle for existence. Rather, the spiritual
regeneration of the entire Jewish People was at stake. Hess could
not see how the Jew could achieve moral freedom apart from a
morally free national Jewish life—possible, he at last realized, only
in the ancestral home of the Jewish People. Moreover, Hess' entire
conception of the Jewish People, its history, its destiny, and its
religion is a corollary of a spiritual world view which was the basis
of all his writings.

Hess was born in Bonn, Germany, in 1812. When he was five
years old his parents moved to Cologne, where his father established a sugar factory. Since Cologne had been closed to the Jews
until 1798, it did not, when his parents arrived in 1817, have the
facilities for an adequate Jewish training. They therefore left
Moses with his maternal grandfather, a learned and kindly man.
The influence of the training the child received from his grandfather remained with him throughout his life and was undoubtedly
the chief motivating factor in his final return to his People. When
he was fourteen, his mother died and his father brought him to
Cologne, with the expectation of training him for the part he was
to take later in the business concern. Young Moritz, as he was
then called, did not take to business, and in other ways could not
get along with his father, who was a strictly observant Jew.

Of a studious nature, as well as of an idealistic turn of mind,
Hess began to move in a revolutionary circle of youths seeking to
combat the reactionary regimes in Germany and elsewhere. That
is the group out of which the Communist movement headed by
Karl Marx and Friedrich Engels finally emerged. Before reaching
the Communist stage, the revolutionary movement derived its
inspiration from the radical thought of the day in philosophy and
religion. Hess had the opportunity to articulate his humanitarian
aspirations. He was a poor speaker but he wrote books, articles,

tracts expounding his views, largely shaped by the thinking of Hegel, Feuerbach and Schleiermacher. But the one thinker who helped Hess synthestize his own thinking was Spinoza. Spinoza had conceived Judaism as a form of nationhood. He had stated that the restoration of the Jewish commonwealth depended upon the courage of the Jews themselves. Hess refers to these ideas in support of his own later interest in the Jewish renaissance.[27] His attitude toward Spinoza may be inferred from his designation of Spinozism as the latest manifestation of Judaism.[28] But it was probably due to his ethnological studies to which Hess turned when he broke with his socialist associates that the Jewish People began "to interest" him and "to enchant" him more and more.[29]

Hess was only twenty-five when he published *Die Heilige Geschichte der Menschheit* (Stuttgart 1837). At that period he seems to have come under the influence of Schleiermacher, the theologian who interpreted Christianity in a manner that appealed to the intellectuals of that day. So imbued was Hess with the Christian spirit that he based his philosophy of history on an idea suggested by a monk of the thirteenth century. According to that philosophy, the history of mankind had gone through three stages, that of God the Father, God the Son, and God the Holy Ghost. Hess assigned to each of those stages a leading figure: Moses represented the first stage, Jesus the second, and Spinoza the third or modern stage. In *Die Heilige Geschichte* Hess found fault with the Jews for having neglected Jesus, but expressed the hope that they would in time wake from their long spiritual sleep.

Hess was then and for many years thereafter preoccupied with the problem of socialism in the study of which he collaborated with Marx and Engels. In the end, however, they repudiated Hess because he could not go along with them in complete rejection of all idealistic considerations in the strategy of socialism. For Marx and Engels, the only legitimate approach to the problem of socialism was the scientific one—this, to them, meant the monistic type of economic determinism.

In the meantime, nationalism on the European continent was changing radically, losing much if not all of its original liberalism, and developing the by-product of anti-Semitism. Ejected from the Socialist movement after it took form in the Communist Manifesto, Hess must have become aware once again of his Jewish origin and heritage. The immediate cause of his Jewish reawakening was undoubtedly his realization that the German people would not permit the Jews to be integrated into the German nation. Hess quotes at length from a tract by his own former publisher, Otto Wiegand, which appeared in Leipzig in 1858: no matter how thoroughly Germanized a Jew may become, wrote Wigand, he can never be a real German, for there is a sleepless guardian angel who watches over racial differences. Hess must have realized that a storm was brewing in Germany which might overwhelm Jewry. "It seems," he said, "that a final race struggle is unavoidable." He blamed the German politicians for failing to grasp the situation and not attempting to stop the growth of reaction which, Hess was sure, would ultimately also entrap the progressive German democrats in the net of romantic demagogy.[30]

Hess states frankly, however, that if he had not lived at one time in France he would never have thought of interesting himself in the revival of Jewish nationhood.[31] Moreover, he needed some contemporary Jewish thinking to help him crystalize in his own mind a constructive conception of the Jewish People relevant to the nationalist climate of opinion. He also required a plan of action capable of arousing the Jews to reassert their nationhood. From the French half-Jew Joseph Salvador, Hess acquired that kind of conception of the Jewish People; Rabbi Zvi Hirsch Kalischer provided him with a plan of action which he quotes at length.[32]

Joseph Salvador was the son of a Sephardic Jew and a Catholic mother. In his *Histoire de la Domination Romaine en Judée et de la Ruine de Jerusalem* (Paris, 1846), Salvador formulated a philosophy of Jewish history where the main outlines of Hess' approach are recognizable. Far from viewing Jewish history as a tragedy, Salvador saw it as a great epic of the spirit, leading ultimately to world unity based on equality and fraternity. Such world unity constituted for him mankind's covenant with God. Christianity, according to Salvador, largely falsified the ideal of Judaism. Rome's conquest of Jerusalem and the subsequent christianization of Rome seemed to point to the ultimate defeat of Judaism. Paris, however, with its 1789 French Revolution, had defeated Rome. That meant the turn of the wheel and the ultimate renaissance of Judaism.

Salvador even envisaged the building of a Suez Canal as part of the rebirth of Palestine. For all we know, Disraeli might himself

have entertained such a hope when he moved heaven and earth to
have England build that canal. In those grandiose dreams of Salvador, the Jewish People comes to figure as the mediator between
East and West, and as destined to give mankind the true religion
dominated neither by Popes nor by Caesars.[33] In his later writings
Salvador developed some strange notions concerning Judaism and
Christianity.[34]

Finally an occasion to declare his new enthusiasm for the Jewish
People presented itself to Hess when he met a Jewish woman from
Frankfort who had lost her husband. Though deeply distressed, she
seemed to find comfort in her loyalty to Judaism. Hess was so impressed that he formulated his ideas on the Jews, their religion, and
their destiny in a series of twelve letters to the widow; these he
published in Cologne in 1862. To Hess the source of the comfort
which the widow drew from her religion was the faith in her husband's immortality. That faith, Hess reasoned, was validated by
the spirit of nationhood which is the foundation of the Jewish religion. Nationhood functioned as a sense of solidarity and social
responsibility, implying that the individual is not regarded as a
separate entity but as part of an organic society. This is in line with
the teaching of both the Jewish sages and Spinoza.[35] The soul of
the individual Jew is merged with the life of his People. He therefore lives on in the life of his People.[36]

A turning point in Hess' thinking was the capture of Rome,
which put an end to the Catholic Church as a world political
power. To him that event marked the end of Medievalism, which
had been responsible for the bondage in which the Jews had been
held throughout Christendom. Free nationhood was beginning to
be consummated for the Jews in the rebuilding of Jerusalem. The
fall of Rome and the unification of Italy represented the outcome
of what Hess regarded as the modern nationalist movement that
arose with the French Revolution.

Unlike the nationalist spirit of Germany, which was marked by
race domination, French nationalism was based on liberty, equality,
and fraternity. France was thus, to Hess, the second nation in the
world to demonstrate the humanizing influence of nationhood; the
first was the Jewish nation. He believed that France was more likely
than any other nation to appreciate the efforts of the Jews to recover their ancient territory. He, therefore, hoped that France

would go so far as to negotiate with the Sultan in behalf of the
Jews.

Hess' idealistic evaluation of nationhood was part of the then-
prevailing assumption that each nation belonged to a particular
historical race, possessing traits transmitted from generation to
generation in accordance with the law of biological heredity. Those
were the years when philosophers of history tried to identify the
distinctive traits of the various nations and to derive from those
traits the particular mission or destiny which fate, or Providence,
had destined each nation to fulfill. Hess, for his part, identified as
specifically Jewish traits the urge to unity, to futurity and to action.

The urge to unity, according to Hess, finds expression in a world
outlook which sees the cosmos in all its three stages—namely, the
physical, the organic, and the spiritual—as impelled by one plan
and purpose. "Judaism," he says, "never severs the individual from
the family, the family from the nation, the nation from mankind,
mankind from the organic and physical creation, creation from the
Creator." [37] He regarded Spinoza as much the incarnation of Jewish
genius as were Moses and Jesus. Spinoza, he maintained, inaugurated the modern era by identifying God with nature.

Hess tried to interpret Spinoza's views in consonance with the
spirit of Jewish tradition, and Jewish tradition in consonance with
Spinoza's philosophy. What he actually did was to read his own
interpretation into both tradition and philosophy. For Hess, Spinozism was the latest manifestation of the religious genius of the
Jews, which in terms of the Spinozist approach he regarded as
divine revelation. That genius manifested itself at "first in prophetic utterances, then in mysticism, and finally in philosophic
speculations." [38]

We evidently have in this three-stage manifestation of the religious genius of the Jews a correspondence with the philosophy of
history, where Hess describes the spiritual development of mankind by Moses typifying the prophetic age, Jesus the mystical and
Spinoza the speculative. It was Spinoza, according to Hess, whose
teachings ushered in the present age, which he characterizes as Messianic. The fulfillment of those teachings began with the French
Revolution. At this point, Hess gives utterance to a daring conception of the future of religion which is generally either overlooked
or ignored. He states that "with the French Revolution, there

began the rebirth of those nations which owe their national historical cult to Judaism." [39]

Hess maintains that the Jews excelled in the appreciation of values that are related to the time sense, as had the Greeks in the appreciation of values that are related to the space sense. Hence, the Jews contributed the historical approach to reality, whereas the main contribution of the Greeks was the esthetic approach to nature. Due to their keen sense of history, the Jews evolved the concept of the millenium. That concept has, in modern times, been given vitality and direction by the French Revolution. It points to a state of society in which the social institutions of all mankind will be so constituted as to afford every individual the opportunity to make the most of his human capacities. Hess designates this as the Sabbath of human evolution.

According to Hess, the Messianic idea in Jewish tradition is intended to negate eschatological notions that are part of the Christian tradition. The Sabbath of history is to be achieved in the world of the here-and-now. Primitive Christianity, he maintains, was merely the Messianic idea in terms of Jewish thinking of that day. Later Christianity, however, departed from the Messianic ideal and lost itself in other-worldly speculations. The French Revolution represented the return of the nations to the Jewish conception of mankind's future; that revolution directed once again the attention of mankind to the possibilities for good that inhere in this world.

Actually, Hess' argument has no foundation in fact. Traditional Judaism, as we have seen, was no less emphatic in stressing the centrality of other-worldliness than was Christianity. Also, the Messianic era in Judaism took on a definitely supernatural character, in that it was to be ushered in by a personal Messiah who was a descendant of King David. To identify it with this-worldly modern utopianism may be valid as *reinterpretation*, but not as *interpretation*.

Hess' idealization of nationalism, both general and Jewish, calls for a word of explanation nowadays, when nationalism has come to play a sinister part in human affairs. Actually Hess was obsessed with the nationalism which was the outcome of the French Revolution of 1791. To him that revolution was an expression of the newly awakened hope for freedom from various forms of oppression, particularly foreign rule, feudalism, and ecclesiasticism. He therefore identified nationalism with the principle òf equality, which conferred upon the common man a share in government. What could be nobler than the spirit of equality! It did not occur to those who advocated it with all the passion of their souls that, by granting to the common man a share in the government, a new energy was released which required intelligent channeling in order that it might lead to beneficent results. The nineteenth century entirely lacked the knowledge of the social forces at work in human life and the technique for bringing them under control.

It was generally assumed that the ethical rightness of equality carried with it a guarantee that it would be administered in keeping with its promise. Only now do we realize that in the hands of clever demagogues equality can be twisted into the kind of regime which has been aptly described as one in which some are "more equal" than others. Equality, unless deliberately fostered in a spirit of freedom, produces the depersonalized mass-man, who transforms war into genocide and converts nations into ravenous beasts seeking to destroy one another. But to dreamer idealists like Hess, who knew equality only as a destroyer of special privilege and as upholding the inalienable rights of the common man, modern nationalism to which democracy gave rise could not but appear as the dawn of the millenium.

In one of Hess' letters he deals with a question raised by his correspondent: Is not cosmopolitanism or humanitarianism a higher ideal than nationalism, in that it extends the principle of equality to include all of mankind? In his reply, to which Hess devotes his "Ninth Letter," he maintains that we only delude ourselves when we imagine that we can improve the condition of human life by appealing to love for mankind as a whole. Only the social forces operating in the solidarity of a nation can help to reduce the amount of suffering and misery in the world. Humanitarian cosmopolitanism can only be preached, not practiced. The creative power in history, like the creative power in nature, has evolved a variety of types. The way to improve the conditions of life is therefore to operate with that creative power, not *against* it. The leveling tendencies of modern industry, by introducing the operation of uniform inorganic mechanism are certain to put a brake on the creative power in history. They must therefore be countered by nationalism, which can release history's creative forces. That power is inherent in Jewish nationhood, which Hess tried hard to call back to life.

Hess was tremendously impressed by Heinrich Graetz's monumental *Geschichte der Juden*. He became fully convinced as a result of reading Graetz that Jews had managed to uphold their nationhood in the face of the most difficult odds. Hess concluded that the nationalist movement in the Europe of his day vindicated the stubbornness of the Jews in maintaining their nationhood at all costs. Jewish firmness had succeeded in keeping alive a force for freedom and equality. Hess assumed that the modern nations, which benefited from their internal unity and freedom from foreign rule through their national renaissance, would be the first to show their appreciation of the tenacity and courage of the Jews and would help them implement Jewish nationhood. Provided, that is, the Jews themselves rose to a proper understanding of their own national "mission," by achieving a thorough awareness of the history and meaning of Judaism.

The mission of the Jewish nation, according to Hess, does not consist, as the Reformists believe, in disseminating the truest and most ethical conception of God. Hess spares no words in denouncing the Reform movement. He characterizes it as a "fantastic illusion of the rationalists and philanthropists, who deny the national character of the Jewish religion." He thinks that Reform does not deserve to be called "liberal." True, in negating much in Judaism that has become obsolete, Reform has taken the first step toward freedom. But positive freedom must be creative; by eliminating the element of nationhood from Judaism, Reform loses the means of being positively free and creative.[40] This of course, does not mean that he approved of the Orthodox, who refuse to develop Judaism along modern lines.[41]

According to Hess, the mission of the Jewish nation consists rather in embodying the type of nationhood which, cherishing no military ambitions of its own, seeks to help other nations to achieve their own high destiny. That is why the Jewish nation needs a country of its own, where those who possess the necessary moral and spiritual qualifications will be in a position to demonstrate the workability of that spiritual nationhood. Their number need not be large; all that is necessary is that they be aware of their mission and dedicate themselves to its fulfillment. Consequently, the first thing Jews have to do is to imbue the most intellectually and spiritually gifted among them with a love for their People, and with the determination to establish in Eretz Yisrael a Jewish community that will live a wholesome and productive life.

Hess thus found the purpose of the reawakened Jewish national spirit in Jewish tradition. He saw in the reclamation of Eretz Yisrael not merely the return of the Jewish People to its former land, but a vindication of its historic martyrdom. He envisaged the Jewish People as destined to become a living channel of communication between Europe and Asia, bringing to the primitive peoples of Asia the sciences and civilization of Europe to which the Jews had made a rich contribution. In addition, they would bring the barren soil of their ancient fatherland under cultivation, rendering it fruitful once again as in days of old. Withal, Hess calls upon the Jews to be grateful to modern France for its anticipated help in making that glorious future possible.[42]

What is striking about his conception of the renaissance of Jewish nationhood in Eretz Yisrael is that Hess realized the impossibility of having the entire Jewish People withdraw from the lands of its dispersion. Instead of adopting the Messianic conception of a complete ingathering of the Jewish People, he preferred to resort to the historical precedent of the return of the Jews from the Babylonian captivity. At that time the majority of the Jewish People remained in Babylon and other countries where they had settled even before the downfall of the First Commonwealth. "So," he adds, "we need not look to a larger concentration of Jews at the future restoration."[43]

AHAD HA-AM (1859-1927)

Ahad Ha-Am's influence on Jewish life, a result of the rationale he developed for the Zionist movement, is probably greater than that of any other Jewish thinker in modern times. That is because his conception of Zionism provides a much needed orientation for the return of the Jewish People to Eretz Yisrael, one that is motivated not by the outer compelling drive of anti-Semitism, but by the inner impelling drive of Judaism. On the other hand, Ahad Ha-Am's Zionism is based not on the traditional belief in the miraculous advent of a personal Messiah, as was the Zionism of Kalischer and Alkalai, nor on the faith which Hess had pinned on liberal nationalism, but on the objective realities of human nature and society.

Ahad Ha-Am was the pen name Asher Ginzberg[44] adopted to indicate that he was not a publicist by profession, but writing only in response to the public call upon him to express his views with regard to the present crisis in Judaism. He was born in 1856 in a small town in South Russia into a rather well-to-do Hasidic family, whose Hasidism was noted for its conscious opposition to Haskalah, or the Jewish Enlightenment movement. Despite every conceivable obstacle, Ahad Ha-Am managed to acquire a wide knowledge of foreign languages, particularly, English, as well as of modern thought. Though he remained rooted in his loyalty to the Jewish People, his conception of the future of Judaism grew to be radically different from that which he had come to know as an expert in Rabbinic lore. He arrived at a social philosophy in which Spencer's sociology and Darwin's evolutionism figured prominently. Bringing that philosophy to bear on his attachment to the Jewish People and his view of Judaism as the people's creation, Ahad Ha-Am saw in the return of the Jewish People to Eretz Yisrael the only alternative to the disappearance of both Jews and Judaism. At the age of thirty-two, he and his family finally broke away from his father's God-forsaken village and moved to Odessa. There he finally found himself amid congenial surroundings and like-minded Jews all of whom were identified with the *Hibbat Tsiyyon* movement. From that time until the end of his life, Ahad Ha-Am was the leading thinker in the Zionist movement.

Ahad Ha-Am's Zionism is based on the specific sense of solidarity which, fluctuate as it may, every individual Jew experiences in relation to his fellow-Jews. The indisputable fact of this we-feeling which Jews have in common was driven home throughout the past in every one of the daily prayers and benedictions that Jews were wont to recite. It gave rise to two well-known principles in Judaism: "All Jews are one fellowship," and "all Jews are responsible for one another."

Ahad Ha-Am became imbued with the Spencerian conception of

society as a living organism, a conception that captured the imagination of most thinking people during the last quarter of the nineteenth century. At that very time Ahad Ha-Am was formulating his own ideas on Zionism. Spencer drew an analogy between the individual living organism and the collectivity of human beings who act as a unitary body for generations. Like all analogies, however, this one tended to overshoot the mark; it evoked misleading inferences. Within limitations, however, that analogy is of service in affording a true insight into how permanent bodies like peoples, nations, and churches function. Ahad Ha-Am kept strictly within those limitations, his critics notwithstanding. He concentrated on the significance of the objective fact that all Jews as such experience a "we-feeling." He noted to what extent this feeling had dominated Jewish life in the past, and how rapidly it was disintegrating as a result of emancipation and enlightenment. Availing himself of the biological interpretation of society made popular by Spencer, Ahad Ha-Am diagnosed the contemporary crisis of the Jewish People as one of a weakening of the collective will-to-live of the Jewish People.

Ahad Ha-Am treated the we-feeling as a psychological manifestation of the social instinct which is part of the mentality of the individual human being, and which functions most potently among those who are related through the consciousness of a common past and who cherish common hopes for the future. A nation consists of individuals who are thus related, and therefore it is held together by the social instinct of its members. Objective truth was not compromised by Ahad Ha-Am's treatment of the "will-to-live of the Jewish People" as an inborn instinct. The term "instinct" merely connoted that this we-feeling functions even more on the unconscious than on the conscious level. Whatever the individual does, thinks, or feels because of his we-feeling he does as a member of a collectivity, and under the collective impact of the interaction of its members. The collectivity is therefore liable to give rise to actions which the conscious ascribes not to the actual but to some imaginary cause.

Ahad Ha-Am, in addition, fully realized that this social instinct, operating as a we-feeling or as the will-to-live, made possible the entire complex of social interaction among Jews, and that out of this complex emerged the Jewish culture or social heritage handed down from generation to generation. Analyzing Jewish culture, Ahad Ha-Am found it to consist of two important factors: one made for a highly ethical sense of justice, and the other, personalizing the will-to-live of the Jewish People, gave that will-to-live the character of a national self. The first factor was expressed in the unique apotheosis of social righteousness in the Jewish tradition, the second, in a glorification of the Jewish People's past and an idealization of its future.

What is distinctive about Ahad Ha-Am's Zionism is that it is so conceived as to form an integral part of a new conception of Judaism and a new program for its future. Zionism for Ahad Ha-Am is no more nor less than a call to thoroughgoing reconstruction of Judaism as a whole.[45] What this implies may be inferred by comparing Ahad Ha-Am's version of Zionism with the ideology of the Reform movement, also a reconstruction of Judaism. In the first place, Reform was motivated mainly by the desire to accommodate Judaism to the expectations of the liberal statesmen who helped to abolish the Medieval disabilities of the Jews. Secondly, Reform cut the Gordian knot of the problem presented by Jewish nationhood by simply renouncing it, thereby removing the very matrix of Judaism. Thirdly, what Reform left of Judaism was a system of ethical monotheism or theistic ethics, based on some of the prophetic writings in the Bible.

To be sure, Reform is based on the conception of the Jews as a race, a conception intended to replace the principle of nationhood. However, Reform was unable to provide a *raison d'être* for Judaism, except on the assumption that certain races are endowed with special talents. Thus, the Greeks were supposed to have possessed an inborn talent for art, the Romans for law and government, and the Jews for religion. Such a rationale for Judaism is descriptive, but not normative. It merely describes what the Jews achieved in the early part of their career, but it throws no light on what enabled the Jews to retain their sense of oneness or nationhood after having lived in dispersion for almost two thousand years. Nor does it account for the Jews' refusal to abandon the hope of returning to their homeland when there was not the least likelihood of such an eventuality in the course of nature.

The foregoing facts were just as much a part of Jewish religion as was the belief in God, and they had nothing to do with any inherent *racial* trait. When a people becomes aware of a sense of unity and passionately cherishes the hope of maintaining that unity, it generally arrives at the idea of having a common ancestry only as an afterthought. The mere fact of deriving from a common ancestry does not *of itself* give rise to a sense of national or religious unity.

It is far more reasonable, therefore, to ascribe the Jewish sense of oneness and the Jewish yearning for a return to Eretz Yisrael to a we-feeling which is an *acquired* social trait; this part is transmitted not through the blood but through social heritage, or the we-feeling which Ahad Ha-Am analogizes with the instinctive will-to-live. Such we-feeling, or collective will-to-live, is not the unique possession of any particular race, but arises within any human group whose members share a common language, a common history, and a common culture. How persistent such we-feeling can be under adverse circumstances depends upon the character of its common culture, and on the extent to which that culture produces in each member of the nation a sense of fellowship with and dependence upon the other members of the nation for his own salvation.

In the past only Jewish culture was capable of producing that effect nationally. Nowadays, when many such cultures are arising among various peoples, mankind is experiencing an upsurge of nationalism. It is only to be expected, therefore, that the Jews whose culture enabled them to retain the we-feeling or the will-to-live under adverse circumstances, should desire when those circumstances are eliminated not to become absorbed by the rest of the world but to reassert their will-to-live as a people. It is not feasible for Jews to do so however when they live among nations which themselves are engaged in evolving a strong we-feeling or will-to-live. Hence Jews must resume their national life in Eretz Yisrael, with the purpose of reviving the prophetic ideal of social righteousness.[46]

Ahad Ha-Am, accordingly, felt that the problem to contend with at present was not principally how to establish a sovereign Jewish State in Palestine, but how to reawaken in Jews the weakening historic we-feeling or will-to-live. The first thing to do was to modernize Jewish culture. The two main elements of traditional Jewish culture, other-worldliness and messianism, prevented that culture from keeping alive the we-feeling or will-to-live. The prospect of salvation in the hereafter tended even in the past to render the individual Jew self-sufficient, morally and spiritually; and the belief in the Messiah was bound up with a supernaturalism that had become obsolete.

Ahad Ha-Am's conception of Judaism as the culture of the Jewish People has to be understood in terms of his conception of the role of a national culture in the life of the individual. It was his view that since mankind is divided into particular nations or peoples, it is possible for an individual to achieve his salvation, or the full measure of his potential humanity, only through the medium of the particular culture or social heritage of the nation to which he belongs. *That culture, or social heritage, which consists of the language, history, ethical and religious values and usages, and which is transmitted from generation to generation, is what gives a people its spiritual character. It is the medium through which the will-to-live of the nation or people functions, and which shapes the basic consciousness and personality of every person who belongs to it. Nationhood, or Peoplehood, is therefore, not a political, but a socio-cultural or spiritual concept.* This is the key principle in Ahad Ha-Am's conception of Judaism, or of that which unites Jews among themselves, distinguishing them from the rest of the world. Judaism is the culture which the Jewish People evolves as a means of articulating its will-to-live. Without such articulation, the will-to-live of the Jewish People can no more function than can the will-to-live of an individual who is unable to articulate his wants, his fears, and his hopes.

What led Ahad Ha-Am to stress the cultural rather than the political conception of nationhood as significant in planning for the future of the Jewish People was undoubtedly the remarkably unique role which culture had played throughout Jewish history. To appreciate that role, we need only contrast it with the role of culture in the life of the rest of mankind. It is a commonplace in the history of culture that education was the privilege only of the ruling classes. Hence, only the well-to-do and the other possessors of power, military and religious, had a stake in the ideals and values through which a people or nation achieved self-awareness, a sense of purpose, and direction for its corporate existence. The toiling masses that sweated for their bare sustenance and to keep the thatched roof over their heads were as unaware of any collective

ideal as were the oxen that pulled their plows. Even as late as the
eighteenth century, education was still confined to the élite. No
wonder, therefore, that even men like Voltaire, Rousseau, Kant,
Goethe, Hume, and Adam Smith hobnobbed for the most part
only with the aristocracy.

Contrast with this the role of religious culture in the life of the
Jewish People. Inherent in the evolution of Torah—a term which
denotes "law," "teaching" and "study," but most of all "religious
culture"—was the mandate that it become the common possession
of the entire "congregation of Jacob or the Jewish People" (Deut.
33:4). Not, however, till the Pharisees took over the spiritual leadership of the Jewish People during the first century before the
Common Era was this mandate carried into effect. From then on
any Jew, no matter how poor in worldly possessions or how humble
his station in life, could rise to the greatest heights in the esteem of
the nation if he availed himself of the opportunity to study Torah.
Such opportunities were open to all, but a special effort was made
to keep them open to the children of the poor and the ignorant.[47]

But Ahad Ha-Am realized that the problem was not merely that
of involving all Jews in the study of Torah in the traditional spirit.
That might be a problem for traditionalist Zionists like the Mizrahi.
He maintained[48] that the time had come when the tradition could
no longer suffice as the sole source of inspiration and guidance in
the cultural life of Jews. In addition to the Written Torah and the
Oral Torah, which constitute the tradition, Jews need· "a living
Torah" (Torah Sh'belev)—an ongoing creative culture, which will
reflect the response of the functioning national spirit to the stream
of living experience, both individual and collective. He deplored
the fact that the Jews were merely "a people of the book" throughout the centuries of exile, shackled by an authoritative tradition to
which every expression of Jewish life had to conform. Ahad Ha-Am
was determined to transform the Jews into "a people of culture" by
activating the national spirit to produce outstanding creators of
culture ("objective culture"), and to evolve the kind of popular
education that would embrace every Jew ("subjective culture").

Ahad Ha-Am's conception of culture ran the whole gamut of
creative self-expression, through philosophy, letters, and the arts.
In modern times Jews have distinguished themselves in all creative
forms, but their contributions have enriched the cultures of other

nations, not that of their own. Ahad Ha-Am dismisses the charge that to express regret over this loss bespeaks small-minded tribalism. "We need not answer those who ask what humanity loses by our loss; it is rather for them to explain what humanity gains by our loss." In illustration, he quotes the case of the Jewish sculptor Antokolsky who, despite his intensive Jewish upbringing in a Jewish environment abounding with themes for his creative genius, chose as his models not Herod but Ivan the Terrible, not the ascetic perpetual student of the Yeshivah, but the Russian chronicler who had been a monk.[49]

Ahad Ha-Am was fully cognizant of the extent to which Traditional Judaism placed the center of reference of human life in the world to come. To him this other-worldly emphasis indicated that, as a result of the destruction of the Second Jewish Commonwealth, Jewish nationhood had been endangered, because the interests of the Jewish nation as a whole no longer coincided with those of the individual Jew. The traditionalists assumed that for the individual Jew to remain loyal to his People, he had to be assured the reward of bliss in the world-to-come. That bliss would compensate for whatever suffering he endured in this life because he adhered to the precepts of the Torah. The Jew was also warned that he could not deviate from that way of life with impunity. Damnation in the world-to-come would counterbalance the success and power he might enjoy in this world.

This appeal to individual interest, according to Ahad Ha-Am was as little in keeping with the Biblical tradition as it was with the outlook of modern man. The rewards promised in the Torah for the observance of its precepts are security, well-being, and prosperity. The penalties for the violation of the divine commandments are war, famine, slavery, and exile. Both rewards and punishments are addressed to the nation as a whole, not to the individual. Nowadays, when the other-worldly appeal can no longer serve as an incentive to loyalty to the Jewish People, some way must be found by which the interests of the individual Jew will again coincide with those of the Jewish People as a whole. Only by identifying himself with the Jewish People can the individual Jew achieve salvation. True, the belief in other-worldly reward and punishment constituted in the past a defense of the Jewish spirit; but, Ahad Ha-Am points out, with the crumbling of that defense, it is necessary to erect another line of defense behind which the Jewish spirit may hold its own.

Three elements are discernable in Ahad Ha-Am's attitude toward Judaism as a culture or way of life based on national self-consciousness: a) passionate love for the Jewish People, which is as implicit and elemental as the will-to-live, b) deep concern and anxiety over the fact that the Jewish People was rapidly disintegrating; and c) implicit faith that the return to Eretz Ysirael would enable the Jewish People to reactivate its ancient prophetic zeal for the ideal of social righteousness.

Ahad Ha-Am's love for the Jewish People was the result of an intimate knowledge of its history and literature. That knowledge acquired a deep emotional tone in the Hasidic environment where he had spent his youth; later it achieved new and relevant significance through Ahad Ha-Am's wide reading in the field of social philosophy. As a Russian Jew, whose government, after having given the Jews a temporary respite from persecution and discriminatory laws, had resumed its anti-Semitic policy with redoubled fury, his love for the Jewish People remained undivided. He owed nothing to Russia. He had no occasion to be troubled by the question of how to combine love for the Jewish People with love for his native country. Hence, there is a lack of charity in the judgment Ahad Ha-Am passed on the Jews of the Western countries. He did not seem to realize that the Jews of those countries could not possibly allow their love for the Jewish People to monopolize their affections, that they had also to find a place in their souls for the nations whose citizens they were.

In defense of Ahad Ha-Am, however, it may be argued that he was too disturbed by the rapid disintegration of the Jewish People and the disruption of its way of life in democratic countries to be objective in his judgment. The spiritual leaders of Western Jewry never frankly admitted that, due to outward pressure they could not resist, they were in fact abandoning one position in Jewish life and thought after another, continually beating a retreat. Instead, they kept pretending that their version of Judaism was on the march. They should have been entirely honest with themselves and with the Jewish People. They should have frankly admitted that they had not found a way of keeping Judaism genuinely alive under the conditions imposed upon them by the Emancipation.

Instead, they pretended to regard the few monotheistic abstractions to which Judaism was reduced, as things for which it was worthwhile to live as a Jew; these, they said, constituted a mission for whose discharge it was necessary only to attend decently to one's own affairs.

This attitude taken by the Western Jewish leaders offended Ahad Ha-Am's sense of reality and intellectual integrity. In 1891, he penned a famous diatribe "Servitude in Freedom," on the jubilee anniversary of a French Jewish scholarly magazine, which happened to coincide with the centenary of the Jewish Emancipation in France. The occasion had been utilized by a number of spiritual leaders in West European Jewry for self-congratulation on the progress achieved by Judaism. Ahad Ha-Am, prophetically devoted to his People, and lamenting its rapid loss of ground, pricked the bubble of self-delusion. Thus he taught the thoughtful Jews not to rely on self-hypnosis to cure their spiritual ills; they must face the situation in all its heart-breaking reality without shrinking.

Yet Ahad Ha-Am possessed unbounded faith in the possibilities of Jewish survival, despite the menacing dangers. He saw no reason for despair. He was sure that there would always be some Jews in whom love for their People would always burn bright, so devoted to the cause of prophetic Judaism that they would succeed in keeping it alive. Ahad Ha-Am realized that there was no *demonstrable* basis for this faith. He could point, however, to the effect of that faith during some of the darkest moments of Jewish history, beginning with the first Babylonian exile.[50] He also found moral support for his attitude in the fact that Maimonides, who had reinterpreted Judaism from the standpoint of the supremacy of reason, included in his Creed the two principles concerning the Messiah and the resurrection, though both principles were out of harmony with the rest of his ideas. Ahad Ha-Am viewed this as Maimonides' way of affirming his faith in the future of the Jewish People.[51] Though Ahad Ha-Am was unable to offer logical proof for his faith, he was determined to translate it into a planned course of action. This planned action dealt with the two centrifugal factors of Jewish life, the Emancipation and the Enlightenment.

The Emancipation had disrupted the unity of the Jewish People. Fearful that the sense of unity with Jews of other lands might impugn their loyalty to their own land, the Jews of Western countries seemed fearful of evincing genuine interest in the well-being of world Jewry. The Jewish People was thus likely to be broken up into many tribes, with no common present or future. But even more fatal was the effect of the Emancipation on each local Jewry. With a natural tendency to identify themselves with the entire cultural life of the country whose citizens they were, Jews were gradually losing their Jewish consciousness; that consciousness was dying for lack of cultural content or activity on which to feed. The few religious ceremonies and occasional prayer services constituted a very frail attachment to the Jewish People. In one or two generations they lost their hold, and the Jew was cast spiritually adrift.

The other centrifugal factor was the Enlightenment, which led to the secularization of life. Salvation, or human self-fulfillment, came to be conceived as realizable in the here-and-now, rather than in the hereafter or in a world-to-come. The other-worldly outlook, regarded as integral to the entire manifold of traditional beliefs in the miracles and the theophanies recorded in the Bible as historical events, was viewed as irrelevant for modern times.

The task confronting the Jews was to counteract these centrifugal forces by setting in motion counter-forces of a centripetal character. This involved discovering motives that would give the Jew a genuine purpose to live for. A program of action had to be devised that would provide a new basis for Jewish nationhood, a new bond of Jewish unity, and a new set of common values in place of those deriving from the traditional other-worldly perspective.

Such a program of action was offered, according to Ahad Ha-Am, by the return of the Jewish People to Eretz Yisrael.[52] Zionism was not to aim merely at the establishment in Eretz Yisrael of a political State to serve as a haven for persecuted Jewry. Ahad Ha-Am did not believe that the political purpose of establishing a Jewish State was realizable within a reasonable future. Moreover, he saw insurmountable obstacles in the way of large-scale migration to Palestine. The main obstacle was the presence of the Arabs, who then occupied Palestine, and of the Turks, who then governed it. Zionism, he maintained, should not undertake to save the Jews, since it was inconceivable that the majority of the Jewish People could be accommodated in Eretz Yisrael. Its main purpose should be to save the Jewish consciousness, or Judaism. This it could do by establishing in Eretz Yisrael as many Jewish settlements as conditions permitted with the view of achieving a permanent Jewish majority in Palestine. To these settlements only those Jews were to be admitted who were fully aware that they were going there to create a new order of Jewish life, and to evolve new incentives for Jews everywhere to live as Jews. The main objective was the conservation of the Jewish spirit. Judaism, which to Ahad Ha-Am was synonymous with Jewish culture, was to find expression in the entire gamut of Jewish cultural values. "Culturally," he wrote, "we left our childhood behind three thousand years ago. We now need an adult's diet, but we are so situated that we have to go to school again and learn the alphabet of national life. What shall we do? The answer is, we have to start from both ends at once—build simultaneously from the bottom and the top. To be sure, this is not the way nations are built, but our case is without precedent." So Ahad Ha-Am urged the establishment of a Hebrew University and the fostering there of arts and letters; this was no less important in Eretz Yisrael than the establishment of colonies.[53]

Spiritual Zionism did not call for less effort and initiative than did political Zionism; but it strove to avoid fanfare and trumped-up propaganda for the sake of winning adherents for the cause. Ahad Ha-Am felt compelled to play the unenviable role of the debunker to tell the unwelcome truth. But his words, like those of the ancient Prophets, while not heeded at the time of their utterance, served as a source of consolation and guidance when some of the evils they had warned against came true.

The above is an attempt to synthesize into an organic orientation the ideas propounded by Ahad Ha-Am in a series of essays, mostly topical and written in response to current events and challenges. That our synthesis does justice to Ahad Ha-Am's version of Zionism is evident from the following brief extract from his introduction to the second edition of *Al Parashat Derakim*:

"Anti-Semitism will never disappear so long as we are dispersed among the nations and there is no way to eradicate it. That is the great *novum* of the Zionists, on which they have built their entire system. . . . We have therefore no alternative but to establish a special 'state' over which our enemies will have no control. . . .

In the midst of all the hurrahs [greeting the 'state' project] along a person comes who says: 'The first thing we must do is achieve the renaissance of Judaism. Even the state needs to be established for the sake of the renaissance of Judaism, using ways and means that can further that purpose.' No wonder that person is set upon by numerous assailants, some with the bitterness of zealots and others with raillery, but all asking in amazement: 'Is now the time to worry about an abstract ideal like Judaism, at this time when Jews are in straits and seeking a haven of safety?' And the younger generation, indignant as usual, cry out: 'Judaism was created for the Jews, and not the Jews for Judaism.'

"This slogan sounds wonderful, but on analysis it turns out to be a boomerang. . . . Since Judaism not only exists for the sake of the Jews but has been fostered by the Jews themselves, who for thousands of years, have devoted their best energies to its preservation, obviously the Jews are badly in need of Judaism and cannot get along without it. It is inconceivable that a people should consistently act on the basis of bad judgment generation after generation. The only explanation is that the people acts as it does at the instinctive command of the will-to-live that dominates it. The truth is that no great ratiocination is necessary to reach the conviction that Jews should worry about Judaism no less than they should worry about themselves. The national feeling is the cause of our survival; the embittered heart cannot be satisfied merely through knowing the cause of our survival. It wants to know the *purpose* of our survival under such terrible conditions as well. . . . The yoke of exile seems unbearable because we lack a national ideal for whose sake we might be reconciled to our sufferings.

"If the state could be established in the near future and accept all of the Jewish People now in exile, we might perhaps ignore for the present the problem of ideals. . . . But even after the state has been established, it can in no way solve the problem of the welfare of the Jews most of whom are bound to remain scattered among the nations and victims of anti-Semitism. On the other hand, we assume that the spiritual salvation of the Jewish People will come from Zion. We have to look for the recovery of our national ideal [Judaism] in the land where it first came into being, since we have lost it in the countries of our exile, and we can no longer bear the yoke of exile without that ideal. Such being the case, how can we sit back quietly when we see Zionism leaving the path to the spiritual ideal and wasting its energy on activities that cannot bring about an encompassing national salvation, either material or spiritual?"

Ahad Ha-Am's contribution to the renaissance of Judaism was not limited to his conception of Zionism. He realized that the renaissance could not wait until conditions in Eretz Yisrael were such as to instil new life in Diaspora Jewry. Ahad Ha-Am called for an immediate revaluation of the spiritual heritage. Since the theurgic and other-worldly assumptions upon which that heritage was based were no longer tenable, it was imperative to reinterpret those assumptions into terms which formed part of the contemporary world outlook. A study of his writings discloses three norms of reinterpretation: 1) the supremacy of reason, 2) the pragmatic test of reality, and 3) conformity with the unique ethical spirit of the Jewish People.

In a brilliant analysis of Maimonides' contribution to Judaism,[54] Ahad Ha-Am points out that Maimonides revolutionized Judaism by making it synonymous with the supremacy of reason. Before Maimonides' influence made itself felt, tradition had been regarded as the main source of religious truth, which had no need to be validated by reason. By the tenth century, however, Judaism had come in contact with the teachings of the ancient Greek philosophers. It then could no longer afford to ignore the challenge of reason. Saadyah Gaon reacted by writing his *Emunot V'deot*. But even Saadyah never got beyond treating reason as subordinate to tradition. It was Maimonides who inaugurated a new development in Judaism, when he insisted that tradition, to be acceptable, must conform with the demands of reason. His basic assumption was that man's distinctive trait consisted in the possession of the intellect. To the extent that man developed his intellect he qualified for unity with the "Active Intellect" of the world, or God. Such unity constituted man's salvation. If Judaism was to lead to salvation, its primary function was to help man live a life of reason.

The Maimonidean Creed, according to Ahad Ha-Am, should be viewed from the standpoint of the historical conditions under which Maimonides lived. Islam in Spain had abandoned its policy of tolerance. The Jews faced the choice of either submitting to conversion or leaving the country. With Islam challenging Judaism and claiming to be a superior revelation, Judaism was bound to lose ground unless it could fortify its position in terms of reason. That is what led Maimonides to formulate his Creed, which is an expression of the rationalism of the thirteenth century. "He who emancipates his reason from outward compulsion," says Ahad Ha-Am, "simultaneously emancipates it from the power of his own inner compulsion; he can regard no idea as necessarily true unless it is rationally acceptable." [55]

Whether Ahad Ha-Am's interpretation of Maimonides is objectively true or not, it is apparent that, *to Ahad Ha-Am, Maimonides was the great emancipator of Judaism from the necessity of accepting Jewish tradition in the form in which it had come down from the past.* The rule of reason which enabled Judaism to weather the crisis in Maimonides' time should help Judaism weather the crisis now. The "inquiring Jew," or the free-thinking Jew, who loves the Jewish People and its spiritual heritage, is better qualified to understand and appreciate Judaism than the "believing Jew." [56]

Then there is the conflict between the Biblical account of the origin of Israel and Israel's religion, on the one hand, and the testimony of historical investigation, on the other. Despite the fact that the problems raised by these conflicts seem to lie within the field of theology, they occupy a large place in Ahad Ha-Am's conception of national Judaism. The principle which Ahad Ha-Am sets up as a means of dealing with the problem of conflict between Jewish tradition and the modern historical approach is: "As historical we may consider only that which produces the forces which operate in the life of human society. A historical personality is one whose effect on human life is evident, though he may be only a product of the imagination. Such a personality is a historical force, and his existence a historical truth." [57] Goethe's Werther, he goes on to say, was only an imaginary person; but since he so impressed himself on the minds of Goethe's generation that many were driven to suicide in imitation of him, Werther was a more genuinely historical personality than any random German who really lived at the time.

Applying this principle, the personality of Moses becomes a

historical fact, regardless of all that archaeological research may say to the contrary, because the Moses who figures in the Jewish consciousness is not the one who is the subject of archaeological research. The Moses of Judaism is a historical reality whose existence cannot be questioned; the evidences of his influence are present in the entire course of Jewish history. Ahad Ha-Am, analyzing this actual "historical" Moses, finds him to have been the incarnation of the Jewish ideal of the Prophet. As such, Moses embodied the synthesis of absolute truth, uncompromising fidelity to the right, and devotion to the ideal of a supreme justice.

Ahad Ha-Am bases this conception of Moses on the various episodes in the life of Moses which are recorded in the Torah and on the laws ascribed to him there. Regardless of whether those episodes actually occurred or not, or whether those laws actually emanated from him, the fact that they were recorded and have been reiterated by the Jewish People throughout the ages, implies an affinity in the Jewish consciousness for what those episodes or laws state and imply. They afford us a deeper insight into the Jewish soul than any cold scientific study of the Jewish past could yield. It is the kind of insight which can do more to shape character and give meaning to life, both individual and collective, than any religious dogma or philosophic principle. Spiritually, such insight is no whit inferior to that of the traditional belief concerning "the man Moses" and the events in which he is said to have figured.

This way of dealing with the problem of conflict between tradition and modern historical approach is a new method of reinterpretation of Jewish values. If applied on a large scale, it can make the basic tradition of Jewish religion a vital factor in the modern Jewish consciousness.

Another norm of reinterpretation proposed by Ahad Ha-Am calls for the development of a system of Jewish ethics. He was fully aware that the great advantage of Traditional Judaism, from a national standpoint, was that, by dint of its religious beliefs and practices, it permeated the entire life of the Jew. Traditional Judaism thus secured the Jew's attachment to his People by rendering him dependent upon it for what he valued most.

The question which Ahad Ha-Am sought to answer was: Can spiritual Zionism create in the Jew who cannot conscientiously live up to the traditional regimen of religious beliefs and practices the same sense of need for his People and the same attachment to it? He knew very well that Zionist activity, supplemented by the study of Hebrew and Jewish history and the cultivation of Hebrew literature, while necessary, cannot be more than a marginal interest in the life of Diaspora Jewry.

Starting from the assumption that each people had its own type of ethics, Ahad Ha-Am insisted that the uniqueness of the Jewish spirit at its highest was reflected in its ethical standards and interests. It was ignorance of the inner spirit of Judaism, he believed, that was responsible for the failure even of some of the foremost Jewish leaders to realize to what extent Judaism emphasized the primacy of ethical behavior.

Ahad Ha-Am therefore centered his hope on the fostering of Jewish ethical activity along the lines he believed were pursued by the Ethical Culture Society founded in the United States by Felix Adler.[58] He maintained that it was incumbent upon Jews to form societies for the promotion of Jewish ethical culture, as zealously as, in the past, they had organized groups for the study of Torah. The pursuit of ethical culture, in a modern spirit, should be the form which the study of Torah should take for the modern nationalist Jew. All problems of right and wrong which the individual encountered in every one of his human relationships should fall within the purview of this modern form of Torah study.

It is regrettable, that, with all his deep insight into both the national and ethical aspects of Judaism, Ahad Ha-Am failed to appreciate the aspect which had contributed most to Judaism's survival under the most adverse circumstances—the religious. Whether due to temperament or to the limited opportunities of his general education, the horizon of Ahad Ha-Am's thinking was limited to the socio-psychological facts of human life. In matters cosmic or metaphysical like Kant, he too was awakened from his dogmatic slumber by Hume; but he was not interested, as Kant had been, in arriving at a deeper understanding of the belief in God. Had he done so, Ahad Ha-Am would have been the Maimonides of our generation, guiding us out of our most troublesome perplexities.

C. POLITICAL ZIONISM

Political Zionism viewed the Jewish situation as an emergency calling for large-scale drastic action of an internationally political character. The emergency was due to the rapidly increasing danger of anti-Semitism. The Jews could not be saved from that danger by the slow process of Jewish colonization of Palestine. Action had to be of an internationally political character; for the homeless condition of the Jewish People had to be ended through their re-acquisition of its ancestral land, to be publicly recognized as its permanent homeland. Involved were political negotiations with those nations which had an interest in that land. Once public recognition was achieved, the Jews would have to engage in a large-scale organized effort for mass migration, settlement, and the establishment of an autonomous government or state.

LEON PINSKER (1821-1891)

Seldom was the title of a book intended to convey such deep feeling as was *Auto-Emancipation*, the title given by Leon Pinsker to the brochure he published in German in 1883.[59] It was meant to be an outcry of bitter disillusionment with the expected release from Medieval disabilities, a passionately prophetic call to Jews to take their fate into their own hands. In his introduction, Pinsker warned his fellow-Jews against permitting the temporary respite from pogroms to pass without finding some more permanent remedy for their ills than was afforded by the palliatives to which they had been resorting. And he borrowed as his motto for the brochure the words of Hillel: "If I do not help myself who can help me?"

Leon Pinsker was the son of one of the few East European scholars who cultivated the scientific study of Judaism. The Pinsker family left Tomashov, a small hamlet in Galicia, and settled finally in the city of Odessa. As a young lad Leon was brought up under the tutelage of his father, who was an instructor in a school where Hebrew studies were secondary to general studies. His basic Jewish training was thus one which had its roots in the *Haskalah,* or Hebrew Enlightenment movement. When he grew up he took advantage of the opportunity opened up to Jews; he studied law in Moscow, and after completing his advanced studies, took up the study of medicine. Pinsker proved to be an excellent physician and recognition and honors came his way.

Those were the years of the reign of Czar Alexander II, who was looked upon as a liberal ruler. Russian Jews were expecting to be emancipated from their Medieval disabilities at the same time the Jews of some of the Western countries were doing their utmost to prove that they deserved the emancipation which had been granted to them. At first the efforts of those Russian Jews, of whom Pinsker was one, were directed toward integrating their fellow-Jews into the life and civilization of the Russian people. Pinsker considered Russia a long-sought-for haven; he was ready to sacrifice all for her welfare. When, however, Russia unleashed the savage pogroms of 1881 against the Jews, and then followed with the discriminatory and oppressive May laws of 1882, Pinsker realized his mistake. His disillusionment led him to repudiate his previous enthusiasm for the Russification of his people, reassessing his hope for their emancipation. He realized that at best Jewish emancipation could only be a *legal* enactment, and even as such an enactment it was due only to *enlightened self-interest* and not to any moral *feeling.* It was merely "a splendid alms willingly or unwillingly flung to the poor, humble beggars whom no one, however, cares to shelter" just because they are homeless.[60] But the general population remained obsessed by the prejudices against Jews which had been inculcated in it for centuries, in addition to xenophobia, an ineradicable tendency of human nature. Pinsker summed up the general attitude of Gentiles to Jews: "For the living, the Jew is a dead man; for the natives, an alien and a vagrant, for the property holders a beggar; for the poor and exploited a millionaire, for patriots a man without a country, for all classes a hated rival." [61]

It then became clear to Pinsker that whatever civil rights were granted to Jews were insecure and could be withdrawn at any time. "The Jew," he wrote, "is not permitted to forget that the daily

bread of civil rights must be given to him. . . . Nowhere have the
Jews succeeded in obtaining from their fellow citizens recognition
as native-born citizens of equal rank . . . What a pitiful figure
we do cut! We do not count as a nation among the other nations,
and we have no voice in the council of the peoples, even in affairs
which concern us." [62] He came to the conclusion that the Jewish
emancipation, even in the Western countries was a broken reed
which, in the words of the Prophet, "pierces the hand of him who
leans upon it." So long as the Jews are dispersed among the nations
and have no land of their own, they are bound to be objects of
contempt, hatred and persecution. Pinsker rebuked his fellow-
Jews however for their loss of self-respect, self-confidence, and
initiative.[63]

The premise upon which Pinsker based this conclusion was that,
human nature being what it is, anti-Semitism was too deep-rooted
ever to be eradicated, so long as the Jews are a homeless people.
It was part of realism not to expect of human nature something
which it had always lacked—humanity. Lacking the sense of
humanity, the human being was subject to xenophobia. Judeo-
phobia was a combination of the fear-inspired hatred of strangers
and fear of imaginary demons and ghosts. The Jews were a kind
of ghost people. Not having a land of their own, their persistence
as a minority among other nations was a disquieting mystery, as
of some demonic being or force. The Jews, failing to grasp the
irrational character of this phobia, or to realize how deeply rooted
it had become after twenty centuries of transmission from generation to generation, hoped to cure the nations by appealing to their
sense of justice. On the other hand, the nations, unwilling to admit
that they were dominated by a phobia, have tried to justify their
cruel treatment of the Jews by all sorts of fanciful and specious
rationalizations.

According to Pinsker, it were better for all concerned that the
truth about human nature were frankly recognized, and that steps
were taken to create the conditions for the Jews which would
eliminate the very cause of the phobia against them. The only
solution was to remove the Jews from all countries where they
were not wanted; this was particularly necessary for the Jewish
proletariat who had become surplus population.[64] The Jews must
be moved to a land of their own where they might become a

nation like all other nations. That land did not necessarily have to be the Holy Land.

It did not seem possible that Palestine might again become the Jewish homeland, because the Turkish government refused to allow the Jews to settle there in large numbers. The immediate need of the Jews, according to Pinsker, was not the Holy Land, "but a land of their own which shall belong to them and from which no one would be able to expel them. It might be a territory in North America, but the main requirement is that it should be a continuous (and as far as possible uniform) stretch of land that would be able to harbor several million Jews.[65] Pinsker did, however, wistfully add: "Perhaps the Holy Land will again be ours. If so, all the better."[66]

But who is to achieve this for the Jews? Only themselves. They have, of course, to count upon the good will of the nations, and especially that of the Government from which they wished to purchase the necessary territory. But the actual undertaking must be planned and executed by the Jews themselves. *Pinsker proposed the convening of an international Jewish congress, with the aid of* "*the societies already in existence,*" *the establishment of a national fund, and the attainment of international recognition for the project.*[67] "The sacred work of national regeneration," he wrote, "may not be left to blind chance." [68]

Those proposals were later embodied in the Zionist movement created by Herzl, who arrived independently at similar conclusions. Pinsker was sure that Jews possessed the organizing talent, energy, and capital needed for the project he outlined. What he feared, however, was that they had lost the will to become a nation again and to achieve real independence through their own efforts. The traditional habit of believing in miraculous redemption, Pinsker feared, had destroyed Jewish initiative. "The belief in a Messiah, the belief in the intervention of a higher power to bring about political resurrection, and the religious assumption that Jews must bear patiently a punishment inflicted upon them by God, caused them to abandon every care for their national liberty, for their unity and independence." [69]

Another factor that Pinsker regarded as contributing to the Jews' loss of will to be a free people was the atomization of Jewish life, which led each Jew to put his personal interests above that of his people. "Care of individual self-preservation," he pointed out, "necessarily nipped in the bud every national thought, every united movement." [70] The misfortunes of the Jews, Pinsker maintained, were due chiefly to their lack of desire for national independence. These misfortunes he sums up in the following lament: "Our fatherland is the other man's country; our unity—dispersion; our solidarity—the general hostility to us; our defense—flight; our individuality—adaptability; our future—tomorrow. What a contemptible role for a people which once had its Maccabees!" [71] Pinsker, however, hoped that the contemporary upsurge of national sentiment in Europe would awaken in the Jews the long dormant national consciousness. He could not imagine that "the great ideas of the eighteenth century" had bypassed the Jewish people without leaving a trace. "We feel not only as Jews; we feel as men. As men, we, too, would fain live and be a nation like the others." [72]

It must be noted that, despite Pinsker's appeal to the Jews to become a nation like the other nations, he took into account the Jewish individuality which had found expression in the high ideals of religion and righteousness. He spurned the assumption of synagogue Judaism that the mission of the Jewish People to teach the truth about God had to be attended by martyrdom; but Pinsker could not conceive of the resurrected Jewish nation as dispensing with the most sacred possessions which had been saved from the wreckage of Israel's ancient homeland, the *God-idea* and the *Bible*.[73] However, in the actual implementation of his idea through the *Hibbat Tziyon* movement and the migration *BILU* movement, the problem of religion was ignored. It is noteworthy, as has been pointed out that the very slogan of BILU (the initial letters of the verse in Isaiah 2:5) standing for the words, "O house of Jacob, come ye, and let us go," stops short before the concluding words of the verse: *"in the light of the Lord."*

Not many Jews responded at first to Pinsker's call. Ahad Ha-Am in his *Reminiscences*[74] mentions that he was present at the meeting of the arrangements committee for the Katowice, (Silesia) Conference in 1884. At that meeting Pinsker read the draft of the presidential address he expected to present at the conference. Wishing to attract Western Jews to the movement for colonization in Palestine he based the need for it on humanitarian reasons.

Pinsker was certain they would fight shy of any movement that avowed nationalism.

A shock was needed to awaken the Jews to a realization of their precarious condition before they could be stirred to take action on a national scale. A democratic nation like France had to prove that it too could furnish mobs who cried "Death to the Jews." And a great leader like the one Pinsker had envisaged[75] had to arise to appeal once more, in the same prophetic vein as had Pinsker, to the conscience and self-respect of his People, before political Zionism could come into being.

THEODOR HERZL (1860-1904)

Herzl had far less Jewish indoctrination as a child than had Pinsker. He was far more alienated as a mature man from Jewish life, and far more integrated into the Western culture of his environment. Herzl was nonetheless as shocked out of his complacency by anti-Semitism as was Pinsker. Herzl, too, concluded that anti-Semitism was ineradicable, threatening the Jews with spiritual and physical extinction. Their only safety, to say nothing of self-respect, lay in acquiring and colonizing a territory of their own. And Herzl, too, realized that such an undertaking called for vast Jewish financial resources and exceptional administrative ability, as well as a high order of statesmanship in dealing with the governments of powerful nations. The differences in *élan*, in scope and in the feeling of urgency between Herzl's conception of the national Jewish renaissance and that of Pinsker were due to the differences in their personalities and in the circumstances under which they expressed their views. Pinsker conceived the Jewish renaissance as a process of long-term colonization; Herzl, on the other hand, conceived of the immediate "restoration of the Jewish State," that is, of the recovery of political status and prestige.

Herzl was born in Budapest, Hungary, in 1860, and grew up with very little knowledge, and still less practice, of Judaism. Though he experienced the sting of anti-Semitism as early as his student years at the University, Herzl regarded himself as fully adjusted to the cosmopolitan society where, as a successful journalist, he moved during his earlier years. As the Paris correspondent of the Vienna *Neue Freie Presse*, he had occasion to report on the Dreyfus case. That gave him an opportunity to learn the truth about the position of the Jews in France, where the idea of Jewish emancipation had first been aired. Herzl became convinced, as Pinsker had been before him, that Europe was determined to get rid of the Jews, and that to escape destruction they must find a homeland of their own.

Herzl, too, did not at first believe that it was at all essential that the Jews return to their ancient homeland.[76] He stressed the need for an international guarantee that whatever land the Jews would adopt as their home would remain theirs forever. Herzl was enough of a realist to know that the political equality and the rights of migration and settlement which an individual government might grant to the Jews might be repudiated by a succeeding government; but he could not be so realistic as to foresee that the time would come when even international guarantees—such as those solemnly pledged to the Jews by the League of Nations—would also be treated as scraps of paper.

Herzl himself added little ideologically to what Pinsker had said before him. His *Jewish State* lacks the prophetic passion of Pinsker's *Auto-Emancipation*. Herzl's greatness lay in what he did, and not in what he said. Had he written nothing, his achievement alone would rank him as a modern Jewish Messiah. During his campaign for the Jewish State, his conception of it deepened and its relationship to Jewish history and destiny grew clearer in his mind. He deplored the fact that Jews were unduly optimistic concerning what lay ahead of them in the countries where they were given political equality. He concluded that only the harsh realities he anticipated would awake the majority of the Jews to the fact that they were everywhere unwanted. "The nations in whose midst we live," he wrote, "are all either covertly or overtly anti-Semites." [77]

Herzl addressed himself at first to those Jews of Western Europe who sought to lose themselves in the general population. They violently opposed the revival of Jewish nationhood because it prevented them from achieving their purpose. Herzl insisted that assimilationism was bankrupt, that Jews, regardless of what they did to hide or erase their Jewish identity, could easily be spotted. It made little difference whether or not they had a common language, a common religion, or common racial characteristics. The object of long-standing universal hostility, Jews were driven in on themselves, united, and converted into a permanently unassimilable body. "Whether we like it or not," he wrote, "we are now, and shall henceforth remain, a historic group with unmistakable characteristics common to all. We are one people—our enemies have made us one without our consent." [78]

One may question the wisdom of asking a people to learn to know itself through the distorted image reflected in the mirror of hate; but such an image, Herzl was convinced, was the only one whose glimpse could convince Jews that all their attempts to refute the grounds for anti-Semitism were futile, and that their only hope lay in escape to a home of their own. There can be nothing worse for a people than to be homeless. If the Jews are to put an end to their homelessness, they must have the courage to come before the world with the just demand that their right to survival as a people be internationally recognized and honored. When that is achieved, it is for the Jews themselves to organize a mass migration, so that all Jews who feel they are not wanted where they happen to live, or who find life there frustrating, might have a place to turn to.

Herzl stressed that modern anti-Semitism was an altogether different species of Jew-hatred from that which had marked the centuries of religious fanaticism. It was rooted in the natural dislike of the foreigner, reinforced by modern exclusivist nationalism and by the need to find a scapegoat on which to pile a nation's failures and sins. He was not deceived by Socialism which treated nationalism as an evil; or by Socialism's claim that it could draw the fang from anti-Semitism. "We are certain to suffer very severely," he wrote, "in the struggle between classes, because we stand in the most exposed position in the camps of both socialists and capitalists." [79]

Herzl pointed out that as soon as the Jews came to any country in considerable numbers, they aroused antagonism, no matter what they did. If, as a result of their poverty, they were forced to accept lower wages, they were accused of lowering the standard of living. If some of them achieved success in their business ventures, they were accused of being exploiters. With a clairvoyance based on insight into the political and economic predicaments of the European nations, he maintained that anti-Semitism was bound to grow in power and virulence. Herzl found the immediate cause of anti-Semitism to be the excessive production of mediocre intellects among the Jews "who cannot find an outlet downward or upward . . . When we sink, we become a revolutionary proletariat, the subordinate officers of all revolutionary parties; and at the same time, when we rise, there rises also our terrible power of the purse." [80]

Testifying in 1902 before a special commission appointed by English Parliament to draw up laws restricting immigration, Herzl stated that the assimilation of the Jew was not feasible; for it to be successful there would have to be unrestricted intermarriage between Jews and Gentiles. The prerequisite for such intermarriage was that the Gentiles regard the Jews as their social equals. Nevertheless, Herzl realized that, despite the obstacles to assimilation, many Jews did somehow manage to make an adjustment, and felt no need for a Jewish homeland. So Herzl assumed that Palestine should be reclaimed only "for Jews who could not or would not be assimilated in the lands of the diaspora." This is a cardinal point in political Zionism, which never shed any tears over those Jews who were destined to be lost to the Jewish People.

Shmarya Levin summed up succinctly the difference between Herzl and Ahad Ha-Am. "Herzl wanted to rebuild the Jewish People through the creation of a Jewish State. Ahad Ha-Am was convinced that the creation of a Jewish State could come only through a Jewish People rebuilt." [81] Nor is that fundamental distinction invalidated by Herzl's introductory remarks at the opening of the first Zionist Congress at Basle, when he said: "Zionism involves a return to Judaism, preceding the return to the Jewish land." [82]

In *Altneuland* (*Old-New Land*), which Herzl wrote later, his interest was centered on having the Jews constitute a "New Society" in Palestine. [83] In that book he depicted what he believed could be realized within a single generation, if the Jews really applied themselves to the task of building a commonwealth along the lines he had suggested in *The Jewish State*. His "commonwealth" is little more than an idealized middle class little republic with all modern improvements. Lotta Levensohn, who translated *Altneuland* into English, finds fault with it for not envisaging "anything creatively Jewish." She then goes on to say, "that he (Herzl) did not and really could not grasp the implications of Ahad Ha-Am's *Merkaz Ruhani*, the cultural spiritual center without which Palestine might at best become a prosperous ghetto, was not only the handicap of a leader without a folk background and traditions, but the tragedy of the Diaspora: that it produced leaders, gifted, valiant champions with such handicaps. . . . The Jews did nothing new in the Old-New Land; merely transplanted facilities and institutions existent in all civilized countries. Culturally and every other way, the country is a collection of copied models." [84]

Herzl's greatest contribution, however, to the Zionist movement was not the formulation of a program but his own personality. At tremendous personal sacrifice of economic security and health, he spent himself in the task, as Nordau puts it, "of forging a people out of scattered, weak-willed aimless human units, of winning a land for that people, without an army, without a navy, without financial resources." [85] He was the first Jew since the destruction of the Second Commonwealth to undertake the herculean task of rousing all world Jewry to common action in its own behalf. On August 29, 1897, 204 Jews who had been sent as delegates from half the countries in the world assembled in Congress in Basle, Switzerland. There they drew up the Platform of the Zionist movement, known as the Basle Platform. At that first Congress Herzl defined Zionism as having for its object "the creation of a home, secured by public rights, for those Jews who either cannot, or will not, be assimilated in the country of their adoption." [86]

The principal turning point in the Zionist movement was the granting of the Balfour Declaration, which was issued on November 2, 1917. In it, the British Government declared that it viewed "with favor the establishment in Palestine of a national home for the Jewish people, and will use their best endeavors to facilitate the achievement of this object, it being clearly understood that nothing shall be done which may prejudice the civil and religious rights of existing non-Jewish communities in Palestine, or the rights and political status enjoyed by Jews in any other country."

On the basis of that declaration, Britain was awarded the mandate over Palestine. The rest belongs to political history and not to any intrinsic trend in Judaism.

The practical task of securing a hearing for political Zionism, both among Jews and Gentiles, constituted Herzl's chief preoccupation. One must therefore look for the exposition of the more theoretic implications of the movement to Max Nordau, who was his first convert, and without whose moral support and cooperation Zionism would have made little headway as a mass movement.

MAX NORDAU (1849-1923)

Nordau, who was born in Pesth, Hungary, in 1849, came of pious Jewish parentage. At the age of fifteen Judaism and Jewry became no more than a memory for him—but a pleasant memory.[87] He settled in Paris, where he practiced medicine and psychiatry, wrote literary criticism, fiction, and drama, and served as a publicist for prominent newspapers. Nordau achieved international fame through his exposure of the "conventional lies" reflecting the decadence in literature and art during the latter half of the nineteenth century. Nordau assailed in particular Tolstoy, Ibsen, Nietzsche and Wagner, because he saw them as a modern expression of the individualism and relativism with which the Sophists had destroyed ancient Greek civilization. Unfortunately, his readers and critics were so enamored of his destructive criticism that they missed entirely his constructive aim to reinstate scientific and ethical standards of truth.

Nordau found himself in the midst of the turmoil that accompanied the Dreyfus trial. He was one of the many assimilated Jews who were shocked out of their indifference to Jewish life and its problems. When Herzl came to him with the manuscript of the *Jewish State*, Nordau at first doubted Herzl's sanity. But after a while he was himself convinced by the irresistible force of Herzl's argument that Western society was incurably anti-Semitic. Whether Nordau's conversion to Zionism was sudden, or whether he had been prepared for it by his own social philosophy,[88] one thing is certain: as Nordau himself admits, anti-Semitism opened his eyes to the need to return to his forgotten Jewishness.[89] He had regarded himself as a full-fledged German; this, in the words of B. Netanyahu, was "a cataract on his far-sighted eyes caused by assimilation which enveloped in darkness a most important part of his field of vision. The growth of anti-Semitism proved to be a powerful operation which removed the cataract forever." [90] In Nordau's own words, "Zionism has given my life its aim and content." [91] With Nordau ready to sponsor the new movement, it was likely to obtain a hearing in non-Jewish circles wielding a powerful political influence.

One element in Nordau's previous cultural interests enabled him to grasp immediately the full significance of Herzl's approach to the Jewish problem: this was his clear realization that nationalism was transforming the life of the European peoples. Armed with this insight Nordau could see forces working in anti-Semitism to intensify the age-old prejudices on which Jew-hatred had been fed for centuries. He was aware that anti-Semitism would be exploited by demagogues to fan the flames of national patriotism; the civil rights of the Jews of Western Europe would be jeopardized. The very progress of the nations economically and culturally was bound to render the position of the Jews more precarious. As long as the economic life of the nations was simple and their culture primitive, the Jews could manage to eke out some mode of adjustment, however fraught with danger. But as soon as the nations' material position improved and they could dispense with the Jews for basic economic functions, the lot of the Jews was certain to become unendurable.

As Nordau envisaged the situation, with the exception of the United States and Britain, in every country where Jews resided a general economic pattern was rendering their position insecure. First, an agricultural economy is gradually replaced by an industrial one. Consequently the nation, requiring foreign markets and capital, invites the Jews who can be useful because of their resources and international connections to the body politic. Emancipated from Medieval disabilities, the Jews are granted civil rights. Before long the country becomes sufficiently industrialized to provide a home market with home consumption. The Jews are no longer necessary to facilitate foreign trade—the home government can now itself obtain foreign credits for its citizens. The banking system following in the wake of industrialization renders the help to be derived from Jews superfluous. This condition becomes aggravated with the adoption of measures to nationalize certain industries and with the formation of trusts, from both of which Jews are excluded.

This economic pattern has its cultural analogue. As the nations advance culturally, their national consciousness becomes intensified. The majority population is then irked by the presence of Jews, who, they fear, may prevent the country from achieving national homogeneity. The long-standing habit of casting the blame on the Jews for everything that goes wrong reasserts itself, and they are made the "whipping boy."

This ineradicable antagonism to Jews on the part of the majority population is the basic explanation of why they are unassimilable. Nothing they may do to hide or deny their Jewish identity is of any avail. "He who wants to be assimilated," says Nordau, "dares not stop half-way. He is compelled to break down all the walls that separate him from the majority population. The first and most important wall is religion. So he must become converted and join the Christian church. He must marry a Christian. Even then he may expect that it will be three or four generations before all signs of Jewish nationality disappear. By half-measures such as shifting the Sabbath to Sunday or eliminating Hebrew from their schools, Jews will only make themselves more conspicuous and ridiculous." [92] It is true, of course, that there are always some individual Jews willing to adopt Christianity and to intermarry. Their grandchildren or great-grandchildren frequently turn out to be the most vicious anti-Semites. It is not likely, however, that the Jews, en masse, will ever renounce their Jewishness for such a prospect.[93]

In his play entitled *Dr. Kohen*, Nordau dramatizes the frustration of the Jew, Moser, who takes the Emancipation seriously. Moser goes the full length of assimilation, even to the point of accepting Christianity. His daughter falls in love with Dr. Kohen, a Jewish physician, whom Moser tries to persuade to do as he has done. It is through Dr. Kohen that Moser discovers that he is barely tolerated by his wife and sons, who hate him in their hearts and are ashamed of his Jewish mannerisms.

As Nordau saw it, the emancipation of the Jews in Western countries gave rise to the belief that the age-old hatred of the Jews would at last relent. It seemed to offer the Jew the opportunity of becoming completely assimilated; but unfortunately emancipation was unaccompanied by frankness on the part of either Jew or Gentile—the result has been disillusioning to both. The states which granted the Jews civil rights did not frankly admit that they expected them to be Christianized within two or three generations; and the Jews deceived themselves into believing that they could remain Jews by reconstituting themselves into a religious community. Nordau saw in the mission idea which the Jewish leaders adopted as a substitute for their historical nationhood nothing more than an adaptation of the Christian legend that the Jews had been dispersed in order to testify, by their misery, to the truth of the New Testament teaching. Instead of being a serious reconstruction of the Jewish religion, with a view to giving the Jew something to live for actively as a Jew, the mission idea, according to Nordau, is an unconscious concession to the Christian conception of the Jews' place in the world, a sort of prelude to their inevitable absorption into Christendom.

As a Zionist champion, Nordau devoted his great skill as orator and debater to demolishing the opposition to Zionism among the Jews. He considered the mission theory advanced by the Jewish Reform movement another "conventional lie," the stalking horse behind which the spiritual leaders of Western Jewry directed their bitter attack against Zionism. He took every available opportunity to denounce it. Nordau maintained that to claim a mission which did not involve the least personal sacrifice—but on the contrary, absolved one of responsibilities and unpleasant duties—was either jejune, or insincere and hollow pretense.

Nordau was equally unsparing in his bitter sarcasm of the opposition to Zionism on so-called ethical and spiritual grounds. That opposition was based on the argument that the curse of our age was the multiplication of small nations, and that the true interests of mankind demanded that the large nations absorb the small. The anti-Zionists claimed that for a people with a three-thousand-year-old history abounding in martyrdom for religion and morality to withdraw into some remote corner of the world, there to lead an obscure vegetative life, would be nothing less than a tragic anti-climax.

On behalf of the Jews of Russia, Rumania, and Galicia, who then constituted the overwhelming majority of the Jewish People, and who still lived under constant fear of government-instigated pogroms, Nordau replied: "We are touched profoundly by your high opinion of us. We feel proud that you expect of us a more exalted fate than that of leading a humble existence in Eretz Yisrael. But before we can hope to realize this great destiny you assign to us, we have to go through something which may appear to you merely a minor formality. We have to eat. To be sure, this is a very prosaic thing; but if we neglect this formality, we shall find it hard to justify the great hopes which you entertain concerning us. And since experience teaches us that nowhere but in Eretz Yisrael is it possible for us to be sure that we shall have enough to eat you must forgive us for wanting to return there. After our daily needs have been met, we shall in all humility wait until it pleases God to give our two-thousand-year-old martyrology the glorious consummation which alone can satisfy your esthetic requirements." [94]

It would be a mistake, however, to infer from the foregoing that Nordau saw in Zionism merely a means of salvaging millions of East European Jews from physical starvation. He emphasized clearly Zionism's different significance for the Jews of Western countries, where they enjoyed civil rights. In Western countries the Jew needed Zionism to fortify his self-respect and moral courage. Without these, no higher life of the spirit was possible.

The truth is that Nordau envisaged a highly ideal future for the Jewish People as a nation reborn. Though mocking what he considered the make-believe mission theory of anti-Zionist Judaism, he nonetheless reveled in a vision of a reconstructed Jewish People, furnishing the world an example of a true kingdom of priests, dedicated to the service of truth, love, and righteousness. When the Jews were a living people again it would be one whose internal relations and relations to mankind would be governed by policies based on the Ten Commandments. According to Nordau, the morally regenerative influence of Zionism did not have to wait for a distant future, but was realizable in the immediate present. Zionism provided the Jewish youth with a spiritual adventure to look forward to. It held out an ideal to Jews of the most diverse temperaments and world-outlooks, to the visionary and the man of action, to the pious and the skeptic, to him whose emotions were rooted in the past, and to him whose social passion impelled him to deal entirely with the present. "Zionism," he said, "is a union of the radical and the conservative sections of Judaism." [95]

Nordau's interest in Jewish life was not monopolized by Zionism. He was also concerned with the future of the Jews in the Western world. Nordau offered some constructive ideas with regard to Jewish life as a whole. Thus, while urging the unqualified participation of Jews in all their civic duties and responsibilities, he deprecated the ambition of Jews to attain high political office when it involved competing against non-Jews. For, Nordau maintained, Jews who rose to political power seldom, if ever, did anything for their fellow-Jews, for fear of being charged with favoritism. At the same time, any ill-will their rivals might entertain against them ultimately spent itself on the rest of the Jews. It was therefore better for all concerned if the abilities of the politically ambitious Jews were utilized by the Jewish community for its internal administration. Jewish activity should not be limited to the synagogue and the cemetery, but should find expression in a variegated cultural life of education, literature, art, and philosophy. The Jewish community should organize schools for general and technical education, establish museums and theatres, and so fill Jewish life with content that the Jew would be cured of the fatal self-contempt gnawing at his heart.

Nordau was not deterred in the least by the expected outcry on the ground that he was reintroducing the Ghetto. No honest critic could equate a voluntary organization of Jewish life, to achieve a healthful and creative togetherness, with imprisonment within unsanitary confines enforced by a hostile government. Nordau envisaged a Jewish environment so clean, sanitary and beautiful as to constitute a sort of town acropolis. So long as anti-Semitism remained deeply rooted in the mentality of Western civilization, some such measure would have to be adopted by Jews if they wished to retain their self-respect.[96]

Nordau realized, however, that, even with all these measures

Jews could hope merely to *retard* the *pace* of their disintegration as a people outside Eretz Yisrael. He was convinced that in the Diaspora Jews would be absorbed by the general population in the course of three or four generations. So Nordau deprecated the efforts of Jews in 1920, during the peace negotiations after World War I, to secure national minority rights in the countries of Central and Eastern Europe. "Jewish nationalism," Nordau maintained, "has no meaning outside of Palestine. If Jews are determined to remain in the Diaspora permanently, Jewish nationalism is sheer nonsense. They can pretend to be followers of the Mosaic persuasion, but their unavoidable fate is assimilation and rapid dissolution in their surroundings." [97]

As a result of events far more violent and shocking than could have been contemplated even by a Nordau, the experiment of the Jews with minority national rights turned out to be a mirage. The very principle of national self-determination upon which that experiment leaned for support proved a broken reed when Fascism raised its head and the League of Nations was dissolved. Then came the Nazi holocaust that exterminated almost all of Jewish life on the European continent. In desperation, World Jewry turned to Eretz Yisrael as the only haven of safety for the Jewish People.

* * *

The main weakness of the foregoing Zionist ideologies is that they fail to reckon with the future of the Jewish People as a whole. They do not take into account the consequences of the fact that a complete ingathering of World Jewry in Eretz Yisrael is inconceivable. Zionism has been narrowly pragmatic, without paying adequate regard to all its involvements in the contemporary world. It has succeeded in providing a precarious measure of *physical* security for about two million Jews, but it has augmented the *spiritual* insecurity of all Jews.

Zionism as a yearning for the return of the Jewish People to Eretz Yisrael and of Eretz Yisrael to the Jewish People was until a century ago an integral part of Judaism. But when the time came for that yearning to be translated into action it had to separate itself from Judaism with all its controversial issues and to concentrate on the achievement of its primary purpose: that of establishing a free and independent State. With the achievement of that purpose, the elan has gone out of Zionism. At the same time, insofar as the existing synagogue movements have become accustomed to treat the restoration of the Land of Israel as outside the purview of their religious activities, Judaism has been deprived of the main source of its vitality and viability, namely the generative and self-renewing potency of Jewish peoplehood.

CHAPTER THIRTEEN

The Greater Judaism

ষ্টে INTRODUCTION

Out of the welter of the four mutually conflicting versions of Judaism there will emerge a Judaism that is certain to be more viable than any of them. It will be a synthesis of those elements in each of those versions which are in keeping with the most advanced knowledge of reality and with what is most likely to enable the Jews as individuals and as a people to contribute their share to the betterment of human life. It will have acquired from Reform the capacity to treat Jewish religion as an evolving historic process. It will have learned from Orthodoxy to treat the Pentateuchal Torah as the *Magna Carta* of the Jewish People and as the Covenant that binds it forever to its homeland. It will have accepted from Conservatism the identification of the Jewish People as the permanent reality to be reckoned with in coping with the present crisis in Judaism. It will have learned from Zionism to treat Judaism as an all-embracing civilization which is rooted in Eretz Yisrael.

That is the Greater Judaism in the making. It is such not only because it is more viable than the existing versions of Judaism, but also because it is an integral part of the world we live in, a world immeasurably greater than the one of our ancestors. It is a greater Judaism not only because of the larger number of its adherents, but also because it is more relevant to mankind's highest spiritual needs and aspirations than Judaism ever could be in the past. To achieve such greatness Judaism has to be conceived as the evolving religious civilization of the Jewish People, and the present crisis in Jewish life has to be interpreted as a challenge to Jews to reconstitute their peoplehood, to revitalize their religion, and to replenish their culture.

To achieve greatness Judaism cannot afford to rest on the laurels of its past; it has to become creative. It should give heed to what a psychologist recently had to say about creativity: "Previous experience," said Nathan Israeli, "is essential up to a point, but it also interferes with creativity. Scholarship and knowledge at times obstruct creativeness; in this respect previous experience clouds the imaginative outlook and impedes the inquiring mind. Scholarship and exploration balance each other: no invention or inquiry without historical knowledge, but historical knowledge alone is insufficient for invention and inquiry."

JUDAISM AS A MODERN
RELIGIOUS CIVILIZATION

The recognition of Judaism as a civilization would remove once and for all a veritable host of false assumptions and distorted notions concerning it. Judaism would then figure in the consciousness of the Jew as the ensemble of all that is generally included in a civilization. It would elicit from him a sense of spiritual rootedness in Eretz Yisrael, a feeling of oneness with the forty-century-old People of Israel, a desire to understand its language and literature, a yearning to cherish its aspirations, and an eagerness to live its way of life, with its mores, laws and arts.

If Jews would try to cope, in this spirit, with their inner and outer problems, they would bring to bear creative intelligence upon whatever task they would undertake, whether it be that of enhancing the State of Israel, of combating anti-Semitism, organizing communal life, promoting Jewish education, establishing congregations, fostering beneficent religion, improving moral standards or encouraging Jewish art. Jews would then no longer content themselves with half-thoughts and compromises which are responsible for the present chaos and demoralization in Jewish life. Their hearts would then be set upon so revitalizing their social heritage, so reconstructing their way of life, and so conditioning their future, that the Jewish People would become a source of spiritual self-realization to the individual Jew, and of marked influence for universal freedom, justice and peace.

If Judaism is to become creative once again, it will have to assimilate the best in contemporary civilization. In the past, this process of assimilating cultural elements from the environment was carried on unawares. Henceforth, that process will have to be carried on in deliberate and planned fashion. In that respect, Judaism will, no doubt, have to depart from its own tradition. That is inevitable, since conscious and purposeful planning is coming to be part of the very life-process of society. No civilization, culture, economy or religion that is content to drift aimlessly has the slightest chance of surviving. It is in the spirit, therefore, of adopting the best in other civilizations and cooperating with them, and not in the spirit of yielding to their superior force or prestige, that Judaism should enter upon what will constitute the next stage in its evolution.

No civilization can afford to become a final and closed system of life. Continuous progress must henceforth be its ruling principle. The realities of the environment and the cultural climate must always be reckoned with. Though this does not preclude the formulation of detailed philosophies and specific lines of conduct, it does preclude their finality, however perfect they may seem at the time of their formulation.

Central to all efforts at Jewish readjustment is the need of clearly defining the status of the Jews in relation to the rest of the world. That status should be based upon the assumption that the dispersion of the Jews must henceforth be accepted as a permanent condition. Jews cannot hope ever again, as a body, to become a nation with a central state to unite them. As citizens of the countries they live in, they cannot aspire to become a trans-national group of a political character, or to function as a political unit. So long as to be a nation means to be a societal unit in which the state is primary and central, Jews throughout the world, including those in Israel, should regard themselves, and be regarded by others, as a "People." A People is not a biological or territorial datum. A People is such by virtue of a cultural pattern which affords it sufficient cohesion to make those who belong to it desire to maintain some kind of unified life.

As a civilization, Judaism requires at least one place in the world where it may be the primary one for its adherents. Everywhere else, Judaism can function only as a secondary civilization for its members, the primary one necessarily being the civilization of the country they live in. Eretz Yisrael will have to serve as both instrument and symbol of the Jewish renascence and as center of Jewish civilization. Without such a center upon which Jews throughout the world may focus their interest, it is impossible for Jews to retain for long the awareness of their unity as a People.

Judaism cannot maintain its character as a civilization, nor can the Jewish People maintain its sense of religio-cultural unity, without a homeland. In Eretz Yisrael, Jewish creativity can express itself in Hebraic form not so easily developed in other lands. There, Jews can attain sufficient autonomy to express their social will in economic and political institutions that might embody their highest ethical aspirations. Albert Einstein once stated the case for Eretz Yisrael succinctly in the following words: "Palestine will become a cultural home for all Jews, a refuge for the worst sufferers from oppression, a field of activity for the best among us, a unifying ideal and a source of spiritual health for the Jews of every country."

What is to be the future of the Jews outside Israel? That is bound up with the following two developments: a) democracy's success in resisting the tendencies that make for a monolithic state, and b) Jewry's success in redefining its own status in conformity with the modern conception of democratic society.

a) The American conception of democracy, which is pertinent to the future of Jews outside Israel, is unmistakably implied in the Federal Constitution. That Constitution, in prohibiting the adoption of any law which would deprive anyone of religious freedom, precludes the totalitarian form of State or Church which would declare, for example, Roman Catholics to be un-American because they insist upon identifying themselves with the Vatican and Papacy. Indeed, Jews would never think of asserting their prerogatives to the same extent that the Roman Catholics do. It could never occur to Jews to ask the State to exempt them from school taxes, even if they undertook to provide for the complete education of their children. Since Jews frankly accord primacy to American civilization, there is no basis whatever for charging them with trying to set up a ghetto, or with halting the process of cultural interpenetration, when they seek to foster their own Jewish heritage.

Religious freedom is meaningless unless it include the recognition of cultural religious autonomy. Cultural-religious autonomy, on the other hand, does not mean segregation or separation from the life of the rest of the population. Western society is so constituted that, if it is to retain the values of individual personality and freedom, it must do nothing to undermine the two associations which have hitherto been the most potent means of social control—namely, the institution of the family and the religious fellowship. The stability of the former depends upon the stability of the latter. Non-Jews need those two social agencies to counteract the totalitarian tendencies of the modern State. By the same token, Jews need to retain the integrity of their family institution and of Jewish peoplehood.

The fear of being charged either with ghetto-ism or with hyphenated loyalty is largely responsible for the failure of the Jews outside Israel to make the most of their Jewish heritage and individuality. The way to come to terms with that fear is not to try to argue it down, but to create a thought-pattern that would remove the very occasion for it. Modern pedagogy teaches that, when a child is afraid of the dark, the best thing to do is to turn on the light. What Jews need at present is such an understanding of their peoplehood as to inspire them with the will to demonstrate the normality of civilizational symbiosis, or living simultaneously in two civilizations, with no less zeal than their ancestors were ready to demonstrate, at all costs, the normality of worshiping only one God. They would manifest such zeal, if they would realize that by fostering their historic civilization simultaneously with their adopted civilization, they have the opportunity of proving, not only in theory, but also in practice, that the diversity of civilizations can become a blessing instead of a curse, and that each civilization should seek not to supplant but to supplement every other, religiously as well as culturally.

b) The present status of world Jewry is so anomalous that its survival outside Israel has been declared an anachronism, which means that Jewish survival does not make sense. The effect of being considered an anomaly cannot but be disruptive and demoralizing. It is impossible to evolve any consistent educational system, any creative cultural pattern, or any inspiring religious beliefs, so long as Jews in the Diaspora are content to remain the enigmatic, anonymous conglomerate they are now. Jews are faced, at present, with a crisis which is succinctly and sharply described in a recent report of the English Zionist Federation. "The State of Israel has solved the problem of Jewish homelessness," says the report. "Any Jew may now enter Israel as of right and will receive a very warm welcome. On the other hand, instead of uniting and consolidating the Jewish people all over the world, there is a real danger that the existence of the state may split them into two camps—Israelis and Diaspora Jews—each speaking a different language, thinking along different lines, living in a different atmosphere and absorbing a different culture. Zionism would then have created the Jewish state, but lost the Jewish people." [1]

The only way to remedy this abnormal situation is to have representative Jews from all parts of the world convene in Jerusalem for the purpose of redefining the status of world Jewry as that of a trans-national people. They will have to indicate the historical, cultural and spiritual factors that constitute the unifying elements in Jewish peoplehood. In addition, they will have to formulate the various duties and responsibilities which Jews, wherever they live, will have to accept, and to state how far diversity in modes of life and organization might be carried without destroying the integral unity of the Jewish People.

All this points to the need of arousing in the Jewish consciousness a demand for the renewal of the covenant by which Jews have lived hitherto as a People. Such renewal will have to prove something more than even the consent of Jews to rededicate themselves to the unity and perpetuation of the Jewish People. It will have to take the form of an impressive demonstration of the fact that Jews still possess a collective will which can be translated into specific amendments to the Torah, and which would be in line of continuity with the various traditional *takkanot*, or Rabbinic provisions, that form part of the Jewish tradition. Those specific amendments would have to define anew the basic rights and duties of Jews throughout the world in their relation to one another.

American Jews have formed all kinds of organizations and federations for specific purposes. These purposes, growing out of the circumstances of Jewish life, are in their very nature interdependent. They are treated, however, as though they had nothing to do with one another. The result is that though each purpose may singly be achieved, it does not further Jewish life as a whole. That is true not only of fraternal organization, social service, overseas relief and Zionist activity, but also of the synagogue and the religious school.

The only way to overcome that fragmentation of Jewish life is to have Jews form themselves into organic communities that would function as the instruments of Jewish life as a whole, and that would meet all its needs, in the order of their urgency and importance. Such a community would have to be democratically organized and represent all Jews who wish to be identified with it. Those who at present serve the various organizations and federations would then serve the entire community. Such reorganized communal life would not only coordinate Jewish activities efficiently, it would also integrate the Jew into the living body of the Jewish People, and give him that inner security which comes from belonging and from being wanted and welcomed.

The Greater Judaism therefore emphasizes the need of finding ways and means of living a maximum Jewish life with the setting of a modern democratic state. Viewing Judaism as a dynamic religious civilization, it addresses itself to the most urgent Jewish needs of our day, which are the following: 1) to restore the spiritual unity of the Jewish people, 2) to reorganize the communal life of the Jews in the Diaspora, 3) to aid the development of Israel, 4) to revitalize Jewish religion, 5) to encourage Jewish cultural creativity in education, literature and the arts, 6) to intensify participation by Jews in all activities that further the ideals of democracy.

RELIGION AS SOCIAL PROCESS

To view Jewish religion as an inseparable function of a living, evolving Jewish civilization carries with it certain implications with regard to the nature of religion in general and of Jewish religion in particular. These we shall here endeavor to set forth.

A *religion is a natural social process which arises from man's intrinsic need of salvation or self-fulfillment.* That conception of a religion is obviously a definite departure from the one held by all the orthodox faiths of the Western World. All of these faiths, in common with Traditional Judaism, have assumed that religious experience is something to which man cannot attain by the exercise of his natural powers, but only by the miraculous intervention of Deity in human affairs in the form of a supernatural revelation of His will.

The considerations that have led great multitudes of men of all religions to abandon faith in miracles and to seek to ground religion in a philosophy of life that accepts ungrudgingly the assumption of the uninterrupted processes of nature are too well-known to need repetition. But among those who accept naturalism and renounce belief in miraculous revelation there is still great confusion as to the true nature of religion, its function in the evolution of human life and the manner in which it must endeavor to realize its purpose.

This is a particularly crucial problem for Jews. Wherever they constitute a minority group, they can preserve their own religious civilization only by much conscious effort. Moreover, Jews feel the widespread antipathy against their People, which exists in the Gentile world, an antipathy that varies in its manifestations from efforts at exterminating them, such as were practiced by the Nazis, to forms of social snobbishness that merely hurt their pride. They know that this antipathy is not directed against them as individuals but against their People, that it is tantamount to a denial of the worth of the Jewish People and its right to a continuing collective existence. If they are to experience their life as worthwhile, they must possess what their fathers possessed before emancipation from the ghetto, a religious faith capable of investing Jewish efforts at collective survival and the cultivation of the Jewish cultural heritage with universal significance. Yet they cannot go back to a belief in the miraculous and supernatural, which was the presupposition of Jewish religion before the Emancipation.

Nor have more modern trends in Jewish religious thinking

afforded them the kind of religious experience that they need. Reform Judaism, which was the first effort on the part of Jews to repudiate the miraculous and supernaturalist formulation of Jewish religion, arose from a misconception of the nature of religion. That misconception was current in the world in the days of the emancipation of Jewry from ghetto conditions and the incorporation of Jews in the bodies politic of the modern nations. It was born of the desire to validate and make possible the toleration of religious differences within the civic community. The notion then prevailed that the different religions were different theistic philosophies, and that one's adherence to a particular religion expressed merely a personal opinion about God and man's relation to him, a predilection for certain theological doctrines. The various religious communions were conceived as societies organized to give effect to their respective theistic philosophies.

The unorthodox among the Jews were therefore inclined to accept the notion that the only thing that mattered in Jewish civilization was Jewish religion, and that the only things that mattered in Jewish religion were the idea of God and the ethical conduct it called for. All else was merely a means to the implementation of the God-idea, and, if its relation to the God-idea could not be demonstrated, it might as well be discarded. It was assumed that the difference between Jewish religion and other religions was based on a difference in the way Jews conceived God.

But a religion is more than the fruit of metaphysical speculation. Metaphysical theory is never the true basis of religious unity. The conclusions of metaphysical schools have always cut across religious denominational lines. All Kantians have more in common in their conception of God than have all Jews or all Christians. A religion is not a philosophical doctrine originating in the mind of an individual and communicated by him to his fellows; it is a product of a people's life, the soul of its civilization. The essence of a religion is the effort to discover what makes life worthwhile, and to bring life into conformity with those laws on which the achievement of a worthwhile life depends. A religion is thus a social institution, a product of man's social life, of his efforts to achieve his salvation through whatever tribe, nation, people or church to which he belongs.

THE FUNCTION OF JEWISH RELIGION

Jewish religion will have to break away from the intellectual limitations within which the traditional conception of God has confined it. For the overwhelming majority of Jews, Jewish religion can no longer be based upon the assumption that the existence of God has been demonstrated by historical events of a miraculous character. It has to be based henceforth upon that faith in God which derives from an understanding of human nature and destiny.

A religion is man's quest for self-fulfillment or salvation, and *the need of self-fulfillment presupposes that Reality is so patterned as to contain the means of satisfying it.* Man is distinguished from the brute by possessing not merely a will-to-live but a will to life abundant and enduring. His quest for abundant life makes him continually aware of his dependence on other persons and objects. He is aware that his conduct will bring him full satisfaction only if the goals he seeks and the means by which he seeks them conform to a law not of his own creation, that his own purposes emanate from and point to a life that transcends his own. That spiritual purpose which transcends his, and which gives significance to the events of life and direction to his own purposes, is what a religion means by the will of God. Faith in God means faith that there is an unfailing Power at work in the universe on which man can depend for salvation or self-fulfillment, if he conforms with the required conditions which constitute the laws of God.

Since all civilizations depend on the willingness of men to cooperate in the pursuit of ends considered to be life-enhancing, at least for their own adherents, they cannot dispense with religion. Even when they avow atheism, their atheism rests on certain unproved assumptions that they consider contributory to the self-fulfillment of the group. The loyalty that they command is essentially a religious loyalty, although they will not admit that it is, for it assumes the inherent and supreme value or holiness of their own civilization.

Different religions result from the fact that every civilization identifies the more important elements of its life as sancta, i.e., as media through which its people can achieve salvation or self-fulfillment.

Among the *sancta* of a civilization are all those institutions, places, historic events, heroes and all other objects of popular reverence to which superlative importance or sanctity is ascribed. These *sancta*, the attitude toward life that they imply and the conduct that they inspire are the religion of that people. In Jewish religion, such *sancta* are, among others, the Torah, Eretz Israel, the synagogue, Sabbaths and holy days, the Hebrew language, Moses and the Patriarchs.

American civilization also has its *sancta*: the Constitution, the Declaration of Independence, Thanksgiving Day, the Fourth of July and other national holidays, the Stars and Stripes. They and what they imply will in time be identified as American religion. The American Jew sees no contradiction in reverencing both groups of *sancta*, any more than American Christians see any contradiction in reverencing these American *sancta* as well as the Cross, the New Testament, the Church and its sacraments and sacred days, which are among the *sancta* of Christian civilization. Religions are not necessarily mutually exclusive; they are so only when their *sancta* are interpreted as denunciatory of other religions. Thus Judaism cannot include the New Testament among its *sancta*, because its fundamental premise is the inadequacy of the Torah, which Judaism holds sacred, as a guide to salvation. Therefore, the Christian and Jewish religions exclude one another; but the American religion excludes neither and neither should exclude the American religion.

If then every civilization has religious *sancta*, what do we mean by speaking of Judaism as specifically a religious civilization? Traditionally, the Jewish People assumed from its early beginnings, that it was the "Chosen People," that it stood in a unique relationship to God, since to it, and to it alone, God miraculously imparted the supreme revelation of His will, the Torah. But that doctrine is inconsistent with our premise that a religion is a natural social process. The need for salvation being inherent in all peoples and the quest of salvation being a natural process evident among all human societies, we must assume that the way of salvation is available to all men and peoples everywhere and on the same terms. We therefore have to renounce all pretensions to Israel's being God's chosen people. While profoundly grateful for all the manifestations of the divine spirit in the history and civilization of Israel, *we cannot assume that Israel must necessarily at all times possess that spirit to a higher degree than any other people.* Loyalty to Judaism and Jewish religion does not require any assumption of the superiority of Jewish religion over all others, any more than an individual's fidelity to his personal ideals, his aspiration to make the most of his personal abilities and talents for the enhancement of human life, requires a belief in his own superiority over other individuals. The worth of one person is incommensurate with the worth of any other, and the same is true of the collective personalities of groups.

What we have in mind when we speak of Judaism as a religious civilization is the historic fact that the Jewish People, under the leadership of its law-givers, prophets and sages, considered the chief function of its collective life to be the fostering if its *sancta*. It sought consciously to make its collective experience yield meaning for the enrichment of the life of the individual Jew and for the spiritual greatness of the Jewish People.

That is how the entire life of the Jew came in time to be invested with *mitzvot*, ritual acts designed to impress on him the moral and spiritual values which had emerged from the process of Jewish living. The performance of every one of these *mitzvot* is preceded by a *berakah* (blessing) which begins with the formula, "Blessed be Thou, O Lord our God, King of the universe, who hast sanctified us by Thy *mitzvot* . . . ," implying that the *mitzvot* are intended to sanctify, that is to confer worth on, Jewish life.

In contrast to certain secularist interpretations of Judaism which have resulted from the reaction against Orthodox dogma on the one hand, and against the Reform movement's repudiation of all the secular aspects of Jewish civilization, on the other, the Greater Judaism stresses the significance of the *mitzvot* as a vital need for modern Jewish life. Without *mitzvot* it is inconceivable that Judaism could have survived in the Diaspora until the present time, or that it will be able to survive in the future. When a people lives on its own soil, its civilization perpetuates itself with a minimum of conscious purpose. Not being challenged by any competing civilization, its *sancta* are taken for granted by its adherents, who think of them only occasionally, while devoting most of their energies to the pursuit of secular, individualistic and materialistic interests. But when the Jewish People was exiled and its state destroyed, the only way in which Judaism could survive at all was by stressing its *sancta* and emphasizing their value for the individual and for the People.

This was true during the Middle Ages, when Jewish communities were autonomous and Jews were excluded from Gentile society. It is even more obviously true in our day, when, in democratic countries, Jews live simultaneously in two civilizations. Under such conditions, Jews have no motive for retaining their connection with the Jewish People unless they derive from that connection values which they cannot find elsewhere. Moreover, these values must be relevant not only to life in an exclusively Jewish environment, but also to life in the two civilizations in which all Jews in the Diaspora are destined to live.

Now, of all Jewish values, the most universal are those that make the Jew feel he has a place in human society, and that help him to understand what he must do to fulfill his destiny as an individual, as a Jew, and as a member of the human race—in a word, the religious values of Judaism. His American inheritance by itself will not suffice to satisfy his need for salvation, because American religion is pluralistic. It assumes that, in addition to being loyal to the *sancta* of Americanism, its adherents will seek salvation through loyalty to one or another of the great religious traditions that existed long before America came into being. The Jew who is out of touch with Jewish life and out of sympathy with its spiritual culture thus feels himself spiritually isolated and generally forlorn. He needs for his salvation *Jewish religion*, for he is conditioned by his early training, his associations and the consciousness of his Jewish identity against accepting as his own the *sancta* of any of the other *historic religion*.

But religious values cannot be realized except in association with all the other elements in the civilization which would embody them. When abstracted from its life, they are mere verbalizations. Religions are not metaphysical schools of thought or the attempts of the adherents of such schools to implement a theoretic doctrine. Religions are not organizations of like-minded individuals; rather are they organic functions of the civilization of some particular societal group or people. Only in relation to the life of that group can their religion be understood, and only in relation to that life can it be effective.

It is therefore incorrect to think of Jewish religion as the elaboration of a specifically Jewish conception of God. There is no single Jewish conception of God. What distinguishes Jewish religion

from all others is that it is a specifically Jewish application of the
God idea, one which associates belief in God with the *sancta* of
Judaism. The Jews have changed their conception of God considerably in the course of Jewish history. In the visions of the Prophets,
God is represented as manifesting himself to the human senses; but
ever since the termination of the controversies between the adherents and opponents of Maimonides, the denial of corporeal attributes to God has become a dogma of Traditional Judaism. Moreover even in any particular age, conceptions of God have varied.
While Maimonides was denying all corporeal attributes to God,
Jewish mystics speculated on God's dimensions. Certainly in our
day, one will find, even among Jewish worshipers in the same
synagogue great variation in their conception of the God they
worship.

The difference between Jewish religion and all others does not
consist so much in the uniqueness of its conception of God as in
the uniqueness of its *sancta*. The distinctive character of Jewish
religion resides in the fact that it is an endeavor to apply the God
idea to the sanctification of Jewish life, to enable the Jew to see
God in the events of his own history, in the products of his own
culture, in the experience of applying ethical standards to the
regulation of Jewish conduct, in the emotional response evoked by
Jewish symbols. Jewish religion, in a word, is the conscious endeavor
of the Jewish People to make its collective experience contribute
to the spiritual growth and self-realization of the individual Jew,
the Jewish People, and all mankind.

THE NEED TO REVITALIZE JEWISH RELIGION

In the light of this analysis of the place of religion in Judaism,
the indifference to religion on the part of many modern Jews becomes intelligible. In part, that indifference is due to the fact that
Jewish religion is identified in the minds of most Jews with a particular traditional doctrine to which they find it intellectually impossible to subscribe, rather than with the entire process by which
a living civilization evolves its *sancta*. In part, it is due to the dis-
organization of Jewish life that resulted from the loss of the communal autonomy which Jews enjoyed in the ghetto, and the con-

stant pressure of the majority culture, making it difficult to maintain such *sancta* as the Jewish Sabbath, the dietary regulations and other elements of Jewish religion. For, since religion is a function of Jewish community life, it thrives or languishes, equally with all other aspects of Jewish civilization, in proportion as that life is vigorous or feeble.

This gives us a clue to what needs to be done to revitalize Jewish religion. In the first place, it must be emancipated from bondage to dogmatism. This bondage arises from the fear that any departure from the specific doctrines that were taught as religion in the past undermines religion itself. But this fear is seen to be groundless, if we regard Jewish religion as a function of Jewish civilization. A living civilization is, of necessity, a changing civilization. But change in a civilization does not mean loss of identity, any more than the individual's growth from childhood to maturity means loss of identity. A religion must change in keeping with the changes in all the other functions of a civilization.

To make this possible, the traditional *sancta* of a religion must be reinterpreted in each generation so that their meanings are kept relevant to the needs of that generation. Tradition must not be a source of authority imposing restrictions on the creativity of later generations, but a source of wisdom and inspiration awakening new creative powers. When *sancta* have become meaningless, they cease, in the nature of the case, to be *sancta*. But this need not trouble us so long as the people lives and creates, for then it will produce new *sancta*. To keep a religion vital, religious thought must be free. It is a sad commentary on the intellectual level of religious thought that a *free thinker* is identified in the popular mind as an atheist.

Freedom of thought will, of course, emancipate religion from all association with magic and supernaturalism. *What is objectionable in supernaturalism is the notion that God's power manifests itself primarily in the suspension or abrogation of natural law.* A revitalized Jewish religion must discountenance the use of ritual for the purpose of influencing the course of events in any other way than by its influence on the mind and heart of the worshiper. Nor should any ritual that is morally or aesthetically offensive be retained merely because in an earlier state of Jewish religion it was legally enjoined.

Stated affirmatively, Jewish worship must be directed to influencing the worshipers to bring their life into harmony with God as the Power that determines the conditions by which man in general, and the Jewish people in particular, can achieve an abundant and harmonious life. All that is not intellectually and emotionally attuned to this purpose should be eliminated. But that is not enough. The liturgy should be enriched by the writing of new prayers, meditations, hymns that express the religious experiences of our generation. Traditional forms should be retained wherever these have something of positive value to contribute to the services; but they must be supplemented by additional material directly relevant to the interests, needs, problems and ideals of the day. Though it is important whenever possible, to reinterpret or revise traditional *sancta* when these have lost their value for considerable numbers of Jews, there must be room for diversity within Jewish religion itself. *The unity of Jewish religion must henceforth be based not on uniformity of theological belief or ritual practice but on a common purpose to sanctify Jewish life.* Those Jews who find that they cannot accept as valid all the tenets of traditional Jewish religion or cannot practice all the traditional religious rites and observances, should seek a new rationale for faith in God and in Jewish spiritual values, and new forms of Jewish religious expression.

All Jewish religious institutions must endeavor to improve human relations and human conduct in accordance with the profoundest religious insights. From time immemorial this has been a major interest of Jewish civilization. The conception of the fatherhood of God, which plays so important a part in Jewish religion, was based on the insight that a community of interests binds together the whole human race, and that this community of interests must transcend all differences. The realization of the ideal unity of the human race cannot be effected by imposing one uniform standard of conduct upon all men. Implied in the concept of brotherhood is the sort of unity that prevails among brothers in a happy family in which all members help one another to achieve each his own purpose. Judaism must strive for the establishment of a social order that satisfies at one and the same time two contradictory requirements: the maximum of human cooperation and the maximum of personal liberty. To this end, Judaism must seek an equitable distribution not merely of the material goods needed for human living, but also of responsibility and power in the control of human affairs.

*   *   *

To summarize: The Greater Judaism provides a rationale and a program that would make possible the survival, progress and beneficent functioning of Judaism, the civilization of the Jewish People, under the conditions of modern life. With this end in view, it is deeply concerned with such social, political and cultural problems as the establishment of the Jewish national home in Eretz Yisrael, the spiritual unity of the Jewish People, the development of the Hebrew language and literature and of Jewish music and art. But it regards the achievement of all these as dependent on religion, on a spiritual attitude toward Jewish life which would invest it with sanctity or supreme importance for the Jew.

Jewish religion cannot meet the needs of modern Jews unless it conforms to a clear and correct understanding of the role of religion in human life and its relation to human civilization. Its function is to point out those elements of Jewish civilization, past and present, which contribute most to making Jewish life worthwhile and to utilize them to this end. In pursuing this common religious purpose, there must be full freedom of thought with its inevitable concomitant, diversity of expression. Freedom of thought should be used to reinterpret the old *sancta* of Judaism in the light of the best spiritual insight of our times. Judaism must renounce all pretensions to superiority or chosenness, and base Jewish loyalty on the need for experiencing the worthwhileness of Jewish life. And it should participate in every human striving for the social and spiritual advancement of the human race.

The principles of Judaism as an evolving religious civilization, though conceived with special reference to Jewish religion and Jewish civilization, can be applied as well to other religions and civilizations. What mankind needs is a way of life that derives inspiration from tradition and guidance from tested experience. That way of life would make it possible for people to retain their allegiance to their religious faiths without surrender of freedom of thought in the interest of any authoritarian dogma. For the civilizational conception of religion renders the survival and development of a religion independent of any notion of the immutability of specfic doctrines. The survival of the religion would be assured by its natural connection with an evolving civilization. There would be no need of insistence on dogmatic adherence to a specific creed, or on conformity to a specific code of ritual practice.

The civilizational conception of religion makes the adherent's loyalty to his faith independent of any pretensions to superiority, and thus affords the only sound basis for interfaith goodwill. Every religion possesses universal values, which it applies to its own group life by relating them to the specific *sancta* of its own civilization. These values are communicable, and can be adopted by other religions without imposing the conditions that the adherents of those religions discard their own *sancta* or adopt those of any other. Unless this viewpoint is universally accepted, religionists must assume that their own religion is the only, or, at any rate, the best religion that there is, an assumption which nullifies mutual respect and frustrates mutual goodwill and interfaith cooperation.

The recognition of the functional character of religion and its relation to all other aspects of a people's civilization answers the charge so often brought against religion that it is concerned only with the hereafter, or with abstract platitudes and not with live issues. Operating with the conception of religion as a functional aspect of a civilization, religions can demonstrate the relevance of the values they cherish to the vital issues which preoccupy the minds of the living generation of their adherents.

THE MEANING OF GOD IN MODERN JEWISH RELIGION

So long as religion permeated every phase of human life, and all human needs and interests had to be brought within its orbit, it could afford to be the chief means of self-expression. Now, however, that the esthetic interests have earned, in their own right, a place in the life of the human spirit, to confine Judaism within the limits of what is exclusively religious in character is to render it irrelevant to most people who are not given to theologizing. *For the very sake of religion, it is necessary to foster other interests besides religion.* Religion is a quality of life, the substance of which consists of the manifold of human interests, with all their satisfactions and their problems. Community life gives rise to, and depends upon, creative self-expression through poetry, drama, music, sculpture, painting and architecture, *belles lettres*, scholarship and philosophy. Only when religion is a quality of such communal living, does it have content, vitality and appeal. Emptied of these concrete manifestations of social and cultural activity, religion is either a form of theurgy or vacuous mysticism.

It is futile to expect all Jews ever again to profess a uniform type of Jewish religion. That was possible only so long as the world around them was dominated not only by religion, but by one kind of religion. Now, however, with the rest of the world in a state of utter confusion in the matter of religion, diversity of religious belief and practice among Jews is inevitable. But that Jews can be altogether religion-less is paradoxical. Such Jews cannot long remain Jews. Frenchmen and Englishmen, regardless of adherence to the Church, will remain loyal to their respective nations. That is because the Church is not an integral part of the life of the Frenchman as Frenchman, or the Englishman as Englishman. The case is otherwise with Jews. Their very peoplehood has always been given a religious significance, and it owes its very survival to that fact. For Jews to try to maintain their peoplehood without their religion is to deprive the former of the principal element by which it can be made into a spiritual asset.

It should not be difficult to render Jewish religion viable in the modern cultural climate. All that is necessary is to accustom the modern-minded Jew to realize that religion is fundamentally a type of human experience which derives from an affirmative and hopeful reaction to life as a whole. So viewed, religion is basically the acceptance of human life as having meaning, that is, as capable of entering into ever-increasing webs of relationship with the rest of reality and of being dominated by purposes of its own choosing. Religion is the ability to discover creative possibilities in the most unpromising aspects of human life. The mystic doctrine that "the sparks of divinity" inhere in all things is what all religion should seek to verify. If we regard human life as deserving that we give it the best that is in us, we necessarily regard it as sacred and divine. If we accept life in that spirit, we are not only religious in the truest and best sense of the term, but we also attain the insight which enables us to appreciate what mankind has sought to achieve through religion. We then begin to understand religion as a dynamic and evolving process, and not as a fixed system of beliefs and ordinances to be either wholly accepted or rejected.

In the past, the Jews looked forward to the acceptance of Jewish religion by all the world as the prerequisite to the coming of the millennium, or to the establishment of the Kingdom of God. Nowadays, however, the very expectation that the religion of any one People or Church can, or should, become the religion of mankind is an anachronism. The main significance of the fact that Judaism is a religious civilization is that Jews cannot expect to function as a People, or keep their historic civilization alive in the Diaspora, unless they make the beneficent functioning of religion their special concern and interest.

In order that the religious aspect of any civilization function beneficently, it has to foster the kind of belief in God that is capable of serving as inspiration and sanction for whatever is likely to render man more fully human. That is his destiny and therein lies his salvation. All the world is at present badly in need of such religion. Only such religion can supply a minority people like the Jews with the moral courage to resist being absorbed by the majority populations. The Prophet who first promulgated the mission idea did not imply that all the people in the world should become Jews. He knew too well that even among his fellow-Jews very few lived by the kind of religion he had in mind. He was fully aware of the spiritual callousness of those he called upon to assume a religious mission. "Who is as blind as my servant, as deaf as my messenger?" he cried out.[2]

The Jews were then already dispersed among the nations. Realizing their plight, the anonymous Prophet whose words are recorded in the second part of Isaiah, pleaded with them to adopt the cause of beneficent religion as the purpose and meaning of their existence as a People. He stated specifically what he regarded as beneficent religion, in the following words: "I the Lord have called thee in righteousness, and have taken thee by the hand, and kept thee as a covenanted people to be a light of the nations; to open eyes that are blind, to free captives from their dungeon, and them that sit in darkness from out of the prison-house." [3] No words could more forcibly convey the truth that the Jew's salvation lay in serving God by furthering the cause of enlightenment and freedom.

The particularity of Jewish religion derives from the experiences which are peculiar to the Jewish People. That particularity has to be preserved in the process of bringing Jewish religion into live contact with the contemporary universe of values. This can be accomplished by taking into account the entire mass of the traditional ideas and practices which belong to the spiritual heritage of the Jewish People, and reinterpreting them from the standpoint of what are felt to be the most urgent moral and spiritual needs in our day. The reason for this is that those traditional values carry with them the accumulated momentum and emotional drive of our People's past efforts to find and render life meaningful. If those values are shown to be relevant to our day, they can transmit that emotional drive. To render them thus relevant, we have to discover what spiritual or ethical urge was latent in the traditional practices, and particularly in the meanings assigned to them.

To illustrate specifically how this approach can revitalize Jewish religion, belief and practice, we shall select from among the traditional Jewish values those of the Sabbath and the Festivals. Those sacred days of the Jewish calendar still have something of a spiritual appeal to all who profess attachment to Jewish life. In the religious tradition, they are assigned meanings which are representative of what that tradition would have us associate with the belief in God.

The following is a tentative attempt to formulate a conception of God in terms that are significant for our day. It is based upon the reinterpretation of the traditional values associated with the Jewish Sabbaths and Festivals.

1. *God as the Power that makes for salvation.* The Sabbath is essentially a symbol of salvation. As such it affirms that all men can achieve salvation if they avail themselves of the resources that inhere in the world about them and make use of their own abilities. This affirmation is supported by the following teachings expressed, or implied, in the meanings which tradition itself

assigns to the Sabbath: a) God is the creative life of the universe; irrevocable fate and absolute evil are deceitful illusions. b) God is manifest in life's holiness, which presupposes the working of divinity in the human person. Man's personality is the instrument through which God, as the creative life of the world, achieves the evolution of the human race. c) God manifests himself in a people's sense of responsibility for contributing creatively to the salvation of mankind. These are the teachings of the Sabbath.

2. *God as the Power that makes for social regeneration.* The modern emphasis upon God's immanence necessitates our reinterpreting the traditional conception of God's sovereignty. As reinterpreted, that conception can function as an aid to the regeneration of society by direct human agency, without reliance on the illusory hope of miraculous intervention. Human initiative and active striving to transform the conditions under which man lives constitute a manifestation of the divine. These are the teachings of Rosh Hashanah.

3. *God as the Power that makes for the regeneration of human nature.* If we identify God with that aspect of reality which confers meaning and value on life, and elicits from us those ideals that determine the course of human progress, then the failure to live up to the best that is in us means that our souls are not in harmony with the divine. That constitutes sin.

Man's striving to achieve and express integrity, responsibility and unity renders life holy. It testifies to the divine possibilities which inhere in human life. Sin is what thwarts this striving. The sins of the individual corrupt the social structure, and the corruption of the social institutions spreads the contagion among individuals. Translated into conduct, the doctrine of the unity of God calls for the integration of all of life's purposes into a consistent pattern of thought and conduct.

Repentance is part of the normal functioning of personality in its effort at progressive self-realization. If human character is to reflect the divine, it must be integrated and self-consistent. This calls for a progressive synthesis of individual self-expression and social cooperation. Such a synthesis is, therefore, evidence of spiritual attainment and the fruit of effective repentance. Whenever we recognize our failure to do justice to the spiritual demands of a new situation, and try to overcome the obstacles that prevent our lives from manifesting the divine, we are practicing repentance, or the return to God. These are the teachings of *Yom Kippur*.

4. *God in nature and in history*. By utilizing the nature festivals to recall historical experiences, the Jews directed the human mind to the consciousness of human history as an ethical and spiritual influence in human life. In contributing to human consciousness the sense of history, the Jews have not only enriched human life, but have also created new problems. Both the creative powers in the physical world and the spiritual forces in the human world that make for personal and social redemption are treated in Jewish religion as manifestations of the divine. Those are the teachings of the Three Pilgrim Festivals.

5. *God as the Power that makes for cooperation*. The tendencies and relationships that augment the unity and value of life, and thus point to the reality of God, are mediated for man chiefly through the organized life of society. Society, therefore, owes it to the individual, in its own interest as well as in his, to give him the opportunity for employing his powers and faculties to the full. Society which deprives men of the opportunity to enjoy and create esthetic values, or which manages its affairs in such a way as to render men godless, bitter and hateful of life, stands self-condemned, as denying men their inalienable right to the pursuit of happiness.

The doctrine of equality does not imply that all men must have identical opportunities for education, employment and esthetic and religious self-expression. It does imply, however, that all have an equal claim to the opportunity to pursue these activities to the limits of their own varying capacities, and in accordance with their own individual interests, insofar as these are not detrimental to the general good. Rights are empty unless they are right to things, or to property. Only those rights to property, however, which emanate from the concept of personality and are indispensable to its fulfillment are sacred and inviolable.

Cooperation is the chief source of happiness; competition, its principal menace. Civilization has become synonymous with the progressive emergence of individuals and groups engaged in internecine struggle for power. The *Sukkot* Festival, with its emphasis on joyous gratitude or happiness, is the protest not against civilization but against its tendency to be a destroyer of happiness. These are the specific teachings of *Sukkot*.

6. *God as the Power that makes for freedom.* The conception of God as the Redeemer of the oppressed has revolutionized the meaning and function of religion, and has placed it at the service of the ethical impulses. Freedom is at the very root of man's spiritual life, and is the primary condition of his self-fulfillment, or salvation. The meaning of religion can be grasped only when social life is based on freedom. The right with which one is born is only potential freedom. Actual freedom is an achievement with the aid of a civilization which is based on the high worth of the human person.

When we look to God as the Power that makes for freedom, we expect that He will give mankind no rest until it puts an end to the order of social living in which human beings drudge and slave for aims in which they have no part or parcel. The freedom which means the release of selfhood consists in the right to be honest, responsible, and creative. These are the specific teachings of Passover.

7. *God, not ourselves, as the Power that makes for righteousness* —The moral law must be regarded not as some prudential arrangement or social convention, but as inherent in the very nature of reality. Jewish religion is unique in clearly recognizing that the chief function of the belief in God is to confirm and fortify the moral law. The word "God" has come to be symbolically expressive of the highest ideals for which men strive. At the same time, it points to the objective fact that nature, both in the world and in man, is so constituted as to make for the realization of those ideals.

Human personality, with its reference to goals of behavior beyond our present capacity, points to a Power not ourselves that makes for righteousness. What God means to us depends mainly upon our ideal of human life, or life as it ought to be. And the way we conceive that ideal depends upon the level of civilization we have attained. God is thus the Power that endorses what we believe *ought* to be, and that guarantees that it *will* be. Just as the will-to-live testifies, in an intuitive sense, to the cosmic support of life, so the will to achieve the abundant, or fully human life, testifies to the ultimate attainment of that life. These are specific teachings of the Festival of *Shavuot*.

HOW TO LIVE IN TWO CIVILIZATIONS

It is incumbent upon American Jews to demonstrate how they expect to solve the problem of living in two civilizations simultaneously. That is a problem which they share with their fellow-Americans who are adherents of other faiths. Each of those faiths has to be lived in its historic civilizational context, if it is not to be reduced to a series of abstract platitudes. Insofar, however, as their adherents wish to integrate their own lives into the general American civilization, they have the task of enriching it by bringing to it some special contribution from their own historic civilizations. That raises the question: What would Jews have to do to excel in the field of religion in such a way as to enrich American life?

To answer that question we must take into consideration the anomalous condition in which the American people finds itself religiously. To prevent the historical religions, which lay claim to being supernaturally revealed and to being the sole means to salvation, from engaging in mutual conflict for political and cultural domination, the American Constitution has adopted the principle of separation of Church and State. So far as domination is concerned, the Constitution has been effective. But that has not prevented the main religious bodies, like the Roman Catholic Church and the outstanding Protestant churches, from seeking to influence legislation and education in favor of their respective ways of life. It has fallen to the lot of the Jews to urge legislation and education in keeping with the principle of separation of Church and State. On the face of it, every such attempt of Jews is made to appear as a move in the direction of secularism and irreligion. In being staunch supporters of the American Constitution, Jews ought to be regarded as good Americans trying to have other Americans live up to their commitment, but life does not work that way.

The fact is that the constitutional amendment pertaining to the separation of Church and State has far-reaching implications which those who enacted it probably never contemplated. That is where all the trouble comes from. Sooner or later, all Americans will have to face up to those implications. American Jews have to do so now, if they wish to do their share as a group in extricating American civilization from the predicament in which it finds itself in relation to religion.

The separation of State and Church means, in effect, that the Founders of the United States were determined that none of the historical religions, which claimed to have been supernaturally revealed, should form an integral part of the life and culture of the newly-born nation. That does not mean that they expected the civilization of the American people to be devoid of all religious spirit. To ascribe that intention to them is to misread their mind. It is true that there are but few references to God in official documents, but those few bespeak deep religious conviction.

The Founding Fathers, undoubtedly, had in mind some kind of naturalistic religion, like that implied in the well-known phrase, "nature's God." They assumed, no doubt, that such religion would evolve out of the life-experience of the American nation. That is the kind of religion practiced, though seldom professed, by so typical and ideal an American as Lincoln. That is the religion that affects people's lives without being authoritarian. When the national hymn "America" invokes "Our fathers' God . . . Author of Liberty," it implies a religious interpretation of American experience. A typically contemporary expression of that same religious spirit of America is to be found in the concluding passage of Adlai E. Stevenson's address in Chicago on Sept. 15, 1953: "We will have to learn to think of the responsibility of leadership . . . as a status in an interdependent world that we Americans . . . must live in, work in, pray for, and pray for in the accents of mercy, justice and faith in a Power greater than ours or any man's."

The framers of the Constitution knew too little about religion as a manifestation of human nature to be able to envisage any practical alternative to the traditional theurgic type of religion. All they could do was to philosophize abstractly about God's being and attributes. Living before the great modern anthropological discoveries, they were sure that institutional religion was either priestcraft or esoteric philosophy. They saw in the growth of modern nationalism the inevitable obsolescence of authoritative religions. But they could not realize that, without free religion to curb and direct modern nationalism, humanity would be re-barbarized. That is why the separation of State and Church has created a religious vacuum, which nothing has been done to fill.

The condition of man has undergone a revolution. The range of his knowledge, ability, and resources has been so enlarged that he can obtain most of what he needs in the way of sustenance, security, and health without the aid of theurgic religion. The blood kinship on which he depended, and which was given importance and sanctity by his religion, is now replaced by his economic organizations and his nationalisms. The description of the pre-modern age as "the Age of Faith" is a misnomer, and based on a misunderstanding. Modern man's faith in science, technology, trade unionism, and nationalism is just as intense and as blind as was his faith in the power of prayer and ritual. To be sure, this modern faith is not faith in God. Does that necessarily mean that man can dispense with faith in God? Certainly not, if the God in whom man is to have faith is one whom the present condition of man renders indispensable.

As a result of the widened range of knowledge and resourcefulness, and the substitution of political and economic association for religiously sanctioned kinship, we find ourselves in a state of perpetual tension and foreboding. The threat of global war and universal devastation hangs like a dark cloud over our lives. We have lost faith in man. We have lost our way in life. We are not sure that there is any real difference between good and evil. We seek in vain to drown our fears and boredoms in a welter of action, excitement and self-indulgence. That is certainly not the way to live; it is only a way to make a mess of life.

In the light of this modern condition of man, the primary task of American Jewry is to have the belief in God motivate the following objectives: 1) the utilization of our material progress for purposes of peace and for the enhancement of human life; 2) the pursuit of the human sciences and arts with a view to the elimination of poverty, ignorance, and disease, and to the creation of opportunities for everybody's material, intellectual, emotional and spiritual self-fulfillment; 3) the limitation of the sovereignty of the nations, and the translation of their economic interdependence into a workable program for the free exchange of goods and services on a world scale; 4) the inculcation in the individual of a sense of responsibility for doing his personal share toward making the world the better and the happier for his having lived in it.

The second task of American Jewry is to advocate an indigenous civic religion for the American people that shall act as a unifying influence, uniting all Americans regardless of race, creed, or status without being authoritative or coercive. That task involves the incorporation into American institutions and practices of those principles in Jewish religion which have a universal import and are therefore transferable to other civilizations.

The universal principles in Jewish religion and their application to American life may be formulated as follows:

1) That God is the God of Israel implies that a People, of which we are a part, should provide the principal experiences on which to base our belief in, or awareness of, God as the Power that makes for salvation. Those experiences constitute the substance which should yield the values that give meaning to human life. As Americans, therefore, we should identify those experiences and strivings in American life and history which would not only give organic character to the American People, but also set it on the road to human progress and perfection. To the extent that American experiences and strivings do that, they reveal God as the Power that makes for salvation, and should be interpreted as such, culturally and educationally.

2) According to the teaching of the Torah and the Prophets, the People of Israel was expected to demonstrate its loyalty to God not merely by worshipping Him, but mainly by practicing justice and righteousness. These are called "the way of the Lord" (Genesis 18:19). In the light of that teaching, failure to walk in that way has brought untold suffering on the People of Israel. Unrighteousness is the offspring of pride which takes the form of rebellion against God, or playing the god. Translated into universal terms, that teaching implies that the religion of a people has to find expression principally in the practice of righteousness in its political, economic, and social affairs. That is the divine law for every people. Violation of that law is bound to lead to failure and disaster.

An illustration of the way those principles should be incorporated in American institutional life is afforded by *The Faith of America*. That book contains programs for the religious observance of American holidays, using for this purpose materials drawn from American literature and historical documents. Each holiday is given a specific religious theme. The theme for Lincoln's Birthday, for example, is the ideal of equality and fraternity; for Washington's Birthday, the promise and responsibility of nationhood, and so on with all the other holidays.

Given the wish to survive as a segment of the Jewish People, that wish is bound to seek an outlet in some effort that would give to our persistence as Jews not merely the significance of inertia, but rather the lift that comes from being dedicated to a high purpose. That high purpose should be to contribute to the spiritual life of America the kind of civic religion that will place America in the spiritual forefront of the world, as she is now in the political and economic. That high purpose should be to achieve for ourselves a conception of Jewish religion that is as free and creative as poetry, literature and art, a Jewish religion that is vitally relevant to reality as we know it and live it.

PEOPLEHOOD AS A DIMENSION OF RELIGION

The Judaism of most Jews is only skin-deep. It is social rather than spiritual. One-half of Jewish identity is the product of Gentile exclusiveness, and the other half is the product of Jewish association. There is no intrinsic connection between Jewish life and spirituality. R. Niebuhr's statement that Jews will find God sooner through their own religion than through Christianity has been challenged in the *Christian Century* magazine by the statement that "many Jews in America scarcely have a religion."

Spirituality is conduct motivated by a sense of values in which not only are the interests of one's ego transcended, but in which also that transcendence is assumed to have cosmic support. For such spirituality to exist in Jewish life, *Jews have to achieve a conception of God which meets the following two requirements: (a) it must make sense, and (b) it must be intrinsically related to the historic experiences of the Jewish People, as well as to its course of action in the future.*

The Secularist Jews deny the need of any but common political and cultural values for the future of the Jewish People.

The Orthodox conception of God does not make sense, because it is based on the assumption that the miraculous events recorded in the Bible are the most authentic evidence of His existence.

The Reform conception of God as embodied in ethical monotheism is, indeed, related to the past of the Jews. Though it makes sense, it points to no specific course of future action for the Jewish People as constituting its destiny. One therefore does not have to be a Jew to live by the Reform conception of God.

The Conservative group recognizes that a definite conception of God is indispensable, but has given little or no thought to what it should be. It is an emotional compound of nostalgia for the Orthodox view and complacency with the Reform view.

The reason a Jewish conception of God has to be related to the past and the future of the Jewish People, is that religion is a process in three dimensions: Divinity, peoplehood and salvation. The three dimensions are interrelated and mutually determined. That is implied in the aphorism that "God, Israel and the Torah are one." The most difficult idea to get across in religion is that while each of the three dimensions is indispensable, it is **not** enough.

Divinity is that cosmic spirit, power or process which enables the individual to achieve his salvation through the medium of the people of which he is a member. Belief in Divinity is the belief that the universe is not indifferent to human behavior, but reacts to it in one form or another. The history of religion is the history of unconscious groping of organic societies for an understanding of the relationship between specific behavior and specific reactions of the universe, or between specific beliefs concerning Divinity and specific notions of the greatest social good.

Salvation is the maximum good which it is assumed men can attain, if they order their lives in accordance with what they interpret to be the will of Divinity. Such maximum good has, throughout the history of religion, been conceived in social terms, or as the greatest social good in which the individual wishes to have a share as a means to his own self-fulfillment. Thus during the Biblical period, salvation was synonymous with the prosperity and prestige of the People of Israel.

Throughout the post-Biblical period until modern times, salvation was conceived as achievable only in the hereafter. In recent times such postponement has come to be regarded as evasion of the duty to improve living conditions and abolish exploitation and war in the here and now. Hence salvation is nowadays to all intents and purposes identified with that political, economic and social structure of society which would enable the individual to become a full-fledged human person.

Of the three dimensions of religion, the conception of salvation is the most decisive in the pattern of spirituality, because a person's conception of it determines his conception of Divinity, and of the kind of social order his people should adopt as a means to his self-fulfillment. The conception of salvation therefore determines one's idea of God, as well as what one's people must do or refrain from doing in order to achieve the greatest social good.

Peoplehood is that social structure of a society from the most primitive to the most advanced, including government, economy, culture and religion, which provides through those organizations and institutions the necessary conditions for salvation, or the self-fulfillment of the individual.

Insofar as the self-fulfillment of the human person is inconsistent with total annihilation at death, it calls for some form of immortality. That demand is satisfied through an organically constituted people, with a common history and common destiny that is the sum of all the individual lives which have been and will be identified with it. A people thus provides its individual lives a kind of continuing radiation or anonymous immortality.

The role of peoplehood as one of the three dimensions of religion is in need of being re-emphasized nowadays to counteract the mental confusion caused by Western political apologetics. Communism treats the individual as expendable, in the interests of the State. Max Eastman, for example, says of Trotsky that "he lives instinctively in a world in which other persons (except in the mass or as classes) do not count." Western civilization, on the other hand, claims to be the champion of the primacy of the individual. In support of its claim, it cites the historic religions. Actually the historic religions have until recently been so insistent upon obedience to authority as to leave little room for individual self-expression. That, however, was not because they regarded the individual as expendable, but because they have found it necessary to emphasize the fact that one cannot achieve individuality except through the medium of the people to which one belongs. Modern democracy merely qualifies, but does not negate, that teaching of the historic religions, by maintaining that a people must not deprive the individual of certain inalienable rights.

GOD AS CREATOR, LAWGIVER, SAVIOR

The Jewish concept of Divinity is related to the past of the Jewish People, insofar as throughout its entire history until modern times the conception of God in terms of relationship and function occupies a position of centrality. As in all other pre-modern civilizations, so in pre-modern Judaism God figured as the "God of" and the "God for." He figures by far less as the God of all the earth, of which He was the Creator, than He does as the God of Abraham, Isaac and Jacob and of the People or House of Israel. Moreover, in Jewish tradition, God figures variously as the God *for* bestowing the following blessings: a) victory in war, b) a land to live in, c) laws to live by, d) prosperity and prestige. It was only during the era of the Second Commonwealth that God came to figure mainly as providing man with e) other-worldly salvation. Those blessings are assumedly withheld when His People disobey His will. The principle of reward and punishment has been integral to the traditional conception of God as far back as Biblical times. That principle, however, is challenged in the Book of Job. In *J.B.*, MacLeish expresses the latest reiteration of that challenge, which implies that the universe is indifferent to human behavior.

That challenge cannot be ignored, if the belief in God is to have a place in human life. It should be met by the reply that mankind has merely been woefully misreading the reaction of the universe to human behavior. The universe may be indifferent to wishful thinking, or to prayer which calls for interference with the laws of nature, but it is not indifferent to intelligence, knowledge, honesty, cooperation, hope, faith, love; nor does it fail to react to their opposites: stupidity, ignorance, dishonesty, exploitation, despair, cynicism and hate. That often the consequences of misbehavior are inflicted on persons other than those guilty of it simply means that we have to change our conception of human individuality, not regard it as encapsulated in a particular body. "No man is an island, entire of itself; every man is a piece of a continent." In that light we should also view the fact that many enjoy benefits they have done nothing to deserve.

These inequities are not altogether beyond man's ability to correct. In time man probably will learn to do so even as he has learned to manufacture satellites for outer space.

If the conception of Divinity is to make sense as well as be related to the past and the future of the Jewish People, it is evident that its association with neither the fortunes of war nor with the supply of rain can be counted on as serving the cause of religion. Two other functions, however, ascribed to God in Jewish tradition have both a universal significance and a particular application to our future as a People. Those are the functions of lawgiver and savior.

The function of lawgiver to the People of Israel accentuates the unique contribution of the Jewish People to the conception of God. Except for the function of salvation, all the other functions —warrior, raingiver, giver of health, prosperity and security—derive from the association of Divinity with *power*. On the other hand, God as lawgiver and savior associates Divinity with the *control* of power to prevent its abuse and to further its use for the spiritual life. Religion is thus assigned the function of regulating the power which human beings possess and acquire, as a means of developing to the maximum the potentialities of the individual for the good life and of society for freedom, justice and peace. That an entire people should come to experience Divinity primarily through lawgiving or Torah is without precedent in the annals of mankind. Had the significance of that fact been sufficiently appreciated by the Apostle Paul, there would have been a different Christianity.

The mission of the Prophets was to persuade the People to see Divinity in the laws which were intended to transform them into a Kingdom of God. They referred to those laws as God's Torah, and what else could God's Torah spell out if not social justice? To what extent the Prophets referred to the Pentateuchal Torah is a moot problem. According to Jewish tradition, God actually revealed Himself to the entire People of Israel as the Author of Torah at the very beginning of its career. *Even if viewed as myth, the assumption that the entire People of Israel was the recipient of God's Torah and committed to it is history, and has made history. That assumption has given the dimension of peoplehood in religion as such a significance which is bound to identify God as the Spirit, or Power, in the Cosmos that impels man to transcend his animal heredity.*

The Prophet Isaiah envisaged the People of Israel as having been created by God for the one purpose of demonstrating the workings of social justice. "Let me sing for my beloved a love song concerning his vineyard: My beloved had a vineyard, a fertile hill. He digged it and cleared it of stones, and planted it with choice vines; he built a watchtower in the midst of it, and hewed out a wine vat in it; and he looked for it to yield grapes but it yielded wild grapes. . . . For the vineyard of the Lord of Hosts is the House of Israel and the men of Judah are His pleasant planting; and He looked for justice, but behold bloodshed; for righteousness, but behold a cry!" [4] Our ancestors, it is true, failed to approximate, to say nothing of living up to, the ideals of the Prophets. But they undoubtedly labored under a sense of guilt because of that failure. That sense of guilt, however, kept the ideals of social justice alive for the day when they would be translated into action.

Social justice as a manifestation of Divinity calls for the existence of a living people with all the appurtenances of a full-fledged civilization: a land, a government, an economy and a culture. These provide those this-worldly conditions which have to be fostered if human society is to achieve this-worldly salvation. What, in the light of that fact, can Jews of the Diaspora do to function as a people?

The inevitable corollary for the individual, of the principle that the civilization of a people should be dedicated to the purpose of demonstrating the existence of Divinity through social justice, is that he must build his own life on the practice of moral responsibility. There can be no social justice in society unless each individual lives up to the awareness that he is accountable for the way he uses his own power (i.e., his abilities and opportunities). The universe is not indifferent to what he is and what he does.

His business in life is not to be merely a fragment of a person or a fragmented person, but a whole and wholesome person. To live for such a purpose is essential to individual salvation. Man can count upon cosmic support or divine help.

In demanding of man that he be godlike or holy, the Jewish tradition implies that, in the same way as social justice is a means of experiencing Divinity in the collective life of a people, so moral responsibility is the means which the individual possesses of experiencing Divinity in his own life, and of realizing that the universe is not indifferent. However, he must be prepared to encounter evil in nature, in society, in human nature—his own included. Moral responsibility then must give rise to moral courage.

The Hellenic tradition has added to the foregoing traits those of a sense of reality, or reason and of intelligence, for the fostering of which man should regard himself as morally responsible. And the modern scientific and esthetic tradition has added the trait of creativity.

Those are the latest developments in the dimension of salvation, both collective and individual, which, as said before, is the decisive one in the process of religion.

THE MITZVOT OF PEOPLEHOOD

In order then that Jewish life recover its spiritual character, Jews have to explore anew their peoplehood and relate it to the dimensions of Divinity and salvation. That means engaging in actions which would activate those relationships, and fostering action-symbols which would render Jews so conscious of their spiritual unity as a People as to raise that consciousness to the level of conscience. *Since those actions and action-symbols aim at relating Jewish peoplehood to Divinity and salvation, they are religious imperatives* or mitzvot, *the mitzvot of peoplehood.*

The primary *mitzvah* of Jewish peoplehood is the rehabilitation of Eretz Yisrael as the spiritual homeland of the Jewish People.

The Arabs contest the Jews' right to the Land, and are biding their time to gather enough strength to invade it and drive the Jews into the sea. The State of Israel finds itself completely isolated. In the present world, where no great or small state considers itself secure unless it is part of some alliance, Israel is left out in the cold. The Western and the Soviet world compete with each other in wooing the Arab nations, whose only bond of unity is the determination to destroy Israel, and who therefore dare not display any great friendship for Israel. Under these circumstances, for Jews in the free countries to justify their interest in the security and wellbeing of Israel merely on humanitarian and philanthropic grounds is to contribute to the growing belief among Western statesmen that the establishment of Israel was a mistake.

Both Jews and non-Jews have to be reoriented to the significance of the Zionist movement. Zionism must become known as the religious or spiritual revival of the Jewish People, whose belief in God is in need of being validated by means of the opportunity to build a full-fledged civilization based on social justice. In the light of this Greater Zionism, the basic *mitzvah* of Jewish peoplehood is to help build the Land—through *Aliyah* for those who can settle there, through economic aid and financial investment for those who cannot.

A series of duties pertaining to pilgrimages, cultural interchange, technical aid, etc., would grow out of the primary one of the rehabilitation of Eretz Yisrael.

Next in order of importance is the establishment of a permanent advisory body, be it in the form of parliament, conference, research institute or forum, that would speak to the entire Jewish People in an advisory capacity concerning the meaning of the spiritual unity of the Jewish People and the most effective ways of translating it into various activities, communal, institutional, educational, cultural, etc.

Thus, a second series of actions as *mitzvot* of peoplehood would be the planning and executing of various techniques to arouse public interest and participation in all efforts leading to the establishment of such an advisory body. This body should develop a method whereby all who would be willing to commit themselves to the acceptance of its recommendations should formalize such commitment by covenanting themselves publicly. The aim should be to make of this ritual or action-symbol a means of Jewish identification.

A third series of actions as *mitzvot* of peoplehood is the reorganization of the present communal structure of Jews in the free countries of the world into organic communities. These communities would have to take on the same spiritual or religious character as world Jewry as a whole. Only they, and not individual congregations, should have the right to be designated by the name of *Kehillah Kedoshah*. That name may properly be borne only by such a segment of the Jewish People as embodies an entire gamut of civilizational functions, and thereby confers reality, even if in miniature form, upon the Jewish People as a whole.

Without going into an analysis of the present structure of American Jewish communities, we may affirm without fear of contradiction that it is inherently not calculated to sustain Jewish life, much less enhance it. Each generation is less Jewish than the preceding. The failure to hold those with a penchant for the reflective life, the self-alienation of the most creatively minded Jews, is a fatal omen for the future of American Judaism. Inherent in the very way in which independent congregations have to manage their economic affairs is their tendency to keep out both the very well-to-do and the lower middle class. That narrowing of the Jewish religious life to the upper middle class is as disruptive of Jewish life and values as the centrifugal pull of the Gentile world.

Nothing but a properly devised organic structure of Jewish communal life may in part counteract those disintegrative forces. The criterion of its organic character would be the extent to which it would result in the kind of creative interaction among Jewish organizations which would eliminate the currently "rasping paradoxes" from Jewish life. Among the important communal activities would be keeping vital statistics, maintaining all-day Jewish schools wherever feasible, providing arbitration and other ways of dealing with problems of social justice, such as those involving unionism, the right to work or to strike, etc., sanctioning marriages and divorces, and being in charge of *Kashrut*. Hence all activities leading to such an organic structure belong to the *mitzvot* of Jewish peoplehood.

A fourth series of actions which should be instituted pertains to spreading a knowledge of Hebrew. There is a definite psychological value to the knowledge of modern Hebrew and the ability to converse in it. For Jewish life in the Diaspora, however, the knowledge of Biblical and liturgical Hebrew is even of greater importance, since it is more likely than vernacular Hebrew to communicate the basic values of Judaism. Without those basic values, Jewish people-hood cannot constitute one of the three dimensions in the process of Jewish religion.

Though by far less potent a factor than Hebrew, the practice of adopting Hebraic personal names has a psychological influence from the standpoint of identification with the Jewish People. Considering it a *mitzvah* to bear a Hebraie name will help to spread the practice.

A fifth series of actions must concern itself with the revitalization of Sabbaths and Festivals. The dimension of peoplehood which is built into the traditional motivation for their observance warrants a special effort to explore all possible ways and means of having them readopted by the masses of our People. A Sabbathless people cannot possibly cultivate the life of the spirit.

All of the foregoing courses of action naturally call for action-symbols. Most of the action-symbols take the form of ritual practices and worship or prayer. The revival of the observance of *Kashrut* and Sabbaths and Festivals would lead to the vitalization of the action-symbols associated with them.

There is one action-symbol, however, which has to be created for the purpose of developing an active awareness of the need of reconstituting and maintaining the spiritual unity of the Jewish People. This would be a ritual of conferring a higher degree upon those who arrive at maturity, just as the elementary degree of *bar* or *bat mitzvah* is conferred at present at the beginning of adolescence. However we may deplore the fact that congregational attendance at Sabbath services has come to depend on *bar* and *bat mitzvah* occasions, those occasions have become indispensable for the upkeep of Jewish life. A similar ritual enacted during the period of maturation would be even more effective in contributing to the intensification of Jewish consciousness and to a sense of responsibility for fostering the spiritual unity of the Jewish People by living a life of *kiddush ha-shem* or spiritual dedication.

*　　*　　*

Two pragmatic consequences follow from the entire discussion. One pertains to the fact of peoplehood, and the other to the concept of *mitzvot*. That peoplehood is a dimension of Jewish religion implies that our vocation as a People coincides with the urgent need of contemporary mankind. The fact is that the world situation is currently fraught with dangers that might lead to the extinction of mankind, due for the most part to the explosive character which nationhood has assumed. The nature of modern warfare is such as to compel nations to form alliances and to limit their own political sovereignty. More nations, however, are coming into being, and each nation is getting to be more conscious of its individuality and intent upon fostering it. By resuming our peoplehood as a dimension of our religion, we Jews have the opportunity of articulating the imperative need of each nation to foster its national individuality as a gift from God, and not as an acquisition of an earthly or demonic power. A nation must be subject to the same divine laws of social justice and moral responsibility in relation to its own citizens and to other nations as is the individual person.

The second pragmatic consequence, of the fact that Jewish peoplehood is a dimension of the Jewish religion bears on the concept of *mitzvot*. It enables the Jew who can no longer accept his tradition in the form in which it has come down to him so to reinterpret that tradition as to render it viable. Literally understood, *mitzvot* means laws commanded by God. According to tradition, all the 613 *mitzvot* were actually dictated by God. That belief had the effect of rendering them immutable. When conditions of life and thought made them obsolete, as was true of the entire sacrificial cult, the traditionalists had to persuade themselves that those *mitzvot* were merely suspended for a time. When, as in the case of other *mitzvot*, the traditional version became restrictive, legal fictions or sophistries were resorted to as a means of overcoming their restrictive character. Neither solution could satisfy those for whom the *mitzvot* had the same kind of human history as the cult practices of all other religions.

On the other hand, to resort to the secularist solution of abolishing the *mitzvot* altogether is to perform a surgical operation that might kill the patient. A third alternative is to transfer them from the dimension of Divinity to the dimension of peoplehood as an indispensable dimension of religion. The *mitzvot* would thus retain their imperative character, not merely because they are the product of collective Jewish life but because they point to the same cosmic or divine drive as that which impels man to transcend his animal heredity. So viewed, *mitzvot* have to be relevant to our spiritual needs. Some traditional *mitzvot* may become obsolete, some may have to be modified, and some may have to be created anew.

If we will deal with the problem of *mitzvot* in that spirit, the Jewish People will experience the fulfillment of the prophetic words which are recited when we perform the *mitzvah* of *tefilin:* "I will betroth you to me forever; I will betroth you to me in righteousness and in justice, in steadfast love and in mercy. I will betroth you to me in faithfulness. Then you will know the Lord." [5]

THE REVELATION OF GOD IN THE HUMAN SPIRIT

The problem of serious-minded religionists is not: How can we get people to become religious? but, how can we get religion to make people better? What should be done to religion to have it exert an impelling influence on people's behavior, an influence that would show itself in their being more honest, more just and more considerate? It is evident, of course, that the best religion in the world cannot make people who have known nothing but poverty, disease and cruelty better. But the fact is that even when these evils are eliminated, human conduct and character are far from being what they should be. Unless the belief in God can contribute to their becoming what they should be it will ultimately become obsolete. The attempt to have religion function mainly as a tranquilizer, affording either peace of mind or peace of soul, will continue to be made so long as the drugs on the market for either purpose have not been perfected or psychoanalysis is too expensive. In the long run, however, the only effort that will save the belief in God from becoming defunct is effort which will be invested in such *rational and communicable* thought as will establish a causal connection between believing in God and being a reliable and kindly person.

If we wish to avoid indulging in vague generalities about religion, we should learn to think of it as concretely embodied in the specific religions of mankind. We must remember that an

institutional or organized religion consists of three elements—
theology, polity and ritual. Theology deals with the conception
of God, polity with the social framework of the religious communion, and ritual with the various practices which the adherents
of the religion have to observe. It is natural for the human association displayed in polity and for the human feelings expressed
in ritual to have a decisive influence on human life both in its
individual and collective capacity. But the nature of that influence, whether it be good or evil, depends, in the final analysis,
upon the conception which the adherents of the religion in question have of God. Insofar therefore as any religion makes a difference in a person's life, the greater part of that difference is to
be ascribed to its theology. Much has unquestionably been wrong
with traditional theology, since so clear-headed and serious a
thinker as Whitehead could have indicted it in the following
fashion: "The notion of God as the 'unmoved mover' is derived
from Aristotle, at least so far as Western thought is concerned.
The notion of God as 'eminently real' is a favorite doctrine of
Christian theology. The combination of the two into the doctrine
of an aboriginal, eminently real, transcendental creator, at whose
fiat the world came into being, and whose imposed will it obeys,
is the fallacy which has infused tragedy into the histories of Christianity and Mahometanism. When the Western world accepted
Christianity, Caesar conquered. . . . The church gave unto God
the attributes which belonged exclusively to Caesar." [6] I may add
that the Synagogue and Islam did the same. That kind of theology
was good enough for a despotically oriented world, but is not good
enough for a democratically oriented one.

For a conception of God to influence the character and conduct of people, it has to be based upon a verifiable conception of
the human spirit. If we want to improve the health and growth
of the human body, we have to learn all about the body and about
the conditions under which it thrives. Engaging in mental gym-
nastics to prove that health and growth really exist and can be
achieved by being praised, glorified and exalted will not have the
least effect on the body. Only when we know the body well enough
to realize what constitutes its health and growth, and we conform
to the conditions necessary to attain them, do they manifest them-

selves in the body. What health and growth are to the human body, God is to the human spirit. If we wish to experience the reality of God, we have to act on the knowledge of the human spirit and of the conditions it has to meet, if it is to function in accordance with its true nature. Only then will God actually reveal Himself to us. This approach negates emphasis on the traditional claim of Jewish religion that the Torah is the only authentic revelation of God's will, of Islam that the Koran is such revelation, and of Christianity that Christ is the actual self-revelation of God Himself. Jews, Moslems and Christians whose world outlook is democratically and scientifically oriented have lost the God of their fathers and have not found a God of their own, one that could give meaning and direction to their lives. The human spirit through which we can behold divinity is certainly not human nature in the raw, in all its stages and in all of its manifestations. The human spirit is only that one aspect of human nature which points to its striving to transform and transcend itself. That aspect properly perceived and apprehended does reveal God in a way that nothing else in the heavens above or on the earth below can.

How does God reveal Himself, or what do we mean by God when we say we experience His reality through the human spirit? The answer is that He reveals Himself as the Cosmic Spirit or Process, both in the universe and in man, that impels man to become fully human, to realize himself, to attain his human destiny, or, in the language of tradition, to achieve salvation. That Cosmic Spirit or Process is, properly speaking, Divinity or Godhood, which, due to the inherent shortcoming or disease of language, we tend to personify. God is thus the personification, not of an abstract idea in the mind of man, but of an actual ongoing process both in the cosmic and in the human order.

To experience, therefore, the reality of God we should concentrate on the nature of the human spirit, or that phase of human nature which has to do with man's becoming fully human, or his achieving salvation. The human spirit is that in the human being which makes of him a person. There is, of course, a variety of ways by which we identify an individual as being a person. There are all kinds of aptitudes, skills and achievements. But there surely must be one denominator common to all whom we designate as persons. What, indeed, constitutes being a person? When we have the answer to that question, we shall have the key to the meaning of salvation, and once we can properly identify salvation, we shall behold the revelation of God in the human spirit.

WHAT CONSTITUTES SALVATION?

To be a person means to have a sense of moral responsibility. One needs no special gift or talent to be a person other than that of being aware of oneself as autonomously accountable for one's behavior. Feeling accountable or responsible on the authority of others, under whatever name they exercise that authority, will not do. Being a person implies an intellectual and emotional maturity which is attained only gradually and which has to keep on enlarging its scope. A person is existentially such by virtue of his sense of moral responsibility, and to the extent that he lives up to it.

The entire structure of Hobbes' philosophy of the state is built on sand, because of his failure to realize that in transferring, as he assumed, all rights to the ruler unconditionally and absolutely, the citizens of the state were abdicating their personality. Ernst Cassirer points out that the political thinkers of the seventeenth century charged Hobbes with a contradiction in terms. "If a man could give up his personality," they said, "he would cease being a moral being. He would become a lifeless thing—and how could it make a promise or enter into a social contract? . . . There is no act of submission by which a man can give up the status of a free agent and enslave himself. For by such an act of renunciation he would give up that very character which constitutes his nature and essence; he would lose his humanity." [7]

Selfish people, those who are heartless, amoral or blasé, are the irresponsible ones with whom one cannot enter into any normal or satisfactory personal relations, even though they may not be psychotic cases. Symptomatic of the age we live in are not only the deterioration of the family institution, juvenile delinquency, and adult criminality and corruption but also what has been termed "America's New Culture Hero." The favorite figure on the stage and in the movies is the rebel and the outcast who is isolated from parents, from friends, from teachers and from society. Those are the characters which occupy the chief role in such motion pictures as *The Wild Ones, Rebel Without a Cause, East of Eden, The Edge of the City*. They apparently cater to the anarchic impulses of the adolescents who constitute the largest percentage of movie fans. The "beatniks" have made of irresponsibility a cult.

To appreciate the role of moral responsibility in transforming human society and remaking human character, we have to take cognizance of its functioning on a grand scale in the lives of the great moral heroes. Human history abounds in exemplars of moral responsibility: the ancient Prophets of Israel, a Buddha, a Jesus, a St. Francis of Assisi. Every age and every land has had equally great personalities, even though history has not always provided them as large a stage. To mention at random but a few outstanding geniuses of the spirit in more recent years, a William Lloyd Garrison, a David Livingston, a Florence Nightingale, and in our own day a Gandhi and a Schweitzer. Thoreau, too, was endowed with a keen sense of responsibility which he displayed when he refused to pay his poll tax, as a protest against the way the American Government was carrying on its business. He was seized and put in jail. Emerson merely protested on the lecture platform and on the printed page. When Emerson visited Thoreau in jail, the latter taught him a lesson in moral responsibility. He said to Emerson: "This is where you should have been." That which in the uncommon man flowers forth as moral genius exists as moral potentiality in the common man, in the same way as the musical genius of a Beethoven implies the capacity for musical appreciation by the average person.

At the present time, for example, when our own South is in the grip of the struggle over the moral issue of desegregation, there are not wanting men and women of moral courage. Lillian Smith of Clayton, Georgia, the well-known author of *Strange Fruit*, herself a symbol of integration in the South during the decade before the Supreme Court decision, reported recently that thousands of white Southerners were quietly working day after day, speaking out in their small towns, their clubs, their churches. She estimates that 2 or 3 per cent of the whites run grave risks of loss of life, job and popularity in order to defend the Negro's right to his full share in our democratic life, not so much for the Negro's sake as for the preservation of human freedom and decency. Another ten per cent, she adds, are trying to get their neighbors to see the light.[8] *The fact is that, but for the divine grace which reveals itself in the moral responsibility of human beings, despite all their assumed and actual depravity, there would have been no mankind.*

On the principle of selection, therefore, whether natural or spiritual, the outstanding moral geniuses, or saints, represent deviants or emergents who in course of time are likely to become the rule. The very esteem in which they are held is bound to become part of the social heritage which slowly but surely moulds the lives of those who cultivate it and cherish its ideals. According to Bergson, the lives of saints are the main source of whatever morality exists in the world. Mankind might have been able to wait for the evolutionary process to take its slow natural course, if it were not for the lethal power of which man has come into possession and which might wipe his entire species off the face of the earth long before the example of the moral geniuses had a chance of transforming the sub-human residue into the humanly spiritual. *No less urgent, therefore, than catching up with Russia in the manufacture of the instruments of death is the problem of what should be done to accelerate in human beings the growth of the sense of moral responsibility.*

Marxism plus Leninism represents the scientific and empirical approach to the problems of human society seen as human nature in the large. That approach is based on what human nature has been hitherto and on the assumption that it is not amenable to change. According to totalitarian communism therefore, the only way to achieve some sort of equality or justice in the distribution of goods and services is to put all economic matters into the hands of a self-chosen elite. Experience has proved that such a goal can be attained only at the price of violating the most elemental rights of human beings. The contemporary leaders of communism do not deny that fact; they claim that, human nature being what it is, the ultimate goal—a just society—can be reached only by wading through rivers of human blood. In the so-called free world, the counter-claim is made that no achievement is ever purged of the bloody means used in attaining it. Far better an evolutionary, even if necessarily bungling, messianism, than one that is revolutionary and brutal. Unfortunately, this preference usually spells dangerous political drifting and repeated economic disasters and social panics.

IS RESPONSIBILITY AN ILLUSION?

The usual remedy is recourse to moral responsibility on a large social, but not governmental, scale. What the application of moral responsibility on such a scale would mean may be illustrated by the statement presented to the Senate Subcommittee on Antitrust and Monopoly, Januray 28, 1956, by Walter P. Reuther, president of the United Automobile Workers. The point of that statement is that one of the main causes of the 1957-58 recession was that not one of the three large automobile companies *"showed the slightest willingness to accept the responsibility of the dominant position in American industry by giving a lead to all industry in a practical program against inflation"* (italics mine). They disregarded his "proposal which not only would have made a price increase unnecessary, but would have made a price cut possible." As with all manifestations of greed, this one too was nothing less than one of stupidity, because a price increase could only have boomeranged in the form of reduced consumer buying, with all the evils in its wake. Strange that so astute a labor leader as Reuther should fail to note that a good deal of the blame falls on him and his men as well, for not using the same strike method against the companies' greed in raising prices as is used against their lowering wages and workers' benefits.

The truth is that comparatively little thought has been given to the very functioning of moral responsibility, despite the seeming emphasis on it in both religion and morals. Religion has been too preoccupied with the supernatural and the other-worldly to pay much attention to morals, and in morals, thinkers have deemed it proper to ignore religion. Actually neither has any meaning without the other. Religion without morals is magic, and morals without religion is a form of expediency. The purpose of this discussion is limited to the exploration of their mutually organic relationship.

Such relationship is due to the following two facts: 1) Man is authentically human only insofar as he has a sense of moral responsibility. 2) Man experiences personally through that sense of responsibility the revelation of God as the source of whatever truth and value there is to any of the historical or institutional religions.

Moral responsibility is a manifestation of the human spirit which the human sciences can study and report on in terms of the situation in which it flourishes or declines. But were psychology and sociology to identify it as the effect of those situations only, they would reduce it to an illusion. The inevitable inference to be drawn from such a procedure would be that the human differential, and the entire structure of civilization made possible by that differential, are nothing but a self-deluding hoax. Rather than accept such a paradoxical and absurd conclusion, most of us who wish to retain our sanity prefer to concede that moral responsibility transcends the narrowly scientific assumption that there must be absolute equality between cause and effect.

The narrowly scientific approach to reality is the one which has come into vogue since the seventeenth century. It has its basis in the assumption that cause and effect, when reducible to quantitative or mathematical terms, must be equal. Its utility in all phases of human life is such as to render it indispensable. But to regard it as sufficient is not only a fallacy but is certain to lead to fateful consequences. Suppose, for example, it were true that juvenile delinquency is due, as a psychiatrist reported to the American Psychiatric Association, to the after effects of encephalitic infection, and that it might be cured by large daily doses of benzedrine, it still remains true that we cannot afford to disregard the various factors which operate in and through consciousness. The very terms in which irresponsible action is described indicate that it involves factors beyond the reach of physical or chemical causes. Delinquents are described as being "overactive, restless, with short attention and concentration span, unpredictable, acting before thinking, destructive and usually not showing any remorse and not learning by experience." Every one of the foregoing terms implies not only life but consciousness, which cannot be ascribed to benzedrine.

The truth is that, though moral responsibility is as vividly concrete an experience as is life itself, it is as little understood and has always puzzled and mystified even the greatest thinkers. Why is that the case? Because to be responsible evidently means to be free to choose. That recalls the interminable discussions of the problem of human freedom, which, like the problem of evil, is still as far from a satisfactory solution as when it was first propounded. Freedom of the will may be doubted theoretically, and even the experience of it considered illusory. But the sense of moral responsibility is something the human being cannot afford to be deprived of either in theory or in practice. To be without it is to be a moral imbecile or psychotic. No mature person would submit to being regarded as irresponsible, unless he could thereby escape imprisonment or death.

The medieval scientists who were sure that the earth could not possibly be a globe, because that would mean that the people on the other side of the one we were on would have to be walking with their feet up and heads down, were mistaken because they argued on the basis of inadequate knowledge of reality. Likewise, those who are sure that man's sense of moral responsibility is a freak or paradox of nature may be arguing from an inadequate knowledge of nature. They assume that man is the product of natural selection, and that natural selection is absolutely devoid of any directive, or creative, factor. On the other hand, the fact is incontestable that at one point in the evolution of life there did emerge a being with enough imagination to conceive of two possible courses of action of which he or it deliberately chose one. The survival power which this capacity contributed to that being confirmed that capacity, which later came to function as moral responsibility.

Under those circumstances it is just as reasonable to regard the capacity to choose among alternatives and the moral responsibility that goes with it as no less built into the reality of nature than the evolutionary process as a whole. Hence, nature, or the cosmos as a whole, has a hand, so to speak, in man's self-aware form of life. *By the same token that the universe has a hand, so to speak, in the emergence of man, it has a hand in impelling him to make the most of his life.* "The last lesson of life," wrote Emerson, "the choral song which rises from all the elements and all angels is a voluntary obedience, a necessitated freedom. Man is made of the same atoms as the world is, he shares the same impressions, pre-dispositions and destiny. When his mind is illuminated, when his heart is kind, he throws himself joyfully into the sublime order, and does with his knowledge what the stones do by structure." [9]

DIVINITY IN THE COSMOS

Accordingly, *insofar as the cosmos is so constituted as to have man in the course of his evolution attain freedom, act responsibly and strive for self-fulfillment or salvation, it is divine, in the same way as man, by virtue of these same traits, is human.* The meta-phor of "dialogue" to identify the interaction between man and cosmos, or between the human and the divine, helps us realize to what extent God is God because of what he means to man, and man is man because of his relationship to God. It is necessary, however, to experience in a literal sense the specific element, or elements, of identity between God and man which make such interaction or "dialogue" possible. To gain such experience we have to do more than affirm the reality and cosmic background of the sense of moral responsibility; we have to probe it for the specific traits which it shares with the cosmos.

When we analyze the sense of moral responsibility, we note in it three constituent factors: a) organicity, b) polarity and c) creativity.

These three factors operate interactively not only in man, but in the entire universe. They are the very making of the universe. They are God and God is they, in their mutually integrated func-tioning. In man, they are his spirit or his soul, and his spirit is they in their mutually integrated functioning. That spirit or soul is a revelation of God which man has sought gropingly and blun-deringly to articulate in his various religious traditions.

a) Organicity

Organicity means that the totality of a thing influences every one of its parts, and that each part is influenced by the rest of the totality. Each such totality is a patterned structure which con-ditions and defines the activity or functioning of each of its parts. All this is implied in the experience of moral responsibility, which is based on the assumption that the person who is subject to it is an organic *continuum*. For that reason he is held accountable for a promise made, a debt contracted, or a crime committed by him, in the past. The ongoing changes in his physical and mental makeup are merely parts held together by the *continuum* of the human person, and their nature and meaning are what they are by reason of their place in the nexus of that *continuum*. Thus in the sense of moral responsibility the human person shares with the entire universe that organicity which makes a universe of whatever swims into the ken of human knowledge.

Only in recent years have scientists come to realize the role of organicity in the more exact decipherment of the mysteries of nature than was possible on the basis of scientific materialism. The facts of radiation have not only substituted energy for the "unfissionable" particles of matter known as atoms, but have assigned to organism a hitherto unsuspected ontological significance. In physics, the atom is now viewed as an organism. In biology, organicity is represented by the cell.

b) Polarity

A second factor in moral responsibility is polarity. All moral responsibility involves two referents, a self and an other, and thus accentuates the bipolar character of the human person. On the one hand, it stresses the individuality, the selfhood, the separateness of the human person, and on the other, it negates emphatically any possible encapsulation of such individuality. Instead, it emphasizes the role of interaction with other persons as integral to being oneself a person. The role of selfhood is the aspect of personal interdependence. The paradoxical character of moral responsibility is in a sense the tension that arises between, on the one hand, the referent of otherhood, with all the conditioning of heredity and environment that it brings to bear upon the human person, and, on the other hand, the referent of selfhood, which refuses to be overwhelmed by all that conditioning and asserts its own right to self-expression. It is only in periods of heightened consciousness that such tension or conflict is experienced. The proper discharge of moral responsibility consists in arriving at a *modus vivendi* between the self and the not-self. That makes it possible for the claims of both to be equally satisfied. As a consequence the human person enters into a relationship with other persons which functions smoothly as habit free from inner tension.

The function of moral responsibility seems thus to be to have man achieve in his own being an equilibrium between selfhood and otherhood. The actual nature of every single thing, from the electron to the stars in their courses, seems to be its endeavor to persevere in its polarity of individuation and interaction. That is true of the entire universe from the minutest particle of matter to the measureless galaxies. For years people considered the existence of an object to be self-evident and independent of its interaction with other objects. It was the development of microphysics which first showed that an object, the "what," acquires its meaning through the interactions, through the "how." That human beings are indeed real "members of one another" does not require laboring in this day and age. "We see ourselves," wrote Arthur Compton, "living increasingly in the lives of each other." [10]

c) Creativity

The third factor in the sense or experience of moral responsibility is *creativity*. The tension between the two poles of the human person, which gives rise to the awareness of human polarity and organicity, is always occasioned by the need to decide between two or more courses of action. Those alternatives are called to mind by the two mental capacities in which man excels all other living beings: memory and imagination. Thus a situation comes into existence which is a complete *novelty* in man's universe: self-consciousness. Self-consciousness is anything but the steady continuing light it is somehow assumed to be because of the fact that it is the primary human differential. From the way most people think of the human person, one might infer it was a kind of bodiless, sleepless, sexless spirit alert so long as it is alive. Nothing of the kind. Self-consciousness is a series of intermittent flashes lighting up various segments of the human landscape. But even as such, self-consciousness is the human differential potent enough to change the face of the earth and almost everything on it. But what is remarkable about it is that it is, so to speak, not in the cards of whatever precedes it. It is a new creation. Of course, the behaviorists refuse to admit creation, and therefore say what the farmer said when he first beheld a camel, "There ain't no such animal." Those who are not behaviorists prefer to recognize the reality of both consciousness and self-consciousness.

But how can we parry the contention of the behaviorist that to ascribe reality to consciousness is to fly in the face of reason, which tells us that there can be no more to the effect than there is to what causes or occasions it? To ascribe reality to consciousness is to affirm the possibility of creation out of nothing. This contention, however, is by no means unanswerable. What the behaviorist overlooks is that reason is not impervious to new experience and is not fixated in any of its own affirmations. Even reason's idea about the mutual relations of cause and effect has changed in the course of time, due to the more reliable experience it has been acquiring.

There was a time when reason assumed that the effect of any cause necessarily represents less potency than its cause, just as light is weaker the further it is away from its source. That assumption of reason has given way to the assumption substantiated by experiments in physics that there is absolute equality between cause and effect. Finally, even that assumption has been upset by the evidence of the biological sciences, which point to life and the evolution of new species as proving that nature does have room for novelty or creativity. That means there can be more potency to the effect than to the cause or occasion which gives rise to it. In the same way as behaviorists deny the reality of consciousness, their forerunners denied the reality of life itself. But that only goes to show how irrational we can become in the name of reason. Why then be surprised to find people acting most ungodly in the name of God? That should teach us that nothing so corrupts either thought or life as fixating them in any one of their stages. It is not too much to expect that before too long an idea like the following which Whitehead expressed will become part of the general climate of thought: "Both God and the world are in grip of the ultimate metaphysical ground, the creative advance into novelty. Either of them, God and the world, is the instrument of novelty for the other." [11]

SELF CONSCIOUSNESS AND RESPONSIBILITY

What has all this to do with moral responsibility? If we have followed the argument concerning creativity, we should realize, first that consciousness, like life itself, represents creation or novelty as a built-in property of nature. Self-consciousness is merely the intensification of that natural or cosmic property developed by man, a development which gives man his differentia. But what is most striking is the fact that the occasion in human life when this new development, or creation, comes into being is when man has to make a decision involving moral responsibility. As Robert Frost put it: "Nature within her inmost self decides / To trouble men with having to take sides." In other words, moral responsibility and self-consciousness are *initially* interchangeable. Thereafter self-consciousness goes off on its own, and attaches itself to art, philosophy, work, business, science or what you will. But it is in moral responsibility that man achieves what Lewis Mumford describes as "a heightened consciousness of what lies beyond the present state in space and time. . . . To act in terms of that consciousness is to acknowledge that no act exists for the actor alone; not even that which seems most private and inviolate." [12] *This heightened consciousness is the revelation of God in the human spirit.*

The sense of moral responsibility is no more fixated than is reason or experience. It is evolving and creative. In it the human will does not operate under the inertia of habit, or follow the path of least resistance. On the contrary, as William James defined morality, in it the will follows the path of *greatest* resistance. Each time the will, acting under the pressure of moral responsibility, comes out victorious, it re-establishes on a higher level the synthesis of the three cosmic tendencies which spell godhood or divinity. In each such instance the human person transforms itself, and approximates more closely the divinity which it shares with the cosmos. That is the pattern of the life-long efforts in which the human being engages in order to attain the full measure of his humanity.

The transformation, or growth, of the human person which has taken place in man from his beginning as a cave dweller to the present day seems to indicate a metamorphosis despite occasional setbacks—away from acceptance of conflict and resort to brute force, however disguised, and toward a growing capacity for symbiosis and compromise, or mutual accommodation; away from coercion, toward consensus. The process of metamorphosis has been subject to acceleration. Westermarck, who made an extensive study of the altruistic or benevolent tendencies in man, arrived at the conclusion that those tendencies have grown in strength and that they have the capacity for "indefinite extension." "A hundred years ago," writes Erich Fromm, "it was a widely accepted belief that no one had the responsibility for his neighbor. It was assumed—and scientifically proved by economics —that the laws of society made it necessary to have a vast army of poor and jobless people in order to keep the economy going. Today hardly anybody would dare voice this principle any longer. It is generally accepted that nobody should be excluded from the wealth of the nation, either by the laws of nature or by those of society." [13] Recently Carl R. Rogers stated that the inescapable conclusion from a quarter-century of his experience in psychotherapy was that "the basic nature of the human being when functioning freely is constructive and trustworthy.[14] According to James Leuba,[15] the continuity of the will-to-salvation with the will-to-live points to the fact that "evolution is directed and sustained by a trans-human cosmic force producing a moral development and culminating in man in the formation of either principles or ideals." He considered the existence of this trans-human urge a sufficient basis "for a minimal religious philosophy acceptable today." So eminent a thelogian as Berdyaev, who is noted for stressing the centrality of the God-idea, nevertheless writes, "Revelation presupposes faith in man and in his higher nature which renders possible that religious upheaval which we call revelation." [16]

Thus we have various authorities confirming the thesis that by identifying in the cosmos the basic elements present in moral responsibility, we can identify in the human spirit that which reveals God.

A character in a play by Tennessee Williams called *Suddenly Last Summer* says that we are all children in a vast kindergarten trying to spell the name of God with the wrong alphabet blocks. What has been wrong with the theologies of the historical religions is the fact that they have all been trying to spell the name of God with the wrong idea blocks, like anthropomorphism, supernaturalism, other-worldliness and human depravity. If we were to use such idea blocks as organicity, polarity and creativity, we might come upon the authentic name of God, that name which the Psalmist had in mind when he said: "Those who know Thy name put their trust in Thee, for Thou, O Lord, has not forsaken those who seek Thee." [17] Moffatt, who is intent upon the inner rather than the literal meaning of that verse, translates it thus: "Those who know what Thou art can trust in Thee, for never wilt Thou abandon those who seek Thee."

THE TORAH AS OUR LIFE AND THE LENGTH OF OUR DAYS

We Jews are urgently in need of recovering our self-awareness as a People. Formerly each generation of Jews cultivated and transmitted that awareness to its successor. To that transmission the Jewish People owes whatever measure of unity and capacity for survival and growth it still possesses. The most potent means of keeping alive that feeling of peoplehood has been the study of the tradition which is rooted in the Bible. If we were to sever the bonds which unite us with the People whose early career and spiritual struggles are reflected in the Bible, we would be left spiritually adrift.

There are various reasons for attachment to the past: there is pride in being able to claim a long ancestry for one's way of life; there is romantic sentiment which leads us to hold dear whatever has gathered patina; and there is worship of the past, on the assumption that those who lived then were in closer communion with God. Common to all of the foregoing reasons is the uncritical acceptance of everything that has come down from the past as necessarily right and of abiding value. Should anything in it be flagrantly unacceptable, it becomes the theme of elaborate apologetics. The most legitimate reason, however, for attachment to the past is that from it emanate those ethical and spiritual tendencies which experience has proved to be indispensable to our self-fulfillment as human beings. The awareness of their early beginnings adds to those humanizing tendencies the dimension of historic depth, thereby reinforcing them with the feeling that they are in keeping with the inherent nature of the human cosmos, or with the will of God.

To recover the feeling of Jewish peoplehood we have to learn to read and interpret our tradition in the light of our modern world outlook. That world outlook is radically different in respect to matters of fact concerning human nature and history from the world outlook implied in the Bible and from the one that was commonly held by Jews and non-Jews until the nineteenth century.

To the Psalmists who used the miracles recorded in the Pentateuch as the theme of their songs of thanksgiving and consolation, those miracles were actual events which could not have been other than the work of God. That has consistently been the traditional approach. The modern critical approach seeks to satisfy the intellectual interest in the actual facts behind the tradition, facts of authorship and historical background. It has no direct bearing on the religious significance of the tradition for our day. To arrive at that significance we have to supplement the modern-critical approach with the pragmatic approach. That involves exploring the sacred writings with a view to identifying the spiritual passion and moral insights which motivated the writing and compilation of the Scriptures. This gives one a glimpse into the extraordinary unfolding of the human spirit.

Granted, for example, that we can no longer accept the traditional belief that God actually dictated the purpose set forth in Exodus: "And ye shall be unto me a kingdom of priests and a holy nation." We cannot, however, help believing that the People whose consciousness was haunted by such a behest was in search of a purpose, and that, in the course of its search, it alighted upon some highly important moral and spiritual discoveries.

Those discoveries grew out of the Jewish People's very struggle for existence. In the literal version of the Pentateuch, the goods for which Israel strove seem for the most part to have been of the earth earthy. They wanted to beget many children, to be secure from attack, to possess great flocks and herds and to live to a ripe old age. But they wanted these goods not each for himself alone, but for all Jews and for the coming generations of their People. They wanted these goods in a way that led to their discovering the relevance of moral and spiritual values. What we experience as discoveries the ancients experienced as divine revelation.

Even though we bypass the belief in the supernatural origin of the Bible, and focus our attention on the Jewish People itself in its struggle to live and grow, we have to accept the traditional hierarchy of the Biblical writings and accord primacy to the Pentateuch. The Pentateuch was the first part of the Bible to be regarded as authoritative by the entire People, or to become Torah. That fact is of inexhaustible significance, from the standpoint not only of the past, but also of the future of the Jewish People. The Pentateuchal Torah may be said to voice what the Jewish People has considered to be the guiding purpose of its existence.

So long as the Pentateuchal Torah continues to be the chief instrument of keeping the Jewish consciousness alive, we shall remain a People. With the changes of climes and times, many of the values which the Torah originally expressed were bound to become irrelevant. Every time that happened the will-to-live of the Jewish People would reassert itself, by discovering such new or implied meanings in those values as rendered them relevant once more. Thus arose the *Midrash* of the Rabbis, the interpretation of Philo, and the *Kabbalah* of the *Zohar*. In our day many of those values seem again to be out of focus in relation to our spiritual needs.

THE MEANING OF THE TORAH FOR OUR DAY

If we wish to recover that unifying and people-making function of the Pentateuchal Torah, in order that it may constitute the basic content of a common Jewish consciousness in our day, we have to achieve a type of *Midrash* that fits into the contemporary world outlook, a kind of reinterpretation that will indicate the Torah's bearing on what profoundly concerns us.

The Pentateuchal Torah should help us identify our People, not so much by its outward history as by the contents of its collective mind and spirit. That Torah should be viewed as reflecting the ancient civilization of our People, insofar as it was geared to the purpose of enabling both the individual and the People to achieve self-fulfillment. The interpretation of the Pentateuchal Torah should, therefore, help to remind us that our People has been concerned with the problem of enabling all who share its life to fulfill their human destiny, to make the most of their lives, or to achieve salvation.

We should not expect to find in the Pentateuchal Torah the last word in philosophical, ethical or religious truth. Nor should we feel called upon to prove that it was meant to be the ultimate source of such truth. We shall then discover that our ancestors had much in common mentally, morally, and spiritually with their contemporaries of other nations. That should lead us to want to know as much as possible of the actual background and mental context of the populations with which our ancestors came into contact and by whom they were influenced.

To recover the way in which the Bible in general, and the Pentateuch in particular, helped to shape the career and the consciousness of the Jewish People, it is necessary to reconstruct as much as possible of the historical context of the text. That calls for the reading of each passage in the setting of the entire pattern of thought and aspiration which prevailed at about the time the text was written. For that reason we have to draw upon as much archaeological information and exegetical understanding of the original meaning of the Biblical text as are available. In addition, we have to reckon with whatever religious experiences throw light upon human nature and society. All such knowledge is necessary to bring into sharp relief the distinctive element in the tradition which the consciousness of the Jewish People evolved, and which, therefore, helps to accentuate the individuality of that People.

* * *

We shall derive the greatest amount of genuine inspiration from an objective approach to the Bible, if we will not mind discovering contradictions in the text and will not feel impelled to explain them away. The Torah is a composite of various documents that emanate from different writers. In the early stages of copying them, copyists probably felt free to make changes in the text to bring it into line with what they had learned from other sources. By the time the documents were put together as authoritative Torah, the scribes were wary of making changes and preferred to allow the contradictions to remain.

Afterward, however, attempts were made to harmonize these contradictions. In the Rabbinic writings these attempts abound. Occasionally, it is possible to reconstruct the very first effort of harmonization. But no harm can come from assuming that the contradictions were never really resolved. We must also be prepared to find much in the life and thought of our ancestors that seems immature, irrational, and, in the light of our present-day standards, even unforgivable. There can be, for example, no moral condonation of genocide, which the Torah purports to have been commanded by God with regard to the aborigines of Canaan. *We should not feel called upon to apologize for the moral immaturity and the spiritual insensitivity of our ancestors.*

An objective study of the text prevents us from following in the footsteps of Philo and the Medieval Jewish philosophers who tried to equate the biblical with the philosophical conceptions of God. The Bible nowhere deprecates picturing God in one's mind as having human form, though it treats the *making* of any image as a cardinal sin.

We must avail ourselves in particular of whatever light is thrown on the contents of the Torah by the discoveries of parallels to its narrative and its legal sections, with a view to emphasizing that which constitutes the unique contribution of the spirit which fashioned the Torah. On the other hand, we should not underestimate the value of whatever ethical or religious concepts of a universal and permanent character our ancestors took over from the world civilizations of their day and transmitted to the rest of the world through our Sacred Scriptures.

THE TORAH REVEALS GOD TO ISRAEL

Apart from any particular values we may derive from each episode or law in the Torah, and as background for such derivation, it is essential to realize that the Pentateuchal Torah was a people-making instrument. It provided our ancestors with an ethnic orientation and an ethnic code of law.

The fact that the two kinds of teaching, namely, narrative and precept, are interwoven into a single integral pattern is preeminently significant. The narrative element of the Pentateuch is centered around the theme of man's obedience to God's will. That obedience is represented as constituting the means to man's self-fulfillment. Man's failure to yield obedience to God is represented as the source of all man's troubles. The precepts constitute what our ancestors believed God expected of the People of Israel as representative of mankind. Divine law is not conveyed as an arbitrarily imposed set of decrees. It is set forth as related to the meaning of human life on earth. That meaning emerges from those events in the career of mankind as a whole, and of Israel in particular, which point to God as the Creator of the world and to man as the crowning purpose of creation.

In addition to being a people-making book, the Pentateuch is a God-revealing book. It reveals those attributes of God which constitute the essence of Godhood: Creator, Redeemer, Lawgiver. Those are the attributes of Cosmic Power which enable man to achieve his destiny as a human being. It also reveals that God's work is far from done, because man keeps on undoing it. God has not yet succeeded, because man has not yet become human. From this emanates the basic contribution of Judaism to the conception of Godhood as manifesting itself primarily in the history of man.

The point in Biblical religion is that God, to be God, needs not only the world but also man, much as the artist needs his creation, or the artisan his handiwork. The mutuality between God and his creation, whether it be the world or man, though not co-ordinate, is nevertheless real. God's relationship to them figures in Scripture as being in the form of a covenant.

Before the Torah was promulgated, the need to integrate human life and give it meaning was felt only sporadically by a few individual saints or thinkers. The Torah represents the first conscious attempt on a large scale to read and understand the destiny of human life in order to learn the direction which man's efforts should take. The Torah is the first product of the awareness that the purpose of religion should be the salvation of the entire man, and of human life as a whole.

The origin and nature of things interested the authors of the Torah primarily from the standpoint of the relation of those things to man's destiny. Likewise with the origin and nature of the world. The main purpose of the opening chapter of the Torah is not to give an account of creation but to teach that the world, as God created it, is a fit place for man to achieve his godlikeness, or salvation.

All ancient peoples except Israel looked to various deities as the source of whatever kind of power they needed. One deity gave power over nature, another over enemies, etc. But to our ancestors, the God of Israel was the only source of all kinds of power, because their spiritual leaders taught them to use power as a means to the achievement of human destiny, and to look to the God of Israel alone as the ordainer of human destiny. That is the real meaning of Jewish monotheism. Its classic formulation is: "God created the world." In the Torah, creation is not a metaphysical but a soterical truth, or a truth which has to do with man's salvation.

Hence *it is not what the Torah text itself teaches that should constitute for us Torah, but what it impels us to affirm as a means of salvation.* What we so affirm may be the very antithesis of what the Torah teaches, yet since we are impelled to do so by the very aim of the Torah as a whole, we are merely extending its scope as did the *Tannaim* and *Amoraim* of old. This is simply another case of the principle that the law is sometimes fulfilled through the very suspension of it *(Bittulah shel torah zehu yissudah)*. The text may state laws and beliefs which we have long outgrown. In recognizing that fact, we necessarily stress the ideas and standards to which we have grown up and which, assumedly, reflect progress in the understanding of salvation.

Even if the standard we choose to live by deviates from the one prescribed in the Torah, so long as that standard is in keeping with the fundamental purpose of the Torah, it is as much entitled to be considered Torah as the rabbinic and philosophic interpretations which read into the Torah a great deal that was not there. The only alternatives to that procedure are either no Torah or some new Torah. The first alternative is unthinkable, because it would put an end to the Jewish People. The second alternative is unthinkable, because it would destroy the spiritual continuity of the Jewish People. We must therefore resort to the evolutionary conception of the Torah as an ongoing process.

That conception, however, is bound to appear labored and artificial, unless we take into account one of the fundamental principles on which the Torah is based—namely, that *God is to be sought in the history of man's effort to learn the meaning of salvation and in the striving to attain it.* In the light of that principle, the very distance we have travelled away from those beginnings which are recorded in the Torah should be treated as history of that kind. The slightest moral or spiritual advance which any law, institution or event recorded in the Torah reflects should be noted as constituting the initial leap into a new dimension of human evolution. But the advance since the one recorded in the Torah should figure equally as Torah, for it marks the growth which the Jewish People has achieved in its efforts to apprehend the meaning of salvation and salvation's God. This is what we mean by saying in our prayers: the Torah is "our life and the length of our days."

Notes

Notes

Chapter I

1. The term "Traditional Judaism" is chosen deliberately in preference to the term "normative Judaism" which has acquired considerable popularity ever since it was coined by George Foot Moore in his classic work *Judaism* (Judaism, Cambridge 1927, 3 Vols). In the first place Moore identifies "normative Judaism" with the beliefs and practices which have become standard since the days of the ancient Rabbis. It ignores the significance of "peoplehood" and the cultural social structure which constituted the framework within which Jewish life functioned. Secondly, there is an implication in the term "normative" which is challenged by the approach in this book. An evolving civilization is one which consists of different stages. Each stage is different both in form and content from the one that precedes and the one that follows it. It is normative only for those who live within it. If, however, we insist upon regarding one stage more authoritative than any other, then the proto-Judaism of the Bible deserves to be regarded as normative rather than Rabbinic Judaism.

2. B. M. 86a.

3. Rashbam, B. B. 130b.

4. Cf. Maimonides' Commentary, Mishnah Sanhedrin, Ch. X, principle 8.

5. Major Trends in Jewish Mysticism, Jerusalem, 1946, p. 313.

6. That development reflected the worsening attitude of Western Christendom toward the Jews in its midst. The more pressure the Christians exerted against participation of the Jews in the life around them, the more inward and parochial the life of the Jews grew and the more they were thrown on their own spiritual resources. This was the case with Jewish mysticism of the Middle Ages, which seemed to ignore the intellectual challenge of non-Jewish thinkers and to concentrate on exploring to the full the resources of the Jewish tradition. In fact, any intimation of reckoning with secular culture was resented as an affront to Judaism.

7. Cf. Midrash Esther Rabbati III, In the Mishnah (Ketubot VII, 6) there occurs the term "dat Moshe v'yehudit." It does not mean Jewish religion, but Jewish custom.

8. B. B. 15a.

9. Deut. 32:39.

10. Sifrē Deut., Haazinu, ed. Friedmann, Wien, 1864, par. 329.

11. Rabbinic Anthology, C. G. Montefiore and H. Loewe, London, 1938, p. 10.

12. Judah Hallevi's Kitab Al Khazari, tr. by H. Hirschfeld, London, 1906, II, p. 16.

13. Sanhed. XI, 1.

14. Cf. Cant. R. on 1:2.

15. Ps. 113: 5,6.

16. Sifrē, Deut., ed. Friedmann, 357.

17. Sanh. 99a, Sifrē, Num., ed. Friedmann, par. 112.

18. Gittin 60a The attempt of apologists to find in this statement an anticipation of the decumentary theory of the Pentateuch is entirely unwarranted.

19. Ibid. and Meg. 27a.

20. Ned. 22b.

21. Jer. Meg. Ch. I, Hal. 5.

22. Cant. R. on 1.2; Maim. Introd. to Commentary on Mishnah Zeraim.

23. Shab. 31a.

24. Cf. Pesik, R. ed. Buber, "Hanukkah," Ch. V, and Jer. Peah., Ch. II, Hal. 4.

25. Sifrē, Deut., ed. Friedmann, ar. 345; cf. Pesik, R., ed. Buber, Lyck, 1868 ch V, 36.

26. Sifrē Deut., ed. Friedmann, par. 47.

27. Cf. Joseph Albo, Sefer Ha-Ikkarim, tr. by Isaac Husik, Phila., 1929, Vol. IV. p. 290.

28. Sanh. X, 1.

29. Is. 60:21.

30. Note: During the last century of the, Second Commonwealth (30 B.C.E.—70 C.E.) the two eschatological beliefs—the one concerning the advent of the Messiah and the other concerning the resurrection and the establishment of the "Kingdom of Heaven"—were blended in the minds of the Jews who did not belong to the Sadducees or the ruling class. That blending is reflected in the Synoptic Gospels, and throws light upon the role of Jesus as he himself and his disciples viewed it.

31. Authorized Daily Prayer Book, trans, by S. Singer. London, 1929, p. 74.

32. Note: Recently a scientific study was made of Jewish life as it was lived in small Jewish towns of Eastern Europe before World War II, while they still retained the structure and character that had been stamped on them by centuries of Traditional Judaism. That study was conducted as part of the Columbia University Research in Contemporary Cultures, begun during World War II and completed in 1949. The outcome is the book Life is With People, N. Y., 1952. There we get an authentic picture of Traditional Judaism as a way of life, with its strains and stresses, when it first felt the shock of modernity.

33. The following letter speaks for itself. For the copy of it I am indebted to Dr. Moshe Davis.

WILLIAM AND PINE STREETS

New York, March 18th, 1910.

Kuhn, Loeb & Co.

My dear Judge Sulzberger:

Since you were good enough to write me so fully recently your views of the Wengeroff Memoirs, I have finished reading the second volume, and I cannot but agree with you in all you say as to the certain danger of placing these Memoirs in the hands of the younger American Jewish generation, with the effect they will no doubt have of impressing younger people that change of faith is permissible, or at least pardonable, when opportunity makes this advisable. As far as I am concerned, I therefore no longer urge the publication of the Memoirs thru the Jewish Publication Society.

With assurances of regard, believe me,

Yours faithfully,

J. Schiff

(In handwriting)

Dear Judge,

Mr. Schiff shows his usual good sense.

C. A.

Hon. Mayer Sulzberger

1303 Girard Avenue

Philadelphia, Pa.

34. The Memoirs of Glueckel of Hameln, tr. from the Judeo-German by M. Lowenthal, Harper. N.Y. 1932.

35. Ibid. pp. 266-267.

36. Ibid. p. 19-20.

37. Ibid. p. 93.

38. "Memoirs of a Jewess" in Studies in Judaism, Second Series, Phila., 1908, p. 139.

39. Ibid. p. 43.

40. Yoma 9b.

41. Memoirs of a Jewess, p.1.

42. Solomon Maimon: An Autobiography, tr. from the German by C. Murray, London, 1888.

43. Ibid. 154.

44. Ibid. 25.

45. Ibid.

46. Ibid. 26.

47. Ibid. 43.

48. Ibid. 13.

49. Ibid. 180.

50. Ibid. 123.

51. Ibid. 130-131.

52. *Ibid.* Ch. XX.
53. Pauline Wengeroff, Memoiren ciner Grossmutter, Berlin 1908.
54. *Ibid.*, II, 134.
55. *Ibid.*, p. 5.
56. *Ibid.*, p. 135.
57. *Ibid.* II, p. 38.
58. Shmarya Levin, Youth in Revolt, tr. by Maurice Samuel, N.Y. 1930.
59. *Ibid.*, p. 3.
60. *Ibid.*, p. 44.
61. *Ibid.*, p. 209.
62. "Reflections on Traditional Jewish Education," in *Jewish Education*, Vol. 8, no. 2.
63. Shmarya Levin, *op. cit.*, p. 225.
64. Russian-Jewish writer born 1842, died 1884. Fought religious obscurantism and sought to reawaken the Hebraic national spirit of the Jews.

Chapter II

1. Gen. 12:2.
2. B.B. 60b.
3. Pes. 116b.
5. Shavuot 39a.
5. Shavuot 39a.
6. Ned. 20a.
7. Cf. B.K. 88a and Mish. Yeb. XI:2.
8. Yeb. 22a, 97b.
9. Sanh. 19 b, Sifrē, ed. Friedmann, Vienna 1948, Deut. par. 34.
10. Ber. 13a.
11. Mish. Ned. III, 11.
12. Betza 32b.
13. Letter to Jost, 1841, Iggeret Shadal V 660, quoted by Salo Baron, A Social and Religious History of the Jews, N.Y. 1937, Vol. II, p. 228.
14. Deut. 7:8.
15. Singer, Authorized Daily Prayer Book, p. 74.
16. Ezk. 34:31, cf. Yeb. 61a.
17. Gen. R. Ch. 1, 4; Ex. R. Ch. 38, 4.
18. Yeb. 38a; Midrash Tanhuma, ed. Buber, p. 55, par. 3.
19. Lam. 1:9.
20. Lev. 16:16.
21. Yoma 57a.
22. Cant. 8:7.
23. Cant. R. ad loc.
24. Ps. 4:3.

25. Mid. Ps. on 4:3.
26. Lam. 3:21.
27. Mid. Lam. R. ad loc.
28. Lev. 26:9.
29. Cf. the dialogue between Roman Christian official and R. Meir, quoted by Bacher in Agadot ha-Tannaim, ed. Rabinowitz, Berlin 1922, Vol. II, Part I. p. 20.
30. Deut. 6:4.
31. Sifrē, Deut. ed. Friedmann, Vienna 1948, par 31.
32. Ezk. 36:22-23.
33. Is. 56:1.
34. Ps. 91:15.
35. Zek. 9:9.
36. Ex. R. ch. 30, par. 24.
37. Mekilta, ed. Lauterbach, Philadelphia 1939, on Ex 12:1.
38. Lev. 18:26-28.
39. Is. 2:2-3, Mic. 4:2.
40. Cf. Yehezkel Kaufman, Golah v' Nekar, Vol. I, ch. 10.
41. Lev. 25:38.
42. I Sam. 26:19.
43. Ket. 110b.
44. Deut. 11:31-32.
45. Sifrē ad loc.
46. Ket. 111a.
47. Sifrē on Deut. 11:17.
48. Horiot 3a.
49. Maimonides, Yad, Hilkot Shegagot, ch. 13, 2.
50. Cf. Judah Hallevi, Kitab Al Khazari tr. by H. Hirschfeld, London, 1906 II, 10, 12, 16, 29-30, and Nahmanides' Comment. on Gen. 26:5, Lev. 18:25, Deut. 4:5, 4:28, 11:18, 17:2.
51. R. Bachya ben Asher, Biur al ha-Torah, Amsterdam 1726, Lek Leka, p. 29 b.
52. Cf. Cecil Roth, A Life of Menasseh ben Israel, Phila. 1934, p. 207.
53. Judah Hallevi, op. cit. II, 24.
54. II Sam. 23:1.
55. I Ki. 8:25.
56. Hos. 8:4.
57. Hos. 3:5.
58. Is. 7:13.
59. Is. 11:1-10.
60. Lam. 4:20.
61. Ps. 89:20-47.
62. Israel Digest, N.Y. June 15, 1956.
63. I Ki. 8:15-20.
64. II Sam. 24:18-25 I Chr. 21:18-30.

65. Is. 10:24-27, 37:33-35.

66. Jer. 7:4.

67. Ps. 137:4.

68. Mekilta, ed. Lauterbach II pp. 78 sq.

69. Mid. Tanhuma, ed. Buber, p. 39b, par. 10.

70. Cf. G.F. Moore, Judaism in the First Centuries of the Christian Era, Cambridge 1927, Vol. II, pp. 14-15.

71. Cf. Lev. R. on Lev. 1:8; Abot d. R. Nathan, ed. S. Schechter, N.Y. 1945, Vers. A, Ch. IV.

72. Ket. 10b.

73. Ber of Bolechow, Zikronot, Berlin 1922, p. 62.

74. Shmarya Levin, Childhood in Exile, trans. by Maurice Samuel, N.Y. 1929, p. 213.

75. Quoted by Carlton Hayes in Essays on Nationalism, N.Y. 1933, p. 53.

76. Ibid. p. 16.

77. This does not refer to the counting by years. For a number of centuries Jews made use of what is known as the minyan shetarot or Seleucidean Calendar, in which 311 B.C.E. was for the Jews the year 1.

78. Memoiren, p. 186.

79. Jer. Peah II, 4.

80. Deut. 6:7.

81. Ned. 81a.

82. Ab. 1:1.

83. B. B. 21a.

84. Maimonides, Yad, Hilkot Talmud Torah, Ch II, 1-5.

85. M. Guedeman, Hatorah v'Hayyim, Warsaw, 1896, I, pp. 72-80.

86. Cf. S. Bernfeld, Toledot ha-Reformatzion, Warsaw 1908, p. 10.

87. Ab. VI:4.

88. Cf. Zikronotai, Warsaw, 1895, 40f.

89. Ab. I:2.

90. Cf. Y'ven Metzula, Nathan Hanover, Venice 1653, and Pinkos shel Vaadē ha-Kehilot Haroshoyot be-Medinat Lita, Berlin 1925.

91. Salo Baron, Menorah Journal, Vol. XIV, p. 519.

92. Git. 88b.

93. Quoted by A.A. Neuman, The Jews in Spain, Phila. 1942, Vol. I, p. 14.

94. Kad ha-Kemah, Warsaw ed., 1878, quoted by I. Bettan in Studies in Jewish Preaching, Cincinnati, 1939, p. 331.

95. Cf. Ba-er Hetev on Orah Hayyim LIII, 25, in reference to civil courts, also Ber. 6a.

96. Shmarya Levin, Childhood in Exile, tr. by Maurice Samuel, N.Y. 1929, p. 194.

97. Ibid., p. 140.

98. Solomon Maimon, Autobiography, tr. by C. Murray, London, 1888, p. 155.

99. Solomon Maimon's Lebensgeschichte, ed. Jacob Fromer, Munich 1911, pp. 107-8.

100. Charles A. Ellwood, Reconstruction of Religion, N.Y. 1922, p. 193.

101. D.M. Schochet, The Jewish Court in the Middle Ages, N.Y. 1931, p. 137.

102. Cf. "Rashi" by Solomon Zeitlin, in A.J.Y.B. Vol. 41, Phila., 1939, p. 120.

103. Claude G. Montefiore and H. Loewe, London 1938, A Rabbinic Anthology, London, 1938, Introd. p. XIII.

104. A. Z., 19b.

105. I.H. Weiss, op. cit., pp. 79-80.

106. Takkanot Rabbenu Tam and his Associates, at the end of the the Responsa of R. Meir of Rothenberg, ed. Prague, and at the end of Kol Bo 117. Cf. Joseph Jacobs, Jews in Angevin England, N.Y. 1893, pp. 47-49.

107. I. Abrahams, J.Q.R. III, 310.

108. Cf. The Memoirs of Ber of Bolechov, transl, by Wishnitzer.

109. Nathan Hanover, in Yeven Metzula, quoted by S. M. Dubnow, History of the Jews in Russia and Poland, tr. from the Russian by I. Friedlaender, Phila., 1916, p. 111.

110. Cf. Solomon Schechter, Some Aspects of Rabbinic Theology, N. Y. 1909, Ch. VI, "The Kingdom of God," pp. 101-2.

111. Mekilta, ed. Lauterbach, Vol. I, p. 6.

112. Ibid., p. 4.

113. Singer, Authorized Prayer Book, p. 48.

114. Is. 126.

115. Author. Prayer Book, p. 46.

116. Meg. 29b.

117. Ber. 34b, Sanh. 99a, Pes. 68a.

118. Sanh. 98a.

119. Is. 60:22.

120. Cant. R. VIII, 12.

120a. Sanh. 97b.

121. Cant. 2:7.

122. Cant. R. on Cant. 2:7.

123. For a contrary view see G.F. Moore, Judaism, Vol. II, p. 371.

124. Dan. 7:27.

125. Cf. Gen R. 68, 14.

126. Cf. Cant. R. on Cant. 2:7.

127. Author. Prayer Book p. 234, Cf. also p. 161.

128. Yom. 86b; cf. Sanh. 97b, 98a.

129. Author. Prayer Book, p. 76.

130. Sanh. 98b.

131. Jer. Ber. Ch. II:Hal 4.

132. Dan. 12:1, 9:24, 26.

133. Cf. Moore, Judaism II, p. 361, J. Klausner, Ha-Rayon ha-Meshihi, Tel Aviv 1956, II p. 215-232.
134. Sanh. 97a, Yom. 10a, Der. Er. Zuta, ch. 10, Pesikta R. ed. Friedmann, Vienna 1863, ch. 15, p. 67, Cant. R. on Cant. 2:13.
135. Deut. 32:36.
136. Sanh. 97a.

The Messianic hope goes back to the early centuries of the First Commonwealth. It was then designated as "The Day of the Lord," and signified the universal recognition of YHWH as God, as a consequence of the greatness and prosperity that would be attained by Israel. Though the Prophets, beginning with Amos changed it to mean the Day of Judgment, when God would summon to judgment the wicked among all the peoples, including those in Israel, the original meaning—that of ultimate vindication of God's elect—was retained.

The concluding chapter in Daniel, the theme of which is "the end of days," marks a new development in the conception of the Messianic hope: the promise of bodily resurrection. (cf. Dan. 12:2-3). This development of the idea concerning "the end of days" finds considerable scope in the Apocryphal literature, of which *Daniel* is the only book that was included in the Canon (cf. Enoch 25: 5; 51:1; 90:33; Jubilees 23:30; Macc. 7:6, 9, 23). In the rest of that literature which was excluded from the Canon, the elements of mystery and supernaturalism figure even more prominently. All these ideas concerning the coming of the Messiah, the world cataclysm, the resurrection and the Kingdom of Heaven—became part of a single eschatological pattern. As such a pattern it figures in the New Testament.

It would be a mistake, however, to regard the figure of the Messiah as occupying a place in the pattern of national redemption analogous to that occupied by Christ in the Christian pattern of salvation. In a class by itself, and therefore unrepresentative of Rabbinic Judaism, is the description of the Messiah given in the Palestinian Aggadah which emanated from the school of R. Yohanan bar Napaha and R. Joshua ben Levi of the 4th century of the common era.

Their thinking had been influenced by the assumption that the world to come and the Messianic age were virtually synchronous. That assumption was closely related to the apocalyptic view of the Messiah which had flourished among Palestinian Jews before the Hadrianic persecutions. It belongs to the mythical type of Midrash literature.

According to that apocalyptic view, the Messiah was created at the same time as the world. When God foresaw what would happen to the Messiah, he stored away for him the original light of creation. Satan, curious to know for whom the light was being stored away, besought God to tell him. Thereupon God replied "For him who will bring shame upon you." "Let me see him," said Satan. When he beheld the Messiah he shook with fear and fell on his face and said: "Surely this is Messiah who will cast me and the heavenly princes of the nations into Gehinnom."

The Midrash then proceeds to record the dialogue that will take place between God and the Messiah. Says God: "The sins of your contemporaries will bring you under an iron yoke, and you will become like a blinded calf and your spirit will be broken."

'Will this suffering last many years?' asks the Messiah.

'A week of years' replies God. 'If your soul is grieved, I am ready to destroy them forthwith.'

'O Master of the world,' answers the Messiah, 'with utmost rejoicing am I ready to endure the suffering to be inflicted on me, only that no Jew shall perish.'

'Not only shall the living be saved, but all who have died since Adam,' replies God.

Then God appoints the Hayyot to carry the throne of the Messiah. (Pesik R. ed. Friedmann, Wien, 1880, pp. 161-162).

Even if we were to deny any Christological influence as responsible for the notion that the Messiah suffered for the sins of mankind, the foregoing description of the Messiah may undoubtedly be traced to the same type of thinking as gave rise to the Christian conception of the Messiah. According to that type of thinking, the Messiah was expected to usher in a new world order, in which all the imperfections of the present world will have been eliminated.

It is said that, with the coming of the Messiah, the world will be rid of whatever corruption it suffered as a result of Adam's sin and will be restored to its original state of perfection. (Gen. R. XII, 6).

We should therefore not be surprised that in course of time this type of thinking gradually disappeared from Jewish life, except in those circles where mysticism kept alive the original apocalyptic notions concerning the Messiah. In Traditional Judaism of the authoritative type, however, the Messiah is merely the concrete symbol of Israel's nationhood. He derives his significance from that fact and not from any supernatural qualities of his own. This may explain why he lost the aura of semidivinity which he began to take on in the Book of Daniel and in most of the apocryphal writings (Daniel 7:3-14). Though he came to be conceived as possessing extraordinary powers of mind and spirit, he nevertheless was thought of as no more than human. Even those extraordinary powers are given him by God to qualify him for his mission, and do not represent intrinsic traits of his own. All this implies that to grasp the full significance of the Messianic advent, we should note what it implied in terms of national redemption. That redemption is the theme of one of the thrice-repeated daily prayers which reads thus: Sound the great horn (as a signal) for our freedom; lift up the standard for the assembling of our exiles. Blessed be thou, O Lord who gatherest the disperesed of Israel. (Auth. Prayer Book, p. 48).

Chapter III

1. Deut. 24:16.
2. II Ki. 14:6.
3. Ezk. 18:2.
4. II Sam. 24:15.
5. I Chr. 21:17.
6. Ps. 92:7-8.
7. Jer. 12:1-2.
8. Hab. 1:13-17.
9. Cf. Ju. 15:18; I Sam. 4:3; 7:8; 14:45; II Sam. 8:14.
10. Ex. 15:1.
11. Sanh. 91b.
12. Kid. 39b.
13. A tanna of the second century, Ab. IV:21.
14. Cf. Moed Katan 9b.
15. Ber. 28b.
16. Mekilta, Lauterbach, Vol. II p. 120.
17. Sanh. X:1.
18. Ab. I:2.
19. Ab. II:8.
20. Ab. II:19.
21. Ab. III:21.
22. Ab. III:20.
23. Ab. IV:21.
24. A.Z. 4b.
25. Ber. 57b.
26. A.Z. 3a.
27. Ber. 17a.
28. Cf. Ab. d'R.N. 28:4.
29. See above, p. 66.
30. Comment. on Mishnah, Sanh. X:1.
31. Author. Prayer Book, p. 129.
32. Commentary by Theodore on Gen R. 74:1, Berlin 1912.
33. B.B. 122a.
34. Is. 7:21-25; 11:6-16; 25:1-8; and most of chs. 40-66.
35. Ezk. 34:11-31; 36:1-2; 22-38; chs. 37-44.
36. Ber. 17a.
37. B.B. 58, Gen. R. ch. 8, par. 1.
38. Albo, Ikkarim, ed. Husik, Phila. 1929. Vol. IV, ch. 31, p. 311.
39. Deut. 7:11.
40. Cf. Erub. 22a; Kid. 39b; Mek. on Ex. 31:12; Ex. R. ch. 52, par. 3.
41. Is. 30:26.
42. Ernst Cassirer, An Essay on Man, New Haven, 1944 p. 84.

43. Sifrē, ed. Friedmann, Deut. p. 138b, par. 323.

44. Pesikta R., ed. Buber 76a; Koh. R. III, 16.

45. Shab. 55a.

46. Gen. R. XVI, 6.

47. Mek. ed. Lauterbach, Vol. II, p. 271.

48. J. Albo, Ikkarim, ed. Husik, IV, ch. 41, p. 399.

49. Mek. Vol. II p. 272; A.Z. 5a.

50. Gen. R. IX, 6-7.

51. According to R. Eleazar b. Pedat (Jer. Shab. XIV Hal. 3) "ninety-nine die of the diseases of the gall, and one by the hand of heaven." That is wrongly interpreted to mean that ninety-nine die a natural death. Such an idea could never have occurred to the Rabbis. The dictum simply reflects R. Pedat's opinion that gall disease is extremely prevalent. He is elsewhere (Lev. R. XVII) wrongly quoted as saying the same about the evil eye (see Bacher, Aggadah der Amoraeer I, 2 in Hebr. transl. p, 25.

52. Cf. Ikkarim IV, pp. 297, 360.

53. Er. 19a.

54. Sifrē, Deut. par. 210.

55. Eliyahu ben R. Abraham of Ismir, Shevet Mussar, ch. 26.

56. Derek Eretz Zuta par. 1.

57. Shab. 33b.

58. Salomon Maimon's Lebensgeschichte, ed. J. Fromer, Munich 1911, p. 90.

59. C. G. Montefiore and H. Loewe, A Rabbinical Anthology, London, 1938, Introd., p. XLIX.

60. Mark Zborowski and Elizabeth Herzog, Life Is With People, N.Y. 1952, Part III, sec. 1.

61. Koran, Sura 2.

62. Al Sharastani, History of Sects, transl. by Haarbruecker, I, p. 231.

63. Cf. S. Baron, Social and Religious History of the Jews, N.Y. 1937 vol. II, p. 45.

64. Cath. Encycl. ed. N.Y. 1908, III, p. 752.

65. Hasting Encyc. Rel. and Eth., N.Y. 1916, VIII, p. 877.

66. "The Religion of the Jews at the Time of Jesus," in The Hebrew College Annual, Vol. I, 1924, p. 310.

67. Tanhuma, ed. Buber, Ex. 95a.

68. Midr. Teh. ed. Buber, Ps. 1, p. 22, par. 21, note 294.

69. Ex. 15:11.

70. Ber. 31b.

71. Cf. Mek. ed. Lauterbach, Vol. II, p. 24. On the question of anthropomorphism, cf. Ab. d 'R.N. version II, ch. 44, p. 123, for Schechter's comment on the saying that some statements about God are expressed euphemistically.

72. Ber. 7a.

73. B.B. 25a.

74. B.B. 58a.

75. Cf. Saadiah, Emunot v'Deot ch.10.
76. Mish. Sanh. VI:5.
77. Cf. Tanhuma on Gen 1:1, par. 4.5.
78. Gen. R. XIX, 4.
79. Meg. 13a, Yalkut on Ex. 18:19, Tanhuma ad loc.
80. Is. 44:6, Ex. R. ch. 29, par. 5.
81. Pes. 56a.
82. Auth. Prayer Book, p. 175e.
83. Tanh. Ex. p. 4b; 40a; Ex. R. ch. 3 par. 6; Pesik. R. ed. Buber. 109b-110a.
84. Deut. 32:39.
85. Is. 44:6.
86. Mek. ed. Lauterbach, Vol. II, p. 31.
87. Sifrē, Deut. p. 132a, par. 306.
88. Hag. 12b.
89. Nid. 31a.
90. Plato's Phaedrus, 246f.
91. Ber. 60b.
92. Author. Prayer Book, p. 5.
93. Ber. 10a.
94. Mid. Teh., ed. Buber, Ps. 103, par 5.
95. Cf. Moore, Judaism, op. cit. I, pp. 371, 373.
96. Gen. R. LXVIII, 9; Mid. Teh. ed. Buber, Ps. 90, par 10.
97. Jer. 23:24.
98. Sifrē, ed. Weiss, Vienna 1862, p. 4a, cf. also Num. R., XII, 4.
99. Claude G. Montefiore and H. Loewe, op. cit. p. 356.
100. Ab. V:8.
101. J. Albo, Ikkarim, op. cit. IV, ch. 8, par. 3.
103. Mek. ed. Lauterbach, Vol. I, pp. 208-209.
104. Is. 41:14.
105. Mek. ibid.
106. Gen. R. ed. Theodore, IX, 3 p. 69; XIV, 3, p. 128.
107. Ab. IV:29.
108. Ab. III:20.
109. Hullin 7b.
110. Yom. 87b.
111. Gen. R. XII, 15.
112. Gen. R.
113. Job 23:13.
114. Gen. R. XXI, 5.
115. I. Bettan, Studies in Jewish Preaching, Cincinnati, 1939, p. 311.
116. Ibid., p. 332; cf. elaborate comment on Deut. 32:4 in Sifrē; also M. Lazarus, Ethics of Judaism, transl. by H. Szold, Philadelphia, 1908-1, pp. 170, 176.
117. Ex. 33:113.

118. Ber. 7a.
119. Ps. 92:9.
120. Ps. 101:1.
121. Job 1:21.
122. Lev. R. XXIV, 2.
123. Ber. IX:5.
124. Ber. 60b.
125. M. Higger, Masseket Semahot, N.Y. 1931, end.
126. Gen. R. III, 9.
127. Mek. ed. Lauterbach, Vol. I, p. 196, Vol. II, p. 178; Gen. R. XX, 9.
128. Author. Prayer Book, p. 45.
129. Ex. 34:6-7.
130. R.H. 17b.
131. Meg. 31a.
132. Deut. 10:17.
133. Tanh. ed. Buber, p. 42b.
134. Gen. R. XXXIX, 6.
135. Gen. R. VIII, 5.
136. Judah Hallevi, op. cit. II, 2.
137. Hos. II:8-9.
138. Ex. R. VI, 2.
139. Sifrē, Num. par. 134.
140. Ps. 25:11. Mid. Teh. ed. Buber, on Ps. XIX, par. 17, p. 86b.
141. T.J. Krotoshin, Peah, 15d; cf. also Gen. R. XXV, 16.
142. Prov. 8:11.
143. Sifrē Deut. par. 33, p. 74.
144. Men. 99b.
145. Cant. R. on Cant. 1:10.
146. Seder Eliyahu Rab, ed. Friedman, Vienna 1898, p. 8.
147. Mid. Teh. on Ps. 30, par. 17, p. 118b.
148. Lev. R. VII, 3.
149. Sifrē on Deut. 11:13.
150. Ber. 63b, cf. also Cant. R. on 2:5.
151. Sifrē, Deut. par. 58, p. 87.
152. Ab. VI:2.
153. Ab. IV:12.
154. Sanh. 7a, Yom. 35b.
155. Ab. II:5.
156. Ab. III:3.
157. Ab. III:4.
158. T. J. Krotoshin, Shab. 15a.
159. Ber. 5a.
160. Sifrē, Deut. par. 34, p. 74.
161. Jos. 1:8.
162. Men. 99b.

163. Sifrē, Deut. 43, p. 81b; Hag. 5b, 9b, 12b; B.B. 79a.
164. Ab. V:25.
165. Num. R. XII, 9.
166. Koh. R. I, 13; cf. also analogies in Lev. R. XIX, 1.
167. Ab. VI:4.
168. Lev. R. XIX, 1.
169. Num. 19:14.
170. Shab. 83b.
171. Ab. VI:6.
172. Erub. 54a; B.M. 85a.
173. Peah I.1.
174. Cant. R. on Cant. 5:14, par. 3.
175. Ber. 5a, Erub. 54a.
176. Sifrē, Deut. par. 45, p. 82b.
177. Ber. 5a, Gen. R. XXII, 6.
178. Ab. d'R. Nath. ch. 20.
179. Ibid. ch. 34; Kid. 30b; Suk. 52b.
180. Ab. VI:2.
181. Sifrē, Num. par. 119, p. 39b.
182. Num. R. XIII, 16 and comment by RDL; B.K. 38a; Sifrā ed. H. Weiss, ch. 13, par. 13.
183. Yalkut Teh. I, 614.
184. Koh. R. IX, 9.
185. Mek. on Exod. 16:4, cf. Mid. Teh. on Ps. 1, par. 16.
186. Shab. 11a.
187. Men. 99b.
188. Cf. also statement of Bar Kappara in Mid. Teh. Ps. 1, par. 17, p. 86.
189. Pr. 3:18.
190. Lev. R. XXV, 2.
191. Deut. 11:19.
192. Ber. 17a.
193. A.Z. 3b.
194. Ab. I:17.
195. Ab. III:10.
196. Ab. III:22.
197. Kid. 40a; cf, also Deut. R. on Deut. 11:6.
198. Ab. IV:6.
199. Ab. VI:5.
200. Deut. R. VII, 4.
201. A.Z. 17b; note Rashi's rather strained interpretation.
202. Ab. I:3.
203. Ber. 17a.
204. J. Albo, Ikkarim, op. cit., Vol. III, 28, par. 7.
205. Cf. R. Nathan in Sifrē, Num. 115 on Num. 15:41.
206. Num. R. on Num. 19:6, pars. 1 and 4.

207. Naz. 23b.
208. Ab. V:23.
209. Judah Hallevi, op cit. I, 62-63.
210. Tanh. Gen. ed. Stettin, 1864, p. 140.
121. Cant. R. on Cant. 4:1.
212. Tanh. Num. ed. Stettin, p. 542.
213. Sot. 5a.
214. Sanh. 92a.
215. Sotah 41a.
216. Lev. R. IX, 3.
217. Ps. 15:1-2, 24:3-4.
218. Yeb. 79a.
219. Sifrē, Deut. ch. 36, p. 75b.

Chapter IV

1. Gershom G. Sholem, Major Trends in Jewish Mysticism, N.Y. 1946, p. 23.

2. Maimonides, Guide for the Perplexed, tr. by M. Friedländer, London, 1910, Part II, ch. 22.

3. Ibid. Part I, ch. 71.

4. Cf. Lev. R. ch. I. par. 1.

5. Maimonides, Guide, Part II, Chs. 36-39; Ibn Daud, Ha-Emannah ha-Ramah, ed. G. Weil, Frankfurt a/M, 1852, p. 73.

6. Maimonides, Guide, Part II, ch. 25 end.

7. Levi ben Gershom, Milhamot Hashem, Berlin 1923, Part II, ch. 12.

8. Cf. Pes. 119a; Sanh. 21b; Rashi, Shab. 120a.

9. Cf. Abraham Ibn Daud, op. cit., p. 102.

10. Cf. I. H. Weiss, Zikronotai, pp. 61, 71.

11. Teshubot ha-Rama, pp. 6-7.

12. She 'elot u-Teshuvot, Bayit Hadash IV, Frankfurt, 1697, Question 4.

13. Yam shel Shlomo, Stettin, 1857, Introd. to Hullin.

14. R. Heschel Levin, Aliyot Eliyahu, quoted by S. Dubnow, Toledot ha-Hasidut, Tel-Aviv, pp. 30-34.

15. Article on "Vitebsk" in Habitzaron Vol. II no. 3.

16. Maim. Yad ha-Hazakah, Hilkot T'shuvah, ch. III, par. 7.

17. Zohar, ed. Jerusalem, 5716, III, 49 b.

18. R. Moses Isserles, Torat ha-Olah, Lemberg 1858, III, 94.

19. R. Solomon Luria, She'elot u-Teshuvot Maharshal, Question 98.

20. Zohar, tr. by Harry Sperling and Maurice Simon, London, 1931, p. 47.

21. G. G. Scholem, op. cit., p. 277.

22. Maimonides, Guide, Part III, ch. 12.

23. Gen. R. X, 6.

24. Cf. E. Schuerer, Geschichte des Jüdischen Volkes im Zeitalter Jesu Christi, 4th ed. II, 651-680, and E. Zeller, Die Philosophie der Griechen, Driete Auf. III, Teil 2, 283-285.

25. Abot VI:1.

26. Cf. Mishnah Hag. II:1.

27. Shab. 30b; Pes. 117a.

28. In the parallel passage in Mid. Teh. (ed. Buber, Vilna 1891) on 24:3, p. 204, the term ruah hakodesh is used instead of Shekinah.

29. Abot III:7.

30. Cf. G. Scholem, op. cit., pp. 41, 47.

31. Mek. I, 252.

32. Sota 20a.

33. Ber. 17a.

34. Cant. R. I, 4.

35. Shab. 67a.

36. Pes. 55a.

37. Jewish Encyclopedia, VIII, p. 256.

38. Hag. 15b.

39. Scholem, op. cit., Notes p. 358.

40. Kid. 71a; J. Yoma, III, 40d; Koh. R. III, 11.

41. Sanh. 65b, 67b.

42. Sanh. 65b, 67b; cf. also Abot d'R. Nathan, XXXIX, ed. Schechter p. 116.

43. Is. 59:2.

44. Ber. 55a, cf. statement concerning Bezalel.

45. Is. 43:28.

46. Cant. R. I, 5.

47. II Sam. 23:3.

48. M.K. 16b.

49. Kid. 71a, J. Yoma III, 40d, Koh. R. on Koh. III, 11.

50. Sifrē, ed. Friedman, p. 357.

51. Pes. 119a., Abot VI:1.

52. Hag. 14b.

53. Judah Hallevi, op cit., IV, 25.

54. Jewish Encyclopedia, XII, p. 603.

55. G. Scholem, op. cit., p. 92.

56. Cf. ibid. p. 89.

57. Cf. R. Hayyim Vital, Sefer ha-Gilgulim, Vilna, 1885, p. 136. Shevet Mussar, Vienna 1864, XIV, 14.

58. Introd. by J. Abelson to translation of The Zohar, London 1931 p. XXIV.

59. M.K. 16b.

60. Cf. Raphael Mahler, Der Kamf zwischen Haskoloh un Hasidus in Galitzie, N.Y. 1942, p. 107.

61. Ibid. p. 80.

62. Harav Mi-Ladi, M. Teitelbaum, Warsaw, 1910.

63. Joseph Weiss, Erke ha-Yahadut, Tel Aviv, 1953, p. 81, ff.
64. Martin Buber, Hasidism, N.Y. 1948, p. 1.
65. Ibid. p. 1.
66. Ps. 34:9.
67. Hul. 92a.
68. Yalkut Shimeoni, Vayigash. 133; Lev. R. ch. 36. par. 2.

Chapter V

1. On a question like the one whether a subject had a right to slay an unjust ruler John of Salisbury advised that the subject should refrain from using poison, because there was no precedent in the Bible for that method of tyrannicide. When Thomas Petrucci published a book on adrenal glands in 1675, he deemed it necessary to quote a text from Leviticus in support of his discovery (cf. A History of Medical Psychology, by G. Zilboorg, N.Y. 1941, p. 250). That frame of mind still persisted in the middle of the twentieth century in those pockets of civilization in which the spirit of the Bible was dominant. In 1958, the South African whites voted into power as Prime Minister Hendrik Verwoerd, a racist who in Hitler's days had been an avowed pro-Nazi and anti-Semite. The irony of it was that he was a pillar of the Calvinist Reformed Church and cited the Old Testament to support the policy of Apartheid, the segregation of the black and colored—or mixed—races from the white race.

2. The Social Contract, tr. by Hafner, p. 123.

3. Louis Biancolli, The Mozart Handbook, N.Y. 1954, p. 80.

4. Emile Durkheim, Suicide, Etude de Sociologie, Paris 1897, pp. 272-288.

5. F.I. Baer has drawn a parallel between R. Judah ha-Hasid (died 1217) and his Christian contemporary St. Francis of Assisi, Cf. Tziyon Vol. III, 1938, pp. 37-40.

6. G. Scholem, op. cit., p. 83.

7. Quoted by S. Dubnow, Toledot ha-Hasidut, Tel Aviv 1932, p. 14.

8. Stuart Chase, in I Believe, N.Y. 1939, pp. 61-69.

9. R.M. MacIver, "The Pattern of Social Change" in Authority and the Individual, Cambridge, Mass., 1937, p. 150.

10. M. Buber, Tales of the Hasidim: The Later Masters, N.Y., 1948, p. 249.

11. Cf. W. Stark, The History of Economics in its Relation to Social Development, London, 1944, p. 9.

12. Preface in M. Samuels' translation of Mendelssohn's Jerusalem, Vol. I, p. 80.

13. R.H. 25b.

14. Cf. Aristotle, Phys. III, 1.

15. Quoted by Jan St. Lewinski, The Founders of Political Economy, London, 1922, p. 23.

16. F.J. Mather, Jr., A History of Italian Paintings, N.Y. 1923, Ch. I.

17. Lewis Mumford, Technics and Civilization, N.Y. 1934, p. 129.

18. Gotthold E. Lessing, Erziehung des Menschengeschlechts, tr. by F.W. Robertson, London, 4th ed. 1896.

Chapter VI

1. In the Archive de la Gironde in Bordeaux there is the Journal of the Bordeaux Jewish Community. The closing entry of that Journal dated February 18, 1790, reads as follows: "Les Juifs de Bordeaux ne pouvent plus être considérés corps de Nation. Comme corps de Nation, l' Assembleé des anciens qui les representaient s'est aussitôt dissoute, et l'on s'est occupé immediatement de la formation d'une association de bien faisance." The date of this concluding entry was the day after the Bordeaux delegation to the Paris Assemblée returned bearing the decree of January 28, 1790 which fully emancipated the Spanish-Portuguese Jews in France. (For the contents of this note I am indebted to Rabbi Arthur Hertzberg).

2. Git. 10b.

3. Cf. N.M. Gelber, Tokniot shel Medinah Yehudit in Keneset I'Zeker Bialik, 1929, p. 293 and M. Teitelbaum in Ha-Rav Miladi Warsaw, 1910, I, ch. 16 p. 155.

4. Cf. A. Geiger in his Wissenschaftliche Zeitschrift für juedsche Theologie, Leipzig, Vol. V, 1844, Die Aufgabe der Gegenwart, p. 1-35.

5. See above, Ch. IV.

6. S. Bernfeld, Toledot ha-Reformatzion, Warsaw, 1923, p. 66.

7. David Philipson, The Reform Movement in Judaism, N.Y., 1931, p. 438, the source of which is the Allgemeine Zeitung des Judentums VIII, 452.

8. Reinhold Niebuhr, The Nature and Destiny of Man, N.Y. 1941, Vol. I, p. 89.

9. Quoted in CCAR Yearbook 1929, by A. Minda, p. 388.

10. Cf. Leopold Zunz, Gottendienstliche Vortraege der Juden, Berlin, 1832. Vorrede X-XII.

11. Cf. Raphael Mahler, Der Kamf zwischen Haskolo un Hasidut in Galitzie N.Y. 1942, p. 69.

12. Cf. Mahler, op. cit., p. 71.

13. Cf. N.M. Gelber, op. cit., p. 309.

14. M. Mendelssohn, Jerusalem, tr. by M. Samuels, Vol. I, p. 50.

15. Ibid., Vol. II, p. 99.

16. Quoted in CCAR vol. XXXIX, p. 345.

17. Luke XX: 25.

18. Cf. M. Mendelssohn, op. cit., Vol. II, pp. 160-4.

19. Ibid., p. 166.

20. Ibid., Vol I, p. 133.

21. Cf. S. Bernfeld, op. cit., pp. 32-33.

22. Quoted in Mendelssohn's Jerusalem, op. cit., Vol. I, p. 287.
23. Ibid., pp. 288-289.
24. G. Scholem, op. cit., p. 296.
25. Leopold Loew, Gesammelte Schriften II, Szegedin, 1890, p. 172.
26. Scholem, op. cit., p. 300.
27. I.H. Weiss, Zikronotai, Warsaw, 1895, p. 15.
28. Ibid., p. 60 ff.
29. See above p. 174.
30. Yesodē, ha-Torah, Warsaw, 1903, p. 39.
31. Ibid., p. 11.
32. Ibid., pp. 39-41.
33. Penine Shadal, Przemysl 1888, p. 411.
34. Quoted by D. Philipson in The Reform Movement in Judaism, N.Y. 1931, p. 80.
35. Quoted, ibid., p. 25.
36. For the reason which the governments gave for refusing to incorporate Reform congregations, see D. Philipson, ibid., p. 256.

Chapter VII

1. Cf. Michael Creizenach's Thesen über den Talmud, and his Shulchan Aruch oder Enzyklopädische Darstellung des Mosaischen Gesetzes, Frankfurt, 1831.
2. Jacob Z. Lauterbach, Rabbinic Essays, with Bibliography of his writings, Cincinnati, 1951, pp 3-20.
3. D. Philipson, op. cit., pp. 307, 327.
4. Holdheim, Uber die Autonomie der Rabbinen und das Prinzip der Juedischen Ehe, zweite Auflage, Schwerin, 1847, p. 15.
5. Maimonides, Yad ha-Hazaka, Hilkot Melakim, 8:11 and Holdheim, op. cit., p. 81.
6. Cf. Tractatus Theologico-politicus, end of ch. VI.
7. Cf. correspondence with his friend Joseph Dérenbourg in Allgemeine Zeitung des Judentums, 1896, p. 165.
8. Ludwig Geiger, Abraham Geiger, Leben und Lebenswerk, Berlin, 1910, p. 227.
9. Jüdische Zeitschrift, II, 84; L. Geiger p. 251.
10. Jüdische Zeitschrift II, 193; L. Geiger, ibid. p. 252.
11. W.Z. f. J.T., IV, 321, L. Geiger ibid. p. 239.
12. J.Z. II, 207; L. Geiger ibid. p. 272ff.
13. J.Z. VIII, 1; L. Geiger ibid. p. 261.
14. Ibid., p. 263.
15. Ibid., p. 226.
16. D. Philipson, op. cit., pp. 136-137. Contrast the view expressed by Spinoza in his Theologico-Politicus, ch. III; in B. Spinoza's Political Works, A.G. Wernham, Oxford 1958, p. 63.
17. J.Z. III, 62.

18. Ket. 110b.
19. J.Z. II, 191ff; I, 249.
20. Cf. K. Kohler, Jewish Theology, N.Y. 1918, p. 445.
21. Ibid., pp. 6-7.
22. C. Montefiore-Loewe, A Rabbinic Anthology, London 1938, Introd. XXXI.
23. D. Philipson, op. cit., p. 5.
24. He-Halutz IV, pp. 83-84.
25. Abraham Krochmal, Ha-Ketab veha-Mikra, Lwow, 1881.

Chapter VIII

1. Cf. Hermann Cohen, "Deutschtum und Judentum" in his Juedische Schriften, Berlin, 1924, Vol. II, pp. 237-291.
2. Cf. Ismar Freund, Die Emanzipation der Juden in Preussen, Vol. II Urkunden, 1912.
3. Benedetto Croce, History as the Story of Liberty, N.Y. 1941, p. 82.
4. W. Windelband, History of Philosophy, N.Y. 1905, p. 573.
5. J.T. Shotwell, Introduction to History, N.Y. 1922, p. 327.
6. John Dewey, Reconstruction in Philosophy, N.Y. 1920, p. 19.
7. G. Fichte, Grundlage der gesamten Wissenschaftslehre, Leipzig 1794.
8. G. Fichte, Addresses to the German Nation, transl. by L.H. Gray, N.Y. 1913.
9. F. Formstecher, Die Religion des Geistes, Frankfurt a/M, 1841, p. 72.
10. J. Schelling, Von der Weltseele, 1798. Erster Entwurf eines Systems der Naturphilosophie 1799. In Gesammelte Werke, Stuttgart-Augsburg 1856-1861.
11. Formstecher, op. cit., IV, p. 36.
12. The full subtitle of Hirsch's work is, in translation: The Principle of the Jewish Religious Outlook and Its Relation to Paganism, Christianity and Absolute Philosophy, expounded and provided with illustrative texts from the Sacred Scriptures, the Talmudim and Midrashim, Leipzig, 1942.
13. Nid. 16b.
14. Git. 10b.
15. S.L. Steinheim, Glaubenslehre der Synagoge, Leipzig 1863, p. 80.
16. K. Kohler, Jewish Theology, N.Y. 1918, p. 389.
17. D. Philipson, The Reform Movement in Judaism, N.Y. 1931, p. 177.
18. Ibid., p. 174.
19. D. Dérenbourg in Wissenschaftliche Zeitschrift für Juedische Theologie. IV, 15.
20. D. Philipson, op. cit., p. 110.

21. Montefiore-Loewe, A Rabbinic Anthology, *op. cit.*, Int. p, XLIX.
22. Hibbert Journal, Vol. XII 2, p. 32.
23. Montefiore-Loewe, *op. cit.*, Introd. passim.
24. Claude G. Montefiore, The Legacy of Israel, Oxford, 1927, pp. 508-522.
25. Montefiore-Loewe, *op. cit.*, Introd. XXII.

Chapter IX

1. Proceedings, Central Conference of American Rabbis, 1909, p. 252.
2. David Einhorn, Memorial Volume, Selected Sermons and Addresses, ed. by K. Kohler. N.Y. 1911 (German), p. 90.
3. I.M. Wise, Reminiscences, transl. and ed. by David Philipson, Cincinnati 1901, p. 49.
4. *Ibid.*, p. 139.
5. Hyman G. Enelow, CCAR, Proceedings, 1900, pp. 131-132.
6. The Hebrew Review, Oct. 1880, p. 19.
7. Dena Wilansky, Sinai to Cincinnati, N.Y. 1937, p. 33.
8. *Ibid.*, p. 33.
9. Spinoza, Tractatus Theologico-Politicus, ch. XI.
10. Dena Wilansky, *op. cit.*, 189.
11. *Ibid.*, p. 194.
12. CCAR, Proceedings, 1937, pp. 97-100.
13. CCAR 1909, Proceedings, pp. 227-228.
14. K. Kohler, Jewish Theology, N.Y. 1918, pp. 445-46 .
15. Robert E. Sherwood, Roosevelt and Hopkins, N.Y. 1948, p. 167.
16. CCAR 1916, p. 207.
17. "The Synagogue," Liberal Judaism, Nov.-Dec. 1948, pp. 51ff.
18. Commentary, July 1952 p. 9.

Chapter X

1. S.R. Hirsch, Horeb, Versuche über Jisroels Pflichten in der Zerstreuung, Frankfurt a/M, Dritte Auflage, 1899, p. 449.
2. B.B. 15a: Maimonides, Introd. to Commentary on Mishnah, Sanhedrin X .
3. Jeschurun, ed. by S.R. Hirsch, 1854-55, I, 17-18.
4. M.H. Luzzatto, Mesillat Yesharim, Phila. 1937, Ch. I (first sentence).
5. S.R. Hirsch, Nineteen Letters of Ben Uziel, transl. by Bernard Drachman, N.Y. 1899, p. 37.
6. Abot I:3, Erub. 31a, Naz. 23a.
7. S.R. Hirsch, Horeb, Altona, 1937, p. 72.

8. "Grundlinien einer jüdischen Symbolik", Jeschurun 1857, III, pp. 352-387.

9. Cf. M.M. Kaplan, Judaism as a Civilization, N.Y. 1957, p. 143.

10. Meg. 20b.

11. S.R. Hirsch, Nineteen Letters, op. cit., p. 67.

12. Ibid., pp. 80, 82.

13. See above p. 57.

14. Git. 10b.

15. S.R. Hirsch, Horeb, op. cit., pp. 305, 313, 314.

16. S.R. Hirsch, Nineteen Letters, op. cit., p. 86.

17. Ibid., p. 162.

18. Sabato Morais also expressed his opposition to Zionism on these grounds. See "The Restoration", Amer. Hebr. Vol. 4, No. 2, Feb. 23, 1883, pp. 18-19.

19. For a lengthy apologia for the sacrificial cult see H. Loewe in "A Rabbinic Anthology", Notes, p. 643, note 3. There he mentions the fact that "the late Mr. Morris Joseph was inhibited by the late Chief Rabbi (Nathan Adler) from being recognized as Minister of the United Synagogue, because he expressed his disbelief in the literal restoration of the sacrifices. The Chief Rabbi's action and the belief in the physical restoration were eloquently upheld by Moses Hyamson in a lengthy article in the Jewish Quarterly Review, April 1893, pp. 469f. in reply to one on "Authority and Dogma in Judaism", by Oswald J. Simon, pp. 231ff.

20. Cf. Louis Ginsberg, Students Scholars and Saints, Phila. 1928, pp. 228-230.

21. S.R. Hirsch, Gesammelte Schriften, Frankfurt a/M, 1908: Das Prinzip der Gewissensfreiheit, 1874, Der Austritt aus der Gemeinde, 295-310.

22. Isaac Breuer, Der Neue Kusari, Frankfurt a/M. 1934.

23. Ibid., p. 225.

24. Ibid., p. 65.

25. Ch. Weizmann, Trial and Error, New York 1949.

26. Ibid., pp. 31-32.

27. Henry Englander, in CCAR Year Book, 1918, pp. 15-216; Occident vols. I-V, 1843-1848.

28. Occident V, pp. 526ff.

29. American Hebrew, Vol. VI, Dec. 19, 1884.

30. Henry Morais, A Memoir, Sabato Morais, Jewish Theological Seminary, 1898, pp. 79-80.

31. Ibid., p. 80.

32. Ibid.

33. Amer. Hebrew, Vol. 61, May 21, 1897.

34. Ibid., Vol. 62, Nov. 19, 1897.

35. Ibid., Vol. IX, Nov. 25, 1881.

36. Ibid., Vol. V, Dec. 3, 1880.

37. Ibid., Vol. XXIII, July 3, 1885.

38. *Ibid.*

39. *Ibid.*, Vol. XXXII, Sep. 2, 1887.

40. *Ibid.*, Vol. XXXII, Sep. 9, 1887.

41. *Ibid.*, Vol. XIII, Jan. 26, 1883.

Chapter XI

1. Cf. his letters to Solis S. Cohen, chairman, Gratz Trust Committee, Feb. 12, 1896.

2. Cf. Cyrus Adler "Sabato Morais" in Jewish Theological Seminary, Semi-centennial N.Y. 1939, pp. 34-36.

3. George Brandes, Main Currents in 19th Century Literature, N.Y. 1906, Vol. II, p. 21.

4. *Ibid.*, pp. 1-4.

5. Ernst Cassirer, The Myth of the State, Yale University, 1946, p.

6. Lord Acton, Historical Essays and Studies, London 1926, p. 346.

7. Quoted by K.S. Pinson, Pietism as a Factor in the Rise of German Nationalism, N.Y. 1934, p. 203.

8. Hans Kohn, Force and Reason, Cambridge 1937, p. 54.

9. Vorstudien der Septuaginta, Leipzig 1841, Vorwort. VII-XII.

10. Three Philosophical Poets, Cambridge Harvard Univ. Press, 1927, p. 144.

11. Berlin 1823, Bd. I, 1-24.

12. Bd. XI, p. 406.

13. L. Ginzberg, Students Scholars and Saints, p. 251.

14. H. Graetz, Geschichte der Juden, Bd. XI, 464.

15. S. Schechter, Studies II, Phila. 1908, p. 199.

16. S. Schechter, Seminary Addresses, Cincinnati 1915, p. 36.

17. G. F. Moore, Judaism, Vol. II, p. 8; Cf. article on "Law-Codification" by Louis Ginzberg, in Jew. Encyc. VIII.

18. S. Schechter, Studies II, p. 195.

19. Orient (ed. Fürst) 1842, nos. 7. 8. 9.

20. Literarische Beilage des Orients 1842, no. 23; Cf. Graetz, Die Fortsetzungen des Jüdischen Stammes, 1864; Cf. article on Heinrich Graetz in Jew. Encyc.

21. S. Schechter, Studies II, p. 185.

22. N. Bentwich, Solomon Schechter, Phila. 1938, p. 295.

23. A. Geiger, Nachgelassene Schriften, Breslau 1885, Vol. I. p. 81.

24. Schechter, Studies I, p. XVIII.

25. *Ibid.*

26. Edmund Wilson, Axel's Castle, N.Y. 1931, p. 126.

27. S. Schechter, Studies I, p. 20.

28. S. Schechter, Some Aspects of Rabbinic Theology, N.Y. 1909, p. 20.

29. Jüdische Apologetik, Glogau 1906, p. 3.

30. Montefiore-Loewe, *op. cit.*, Intr., p. LXI.

31. S. Schechter, Studies I, p. 180.

32. Ibid., Intr. 1. p. XVII.

33. Louis Ginzberg, Students Scholars and Saints, pp. 206-207.

34. Ibid., p. 208.

35. Ibid., p. 237.

36. Ibid.

37. Ibid.

38. Ibid., p. 206.

39. Ibid.

40. Cf. Graetz, Geschichte, Bd. XI, 329.

41. Cf. Z. Frankel, Zur Orientierung in der Cultusfrage, 1867.

42. M.R. Cohen, Nature and Reason, N.Y. 1931, p. 375.

43. Quoted by B. Croce, History as the Story of Liberty, London 1941, p. 84.

44. Cf. United Synagogue of America, Fifth Annual Report, 1918, pp. 44-45.

Chapter XII

1. Salo W. Baron, Modern Nationalism and Religion, N.Y., 1947, ch. II.

2. Simon M. Dubnow, Nationalism and Its History, ed. by K. B. Pinson, Phila., p. 103.

3. G. Theune, Volk und Nation, Berlin, 1937.

4. Alex Bein, Theodor Herzl, trans. from the German by Maurice Samuel, Phila., 1940, p. 37.

5. Simon M. Dubnow, op. cit., p. 108.

6. Were the Minorities Treaties a Failure?, by Jacob Robinson, Oscar Karback, Max M. Laserson, Nehemiah Robinson, Marc Vichniak, N.Y., 1943, pp. 244, 255.

7. Ketubot 111a, Cant. R. on Cant. 2:7.

8. The references in this chapter to the writings of R. Judah Alkalai and R. Zvi Hirsch Kalischer are based on an accessible Hebrew text of selections from those writings. That text gives the sources of those selections. The Hebrew text is R. Yehudah Alkalai—R. Zvi Hirsch Kalischer, ed. G. Kresel, Tel-Aviv, 1943. Ibid., p. 132.

9. Ibid., p. 137.

10. Ibid., p. 126.

11. Ibid., p. 127.

12. Ibid., p. 128.

13. Ibid., pp. 127-128.

14. Ibid., p. 134.

15. Ibid., p. 136.

16. Ibid., pp. 144-145.

17. Ibid., pp. 133-137.

18. I. Werfel, "Religious Zionist Miniatures," in Iggeret Lagolah, July 1947.

19. G. Kresel, op. cit., 62.

20. Ibid., pp. 44, 61.

21. Ibid., p. 69.

22. Ibid., p. 8.

23. Ibid., p. 10.

24. Ketubot, 110a.

25. G. Kresel, op. cit., 43-45.

26. Ibid., p. 54.

27. M. Hess, Rom und Jerusalem, M. W. Kaufmann, Leipzig, 1899, 15.

28. Moses Hess, Rome and Jerusalem, tr. from the German by Meyer Waxman, N.Y., p. 106.

29. Ibid., p. 62.

30. Ibid., p. 211 ff.

31. Ibid., p. 50.

32. M. Hess, Rom und Jerusalem, op. cit., pp. 200-201.

33. Moses Hess, Rome and Jerusalem, op. cit., p. 43.

34. Ibid., p. 101.

35. Ibid., third letter.

36. Ibid.

37. Rom und Jerusalem, op. cit., p. 4.

38. Moses Hess, Rome and Jerusalem, op. cit., p. 119.

39. Rom und Jerusalem, op. cit., p. 70.

40. Moses Hess, Rome and Jerusalem, op. cit., p. 90.

41. Ibid.

42. Ibid., pp. 139-141.

43. Ibid., p. 103.

44. Essays, Letters, Memoirs of Ahad Ha-Am, trans. & ed. by Leon Simon, Oxford, 1946; Al Parashat Derakim, I-IV, Berlin, 1904.

45. Ahad Ha-Am, Al Parashat Derakim, Berlin 1913, IV, 133-181.

46. Ibid., II 79-91.

47. Sanhedrin 96a, and Nedarim 81a.

48. Ahad Ha-Am, op. cit., 192 ff.

49. Ibid., II, 111, ff.

50. Ibid., I, 160 ff.

51. Ibid., IV, 34.

52. Ibid., II, 28.

53. Ibid., II, 130.

54. Ibid., IV, 1 ff.

55. Ibid., IV, 30.

56. Ibid., III, 93.

57. Ibid., III, 210; IV, 127.

58. Ibid., II, 89.

59. Auto-Emancipation, trans. from the German by D. S. Blondheim, N.Y., 1906.

60. *Ibid.*, p. 82.
61. *Ibid.*, p. 83.
62. *Ibid.*, p. 87.
63. *Ibid.*, p. 89.
64. *Ibid.*, p. 99.
65. *Ibid.*, pp. 99, 101 ff.
66. *Ibid.*, p. 95.
67. *Ibid.*, p. 102.
68. *Ibid.*, p. 101.
69. *Ibid.*, p. 89.
70. *Ibid.*, p. 88.
71. *Ibid.*, p. 87.
72. *Ibid.*, p. 96 ff.
73. *Ibid.*, p. 95.
74. Essays, Letters, Memoirs by Ahad Ha-Am, trans. and ed. by Leon Simon, Oxford, 1946, p. 352.
75. *Ibid.*, p. 98.
76. Theodor Herzl, The Jewish State, N.Y., 1946, p. 95.
77. *Ibid.*, p. 86.
78. *Ibid.*, p. 92.
79. *Ibid.*, p. 87.
80. *Ibid.*, p. 91.
81. Shmarya Levin, trans. by M. Samuel, *The Arena*, N.Y., 1932, p. 151; Cf. Leib Jaffe "The Springtide of Zionism" in *Jewish Forum*, August, 1947.
82. Quoted by Nordau in his address at the Eighth Zionist Congress in August, 1907. Old-New Land, trans. by Lotta Levensohn, N.Y., 1941, p. 161.
83. Old-New Land, trans. from the German by Lotta Levensohn, N.Y., 1941, pp. 79, 151, ff.
84. *Ibid.*, XII.
85. Max Nordau to His People, N.Y., 1941, p. 153.
86. "The Zionist Congress," in *Contemporary Review*, Vol. 24, p. 587.
87. From a letter to Reuben Brainin dated June 16, 1896 in *New Palestine*, Jan. 26, 1923.
88. Cf. Meir Ben-Horim, Max Nordau, N.Y., 1956, p. 175.
89. *Ibid.*
90. B. Netanyahu, Max Nordau and His People, N.Y., 1941, p. 42.
91. Quoted in *Ibid.*, p. 47.
92. Maks Nordau el Ammo, Tel Aviv, 1936, Vol. II, Book 1, 144; Cf. also *Ibid.*, 14.
93. *Ibid.*, 108.
94. *Ibid.*, Vol. II, Book 1, 104.
95. *Ibid.*, 163.
96. *Ibid.*, 200-209.
97. Quoted in *Menorah Journal*, March, 1929, p. 196, source not given.

Chapter XIII

1. N.Y. Times, Sunday, March 30, 1952.
2. Is. 42:19.
3. *Ibid.*, 42:6-7.
4. *Ibid.*, 5:1-2, 7.
5. Hos., 2:21-22.
6. A.N. Whitehead, Process and Reality, N.Y. 1929, p. 519.
7. Ernst Cassirer, The Myth of the State, Anchor Book, N.Y. 1955, p. 219.
8. The Christian Century, Oct. 2, 1957.
9. R. W. Emerson, The Conduct of Life, Cambridge, 1904, p. 204.
10. Arthur Compton, "The Case for Hope," *Sat. Rev.*, June 18, 1955.
11. A.N. Whitehead, *op. cit.*, p. 529.
12. Lewis Mumford, The Conduct of Life, N.Y. 1951, p. 87.
13. Erich Fromm, The Sane Society, N.Y. 1955, p. 335.
14. Carl R. Rogers, "A Therapist's View of the Good Life." Humanist, 1957, No. 5.
15. James Leuba, Standard, Jan., 1944.
16. Nicolas Berdyaev, Spirit and Freedom, New York, 1935, p. 94.
17. Ps. 9:11.
18. Men. 99b.

Index

543

4; infinitude, 235; interpretation of, 236; Islamic, 450; Jewish and pagan, 256-57; Judge of man, 94; justice, 96, 322, 323; Kingdom of God, 68, 69, 253, 261, 280, 283, 297, 324, 373, 412, 413, 469; knowledge of, 256; law of, see: Law; Lawgiver, 279, 482; life of man's spirit, 364; living God; faith in, 287; love, 322, 323; love of, and fear of, 97; 260; loyalty to, 477; *Makom*, 91; manifestation of, 88, 92, 462; in the People of Israel, 87; meaning of, in modern Judaism, 467-74; modern meaning of revelation, 252; monotheism, 35, 41, 67, 84, 89-90, 226, 235, 246, 256, 264, 268, 283, 292, 386, 418, 419, 424, 454, 479, 510; name of, 504; sanctification of, 38, 110; Name, Ineffable, 133, 135; nature of, 133-34, 322; need for the world, 509; obedience to, 509; pantheism, 91; Hasidic conception, 141; place in religion, 459; Power, cosmic, 491, 509; Presence of, 90-95; omnipresence (ubiquity), 94, 140; prestige, and the greatness of Israel, 38; providence, and man's destiny, 15-16, 119; reality of, 91; Reason, Divine, 253-54; Redeemer, 473, relationship to, 498; repudiation by, 36, return to, 405-06; revelation of, 352, 491, 496, 502-04, 506, 509; in the human spirit, 489-92; in the Pentateuch, 509, in *Torah*, 508-10; salvation; source of, 86-100; 311-12; Savior, 482; self-manifestation, 35, 236, 256; *Shekinah*, 36, 37, 43, 58, 64, 77, 78, 89, 92, 98, 118, 131, 132, 491; concept of, 88; solity, 89-90; source of power, 510; source of salvation, 86-100; 311-12; Spinozist view, 252; spirituality, 90; theism, 91, 270, 458, theocracy, 162, 178, 358; theodicies, 16; theurgy, 94; *Torah*; dictated by God, 101-02, 483; transcendence and immanence, 137; unchanging, 90; universality, and relation to Israel, 37; "unmoved mover," 490; views of Judah Hallevi, 9; vindication of, by Glueckl of Hameln, 17; "way of the Lord," 477; "We Thou" and "I-Thou" relationship, 31; will, Divine, 257, 326, 505; expression of God's will in *Torah*, 15-16; obedience to, 108, 117; revelation of, 83, 164; YHWH, 45, 47; Yah, the Lord of Hosts, 88.

God-consciousness, 39; and ethnic consciousness, 46.
God-idea, 38, 247, 436, 458, 503.
Godliness, 287.
God-man (Jesus), 251.
Gods, ancient, 510; deified potentates, 67-68.
Goethe, 173, 351, 421, 429.
"Golden Era" in Arabic Spain, 169.
"Golden Mean" of Aristotle, 119, 201, 211.
Golem, 153.
Good and evil, 137, 255, 259, 261, 288, 326, 476, 489, 491.
Gospel, see: Christianity.
Gottesdienstliche Vortraege, by Leopold Zunz, 179.
Gottlober, A. B., 180.
Government, self, see: Autonomy.
Graetz, Heinrich, 233, 338-39, 356-58, 360-61, 414; *History of the Jews*, 180.
Great Britain, see: England.
Greatness of Israel and prestige of God, 38.
Greek Bible, 73.
Greeks, see: Hellenism.
Grillparzer, 173.
Group-life, see: Peoplehood.
Guedemann, Moritz, 373; on Jews in the Middle Ages, 148.
Guide for the Perplexed, see: Maimonides.
Guide for the Perplexed (Contemporary), by Nachman Krochmal, 200.
"Guiding Principles of Reform Movement", 298, 304-05.

H

HA-ARI, see: Luria, Isaac.
Ha Ba D, see: Hasidism.
Ha-Measef, 196.
Ha-olam ha-ba, see: Other-worldliness.
Habakkuk, 72.
Hagiographa, 10.
Halakah, see: Law-Jewish.
Hallevi, Judah, 42, 44; on God, in *Al-Khazari*, 9, 115, 233-34.
Halizah, 347, 348.
Hametz, see: Passover.
Happiness, 323, 472; pursuit of, 312.
Hardenburg, Prince Friedrich von, 173, 193, 213.
Hasidism, 7, 21, 22, 112, 124, 135, 139, 140, 153, 176, 197, 199, 205, 329,

M

Tolerance, 159.
Tolerance Edict of Joseph 11, 172.
Tolstoy, Leo, 442.
Torah, 83, 90, 98, 113, 116-19, 121,
122, 128, 131, 133, 141, 189, 207, 211,
212, 228-30, 238, 264, 267, 298-308,
320-26, 328, 329, 332, 335, 336, 357,
366-68, 372, 373, 396, 406, 421, 422,
430, 431, 450, 455, 460, 477, 482,
491, 504-12; acceptance of, 33; and
philosophy, 113; authority of, challenges to, 124; authorship of, 507-08,
510; views of Rabbi Meir, 9; basis of,
512; belief in, and salvation, 9, canon-
ization, 511; claim to, as exclusively
Jewish, 10; concept, Reform version,
298; in Traditional Judaism, 5; dedication to, 59-60; deviation from, 511-
12; divine authorship of, 101-02, 483;
evaluation of, 16-17; expression of
God's will, 15-16; function of in
Jewish life, 30; twofold, 11, 12; "God,
Israel and Torah," 479; immutability
of, 369, 376; in the making, 510-12;
inculcation of, 54; influence of on life,
22; interpretations of, 53, 123, 125,
377; pragmatic, 12; "interruption of
reading," 59; knowledge of, traits required, 104; learning and doing, 106-
07; link with the past, 511; "living,"
421, 511; meaning for our day, 506-
07; meanings, hidden, 130; Mosaic,
292, 368, 369, 483; norms not in
Torah, 511; on reward and punishment, 13, 422; Oral and Written Law,
10, 63, 125, 318, 320-21, 334, 372,
385, 421, 411; origin, 190, 204, 213,
318, 362; supernatural, 119, 375; promulgation of religious and national
unity, 23; reinstatement of sanctions,
65; reinterpretation, 506-07; by the
Pharisees, 86; revelation of, 147; revelation of God in, 10; salvation
through, 38, 75; spirit of, 508; study
of, 55, 100-06, 164, 198; Chapters of
the Fathers, 12; effect of, 104-05;
primacy of, 76; reward for, 104; for
women, 15, 106; symbol and instrument of religion, 511.
Totolitarianism, 160, 454.
Tradition, 129-30, 200, 204, 236-37,
243-44, 246, 248, 252, 254, 262, 273,
293, 304, 317, 318, 320, 321, 323-36,
332-35, 342, 347, 359, 370, 374,
376-78, 411, 415, 422, 425, 428, 429,
452, 455, 460, 463-65, 470, 484, 488,
491; and history, 430; and modernism,
5, 263; and nature, 123; and personal
memories, 33; and reason, 77; failure
of, 222; historical approach, 204; history of, 360; interpretation of, 504-06;
literature of, 405; loyalty to, 23, 113-
114; national, 353, 354; values, 360.
Traditional (Rabbinic) Judaism, 3-10,
18, 32, 194, 198, 205, 222, 223, 227,
233-34, 235, 236, 252, 258, 263, 264,
267, 269, 273, 325, 341, 343-46, 348,
354, 356, 358, 361, 363-65, 367, 368,
373, 374, 376-78, 386, 394, 396, 397,
401, 402, 404, 412, 419, 430, 457,
459, 463; adherence to, cost of, 190;
and modernism, 7; and Orthodoxy,
316-20, 332-41; and the family, 61;
and today's needs, 5; aspect, ethnic,
30-69; authority of, 319; change in,
240-41; collaboration with the State,
205-06; continuity of, 86; defense of,
205; definition of, 5; deprecation of
other-worldliness, 83, 422; early, 62;
faith in, pre-modern, 7-8; function,
twofold, 11; God-consciousness and
ethnic consciousness, 46; Hasidism,
see: Hasidism; in the United States,
275-76; salvational aspect of, 70-111.
Transcendence of the ego, 478-79.
Transgression, see: Sin.
Trans-nationalism, 452, 455, 458, 474-
78.
Transition to modern era, 144 ff., 214.
Treitschke, Heinrich von, 388-89.
Trends in modern Judaism, 4-5.
Tribalism, 422.
Tsaddikim, 133, 138-49, 143.
Turim, by Jacob ben Asher, 59-60.

U

UKRAINE, The, 124; persecution in,
139.
Union of American Hebrew Congregations, 274, 283, 295, 309, 313, 341.
Union Prayer Book, 285, 302, 307;
Union Hymnal, 302.
Unions, labor, 486.
United States, 443; American Council
for Judaism, 291; American Jewish
Committee, 296, 310; American Jewish Congress, 310; anti-Semitism in,
308; civilizations, two; how to live in,
474-78; Conservative Judaism, 350-80;
shortcomings, 369-78; culture hero,
new, 49; democracy in, 453; divorce

Will, free, of man, 117, 257, 326, 497, 500.
"Will, General," 5, 216, 224, 228.
Will-to-live, 204, 221, 222, 226, 383, 385-86, 417-20, 423, 427, 435, 436, 455, 459, 473-74, 503, 506.
Wise, Isaac M., 274,-82, 283, 285, 286, 295, 301, 344; *Minhag America*, 301; *Reminiscences*, 276.
Wissenschaft des Judentums, 321, founders of, 356.
Wolf, Immanuel, 357.
Wolff, Christian, philosophy of, 18.
Women, nineteenth-century, 21-4; Medieval, religious inspiration, 15; part in study of Torah, 106; see: Marriage.
World, cataclysm, 358; domination, accusation of, 220; lower, 133; see: Hell; origin and nature of, 510; religion, 238, 287, 301-02.
World-to-come, see: Other-Worldliness.
World War I, 392, 448.
World War II, 69, 395-96.
Worship, 40, 216-18, 247-48, 324, 327, 342, 364, 367, 487; Hasidic, 141; idol worship, see: Paganism; of the past, 504; purpose, 31; requirement of Minyan, 31; see: Prayer, Ritual.
Written and Oral Law, see: Torah.
Wrong and right, 167-68; see Evil and good.

X

XENOPHOBIA, 433, 434, 439-40.

Y

YAHADUT (Judaism), 8.
Yemen, Jews of, 33.
Yeshiva, 28, 55, 63, 205, 356.

Yetzer, good and evil, 78, 80, 104, 132.
Yiddish, 3, 15, 183, 184, 311; origin, 14.
Yisroel-Mensch, 320-35.
Yohanan, Rabbi, 36-7, 98; on study of the Torah, 10.
Yohanan ben Zakkai, 6, 48, 131.
Yom Kippur, 43, 95, 472, 511; prayer for social justice, 307.
Yoreh Deah, code, 29.

Z

ZADOK, 237, 238.
Zadokites, 237.
Zekut avot (merit of the Patriarchs), 32.
Zeitgeist, 249, 252-53, 319, 320, 324, 351, 359, German, 247-71.
Zion College, 277.
Zion, Hill of, 81.
Zionism, 161-62, 216, 245, 281-82, 284, 291, 337-38, 348, 365; and peoplehood, 365, 381ff., 394; and religion, 449; Einstein's view of, 453; Federation, English, 455; Greater, 485; *Hatikvah*, 302; *Hibbat Tsiyon*, 416, 436; influence of, 447; *Mizrachi*, 396, 402, 404, 421; opposition to, 445-46; Nationalism a threat to Judaism, 381ff., Political, 392, 394, 395, 432-49; pre-Messianic, 384-97, 399; *Rome and Jerusalem*, 406-07; significance, 446, 485; Spiritual, 365, 394, 395, 406-31; traditional, 421.
Zohar, and study of, 125, 126, 138, 214, 506.
Zoroaster and Zoroastrianism, 12, 72, 89, 130.
Zunz, Leopold, 200, 233, 247, 286, 356, 359, 367; *Gottesdienstliche Vorträge*, 179.